Guide to Assembly Language Programming in Linux

T0181625

Sivarama P. Dandamudi

Guide to Assembly Language
Programming in Linux

 Springer

Sivarama P. Dandamudi
School of Computer Science
Carleton University
Ottawa, ON K1S 5B6
Canada
sivarama@scs.carleton.ca

Library of Congress Cataloging-in-Publication Data

Dandamudi, Sivarama P., 1955–
    Guide to assembly language programming in Linux / Sivarama P. Dandamudi.
        p.   cm.
    Includes bibliographical references and index.
    ISBN 978-0387-25897-3 (alk. paper)

    1. Assembler language (Computer program language) 2. Linux. I. Title.

    QA76.73.A8D34 2005
    005.13'6—dc22
                                                                    2005049758

9 8 7 6 5 4 3 2 1   SPIN 11302087

springeronline.com

To
my parents, **Subba Rao** and **Prameela Rani**,
my wife, **Sobha**,
and
my daughter, **Veda**

Preface

The primary goal of this book is to teach the IA-32 assembly language programming under the Linux operating system. A secondary objective is to provide a gentle introduction to the Fedora Linux operating system. Linux has evolved substantially since its first appearance in 1991. Over the years, its popularity has grown as well. According to an estimate posted on http://counter.li.org/, there are about 18 million Linux users worldwide. Hopefully, this book encourages even more people to switch to Linux.

The book is self-contained and provides all the necessary background information. Since assembly language is very closely linked to the underlying processor architecture, a part of the book is dedicated to giving computer organization details. In addition, the basics of Linux are introduced in a separate chapter. These details are sufficient to work with the Linux operation system.

The reader is assumed to have had some experience in a structured, high-level language such as C. However, the book does not assume extensive knowledge of any high-level language—only the basics are needed.

Approach and Level of Presentation

The book is targeted for software professionals who would like to move to Linux and get a comprehensive introduction to the IA-32 assembly language. It provides detailed, step-by-step instructions to install Linux as the second operating system.

No previous knowledge of Linux is required. The reader is introduced to Linux and its commands. Four chapters are dedicated to Linux and NASM assembler (installation and usage). The accompanying DVD-ROMs provide the necessary software to install the Linux operating system and learn assembly language programming.

The assembly language is presented from the professional viewpoint. Since most professionals are full-time employees, the book takes their time constraints into consideration in presenting the material.

Summary of Special Features

Here is a summary of the special features that sets this book apart:

- The book includes the Red Hat Fedora Core 3 Linux distribution (a total of two DVD-ROMs are included with the book). Detailed step-by-step instructions are given to install Linux on a Windows machine. A complete chapter is used for this purpose, with several screenshots to help the reader during the installation process.

- Free NASM assembler is provided so that the readers can get hands-on assembly language programming experience.

- Special I/O software is provided to simplify assembly language programming. A set of input and output routines is provided so that the reader can focus on writing assembly language programs rather than spending time in understanding how the input and output are done using the basic I/O functions provided by the operating system.

- Three chapters are included on computer organization. These chapters provide the necessary background to program in the assembly language.

- Presentation of material is suitable for self-study. To facilitate this, extensive programming examples and figures are used to help the reader grasp the concepts. Each chapter contains a simple programming example in "Our First Program" section to gently introduce the concepts discussed in the chapter. This section is typically followed by "Illustrative Examples" section, which gives more programming examples.

- This book does not use fragments of code in examples. All examples are complete in the sense that they can be assembled and run, giving a better feeling as to how these programs work. These programs are on the accompanying DVD-ROM (DVD 2). In addition, you can also download these programs from the book's Web site at the following URL: http://www.scs.carleton.ca/~sivarama/linux_book.

- Each chapter begins with an overview and ends with a summary.

Overview of the Book

The book is divided into seven parts. Part I provides introduction to the assembly language and gives reasons for programming in the assembly language. Assembly language is a low-level language. To program in the assembly language, you should have some basic knowledge about the underlying processor and system organization. Part II provides this background on computer organization. Chapter 2 introduces the digital logic circuits. The next chapter gives details on memory organization. Chapter 4 describes the Intel IA-32 architecture.

Part III covers the topics related to Linux installation and usage. Chapter 5 gives detailed information on how you can install the Fedora Core Linux provided on the accompanying DVD-ROMs. It also explains how you can make your system dual bootable so that you can select the operating system (Windows or Linux) at boot time. Chapter 6 gives a brief introduction to the Linux operating system. It gives enough details so that you feel comfortable using the Linux operating system. If you are familiar with Linux, you can skip this chapter.

Part IV also consists of two chapters. It deals with assembling and debugging assembly language programs. Chapter 7 gives details on the NASM assembler. It also describes the I/O routines developed by the author to facilitate assembly language programming. The next chapter looks at the debugging aspect of program development. We describe the GNU debugger (gdb), which is a command-line debugger. This chapter also gives details on Data Display Debugger (DDD), which is a nice graphical front-end for gdb. Both debuggers are included on the accompanying DVD-ROMs.

After covering the setup and usage details of Linux and NASM, we look at the assembly language in Part V. This part introduces the basic instructions of the assembly language. To facilitate modular program development, we introduce procedures in the third chapter of this part. The remaining chapters describe the addressing modes and other instructions that are commonly used in assembly language programs.

Part VI deals with advanced assembly language topics. It deals with topics such as string processing, recursion, floating-point operations, and interrupt processing. In addition, Chapter 21 explains how you can interface with high-level languages. By using C, we explain how you can call assembly language procedures from C and vice versa. This chapter also discusses how assembly language statements can be embedded into high-level language code. This process is called inline assembly. Again, by using C, this chapter shows how inline assembly is done under Linux.

The last part consists of five appendices. These appendices give information on number systems and character representation. In addition, Appendix D gives a summary of the IA-32 instruction set. A comprehensive glossary is given in Appendix E.

Acknowledgments

I want to thank Wayne Wheeler, Editor and Ann Kostant, Executive Editor at Springer for suggesting the project. I am also grateful to Wayne for seeing the project through.

My wife Sobha and daughter Veda deserve my heartfelt thanks for enduring my preoccupation with this project! I also thank Sobha for proofreading the manuscript. She did an excellent job!

I also express my appreciation to the School of Computer Science at Carleton University for providing a great atmosphere to complete this book.

Feedback

Works of this nature are never error-free, despite the best efforts of the authors and others involved in the project. I welcome your comments, suggestions, and corrections by electronic mail.

Ottawa, Canada   Sivarama P. Dandamudi
January 2005   sivarama@scs.carleton.ca
                                                                                    http://www.scs.carleton.ca/~sivarama

Contents

PART I

Overview

1

Assembly Language

The main objective of this chapter is to give you a brief introduction to the assembly language. To achieve this goal, we compare and contrast the assembly language with high-level languages you are familiar with. This comparison enables us to take a look at the pros and cons of the assembly language vis-à-vis high-level languages.

Introduction

A user's view of a computer system depends on the degree of abstraction provided by the underlying software. Figure 1.1 shows a hierarchy of levels at which one can interact with a computer system. Moving to the top of the hierarchy shields the user from the lower-level details. At the highest level, the user interaction is limited to the interface provided by application software such as spreadsheet, word processor, and so on. The user is expected to have only a rudimentary knowledge of how the system operates. Problem solving at this level, for example, involves composing a letter using the word processor software.

At the next level, problem solving is done in one of the *high-level languages* such as C and Java. A user interacting with the system at this level should have detailed knowledge of software development. Typically, these users are application programmers. Level 4 users are knowledgeable about the application and the high-level language that they would use to write the application software. They may not, however, know internal details of the system unless they also happen to be involved in developing system software such as device drivers, assemblers, linkers, and so on.

Both levels 4 and 5 are *system independent*, that is, independent of a particular processor used in the system. For example, an application program written in C can be executed on a system with an Intel processor or a PowerPC processor without modifying the source code. All we have to do is recompile the program with a C compiler native to the target system. In contrast, software development done at all levels below level 4 is *system dependent*.

Assembly language programming is referred to as *low-level programming* because each assembly language instruction performs a much lower-level task compared to an instruction in a high-level language. As a consequence, to perform the same task, assembly language code tends to be much larger than the equivalent high-level language code.

Assembly language instructions are native to the processor used in the system. For example, a program written in the Intel assembly language cannot be executed on the PowerPC processor.

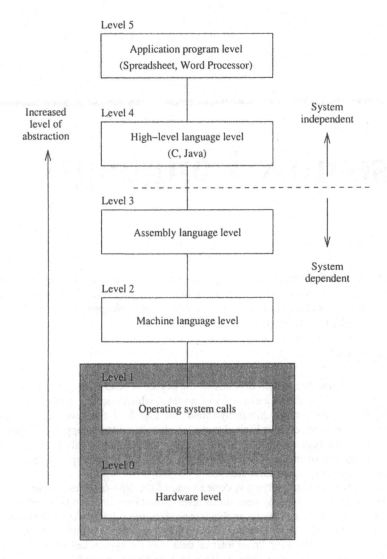

Figure 1.1 A user's view of a computer system.

Programming in the assembly language also requires knowledge about system internal details such as the processor architecture, memory organization, and so on.

Machine language is a close relative of the assembly language. Typically, there is a one-to-one correspondence between the assembly language and machine language instructions. The processor understands only the machine language, whose instructions consist of strings of 1s and 0s. We say more on these two languages in the next section.

Even though assembly language is considered a low-level language, programming in assembly language will not expose you to all the nuts and bolts of the system. Our operating system hides several of the low-level details so that the assembly language programmer can breathe easy. For example, if we want to read input from the keyboard, we can rely on the services provided by the operating system.

Well, ultimately there has to be something to execute the machine language instructions. This is the system hardware, which consists of digital logic circuits and the associated support electronics. A detailed discussion of this topic is beyond the scope of this book. Books on computer organization discuss this topic in detail.

What Is Assembly Language?

Assembly language is directly influenced by the instruction set and architecture of the processor. In this book, we focus on the assembly language for the Intel 32-bit processors like the Pentium. The assembly language code must be processed by a program in order to generate the machine language code. *Assembler* is the program that translates the assembly language code into the machine language.

NASM (Netwide Assembler), MASM (Microsoft Assembler), and TASM (Borland Turbo Assembler) are some of the popular assemblers for the Intel processors. In this book, we use the NASM assembler. There are two main reasons for this selection: (i) It is a free assembler; and (ii) NASM supports a variety of formats including the formats used by Microsoft Windows, Linux and a host of others.

Are you curious as to how the assembly language instructions look like? Here are some examples:

```
inc    result
mov    class_size,45
and    mask1,128
add    marks,10
```

The first instruction increments the variable result. This assembly language instruction is equivalent to

```
result++;
```

in C. The second instruction initializes class_size to 45. The equivalent statement in C is

```
class_size = 45;
```

The third instruction performs the bitwise and operation on mask1 and can be expressed in C as

```
mask1 = mask1 & 128;
```

The last instruction updates marks by adding 10. In C, this is equivalent to

```
marks = marks + 10;
```

These examples illustrate several points:

1. Assembly language instructions are cryptic.

2. Assembly language operations are expressed by using mnemonics (like `and` and `inc`).

3. Assembly language instructions are low level. For example, we cannot write the following in the assembly language:

   ```
   add     marks,value
   ```

   This instruction is invalid because two variables, `marks` and `value`, are not allowed in a single instruction.

We appreciate the readability of the assembly language instructions by looking at the equivalent machine language instructions. Here are some machine language examples:

Assembly language		Operation	Machine language (in hex)
`nop`		No operation	`90`
`inc`	`result`	Increment	`FF060A00`
`mov`	`class_size,45`	Copy	`C7060C002D00`
`and`	`mask,128`	Logical and	`80260E0080`
`add`	`marks,10`	Integer addition	`83060F000A`

In the above table, machine language instructions are written in the hexadecimal number system. If you are not familiar with this number system, see Appendix A for a quick review of number systems.

It is obvious from these examples that understanding the code of a program in the machine language is almost impossible. Since there is a one-to-one correspondence between the instructions of the assembly language and the machine language, it is fairly straightforward to translate instructions from the assembly language to the machine language. As a result, only a masochist would consider programming in a machine language. However, life was not so easy for some of the early programmers. When microprocessors were first introduced, some programming was in fact done in machine language!

Advantages of High-Level Languages

High-level languages are preferred to program applications, as they provide a convenient abstraction of the underlying system suitable for problem solving. Here are some advantages of programming in a high-level language:

1. *Program development is faster.*
   Many high-level languages provide structures (sequential, selection, iterative) that facilitate program development. Programs written in a high-level language are relatively small compared to the equivalent programs written in an assembly language. These programs are also easier to code and debug.

2. *Programs are easier to maintain.*
   Programming a new application can take from several weeks to several months and the lifecycle of such an application software can be several years. Therefore, it is critical that software development be done with a view of software maintainability, which involves activities ranging from fixing bugs to generating the next version of the software. Programs

written in a high-level language are easier to understand and, when good programming practices are followed, easier to maintain. Assembly language programs tend to be lengthy and take more time to code and debug. As a result, they are also difficult to maintain.

3. *Programs are portable.*
High-level language programs contain very few processor-specific details. As a result, they can be used with little or no modification on different computer systems. In contrast, assembly language programs are processor-specific.

Why Program in Assembly Language?

The previous section gives enough reasons to discourage you from programming in the assembly language. However, there are two main reasons why programming is still done in assembly language: (i) efficiency, and (ii) accessibility to system hardware.

Efficiency refers to how "good" a program is in achieving a given objective. Here we consider two objectives based on space (space-efficiency) and time (time-efficiency).

Space-efficiency refers to the memory requirements of a program, that is, the size of the executable code. Program A is said to be more space-efficient if it takes less memory space than program B to perform the same task. Very often, programs written in the assembly language tend to be more compact than those written in a high-level language.

Time-efficiency refers to the time taken to execute a program. Obviously a program that runs faster is said to be better from the time-efficiency point of view. If we craft assembly language programs carefully, they tend to run faster than their high-level language counterparts.

As an aside, we can also define a third objective: how fast a program can be developed (i.e., write code and debug). This objective is related to the *programmer productivity*, and assembly language loses the battle to high-level languages as discussed in the last section.

The superiority of assembly language in generating compact code is becoming increasingly less important for several reasons. First, the savings in space pertain only to the program code and not to its data space. Thus, depending on the application, the savings in space obtained by converting an application program from some high-level language to the assembly language may not be substantial. Second, the cost of memory has been decreasing and memory capacity has been increasing. Thus, the size of a program is not a major hurdle anymore. Finally, compilers are becoming "smarter" in generating code that is both space- and time-efficient. However, there are systems such as embedded controllers and handheld devices in which space-efficiency is important.

One of the main reasons for writing programs in an assembly language is to generate code that is time-efficient. The superiority of assembly language programs in producing efficient code is a direct manifestation of *specificity*. That is, assembly language programs contain only the code that is necessary to perform the given task. Even here, a "smart" compiler can optimize the code that can compete well with its equivalent written in the assembly language. Although the gap is narrowing with improvements in compiler technology, assembly language still retains its advantage for now.

The other main reason for writing assembly language programs is to have direct control over system hardware. High-level languages, on purpose, provide a restricted (abstract) view of the underlying hardware. Because of this, it is almost impossible to perform certain tasks that require access to the system hardware. For example, writing a device driver for a new scanner on the market almost certainly requires programming in assembly language. Since assembly language does not impose any restrictions, you can have direct control over the system hardware. If you are developing system software, you cannot avoid writing assembly language programs.

Typical Applications

We have identified three main advantages to programming in an assembly language.

1. Time-efficiency
2. Accessibility to hardware
3. Space-efficiency

Time-efficiency: Applications for which the execution speed is important fall under two categories:

1. Time convenience (to improve performance)
2. Time critical (to satisfy functionality)

Applications in the first category benefit from time-efficient programs because it is convenient or desirable. However, time-efficiency is not absolutely necessary for their operation. For example, a graphics package that scales an object instantaneously is more pleasant to use than the one that takes noticeable time.

In *time-critical applications*, tasks have to be completed within a specified time period. These applications, also called *real-time applications*, include aircraft navigation systems, process control systems, robot control software, communications software, and target acquisition (e.g., missile tracking) software.

Accessibility to hardware: System software often requires direct control over the system hardware. Examples include operating systems, assemblers, compilers, linkers, loaders, device drivers, and network interfaces. Some applications also require hardware control. Video games are an obvious example.

Space-efficiency: As mentioned before, for most systems, compactness of application code is not a major concern. However, in portable and handheld devices, code compactness is an important factor. Space-efficiency is also important in spacecraft control systems.

Summary

We introduced assembly language and discussed where it fits in the hierarchy of computer languages. Our discussion focused on the usefulness of high-level languages vis-à-vis the assembly language. We noted that high-level languages are preferred, as their use aids in faster program development, program maintenance, and portability. Assembly language, however, provides two chief benefits: faster program execution, and access to system hardware. We give more details on the assembly language in Parts V and VI.

PART II

Computer Organization

2

Digital Logic Circuits

Viewing computer systems at the digital logic level exposes us to the nuts and bolts of the basic hardware. The goal of this chapter is to cover the necessary digital logic background. Our discussion can be divided into three parts. In the first part, we focus on the basics of digital logic circuits. We start off with a look at the basic gates such as AND, OR, and NOT gates. We introduce Boolean algebra to manipulate logical expressions. We also explain how logical expressions are simplified in order to get an efficient digital circuit implementation.

The second part introduces combinational circuits, which provide a higher level of abstraction than the basic circuits discussed in the first part. We review several commonly used combinational circuits including multiplexers, decoders, comparators, adders, and ALUs.

In the last part, we review sequential circuits. In sequential circuits, the output depends both on the current inputs as well as the past history. This feature brings the notion of time into digital logic circuits. We introduce system clock to provide this timing information. We discuss two types of circuits: latches and flip-flops. These devices can be used to store a single bit of data. Thus, they provide the basic capability to design memories. These devices can be used to build larger memories, a topic covered in detail in the next chapter.

Introduction

A computer system has three main components: a central processing unit (CPU) or processor, a memory unit, and input/output (I/O) devices. These three components are interconnected by a *system bus*. The term bus is used to represent a group of electrical signals or the wires that carry these signals. Figure 2.1 shows details of how they are interconnected and what actually constitutes the system bus. As shown in this figure, the three major components of the system bus are the address bus, data bus, and control bus.

The width of address bus determines the memory addressing capacity of the processor. The width of data bus indicates the size of the data transferred between the processor and memory or I/O device. For example, the 8086 processor had a 20-bit address bus and a 16-bit data bus. The amount of physical memory that this processor can address is 2^{20} bytes, or 1 MB, and each data transfer involves 16 bits. The Pentium processor, for example, has 32 address lines and 64 data lines. Thus, it can address up to 2^{32} bytes, or a 4 GB memory. Furthermore, each data transfer can

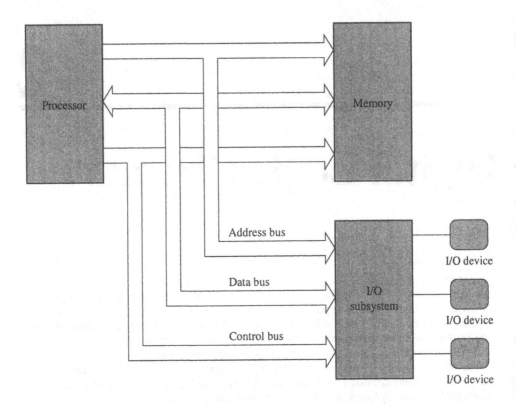

Figure 2.1 Simplified block diagram of a computer system.

move 64 bits. In comparison, the Intel 64-bit processor Itanium uses 64 address lines and 128 data lines.

The control bus consists of a set of control signals. Typical control signals include memory read, memory write, I/O read, I/O write, interrupt, interrupt acknowledge, bus request, and bus grant. These control signals indicate the type of action taking place on the system bus. For example, when the processor is writing data into the memory, the memory write signal is asserted. Similarly, when the processor is reading from an I/O device, the I/O read signal is asserted.

The system memory, also called *main memory* or *primary memory*, is used to store both program instructions and data. I/O devices such as the keyboard and display are used to provide user interface. I/O devices are also used to interface with secondary storage devices such as disks.

The system bus is the communication medium for data transfers. Such data transfers are called *bus transactions*. Some examples of bus transactions are memory read, memory write, I/O read, I/O write, and interrupt. Depending on the processor and the type of bus used, there may be other types of transactions. For example, the Pentium processor supports a burst mode of data transfer in which up to four 64 bits of data can be transferred in a burst cycle.

Every bus transaction involves a *master* and a *slave*. The master is the initiator of the transaction and the slave is the target of the transaction. For example, when the processor wants to read data from the memory, it initiates a bus transaction, also called a bus cycle, in which the processor is the bus master and memory is the slave. The processor usually acts as the master of the system bus, while components like memory are usually slaves. Some components may act as slaves for some transactions and as masters for other transactions.

When there is more than one master device, which is typically the case, the device requesting the use of the bus sends a *bus request* signal to the bus arbiter using the bus request control line. If the bus arbiter grants the request, it notifies the requesting device by sending a signal on the *bus grant* control line. The granted device, which acts as the master, can then use the bus for data transfer. The bus-request-grant procedure is called *bus protocol*. Different buses use different bus protocols. In some protocols, permission to use the bus is granted for only one bus cycle; in others, permission is granted until the bus master relinquishes the bus.

The hardware that is responsible for executing machine language instructions can be built using a few basic building blocks. These building blocks are called *logic gates*. These logic gates implement the familiar logical operations such as AND, OR, NOT, and so on, in hardware. The purpose of this chapter is to provide the basics of the digital hardware. The next two chapters introduce memory organization and architecture of the Intel IA-32 processors.

Our discussion of digital logic circuits is divided into three parts. The first part deals with the basics of digital logic gates. Then we look at two higher levels of abstractions—combinational and sequential circuits. In combinational circuits, the output of the circuit depends solely on the *current* inputs applied to the circuit. The adder is an example of a combinational circuit. The output of an adder depends only on the current inputs. On the other hand, the output of a sequential circuit depends not only on the current inputs but also on the past inputs. That is, output depends both on the current inputs as well as on how it got to the current state. For example, in a binary counter, the output depends on the current value. The next value is obtained by incrementing the current value (in a way, the current state represents a snapshot of the past inputs). That is, we cannot say what the output of a counter will be unless we know its current state. Thus, the counter is a sequential circuit. We review both combinational and sequential circuits in this chapter.

Simple Logic Gates

You are familiar with the three basic logical operators: AND, OR, and NOT. Digital circuits to implement these and other logical functions are called gates. Figure 2.2a shows the symbol notation used to represent the AND, OR, and NOT gates. The NOT gate is often referred to as the inverter. We have also included the truth table for each gate. A *truth table* is a list of all possible input combinations and their corresponding output. For example, if you treat a logical zero as representing false and a logical 1 truth, you can see that the truth table for the AND gate represents the logical AND operation.

Even though the three gates shown in Figure 2.2a are sufficient to implement any logical function, it is convenient to implement certain other gates. Figure 2.2b shows three popularly used gates. The NAND gate is equivalent to an AND gate followed by a NOT gate. Similarly, the NOR gates are a combination of the OR and NOT gates. The exclusive-OR (XOR) gate generates a 1 output whenever the two inputs differ. This property makes it useful in certain applications such as parity generation.

Logic gates are in turn built using transistors. One transistor is enough to implement a NOT gate. But we need three transistors to implement the AND and OR gates. It is interesting to note that, contrary to our intuition, implementing the NAND and NOR gates requires only two transistors. In this sense, transistors are the basic electronic components of digital hardware circuits. For example, the Pentium processor introduced in 1993 consists of about 3 million transistors. It is now possible to design chips with more than 100 million transistors.

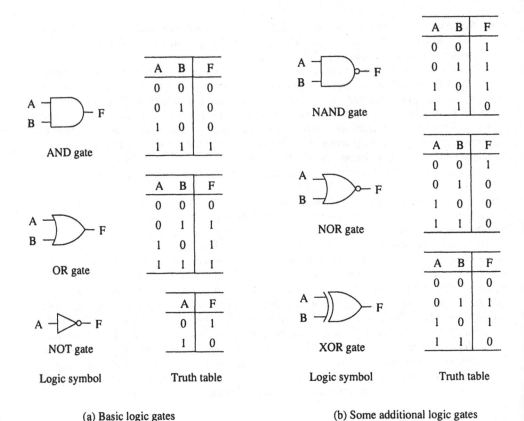

Figure 2.2 Simple logic gates: Logic symbols and truth tables.

There is a *propagation delay* associated with each gate. This delay represents the time required for the output to react to an input. The propagation delay depends on the complexity of the circuit and the technology used. Typical values for the TTL gates are in the range of a few nanoseconds (about 5 to 10 ns). A nanosecond (ns) is 10^{-9} second.

In addition to propagation delay, other parameters should be taken into consideration in designing and building logic circuits. Two such parameters are fanin and fanout. *Fanin* specifies the maximum number of inputs a logic gate can have. *Fanout* refers to the driving capacity of an output. Fanout specifies the maximum number of gates that the output of a gate can drive.

A small set of independent logic gates (such as AND, NOT, NAND, etc.) are packaged into an integrated circuit (IC) chip, or "chip" for short. These ICs are called small-scale integrated (SSI) circuits and typically consist of about 1 to 10 gates. Medium-scale integrated (MSI) circuits represent the next level of integration (typically between 10 and 100 gates). Both SSI and MSI were introduced in the late 1960s. LSI (large-scale integration), introduced in early 1970s, can integrate between 100 and 10,000 gates on a single chip. The final degree of integration, VLSI (very large scale integration), was introduced in the late 1970s and is used for complex chips such as microprocessors that require more than 10,000 gates.

Table 2.1 Truth tables for the majority and even-parity functions

Majority function					Even-parity function			
A	B	C	F_1		A	B	C	F_2
0	0	0	0		0	0	0	0
0	0	1	0		0	0	1	1
0	1	0	0		0	1	0	1
0	1	1	1		0	1	1	0
1	0	0	0		1	0	0	1
1	0	1	1		1	0	1	0
1	1	0	1		1	1	0	0
1	1	1	1		1	1	1	1

Logic Functions

Logic functions can be specified in a variety of ways. In a sense their expression is similar to problem specification in software development. A logical function can be specified verbally. For example, a majority function can be specified as: Output should be 1 whenever the majority of the inputs is 1. Similarly, an even-parity function can be specified as: Output (parity bit) is 1 whenever there is an odd number of 1s in the input. The major problem with verbal specification is the imprecision and the scope for ambiguity.

We can make this specification precise by using a truth table. In the truth table method, for each possible input combination, we specify the output value. The truth table method makes sense for logical functions as the alphabet consists of only 0 and 1. The truth tables for the 3-input majority and even-parity functions are shown in Table 2.1.

The advantage of the truth table method is that it is precise. This is important if you are interfacing with a client who does not understand other more concise forms of logic function expression. The main problem with the truth table method is that it is cumbersome as the number of rows grows exponentially with the number of logical variables. Imagine writing a truth table for a 10-variable function—it requires $2^{10} = 1024$ rows!

We can also use logical expressions to specify a logical function. Logical expressions use the dot, +, and overbar to represent the AND, OR, and NOT operations, respectively. For example, the output of the AND gate in Figure 2.2 is written as $F = A \cdot B$. Assuming that single letters are used for logical variables, we often omit the dot and write the previous AND function as $F = A B$. Similarly, the OR function is written as $F = A + B$. The output of the NOT gate is expressed as $F = \overline{A}$. Some authors use a prime to represent the NOT operation as in $F = A'$ mainly because of problems with typesetting the overbar.

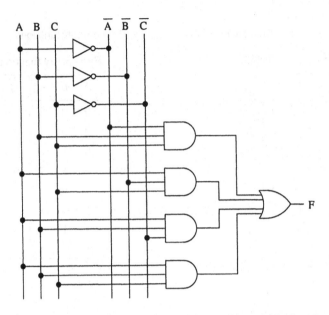

Figure 2.3 Logical circuit to implement the 3-input majority function.

The logical expressions for our 3-input majority and even-parity functions are shown below:

- 3-input majority function = A B + B C + A C,
- 3-input even-parity function = $\overline{A}\,\overline{B}\,C + \overline{A}\,B\,\overline{C} + A\,\overline{B}\,\overline{C} + A\,B\,C$.

An advantage of this form of specification is that it is compact while it retains the precision of the truth table method. Another major advantage is that logical expressions can be manipulated to come up with an efficient design. We say more on this topic later.

The final form of specification uses a graphical notation. Figure 2.3 shows the logical circuit to implement the 3-input majority function. As with the last two methods, it is also precise but is more useful for hardware engineers to implement logical functions.

A logic circuit designer may use all the three forms during the design of a logic circuit. A simple circuit design involves the following steps:

- First we have to obtain the truth table from the input specifications.
- Then we derive a logical expression from the truth table.
- We do not want to implement the logical expression derived in the last step as it often contains some redundancy, leading to an inefficient design. For this reason, we simplify the logical expression.
- In the final step, we implement the simplified logical expression. To express the implementation, we use the graphical notation.

The following sections give more details on these steps.

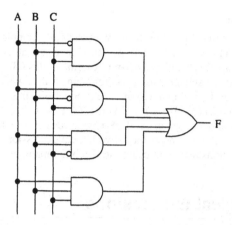

Figure 2.4 Logic circuit for the 3-input majority function using the bubble notation.

Bubble Notation

In large circuits, drawing inverters can be avoided by following what is known as the "bubble" notation. The use of the bubble notation simplifies the circuit diagrams. To appreciate the reduced complexity, compare the bubble notation circuit for the 3-input majority function in Figure 2.4 with that in Figure 2.3.

Deriving Logical Expressions

We can write a logical expression from a truth table in one of two forms: *sum-of-products* (SOP) and *product-of-sums* (POS) forms. In sum-of-products form, we specify the combination of inputs for which the output should be 1. In product-of-sums form, we specify the combinations of inputs for which the output should be 0.

Sum-of-Products Form

In this form, each input combination for which the output is 1 is expressed as an **and** term. This is the *product term* as we use · to represent the AND operation. These product terms are ORed together. That is why it is called sum-of-products as we use + for the OR operation to get the final logical expression. In deriving the product terms, we write the variable if its value is 1 or its complement if 0.

Let us look at the 3-input majority function. The truth table is given in Table 2.1. There are four 1 outputs in this function. So, our logical expression will have four product terms. The first product term we write is for row 4 with a 1 output. Since A has a value of 0, we use its complement in the product term while using B and C as they have 1 as their value in this row. Thus, the product term for this row is $\overline{A}\,B\,C$. The product term for row 6 is $A\,\overline{B}\,C$. Product terms for rows 7 and 8 are $A\,B\,\overline{C}$ and $A\,B\,C$, respectively. ORing these four product terms gives the logical expression as $\overline{A}\,B\,C + A\,\overline{B}\,C + A\,B\,\overline{C} + A\,B\,C$.

Product-of-Sums Form

This is the dual form of the sum-of-products form. We essentially complement what we have done to obtain the sum-of-products expression. Here we look for rows that have a 0 output. Each such row input variable combination is expressed as an OR term. In this OR term, we use the variable if its value in the row being considered is 0 or its complement if 1. We AND these sum terms to get the final product-of-sums logical expression. The product-of-sums expression for the 3-input majority function is $(A + B + C)(A + B + \overline{C})(A + \overline{B} + C)(\overline{A} + B + C)$.

This logical expression and the sum-of-products expressions derived before represent the same truth table. Thus, despite their appearance, these two logical expressions are logically equivalent. We can prove this logical equivalence by using the algebraic manipulation method described in the next section.

Simplifying Logical Expressions

The sum-of-products and product-of-sums logical expressions can be used to come up with a crude implementation that uses only the AND, OR, and NOT gates. The implementation process is straightforward. We illustrate the process for sum-of-products expressions. Figure 2.3 shows the brute force implementation of the sum-of-products expression we derived for the 3-input majority function. If we simplify the logical expression, we can get a more efficient implementation (see Figure 2.5).

Let us now focus on how we can simplify the logical expressions obtained from truth tables. Our focus is on sum-of-products expressions. There are three basic techniques: the algebraic manipulation, Karnaugh map, and Quine–McCluskey methods. Algebraic manipulation uses Boolean laws to derive a simplified logical expression. The Karnaugh map method uses a graphical form and is suitable for simplifying logical expressions with a small number of variables. The last method is a tabular method and is particularly suitable for simplifying logical expressions with a large number of variables. In addition, the Quine–McCluskey method can be used to automate the simplification process. In this section, we discuss the first two methods (for details on the last method, see *Fundamentals of Computer Organization and Design* by Dandamudi).

Algebraic Manipulation

In this method, we use the Boolean algebra to manipulate logical expressions. We need Boolean identities to facilitate this manipulation. These are discussed next. Following this discussion, we show how the identities developed can be used to simplify logical expressions.

Table 2.2 presents some basic Boolean laws. For most laws, there are two versions: an **and** version and an **or** version. If there is only one version, we list it under the **and** version. We can transform a law from the **and** version to the **or** version by replacing each 1 with a 0, 0 with a 1, + with a ·, and · with a +. This relationship is called *duality*.

We can use the Boolean laws to simplify the logical expressions. We illustrate this method by looking at the sum-of-products expression for the majority function. A straightforward simplification leads us to the following expression:

$$\text{Majority function} = \overline{A}BC + A\overline{B}C + \underbrace{AB\overline{C} + ABC}_{AB}$$

$$= \overline{A}BC + A\overline{B}C + AB.$$

Table 2.2 Boolean laws

Name	**and** version	**or** version
Identity	$x \cdot 1 = x$	$x + 0 = x$
Complement	$x \cdot \overline{x} = 0$	$x + \overline{x} = 1$
Commutative	$x \cdot y = y \cdot x$	$x + y = y + x$
Distribution	$x \cdot (y + z) = (x \cdot y) + (x \cdot z)$	$x + (y \cdot z) = (x + y) \cdot (x + z)$
Idempotent	$x \cdot x = x$	$x + x = x$
Null	$x \cdot 0 = 0$	$x + 1 = 1$
Involution	$\overline{\overline{x}} = x$	—
Absorption	$x \cdot (x + y) = x$	$x + (x \cdot y) = x$
Associative	$x \cdot (y \cdot z) = (x \cdot y) \cdot z$	$x + (y + z) = (x + y) + z$
de Morgan	$\overline{x \cdot y} = \overline{x} + \overline{y}$	$\overline{x + y} = \overline{x} \cdot \overline{y}$

Do you know if this is the final simplified form? This is the hard part in applying algebraic manipulation (in addition to the inherent problem of which rule should be applied). This method definitely requires good intuition, which often implies that one needs experience to know if the final form has been derived. In our example, the expression can be further simplified. We start by rewriting the original logical expression by repeating the term A B C twice and then simplifying the expression as shown below.

$$\text{Majority function} = \overline{A}\,B\,C + A\,\overline{B}\,C + A\,B\,\overline{C} + A\,B\,C + \underbrace{A\,B\,C + A\,B\,C}_{\text{Added extra}}$$

$$= \underbrace{\overline{A}\,B\,C + A\,B\,C}_{B\,C} + \underbrace{A\,\overline{B}\,C + A\,B\,C}_{A\,C} + \underbrace{A\,B\,\overline{C} + A\,B\,C}_{A\,B}$$

$$= B\,C + A\,C + A\,B.$$

This is the final simplified expression. In the next section, we show a simpler method to derive this expression. Figure 2.5 shows an implementation of this logical expression.

We can see the benefits of implementing the simplified logical expressions by comparing this implementation with the one shown in Figure 2.3. The simplified version reduces not only the gate count but also the gate complexity.

Karnaugh Map Method

This is a graphical method and is suitable for simplifying logical expressions with a small number of Boolean variables (typically six or less). It provides a straightforward method to derive minimal sum-of-products expressions. This method is preferred to the algebraic method as it takes the guesswork out of the simplification process. For example, in the previous majority function example, it was not straightforward to guess that we have to duplicate the term A B C twice in order to get the final logical expression.

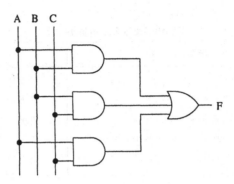

Figure 2.5 An implementation of the simplified 3-input majority function.

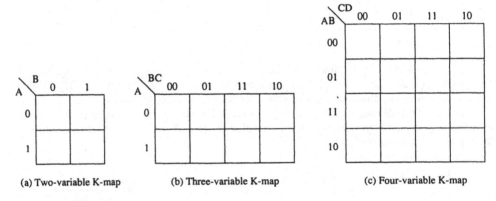

(a) Two-variable K-map   (b) Three-variable K-map   (c) Four-variable K-map

Figure 2.6 Maps used for simplifying 2-, 3-, and 4-variable logical expressions using the Karnaugh map method.

The Karnaugh map method uses maps to represent the logical function output. Figure 2.6 shows the maps used for 2-, 3-, and 4-variable logical expressions. Each cell in these maps represents a particular input combination. Each cell is filled with the output value of the function corresponding to the input combination represented by the cell. For example, the bottom left-hand cell represents the input combination $A = 1$ and $B = 0$ for the two-variable map (Figure 2.6a), $A = 1$, $B = 0$, and $C = 0$ for the three-variable map (Figure 2.6b), and $A = 1$, $B = 0$, $C = 0$, and $D = 0$ for the four-variable map (Figure 2.6c).

The basic idea behind this method is to label cells such that the neighboring cells differ in only one input bit position. This is the reason why the cells are labeled 00, 01, 11, 10 (notice the change in the order of the last two labels from the normal binary number order). What we are doing is labeling with a Hamming distance of 1. Hamming distance is the number of bit positions in which

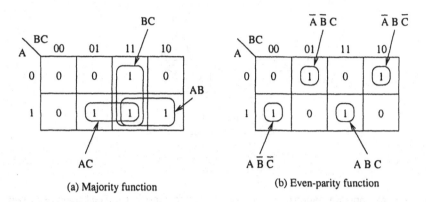

(a) Majority function   (b) Even-parity function

Figure 2.7 Three-variable logical expression simplification using the Karnaugh map method: (a) majority function; (b) even-parity function.

two binary numbers differ. This labeling is also called *gray code*. Why are we so interested in this gray code labeling? Simply because we can then eliminate a variable as the following holds:

$$AB\overline{C}D + ABCD = ABD.$$

Figure 2.7 shows how the maps are used to obtain minimal sum-of-products expressions for three-variable logical expressions. Notice that each cell is filled with the output value of the function corresponding to the input combination for that cell. After the map of a logical function is obtained, we can derive a simplified logical expression by grouping neighboring cells with 1 into areas. Let us first concentrate on the majority function map shown in Figure 2.7a. The two cells in the third column are combined into one area. These two cells represent inputs $\overline{A}$B C (top cell) and A B C (bottom cell). We can, therefore, combine these two cells to yield a product term B C. Similarly, we can combine the three 1s in the bottom row into two areas of two cells each. The corresponding product terms for these two areas are A C and A B as shown in Figure 2.7a. Now we can write the minimal expression as B C + A C + A B, which is what we got in the last section using the algebraic simplification process. Notice that the cell for A B C (third cell in the bottom row) participates in all three areas. This is fine. What this means is that we need to duplicate this term two times to simplify the expression. This is exactly what we did in our algebraic simplification procedure.

We now have the necessary intuition to develop the required rules for simplification. These simple rules govern the simplification process:

1. Form regular areas that contain 2^i cells, where $i \geq 0$. What we mean by a regular area is that they can be either rectangles or squares. For example, we cannot use an "L" shaped area.

2. Use a minimum number of areas to cover all cells with 1. This implies that we should form as large an area as possible and redundant areas should be eliminated.

Once minimal areas have been formed, we write a logical expression for each area. These represent terms in the sum-of-products expressions. We can write the final expression by connecting the terms with OR.

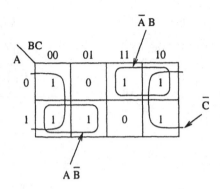

Figure 2.8 An example Karnaugh map that uses the fact that the first and last columns are adjacent.

In Figure 2.7a, we cannot form a regular area with four cells. Next we have to see if we can form areas of two cells. The answer is yes. Let us assume that we first formed a vertical area (labeled B C). That leaves two 1s uncovered by an area. So, we form two more areas to cover these two 1s. We also make sure that we indeed need these three areas to cover all 1s. Our next step is to write the logical expression for these areas.

When writing an expression for an area, look at the values of a variable that is 0 as well as 1. For example, for the area identified by B C, the variable A has 0 and 1. That is, the two cells we are combining represent $\overline{A}$ B C and A B C. Thus, we can eliminate variable A. The variables B and C have the same value for the whole area. Since they both have the value 1, we write B C as the expression for this area. It is straightforward to see that the other two areas are represented by A C and A B.

If we look at the Karnaugh map for the even-parity function (Figure 2.7b), we find that we cannot form areas bigger than one cell. This tells us that no further simplification is possible for this function.

Note that, in the three-variable maps, the first and last columns are adjacent. We did not need this fact in our previous two examples. You can visualize the Karnaugh map as a tube, cut open to draw in two dimensions. This fact is important because we can combine these two columns into a square area as shown in Figure 2.8. This square area is represented by $\overline{C}$.

You might have noticed that we can eliminate $\log_2 n$ variables from the product term, where n is the number of cells in the area. For example, the four-cell square in Figure 2.8 eliminates two variables from the product term that represents this area.

Figure 2.9 shows an example of a four-variable logical expression simplification using the Karnaugh map method. *It is important to remember the fact that first and last columns as well as first and last rows are adjacent.* Then it is not difficult to see why the four corner cells form a regular area and are represented by the expression $\overline{B}\,\overline{D}$. In writing an expression for an area, look at the input variables and ignore those that assume both 0 and 1. For example, for this weird square area, looking at the first and last rows, we notice that variable A has 0 for the first row and 1 for the last row. Thus, we eliminate A. Since B has a value of 0, we use $\overline{B}$. Similarly, by looking at the first and last columns, we eliminate C. We use $\overline{D}$ as D has a value of 0. Thus, the expression for this area is $\overline{B}\,\overline{D}$. Following our simplification procedure to cover all cells with 1, we get the

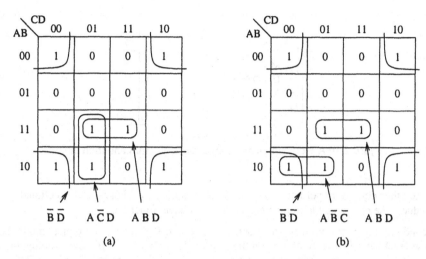

Figure 2.9 Different minimal expressions will result depending on the groupings.

following minimal expression for Figure 2.9a:

$$\overline{B}\overline{D} + A\overline{C}D + ABD.$$

We also note from Figure 2.9 that a different grouping leads to a different minimal expression. The logical expression for Figure 2.9b is

$$\overline{B}\overline{D} + A\overline{B}\overline{C} + ABD.$$

Even though this expression is slightly different from the logical expression obtained from Figure 2.9a, both expressions are minimal and logically equivalent.

The best way to understand the Karnaugh map method is to practice until you develop your intuition. After that, it is unlikely you will ever forget how this method works even if you have not used it in years.

Combinational Circuits

So far, we have focused on implementations using only the basic gates. One key characteristic of the circuits that we have designed so far is that the output of the circuit is a function of the inputs. Such devices are called *combinational circuits* as the output can be expressed as a combination of the inputs. We continue our discussion of combinational circuits in this section.

Although gate-level abstraction is better than working at the transistor level, a higher level of abstraction is needed in designing and building complex digital systems. We now discuss some combinational circuits that provide this higher level of abstraction.

Higher-level abstraction helps the digital circuit design and implementation process in several ways. The most important ones are the following:

1. Higher-level abstraction helps us in the logical design process as we can use functional building blocks that typically require several gates to implement. This, therefore, reduces the complexity.

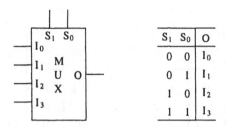

Figure 2.10 A 4-data input multiplexer block diagram and truth table.

2. The other equally important point is that the use of these higher-level functional devices reduces the chip count to implement a complex logical function.

The second point is important from the practical viewpoint. If you look at a typical motherboard, these low-level gates take a lot of area on the printed circuit board (PCB). Even though the low-level gate chips were introduced in the 1970s, you still find them sprinkled on your PCB along with your Pentium processor. In fact, they seem to take more space. Thus, reducing the chip count is important to make your circuit compact. The combinational circuits provide one mechanism to incorporate a higher level of integration.

The reduced chip count also helps in reducing the production cost (fewer ICs to insert and solder) and improving the reliability. Several combinational circuits are available for implementation. Here we look at a sampler of these circuits.

Multiplexers

A multiplexer (MUX) is characterized by 2^n data inputs, n selection inputs, and a single output. The block diagram representation of a 4-input multiplexer (4-to-1 multiplexer) is shown in Figure 2.10. The multiplexer connects one of 2^n inputs, selected by the selection inputs, to the output. Treating the selection input as a binary number, data input I_i is connected to the output when the selection input is i as shown in Figure 2.10.

Figure 2.11 shows an implementation of a 4-to-1 multiplexer. If you look closely, it somewhat resembles our logic circuit used by the brute force method for implementing sum-of-products expressions (compare this figure with Figure 2.3 on page 16). This visual observation is useful in developing our intuition about one important property of the multiplexers: we can implement any logical function using only multiplexers. The best thing about using multiplexers in implementing a logical function is that you don't have to simplify the logical expression. We can proceed directly from the truth table to implementation, using the multiplexer as the building block.

How do we implement a truth table using the multiplexer? Simple. Connect the logical variables in the logical expression as the selection inputs and the function outputs as constants to the data inputs. To follow this straightforward implementation, we need a 2^b data input multiplexer with b selection inputs to implement a b variable logical expression. The process is best illustrated by means of an example.

Figure 2.12 shows how an 8-to-1 multiplexer can be used to implement our two running examples: the 3-input majority and 3-input even-parity functions. From these examples, you can see that the data input is simply a copy of the output column in the corresponding truth table. You just need to take care how you connect the logical variables: connect the most significant variable in the truth table to the most significant selection input of the multiplexer as shown in Figure 2.12.

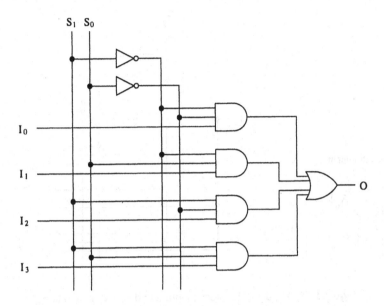

Figure 2.11 A 4-to-1 multiplexer implementation using the basic gates.

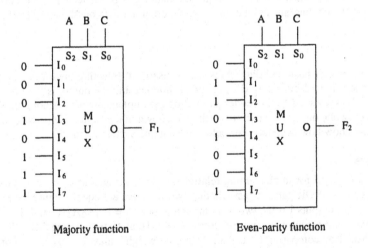

Figure 2.12 Two example implementations using an 8-to-1 multiplexer.

Demultiplexers

The demultiplexer (DeMUX) performs the complementary operation of a multiplexer. As in the multiplexer, a demultiplexer has n selection inputs. However, the roles of data input and output are reversed. In a demultiplexer with n selection inputs, there are 2^n data outputs and one data input.

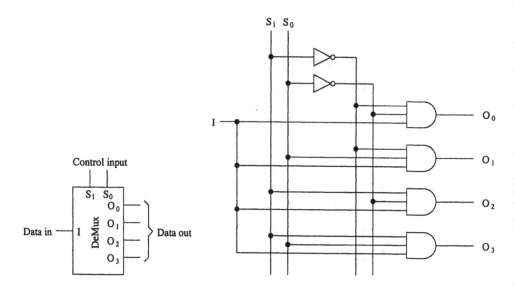

Figure 2.13 Demultiplexer block diagram and its implementation.

Depending on the value of the selection input, the data input is connected to the corresponding data output. The block diagram and the implementation of a 4-data out demultiplexer is shown in Figure 2.13.

Decoders

The decoder is another basic building block that is useful in selecting one-out-of-N lines. The input to a decoder is an I-bit binary (i.e., encoded) number and the output is 2^I bits of decoded data. Figure 2.14 shows a 2-to-4 decoder and its logical implementation. Among the 2^I outputs of a decoder, only one output line is 1 at any time as shown in the truth table (Figure 2.14). In the next chapter we show how decoders are useful in designing system memory.

Comparators

Comparators are useful for implementing relational operations such as =, <, >, and so on. For example, we can use XOR gates to test whether two numbers are equal. Figure 2.15 shows a 4-bit comparator that outputs 1 if the two 4-bit input numbers $A = A_3A_2A_1A_0$ and $B = B_3B_2B_1B_0$ match. However, implementing < and > is more involved than testing for equality. While equality can be established by comparing bit by bit, positional weights must be taken into consideration when comparing two numbers for < and >. We leave it as an exercise to design such a circuit.

Adders

We now look at adder circuits that provide the basic capability to perform arithmetic operations. The simplest of the adders is called a *half-adder*, which adds two bits and produces a sum and carry output as shown in Figure 2.16a. From the truth table it is straightforward to see that the

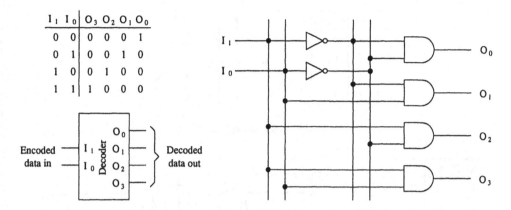

I_1	I_0	O_3	O_2	O_1	O_0
0	0	0	0	0	1
0	1	0	0	1	0
1	0	0	1	0	0
1	1	1	0	0	0

Figure 2.14 Decoder block diagram and its implementation.

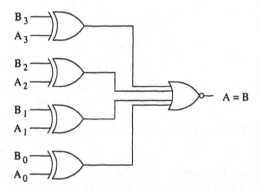

Figure 2.15 A 4-bit comparator implementation using XOR gates.

carry output C_{out} can be generated by a single AND gate and the sum output by a single XOR gate.

The problem with the half-adder is that we cannot use it to build adders that can add more than two 1-bit numbers. If we want to use the 1-bit adder as a building block to construct larger adders that can add two N-bit numbers, we need an adder that takes the two input bits and a potential carry generated by the previous bit position. This is what the *full-adder* does. A full adder takes three bits and produces two outputs as shown in Figure 2.16b. An implementation of the full-adder is shown in Figure 2.16.

Using full adders, it is straightforward to build an adder that can add two N-bit numbers. An example 16-bit adder is shown in Figure 2.17. Such adders are called *ripple-carry adders* as the carry ripples through bit positions 1 through 15. Let us assume that this ripple-carry adder is using the full adder shown in Figure 2.16b. If we assume a gate delay of 5 ns, each full adder takes three gate delays (=15 ns) to generate C_{out}. Thus, the 16-bit ripple-carry adder shown in Figure 2.17

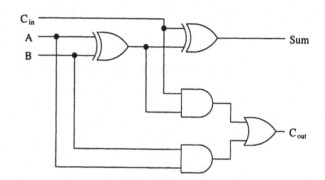

A	B	Sum	C_out
0	0	0	0
0	1	1	0
1	0	1	0
1	1	0	1

(a) Half-adder truth table and implementation

A	B	C_{in}	Sum	C_out
0	0	0	0	0
0	0	1	1	0
0	1	0	1	0
0	1	1	0	1
1	0	0	1	0
1	0	1	0	1
1	1	0	0	1
1	1	1	1	1

(b) Full-adder truth table and implementation

Figure 2.16 Full- and half-adder truth tables and implementations.

takes $16 \times 15 = 240$ ns. If we were to use this type of adder circuit in a system, it cannot run more than $1/240$ ns $= 4$ MHz with each addition taking about a clock cycle.

How can we speed up multibit adders? If we analyze the reasons for the "slowness" of the ripple-carry adders, we see that carry propagation is causing the delay in producing the final N-bit output. If we want to improve the performance, we have to remove this dependency and determine the required carry-in for each bit position independently. Such adders are called *carry lookahead adders*. The main problem with these adders is that they are complex to implement for long words. To see why this is so and also to give you an idea of how each full adder can generate its own carry-in bit, let us look at the logical expression that should be implemented to generate the carry-in. Carry-out from the rightmost bit position C_0 is obtained as

$$C_0 = A_0 B_0 .$$

C_1 is given by

$$C_1 = C_0 (A_1 + B_1) + A_1 B_1 .$$

By substituting $A_0 B_0$ for C_0, we get

$$C_1 = A_0 B_0 A_1 + A_0 B_0 B_1 + A_1 B_1 .$$

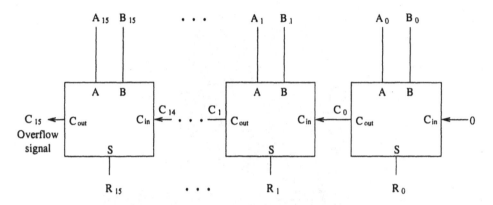

Figure 2.17 A 16-bit ripple-carry adder using the full adder building blocks.

Similarly, we get C_2 as

$$C_2 = C_1 (A_2 + B_2) + A_2 B_2$$
$$= A_2 A_0 B_0 A_1 + A_2 A_0 B_0 B_1 + A_2 A_1 B_1$$
$$+ B_2 A_0 B_0 A_1 + B_2 A_0 B_0 B_1 + B_2 A_1 B_1 + A_2 B_2 .$$

Using this procedure, we can generate the necessary carry-in inputs independently. The logical expression for C_i is a sum-of-products expression involving only A_k and B_k, $i \leq k \leq 0$. Thus, independent of the length of the word, only two gate delays are involved, assuming a single gate can implement each product term. The complexity of implementing such a circuit makes it impractical for more than 8-bit words. Typically, carry lookahead is implemented at the 4- or 8-bit level. We can apply our ripple-carry method of building higher word length adders by using these 4- or 8-bit carry lookahead adders.

Programmable Logic Devices

We have seen several ways of implementing sum-of-products expressions. Programmable logic devices provide yet another way to implement these expressions. There are two types of these devices that are very similar to each other. The next two subsections describe these devices.

Programmable Logic Arrays (PLAs)

PLA is a field programmable device to implement sum-of-product expressions. It consists of an AND array and an OR array as shown in Figure 2.18. A PLA takes N inputs and produces M outputs. Each input is a logical variable. Each output of a PLA represents a logical function output. Internally, each input is complemented, and a total of $2N$ inputs is connected to each AND gate in the AND array through a fuse. The example PLA, shown in Figure 2.18, is a 2×2 PLA with two inputs and two outputs. Each AND gate receives four inputs: I_0, $\bar{I}_0$, I_1, and $\bar{I}_1$. The fuses are shown as small white rectangles. Each AND gate can be used to implement a product term in the sum-of-products expression.

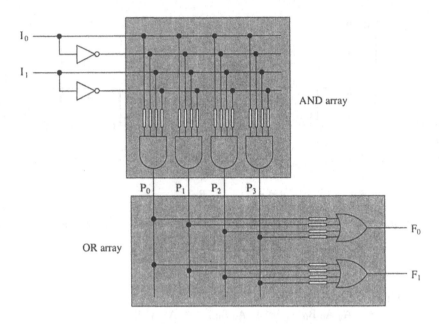

Figure 2.18 An example PLA with two inputs and two outputs.

The OR array is organized similarly except that the inputs to the OR gates are the outputs of the AND array. Thus, the number of inputs to each OR gate is equal to the number of AND gates in the AND array. The output of each OR gate represents a function output.

When the chip is shipped from the factory, all fuses are intact. We program the PLA by selectively blowing some fuses (generally by passing a high current through them). The chip design guarantees that an input with a blown fuse acts as 1 for the AND gates and as 0 for the OR gates.

Figure 2.19 shows an example implementation of functions F_0 and F_1. The rightmost AND gate in the AND array produces the product term $A\,B$. To produce this output, the inputs of this gate are programmed by blowing the second and fourth fuses that connect inputs $\overline{A}$ and $\overline{B}$, respectively. Programming a PLA to implement a sum-of-products function involves implementing each product term by an AND gate. Then a single OR gate in the OR array is used to obtain the final function. In Figure 2.19, we are using two product terms generated by the middle two AND gates (P_1 and P_2) as inputs to both OR gates as these two terms appear in both F_0 and F_1.

To simplify specification of the connections, the notation shown in Figure 2.20 is used. Each AND and OR gate input is represented by a single line. A × is placed if the corresponding input is connected to the AND or OR gates as shown in this figure.

Programmable Array Logic Devices (PALs)

PLAs are very flexible in implementing sum-of-products expressions. However, the cost of providing a large number of fuses is high. For example, a 12×12 PLA with a 50-gate AND array and 12-gate OR array requires $24 \times 50 = 1200$ fuses for the AND array and $50 \times 12 = 600$ fuses for the OR array for a total of 1800 fuses. We can reduce this complexity by noting that we can

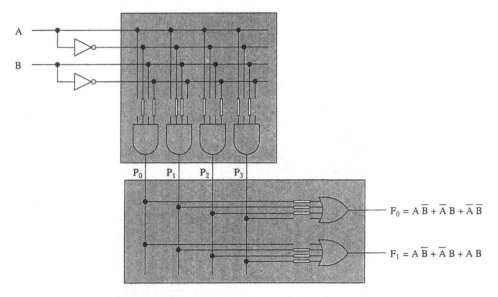

Figure 2.19 Implementation of functions F_0 and F_1 using the example PLA.

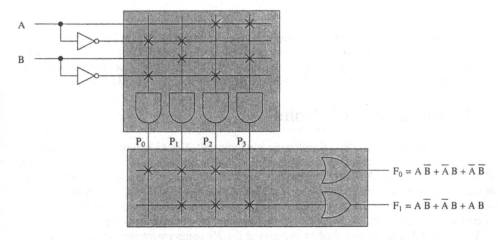

Figure 2.20 A simplified notation to show implementation details of a PLA.

retain most of the flexibility by cutting down the set of fuses in the OR array. This is the rationale for PALs. Due to their cost advantage, most manufacturers produce only PALs.

PALs are very similar to PLAs except that there is no programmable OR array. Instead, the OR connections are fixed. Figure 2.21 shows a PAL with the bottom OR gate connected to the leftmost two product terms and the other OR gate connected to the other two product terms. As a

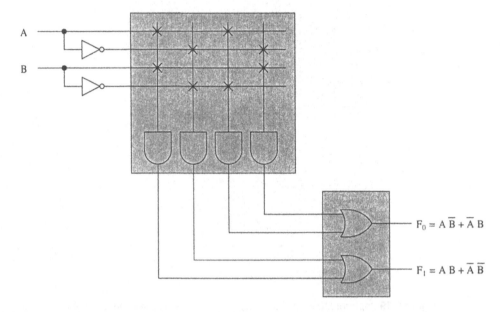

Figure 2.21 Programmable array logic device with fixed OR gate connections. We have used the simplified notation to indicate the connections in the AND array.

result of these connections, we cannot implement the two functions shown in Figure 2.20. This is the loss of flexibility that sometimes may cause problems but in practice is not such a big problem. But the advantage of PAL devices is that we can cut down all the OR array fuses that are present in a PLA. In the last example, we reduce the number of fuses by a third—from 1800 fuses to 1200.

Arithmetic and Logic Units

We are now ready to design our own arithmetic and logic unit. The ALU forms the computational core of a processor, performing basic arithmetic and logical operations such as integer addition, subtraction, and logical AND and OR functions. Figure 2.22 shows an example ALU that can perform two arithmetic functions (addition and subtraction) and two logical functions (AND and OR). We use a multiplexer to select one of the four functions. The implementation is straightforward except that we implement the subtractor using a full adder by negating the B input.

To see why this is so, you need to understand the 2's complement representation for negative numbers. A detailed discussion of this number representation is given in Appendix A (see page 468). Here we give a brief explanation. The operation $(x - y)$ is treated as adding $-y$ to x. That is, $(x - y)$ is implemented as $x + (-y)$ so that we can use an adder to perform subtraction. For example, $12 - 5$ is implemented by adding -5 to 12. In the 2's complement notation, -5 is represented as 1011B, which is obtained by complementing the bits of number 5 and adding 1. This operation produces the correct result as shown below:

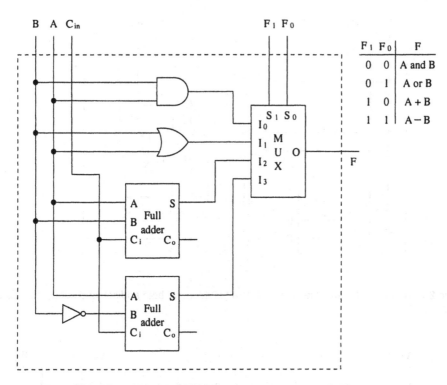

Figure 2.22 A simple 1-bit ALU that can perform addition, subtraction, AND, and OR operations. The carry output of the circuit is incomplete in this figure as a better and more efficient circuit is shown in the next figure. Note: "+" and "−" represent arithmetic addition and subtraction operations, respectively.

$$12D = 1100B$$
$$-5D = 1011B$$
$$\overline{0111B} = 7D$$

To implement the subtract operation, we first convert B to −B in 2's complement representation. We get the 2's complement representation by complementing the bits and adding 1. We need an inverter to complement. The required 1 is added via C_{in}.

Since the difference between the adder and subtractor is really the negation of the one input, we can get a better circuit by using a programmable inverter. Figure 2.23 shows the final design with the XOR gate acting as a programmable inverter. Remember that, when one of the inputs is one, the XOR gate acts as an inverter for the other input. We can use these 1-bit ALUs to get word-length ALUs. Figure 2.24 shows an implementation of a 16-bit ALU using the 1-bit ALU of Figure 2.23.

To illustrate how the circuit in Figure 2.24 subtracts two 16-bit numbers, let us consider an example with A = 1001 1110 1101 1110 and B = 0110 1011 0110 1101. Since B is internally complemented, we get $\overline{B}$ = 1001 0100 1001 0010. Now we add A and $\overline{B}$ with the carry-in to the rightmost bit set to 1 (through the F_0 bit):

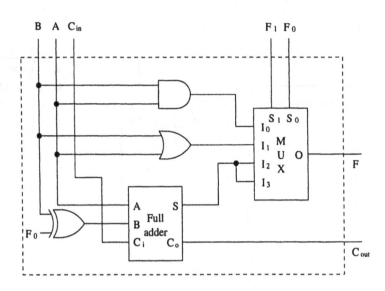

Figure 2.23 A better 1-bit ALU that uses a single full adder for both addition and subtraction operations.

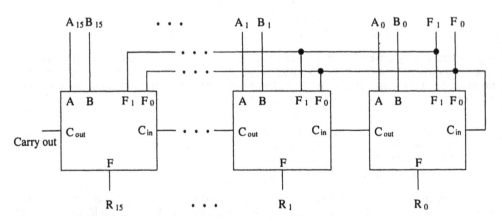

Figure 2.24 A 16-bit ALU built with the 1-bit ALU: The F_0 function bit sets C_{in} to 1 for the subtract operation. Logical operations ignore the carry bits.

$$1 \leftarrow \text{carry-in from } F_0$$

$$
\begin{array}{lcl}
A & = & 1001\ 1110\ 1101\ 1110 \\
\overline{B} & = & 1001\ 0100\ 1001\ 0010 \\
\hline
A - B & = & 0011\ 0011\ 0111\ 0001
\end{array}
$$

which is the correct value. If B is larger than A, we get a negative number. In this case, the result

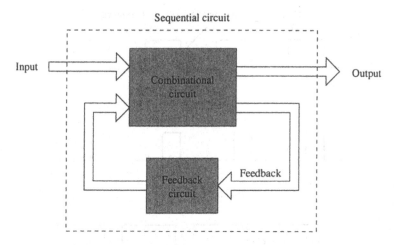

Figure 2.25 Main components of a sequential circuit.

will be in the 2's complement form. Also note that, in the 2's complement representation, we ignore any carry generated out of the most significant bit.

Sequential Circuits

The output of a combinational circuit depends only on the current inputs. In contrast, the output of a sequential circuit depends both on the current input values as well as the past inputs. This dependence on past inputs gives the property of "memory" for sequential circuits.

In general, the sequence of past inputs is encoded into a set of state variables. There is a feedback path that feeds these variables to the input of a combinational circuit as shown in Figure 2.25. Sometimes, this feedback consists of a simple interconnection of some outputs of the combinational circuit to its inputs. For the most part, however, the feedback circuit consists of elements such as flip-flops that we discuss later. These elements themselves are sequential circuits that can remember or store the state information. Next we introduce system clock to incorporate time into digital circuits.

System Clock

Digital circuits can operate in *asynchronous* or *synchronous* mode. Circuits that operate in asynchronous mode are independent of each other. That is, the time at which a change occurs in one circuit has no relation to the time a change occurs in another circuit. Asynchronous mode of operation causes serious problems in a typical digital system in which the output of one circuit goes as input to several others. Similarly, a single circuit may receive outputs of several circuits as inputs. Asynchronous mode of operation implies that all required inputs to a circuit may not be valid at the same time.

To avoid these problems, circuits are operated in synchronous mode. In this mode, all circuits in the system change their state at some precisely defined instants. The clock signal provides such

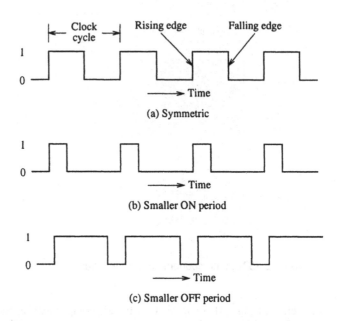

Figure 2.26 Three types of clock signals with the same clock period.

a global definition of time instants at which changes can take place. Implicit in this definition is the fact that the clock signal also specifies the speed at which a circuit can operate.

A clock is a sequence of 1s and 0s as shown in Figure 2.26. We refer to the period during which the clock is 1 as the ON period and the period with 0 as the OFF period. Even though we normally use symmetric clock signals with equal ON and OFF periods as in Figure 2.26a, clock signals can take asymmetric forms as shown in Figures 2.26b and c.

The clock signal edge going from 0 to 1 is referred to as the *rising edge* (also called the positive or leading edge). Analogously, we can define a *falling edge* as shown in Figure 2.26a. The falling edge is also referred to as a negative or trailing edge.

A clock cycle is defined as the time between two successive rising edges as shown in Figure 2.26. You can also treat the period between successive falling edges as a clock cycle.

Clock rate or frequency is measured in number of cycles per second. This number is referred to as Hertz (Hz). The clock period is defined as the time represented by one clock cycle. All three clock signals in Figure 2.26 have the same clock period.

$$\text{Clock period} = \frac{1}{\text{Clock frequency}}.$$

For example, a clock frequency of 1 GHz yields a clock period of

$$\frac{1}{1 \times 10^9} = 1 \text{ ns}.$$

Note that one nanosecond (ns) is equal to 10^{-9} second.

The clock signal serves two distinct purposes in a digital circuit. It provides the global synchronization signal for the entire system. Each clock cycle provides three distinct epochs: start of

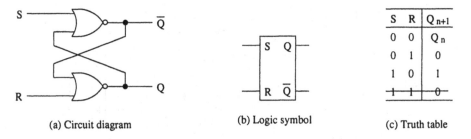

(a) Circuit diagram	(b) Logic symbol	(c) Truth table

S	R	Q_{n+1}
0	0	Q_n
0	1	0
1	0	1
~~1~~	~~1~~	~~0~~

Figure 2.27 A NOR gate implementation of the SR latch.

a clock cycle, end of a clock cycle, and an intermediate point at which the clock signal changes levels. This intermediate point is in the middle of a clock cycle for symmetric clock signals. The other equally important purpose is to provide timing information in the form of a clock period.

Latches

It is time to look at some simple sequential circuits that can remember a single bit value. We discuss latches in this section. Latches are level-sensitive devices in that the device responds to the input signal levels (high or low). In contrast, flip-flops are edge-triggered. That is, output changes only at either the rising or falling edge. We look at flip-flops in the next section.

SR Latch

The SR latch is the simplest of the sequential circuits that we consider. It requires just two NOR gates. The feedback in this latch is a simple connection from the output of one NOR gate to the input of the other NOR gate as shown in Figure 2.27a. The logic symbol for the SR latch is shown in Figure 2.27b.

A simplified truth table for the SR latch is shown in Figure 2.27c. The outputs of the two NOR gates are labeled Q and $\overline{Q}$ because these two outputs should be complementary in normal operating mode. We use the notation Q_n to represent the current value (i.e., current state) and Q_{n+1} to represent the next value (i.e., next state).

Let us analyze the truth table. First consider the two straightforward cases. When S = 0 and R = 1, we can see that independent of the current state, output Q is forced to be 0 as R is 1. Thus, the two inputs to the upper NOR gate are 0. This leads $\overline{Q}$ to be 1. This is a stable state. That is, Q and $\overline{Q}$ can stay at 0 and 1, respectively. You can verify that when S = 1 and R = 0, another stable state Q = 1 and $\overline{Q}$ = 0 results.

When both S and R are zero, the next output depends on the current output. Assume that the current output is Q = 1 and $\overline{Q}$ = 0. Thus, when you change inputs from S = 1 and R = 0 to S = R = 0, the next state Q_{n+1} remains the same as the current state Q_n. Now assume that the current state is Q = 0 and $\overline{Q}$ = 1. It is straightforward to verify that changing inputs from S = 0 and R = 1 to S = R = 0, leaves the output unchanged. We have summarized this behavior by placing Q_n as the output for S = R = 0 in the first row of Figure 2.27c.

What happens when both S and R are 1? As long as these two inputs are held high, both outputs are forced to take 0. We struck this state from the truth table to indicate that this input combination is undesirable. To see why this is the case, consider what happens when S and R

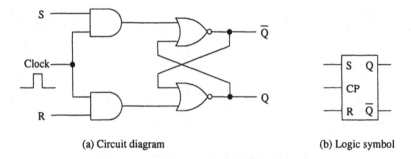

(a) Circuit diagram   (b) Logic symbol

Figure 2.28 Clocked SR latch.

inputs are changed from S = R = 1 to S = R = 0. It is only in theory that we can assume that both inputs change simultaneously. In practice, there is always some finite time difference between the two signal changes. If the S input goes low earlier than the R signal, the sequence of input changes is SR = 11 → 01 → 00. Because of the intermediate state SR = 01, the output will be Q = 0 and $\overline{Q}$ = 1.

If, on the other hand, the R signal goes low before the S signal does, the sequence of input changes is SR = 11 → 10 → 00. Because the transition goes through the SR = 10 intermediate state, the output will be Q = 1 and $\overline{Q}$ = 0. Thus, when the input changes from 11 to 00, the output is indeterminate. This is the reason we want to avoid this state.

The inputs S and R stand for "Set" and "Reset," respectively. When the set input is high (and reset is low), Q is set (i.e., Q = 1). On the other hand, if set is 0 and reset is 1, Q is reset or cleared (i.e., Q = 0).

From this discussion, it is clear that this latch is level sensitive. The outputs respond to changes in input levels. This is true for all the latches.

We notice that this simple latch has the capability to store a bit. To write 1 into this latch, set SR as 10; to write 0, use SR = 01. To retain a stored bit, keep both S and R inputs at 0. In summary, we have the capacity to write 0 or 1 and retain it as long as there is power to the circuit. This is the basic 1-bit cell that static RAMs use. Once we have the design to store a single bit, we can replicate this circuit to store wider data as well as multiple words. We look at memory design issues in the next chapter.

Clocked SR Latch

A basic problem with the SR latch is that the output follows the changes in the input. If we want to make the output respond to changes in the input at specific instants in order to synchronize with the rest of the system, we have to modify the circuit as shown in Figure 2.28a. The main change is that a clock input is used to gate the S and R inputs. These inputs are passed onto the original SR latch only when the clock signal is high. The inputs have no effect on the output when the clock signal is low. When the clock signal is high, the circuit implements the truth table of the SR latch given in Figure 2.27c. This latch is level sensitive as well. As long as the clock signal is high, the output responds to the SR inputs.

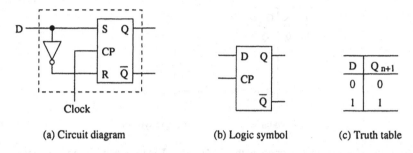

| | (a) Circuit diagram | (b) Logic symbol | (c) Truth table |

Figure 2.29 D latch uses an inverter to avoid the SR = 11 input combination.

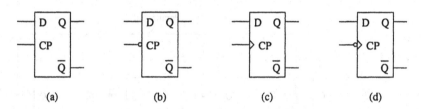

(a)   (b)   (c)   (d)

Figure 2.30 Logic symbol notation for latches and flip-flops: (a) high level-sensitive latch; (b) low level-sensitive latch; (c) positive edge-triggered flip-flop; (d) negative edge-triggered flip-flop.

D Latch

A problem with both versions of SR latches is that we have to avoid the SR = 11 input combination. This problem is solved by the D latch shown in Figure 2.29a. We use a single inverter to provide only complementary inputs at S and R inputs of the clocked SR latch. To retain the value, we maintain the clock input at 0. The logic symbol and the truth table for the D latch clearly show that it can store a single bit.

Storing a bit in the D-latch is straightforward. All we have to do is feed the data bit to the D input and apply a clock pulse to store the bit. Once stored, the latch retains the bit as long as the clock input is zero. This simple circuit is our first 1-bit memory. In the next chapter, we show how we can use this basic building block to design larger memories.

Flip-Flops

We have noted that flip-flops are edge-triggered devices whereas latches are level sensitive. In the logic symbol, we use an arrowhead on the clock input to indicate a positive edge-triggered flip-flop as shown in Figure 2.30c. The absence of this arrowhead indicates a high level-sensitive latch (see Figure 2.30a). We add a bubble in front of the clock input to indicate a negative edge-triggered flip-flop (Figure 2.30d) or a low level-sensitive latch (Figure 2.30b).

As is obvious from the bubble notation, we can convert a high level-sensitive latch to a low level-sensitive one by feeding the clock signal through an inverter. Recall that the bubble represents an inverter (see page 17). Similarly, we can invert the clock signal to change a negative edge-triggered flip-flop to a positive edge-triggered one.

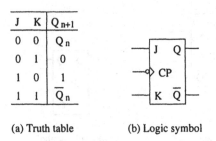

J	K	Q_{n+1}
0	0	Q_n
0	1	0
1	0	1
1	1	$\overline{Q}_n$

(a) Truth table   (b) Logic symbol

Figure 2.31 Truth table and logic symbol of the JK flip-flop. The logic symbol is for a negative edge triggered flip-flop. For a negative flip-flop, delete the bubble on the clock input.

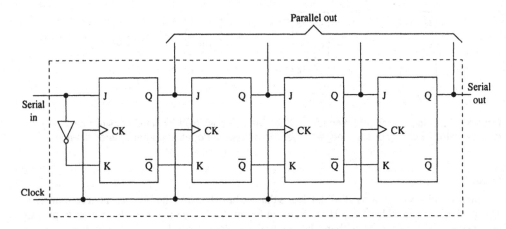

Figure 2.32 A 4-bit shift register using JK flip-flops.

In this section, we look at JK flip-flops. The truth table and logic symbol of this flip-flop is shown in Figure 2.31. Unlike the SR latch, the JK flip-flop allows all four input combinations. When JK = 11, the output toggles. This characteristic is used to build counters. Next we show couple of example sequential circuits that use the JK flip-flops.

Shift Registers

Shift registers, as the name suggests, shift data left or right with each clock pulse. Designing a shift register is relatively straightforward as shown in Figure 2.32. This shift register, built with positive edge-triggered JK flip-flops, shifts data to the right. For the first JK flip-flop, we need an inverter so that the K input is the complement of the data coming in ("Serial in" input). The data out, taken from the Q output of the rightmost JK flip-flop, is a copy of the input serial signal except that this signal is delayed by four clock periods. This is one of the uses of the shift registers.

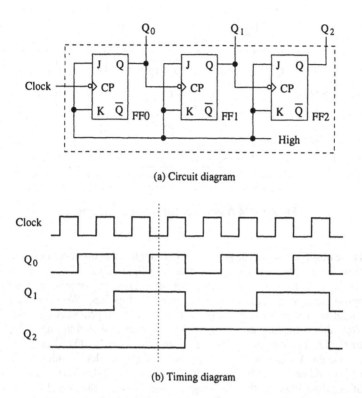

(a) Circuit diagram

(b) Timing diagram

Figure 2.33 A binary ripple counter implementation using negative edge-triggered JK flip-flops.

We can also use a shift register for serial-to-parallel conversion. For example, a serial signal, given as input to the shift register in Figure 2.32, produces a parallel 4-bit output (taken from the four Q outputs of the JK flip-flops) as shown in Figure 2.32. Even though we have not shown it here, we can design a shift register that accepts input in parallel (i.e., parallel load) as well as serial form. Shift registers are also useful in implementing logical bit shift operations in the ALU of a processor.

Counters

A counter is another example of a sequential circuit that is often used in digital circuits. To see how we can build a counter, let us consider the simplest of all counters: the binary counter. A binary counter with B bits can count from 0 to $2^B - 1$. For example, a 3-bit binary counter can count from 0 to 7. After counting eight (with a count value of 7), the count value wraps around to zero. Such a counter is called a modulo-8 counter.

We know that a modulo-8 counter requires 3 bits to represent the count value. In general, a modulo-2^B counter requires B bits (i.e., $\log_2 2^B$ bits). To develop our intuition, it is helpful to look at the values 0 through 7, written in the binary form in that sequence. If you look at the rightmost bit, you will notice that it changes with every count. The middle bit changes whenever the rightmost bit changes from 1 to 0. The leftmost bit changes whenever the middle bit changes

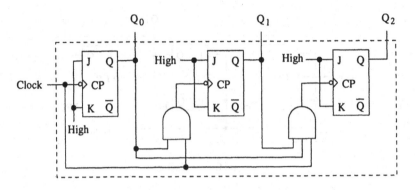

Figure 2.34 A synchronous modulo-8 counter.

from 1 to 0. These observations can be generalized to counters that use more bits. There is a simple rule that governs the counter behavior: a bit changes (flips) its value whenever its immediately preceding right bit goes from 1 to 0. This observation gives the necessary clue to design our counter. Suppose we have a negative edge-triggered JK flip-flop. We know that this flip-flop changes its output with every negative edge on the clock input, provided we hold both J and K inputs high. Well, that is the final design of our 3-bit counter as shown in Figure 2.33.

We operate the JK flip-flops in the "toggle" mode with JK = 11. The Q output of one flip-flop is connected as the clock input of the next flip-flop. The input clock, which drives our counter, is applied to FF0. When we write the counter output as $Q_2Q_1Q_0$, the count value represents the number of negative edges in the clock signal. For example, the dotted line in Figure 2.33b represents $Q_2Q_1Q_0 = 011$. This value matches the number of falling edges to the left of the dotted line in the input clock.

Counters are also useful in generating clocks with different frequencies by dividing the input clock. For example, the frequency of the clock signal at Q_0 output is half of the input clock. Similarly, frequencies of the signals at Q_1 and Q_2 are one-fourth and one-eighth of the counter input clock frequency.

The counter design shown in Figure 2.33 is called a *ripple counter* as the count bits ripple from the rightmost to the leftmost bit (i.e., in our example, from FF0 to FF2). A major problem with ripple counters is that they take a long time to propagate the count value. We have had a similar discussion about ripple carry adders on page 28.

How can we speed up the operation of the ripple binary counters? We apply the same trick that we used to derive the carry lookahead adder on page 28. We can design a counter in which all output bits change more or less at the same time. These are called *synchronous counters*. We can obtain a synchronous counter by manipulating the clock input to each flip-flop. We observe from the timing diagram in Figure 2.33b that a clock input should be applied to a flip-flop if all the previous bits are 1. For example, a clock input should be applied to FF1 whenever the output of FF0 is 1. Similarly, a clock input for FF2 should be applied when the outputs of FF0 and FF1 are both 1. A synchronous counter based on this observation is shown in Figure 2.34.

Sequential circuit design is relatively more complex than designing a combinational circuit. A detailed discussion of this topic is outside the scope of this book. If you are interested in this topic, you can refer to *Fundamentals of Computer Organization and Design* by Dandamudi for more details.

Summary

A computer system consists of three main components: processor, memory, and I/O. These three components are glued together by a system bus. The system bus consists of three buses: data bus, address bus, and control bus. The address bus is used to carry the address information. The width of this bus determines the memory address space of the processor. The data bus is used for transferring data between these components (e.g., from memory to processor). The data bus width determines the size of the data moved in one transfer cycle. The control bus provides several control signals to facilitate a variety of activities on the system bus. These activities include memory read, I/O write, and so on.

The remainder of the chapter looked at the digital logic circuits in detail. We introduced several simple logic gates such as AND, OR, NOT gates as well as NAND, NOR, and XOR gates. Although the first three gates are considered as the basic gates, we often find that the other three gates are useful in practice.

We described three ways of representing logical functions: truth table, logical expression, and graphical form. The truth table method is cumbersome for logical expressions with more than a few variables. Logical expression representation is useful to derive simplified expressions by applying Boolean identities. The graphical form is useful to implement logical circuits.

Logical expressions can be written in one of two basic forms: sum-of-products or product-of-sums. From either of these expressions, it is straightforward to obtain logic circuit implementations. However, such circuits are not the best designs as simplifying logical expressions can minimize the component count. Several methods are available to simplify logical expressions. We have discussed two of them: the algebraic and Karnaugh map methods.

Combinational circuits provide a higher level of abstraction than the basic logic gates. Higher-level logical functionality provided by these circuits helps in the design of complex digital circuits. We have discussed several commonly used combinational circuits including multiplexers, demultiplexers, decoders, comparators, adders, and ALUs.

We also presented details about two types of programmable logic devices: PLAs and PALs. These devices can also be used to implement any logical function. Both these devices use internal fuses that can be selectively blown to implement a given logical function. PALs reduce the complexity of the device by using fewer fuses than PLAs. As a result, most commercial implementations of programmable logic devices are PALs.

Our discussion of ALU design suggests that complex digital circuit design can be simplified by using the higher level of abstraction provided by the combinational circuits.

In combinational circuits, the output depends only on the current inputs. In contrast, output of a sequential circuit depends both on the current inputs as well as the past history. In other words, sequential circuits are state-dependent whereas the combinational circuits are stateless.

Design of a sequential circuit is relatively more complex than designing a combinational circuit. In sequential circuits, we need a notion of time. We introduced the clock signal to provide this timing information. Clocks also facilitate synchronization of actions in a large, complex digital system that has both combinational and sequential circuits.

We discussed two basic types of circuits: latches and flip-flops. The key difference between these two devices is that latches are level sensitive whereas flip-flops are edge-triggered. These devices can be used to store a single bit of data. Thus, they provide the basic capability to design memories. We discuss memory design in the next chapter.

We presented some example sequential circuits—shift registers and counters—that are commonly used in digital circuits. There are several other sequential circuit building blocks that are commercially available.

3

Memory Organization

In the last chapter, we have seen how flip-flops and latches can be used to store a bit. This chapter builds on this foundation and explains how we can use these basic devices and build larger memory blocks and modules. We start off with an overview of memory operations and the types of memory. The following section discusses how larger memories can be built using memory chips. The design process is fairly intuitive. The basic technique involves using a two-dimensional array of memory chips. A characteristic of these designs is the use of chip select. Chip select input can be used to select or deselect a chip or a memory module. Chip select allows us to connect multiple devices to the system bus. Appropriate chip select signal generation facilitates communication among the entities connected to the system bus.

Chip select logic is also useful in mapping memory modules to memory address space. We present details about two ways of mapping a memory module to the address space. Before ending the chapter, we describe how multibyte data are stored in memory and explain the reasons why data alignment leads to improved application performance. We end the chapter with a summary.

Introduction

The memory of a computer system consists of tiny electronic switches, with each switch set in one of two states: *open* or *closed*. It is, however, more convenient to think of these states as 0 and 1 rather than open and closed. A single such switch can be used to represent two (i.e., binary) numbers: a zero and a one. Thus, each switch can represent a *binary digit* or *bit*, as it is known. The memory unit consists of millions of such bits. In order to make memory more manageable, bits are organized into groups of eight bits called *bytes*. Memory can then be viewed as consisting of an ordered sequence of bytes. Each byte in this memory can be identified by its sequence number starting with 0, as shown in Figure 3.1. This is referred to as the *memory address* of the byte. Such memory is called *byte addressable* memory.

The amount of memory that a processor can address depends on the address bus width. Typically, 32-bit processors support 32-bit addresses. Thus, these processors can address up to 4 GB (2^{32} bytes) of main memory as shown in Figure 3.1. This number is referred to as the *memory address space*. The actual memory in a system, however, is always less than or equal to the memory address space. The amount of memory in a system is determined by how much of this memory address space is *populated* with memory chips.

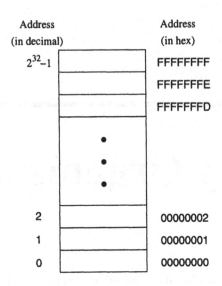

Figure 3.1 Logical view of the system memory.

This chapter gives details about memory organization. In the next section we give details about the two basic memory operations—read and write. Memory can be broadly divided into read-only and read/write types. Details about the types of memory are given next. After giving these details, we look at the memory design issues. Towards the end of the chapter, we describe two ways of storing multibyte data and the reasons why data alignment results in improved performance.

Basic Memory Operations

The memory unit supports two fundamental operations: *read* and *write*. The *read operation* reads a previously stored data and the *write operation* stores a value in memory. Both of these operations require an address in memory from which to read a value or to which to write a value. In addition, the write operation requires specification of the data to be written. The block diagram of the memory unit is shown in Figure 3.2. The address and data of the memory unit are connected to the address and data buses of the system bus, respectively. The read and write signals come from the control bus.

Two metrics are used to characterize memory. *Access time* refers to the amount of time required by the memory to retrieve the data at the addressed location. The other metric is the *memory cycle time*, which refers to the minimum time between successive memory operations. Memory transfer rates can be measured by the bandwidth metric, which specifies the number of bytes transferred per second.

The read operation is nondestructive in the sense that one can read a location of the memory as many times as one wishes without destroying the contents of that location. The write operation, on the other hand, is destructive, as writing a value into a location destroys the old contents of that memory location.

Figure 3.2 Block diagram of the system memory.

Steps in a typical read cycle

1. Place the address of the location to be read on the address bus;

2. Activate the memory read control signal on the control bus;

3. Wait for the memory to retrieve the data from the addressed memory location and place it on the data bus;

4. Read the data from the data bus;

5. Drop the memory read control signal to terminate the read cycle.

For example, a simple Pentium read cycle takes three clock cycles. During the first clock cycle, steps 1 and 2 are performed. The processor waits until the end of the second clock and reads the data and drops the read control signal. If the memory is slower (and therefore cannot supply data within the specified time), the memory unit indicates its inability to the processor and the processor waits longer for the memory to supply data by inserting *wait cycles*. Note that each wait cycle introduces a waiting period equal to one system clock period and thus slows down the system operation.

Steps in a typical write cycle

1. Place the address of the location to be written on the address bus;

2. Place the data to be written on the data bus;

3. Activate the memory write control signal on the control bus;

4. Wait for the memory to store the data at the addressed location;

5. Drop the memory write signal to terminate the write cycle.

As with the read cycle, Pentium requires three clock cycles to perform a simple write operation. During the first clock cycle, steps 1 and 3 are done. Step 2 is performed during the second clock cycle. The processor gives memory time until the end of the second clock and drops the memory write signal. If the memory cannot write data at the maximum processor rate, wait cycles can be introduced to extend the write cycle.

Types of Memory

The memory unit can be implemented using a variety of memory chips—different speeds, different manufacturing technologies, and different sizes. The two basic types of memory are the *read-only memory* and *read/write memory*.

A basic property of memory systems is, they are random access memories in that accessing any memory location (for reading or writing) takes the same time. Contrast this with data stored on a magnetic tape. Access time on the tape depends on the location of the data.

Volatility is another important property of a memory system. A *volatile* memory requires power to retain its contents. A *nonvolatile* memory can retain its values even in the absence of power.

Read-Only Memories   Read-only memory (ROM) allows only read operations to be performed. As the name suggests, we cannot write into this memory. The main advantage of ROM is that it is nonvolatile. Most ROM is factory programmed and cannot be altered. The term *programming* in this context refers to writing values into a ROM. This type of ROM is cheaper to manufacture in large quantities than other types of ROM. The program that controls the standard input and output functions (called BIOS), for instance, is kept in ROM. Current systems use the flash memory rather than a ROM (see our discussion later).

Other types include *programmable ROM* (PROM) and *erasable PROM* (EPROM). PROM is useful in situations where the contents of ROM are not yet fixed. For instance, when the program is still in the development stage, it is convenient for the designer to be able to program the ROM locally rather than at the time of manufacture.

In PROM, a fuse is associated with each bit cell. If the fuse is on, the bit cell supplies a 1 when read. The fuse has to be burned to read a 0 from that bit cell. When PROM is manufactured, its contents are all set to 1. To program a PROM, selective fuses are burned (to introduce 0s) by sending high current. This is the writing process and is not reversible (i.e., a burned fuse cannot be restored). EPROM offers further flexibility during system prototyping. Contents of EPROM can be erased by exposing them to ultraviolet light for a few minutes. Once erased, EPROM can be reprogrammed again.

Electrically erasable PROMs (EEPROMs) allow further flexibility. By exposing to ultraviolet light, we erase *all* the contents of an EPROM. EEPROMs, on the other hand, allow the user to selectively erase contents. Furthermore, erasing can be done in place; there is no need to place it in a special ultraviolet chamber.

Flash memory is a special kind of EEPROM. One main difference between the EEPROM and flash memory lies in how the memory contents are erased. The EEPROM is byte-erasable whereas the flash memory is block-erasable. Thus, writing in the flash memory involves erasing a block and rewriting it.

Current systems use the flash memory for BIOS so that changing BIOS versions is fairly straightforward (You just have to "flash" the new version). Flash memory is also becoming very popular as a removable media. The SmartMedia, CompactFlash, Sony's Memory Stick are all examples of various forms of removable flash media.

Flash memory, however, is slower than the RAMs we discuss next. For example, flash memory cycle time is about 80 ns whereas the corresponding value for RAMs is about 10 ns. Nevertheless, since flash memories are nonvolatile, they are used in applications where this property is important. Apart from BIOS, we see them in devices like digital cameras and video game systems.

Read/Write Memory   Read/write memory is commonly referred to as *random access memory* (RAM), even though ROM is also a random access memory. This terminology is so entrenched in the literature that we follow it here with a cautionary note that RAM actually refers to RWM.

Read/write memory can be divided into *static* and *dynamic* categories. Static random access memory (SRAM) retains the data, once written, without further manipulation so long as the source of power holds its value. SRAM is typically used for implementing the processor registers and cache memories.

The bulk of main memory in a typical computer system, however, consists of dynamic random access memory (DRAM). DRAM is a complex memory device that uses a tiny capacitor to store a bit. A charged capacitor represents 1 bit. Since capacitors slowly lose their charge due to leakage, they must be periodically *refreshed* to replace the charges representing 1 bit. A typical refresh period is about 64 ms. Reading from DRAM involves testing to see if the corresponding bit cells are charged. Unfortunately, this test destroys the charges on the bit cells. Thus, DRAM is a destructive read memory.

For proper operation, a read cycle is followed by a restore cycle. As a result, the DRAM cycle time, the actual time necessary between accesses, is typically about twice the read access time, which is the time necessary to retrieve a datum from the memory.

Several types of DRAM chips are available. We briefly describe some of most popular types DRAMs next.

FPM DRAMs   Fast page mode (FPM) DRAMs are an improvement over the previous generation DRAMs. FPM DRAMs exploit the fact that we access memory sequentially, most of the time. To know how this access pattern characteristic is exploited, we have to look at how the memory is organized. Internally, the memory is organized as a matrix of bits. For example, a 32 Mb memory could be organized as 8 K rows (i.e., 8192 since K = 1024) and 4 K columns. To access a bit, we have to supply a row address and a column address. In the FPM DRAM, a page represents part of the memory with the same row address. To access a page, we specify the row address only once; we can read the bits in the specified page by changing the column addresses. Since the row address is not changing, we save on the memory cycle time.

EDO DRAMs   Extended Data Output (EDO) DRAM is another type of FPM DRAM. It also exploits the fact that we access memory sequentially. However, it uses pipelining to speed up memory access. That is, it initiates the next request before the previous memory access is completed. A characteristic of pipelining inherited by EDO DRAMs is that single memory reference requests are not speeded up. However, by overlapping multiple memory access requests, it improves the memory bandwidth.

SDRAMs   Both FPM DRAMs and EDO DRAMs are asynchronous in the sense that their data output is not synchronized to a clock. The synchronous DRAM (SDRAM) uses an external clock to synchronize the data output. This synchronization reduces delays and thereby improves the memory performance. The SDRAM memories are used in systems that require memory satisfying the PC100/PC133 specification. SDRAMs are dominant in low-end PC market and are cheap.

DDR SDRAMs   The SDRAM memories are also called single data rate (SDR) SDRAMs as they supply data once per memory cycle. However, with increasing processor speeds, the processor bus (also called front-side bus or FSB) frequency is also going up. For example, PCs now have a 533 MHz FSB that supports a transfer rate of about 4.2 GB/s. To satisfy this transfer rate, SDRAMs have been improved to provide data at both rising and falling edges of the clock. This effectively doubles the memory bandwidth and satisfies the high data transfer rates of faster processors.

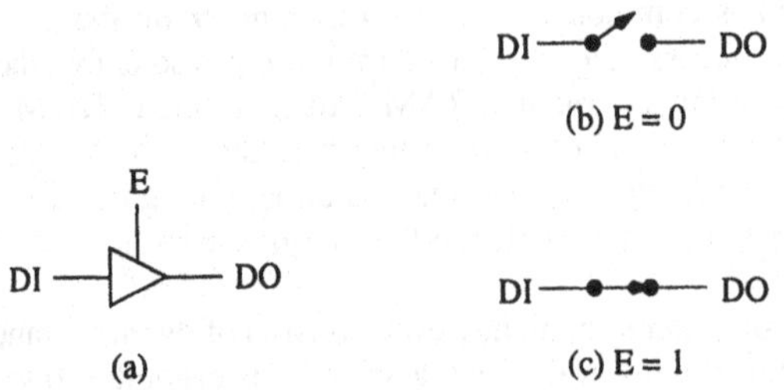

DI —⚡•— DO

(b) E = 0

E

DI —▷— DO

DI —•—••— DO

(c) E = 1

Inputs		Output
E	DI	DO
1	0	0
1	1	1
0	X	Z

(a)

(d)

Figure 3.3 Tristate buffer: (a) logic symbol; (b) it acts as an open circuit when the enable input is inactive (E = 0); (c) it acts as a closed circuit when the enable input is active (E = 1); (d) truth table (X = don't care input, and Z = high impedance state).

RDRAMs Rambus DRAM (RDRAM) takes a completely different approach to increase the memory bandwidth. A technology developed and licensed by Rambus, it is a memory subsystem that consists of the RAM, RAM controller, and a high-speed bus called the Rambus channel. Like the DDR DRAM, it also performs two transfers per cycle. In contrast to the 8-byte wide data bus of DRAMs, Rambus channel is a 2-byte data bus. However, by using multiple channels, we can increase the bandwidth of RDRAMs. For example, a dual-channel RDRAM operating at 533 MHz provides a bandwidth of 533 * 2 * 4 = 4.2 GB/s, sufficient for the 533 MHz FSB systems.

From this brief discussion it should be clear that DDR SDRAMs and RDRAMs compete with each other in the high-end market. The race between these two DRAM technologies continues as Intel boosts its FSB to 800 MHz.

Building a Memory Block

In the last chapter, we discussed several basic building blocks such as flip-flops, multiplexers, and decoders. For example, flip-flops provide the basic capability to store a bit of data. These devices can be replicated to build larger memory units. For example, we can place 16 flip-flops together in a row to store a 16-bit word. All the 16 flip-flops would have their clock inputs tied together to form a single common clock to write a 16-bit word. We can place several such rows in a memory chip to store multiple words of data. In this organization, each row supplies a word. To build even larger memories, we can use multiple chips such that all their data lines are connected to the data bus. This implies that we need to find a way to connect these outputs together. Tristate buffers are used for this purpose.

Tristate Buffers

The logic circuits we have discussed in the last chapter have two possible states: 0 or 1. The devices we discuss here are called tristate buffers as they can be in three states: 0, 1, or Z state. A tristate buffer output can be in state 0 or 1 just as with a normal logic gate. In addition, the output can also be in a high impedance (Z) state, in which the output floats. Thus, even though the output is physically connected to the bus, it behaves as though it is electrically and logically disconnected from the bus.

Tristate buffers use a separate control signal to float the output independent of the data input (see Figure 3.3a). This particular feature makes them suitable for bus connections. Figure 3.3a shows the logic symbol for a tristate buffer. When the enable input (E) is low, the buffer acts as an open circuit (i.e., output is in the high impedance state Z) as shown in Figure 3.3b; otherwise, it acts as a short circuit (Figure 3.3c). The enable input must be high in order to pass the input data to output, as shown in the truth table (see Figure 3.3d).

Memory Design with D Flip-Flops

We begin our discussion with how one can build memories using the D flip-flops. Recall that we use flip-flops for edge-triggered devices and latches for level-sensitive devices. The principle of constructing memory out of D flip-flops is simple. We use a two-dimensional array of D flip-flops, with each row storing a word. The number of rows is equal to the number of words the memory should store. Thus, this organization uses "horizontal" expansion to increase the word width and "vertical" expansion to increase the number of words.

In general, the number of columns and the number of rows is a power of two. We use the notation M × N memory to represent a memory that can store M words, where each word is N-bits long.

Figure 3.4 shows a 4 × 3 memory built with 12 D flip-flops organized as a 4 × 3 array. Since all flip-flops in a row store a word of data, each row of flip-flops has their clock signals tied together to form a single clock signal for each row. All flip-flops in a column receive input from the same input data line. For example, the rightmost column D inputs are connected to the input data D0.

This memory requires two address lines to select one of the four words. The two address lines are decoded to select a specific row by using a 2-to-4 decoder. The low-active write signal ($\overline{WR}$) is gated through an AND gate as shown in Figure 3.4. Depending on the address, only one of the four decoder output lines will be high, permitting the $\overline{WR}$ signal to clock the selected row to write the 3-bit data present on D0 to D2 lines. Note that the decoder along with the four AND gates forms a demultiplexer that routes the $\overline{WR}$ signal to the row selected by the address lines A1 and A0.

The design we have done so far allows us to write a 3-bit datum into the selected row. To complete the design, we have to find a way to read data from this memory. As each bit of data is supplied by one of the four D flip-flops in a column, we have to find a way to connect these four outputs to a single data out line. A natural choice for the job is a 4-to-1 multiplexer. The MUX selection inputs are connected to the address lines to allow appropriate data on the output lines D0 through D2. The final design is shown in Figure 3.4.

We need to pass the outputs of the multiplexers through tristate buffers as shown in Figure 3.4. The enable input signal for these output tristate buffers is generated by ANDing the chip select and read signals. Two inverters are used to provide low-active chip select ($\overline{CS}$) and memory read ($\overline{RD}$) inputs to the memory block.

With the use of the tristate buffers, we can tie the corresponding data in and out signal lines together to satisfy the data bus connection requirements. Furthermore, we can completely disconnect the outputs of this memory block by making $\overline{CS}$ high.

We can represent our design using the logic symbol shown in Figure 3.5. Our design uses separate read and write signals. These two signals are part of the control bus (see Figure 2.1). It is also possible to have a single line to serve as a read and write line. For example, a 0 on this line can be interpreted as write and a 1 as read. Such signals are represented as the $\overline{WR}$/RD line, indicating low-active write and high-active read.

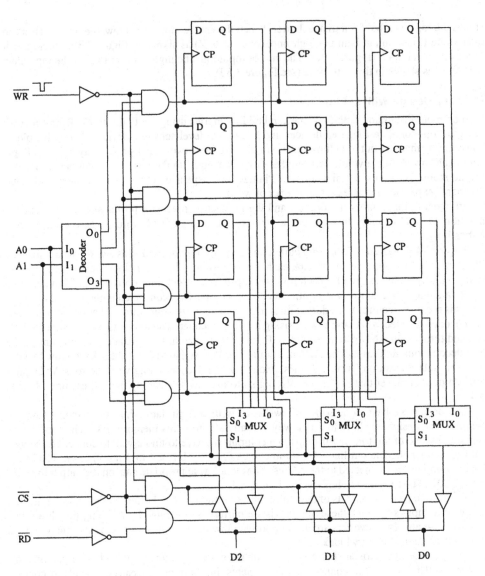

Figure 3.4 A 4 × 3 memory design using D flip-flops.

Building Larger Memories

Now that we know how to build memory blocks using devices that can store a single bit, we move on to building larger memory units using these memory blocks. We explain the design process by using an example. Before discussing the design procedure, we briefly present details about commercially available memory chips.

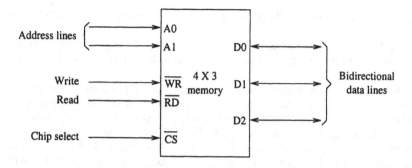

Figure 3.5 Block diagram representation of a 4 × 3 memory.

Memory Chips

Several commercial memory chips are available to build larger memories. Here we look at two example chips—a SRAM and a DRAM—from Micron Technology.

The SRAM we discuss is an 8-Mb chip that comes in three configurations: 512 K × 18, 256 K × 32, or 256 K × 36. Note that, in the first and last configurations, word length is not a multiple of 8. These additional bits are useful for error detection/correction. These chips have an access time of 3.5 ns. The 512 K × 18 chip requires 19 address lines, whereas the 256 K × 32/36 versions require 18 address lines.

An example DRAM (it is a synchronous DRAM) is the 256-Mb capacity chip that comes in word lengths of 4, 8, or 16 bits. That is, this memory chip comes in three configurations: 64 M × 4, 32 M × 8, or 16 M × 16. The cycle time for this chip is about 7 ns.

In the days when the data bus widths were small (8 or 16), DRAM chips were available in 1-bit widths. Current chips use a word width of more than 1 as it becomes impractical to string 64 1-bit chips to get 64-bit word memories for processors such as the Pentium.

From the details of these two example memory chips, we see that the bit capacity of a memory chip can be organized into several configurations. If we focus on the DRAM chip, for example, what are the pros and cons of the various configurations? The advantage of wider memory chips (i.e., chips with larger word size) is that we require fewer of them to build a larger memory. As an example, consider building memory for your Pentium-based PC. Even though the Pentium is a 32-bit processor, it uses a 64-bit wide data bus. Suppose that you want to build a 16 M × 64 memory. We can build this memory by using four 16 M × 16 chips, all in a single row. How do we build such a memory using, for example, the 32 M × 8 version of the chip? Because our word size is 64, we have to use 8 such chips in order to provide 64-bit wide data. That means we get 32 M × 64 memory as the minimum instead of the required 16 M × 64. The problem becomes even more serious if we were to use the 64 M × 4 version chip. We have to use 16 such chips, and we end up with a 64 M × 64 memory. This example illustrates the tradeoff between using "wider" memories versus "deeper" memories.

Larger Memory Design

Before proceeding with the design of a memory unit, we need to know if the memory address space (MAS) supported by the processor is byte addressable or not. In a byte-addressable space, each address identifies a byte. All popular processors—the Pentium, PowerPC, SPARC, and MIPS—

support byte-addressable space. Therefore, in our design examples, we assume byte-addressable space.

We now discuss how one can use memory chips, such as the ones discussed before, to build system memory. The procedure is similar to the intuitive steps followed in the previous design example.

First we have to decide on the configuration of the memory chip, assuming that we are using the DRAM chip described before. As described in the last section, independent of the configuration, the total bit capacity of a chip remains the same. That means the number of chips required remains the same. For example, if we want to build a 64 M $\times$ 32 memory, we need eight chips. We can use eight 64 M $\times$ 4 in a single row, eight 32 M $\times$ 8 in 2 $\times$ 4 array, or 16 M $\times$ 16 in 4 $\times$ 2 array. Although we have several alternatives for this example, there may be situations where the choice is limited. For example, if we are designing a 16 M $\times$ 32 memory, we have no choice but to use the 16 M $\times$ 16 chips.

Once we have decided on the memory chip configuration, it is straightforward to determine the number of chips and the organization of the memory unit. Let us assume that we are using D $\times$ W chips to build an M $\times$ N memory. Of course, we want to make sure that D $\leq$ M and W $\leq$ N.

$$\text{Number of chips required} \quad = \quad \frac{M \times N}{D \times W},$$

$$\text{Number of rows} \quad = \quad \frac{M}{D},$$

$$\text{Number of columns} \quad = \quad \frac{N}{W}.$$

The read and write lines of all memory chips should be connected to form a single read and write signal. These signals are connected to the control bus memory read and write lines. For simplicity, we omit these connections in our design diagrams.

Data bus connections are straightforward. Each chip in a row supplies a subset of data bits. In our design, the right chip supplies D0 to D15, and the left chip supplies the remaining 16 data bits (see Figure 3.6).

For each row, connect all chip select inputs as shown in Figure 3.6. Generating appropriate chip select signals is the crucial part of the design process. To complete the design, partition the address lines into three groups as shown in Figure 3.7.

The least significant Z address bits, where Z = $\log_2$(N/8), are not connected to the memory unit. This is because each address going into the memory unit will select an N-bit value. Since we are using byte-addressable memory address space, we can leave the Z least significant bits that identify a byte out of N/8 bytes. In our example, N = 32, which gives us Z = 2. Therefore, the address lines A0 and A1 are not connected to the memory unit.

The next Y address bits, where Y = $\log_2$D, are connected to the address inputs of all the chips. Since we are using 16 M chips, Y = 24. Thus, address lines A2 to A25 are connected to all the chips as shown in Figure 3.6.

The remaining most significant address bits X are used to generate the chip select signals. This group of address bits plays an important role in mapping the memory to a part of the memory address space. We discuss this mapping in detail in the next section. The design shown in Figure 3.6 uses address lines A26 and A27 to generate four chip select signals, one for each row of chips. We are using a low-active 2-to-4 decoder to generate the $\overline{\text{CS}}$ signals.

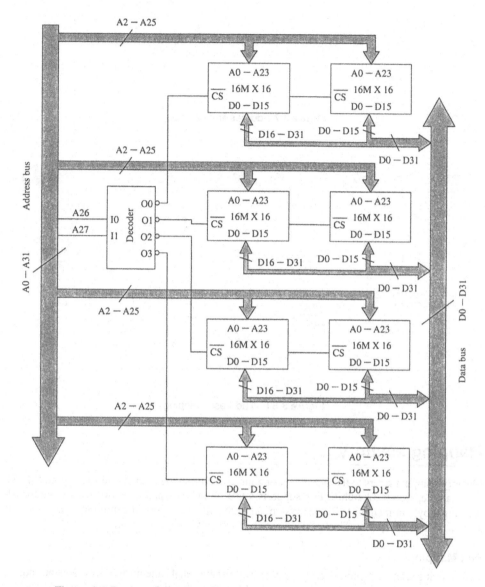

Figure 3.6 Design of a 64 M × 32 memory using 16 M × 16 memory chips.

The top row of chips in Figure 3.6 is mapped to the first 64-MB address space (i.e., from addresses 0 to $2^{26} - 1$). The second row is mapped to the next 64-MB address space, and so on. After reading the next section, you will realize that this is a partial mapping.

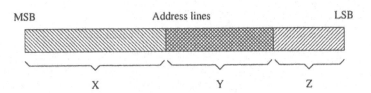

Figure 3.7 Address line partition.

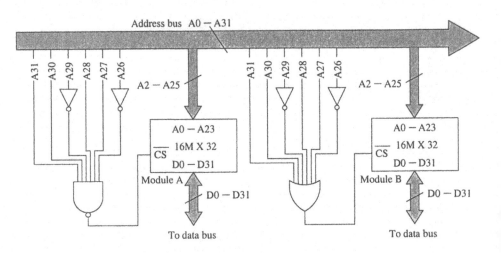

Figure 3.8 Full address mapping.

Mapping Memory

Memory mapping refers to the placement of a memory unit in the memory address space (MAS). For example, the IA-32 architecture supports 4 GB of address space (i.e., it uses 32 bits for addressing a byte in memory). If your system has 128 MB of memory, it can be mapped to one of several address subspaces. This section describes how this mapping is done.

Full Mapping

Full mapping refers to a one-to-one mapping function between the memory address and the address in MAS. This means, for each address value in MAS that has a memory location mapped, there is one and only one memory location responding to the address.

Full mapping is done by completely decoding the higher-order X bits of memory (see Figure 3.7) to generate the chip select signals. Two example mappings of 16 M × 32 memory modules are shown in Figure 3.8. Both these mappings are full mappings as all higher-order X bits participate in generating the $\overline{CS}$ signal.

Logically we can divide the 32 address lines into two groups. One group, consisting of address lines Y and Z, locates a byte in the selected 16 M × 32 memory module. The remaining higher-

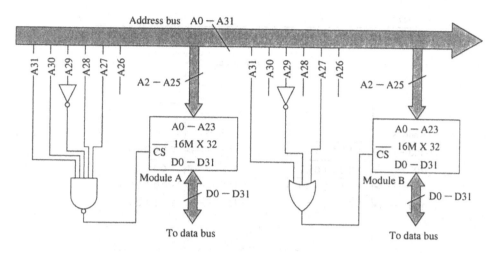

Figure 3.9 Partial address mapping.

order bits (i.e., the X group) are used to generate the $\overline{CS}$ signal. Given this delineation, it is simple to find the mapping.

We illustrate the technique by using the two examples shown in Figure 3.8. Since the memory modules have a low-active chip select input, a given module is selected if its $\overline{CS}$ input is 0. For Module A, the NAND gate output is low when A26 and A29 are low and the remaining four address lines are high. Thus, this memory module responds to memory read/write activity whenever the higher-order six address bits are 110110. From this, we can get the address locations mapped to this module as D8000000H to DBFFFFFFH. For convenience, we have expressed the addresses in the hexadecimal system (as indicated by the suffix letter H). The address D8000000H is mapped to the first location and the address DBFFFFFFH to the last location of Module A. For addresses that are outside this range, the $\overline{CS}$ input to Module A is high and, therefore, it is deselected.

For Module B, the same inputs are used except that the NAND gate is replaced by an OR gate. Thus, the output of this OR gate is low when the higher-order six address bits are 001001. From this, we can see that mapping for Module B is 24000000H to 27FFFFFFH. As these two ranges are mutually exclusive, we can keep both mappings without causing conflict problems.

Partial Mapping

Full mapping is useful in mapping a memory module; however, often the complexity associated with generating the $\overline{CS}$ signal is not necessary. For example, we needed a 6-input NAND or OR gate to map the two memory modules in Figure 3.8. Partial mapping reduces this complexity by mapping each memory location to more than one address in MAS. We can obtain simplified $\overline{CS}$ logic if the number of addresses a location is mapped to is a power of 2.

Let us look at the mapping of Module A in Figure 3.9 to clarify some of these points. The $\overline{CS}$ logic is the same except that we are not connecting the A26 address line to the NAND gate. Because A26 is not participating in generating the signal, it becomes a don't care input. In this mapping, Module A is selected when the higher-order six address bits are 110110 or 110111. Thus, Module A is mapped to the address space D8000000H to DBFFFFFFH and DC000000H

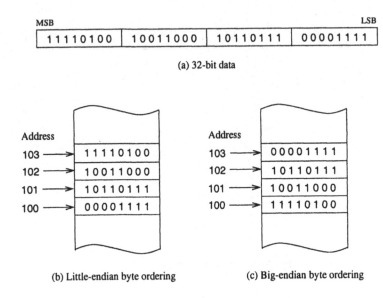

(a) 32-bit data

(b) Little-endian byte ordering   (c) Big-endian byte ordering

Figure 3.10 Two byte ordering schemes.

to DFFFFFFFH. That is, the first location in Module A responds to addresses D8000000H and DC000000H. Since we have left out one address bit A26, two (i.e., 2^1) addresses are mapped to a memory location. In general, if we leave out k address bits from the chip select logic, we map 2^k addresses to each memory location. For example, in our memory design of Figure 3.6, four address lines (A28 to A31) are not used. Thus, $2^4 = 16$ addresses are mapped to each memory location.

We leave it as an exercise to verify that each location in Module B is mapped to eight addresses as there are three address lines that are not used to generate the $\overline{CS}$ signal.

Storing Multibyte Data

Storing data often requires more than a byte. For example, we need four bytes of memory to store an integer variable that can take a value between 0 and $2^{32} - 1$. Let us assume that the value to be stored is the one shown in Figure 3.10a.

Suppose that we want to store these 4-byte data in memory at locations 100 through 103. How do we store them? Figure 3.10 shows two possibilities: least significant byte (Figure 3.10b) or most significant byte (Figure 3.10c) is stored at location 100. These two byte ordering schemes are referred to as the *little endian* and *big endian*. In either case, we always refer to such multibyte data by specifying the lowest memory address (100 in this example).

Is one byte ordering scheme better than the other? Not really! It is largely a matter of choice for the designers. For example, the IA-32 processors use the little-endian byte ordering. However, most processors leave it up to the system designer to configure the processor. For example, the MIPS and PowerPC processors use the big-endian byte ordering by default, but these processors can be configured to use the little-endian scheme.

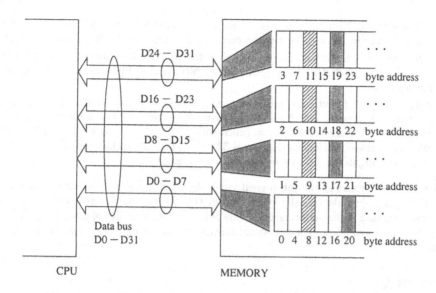

Figure 3.11 Byte-addressable memory interface to the 32-bit data bus.

The particular byte-ordering scheme used does not pose any problems as long as you are working with machines that use the same byte-ordering scheme. However, difficulties arise when you want to transfer data between two machines that use different schemes. In this case, conversion from one scheme to the other is required. For example, the IA-32 instruction set provides two instructions to facilitate such conversion: one to perform 16-bit data conversions and the other for 32-bit data. Later chapters give details on these instructions.

Alignment of Data

We can use our memory example to understand why data alignment improves the performance of applications. Suppose we want to read 32-bit data from the memory shown in Figure 3.6. If the address of these 32-bit data is a multiple of four (i.e., address lines A0 and A1 are 0), the 32-bit data are stored in a single row of memory. Thus the processor can get the 32-bit data in one read cycle. If this condition is not satisfied, then the 32-bit data item is spread over two rows. Thus the processor needs to read two 32-bits of data and extract the required 32-bit data. This scenario is clearly demonstrated in Figure 3.11.

In Figure 3.11, the 32-bit data item stored at address 8 (shown by hashed lines) is aligned. Due to this alignment, the processor can read this data item in one read cycle. On the other hand, the data item stored at address 17 (shown shaded) is unaligned. Reading this data item requires two read cycles: one to read the 32 bits at address 16 and the other to read the 32 bits at address 20. The processor can internally assemble the required 32-bit data item from the 64-bit data read from the memory.

You can easily extend this discussion to the Pentium's 64-bit data bus. It should be clear to you that aligned data improve system performance.

- *2-Byte Data*: A 16-bit data item is aligned if it is stored at an even address (i.e., addresses that are multiples of two). This means that the least significant bit of the address must be 0.
- *4-Byte Data*: A 32-bit data item is aligned if it is stored at an address that is a multiple of four. This implies that the least significant two bits of the address must be 0 as discussed in the last example.
- *8-Byte Data*: A 64-bit data item is aligned if it is stored at an address that is a multiple of eight. This means that the least significant three bits of the address must be 0. This alignment is important for Pentium processors, as they have a 64-bit wide data bus. On 80486 processors, since their data bus is 32-bits wide, a 64-bit data item is read in two bus cycles and alignment at 4-byte boundaries is sufficient.

The IA-32 processors allow both aligned and unaligned data items. Of course, unaligned data cause performance degradation. Alignment constraints of this type are referred to as *soft alignment* constraints. Because of the performance penalty associated with unaligned data, some processors do not allow unaligned data. This alignment constraint is referred to as the *hard alignment* constraint.

Summary

We have discussed the basic memory design issues. We have shown how flip-flops can be used to build memory blocks. Interfacing a memory unit to the system bus typically requires tristate buffers. We have described by means of an example how tristate buffers are useful in connecting the memory outputs to the data bus.

Building larger memories requires both horizontal and vertical expansion. Horizontal expansion is used to expand the word size, and vertical expansion provides an increased number of words. We have shown how one can design memory modules using standard memory chips. In all these designs, chip select plays an important role in allowing multiple entities to be attached to the system bus.

Chip select logic also plays an important role in mapping memory modules into the address space. Two basic mapping functions are used: full mapping and partial mapping. Full mapping provides a one-to-one mapping between memory locations and addresses. In partial mapping, each memory location is mapped to a number of addresses equal to a power of 2. The main advantage of partial mapping is that it simplifies the chip select logic.

We have described the big-endian or little-endian formats to store multibyte data. We have also discussed the importance of data alignment. Unaligned data can lead to performance degradation. We have discussed the reasons for improvement in performance due to alignment of data.

4

The IA-32 Architecture

When you are programming in a high-level language like C, you don't have to know anything about the underlying processor and the system. However, when programming in an assembly language, you should have some understanding of how the processor is organized and the system is put together. This chapter provides these details for the Intel IA-32 architecture. The Pentium processor is an implementation of this architecture. Of course, several other processors such as Celeron, Pentium 4, and Xeon also belong to this architecture. We present details of its registers and memory architecture. It supports two memory architectures: protected-mode and real-mode. Protected-mode architecture is the native mode and the real-mode is provided to mimic the 16-bit 8086 memory architecture. Both modes support segmented memory architecture. It is important for the assembly language programmer to understand the segmented memory organization. Other details of this architecture are given in later chapters.

Introduction

Intel introduced microprocessors way back in 1969. Their first 4-bit microprocessor was the 4004. This was followed by the 8080 and 8085 processors. The work on these early microprocessors led to the development of the Intel architecture (IA). The first processor in the IA family was the 8086 processor, introduced in 1979. It has a 20-bit address bus and a 16-bit data bus.

The 8088 is a less expensive version of the 8086 processor. The cost reduction is obtained by using an 8-bit data bus. Except for this difference, the 8088 is identical to the 8086 processor. Intel introduced segmentation with these processors. These processors can address up to four segments of 64 KB each. This IA segmentation is referred to as the real-mode segmentation and is discussed later in this chapter.

The 80186 is a faster version of the 8086. It also has a 20-bit address bus and 16-bit data bus, but has an improved instruction set. The 80186 was never widely used in computer systems. The real successor to the 8086 is the 80286, which was introduced in 1982. It has a 24-bit address bus, which implies 16 MB of memory address space. The data bus is still 16 bits wide, but the 80286 has some memory protection capabilities. It introduced the protection mode into the IA architecture. Segmentation in this new mode is different from the real-mode segmentation. We present details on this new segmentation later. The 80286 is backward compatible in that it can run the 8086-based software.

Intel introduced its first 32-bit processor—the 80386—in 1985. It has a 32-bit data bus and 32-bit address bus. It follows their 32-bit architecture known as IA-32. The memory address space has grown substantially (from 16 MB address space to 4 GB). This processor introduced paging into the IA architecture. It also allowed definition of segments as large as 4 GB. This effectively allowed for a "flat" model (i.e., effectively turning off segmentation). Later sections present details on this aspect. Like the 80286, it can run all the programs written for 8086 and 8088 processors.

The Intel 80486 processor was introduced in 1989. This is an improved version of the 80386. While maintaining the same address and data buses, it combined the coprocessor functions for performing floating-point arithmetic. The 80486 processor has added more parallel execution capability to instruction decode and execution units to achieve a scalar execution rate of one instruction per clock. It has an 8 KB onchip L1 cache. Furthermore, support for the L2 cache and multiprocessing has been added. Later versions of the 80486 processors incorporated features such as energy saving mode for notebooks.

The latest in the family is the Pentium series. It is not named 80586 because Intel found belatedly that numbers couldn't be trademarked! The first Pentium was introduced in 1993. The Pentium is similar to the 80486 but uses a 64-bit wide data bus. Internally, it has 128- and 256-bit wide datapaths to speed up internal data transfers. However, the Pentium instruction set supports 32-bit operands like the 80486 processor. It has added a second execution pipeline to achieve superscalar performance by having the capability to execute two instructions per clock. It has also doubled the onchip L1 cache, with 8 KB for data and another 8 KB for the instructions. Branch prediction has also been added.

The Pentium Pro processor has a three-way superscalar architecture. That is, it can execute three instructions per clock cycle. The address bus has been expanded to 36 bits, which gives it an address space of 64 GB. It also provides dynamic execution including out-of-order and speculative execution. In addition to the L1 caches provided by the Pentium, the Pentium Pro has a 256 KB L2 cache in the same package as the CPU.

The Pentium II processor has added multimedia (MMX) instructions to the Pentium Pro architecture. It has expanded the L1 data and instruction caches to 16 KB each. It has also added more comprehensive power management features including Sleep and Deep Sleep modes to conserve power during idle times.

The Pentium III processor introduced streaming SIMD extensions (SSE), cache prefetch instructions, and memory fences, and the single-instruction multiple-data (SIMD) architecture for concurrent execution of multiple floating-point operations. Pentium 4 enhanced these features further.

Intel's 64-bit Itanium processor is targeted for server applications. For these applications, the 32-bit memory address space is not adequate. The Itanium uses a 64-bit address bus to provide substantially larger address space. Its data bus is 128 bits wide. In a major departure, Intel has moved from the CISC designs used in their 32-bit processors to RISC orientation for their 64-bit Itanium processors. The Itanium also incorporates several advanced architectural features to provide improved performance for the high-end server market.

In the rest of the chapter, we look at the basic architectural details of the IA-32 architecture. Our focus is on the internal registers and memory architecture. Other details are covered in later chapters.

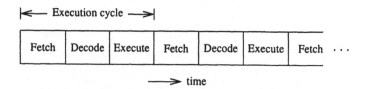

Figure 4.1 Execution cycle of a typical computer system.

Processor Execution Cycle

The processor acts as the controller of all actions or services provided by the system. It can be thought of as executing the following cycle forever:

1. Fetch an instruction from the memory;

2. Decode the instruction (i.e., identify the instruction);

3. Execute the instruction (i.e., perform the action specified by the instruction).

This process is often referred to as the *fetch-decode-execute* cycle, or simply the *execution* cycle.

The execution cycle of a processor is shown in Figure 4.1. As discussed in the last chapter, *Fetching* an instruction from the main memory involves placing the appropriate address on the address bus and activating the memory read signal on the control bus to indicate to the memory unit that an instruction should be read from that location. The memory unit requires time to read the instruction at the addressed location. The memory then places the instruction on the data bus. The processor, after instructing the memory unit to read, waits until the instruction is available on the data bus and then reads the instruction.

Decoding involves identifying the instruction that has been fetched from the memory. To facilitate the decoding process, machine language instructions follow a particular instruction-encoding scheme.

To *execute* an instruction, the processor contains hardware consisting of control circuitry and an arithmetic and logic unit (ALU). The control circuitry is needed to provide timing controls as well as to instruct the internal hardware components to perform a specific operation. As described in Chapter 2, the ALU is mainly responsible for performing arithmetic operations (such as add and divide) and logical operations (such as and, or) on data.

In practice, instructions and data are not fetched, most of the time, from the main memory. There is a high-speed cache memory that provides faster access to instructions and data than the main memory. For example, the Pentium processor provides a 16 KB on-chip cache. This is divided equally into data cache and instruction cache. The presence of on-chip cache is transparent to application programs—it helps improve application performance.

Processor Registers

The IA-32 architecture provides ten 32-bit and six 16-bit registers. These registers are grouped into general, control, and segment registers. The general registers are further divided into data, pointer, and index registers as shown in Figures 4.2 and 4.3.

32-bit registers   16-bit registers

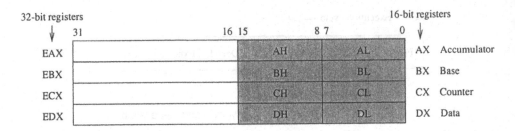

Figure 4.2 Data registers (the 16-bit registers are shown shaded).

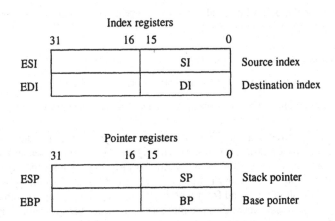

Figure 4.3 Index and pointer registers.

Data Registers

There are four 32-bit data registers that can be used for arithmetic, logical, and other operations (see Figure 4.2). These four registers are unique in that they can be used as follows:

- Four 32-bit registers (EAX, EBX, ECX, EDX); or
- Four 16-bit registers (AX, BX, CX, DX); or
- Eight 8-bit registers (AH, AL, BH, BL, CH, CL, DH, DL).

As shown in Figure 4.2, it is possible to use a 32-bit register and access its lower half of the data by the corresponding 16-bit register name. For example, the lower 16 bits of EAX can be accessed by using AX. Similarly, the lower two bytes can be individually accessed by using the 8-bit register names. For example, the lower byte of AX can be accessed as AL and the upper byte as AH.

The data registers can be used without constraint in most arithmetic and logical instructions. However, some registers in this group have special functions when executing specific instructions. For example, when performing a multiplication operation, one of the two operands should be in the EAX, AX, or AL register depending on the operand size. Similarly, the ECX or CX register is assumed to contain the loop count value for iterative instructions.

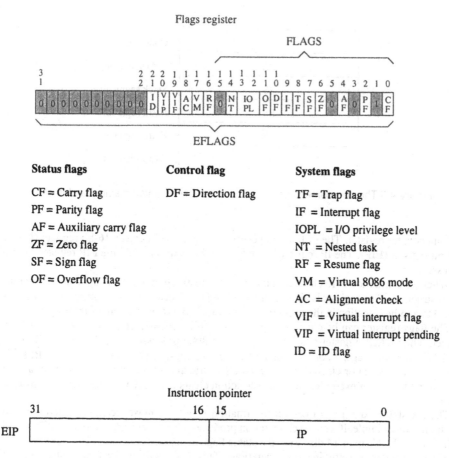

Figure 4.4 Flags and instruction pointer registers.

Pointer and Index Registers

Figure 4.3 shows the four 32-bit registers in this group. These registers can be used either as 16- or 32-bit registers. The two index registers play a special role in the string processing instructions (these instructions are discussed in Chapter 17). In addition, they can be used as general-purpose data registers.

The pointer registers are mainly used to maintain the stack. Even though they can be used as general-purpose data registers, they are almost exclusively used for maintaining the stack. The stack implementation is discussed in Chapter 11.

Control Registers

This group of registers consists of two 32-bit registers: the instruction pointer register and the flags register (see Figure 4.4). The processor uses the instruction pointer register to keep track of the location of the next instruction to be executed. Instruction pointer register is sometimes called the

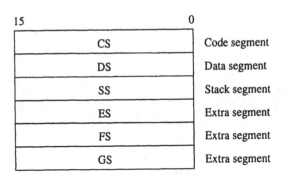

Figure 4.5 The six segment registers support the segmented memory architecture.

program counter register. The instruction pointer can be used either as a 16-bit register (IP), or as a 32-bit register (EIP). The IP register is used for 16-bit addresses and the EIP register for 32-bit addresses.

When an instruction is fetched from memory, the instruction pointer is updated to point to the next instruction. This register is also modified during the execution of an instruction that transfers control to another location in the program (such as a jump, procedure call, or interrupt).

The flags register can be considered as either a 16-bit FLAGS register, or a 32-bit EFLAGS register. The FLAGS register is useful in executing 8086 processor code. The EFLAGS register consists of 6 *status* flags, 1 *control* flag, and 10 *system* flags, as shown in Figure 4.4. Bits of this register can be set (1) or cleared (0). The IA-32 instruction set has instructions to set and clear some of the flags. For example, the `clc` instruction clears the carry flag, and the `stc` instruction sets it.

The six status flags record certain information about the most recent arithmetic or logical operation. For example, if a subtract operation produces a zero result, the zero flag (ZF) would be set (i.e., ZF = 1). Chapter 14 discusses the status flags in detail.

The control flag is useful in string operations. This flag determines whether a string operation should scan the string in the forward or backward direction. The function of the direction flag is described in Chapter 17, which discusses the string instructions.

The 10 system flags control the operation of the processor. A detailed discussion of all 10 system flags is beyond the scope of this book. Here we briefly discuss a few flags in this group. The two interrupt enable flags—the trap enable flag (TF) and the interrupt enable flag (IF)—are useful in interrupt-related activities. For example, setting the trap flag causes the processor to single-step through a program, which is useful in debugging programs. These two flags are covered in Chapter 20, which discusses the interrupt processing mechanism.

The ability to set and clear the identification (ID) flag indicates that the processor supports the CPUID instruction. The CPUID instruction provides information to software about the vendor (Intel chips use a "GenuineIntel" string), processor family, model, and so on. The virtual-8086 mode (VM) flag, when set, emulates the programming environment of the 8086 processor.

The last flag that we discuss is the alignment check (AC) flag. When this flag is set, the processor operates in alignment check mode and generates exceptions when a reference is made to an unaligned memory address. We discussed data alignment in the last chapter.

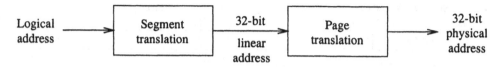

Figure 4.6 Logical to physical address translation process in the protected mode.

Segment Registers

The six 16-bit segment registers are shown in Figure 4.5. These registers support the segmented memory organization. In this organization, memory is partitioned into segments, where each segment is a small part of the memory. The processor, at any point in time, can only access up to six segments of the main memory. The six segment registers point to where these segments are located in the memory.

A program is logically divided into two parts: a code part that contains only the instructions, and a data part that keeps only the data. The code segment (CS) register points to where the program's instructions are stored in the main memory, and the data segment (DS) register points to the data part of the program. The stack segment (SS) register points to the program's stack segment (further discussed in Chapter 11).

The last three segment registers—ES, FS, and GS—are additional segment registers that can be used in a similar way as the other segment registers. For example, if a program's data could not fit into a single data segment, we could use two segment registers to point to the two data segments. We will say more about these registers later.

Protected Mode Memory Architecture

The IA-32 architecture supports a sophisticated memory architecture under real and protected modes. The real mode, which uses 16-bit addresses, is provided to run programs written for the 8086 processor. In this mode, it supports the segmented memory architecture of the 8086 processor. The protected mode uses 32-bit addresses and is the native mode of the IA-32 architecture. In the protected mode, both segmentation and paging are supported. Paging is useful in implementing virtual memory; it is transparent to the application program, but segmentation is not. We do not look at the paging features here. We discuss the real-mode memory architecture in the next section, and devote the rest of this section to describing the protected-mode segmented memory architecture.

In the protected mode, a sophisticated segmentation mechanism is supported. In this mode, the segment unit translates a logical address into a 32-bit linear address. The paging unit translates the linear address into a 32-bit physical address, as shown in Figure 4.6. If no paging mechanism is used, the linear address is treated as the physical address. In the remainder of this section, we focus on the segment translation process only.

Protected mode segment translation process is shown in Figure 4.7. In this mode, contents of the segment register are taken as an index into a segment descriptor table to get a descriptor. Segment descriptors provide the 32-bit segment base address, its size, and access rights. To translate a logical address to the corresponding linear address, the offset is added to the 32-bit base address. The offset value can be either a 16-bit or 32-bit number.

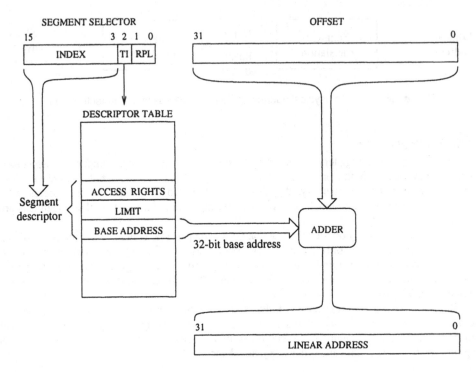

Figure 4.7 Protected mode address translation.

Visible part	Invisible part	
Segment selector	Segment base address, size, access rights, etc.	CS
Segment selector	Segment base address, size, access rights, etc.	SS
Segment selector	Segment base address, size, access rights, etc.	DS
Segment selector	Segment base address, size, access rights, etc.	ES
Segment selector	Segment base address, size, access rights, etc.	FS
Segment selector	Segment base address, size, access rights, etc.	GS

Figure 4.8 Visible and invisible parts of segment registers.

Segment Registers

Every segment register has a "visible" part and an "invisible" part, as shown in Figure 4.8. When we talk about segment registers, we are referring to the 16-bit visible part. The visible part is referred to as the segment selector. There are direct instructions to load the segment selector. These instructions include mov, pop, lds, les, lss, lgs, and lfs. Some of these instructions

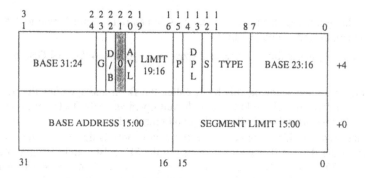

Figure 4.9 A segment descriptor.

are discussed in later chapters and in Appendix D. The invisible part of the segment registers is automatically loaded by the processor from a descriptor table (described next).

As shown in Figure 4.7, the segment selector provides three pieces of information:

- *Index:* The index selects a segment descriptor from one of two descriptor tables: a local descriptor table or a global descriptor table. Since the index is a 13-bit value, it can select one of $2^{13} = 8192$ descriptors from the selected descriptor table. Since each descriptor, shown in Figure 4.9, is 8 bytes long, the processor multiplies the index by 8 and adds the result to the base address of the selected descriptor table.

- *Table Indicator (TI):* This bit indicates whether the local or global descriptor table should be used.

    0 = Global descriptor table,
    1 = Local descriptor table.

- *Requester Privilege Level (RPL):* This field identifies the privilege level to provide protected access to data: the smaller the RPL value, the higher the privilege level. Operating systems don't have to use all four levels. For example, Linux uses level 0 for the kernel and level 3 for the user programs. It does not use levels 1 and 2.

Segment Descriptors

A segment descriptor provides the attributes of a segment. These attributes include its 32-bit base address, 20-bit segment size, as well as control and status information, as shown in Figure 4.9. Here we provide a brief description of some of the fields shown in this figure.

- *Base Address:* This 32-bit address specifies the starting address of a segment in the 4 GB physical address space. This 32-bit value is added to the offset value to get the linear address (see Figure 4.7).

- *Granularity (G):* This bit indicates whether the segment size value, described next, should be interpreted in units of bytes or 4 KB. If the granularity bit is zero, segment size is interpreted in bytes; otherwise, in units of 4 KB.

- *Segment Limit:* This is a 20-bit number that specifies the size of the segment. Depending on the granularity bit, two interpretations are possible:

1. If the granularity bit is zero, segment size can range from 1 byte to 1 MB (i.e., 2^{20} bytes), in increments of 1 byte.

2. If the granularity bit is 1, segment size can range from 4 KB to 4 GB, in increments of 4 KB.

- *D/B Bit:* In a code segment, this bit is called the D bit and specifies the default size for operands and offsets. If the D bit is 0, default operands and offsets are assumed to be 16 bits; for 32-bit operands and offsets, the D bit must be 1.

  In a data segment, this bit is called the B bit and controls the size of the stack and stack pointer. If the B bit is 0, stack operations use the SP register and the upper bound for the stack is FFFFH. If the B bit is 1, the ESP register is used for the stack operations with a stack upper bound of FFFFFFFFH. Recall that numbers expressed in the hexadecimal number system are indicated by suffix H (see Appendix A).

  Typically, this bit is cleared for the real-mode operation and set for the protected-mode operation. Later we describe how 16- and 32-bit operands and addresses can be mixed in a given mode of operation.

- *S Bit:* This bit identifies whether the segment is a system segment or an application segment. If the bit is 0, the segment is identified as a system segment; otherwise, as an application (code or data) segment.

- *Descriptor Privilege Level (DPL):* This field defines the privilege level of the segment. It is useful in controlling access to the segment using the protection mechanisms of the processor.

- *Type:* This field identifies the type of segment. The actual interpretation of this field depends on whether the segment is a system or application segment. For application segments, the type depends on whether the segment is a code or data segment. For a data segment, type can identify it as a read-only, read-write, and so on. For a code segment, type identifies it as an execute-only, execute/read-only, and so on.

- *P bit:* This bit indicates whether the segment is present. If this bit is 0, the processor generates a segment-not-present exception when a selector for the descriptor is loaded into a segment register.

Segment Descriptor Tables

A segment descriptor table is an array of segment descriptors shown in Figure 4.9. There are three types of descriptor tables:

- The global descriptor table (GDT);
- Local descriptor tables (LDT);
- The interrupt descriptor table (IDT).

All three descriptor tables are variable in size from 8 bytes to 64 KB. The interrupt descriptor table is used in interrupt processing and is discussed in Chapter 20. Both LDT and GDT can contain up to $2^{13} = 8192$ 8-bit descriptors. As shown in Figure 4.7, the upper 13 bits of a segment selector are used as an index into the selected descriptor table. Each table has an associated register that holds the 32-bit linear base address and a 16-bit size of the table. The LDTR and GDTR registers are used for this purpose. These registers can be loaded using the lldt and lgdt instructions. Similarly, the values of the LDTR and GDTR registers can be stored by the sldt and sgdt instructions. These instructions are typically used by the operating system.

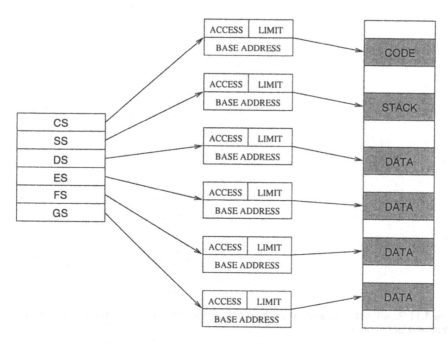

Figure 4.10 Segments in a multisegment model.

The global descriptor table contains descriptors that are available to all tasks within the system. There is only one GDT in the system. Typically, the GDT contains code and data used by the operating system. The local descriptor table contains descriptors for a given program. There can be several LDTs, each of which may contain descriptors for code, data, stack, and so on. A program cannot access a segment unless there is a descriptor for the segment in either the current LDT or GDT.

Segmentation Models

The segments can span the entire memory address space. As a result, we can effectively make the segmentation invisible by mapping all segment base addresses to zero and setting the size to 4 GB. Such a model is called a *flat model* and is used in programming environments such as UNIX and Linux.

Another model that uses the capabilities of segmentation to the full extent is the *multisegment model*. Figure 4.10 shows an example mapping of six segments. A program, in fact, can have more than just six segments. In this case, the segment descriptor table associated with the program will have the descriptors loaded for all the segments defined by the program. However, at any time, only six of these segments can be active. Active segments are those that have their segment selectors loaded into the six segment registers. A segment that is not active can be made active by loading its selector into one of the segment registers, and the processor automatically loads the associated descriptor (i.e., the "invisible part" shown in Figure 4.8). The processor generates a general-protection exception if an attempt is made to access memory beyond the segment limit.

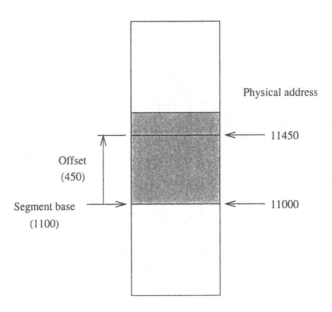

Figure 4.11 Relationship between the logical and physical addresses of memory in the real mode (all numbers are in hex).

Real Mode Memory Architecture

In the real mode, an IA-32 processor such as the Pentium behaves like a faster 8086. The memory address space of the 8086 processor is 1 MB. To address a memory location, we have to use a 20-bit address. The address of the first location is 00000H; the last addressable memory location is at FFFFFH.

Since all registers in the 8086 are 16 bits wide, the address space is limited to 2^{16}, or 65,536 (64 K) locations. As a consequence, the memory is organized as a set of segments. Each segment of memory is a linear contiguous sequence of up to 64 K bytes. In this segmented memory organization, we have to specify two components to identify a memory location: a *segment base* and an *offset*. This two-component specification is referred to as the *logical address*. The segment base specifies the start address of a segment in memory and the offset specifies the address relative to the segment base. The offset is also referred to as the *effective address*. The relationship between the logical and physical addresses is shown in Figure 4.11.

It can be seen from Figure 4.11 that the segment base address is 20 bits long (11000H). So how can we use a 16-bit register to store the 20-bit segment base address? The trick is to store the most significant 16 bits of the segment base address and assume that the least significant four bits are all 0. In the example shown in Figure 4.11, we would store 1100H as the segment base. The implied four least significant zero bits are not stored. This trick works but imposes a restriction on where a segment can begin. Segments can begin only at those memory locations whose address has the least significant four bits as 0. Thus, segments can begin at 00000H, 00010H, 00020H, ..., FFFE0H, FFFF0H. Segments, for example, cannot begin at 00001H or FFFEEH.

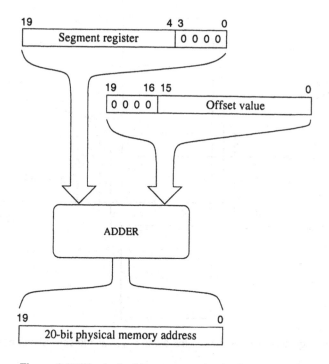

Figure 4.12 Physical address generation in the real mode.

In the segmented memory organization, a memory location can be identified by its logical address. We use the notation *segment:offset* to specify the logical address. For example, 1100:450H identifies the memory location 11450H, as shown in Figure 4.11. The latter value to identify a memory location is referred to as the *physical memory address*.

Programmers have to be concerned with the logical addresses only. However, when the processor accesses the memory, it has to supply the 20-bit physical memory address. The conversion of logical address to physical address is straightforward. This translation process, shown in Figure 4.12, involves adding four least significant zero bits to the segment base value and then adding the offset value. When using the hexadecimal number system, simply add a zero to the segment base address at the right and add the offset value. As an example, consider the logical address 1100:450H. The physical address is computed as follows.

```
  11000    (add 0 to the 16-bit segment base value)
+   450    (offset value)
  11450    (physical address).
```

For each logical memory address, there is a unique physical memory address. The converse, however, is not true. More than one logical address can refer to the same physical memory address. This is illustrated in Figure 4.13, where logical addresses 1000:20A9H and 1200:A9H refer to the same physical address 120A9H. In this example, the physical memory address 120A9H is mapped to two segments.

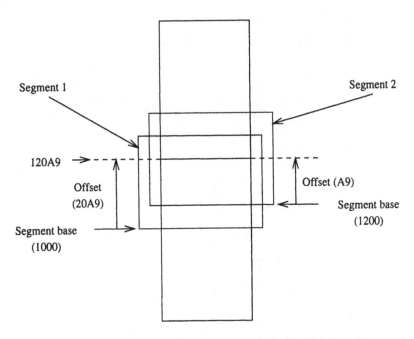

Figure 4.13 Two logical addresses map to the same physical address (all numbers are in hex).

In our discussion of segments, we never said anything about the actual size of a segment. The main factor limiting the size of a segment is the 16-bit offset value, which restricts the segments to at most 64 KB in size. In the real mode, the processor sets the size of each segment to exactly 64 KB. At any instance, a program can access up to six segments. The 8086 actually supported only four segments: segment registers FS and GS were not present in the 8086 processor.

Assembly language programs typically use at least two segments: code and stack segments. If the program has data (which almost all programs do), a third segment is also needed to store data. Those programs that require additional memory can use the other segments.

The six segment registers point to the six active segments, as shown in Figure 4.14. As described earlier, segments must begin on 16-byte memory boundaries. Except for this restriction, segments can be placed anywhere in memory. The segment registers are independent and segments can be contiguous, disjoint, partially overlapped, or fully overlapped.

Mixed-Mode Operation

Our previous discussion of protected and real modes of operation suggests that we can use either 16-bit or 32-bit operands and addresses. The D/B bit indicates the default size. The question is: Is it possible to mix these two? For instance, can we use 32-bit registers in the 16-bit mode of operation? The answer is yes!

The instruction set provides two size override prefixes—one for the operands and the other for the addresses—to facilitate such mixed mode programming. Details on these prefixes are provided in Chapter 13.

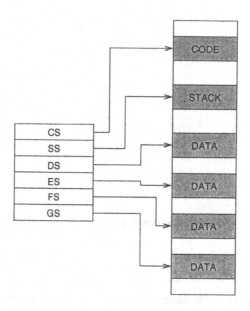

Figure 4.14 The six active segments of the memory system.

Which Segment Register to Use

This discussion applies to both real and protected modes of operation. In generating a physical memory address, the processor uses different segment registers depending on the purpose of the memory reference. Similarly, the offset part of the logical address comes from a variety of sources.

Instruction Fetch: When the memory access is to read an instruction, the CS register provides the segment base address. The offset part is supplied either by the IP or EIP register, depending on whether we are using 16-bit or 32-bit addresses. Thus, CS:(E)IP points to the next instruction to be fetched from the code segment.

Stack Operations: Whenever the processor is accessing the memory to perform a stack operation such as push or pop, the SS register is used for the segment base address, and the offset value comes from either the SP register (for 16-bit addresses) or the ESP register (for 32-bit addresses). For other operations on the stack, the BP or EBP register supplies the offset value. A lot more is said about the stack in Chapter 11.

Accessing Data: If the purpose of accessing memory is to read or write data, the DS register is the default choice for providing the data segment base address. The offset value comes from a variety of sources depending on the addressing mode used. Addressing modes are discussed in Chapter 13.

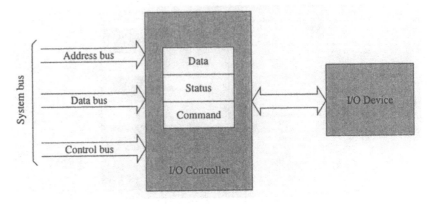

Figure 4.15 Block diagram of a generic I/O device interface.

Input/Output

Input/Output (I/O) devices provide the means by which a computer system can interact with the outside world. An I/O device can be a purely input device (e.g., keyboard, mouse), a purely output device (e.g., printer, display screen), or both an input and output device (e.g., disk). Here we present a brief overview of the I/O device interface. Chapter 20 provides more details on I/O interfaces.

Computers use I/O devices (also called *peripheral devices*) for two major purposes—to communicate with the outside world, and to store data. I/O devices such as printers, keyboards, and modems are used for communication purposes and devices like disk drives are used for data storage. Regardless of the intended purpose of an I/O device, all communications with these devices must involve the system bus. However, I/O devices are not directly connected to the system bus. Instead, there is usually an *I/O controller* that acts as an interface between the system and the I/O device.

There are two main reasons for using an I/O controller. First, different I/O devices exhibit different characteristics and, if these devices were connected directly, the processor would have to understand and respond appropriately to each I/O device. This would cause the processor to spend a lot of time interacting with I/O devices and spend less time executing user programs. If we use an I/O controller, this controller could provide the necessary low-level commands and data for proper operation of the associated I/O device. Often, for complex I/O devices such as disk drives, there are special I/O controller chips available.

The second reason for using an I/O controller is that the amount of electrical power used to send signals on the system bus is very low. This means that the cable connecting the I/O device has to be very short (a few centimeters at most). I/O controllers typically contain driver hardware to send current over long cables that connect the I/O devices.

I/O controllers typically have three types of internal registers—a data register, a command register, and a status register—as shown in Figure 4.15. When the processor wants to interact with an I/O device, it communicates only with the associated I/O controller.

To focus our discussion, let us consider printing a character on the printer. Before the processor sends a character to be printed, it has to first check the status register of the associated I/O controller to see whether the printer is online/offline, busy or idle, out of paper, and so on. In the status register, three bits can be used to provide this information. For example, bit 4 can be used to indicate whether the printer is online (1) or offline (0), bit 7 can be used for busy (1) or not busy (0) status indication, and bit 5 can be used for out of paper (1) or not (0).

The data register holds the character to be printed and the command register tells the controller the operation requested by the processor (for example, send the character in the data register to the printer). The following summarizes the sequence of actions involved in sending a character to the printer:

- Wait for the controller to finish the last command;
- Place a character to be printed in the data register;
- Set the command register to initiate the transfer.

The processor accesses the internal registers of an I/O controller through what are known as *I/O ports*. An I/O port is simply the address of a register associated with an I/O controller.

There are two ways of mapping I/O ports. Some processors such as the MIPS map I/O ports to memory addresses. This is called *memory-mapped I/O*. In these systems, writing to an I/O port is similar to writing to a memory address. Other processors like the Pentium have an *I/O address space* that is separate from the memory address space. This technique is called *isolated I/O*. In these systems, to access the I/O address space, special I/O instructions are needed. The IA-32 instruction set provides two instructions—in and out—to access I/O ports. The in instruction can be used to read from an I/O port and the out for writing to an I/O port. Chapter 20 gives more details on these instructions.

The IA-32 architecture provides 64 KB of I/O address space. This address space can be used for 8-bit, 16-bit, and 32-bit I/O ports. However, the combination cannot be more than the I/O address space. For example, we can have 64 K 8-bit ports, 32 K 16-bit ports, 16 K 32-bit ports, or a combination of these that fits the 64 K address space.

Systems designed with processors supporting the isolated I/O have the flexibility of using either the memory-mapped I/O or the isolated I/O. Typically, both strategies are used. For instance, devices like printer or keyboard could be mapped to the I/O address using the isolated I/O strategy; the display screen could be mapped to a set of memory addresses using the memory-mapped I/O.

Accessing I/O Devices   As a programmer, you can have direct control on any of the I/O devices (through their associated I/O controllers) when you program in the assembly language. However, it is often a difficult task to access an I/O device without any help. Furthermore, it is a waste of time and effort if everyone has to develop their own routines to access I/O devices (called *device drivers*). In addition, system resources could be abused, either unintentionally or maliciously. For instance, an improper disk driver could erase the contents of a disk due to a bug in the driver routine.

To avoid these problems and to provide a standard way of accessing I/O devices, operating systems provide routines to conveniently access I/O devices. Linux provides a set of system calls to access system I/O devices. In Windows, access to I/O devices can be obtained from two layers of system software: the basic I/O system (BIOS), and the operating system. BIOS is ROM resident and is a collection of routines that control the basic I/O devices. Both provide access to routines that control the I/O devices though a mechanism called *interrupts*. Interrupts are discussed in detail in Chapter 20.

Summary

We described the Intel IA-32 architecture in detail. Implementations of this architecture include processors such as Pentium, Celeron, Pentium 4, and Xeon. These processors can address up to 4 GB of memory. This architecture provides protected- and real-mode memory architectures. The protected mode is the native mode of this architecture. In this mode, it supports both paging and segmentation. Paging is useful in implementing virtual memory and is not discussed here.

In the real mode, 16-bit addresses and the memory architecture of the 8086 processor are supported. We discussed the segmented memory architecture in detail, as these details are necessary to program in the assembly language.

PART III
Linux

PART III

INDEX

5

Installing Linux

This chapter gives detailed information on installing Fedora Linux on your system. If your system already has another operating system such as Windows XP, you can install Fedora Linux as the second operating system. At the boot time, you can select one of the operating systems to boot. Such systems are called dual-boot systems. If you want to install it as the only operating system, you can skip some of the steps described in this chapter.

The default software packages installed do not include the compilers and assemblers that we need for the assembly language programming. We show how software packages can be installed and removed by using the package management tool provided by Fedora Linux.

We also discuss how files can be shared between the Windows and Linux operating systems. To share files between these two operating systems, you need to mount a Windows partition so that it is accessible under Linux. We provide detailed instructions to mount Windows partitions. Toward the end of the chapter, we give information on how you can get help if you run into installation problems.

Introduction

This chapter describes the Fedora Core 3 Linux operating system installation process. The book comes with two DVD-ROMs. The first DVD-ROM (DVD 1) contains the complete Fedora 3 distribution. It is a copy of the distribution available at the Red Hat's Fedora Web site (www.fedora. redhat.com). The second DVD-ROM (DVD 2) contains the source code and CD-ROM images. If you have a DVD-ROM drive, you can install Fedora Core 3 using DVD 1.

If your system does not have a DVD-ROM drive, you can make installation CD-ROMs from the image files on DVD 2. This DVD-ROM contains three CD-ROM ISO image files: FC3-i386-disc1.iso, FC3-i386-disc2.iso, and FC3-i386-disc3.iso. You can use these files to burn three CDs. Note that you should *not* copy these ISO files onto the CDs as if they are data files. Instead, you have to let the CD writer software know that these are ISO image files. If you do not have a CD writer application that allows you burning of CD image files, several utilities are available in the public domain. For example, the BurnCDCC utility from Terabyte Unlimited (http://www.terabyteunlimited.com/utilities.html) is a freeware that allows you to burn an ISO file to a CD or DVD. In the rest of the chapter, we assume that you are using DVD 1 to install the Fedora Linux.

To install the Linux operating system from the accompanying DVD-ROM, you need to have a DVD-ROM drive supported by Linux. Linux supports a variety of DVD-ROM drives. In all probability, your drive is supported. In this chapter, we describe installation of *Personal Desktop*, which is a compact system that is targeted for new users. Unfortunately, it does not install all the software we need. For example, development tools like compilers, assemblers, and debuggers are not installed. It is, however, simple to add additional software packages using the package management tool provided by the Fedora 3 distribution. We give detailed instructions on how the missing packages can be installed.

The installation can be done in several different ways depending on the state of your current system. If you want to install Linux as the only operating system, it is relatively straightforward. In fact, you will perform only some of the steps described here.

A most likely scenario is that you want to keep your current Windows operating system such as XP. This is what we assume in the remainder of this chapter. The steps we describe here will add Linux as the second operating system. At boot time you can select the operating system you want to start.

The installation process involves two steps: (i) create enough disk space for the Linux operating system, and (ii) install the Linux system. Between these two steps, the first step is a critical one. Several scenarios are possible here. You may want to isolate your Windows system from Linux by using a second hard drive. In this case, creating space for Linux is not a problem. Often, you find that there is a lot of disk space in your existing hard drive. This is typically the case if you have a recent system with a large disk drive. In this case, you may want to partition your hard drive to make room for Linux. This is the scenario we describe here. If your situation is different from what is described here, you may want to get on the Internet for the information that applies to your system configuration. You can refer to the "Getting Help" section at the end of the chapter for details on where you can get help. This chapter gives detailed instructions on how you can partition your hard disk, install the Fedora distribution, and add additional software packages we need.

When you have more than one operating system, it is often convenient to share files between the operating systems. One way to share the files is to explicitly copy using a removable medium such as a memory stick or floppy disk. However, it would be better if we can share the files without such explicit copying. Before closing the chapter, we describe the procedure involved in mounting a Windows partition under the Linux operating system to facilitate file sharing.

Partitioning Your Hard Disk

If you decide to partition your existing hard disk for Linux, you can use a commercial product such as `PartitionMagic`. It allows you to create new partitions or resize an existing partition. If your file system is FAT32 (not NTFS), you can also use the `parted` utility provided on the accompanying DVD-ROM. If you decide to follow this path, make sure to read the `parted` documentation.

> **Important**
>
> Irrespective of how you plan to partition your hard disk, make sure to backup all your files in case you run into problems. Before you proceed, ensure that the backup is readable. If you want some degree of added safety, you may want to make two backup copies.

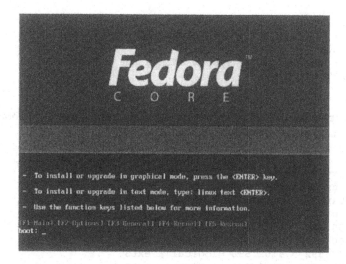

Figure 5.1 Fedora Core 3 initial screenshot. Type linux rescue to access the parted utility to partition your hard disk.

In this section, we describe three ways of partitioning your hard disk. The first one uses the parted utility that comes with the Fedora Core Linux distribution. Next we describe how you can use the QTparted utility on DVD 2. Lastly, we describe Partition Magic to partition your hard disk. You can use parted to partition FAT32 partitions. If your file system uses NTFS, you can use either QTparted or PartitionMagic.

Using PARTED

To use parted, insert DVD 1 into your DVD-ROM drive and reboot your system. For this to work, your system should be bootable from the DVD-ROM drive. If not, get into your system's BIOS to change the boot sequence to include DVD-ROM first or after the floppy drive A (see the boxed note on page 93 for details on making your system bootable from the DVD-ROM drive).

To access parted, you need to boot in the rescue mode. After booting off the DVD, you will see a boot prompt screen shown in Figure 5.1. To enter the rescue mode, type linux rescue. After this, you will be prompted for some hardware choices (keyboard, mouse, and so on). Finally when you get the prompt, type parted. You get (parted) prompt after displaying the GNU copyright information as shown here:

```
[root@veda root]# parted
GNU Parted 1.6.3
Copyright (C) 1998, 1999, 2000, 2001, 2002 Free Software
Foundation, Inc.
This program is free software, covered by the GNU General
Public License.

This program is distributed in the hope that it will be useful,
but WITHOUT ANY WARRANTY; without even the implied warranty of
MERCHANTABILITY or FITNESS FOR A PARTICULAR PURPOSE.  See the
```

GNU General Public License for more details.

Using /dev/hda
Information: The operating system thinks the geometry on
/dev/hda is 784/255/63.
(parted)

At the parted prompt, type p or print to see the current partition information. In our example system, we got the following:

```
(parted) p
Disk geometry for /dev/hda: 0.000-6149.882 megabytes
Disk label type: msdos
Minor    Start       End      Type      Filesystem  Flags
1           0.031   2000.280  primary   fat32       boot
2        2000.281   6142.038  extended
5        2000.312   4000.561  logical   fat32
6        4000.592   4102.536  logical   ext3
7        4102.567   5828.269  logical   ext3
8        5828.300   6142.038  logical   linux-swap
(parted)
```

The partition information consists of a minor number, start and end along with the type of partition and the file system. In our example, Windows XP is on the primary partition (minor 1). The file system on this partition is FAT32 (this is our drive C:). The other FAT32 partition (drive D:) is about 2 GB. Let's assume that this is the partition that we want to resize to make room for Linux. We can use the resize command for this purpose. You can type help to get a command list:

```
(parted) help
  check MINOR                            do a simple check on the filesystem
  cp [FROM-DEVICE] FROM-MINOR TO-MINOR      copy filesystem to another partition
  help [COMMAND]                         prints general help, or help on COMMAND
  mklabel LABEL-TYPE                     create a new disklabel (partition table)
  mkfs MINOR FS-TYPE                     make a filesystem FS-TYPE on partititon MINOR
  mkpart PART-TYPE [FS-TYPE] START END      make a partition
  mkpartfs PART-TYPE FS-TYPE START END      make a partition with a filesystem
  move MINOR START END                   move partition MINOR
  name MINOR NAME                        name partition MINOR NAME
  print [MINOR]                          display the partition table, or a partition
  quit                                   exit program
  rescue START END                       rescue a lost partition near START and END
  resize MINOR START END                 resize filesystem on partition MINOR
  rm MINOR                               delete partition MINOR
  select DEVICE                          choose the device to edit
  set MINOR FLAG STATE                   change a flag on partition MINOR
(parted)
```

You can also get information on a specific command. For example, if you want to know the format of resize, you can type help resize as shown here.

```
(parted) help resize
  resize MINOR START END          resize filesystem on partition MINOR

        MINOR is the partition number used by Linux.  On msdos disk labels, the
        primary partitions number from 1-4, and logical partitions are 5
        onwards.
        START and END are in megabytes.
(parted)
```

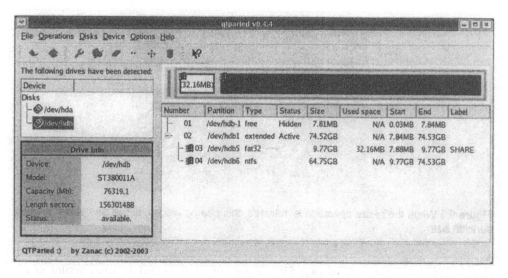

Figure 5.2 QTparted provides a nice, user-friendly interface similar to the PartitionMagic tool.

To create space for Linux, we resize the minor 5 partition from 2 GB to about 1 GB. This is done by the following resize command.

```
(parted) resize 5 2000.312 3000
```

Notice that we specify 5 as the minor identifying the partition, and its start and end points. To verify that the partition size has been reduced, we use the print command:

```
(parted) p
Disk geometry for /dev/hda: 0.000-6149.882 megabytes
Disk label type: msdos
Minor    Start        End        Type       Filesystem  Flags
1         0.031      2000.280    primary    fat32       boot
2        2000.281    6142.038    extended
5        2000.312    2996.499    logical    fat32
6        4000.592    4102.536    logical    ext3
7        4102.567    5828.269    logical    ext3
8        5828.300    6142.038    logical    linux-swap
(parted)
```

Clearly, the partition has been reduced in size to about 1 GB. Now we can use the freed space for installing another operating system. Of course, in our example system, Linux is already installed. But you get the idea of what is involved in resizing a partition to create free space.

Using QTparted

The QTparted partitioning tool provides a nice user interface to parted and other partition programs (see Figure 5.2). The best way to get QTparted is to get the SystemRescueCD ISO image. For your convenience, this ISO image is on DVD 2. It is distributed under the GNU

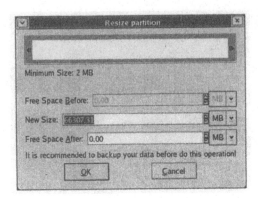

Figure 5.3 When the resize operation is selected, this pop-up window allows us specify the new partition size.

General Public License given on page 539. If you want to download the latest version of this image, which is about 100 MB, you can do so from www.sysresccd.org. Irrespective of how you got the ISO file, you need to create a CD by burning this image.

You can use this CD to boot into a variety of tools, including QTparted. After the booting is completed, enter run_qtparted to launch QTparted. It displays the drives found in your system. Once you select a drive, it gets the partition information. In our example system there are two hard disks, /dev/hda and /dev/hdb, as shown in Figure 5.2. By selecting the second hard disk hdb, we get its partition information shown in this figure. As shown in this screenshot, the window is divided into three parts: the left side gives a list of disk drives and information on the selected disk drive (in our example, on /dev/hdb). The partition information is displayed in the main window.

The operations pull-down menu can be used to select an operation. Some of the common operations are also shown on the toolbar. To illustrate the working of QTparted, we split the NTFS partition /dev/hdb6 to create about 30 GB of free space. To do this task, we select the /dev/hdb6 partition and apply the Resize operation from the Operations menu. You could also apply the resize operation from the toolbar by selecting the icon ↔. This pops up the Resize partition window shown in Figure 5.3. This window shows the free space before as well after the partition. In our example, there is no free space on either end. We can specify the new size of the partition by changing the value or by sliding the size window at the top. In our example, we reduce the partition to about 35 GB, leaving about 30 GB of free space as shown in Figure 5.4.

Once you click OK, the main window shows the new partition information. However, actual partitioning is not done. The necessary operations are queued for execution. If you want to proceed with the resizing operation, you have to commit the changes by selecting Commit from the File pull-down menu. You can undo the changes by selecting the Undo command from this menu. In our case, we proceed to commit the resize operation. After this, we get one last chance to change our mind. Before proceeding to resize the partition, QTparted gives us the warning message shown in Figure 5.5. If we click "Yes" the operations are executed to resize the partition. The screenshot in Figure 5.6 clearly shows the free space created by this operation.

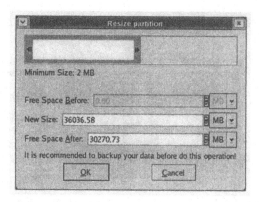

Figure 5.4 The resize partition window shows that we want to reduce the NTFS partition to about 36036 MB, or about 35 GB.

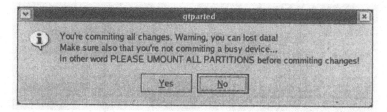

Figure 5.5 When we want to proceed with the partition operations, this warning is given before committing the changes.

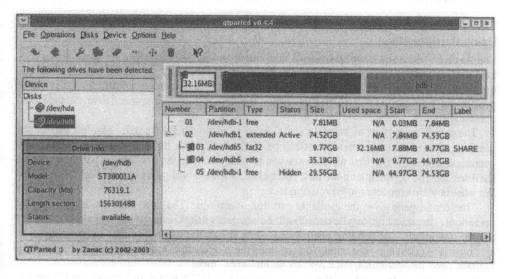

Figure 5.6 This screenshot clearly shows the reduced NTFS partition.

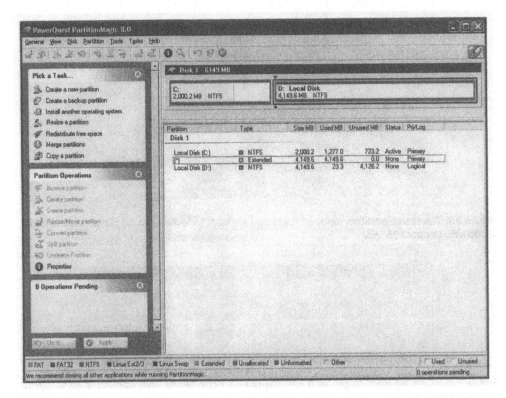

Figure 5.7 A screenshot of `PartitionMagic` showing the tasks that it can perform.

Using PartitionMagic

The `PartitionMagic` tool provides a convenient and friendly interface for partitioning your hard disk. The `QTparted` interface is designed to be a clone of `PartitionMagic`. We can use `PartitionMagic` to create a new partition, resize, delete or move a partition, and so on. In this section, we describe how an NTFS partition is divided to create free space to install the Linux operating system.

The initial screenshot of `PartitionMagic` is shown in Figure 5.7. The left part of the screen is divided into three panes that can be used to select the tasks, partition operations, and pending operations. The first pane allows you to pick a task such as resizing a partition. As we shall see shortly, depending on the task you picked, a wizard will guide you through the process. We will show this process for the resizing task.

The second pane gives the available partition operations. The third pane shows the pending operations. `PartitionMagic` collects all the necessary information before actually implementing the operation. The pending operation window shows the operations that are pending to be executed. If you change your mind, you can undo these operations easily. If you want to go ahead with the pending operations, click `Apply` to implement them.

In our example, we use a 6 GB disk that contains two NTFS partitions as shown in Figure 5.7.

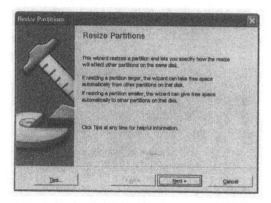

Figure 5.8 The Resize wizard helps you with the resizing task.

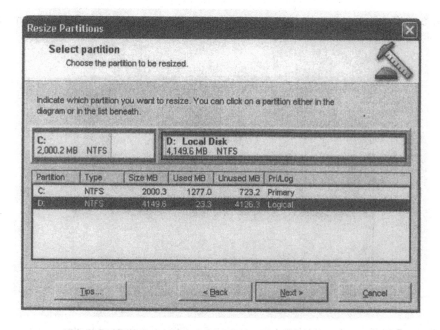

Figure 5.9 The Resize wizard allows you to select the partition.

In the remainder of this section, let us focus on dividing the second partition (Local Disk D) to make free space. To do this, we select the Resize task in "Pick a Task..." pane. This selection invokes the Resize wizard shown in Figure 5.8.

The wizard lets you select the partition that is to be resized. In our example, we select the D: partition (see Figure 5.9). Any time you need help, you can select Tips... for information and

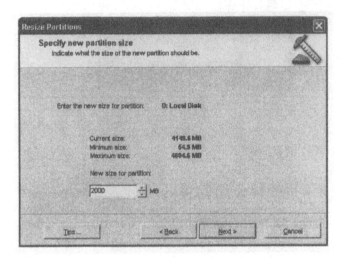

Figure 5.10 The wizard gives the partition information, including the minimum and maximum sizes of the partition.

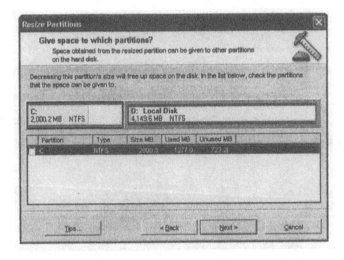

Figure 5.11 The space obtained from resizing a partition can be given to other partitions.

help. The wizard then asks for the size of the new partition. To help you with the selection, it specifies the minimum and maximum sizes possible for the given partition along with the current partition size. In our example, the current partition size is about 4 GB. We can resize this partition to a size that is between the minimum and maximum sizes given in Figure 5.10. We selected a partition size of about 2 GB for the current partition (i.e., we are reducing it from about 4 GB to 2 GB).

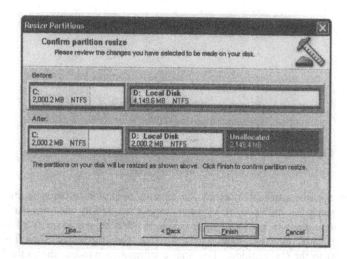

Figure 5.12 Final confirmation window shows the partition information.

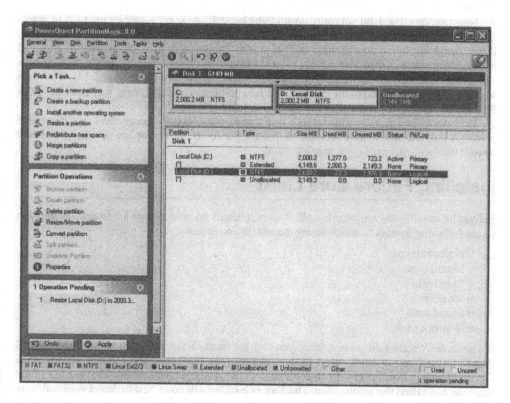

Figure 5.13 Main window with a pending operation to resize the partition.

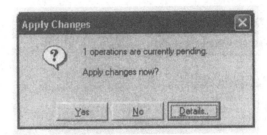

Figure 5.14 Confirmation window before applying the changes.

We can give the free space obtained by the resizing operation to other partitions. The next window lets us specify this information. In our example, there is only one other partition (partition C:), which appears in the window (see Figure 5.11). In our case, we do not want to give the free space to any other partition, as we want to keep the free space for Linux. Therefore, we deselect the checkbox next to the C: partition. The final confirmation window shows the "Before" and "After" picture of the partition (see Figure 5.12). As shown in this figure, we have more than 2 GB of free space.

Note that the wizard did not really do anything but collect the necessary information in preparation for resizing the partition. As can be seen from Figure 5.13 the resize operation is pending. If we change our mind, we can undo this operation. On the other hand, if we want to go ahead with applying these changes, we can apply these changes by clicking Apply button. Before these changes are permanently applied, we get one last chance to confirm (see Figure 5.14). The main window in Figure 5.15 shows the creation of a free partition to install Linux. It is clear from this description that QTparted clones the PartitionMagic tool.

We have looked at one particular task that PartitionMagic can perform. As mentioned before, it provides many more services to manage partitions. For complete details, you should consult the PartitionMagic user's manual.

Installing Fedora Core Linux

Before the installation, you need to collect certain details on your system hardware. Information on the following devices is useful during the installation process:

- Keyboard type
- Mouse type
- Video card
- Monitor
- Sound card
- Network card

If you have Windows on your system, you can get most of this information from the Control Panel. In the Control Panel, select System and then the Hardware tab. On this window click Device Manager. Don't worry if you don't have all the information mentioned above. Most of the time you don't need this information. The Fedora installer will do its best to detect your hardware but sometimes it fails to recognize your hardware. In that case, it helps if you have this information handy.

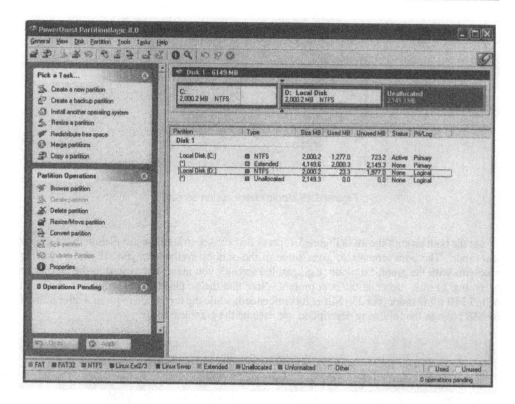

Figure 5.15 This window clearly shows the unallocated partition to install Linux.

Booting

You begin the installation process by inserting DVD 1 into the DVD-ROM drive and starting your computer. Note that you should to be able to boot off the DVD-ROM drive for the installation process to proceed. If successful, you will see the boot screen shown in Figure 5.1.

No Boot Screen?

If you don't see the boot screen, it is likely that you are not able to boot off the DVD-ROM drive. In this case, if you have Windows on your system, it proceeds with booting the Windows operating system. To make the DVD-ROM drive bootable, restart your computer. As it starts, check for a message that tells you how to get into BIOS setup (e.g., pressing Del, F1, or F2 key). Once you are into the BIOS setup, look for "Boot Options", or something similar. It tells you the order in which the devices are used for booting. It probably has "A" first and then "C". That is, it first tries to boot from the floppy drive. If no floppy disk is present, it boots from the hard disk (drive C). What you need to do is make the DVD-ROM as either the first in the list, or after the floppy drive. This should make your system DVD-ROM bootable.

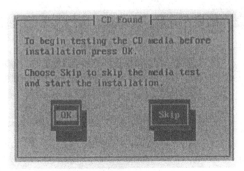

Figure 5.16 Media check option screen.

At the boot prompt shown in Figure 5.1, press Enter key to start the installation in the graphical mode. The boot screen also gives some of the options available to you. If you are having problems with the graphical mode (e.g., garbled screen), you may want to start in the text mode by typing linux text at the boot prompt. Note that the graphical mode requires a minimum of 192 MB of memory (but 256 MB is recommended) while the text mode requires a minimum of 64 MB only. In the following description, we assume the graphical mode.

> **Installation Problems?**
>
> Sometimes the installation process hangs up, particularly if you have an LCD monitor, or installing on a laptop. If this happens, try using linux nofb to turn off the frame buffer. For more details, see the release notes at www.fedora.redhat.com/docs/release-notes/fc3/x86/.

Once the mode is selected, you will see a flurry of messages and the boot up process stays in the text mode for a while. During this time, it performs some simple checks and determines your basic hardware (keyboard, mouse type, video card). It then launches the graphical mode to begin the media check process.

Media Check

Before proceeding with the installation process, you are given an option to check the media (see Figure 5.16). If you are using the media for the first time, you should click OK to allow media check. It may take several minutes to complete the check. At the end of the test, it will let you know the media test result (PASS or FAIL). If the media check failed, you need to get a replacement. If you know that the media is not defective, you can skip this check.

Once the media has passed the test (or if you skipped), you can press continue to proceed with the installation. Next you will see the installation welcome screen shown in Figure 5.17. If your hardware (mouse, monitor, and video card) is not properly recognized, the Fedora installer will use defaults that should work, though these default settings may not give the best performance.

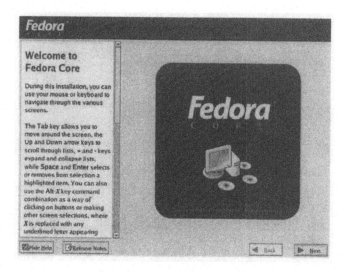

Figure 5.17 Welcome screen.

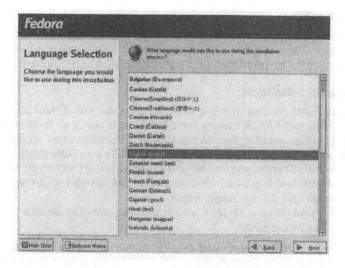

Figure 5.18 Language selection screen.

Select the Installation Language

The language selection screen, shown in Figure 5.18, allows you to select a language that you would like to use during the installation. As you can see from this screenshot, Fedora supports several languages to facilitate installation. If needed, other languages can be added later. After your selection, click next to proceed with the keyboard selection.

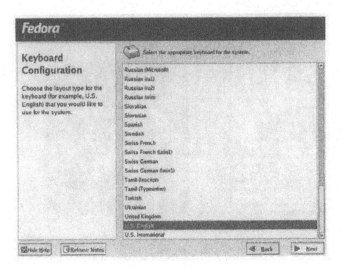

Figure 5.19 Keyboard selection screen.

Select the Keyboard

The installer presents you with the screen shown in Figure 5.19 to allow you select the keyboard layout of your choice. The selection in this screenshot is the default generic 101-key U.S. English layout. After selecting the keyboard layout for your system, click next to proceed.

Select the Type of Installation

Having selected the basic devices, your next step is to select the type of installation you want. At this point, the installer looks for an existing version. If there is one (e.g., Fedora Core 1), you are given the option of either upgrading the previous version or installing a new version. If you have a previous version, select the upgrade option, as it would preserve your current data in the system. If you select the new install option, you lose all your existing data. Whatever you want to do, make your selection and press next to proceed. Here we assume that you did not have a previous version of Fedora and proceed with the new install option.

Next you have to decide on the type of installation you want. The installer supports the following four types (see Figure 5.20):

- *Personal Desktop:* This type of installation is suitable for a home PC or laptop. It requires 2.3 GB of disk space and installs the GNOME desktop and other tools appropriate for a home PC. This is the installation type we would use. However, it does not install system development tools such as compilers, assemblers, and debuggers. We need these tools for the assembly language programming. We will install these packages later.
- *Workstation:* This install type is similar to the personal desktop installation except that it installs software development and system administration tools. It requires about 3 GB of disk space.
- *Server:* This type installs packages that are needed to run the machine as a server (such as a file server, print server, and Web server). By default, it does not install the graphical environment. It needs about 1.1 GB of disk space.

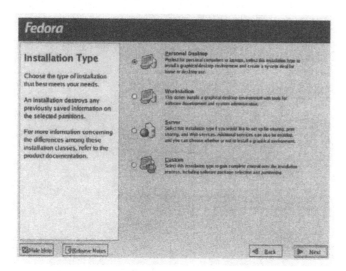

Figure 5.20 Installation type selection screen.

- *Custom System:* This option lets you decide what you want to install on the system. This option is typically meant for advanced users. One can elect to install everything, a minimum set of packages, or a combination between these two extremes. A minimal install requires only 620 MB of disk space. A full install has the advantage of having everything available after the install but requires about 6.9 GB of disk space. On the down side, it takes quite a bit of disk space and longer installation time. If you don't use most of the packages or plan to use Linux only occasionally, you don't want to install everything.

As mentioned earlier, select the Personal Desktop install type and click next.

Disk Partitioning

This is a major step in the installation process. Fortunately you have done most of the work before starting the installation process. You created a free partition for the Fedora Linux. The installer gives you two options: automatic or manual (see Figure 5.21). Assuming that you have a free partition on your disk, select the `Automatically partition` option and press next. This option takes the free space and automatically partitions the disk.

On the next screen, shown in Figure 5.22, you will be given further options on how the installation program should use the disk space. The three options are as follows.

- The first option removes all the existing Linux partitions. This option is good if you want to remove an existing Linux installation while keeping the Windows installation.

- The second option removes all the partitions. You don't want to select this if you have other partitions. For example, you may have several NTFS partitions for the Windows operating system that you want to keep.

- The last option will not touch any of the existing partitions. It uses only the free space on your disk. Of course, you have to make free space available to use this option. This option is appropriate, for example, if you want to keep the existing Windows and Linux installations.

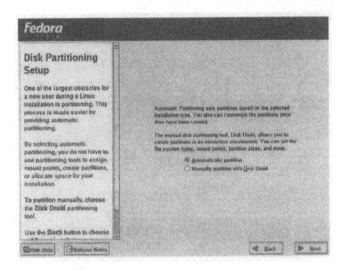

Figure 5.21 Disk partition strategy selection screen.

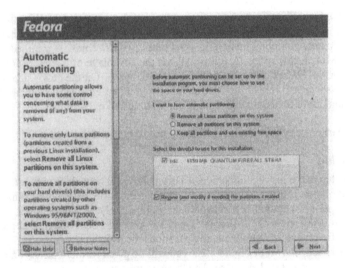

Figure 5.22 Disk partitioning screen.

If you have only Windows on your system, the first or the last option is okay. Before clicking `Next`, select the `Review...` checkbox if you want to review the partitions created by the automatic partitioning tool. The installer cautions you that you are removing some of the partitions (Figure 5.23). If you checked the `Review...` checkbox, you will see a screen with the partition details (see Figure 5.24).

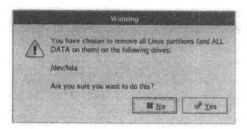

Figure 5.23 Linux partition warning message.

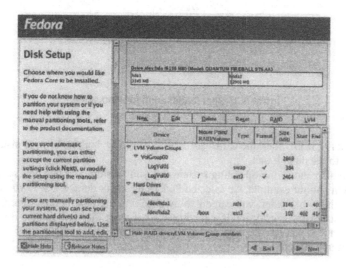

Figure 5.24 Disk partition details.

The automatic partitioning provides you with three partitions: a small `boot` partition of about 100 MB and a root partition (/) that is large enough for the selected installation as well as your files. In addition, it provides a swap partition that is about twice the size of the main memory on your system. For example, if the system has 256 MB, the swap partition should be about 512 MB.

You can change the size of any of these partitions by selecting the manual partition option and then using the Disk Druid tool. If this is the first time you are installing Linux and you are not comfortable with creating your own partitions, accept the partitions created by the automatic partition tool. Click next to go to the next step.

Boot Loader Configuration

This screen allows you to configure the boot loader, which is required when you have multiple operating systems as in our case. When you start your system, the boot loader gives you a list of the available operating systems. You can select the operating system you want to boot. The default boot loader is set to GRUB (GRand Unified Boot loader). If you want to change to the

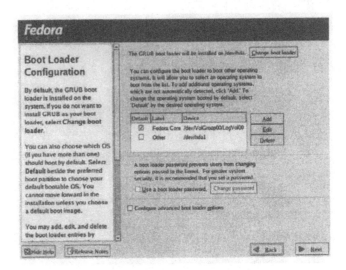

Figure 5.25 Boot loader configuration screen.

other boot loader (LILO), click the `Change boot loader` button. In your installation, leave the boot loader to the default one.

This screen also shows the operating systems on your system and lets you select the default operating system. In our example, we selected Fedora to be our default OS. If you want to set up a password for the boot loader, you can do so by checking the box on this screen. Setting up a password provides extra security and is a good practice if more than one person uses your system. On the other hand, if you are the only one using the system (for example, your home machine) you can leave it unchecked.

Network Configuration

This step allows you to configure your local area network. If your computer does not have an Ethernet interface, or if you are using a dialup connection, you can skip this step. The installer automatically detects the available network interfaces as shown in Figure 5.26. In our example system, we have two network interfaces: `eth0` and `eth1`. You can click the check box next to a network interface if you want that network to be active when the system boots. The `Edit` button can be used to change the parameters for the selected network interface.

If your ISP or access point supports DHCP (most do), you can let the system get the network parameters from the server. In this case, keep the default DHCP selection. On the other hand, if you are using a static IP address, you can enter these values by deselecting the DHCP option.

You can setup the hostname via the DHCP or manually. If you want the hostname to be setup via DHCP, select the "automatically via DHCP" option.

Firewall Setup

If your system is connected to the Internet, it is important that you enable the firewall option (see Figure 5.27). A firewall can significantly reduce the chances of an intruder attacking your system. The installer gives you two options for configuring a firewall during installation:

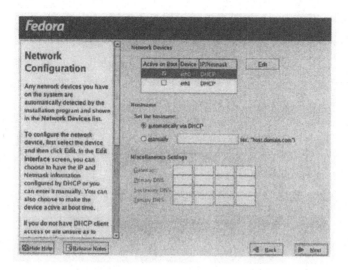

Figure 5.26 Network configuration screen.

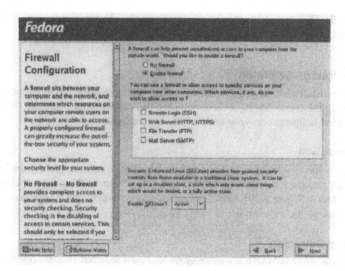

Figure 5.27 Firewall setup screen.

- **Enable firewall:** If you are connected to the Internet or to a public network, you should select this option. This option does not allow any incoming network traffic. If you want to allow a specific service, you have to explicitly list it. However, if the system does not allow any incoming connections, it cannot establish service connections on the Internet. Thus, to allow basic network setup and Web browsing, it allows DHCP and DNS replies.

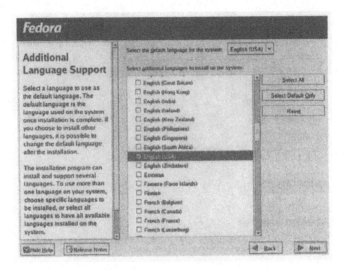

Figure 5.28 Additional language selection screen.

- **No firewall:** This option is appropriate, for example, if your computer is not connected to the Internet.

Additional Language Selection

In addition to the installation language selected before, you can install support for additional languages by clicking the check boxes of the languages. By clicking the `Select All` button, you install all supported languages on your system (see Figure 5.28).

Time Zone Selection

This screen allows you to select the time zone of your location. You can specify the location in one of two ways. You can click a yellow dot on the interactive map to identify your city. (These dots appear as white dots in Figure 5.29) A red X would appear to indicate your selection. Alternatively, you can scroll through the location list to select your location.

Root Password Selection

This screen can be used to select a password for the root account (see Figure 5.30). The root account is special in that it can be used for system administration. It is always a good idea to keep another account for your day-to-day activities and reserve the root account for administration purposes only.

Package Selection

The next step in the installation process involves the selection of the packages you want to install. The installer selects a default set of packages depending on the installation type. The default package selection for the Personal Desktop type installation is shown in Figure 5.31.

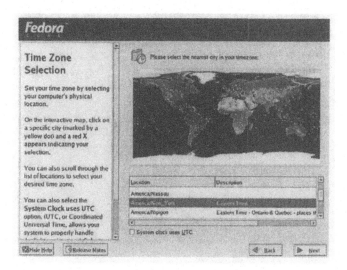

Figure 5.29 Time zone selection screen.

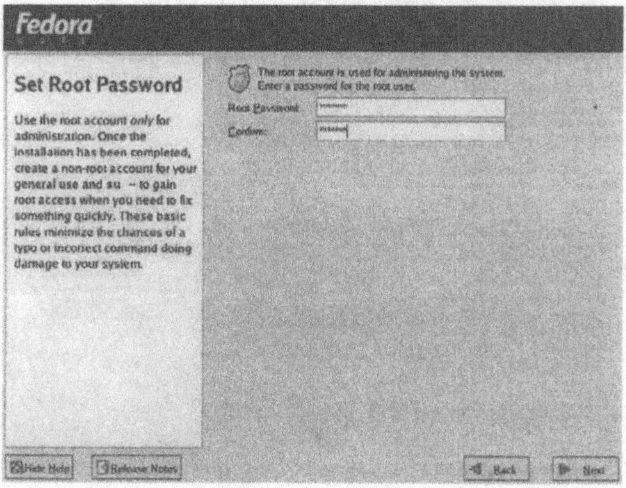

Figure 5.30 Root password selection screen.

If you want to select a different set of packages, or if you want to add some extra packages, you can choose the "Customize software package to be installed" option. For example, the default selection does not install NASM or DDD that we need. However, in our installation, we stick with the default selection as we can easily add the missing packages later.

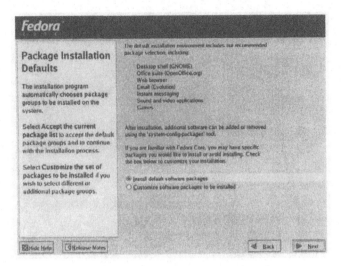

Figure 5.31 Default package selection screen

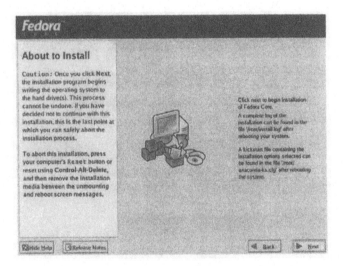

Figure 5.32 About to install screen.

Installation Process Continues

If you are using the CD-ROMs for the installation, the installer informs you that three Fedora Core CDs are required for the installation to proceed. It gives an option of either continuing with the installation or to reboot as shown in Figure 5.33.

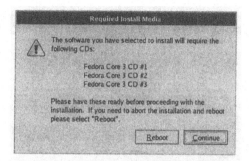

Figure 5.33 Before starting the actual installation process, the installer displays the required media information (if you are using the CD-ROM media).

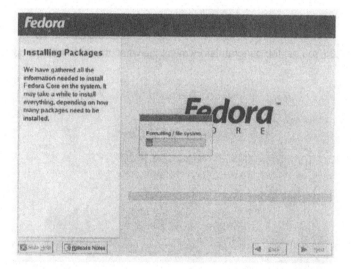

Figure 5.34 Installation process begins by formatting file systems.

The installer has collected the necessary information and is ready to start the installation. This is your last chance to safely abort the installation process. Click "Next" to proceed with the installation. After this, the installation proceeds automatically. If you are using the CDs, the installer prompts you to change the CD a couple of times.

The installation begins by formatting the file system (Figure 5.34). Once the installation is done, you are prompted to reboot (Figure 5.35). Make sure to remove the media (DVD or CD) before clicking the reboot button.

Post-Install Configuration

After rebooting the system, you are presented with the screen shown in Figure 5.36. There are a few more steps to go through before the system is ready for use. These steps are:

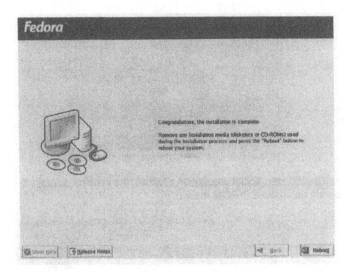

Figure 5.35 You get the congratulatory message when the installation is completed.

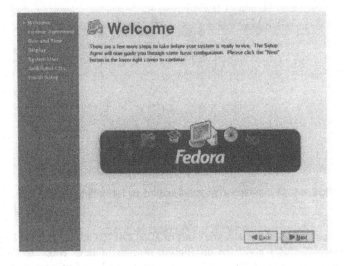

Figure 5.36 Post-install configuration is the last step involved in completing the installation process.

- Accepting licensing agreement;
- Setting/confirming the time and date information;
- Setting the display properties including the resolution;
- Creating a system user: You should not use the `root` account created during the installation as your regular account. This account should be reserved for system maintenance

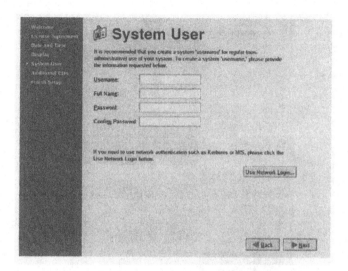

Figure 5.37 You can create a system user account as part of the post-install operations.

activities only. It is strongly recommended that you create an account for your routine use (see Figure 5.37). Alternatively, you can do this later by using a system tool.

- If you want to load additional packages, you can do here. But we prefer to do this later by using the package management tool provided by Fedora.

Congratulations! Your long wait is over. When you start Fedora the next time, it boots up normally and presents you with a login screen. This requests you to enter your user name and password. After you have successfully logged into your account, the system will display the GNOME desktop (for a quick peek at this desktop, see Figure 6.1 on page 116).

Installing and Removing Software Packages

The default software packages installed for the "Personal Desktop" do not include the "Development Tools" group that includes compilers such as gcc, nasm assembler, and ddd debugger. In this section we show how software packages can be installed and removed. Since we need these development tools to program in the assembly language, we install them to illustrate package management.

You can add or remove packages by the package management tool that comes with the Fedora Linux system. It can be invoked from the Applications pull-down menu. From this menu, select System Settings and then Add/Remove Applications as shown in Figure 5.38. If you are not logged in as the root user, which is recommended, it will first ask you for the root password. The package management tool then scans the packages for their status and displays this information as shown in Figure 5.39. For example, we have installed the X Window System and the GNOME Desktop but not the KDE and XFCE desktops.

Scroll down this list until you find the Development Tools package group and check the box to select this group of tools for installation (see Figure 5.40). A package group consists of

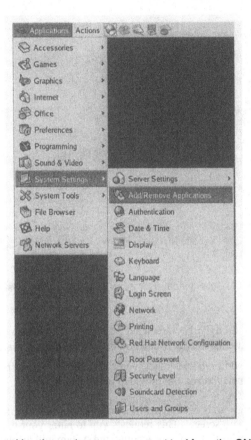

Figure 5.38 Invoking the package management tool from the GNOME desktop.

several standard packages and some extra packages. The standard packages are always selected by default. These packages, which include the gcc C compiler and the gdb debugger, are always available when the group is installed. In addition, several extra packages are also selected by default. However, nasm and ddd are not part of the default extra packages selected for installation. To see the package details for the selected group, click details. This opens a Package Details window that gives details on the standard packages selected and the extra packages available along with their default selection. We scroll down this list to select nasm and ddd as shown in Figure 5.41.

To install these packages, close the package details window and click Update in the Package Management window. The tool collects the necessary information and prepares to install the packages. During this stage, it checks for package dependencies and collects a list of packages. This list includes the actual packages you have selected and any other packages that are required by the selected packages. Once this analysis is done and a package list has been prepared, you will see the prompt shown in Figure 5.42. It gives you information on the number of packages selected and the amount of disk space required. If for some reason you want to abort the installation, this is a good time. If you want to see the packages selected, click the Show Details button.

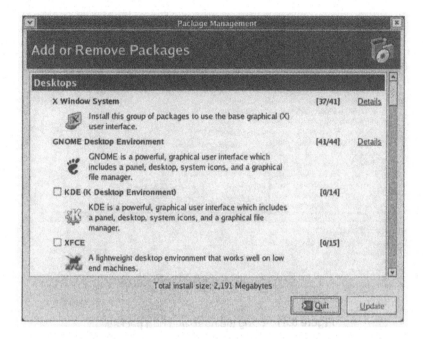

Figure 5.39 Initial screen of the package management tool.

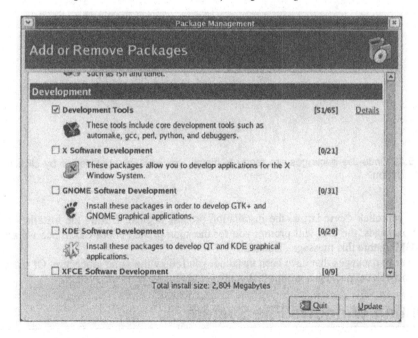

Figure 5.40 Tools available under the Development category.

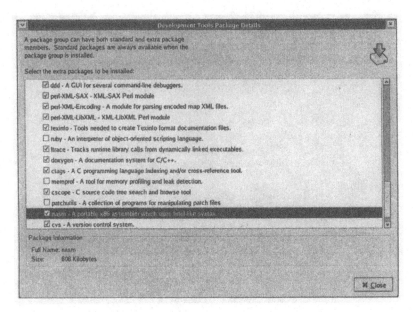

Figure 5.41 Adding the `nasm` and `ddd` packages.

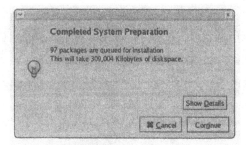

Figure 5.42 Once the packages are ready to install, you can view the details by clicking `Show Details` button.

Once you click `Continue`, the installation process begins. During the installation of the selected packages, the tool will prompt you for the appropriate Fedora CD. Since we are using DVD-ROM, ignore this message. That's it!

To remove packages that have been installed, you follow the same procedure. Of course, you have to uncheck the packages/groups that you want to remove from the system.

Mounting Windows File System

When you have two operating systems, you would like to share files between the two systems. Of course, you can always use a removable medium such as a floppy disk or a memory stick to

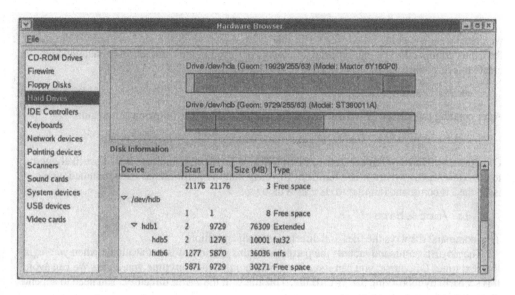

Figure 5.43 You can use the hardware browser to get information on the partitions.

transfer files between the two systems. There is a better solution that eliminates the need for file copying. In this section we show how you can mount a Windows partition so that Linux can access this partition.

There is one restriction—Linux is not able to read NTFS partitions, at least not yet. So the partition that you want to share between the Windows and Linux operating systems has to be a FAT32 partition. Even if you are using FAT32 for your Windows, you do not want to make it sharable for security reasons. For example, a single command in Linux can wipe out all the Windows files. Your Windows operating system, on purpose, hides some system files that you should not normally access. One such example is the boot.ini file to manage the boot process. In Linux, you see all the Windows files and you may accidentally modify the contents or delete a file. This is particularly so during the initial learning stages. Therefore, it is a good idea to create a separate partition that you want to use for sharing. In our example system, we created a 10 GB partition to facilitate this sharing. We would like to mount this partition under Linux so that we could access the files from the Windows system.

As a first step we have to find out the device number assigned to the shared partition. We can use the Hardware Browser to get this information. The Hardware Browser can be invoked from the Applications menu by selecting System Tools and then Hardware Browser. We can use this browser to get information on the system hardware such as CD-ROM drives, floppy disks, hard drives, keyboard, and so on.

In order to run this browser, you need administrative privileges. That means, if you are not running it as the root, you will be asked for the root password. To get the partition information that we are interested here, we select Hard Drives as shown in Figure 5.43. From this information we notice that the 10 GB FAT32 shared partition is assigned \dev\hdb5. To share this partition, we need to mount this partition.

Mounting a partition involves creating a mount point, which is a directory. In our example, we create a mount point called share in the \mnt directory. Since we have not yet discussed the Linux commands, you can type the following command in the command terminal window [1] to create this directory:

```
mkdir /mnt/share
```

After creating this directory we can mount the partition using the following command:

```
mount -t vfat /dev/hdb5 /mnt/share
```

Of course, you have to replace /dev/hdb5 with your partition number. It is most likely going to be /dev/hdaX where X is a number. To verify that the partition has been mounted, you can issue the ls command (similar to dir in Windows).

```
ls /mnt/share
```

This command displays the files and directories in this partition.

The mount command mounts the partition for this session. It is not available when you login the next time. Of course, you can issue the mount command every time you login. We can avoid this scenario by modifying the fstab file. This file is in the /etc directory. You need to append the following line to this file:

```
/dev/hdb5       /mnt/share      vfat      auto,umask=0 0 0
```

Once this step is done, the partition is mounted automatically as the system reads this file every time you log into the system.

To edit the /etc/fstab file, use the text editor available under Applications pull-down menu by following Accessories ⇒ Text Editor. This is a simple text editor that resembles the Windows Wordpad editor. We discuss this editor in the next chapter.

To open the fstab file you need administrative privileges, which means you must be root to open this file in read-write mode. All other users can open this file in read-only mode. So be sure to login as the root to modify this file.

You can use the Open icon to open a file for editing (see Figure 5.44). This pops up the Open File... window to select the file (see Figure 5.45). You can start by double-clicking the Filesystem, then etc directory, and finally the fstab file to open it for editing. The contents of the fstab file in our example system are shown in Figure 5.44.

There are several other editors available in Linux. Some of the popular ones are the vi and emacs editors. We describe the vi editor in the next chapter.

Summary

We have provided a detailed step-by-step description of the Fedora Core 3 installation process. The installation is a two-step process: creating sufficient disk space for the Fedora system and installing the operating system. The first step is not required if Linux is the only operating system you want to install. However, if you want to keep the existing Windows operating system and install Linux as the second operating system, the first step is necessary. It often involves partitioning the disk to make room for Linux.

We have introduced three partitioning tools for this purpose:

---

[1] The command terminal can be invoked from the Applications menu under System Tools submenu. More details on the command terminal are on page 132.

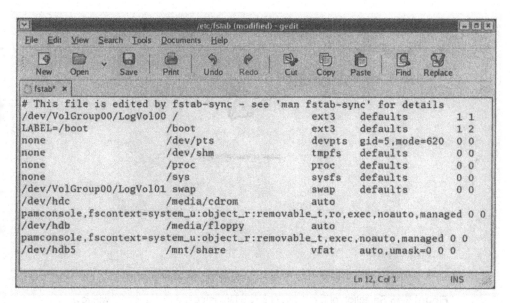

Figure 5.44 Contents of the /etc/fstab file after adding the last line to mount the shared partition.

- The parted tool that comes with Fedora is a text-based partitioning tool. It can be used on FAT32 and other types of partitions but not on NTFS partitions. For NTFS partitions, you can use one of the other two tools.

- The second tool, QTparted, works on NTFS partitions as well as others. It provides a nice user-friendly graphical interface and uses a variety of partitioning tools including parted. Its user interface closely resembles that of the ParttionMagic tool.

- The last tool we presented in this chapter, PartitionMagic, is a commercial partitioning tool. This tool works with different file systems including NTFS partitions.

The Fedora Core 3 Linux can be installed from the DVD-ROM accompanying this book. If your system does not have a DVD-ROM drive, you can burn CDs from the CD image files provided in the second DVD. We have given detailed instructions to install Personal Desktop system that is suitable for new users.

The default software packages selected for this installation type do not include all the software we need. Specifically, the Personal Desktop installation excludes the development tools group. This group includes the C compilers, assemblers, and debuggers that we need for our assembly language programming. However, using the Fedora's package management tool, it is rather straightforward to install these developmental tools. We have given detailed instructions on how you can do this.

Finally, we presented details on sharing files between the Windows and Linux operating systems. The Linux operating system can see the FAT32 partitions but not the NTFS partitions. For this reason, we suggested a small partition for sharing the files between the two operating systems. In our example, we set this partition to 10 GB, but you can set it to whatever size is appropriate in your case. We have given step-by-step instructions to mount such shared partitions.

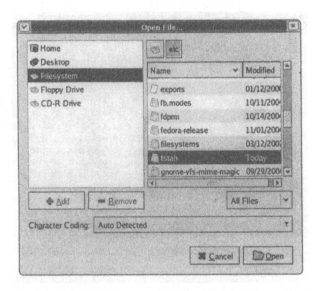

Figure 5.45 Selection of the /etc/fstab file using the open file window.

Getting Help

The Fedora Linux has been installed on five different systems (desktops and laptops) using the procedure described in this chapter. In all these systems, the installation proceeded smoothly. Even though we have given detailed instructions to install the Fedora Linux operating system, it is still possible that you encounter installation problems. There are several places you can turn to for help.

A good starting point is the extensive and detailed bug report database maintained by Red Hat at http://bugzilla.redhat.com. Here you can enter the bug number (if you know it) or keywords to search for information on your problem.

Several online sources are also available to help resolve installation problems. For example, LinuxQuestions.org maintains several forums for Linux-related issues including installation problems at http://www.linuxquestions.org/questions. Another good source is the mailing list maintained by Red Hat at http://www.redhat.com/mailman/listinfo/fedora-list.

You can also use a good search engine such as Google (http://www.google.com) to search the Internet on how others solved your installation problem.

6

Using Linux

Now that you have installed the Fedora Linux on your system, it is time to learn the basics of the Linux operating system. This chapter assumes that you are familiar with another operating system such as Windows XP. Our focus is on the Fedora 3 Linux. We look at both the graphical user interface (GUI) and the command line interface (CLI) provided by the system. For new users, the GUI provides an easy-to-use, point-and-click type of interface. However, as you get familiar with the system, the command line interface tends to be more efficient. We discuss the basics of the command line interface and several simple but useful commands. The overview presented here is sufficient to proceed with our goal of learning the assembly language programming.

Introduction

Assuming that you are new to the Linux operating system, this chapter gives more details on using the Fedora 3 Linux. You have to login to an account in order to use the Linux system. To log into the system, the login screen first prompts you for your login username. Then you will be asked to enter your password for the account. This brings up the GNOME desktop shown in Figure 6.1. This is the default desktop in Fedora 3. The panel at the top contains two pull-down menus: Applications and Actions. The Applications menu provides various applications and systems tools. It provides several useful GUI applications including games, graphics, system tools, and system settings (see Figure 6.2a). The Actions menu can be used to run applications, search for files, lock the screen, and logout as shown in Figure 6.2b.

The icons next to the Actions menu can be used to launch applications quickly. You can click these launch panel icons to launch a Web browser, email reader, word processor, presentations creator, or a spreadsheet. You can customize the launch panel by adding applications of your choice. For example, we have added the command terminal to the launch panel shown in Figure 6.1 (see the icon next to Actions menu).

The workspace, appears as black in Figure 6.1, displays four shortcuts: Computer, your home directory, trash, and a USB hard drive labeled PORTABLE. By clicking the Computer, you will see the various drives (floppy drive, CD-ROM drives, and hard disks), your file system, and networks. It is a good idea to get familiar with the desktop by playing with the various menus and icons. Later we describe some of the applications available to perform commonly required tasks.

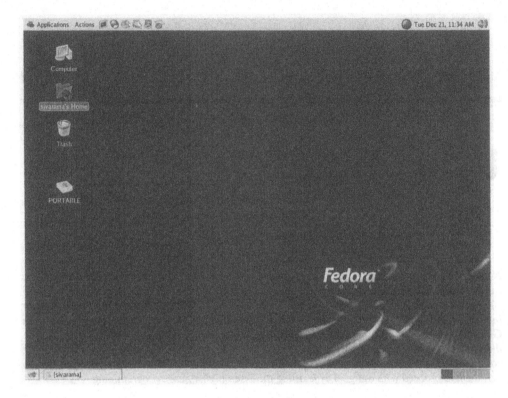

Figure 6.1 Initial Fedora screen with a USB hard drive (PORTABLE).

To logout of your account, you can use the Actions menu as shown in Figure 6.2b. When you select Logout from the Actions menu, a popup window appears with three options: logout of the account, shutdown the system, or restart the system. If you opt for logout, it will bring the login screen. The other options can be selected to either shutdown or restart the system.

Which Account to Use?

During the installation, you created two accounts for yourself: a root account and a system user account. Always use your system user account for non-administrative activities and reserve the root account for special administrative tasks. Note that most administrative tasks can also be done from your system user account. If a task requires administrative privileges, the system will ask you for the root password. On the other hand, if you login as the root, the system gives you permission to do whatever you want. This can lead to mishaps that you did not anticipate.

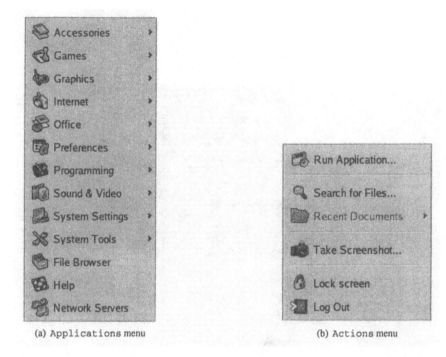

(a) Applications menu   (b) Actions menu

Figure 6.2 The Applications and Actions pull-down menus of the GNOME desktop.

You can run your programs either by using the desktop or from the command line interface. The first part of the chapter describes several applications to manage the system. Later part concentrates on the command line interface.

Setting User Preferences

When you installed the Fedora Linux, you have already configured several of your system devices such as the display and keyboard. It is also straightforward to configure these devices after the installation. This configuration can be done from the Applications pull-down menu under the Preferences menu as shown in Figure 6.3. Next we look at some of these tools.

Keyboard Configuration Tool

Figure 6.4 shows the keyboard configuration tool window. It provides four functional areas: Keyboard, Layouts, Layout Options, and Typing Break. In the Keyboard area, you can set two main options:

- You can decide if you want the repeat-key functionality when a key pressed and held down. To enable this functionality, select the first checkbox as shown in Figure 6.4. If this option is enabled, you can select the initial delay and the rate of repetition by using the two sliders.

Figure 6.3 The Preferences menu.

- The second checkbox allows you to enable the cursor to blink in the fields and text boxes. You can use the slider to select the cursor blink frequency. You can test the setting by typing a sample text in the test area.

The Layouts tabbed window can be used to select your keyboard model. The default is the generic 105-key PC keyboard. This window also allows you to add or remove keyboard layouts. By default, the U. S. English layout is selected.

The Layouts Options window allows you to select several options for the behavior of the various keys such as Alt and CapsLock.

The Typing Break tabbed window can be used to set typing break preferences. You can set how long you want to work and how long the breaks should be. For example, you can select to work 30 minutes and take a break for 3 minutes. The system will lock the screen to force you to take the 3-minute break after 30 minutes of typing. There is also a checkbox that allows you to postpone the breaks.

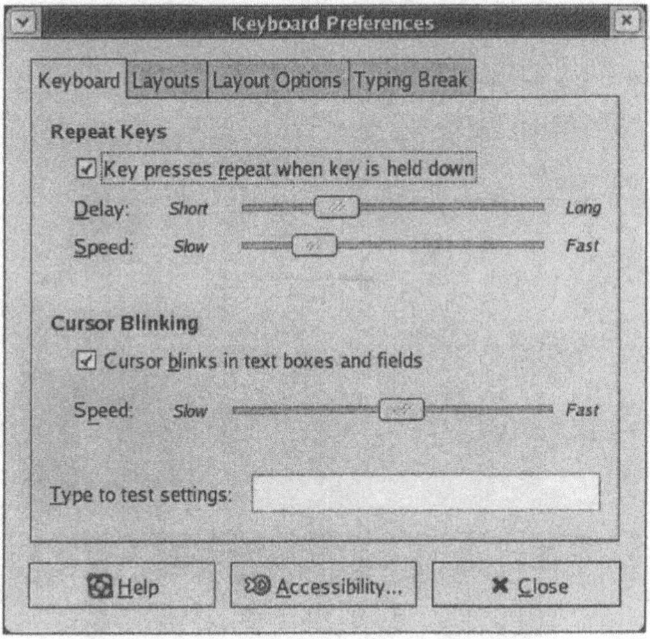

Figure 6.4 The keyboard configuration window.

Mouse Configuration Tool

The mouse configuration tool window is shown in Figure 6.5. It has three functional areas to set the preferences. The Buttons window can be used to set the mouse orientation (left-handed or right-handed) as well as the double-click timeout period.

Use the Cursors tabbed window to select the cursor size (small, medium, or large). The changes you make will take effect when you login the next time. You can also select the option that highlights the cursor when you press the Ctrl key. This option is helpful to locate the cursor.

The Motion window can be used to set the motion preferences. It provides two sliders to set the speed of the mouse pointer and the sensitivity of the mouse pointer to the movement of the mouse. It also has a third slider to specify the distance you must move an item in order to interpret the move as the drag-and-drop action.

Screen Resolution Configuration

You can use the screen resolution tool to set the resolution of your screen. It allows you to select the resolution from the drop-down list (see Figure 6.6). You can also set the refresh rate for your screen. Once the selection is made, you can click the Apply button. The screen will reflect your selection and prompts you if you want to keep the new resolution or revert back to the previous resolution. In general, the installer does a good job in selecting the resolution and refresh rates appropriate for your screen during the installation.

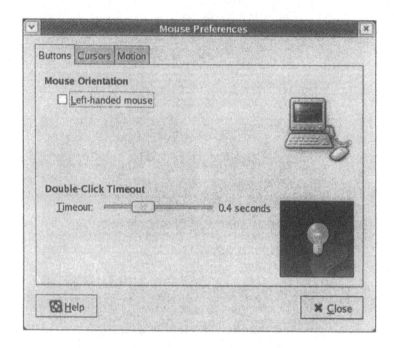

Figure 6.5 The mouse configuration window.

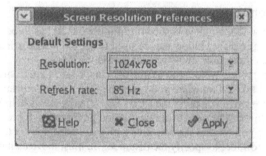

Figure 6.6 The screen resolution window.

Changing Password

You can use the password tool to change the user password. If you want to change your root account password, you should use the root password change tool available in the System Setting menu. The tool first requests your current password (see Figure 6.7). It then prompts you to enter the new password as shown in Figure 6.8. You are asked to reenter the new password to make sure that you did not make a mistake in entering your new password (Figure 6.9). The new password will be effective for your next login.

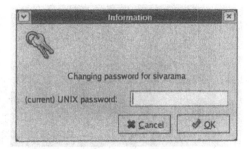

Figure 6.7 Changing the user password—screen 1.

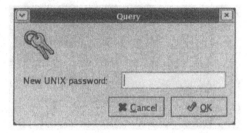

Figure 6.8 Changing the user password—screen 2.

Screensaver

The screensaver tool can be used to control the behavior of the screensaver, display power management, and so on. The functionality is divided into two groups: Display Modes and Advanced as shown in Figure 6.10. The Display Modes tabbed window is used to enable and control the behavior of the screensaver. The screensaver is activated either when the system is idle (when there is no mouse or keyboard activity) for a specified period of time, or when the screen is locked. Note that you can lock your screen by using the Actions menu (see Figure 6.2b on page 117).

The Mode drop-down menu gives you four options:

- *Disable Screen Saver:* Select this option if you don't want the screensaver.

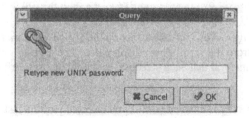

Figure 6.9 Changing the user password—screen 3.

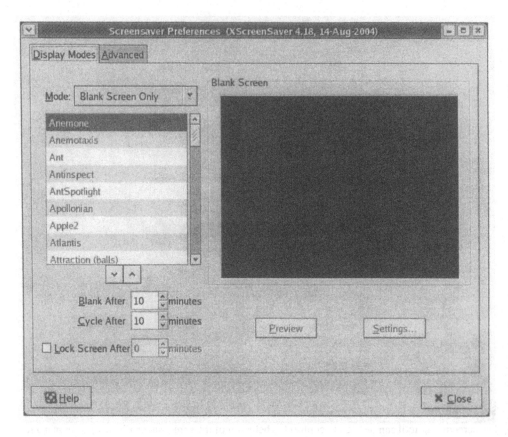

Figure 6.10 The Display Modes tabbed window can be used to enable and control the screen-saver behavior.

- *Blank Screen Only:* This option not only enables the screensaver but also selects blank screen as your screensaver. This option is shown in Figure 6.10.
- *Only One Screen Saver:* This option allows you to select a single screensaver from the scroll-down display list. The selected screensaver is displayed in the test area. The Settings button allows you to customize the parameters of the selected screensaver. You can preview the selected screensaver by clicking the Preview button. You can exit the preview mode by pressing any key or clicking a mouse button.
- *Random Screen Saver:* You can select this option if you want more than one screensaver display, selected from the scroll-down display list. The Cycle After field allows you to select the time interval that each screensaver should be used before switching to another screensaver.

When the screensaver display is enabled (i.e., if you select any of the last three options), you can specify the idle time period before the screensaver is activated. You can set this period in minutes in the Blank After field.

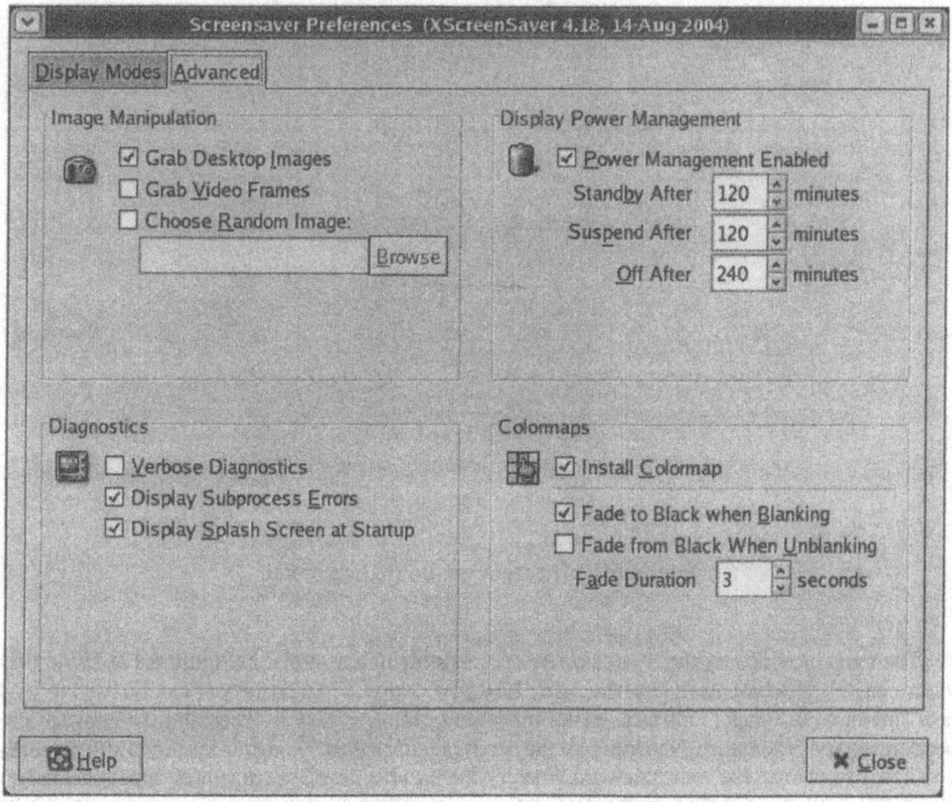

Figure 6.11 The Advanced tabbed window can be used to select the display power management options.

If you want to lock your screen after the screensaver is activated, select the Lock Screen After checkbox and enter the delay between screensaver activation and locking of the screen.

The Advanced tabbed window can be used to specify the display power management options as well as others shown in Figure 6.11. If you enable the power management, you can specify the standby, suspend, and off periods. In the standby mode, the screen is blank. In the suspend mode, the display enters the power-saving mode. The off period indicate the waiting time before the display is turned off.

System Settings

The system settings menu provides several services to control the system behavior. Since most of the tools in this menu control the behavior at the system level, these tools require root privileges. If you are logged into the system using your system user account, you will be prompted for the root account password before proceeding with the changes.

Figure 6.12 The System Settings menu.

The tools provided by the System Settings menu are shown in Figure 6.12. In the previous chapter, you have seen how the Add/Remove Applications tool can be used to load new software packages. This tool makes managing packages easy by checking the package dependencies and automatically loading all the necessary packages. Using the system settings menu, you can also change the root password, specify the security level, manage user accounts, and so on. In this section we show how the date and time as well as display properties can be set. We let you play with the other services available in this menu.

Setting Date and Time

You can set the date and time by using the Date & Time properties tool. It provides a very nice calendar interface to set these properties (see Figure 6.13). You have seen this type of interface during the post-installation setup. As shown in this figure, there are three tabbed windows. The first window can be used to set the time and date. The date can be specified by using the left and right arrows on the month and year. The time can be set by entering the three components: hour, minutes, and seconds.

The second tabbed window allows you to specify the network time protocol that should be used to synchronize your computer clock. This synchronization is useful as your computer clock drifts away from the actual time. The amount of drift depends on various factors including the temperature. The drift is measured in PPM (parts per million), which corresponds to 0.0001%. Since a day has 86,400 seconds, a drift of approximately 11.57 PPM means a difference of 1 second per day. The Network Time Protocol (NTP) is designed to synchronize computer clocks, which is important when communicating with other computers. NTP uses UTC (Universal Time Coordinated) as the reference time. UTC is an official standard that evolved from the GMT (Greenwich Mean Time). You can use this tabbed window to specify several options including whether you want to use NTP and so on.

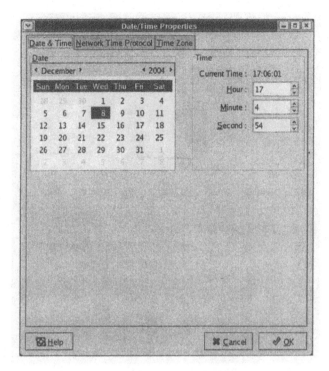

Figure 6.13 Setting the date and time.

The third tabbed window can be used to specify the time zone. You have set the time zone during the installation (see Figure 5.29 on page 103). This window provides the same screen as that in Figure 5.29.

Setting Display

As in the Date and Time tool, setting the display properties requires root privileges. It has three tabbed windows: Settings, Hardware, and Dual head as shown in Figure 6.14. The settings window lets you specify the screen resolution and color depth. You have seen a similar screen during the post-installation setup. You have also set the display resolution at the user-level before (see Figure 6.6).

The Hardware tabbed window allows you to configure the monitor type and the video card. The Configure... button displays a large list of monitors and video cards supported by Fedora 3. If your display and video card are not supported, use a generic type that closely matches your hardware. In general, though, the installer does a pretty good job in detecting your monitor type and video card or selecting an appropriate generic settings.

The third tabbed window can be used to enable and configure two displays. This window lets you configure the second video card and set the second screen resolution and color depth. In addition, you can select a desktop layout for the two screens—either individual desktops or spanned desktop. In the spanned desktop, your desktop is split between the two screens.

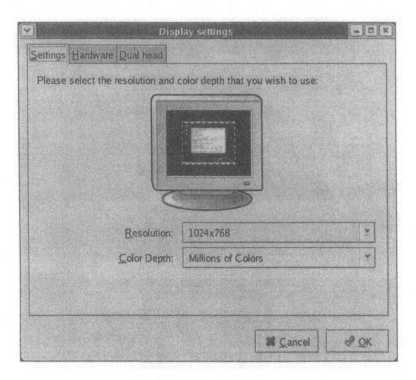

Figure 6.14 The display configuration window.

Working with the GNOME Desktop

Fedora 3 supports two types of desktops: GNOME and KDE. The GNOME desktop is the default desktop and this is the one you have installed. Let's get familiar with this desktop before looking at the command line interface details.

If you have used My Computer in Windows XP, you have an equivalent one here (see the Computer icon in Figure 6.1). You can launch the Nautilus graphical tool by double-clicking the Computer icon. This tool provides an intuitive interface to manage the file system and other resources in your computer. In our example system, this tool shows four icons as we have a USB hard disk drive (PORTABLE) attached to the system (see Figure 6.15).

Browsing the File System

You invoke the Nautilus file manager by selecting File Browser from the Applications main menu (see Figure 6.2a). The file manager is useful to navigate and manage the file system; you can also use it to browse Web pages and play multimedia content.

This interface looks somewhat similar to the Windows Explorer you are familiar with (see Figure 6.16). The File menu allows you to create a new folder or a document, open or browse a folder, and so on. The Edit menu supports the standard editing actions such as cut, copy, paste, rename, and so on. In addition, you can use Preferences to set the file management

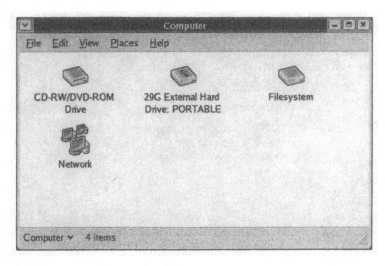

Figure 6.15 The Nautilus file manager can be used to manage resources in your computer system.

preferences. For example, it is possible to select single-click or double-click to activate an item. Similarly, you can specify to run executable files when they are clicked.

You can customize the window by using the view menu. This menu lets you specify how the contents of the window should be viewed (as a list, icons, or catalog). In addition, it allows you to specify whether you want the Location bar above the main area, Sidepane on the lefthand side, and Status bar at the bottom of the window. The Go menu provides services to visit different locations in your file system, various Web sites, create CDs, and so on. The Bookmarks menu can be used to add and edit bookmarks.

You can use the Location bar to specify the location you want to go. You could enter here the URL of a Web site or a location in your file system. For example, in Figure 6.16, the location bar shows /home/sivarama and the main window shows the contents of this location.

The icons in the toolbar let you move around the directories and Web sites you visited. The Up arrow can be used to move up in the directory structure. The Back and Forward buttons work as in a typical Web browser. The Reload button is for refreshing the content. The Home button takes you to your home directory (in our example, /home/sivarama is the home directory). The Computer button displays the content shown in Figure 6.15.

Editing with GEDIT

The gedit is a simple text editor that provides functionality somewhat similar to the Wordpad in Windows. It can be invoked from the Accessories submenu available from the Applications main menu as shown in Figure 6.17.

The gedit window, shown in Figure 6.18, consists of the following components.

* The Menubar at the top of the window contains several pull-down menus that provide commands to open and edit text files. The File menu has commands to manipulate files (open, create, save, or save as), print files, page setup, print preview, and quit. The Edit menu has the standard edit commands such as undo, redo, cut, paste, copy, and delete. In addition,

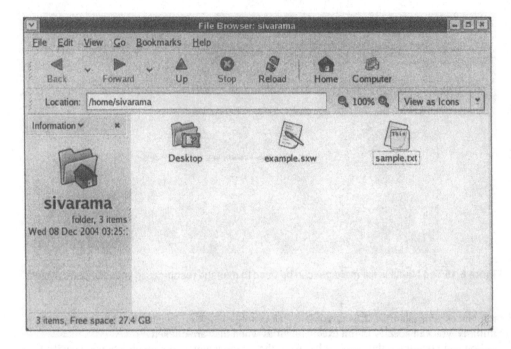

Figure 6.16 The Nautilus file manager can be used to access the file system, Web pages, FTP sites as well as to run applications and create CDs.

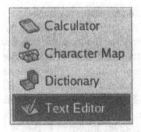

Figure 6.17 The Accessories pull-down menu.

you can also set the editor preferences. The View menu can be used to customize the toolbars. The Search menu provides commands to search and replace text. The spelling check functionality is in the Tools menu. The Documents menu has save and close commands that affect all the open documents.

- The Toolbar provides several icons for some of the common tasks such as creating a new file, opening an existing file, saving a modified file, printing a file, and several editing commands such as undo, redo, cut and so on.
- The Display area is for the contents of the file that is being edited.

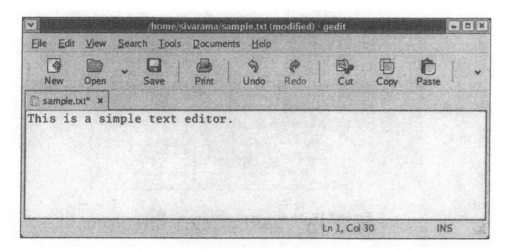

Figure 6.18 The gedit window.

- The Status bar at the bottom of the window gives information on the current activity. It also provides contextual information on the menu commands. In addition, it displays the cursor position (line number and column number) and the edit mode. The edit mode can be either overwrite (OVR) or insert (INS). In our example, it is in the insert mode. You can switch the edit mode by pressing the Insert key.

In Figure 6.18 we didn't show another component—the output window. This window, which appears above the status bar, captures the output of the shell command plugin.

Running Applications

The Run... equivalent of Windows is available as the Run Application... command in the Actions menu (see Figure 6.2b). The run application window, shown in Figure 6.19, allows you to enter the command to execute in the command field. If you want to run a previously executed command, use the arrow button next to the command field to select the command. You can also pick an application from the list displayed by selecting the Show list... option.

Select the Run in terminal checkbox if you want to run the command in a terminal window. You can use the Run with file... button if you want to include a file to the command. For example, if you want to open sample.txt file using the gedit, type gedit in the command field and click the Run with file... button. This pops up a window to browse and select the file to be edited.

Office Tools

The Fedora 3 Linux has several office applications that mimic the Microsoft office suite. These applications are available from the Office menu as shown in Figure 6.20. The OpenOffice Writer is a word processor application that can read and modify the Microsoft Word documents. It can also save files in several formats including the Word format. A nice feature of this application is that you can password protect the file. This feature, however, is not available for all formats. This

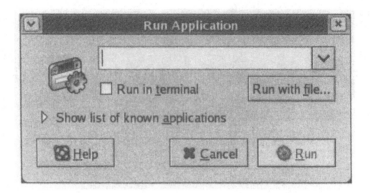

Figure 6.19 The Run application window.

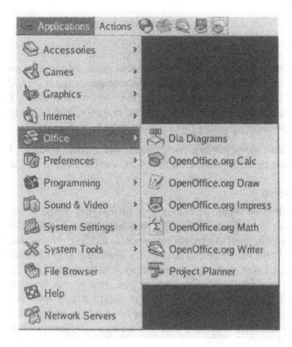

Figure 6.20 The office applications software suite.

application allows you to open and process Word documents conveniently without going back to your Windows system.

The OpenOffice Calc is a spreadsheet application that can import and modify Microsoft Excel spreadsheets. As with the OpenOffice Writer, Calc can also save a spreadsheet in the Excel format. When stored in the native format, you can password protect the file.

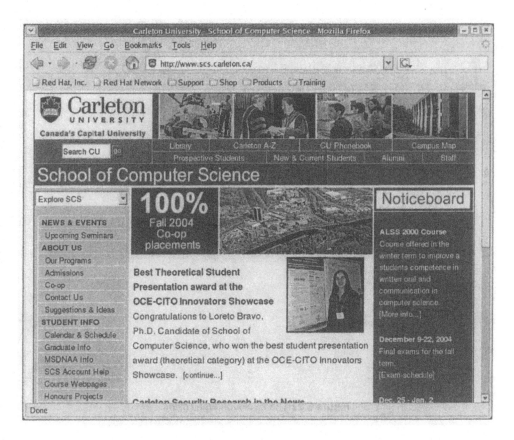

Figure 6.21 The Mozilla Fire Fox Web browser.

Are you wondering if there is a Microsoft PowerPoint equivalent? The answer is the OpenOffice Impress, which lets you create presentations. It can read the PowerPoint files and you can save your presentation in the PowerPoint format as well. As with the last two applications, you can password protect the files stored in the native format.

As shown in Figure 6.20, there are also other applications such as Draw for drawings, Math for equations, Dia for flowcharts, and Project Planner. For example, the Dia application is convenient to draw technical diagrams such as UML diagrams, flowcharts, and so on.

Connecting to the Internet

The applications to connect to the Internet are available under the `Internet` submenu of the `Applications` menu (see Figure 6.2a on page 117). Here we briefly mention two common applications that are often used: a Web browser and an email client. The system installs the default Web browser Mozilla Firefox, which can be invoked either from the Panel or from the Internet submenu. To invoke from the Panel, click the globe-and-mouse icon at the top of the desktop. This Web browser is a derivative of the Netscape Web browser (see Figure 6.21). Because

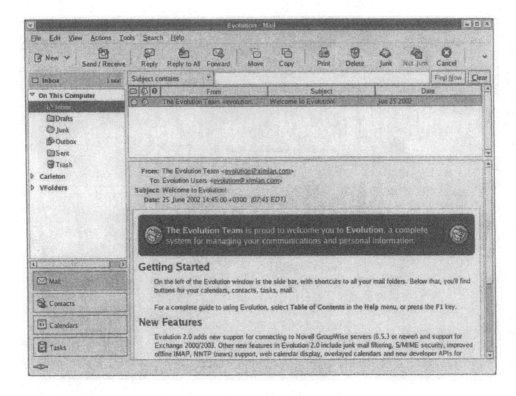

Figure 6.22 The Evolution email client.

of this relationship, you see a lot of similarities between the Mozilla and Netscape browsers. You can also run Firefox on your Windows system by downloading the Windows version from `http://www.mozilla.org`.

The other application we mention here is the Evolution email client to access your email (see Figure 6.22 for its screenshot). Again, you will see similarities between this client and the Netscape's email client. If you are interested, Mozilla has its own version of the email client called Thunderbird. You can download Thunderbird from the Mozilla site mentioned before.

Command Terminal

Once you are familiar with the Linux operating system you are likely to spend more time with the terminal emulator shown in Figure 6.23. This is the equivalent of the Command Prompt in the Windows system. The terminal window can be invoked from the `Applications` menu under `System Tools` submenu. Since this interface is preferred as you get experience with the system and its commands, you may want to add it to the panel for single-click invocation as in Figure 6.1. Note that you can add an application to the panel by right-clicking on it and selecting `Add this launcher to panel` option.

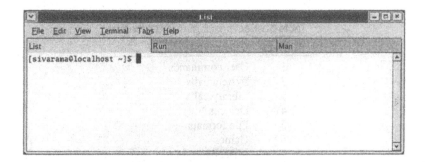

Figure 6.23 The terminal emulator window.

The terminal emulator is much more flexible than the Windows Command Prompt. Each terminal can be defined to have its own profile. A default profile is used to open the initial terminal. A profile defines the various characteristics of the terminal window including the colors, font, scrollbar type, and so on. The `File` menu can be used to open a new terminal, define a new profile, and close a window.

The terminal emulator supports a tabbed window feature that allows multiple terminals to share a single window. For example, Figure 6.23 has three terminals sharing the same window: `List` is used to display a program's source code, `Run` is used to execute the program and check its output, and `Man` is used to look at help information ("man" pages are discussed in the next section). You can easily switch from one terminal to another by selecting the window tab. You can use the `File` menu to close each individual terminal as well as open a tabbed terminal.

The `Edit` menu can be used to edit the current profile, copy and paste, as well as to manage profiles and keyboard shortcuts. The `View` menu is useful to specify the font size (zoom in, zoom out, normal size), whether you want the menubar to appear, or if you want a full screen terminal.

You can use the `terminal` menu to change the profile and title (for example, we used `List` as our title for a terminal in Figure 6.23). In addition, you can use this menu to specify character encoding and reset the state of the terminal if you are having problems with terminals. The `Tabs` menu lists all the tabbed terminals and allows you to navigate through the tabbed terminals.

The terminal window is useful to enter commands to invoke both GUI and non-GUI applications. For example, you can invoke `gedit` to edit `sample.txt` file by entering the following command in the terminal window:

```
gedit sample.txt
```

Here is another example. The command

```
gnome-terminal
```

launches another terminal window. Since the terminal emulator requires commands to specify the work to be done, this interface is often called command-line interface (CLI). Thus, we have two main interfaces to interact with the system: GUI and CLI.

What are the pros and cons of these interfaces? For beginners, GUI is easier to use than CLI because of the point-and-click strategy. The main problem with CLI is the learning curve associated with it—you need to remember various commands and their syntax. In contrast, GUI makes the available options visible to the user. However, it is time consuming as the selection

Table 6.1 Sections of the LINUX manual

Section	Description
1	User commands
2	System calls
3	Library calls
4	Devices
5	File formats
6	Games
7	Miscellaneous
8	System administration tools

of these options often requires traversing a hierarchy of menus. In particular, if you know which command to use and its syntax, it is faster to type the command than using menus. This is typically the case with experienced users. As we shall see in the rest of the chapter, it is fairly straightforward to develop simple scripts that combine several commands to accomplish a complex task. For example, you can feed the output of one command as input to another command. In general, experienced users tend to prefer CLI whereas new users prefer GUI for its ease of use.

In the remainder of the chapter, we focus on the command line interface and look at various commands you can use in the terminal window.

Getting Help

Help on the Linux commands is particularly needed with the command line interface. The Linux manual pages ("man pages") provide information on the various commands. These man pages are divided into several sections as shown in Table 6.1. Most of the commands executed by the users are placed in Section 1. The next section gives information on the system calls provided by the kernel. Section 3 describes the language library functions in C, FORTRAN, and so on. Special files in the /dev directory are described in Section 4. Section 5 describes the file formats and protocols. The next section gives information on the games available. Section 7 describes conventions, character set standards, file system layout, and other miscellaneous items. The system administrative commands, described in Section 8, can only be used by the root or superuser.

The man command can be used to access the man pages. Its syntax is simple—just type man and the command name. For example, to get information on gedit, you can enter the man command as

    man gedit

Of course, you can use

    man man

to get information on how to use the man command itself. This command displays the information shown in Figure 6.24. You can use the Spacebar key to scroll forward through the document and the b key to scroll backwards (up and down arrow keys also work). You can use the Enter key to scroll line by line. If you want to quit the document, press q key.

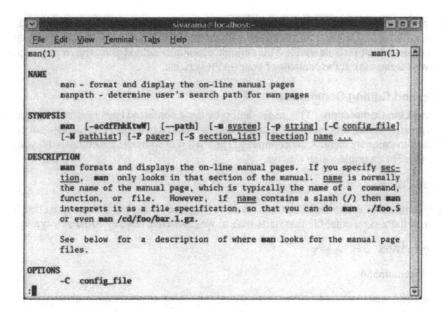

Figure 6.24 Manual page entry for the man command.

Some commands appear in more than one section. For example, the passwd command can be used by the user to change his/her account password. Thus, information on this command is included in Section 1. There is also another entry for passwd in Section 5. This entry describes the /etc/passwd file maintained by the system. To clarify this ambiguity, you can include the section number in the man command. For example, to get information on the passwd file in Section 5, we enter the man command as

```
man 5 passwd
```

All man pages follow a very simple format. Often, the description given is very cryptic. As a new user, you may not find the man pages all that helpful. But as you get used to the various commands, you will find man pages useful as a reference document that gives concise information on the command syntax and the various options available.

Some General-Purpose Commands

In this section, we introduce some of the common commands that are useful for a beginner. Our description of these commands is rather brief. Of course, you can use the man command to get more information on these commands.

Before we proceed further, we need to introduce the shell. For our purposes, the shell can be thought of as the user's interface to the operating system. It acts as the command line interpreter. Several popular shells including the Bourne shell (sh), C-shell (csh), Korn shell (ksh), and Bourne Again shell (bash) are available. Since bash is the preferred shell in the Linux systems, we assume that you are using this shell. Furthermore, bash is the default shell in Fedora 3.

When you type a command, you don't have to specify the location of its executable program. The shell searches for the program associated with the command among the locations specified by a special environment variable PATH. This variable essentially defines your search path. Later we show how you can look at the contents of your PATH variable.

Entering and Editing Commands

Command Line Completion   The bash shell provides a command line completion feature that helps us greatly. Using this feature you don't need to type the complete command—just enough for the shell to uniquely identify the command. The shell will complete the command if you press the tab key. For example, when we type

```
ged<TAB>
```

the shell completes the command name as gedit. Suppose we have a file sample.txt in our directory. If there is no other file that starts with s, we can save a few key strokes by typing

```
ged<TAB> s<TAB>
```

to enter the command

```
gedit sample.txt
```

Recalling a Command   The shell maintains a record of all your commands in a history file. Every time you enter a command, the complete command is stored in this file. This list is maintained in the reverse chronological order (i.e., with the most recent command at the head of the list). You can take a peek into this list by using the history command. When this command is used without any options, it gives the full list of commands from the history file. However, if you want to see the most recent n commands, enter history n. For example, the command

```
history 4
```

display the last four commands including the current history command:

```
93 man man
94 man 5 passwd
95 gedit sample.txt
96 history 4
```

Each command is displayed with a line number in the history file. You can use these line numbers to execute the corresponding command. For example, to run the man 5 passwd command, you type !94 at the prompt. You can run the last command by typing !!. To run a command that contains a string, just type ?string? where ? is a wildcard (that is, it matches zero or more characters). For example, given the previous history, the command

```
!dit
```

results in the following error:

```
bash: !dit: event not found
```

However, by modifying the command to

```
!?dit
```

the shell successfully executes the command

```
gedit sample.txt
```

You can also access the commands from the history list with the keys. Here are some examples:

- Use the up (↑) and down (↓) arrow keys to navigate the history list. Alternatively, use `ctrl-p` to go to the previous command and `ctrl-n` to go to the next command.
- You can use `ctrl-r` to incrementally reverse search the command history. Once you press `ctrl-r`, you are prompted for a search string. As you enter the search string, a matching command appears. This is the reason for calling it "incremental search" as it does not wait for the complete string to be typed.

Sometimes you don't want to execute the command as is. You may want to modify it before running it again. To do this, you need to edit the command. This is what we are going to discuss next.

Editing Commands   The shell provides several shortcuts for editing a command line. Use the left (←) and right (→) arrow keys to move cursor on your command line. You can also use `Ctrl-b` to move cursor back by one character and `Ctrl-f` to move it forward by one character. When you enter text, it is inserted at the current cursor position. The backspace key erases the character before the cursor. For example, suppose you typed the following command:

```
gedit samples.txt
```

Then you notice that you entered the wrong file name (`samples` instead of `sample`). To delete the s, use the left arrow key to move the cursor to the period and press the backspace key. Then you can simply press `Enter` to execute the command. Table 6.2 gives a list of keystrokes that allow you to navigate and edit command lines.

Changing Password

You have seen how your password can be changed by using the `Applications` main menu from the GNOME desktop. You can also change your password from the command line interface. To change your current account password, just type the command `passwd`. It first asks for your current password and then prompts you to enter the new password twice. If you are the root, you can specify the user name. Thus, as the root, you can change the password of any account in the system.

Locating a Program

Two commands are available to find the location of a program. The `which` command finds the location of a file within the directories listed in your `PATH` variable. The `whereis` command can find the files that are located in the standard directories. It is not restricted searching only the directories listed in your `PATH` variable.

Miscellaneous Commands

If you want to find out the users logged into your system, use the `who` command. The `uname` command gives the operating system running on your system. The `echo` command displays a line of text. For example, the command

Table 6.2 Some of the keystrokes for navigating and editing command lines

Keystroke	Action
Ctrl-b	Move cursor back by one character
Ctrl-f	Move cursor forward by one character
Alt-b	Move cursor back by one word
Alt-f	Move cursor forward by one word
Ctrl-a	Move cursor to the beginning of the command line
Ctrl-e	Move cursor to the end of the command line
Ctrl-l	Clear the screen and leave the command line at the top of the screen
Ctrl-d	Delete the character at the cursor position
Backspace	Delete the character before the cursor position
Ctrl-t	Transpose the current and previous characters

```
echo $PATH
```

can be used to see the directories listed in your PATH variable.

The ps command can be used to see the processes running on the system. By default, it gives information about all processes with the same user id as the current user. It displays the process id (PID), the terminal associated with the process (TTY), the cumulative CPU time (TIME), and the command name (CMD). You can also specify several options to get more detailed information.

The last command we discuss here allows you to become super user (i.e., root) without explicitly logging in as the root. Often, when you are in your system user account, you may need to do a small administrative chore that requires root privileges. Instead of logging out of your current account and logging in as the root, the su command allows you to assume the root identity. For example, you can use the su command as shown below:

```
$ su -
Password: ********
#
```

The su command asks for the root password. If you give the correct password, it changes the prompt from $ to # to indicate that you are now the root. Then, for example, you can edit the fstab file. Recall from Chapter 5 that only the root can modify this file. To edit the file, you can use the following command:

```
gedit /etc/fstab
```

To leave the super user shell and return to your previous shell, use either exit or ctrl-d. As usual, you can get more details on this command by using the man command.

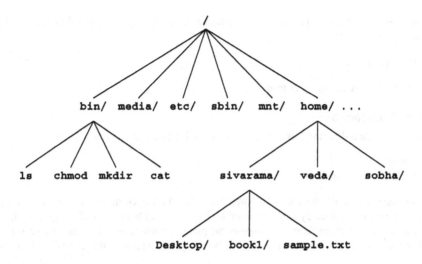

Figure 6.25 The file system is a hierarchy of directories. The root directory is represented by a slash (/).

File System

The Fedora 3 file system provides the necessary structure to store information. While the file system supports several types of files, here we focus on ordinary files and directories. The file system is organized as a hierarchy of directories (similar to that in Windows). Since you are familiar with hierarchical file systems, we briefly present details of the Fedora file system.

The root directory of the file system is represented by a slash / as shown in Figure 6.25. At the next level, you see a set of common directories such as bin/, etc/, home/, and so on. The /home directory contains the user directories. In the example, we show three user directories: sivarama/, veda/, and sobha/. Each of these directories may have other directories or files. Figure 6.25 shows the subdirectories under the sivarama directory.

Path Names

You can uniquely specify the files and directories in the file system by its path. A path is simply the list of directories from the root directory (/). For example, the path of sample.txt in Figure 6.25 is

```
/home/sivarama/sample.txt
```

This is called the *absolute path* because it specifies where the sample.txt file is within the file system. Absolute path always begins with the root directory (/). In contrast, a relative path specifies the path relative to your current directory. We discuss later how you can specify a relative path.

You can always find your home directory by displaying the value of HOME environment variable as in the following command:

```
$ echo $HOME
/home/sivarama
```

In the command line, tilde (˜) represents your home directory. For example, you can specify the path of `sample.txt` as

```
~/sample.txt
```

Next we look at a few directory commands.

Directory Commands

To know your current directory, use the pwd command. For example, you will see

```
$ pwd
/home/sivarama
```

if you are currently in the `sivarama` directory. Use the cd command to change the current directory. The current directory is represented by a dot (`.`) and the parent of the current directory by two dots (`..`). For example cd `..` makes the parent directory as your current directory. Here is another example. If your current directory is `bin/`, you can refer to the `sample.txt` file as

```
../home/sivarama/sample.txt
```

This is a *relative path* as opposed to the absolute path we had given before.

Next we look at some commands to navigate and access the directories and files. The ls command lists the contents of a directory. If you don't specify a directory, the current directory is the default.

To create a new directory, you can use the mkdir (make directory) command. Here is an example.

```
mkdir courses
```

creates the `courses` directory in your current directory. If you want to remove an empty directory, you can do so with the rmdir (remove directory) command. For example, the command

```
rmdir courses
```

deletes the directory we just created. If the directory specified is not *empty*, rmdir will not delete the directory. To delete a non-empty directory, you can first empty the directory by deleting its contents (files and other sub-directories) and then delete the directory. There is also a convenient way of deleting a non-empty directory by using the rm command, which is discussed in the next section.

File Commands

Several commands are available to view the contents of files. The cat (concatenate) command displays the contents of the specified files. You can specify more than one file. For example, the command

```
cat sample.txt test
```

displays the contents of the files (`sample.txt`) and `test`.

If the file is large, you may want to control how its contents are displayed. There are several commands that allow you controlled view of the contents. The more command displays the contents of a file one screen at a time. To scroll the screen by a single line, press the Enter key. To scroll to the next screen, use the Spacebar key.

A problem with more is that it allows only forward movement—you cannot go back. This is remedied by the less command. This command allows both forward and backward movement. In addition, the less command doesn't wait to read the whole file before displaying the contents. Thus, it is faster if the file is very large. For large files, you can also use head to view the first part of the file and tail to view the last part. You can use the man command to find out more details on these commands.

The cp (copy) command copies files and has the following format:

```
cp from to
```

A path can be specified for from and to. If no path is given, the current directory is the default. Here is an example that copies sample.txt to test.

```
cp sample.txt test
```

Instead of copying a file, sometimes you may want to move a file. The mv (move) command performs this job. For example, the command

```
mv test test1
```

moves the file test to test1. This operation is effectively renaming the file. Thus, you can use mv to move and rename files. To delete a file, use rm (remove) as in the following example:

```
rm test
```

This command deletes the test file. To specify a group of files, you can use wildcards: * to match zero or more characters, and ? to match a single character. The command

```
rm *
```

deletes all the files in the current directory. It does not delete the directories. For that, you need to use the -r option mentioned below.

This last command (rm *) can be quite dangerous—it silently deletes all the files. If you want the delete process to be interactive, use the -i (interactive) option. With this option, the rm command asks whether to delete a file; depending on what you say (y or n), the process proceeds.

The mv command works on directories as well as files. However, cp and rm cannot be used on a directory without options. To work on the directories, you have to use the -r (recursive) option. As an example, if you want to remove a non-empty directory (say, courses), you can use

```
rm -r courses
```

Similarly, if you want copy a directory, the cp command with -r would do the job.

Access Permissions

Linux provides a sophisticated security mechanism to control access to individual files and directories. Each file and directory has certain access permissions that indicate who can access and in what mode (read-only, read/write, and so on). With these permissions the system can protect,

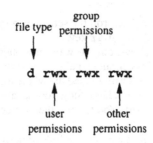

Figure 6.26 Details of the access permissions.

for example, users from accessing other user's files. However, sometimes, we do need to share files. For example, a group of software developers working on a project may need to share each other's files. If we strictly do not allow any sharing of files, the group members would have to share passwords so that one can login as another user to access the files, or use explicit copying of files between the user accounts.

To avoid these problems, each Linux user belongs to a group of users as determined by the system administrator when the account was created. You can verify this information on your system by going to the Applications→System Settings→Users and Groups menu. If you are not logged in as root, it will ask you for the root password and then opens a tabbed window. The Users tabbed window gives information on the user accounts in the system. If you click the Groups window, it gives the group information: group name to identify the group, group id, and the group members. In the toolbar of this window, you see icons to add groups and to modify group membership. The group id is an integer. Fedora reserves group ids less than 500 for system groups. Thus, for user groups, group id starts at 500.

Typically, a user belongs to a single group. However, a user may belong to multiple groups. From the access permission point of view, there are three types of users: owner, group, and others. The last group represents everyone else.

Linux, like the UNIX systems, associates three types of access permissions to files and directories in the file system: read (r), write (w), and execute (x). As the names indicate, the read permission allows read access and the write permission allows writing into the file or directory. The execute permission is required to execute a file and, for obvious reasons, should be used with binary and script files that contain executable code or commands.

The Linux system uses nine bits to keep the access permissions as there are three types of users, each of which can have three types of permissions. The ls command with -l (long) option gives the access permission information, as in the following example.

```
$ ls -l
drwxr-xr-x 2 sivarama project1 4096 Dec 24 13:56 Desktop
-rw-rw-r-- 1 sivarama project1 5610 Dec 30 12:53 sample.txt
-rw-r--r-- 1 sivarama project1 5610 Dec 30 12:53 test
```

Each line in this list contains the following information (from left to right):

- The first column displays the permissions for each file/directory. Figure 6.26 shows details of this column. The first letter before the nine permission letters identifies the file type. In our example, the first line with d identifies that Desktop is a directory. A dash (-) is used for a regular file as in lines 2 and 3. The next nine letters are divided into three fields.

- The first three letters give information on the permissions for the user (that is, the owner).
- The second set of three letters indicates the permissions for the user group.
- The last three letters represent the permissions for everyone else.

If a permission is off, it is indicated by a dash (-); otherwise, the corresponding letter is used.

- The integer in the second column gives the number of links. For example, if you give permission to share your file to another user in your group, a link to this file will be placed for the other user. For most files, the link count is 1.
- The next column (sivarama in our example) gives the owner of the file. This is usually the person who created the file.
- The next entry (project1 here) is the group that has the group access to the file/directory.
- The next number gives the size of the file in bytes (characters). In our example, the size of sample.txt file is 5610 characters long.
- The date and time stamp of the file (when it was created or last modified) are given next.
- The last column gives the name of the file/directory.

In our example, the first line indicates that the owner can read, write, and execute the Desktop directory. The group and others have read and execute permissions but not the write permission.

Note that the read permission on a directory allows you to read its contents. The write permission for a directory means you can write into the directory (e.g., create a subdirectory in it). What does execute permission on a directory mean? The execute permission for a directory is redefined from its file definition. If a directory has the execute permission, it allows you to use the cd command to make it your current directory and/or look at the files in that directory. However, it will not allow you to read from or write into the directory. For example, the ls command will not list the files in the directory if you don't have the execute permission. However, if you know the name of a file, you can get details about it or look at its contents.

In the second line, the dash in the file type suggests that sample.txt is a regular file. Of course, we know that it is a text file. Therefore, it does not make sense to use execute permissions. On this file, the owner and the group have read and write permissions whereas others have only the read permission. From the third line in this example, we can gather that test is a regular file. In addition, only the owner has the read/write access. All the others can only read this file.

Setting Access Permissions

The chmod (change mode) command changes the access permissions. The owner of a file can determine who can access the file. There are two ways of specifying the access permissions: in octal or symbolic mode.

In the octal mode, you convert the three permission bits for each user type into an octal number. In this method, the 9-bit permissions can range from 000 to 777. The permissions are represented in the octal notation by writing a 1 for the permission bit that is on and 0 for the off bit. Following this procedure, the Desktop directory permissions from our previous example (rwx r-x r-x) are represented in the octal notation as 111 101 101, which is 755 in octal. Similarly, the permissions for the sample.txt file rw-rw-r-- can be expressed in octal as 664. The octal

Table 6.3 Values for the symbolic mode fields

Field	Value	Description
Who		
	u	User
	g	Owner's group
	o	All others not in the group
	a	All users
Operator		
	+	Add the permission
	−	Remove the permission
	=	Set the permission
Permission		
	r	Set the read permission
	w	Set the write permission
	x	Set the execute permission
	u	Set to the file owner's current permissions
	g	Set to the file group's current permissions
	o	Set to the file other's current permissions

string 644 expresses the permissions (rw-r--r--) for the test files in our example. Since you specify the actual permissions, this mode is also called the absolute mode.

In the symbolic mode, mode control words are used to express the access privileges, mostly relative to the current privileges. For example, you may add the write privilege to your group. Mode control words consist of three fields and take the form <who><operator><permission>. These fields can take the values shown in Table 6.3.

The format of chmod is

```
chmod access-mode file-list
```

The access-mode can be expressed in the octal or symbolic mode. Here are some examples. The command

```
chmod 660 test
```

changes the permissions to the test file as rw- rw- ---. This means that only the owner and his/her group can read or write test; all others cannot access the file. If you use the * wildcard, permissions for all the files and directories are changed. You can also use other metacharacters like ? to specify file-list. If you want to allow others to read the test file, you can do so by the following command:

```
chmod o+r test
```

To change the permissions of all the files in a directory and in all of its subdirectories, use the -R (recursive) option. For example, if temp is a directory, the command

```
chmod -R 764 temp
```

recursively changes the permissions for all the files and directories in temp and its subdirectories.

Redirection

In Linux, three standard files are automatically opened for you. These default files are used by your command to read its input and to send its output and error messages. The stdin (standard input) file supplies the data needed by the command. This file is mapped to your keyboard. The stdout (standard output) file receives the program's output. The error messages are directed to stderr (standard error) file. These last two standard files are mapped to the terminal running the command. This default association with files can be changed using redirection operators.

To redirect output of a command to a file, use the > (greater-than) symbol as shown here:

```
command > out-file
```

As an example, consider the following command:

```
ls -l > list
```

This command sends the output to the list file. Here is a simple way to create a text file without using a text editor.

```
cat > simple.txt
```

Since we did not specify the file in the cat command, it expects the input to come from the default input file (stdin). The output of this command is redirected to the simple.txt file. You can terminate the input by typing Ctrl-d.

The redirect the input of a command, you can use the < (less-than) symbol as shown below:

```
command < in-file
```

Before giving an example of the input redirection, let's first look at a new command. The word count (wc) command can be used to print the line, word, and byte counts of a file. In fact, you can specify more than one file on the command line. If no file is specified on the command line, it reads from the standard input file stdin. For example, the following command

```
$ wc < simple.txt
  22   191   1327
```

uses input redirection to print the three counts for the simple.txt file. The three numbers give the line count (22), word count (191), and byte count (1327).

Both input and output redirections can be used in a single command. For example, if you want to store the output of the previous command in a file (say, count), the following command will do the job.

```
$ wc < simple.txt > count
```

When we use the output redirection, if the output file already exists, the contents are erased and the command's output is placed in the file. Instead, if you want the command output to be appended to the file contents, use the append output symbol (>>). The command sequence

```
$ cat < sample1.txt > test
$ cat < sample2.txt >> test
```

copies the contents of the files `sample1.txt` and `sample2.txt` into the `test` file.

Before closing this section, we note that the output redirect command (`>`) overwrites the file with the command output. This has the unfortunate side effect of overwriting files by accident (for example, if a wrong file name is given). You can set the `noclobber` variable to avoid this problem. You can set this variable by using the `set` command as shown below:

```
set -o noclobber
```

When the `noclobber` variable is set, you can force overwriting a file by using a pipe symbol (discussed next) after the redirection (`>|`) or append symbol ((`>>|`). To unset the `noclobber` variable, you can use the following command:

```
set +o noclobber
```

This command allows overwriting of files as before.

Pipes

As we have seen, the Linux system provides several commands. These commands can be treated as the basic building blocks. While a simple task can be done by using a single command, we may need several commands to accomplish a complicated task. We may have to feed the output of one command as input to another to accomplish the task. Of course, we can store the output of the first command in a temporary file and use this file as the input to the next command. The shell provides the pipe operator (`|`) to achieve this without any temporary files. The syntax is

```
command1 | command2
```

The output of the first command (`command1`) is fed as input to the second command (`command2`). The output of `command2` is the final output. Of course, we can connect several commands using the pipes:

```
command1 | command2 | command3 | command4 | command5
```

Here is an example that uses a pipe to sort the output of the `ls` command.

```
ls | sort
```

As another example, let's look at a different way to get the three counts (line, word, and byte) for the `simple.txt` file. We can use the `cat` and `wc` commands connected by a pipe as shown below:

```
cat simple.txt | wc
```

`grep` is another useful command that allows you to find a string in one or more files. For example, the command

```
ls -l | grep simple
```

displays the lines in the output of `ls -l` command that contain the string `simple`.

We have briefly introduced several basic commands. However, this is only a small sample of the commands that are available. If you are intrigued by this introduction, you can get more information from several online resources. You can also visit your favorite bookstore for books dedicated to the Linux operating system.

Editing Files with Vim

Two text editors, vi and emacs, are commonly used in the Linux system. The Fedora system you installed has an improved version of vi called vim (vi improved). In this section we briefly describe the vim text editor.

You can invoke vim to edit a file (say, simple.txt) by typing vim simple.txt. The vim editor works in two modes:

- *Command Mode:* In this mode, the input is interpreted as a command to the editor. Some examples of these commands are: save the file, exit vim, move the cursor, delete and search for text.

- *Input Mode:* This mode allows you to input text. When you start vim, it is in the command mode. You can switch to the input mode by several commands. For example, the i command switches it to the input mode.

If the editor is in the insert mode, the bottom line indicates this (see Figure 6.27). The empty lines are indicated with the tilde characters (~). You can exit vim in one of several ways as shown here:

ZZ	—	Save the buffer and quit
:x	—	Save the buffer and quit (same as ZZ)
:wq	—	Save the buffer and quit (same as ZZ)
:q	—	Quit (works only if you don't have any unsaved changes)
:q!	—	Quit without saving the changes in the buffer

The first three commands perform the same action—write the changes in the buffer and quit. The vim editor has the following commands to write the buffer.

:w	—	Save the buffer to the current file
:w filename	—	Save the buffer to filename; it does not overwrite if the file exists
:w! filename	—	Save the buffer to filename; it overwrites if the file exists

The first command saves the buffer to the current file that vim is editing. The second and the third commands allow you to write the buffer to a new file.

You can move the cursor using the four arrow keys. You can also use the h, j, k, and l keys to move the cursor left, down, up, and right, respectively. In addition, the following commands are available to move the cursor:

G	—	Move cursor to the first line of the file
1G	—	Move cursor to the last line of the file
0 (zero)	—	Move cursor to the first character of the current line
$	—	Move cursor to the last character of the current line
w	—	Move cursor forward by one word
b	—	Move cursor backward by one word

Note that you have to be in the command mode to issue commands to vim. Also in the command mode, you can do simple text editing using the following commands:

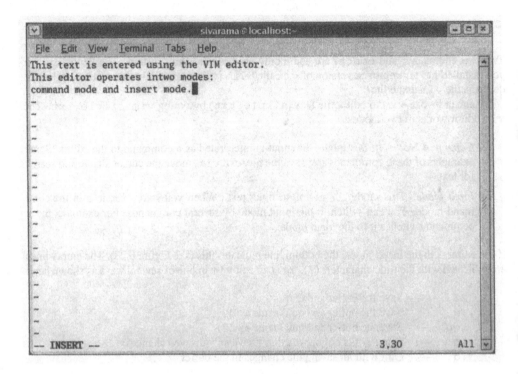

Figure 6.27 The VIM editor in the input mode.

```
x    —   Delete the character at the cursor
X    —   Delete the character before the cursor
dd   —   Delete the line at the cursor
u    —   Undo the most recent change
r    —   Replace the character at the cursor by the character typed next
```

The replace command places vim in the Input mode and the character you type after the r command replaces the current character. After that the editor returns to the Command mode.

In addition to the replace command, you can put vim in the Input mode by any of the following commands: insert (i), append (a), or open (o). When you are done entering the text, press the Esc (Escape) key to return to the command mode. The insert command places vim in the Input mode and the text entered will go before the cursor. The append command is similar to the i command except that it places the text after the cursor. The open command opens a blank line and places the cursor at the beginning of the blank line.

To search forward, you can use the / command. For example, /text looks for the string text in the forward direction (that is, from the current cursor position to the end of the file). To do the reverse search, use ? in place of the slash. For example, ?text searches backward from the current cursor position to the beginning of the file.

The last command we discuss here is the substitute (s) command. It lets you replace text conveniently. The format of this command is

```
: [range] s/old_string/new_string/option
```

The old_string is substituted by new_string in the range of lines specified by the optional range. The range is specified in the format "from,to". If no range is given in the command, the current line is the default. The option is a modifier to the command. Usually, g is used for global substitutions. The following examples give an idea of how this command works. The command

```
:s/test/text
```

replaces the first occurrence of test in the current line by text. If you want to replace all occurrences in the current line, use the g option as in the following command:

```
:s/test/text/g
```

The command

```
:1,10s/test/text
```

replaces the first occurrence of test in each of the ten lines specified (i.e., lines 1 through 10) by text. To change all occurrences in these ten lines, add the g option to the previous command.

We have covered only the basic commands available in the vim editor. It has several very powerful and sophisticated commands. If you decide to use vim you can look at these advanced commands after you gain some degree of familiarity with the editor.

Summary

This chapter introduced the basics of the Linux system. If you are new to Linux, the material presented here should get you started with the Fedora 3 system you have installed. We started the chapter with a discussion of the graphical user interface provided by the system. Specifically, we focused on the GNOME desktop. For new users, GUI provides an easy, point-and-click interface. However, as you get familiar with the system, the command line interface tends to be more efficient. We have provided the basics of the command line interface and discussed several basic commands that are useful. The material presented in this chapter is sufficient to proceed with our main goal of learning assembly language programming using the Linux tools.

PART IV
NASM

7

Installing and Using NASM

In this chapter, we introduce the necessary mechanisms to write and execute assembly language programs. We begin by taking a look at the structure of assembly language programs we use in this book. To make the task of writing assembly language programs easier, we provide a simple template to structure the stand-alone assembly language programs used in this book.

Unlike the high-level languages, assembly language does not provide a convenient mechanism to do input and output. To overcome this deficiency, we have developed a set of I/O routines to facilitate character, string, and numeric input and output. These routines are described after introducing the assembly language template.

Once we have written an assembly language program, we have to transform it into its executable form. Typically, this takes two steps: we use an assembler to translate the source program into what is called an object program and then use a linker to transform the object program into an executable version. We give details of these steps in the "Assembling and Linking" section. However, this section uses an assembly language program example. Since we have not yet discussed the assembly language, you may want to skip this section on the first reading and come back to it after you have read Chapters 9 and 10, which provide an overview of the assembly language.

Introduction

Writing an assembly language program is a complicated task, particularly for a beginner. We make this daunting task simple by hiding those details that are irrelevant. A typical assembly language program consists of three parts. The code part of the program defines the program's functionality by a sequence of assembly language instructions. The code part of the program, after translating it to the machine language code, is placed in the code segment. The data part reserves memory space for the program's data. The data part of the program is mapped to the data segment. Finally, we also need the stack data structure, which is mapped to the stack segment. The stack serves two main purposes: it provides temporary storage, and acts as the medium to pass parameters in procedure calls. We introduce a template for writing stand-alone assembly language programs, which are written completely in the assembly language.

We rarely write programs that do not input and/or output data. High-level languages provide facilities to input and output data. For example, C provides the `scanf` and `printf` functions to input and output data, respectively. Typically, high-level languages can read numeric data (integers, floating-point numbers), characters, and strings.

Assembly language, however, does not provide a convenient mechanism to input and output data. The operating system provides some basic services to read and write data, but these are fairly limited. For example, there is no function to read an integer from the user.

In order to facilitate I/O in assembly language programs, we have developed a set of I/O routines to read and display characters, strings, and signed integers. Each I/O routine call looks like an assembly language instruction. This similarity is achieved by using macros. Each macro call typically expands to several assembly language statements and includes a call to an appropriate procedure. These macros are all defined in the `io.mac` file and the assembled procedures are in the `io.obj` file. We use an example program to illustrate the use of these I/O routines as well as the assembly language template.

Installing NASM

NASM, which stands for netwide assembler, is a portable, public-domain, IA-32 assembler that can generate a variety of object file formats. In this chapter, we restrict our discussion to a Linux system running on an Intel PC.

The accompanying CD-ROM has a copy of NASM. If you followed the Linux installation directions given in Chapter 5, it is already installed. However, if you did not install NASM as part of the Linux installation, or if you want the latest version, this section explains how you can install it.

The latest version of NASM can be downloaded from several sources (see the book's Web page for details). The NASM manual has clear instructions on how to install NASM under Linux. (To get the NASM manual, see the "Web Resources" section at the end of this chapter.) Here is a summary extracted from this manual:

1. Download the Linux source archive `nasm-X.XX.tar.gz`, where `X.XX` is the NASM version number in the archive.

2. Unpack the archive into a directory, which creates a subdirectory `nasm-X.XX`.

3. `cd` to `nasm-X.XX` and type `./configure`. This shell script will find the best C compiler to use and set up Makefiles accordingly.

4. Type `make` to build the `nasm` and `ndisasm` binaries.

5. Type `make install` to install `nasm` and `ndisasm` in `/usr/local/bin` and to install the man pages.

This should install NASM on your system. Alternatively, you can use an RPM distribution for the Fedora Linux. This version is simpler to install—just double-click the RPM file.

Generating the Executable File

The NASM assembler supports several object file formats including ELF (execute and link format) used by Linux. The assembling and linking process is simple. For example, to assemble the `sample.asm` program, we use

```
;brief title of program                    file name
;
;              Objectives:
;                  Inputs:
;                 Outputs:
;
%include  "io.mac"

.DATA
(initialized data go here)

.UDATA
(uninitialized data go here)

.CODE
        .STARTUP                ; setup
           . . .
           . . .
     (code goes here)
           . . .
           . . .
         .EXIT                  ; returns control
```

Figure 7.1 Template for the assembly language programs used in the book.

```
nasm -f elf sample.asm
```

This generates the sample.o object file. To generate the executable file sample, we have to link this file with our I/O routines. This is done by

```
ld -s -o sample sample.o io.o
```

Note that nasm requires the io.mac file and ld needs the io.o file. Make sure that you have these two files in your current directory. We give details about the assembly process towards the end of the chapter.

Assembly Language Template

To simplify writing assembly language programs, we use the template shown in Figure 7.1. We include the io.mac file by using the %include directive. This directive allows us to include the contents of io.mac in the assembly language program. If you had used other assemblers like TASM or MASM, it is important to note that NASM is case-sensitive.

The data part is split into two: the .DATA macro is used for initialized data and the .UDATA for uninitialized data. The code part is identified by the .CODE macro. The .STARTUP macro handles the code for setup. The .EXIT macro returns control to the operating system.

Now let us dissect the statements in this template. This template consists of two types of statements: executable instructions and assembler directives. Executable instructions generate machine code for the processor to execute when the program is run. Assembler directives, on the other hand, are meant only for the assembler. They provide information to the assembler on the various aspects of the assembly process. In this book, all assembler directives are shown in uppercase letters, while the instructions are shown in lowercase.

The %include directive causes the assembler to include the source code from another file (io.mac in our case). This file contains macros for the I/O routines we will discuss in the next section.

The data section is used to define the program's variables. It is divided into two parts: *initialized* and *uninitialized*. The .DATA macro is used to define initialized variables while the .UDATA macro is used to define uninitialized variables of the assembly language program. Chapter 9 discusses various assembler directives to define and initialize variables used in assembly language programs.

The .CODE macro terminates the data segment and starts the code section. The .STARTUP macro sets up the starting point. If you want, you can use the following code in its place.

```
        global    _start
   _start:
```

To return control from the assembly program, we use the .EXIT macro, which places the code to call the int 21H function 4CH to return control. In place of the .EXIT macro, you can write your own code to call int 21H, as shown below.

```
    mov    AX,4C00H
    int    21H
```

Control is returned to the operating system by the interrupt 21H service 4CH. The service required under interrupt 21H is indicated by moving 4CH into the AH register. This service also returns an error code that is given in the AL register. It is a good practice to set AL to 0 to indicate normal termination of the program. We discuss interrupts in Chapter 20.

Input/Output Routines

This section describes the I/O routines we developed to input and output characters, strings, and signed integers. A summary of these routines is given in Table 7.1.

Character I/O

Two macros are defined to input and output characters: PutCh and GetCh. The format of PutCh is

```
    PutCh    source
```

where source can be any general-purpose, 8-bit register, or a byte in memory, or a character value. Some examples follow.

```
    PutCh    'A'          ; displays character A
    PutCh    AL           ; displays the character in AL
    PutCh    response     ; displays the character located in
                          ; memory (labeled response)
```

The format of GetCh is

```
    GetCh    destination
```

Table 7.1 Summary of I/O routines defined in the `io.mac` file

name	operand(s)	operand location	size	what it does
PutCh	source	value register memory	8 bits	Displays the character located at `source`
GetCh	dest	register memory	8 bits	Reads a character into `dest`
nwln	none	—	—	Displays a newline
PutStr	source	memory	variable	Displays the NULL-terminated string at `source`
GetStr	dest [,buf_size]	memory	variable	Reads a carriage-return-terminated string into `dest` and stores it as a NULL-terminated string. Maximum string length is `buf_size−1`.
PutInt	source	register memory	16 bits	Displays the signed 16-bit number located at `source`
GetInt	dest	register memory	16 bits	Reads a signed 16-bit number into `dest`
PutLInt	source	register memory	32 bits	Displays the signed 32-bit number located at `source`
GetLInt	dest	register memory	32 bits	Reads a signed 32-bit number into `dest`

where `destination` can be either an 8-bit, general-purpose register or a byte in memory. Some examples are given here.

```
GetCh    DH
GetCh    response
```

In addition, a `nwln` macro is defined to display a newline. It takes no operands.

String I/O

The `PutStr` and `GetStr` macros are defined to display and read strings, respectively. The strings are assumed to be in the NULL-terminated format. That is, the last character of the string is the NULL character, which signals the end of the string. Strings are discussed in Chapter 17.

The format of `PutStr` is

```
PutStr    source
```

where `source` is the name of the buffer containing the string to be displayed. For example,

```
PutStr    message
```

displays the string stored in the buffer `message`. Strings are limited to 80 characters. If the buffer does not contain a NULL-terminated string, a maximum of 80 characters are displayed.

The format of `GetStr` is

```
GetStr    destination [, buffer_size]
```

where `destination` is the buffer name into which the string from the keyboard is read. The input string can be terminated by a carriage-return. You can also specify an optional value for `buffer_size`. If it is not specified, a buffer size of 81 is assumed. Thus, in the default case, a maximum of 80 characters are read into the string. If a value is specified, `buffer_size`−1 characters are read. The string is stored as a NULL-terminated string. While entering a string, you can backspace to correct the input. Here are some examples.

```
GetStr    in_string    ; reads at most 80 characters
GetStr    TR_title,41   ; reads at most 40 characters
```

Numeric I/O

There are four macros for performing integer I/O: two are used for 16-bit integers and the other two for 32-bit integers. First we look at the 16-bit integer I/O routines—`PutInt` and `GetInt`. The formats are

```
PutInt    source
GetInt    destination
```

where `source` and `destination` can be a 16-bit, general-purpose register or the label of a memory word.

The `PutInt` macro displays the signed number at `source`. It suppresses all leading 0s. The `GetInt` macro reads a 16-bit signed number into destination. You can backspace while entering a number. The valid range of input numbers is −32,768 to +32,767. If an invalid input (such as typing a nondigit character) or out-of-range number is given, an error message is displayed and the user is asked to type a valid number. Some examples are given below.

```
PutInt    AX
PutInt    sum
GetInt    CX
GetInt    count
```

Long integer I/O is similar except that the source and destination must be a 32-bit register or a label of a memory doubleword (i.e., 32 bits). For example, if `total` is a 32-bit number in memory, we can display it by

```
PutLInt   total
```

and read a long integer from the keyboard into `total` by

```
GetLInt   total
```

Some examples that use registers are:

```
PutLInt   EAX
GetLInt   EDX
```

An Example Program

Program 7.1 gives a simple example to demonstrate how some of these I/O routines can be used to facilitate input and output. The program requests the user for a name and a repeat count. After confirming the repeat count, it displays a welcome message repeat count times.

The program uses the db (define byte) assembly language directive to declare several strings (lines 11–15). All these strings are terminated by a 0, which is the ASCII value for the NULL character. Similarly, in the uninitialized data area, we use the resb directive to allocate 16 bytes for a buffer to store the user name and another byte to store the user response to the repeat count confirmation message (lines 18 and 19). These assembler directives are discussed in Chapter 9.

We use PutStr on line 23 to prompt the user for her or his name. The name is read as a string using GetStr into the user_name buffer (line 24). Since we allocated only 16 bytes for the buffer, the name cannot be more than 15 characters. We enforce this by specifying the optional buffer size parameter in the GetStr macro. The PutStr on line 26 requests a repeat count, which is read by GetInt on line 27.

Program 7.1 An example assembly program (for now, you can safely ignore the assembly language statements on lines 32, 33, and 38)

```
 1:  ;An example assembly language program        SAMPLE.ASM
 2:  ;
 3:  ;           Objective: To demonstrate the use of some I/O
 4:  ;                      routines and to show the structure
 5:  ;                      of assembly language programs.
 6:  ;              Inputs: As prompted.
 7:  ;             Outputs: As per input.
 8:  %include   "io.mac"
 9:
10:  .DATA
11:  name_msg       db    'Please enter your name: ',0
12:  query_msg      db    'How many times to repeat welcome message? ',0
13:  confirm_msg1   db    'Repeat welcome message ',0
14:  confirm_msg2   db    ' times? (y/n) ',0
15:  welcome_msg    db    'Welcome to Assembly Language Programming ',0
16:
17:  .UDATA
18:  user_name      resb  16              ; buffer for user name
19:  response       resb  1
20:
21:  .CODE
22:      .STARTUP
23:      PutStr   name_msg               ; prompt user for his/her name
24:      GetStr   user_name,16           ; read name (max. 15 characters)
25:  ask_count:
26:      PutStr   query_msg              ; prompt for repeat count
27:      GetInt   CX                     ; read repeat count
28:      PutStr   confirm_msg1           ; confirm repeat count
29:      PutInt   CX                     ; by displaying its value
30:      PutStr   confirm_msg2
```

```
31:        GetCh   [response]            ; read user response
32:        cmp     byte [response],'y'   ; if 'y', display welcome message
33:        jne     ask_count             ; otherwise, request repeat count
34: display_msg:
35:        PutStr  welcome_msg           ; display welcome message
36:        PutStr  user_name             ; display the user name
37:        nwln
38:        loop    display_msg           ; repeat count times
39:        .EXIT
```

The confirmation message is displayed by lines 28–30. The response of the user y or n is read by GetCh on line 31. If the response is y, the loop (lines 34–38) displays the welcome message repeat count times. A sample interaction with the program is shown below.

```
Please enter your name: Veda
How many times to repeat welcome message? 5
Repeat welcome message 5 times? (y/n) y
Welcome to Assembly Language Programming Veda
Welcome to Assembly Language Programming Veda
Welcome to Assembly Language Programming Veda
Welcome to Assembly Language Programming Veda
Welcome to Assembly Language Programming Veda
```

Assembling and Linking

Figure 7.2 shows the steps involved in converting an assembly language program into an executable code. It uses the sample.asm file as an example. The source assembly language file sample.asm is given as input to the assembler. The assembler translates the assembly language program into an object program sample.o. The linker takes one or more object programs (in our example the sample.o and io.o files) and combines them into an executable program sample. The following subsections describe each of these steps in detail.

The Assembly Process

The general format to assemble a program is

```
nasm  -f <format> <source-file> [-o <object-file>] [-l <list-file>]
```

where the specification of fields in [ ] is optional. If we specify only the source file, NASM produces only the object file. Thus to assemble our example source file sample.asm, we can use the command

```
nasm -f elf  sample.asm
```

After successfully assembling the source program, NASM generates an object file with the same file name as the source file but with .o extension. Thus, in our example, it generates the sample.o file. You can also specify a file name for the object file using the -o option.

If you want the assembler to generate the listing file, you can use

```
nasm   -f elf sample.asm -l sample.lst
```

This command produces two files: sample.o and sample.lst. The list file contains detailed information as we shall see next.

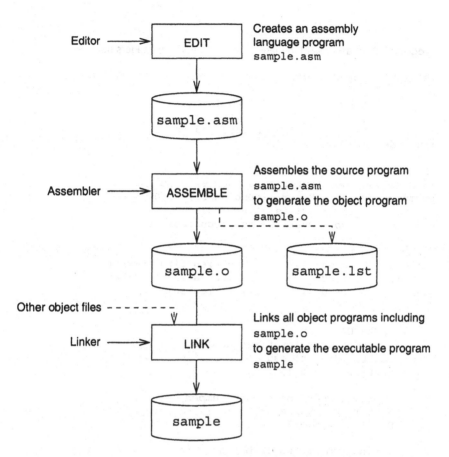

Figure 7.2 Assembling and linking assembly language programs (optional inputs and outputs are shown by dashed lines).

The List File   Program 7.2 gives a simple program that reads two signed integers from the user and displays their sum if there is no overflow; otherwise, it displays an error message. The input numbers should be in the range −2,147,483,648 to +2,147,483,647, which is the range of a 32-bit signed number. The program uses PurStr and GetLInt to prompt and read the input numbers (see lines 22, 23 and 26, 27). The sum of the input numbers is computed on lines 30–32.

If the resulting sum is outside the range of a signed 32-bit integer, the overflow flag is set by the add instruction. In this case, the program displays the overflow message (line 36). If there is no overflow, the sum is displayed (lines 42 and 43).

The list file for the source program sumprog.asm is shown in Program 7.3. In addition to the original source code lines, it contains a lot of useful information about the results of the assembly. This additional information includes the actual machine code generated for the executable statements and the offset of each statement.

Program 7.2 An assembly language program to add two integers `sumprog.asm`

```
1: ;Assembly language program to find sum    SUMPROG.ASM
2: ;
3: ;         Objective: To add two integers.
4: ;            Inputs: Two integers.
5: ;            Output: Sum of input numbers.
6: %include  "io.mac"
7:
8: .DATA
9: prompt1_msg  db  'Enter first number: ',0
10: prompt2_msg  db  'Enter second number: ',0
11: sum_msg      db  'Sum is: ',0
12: error_msg    db  'Overflow has occurred!',0
13:
14: .UDATA
15: number1      resd  1        ; stores first number
16: number2      resd  1        ; stores first number
17: sum          resd  1        ; stores sum
18:
19: .CODE
20:       .STARTUP
21:       ; prompt user for first number
22:       PutStr  prompt1_msg
23:       GetLInt [number1]
24:
25:       ; prompt user for second number
26:       PutStr  prompt2_msg
27:       GetLInt [number2]
28:
29:       ; find sum of two 32-bit numbers
30:       mov     EAX,[number1]
31:       add     EAX,[number2]
32:       mov     [sum],EAX
33:
34:       ; check for overflow
35:       jno     no_overflow
36:       PutStr  error_msg
37:       nwln
38:       jmp     done
39:
40:       ; display sum
41: no_overflow:
42:       PutStr  sum_msg
43:       PutLInt [sum]
44:       nwln
45: done:
46:       .EXIT
```

List File Contents   The format of the list file lines is

    line# offset machine-code nesting-level source-line

line#: is the listing file line number. These numbers are different from the line numbers in the source file. This can be due to include files, macros, and so on, as shown in Program 7.3.

offset: is an 8-digit hexadecimal offset value of the machine code for the source statement. For example, the offset of the first instruction (line 187) is 00000000H, and that of the add instruction on line 219 is 00000035H. Source lines such as comments do not generate any offset.

machine-code: is the hexadecimal representation of the machine code for the assembly language instruction. For example, the machine language encoding of

    mov   EAX, [number1]

is A1[00000000] (line 218) and requires five bytes. The value zero in [ ] is the offset of number1 in the data segment (see line 173).
   Similarly, the machine language encoding of

    jmp   done

is E91D000000 (line 231), requiring five bytes.

nesting-level: is the level of nesting of "include files" and macros.

source-line: is a copy of the original source code line. As you can see from Program 7.3, the number of bytes required for the machine code depends on the source instruction. When operands are in memory (e.g., number1), their relative address is used in the instruction encoding. The actual value is fixed up by the linker after all the object files are combined (for example, io.o in our example). Also note that the macro definitions are expanded. For example, the PutStr on line 186 is expanded on lines 187 through 190.

Program 7.3 The list file for the example assembly program sumprog.asm

```
 1                              ;Assembly language program to find sum. . .
 2                              ;
 3                              ;         Objective: To add two integers.
 4                              ;            Inputs: Two integers.
 5                              ;            Output: Sum of input numbers.
 6                              %include  "io.mac"
 7                     <1> extern    proc_nwln, proc_PutCh, proc_PutStr
 8                     <1> extern    proc_GetStr, proc_GetCh
 9                     <1> extern    proc_PutInt, proc_GetInt
10                     <1> extern    proc_PutLInt, proc_GetLInt
11                     <1>
12                     <1> ;;----------------------------------
13                     <1> %macro   .STARTUP  0
14                     <1> ;group dgroup .data .bss
15                     <1>          global    _start
16                     <1> _start:
17                     <1> %endmacro
18                     <1> ;;----------------------------------
```

```
 19                                    <1>
 20                                    <1>
 21                                    <1> ;;-------------------------------------
 22                                    <1> %macro  .EXIT  0
 23                                    <1>      mov    EAX,1
 24                                    <1>      xor    EBX,EBX
 25                                    <1>      int    0x80
 26                                    <1> %endmacro
 27                                    <1> ;;-------------------------------------
 28                                    <1>
 29                                    <1>
 30                                    <1> ;;-------------------------------------
 31                                    <1> %macro  .DATA  0
 32                                    <1>      segment .data
 33                                    <1> %endmacro
 34                                    <1> ;;-------------------------------------
 35                                    <1>
 36                                    <1> ;;-------------------------------------
 37                                    <1> %macro  .UDATA  0
 38                                    <1>      segment .bss
 39                                    <1> %endmacro
 40                                    <1> ;;-------------------------------------
. . .            . . . . . . .                . . . . . . . . .
158                                        .DATA
159                                    <1>  segment .data
160 00000000 456E74657220666972-        prompt1_msg  db  'Enter first number: ',0
161 00000009 7374206E756D626572-
162 00000012 3A2000
163 00000015 456E74657220736563-        prompt2_msg  db  'Enter second number: ',0
164 0000001E 6F6E64206E756D6265-
165 00000027 723A2000
166 0000002B 53756D2069733A2000         sum_msg      db  'Sum is: ',0
167 00000034 4F766572666C6F7720-        error_msg    db  'Overflow has occurred!',0
168 0000003D 686173206F63637572-
169 00000046 7265642100
170
171                                        .UDATA
172                                    <1>  segment .bss
173 00000000 <res 00000004>             number1      resd  1   ; stores first number
174 00000004 <res 00000004>             number2      resd  1   ; stores first number
175 00000008 <res 00000004>             sum          resd  1   ; stores sum
176
177                                        .CODE
178                                    <1>  segment .data
179                                    <1>  segment .bss
180                                    <1>  segment .text
181                                             .STARTUP
182                                    <1>
183                                    <1>  global _start
184                                    <1>  _start:
185                                             ; prompt user for first number
186                                             PutStr  prompt1_msg
187 00000000 51                        <1>  push ECX
188 00000001 B9[00000000]              <1>  mov ECX,%1
189 00000006 E8(00000000)              <1>  call proc_PutStr
190 0000000B 59                        <1>  pop ECX
191                                             GetLInt [number1]
192                                    <1> %ifnidni %1,EAX
193 0000000C 50                        <1>  push EAX
```

```
194  0000000D E8(00000000)          <1>   call proc_GetLInt
195  00000012 A3[00000000]          <1>   mov  %1,EAX
196  00000017 58                    <1>   pop  EAX
197                                  <1>   %else
198                                  <1>   call proc_GetLInt
199                                  <1>   %endif
200
201                                        ; prompt user for second number
202                                        PutStr  prompt2_msg
203  00000018 51                    <1>   push ECX
204  00000019 B9[15000000]          <1>   mov  ECX,%1
205  0000001E E8(00000000)          <1>   call proc_PutStr
206  00000023 59                    <1>   pop  ECX
207                                        GetLInt [number2]
208                                  <1>   %ifnidni %1,EAX
209  00000024 50                    <1>   push EAX
210  00000025 E8(00000000)          <1>   call proc_GetLInt
211  0000002A A3(04000000)          <1>   mov  %1,EAX
212  0000002F 58                    <1>   pop  EAX
213                                  <1>   %else
214                                  <1>   call proc_GetLInt
215                                  <1>   %endif
216
217                                        ; find sum of two 32-bit numbers
218  00000030 A1[00000000]                 mov     EAX, [number1]
219  00000035 0305[04000000]                add     EAX, [number2]
220  0000003B A3[08000000]                 mov     [sum], EAX
221
222                                        ; check for overflow
223  00000040 7116                         jno     no_overflow
224                                        PutStr  error_msg
225  00000042 51                    <1>   push ECX
226  00000043 B9[34000000]          <1>   mov  ECX,%1
227  00000048 E8(00000000)          <1>   call proc_PutStr
228  0000004D 59                    <1>   pop  ECX
229                                        nwln
230  0000004E E8(00000000)          <1>   call proc_nwln
231  00000053 E91D000000                   jmp     done
232
233                                        ; display sum
234                                  no_overflow:
235                                        PutStr  sum_msg
236  00000058 51                    <1>   push ECX
237  00000059 B9[2B000000]          <1>   mov  ECX,%1
238  0000005E E8(00000000)          <1>   call proc_PutStr
239  00000063 59                    <1>   pop  ECX
240                                        PutLInt [sum]
241  00000064 50                    <1>   push EAX
242  00000065 A1[08000000]          <1>   mov  EAX,%1
243  0000006A E8(00000000)          <1>   call proc_PutLInt
244  0000006F 58                    <1>   pop  EAX
245                                        nwln
246  00000070 E8(00000000)          <1>   call proc_nwln
247                                  done:
248                                        .EXIT
249  00000075 B801000000            <1>   mov  EAX,1
250  0000007A 31DB                  <1>   xor  EBX,EBX
251  0000007C CD80                  <1>   int  0x80
```

Linking Object Files

Linker is a program that takes one or more object programs as its input and produces executable code. In our example, since I/O routines are defined separately, we need two object files—sample.o and io.o—to generate the executable file sample (see Figure 7.2). To do this, we use the command

```
ld -s -o sample sample.o io.o
```

If you intend to debug your program using gdb, you should use the stabs option during the assembly in order to export the necessary symbolic information. We discuss this option in the next chapter, which deals with debugging.

Summary

We presented details about the NASM assembler. We also presented the template used to write stand-alone assembly language programs. Since the assembly language does not provide a convenient mechanism to do input and output, we defined a set of I/O routines to help us in performing simple character, string, and numeric input and output. We used simple examples to illustrate the use of these I/O routines in a typical stand-alone assembly language program.

To execute an assembly language program, we have to first translate it into an object program by using an assembler. Then we have to pass this object program, along with any other object programs needed by the program, to a linker to produce the executable code. We used NASM to assemble the programs. Note that NASM produces additional files that provide information on the assembly process. The list file is the one we often use to see the machine code and other details.

Web Resources

Documentation (including the NASM manual) and download information on NASM are available from http://sourceforge.net/projects/nasm.

8

Debugging Assembly Language Programs

Debugging assembly language programs is more difficult and time-consuming than debugging high-level language programs. However, the fundamental strategies that work for high-level languages also work for assembly language programs. We start this chapter with a discussion of these strategies. Since you are familiar with debugging programs written in a high-level language, this discussion is rather brief.

The following section discusses the GNU debugger (GDB). This is a command-line debugger. A nice visual interface to GDB is provided by Dynamic Data Display (DDD), which is described toward the end of the chapter. We use a simple example to explain some of the commands of GDB and DDD. The chapter concludes with a summary.

As we have not yet covered the assembly language programming, you may want to read this chapter in two passes. In the first pass, your goal is to get an overview of the two debuggers and some hands-on experience in invoking and using them. In this pass, you can skip the material that specifically deals with assembly language program statements. In the second pass, you can look at the skipped material. Ideally, you can come back to this chapter after you are familiar with the material presented in Chapters 9 through 11.

Strategies to Debug Assembly Language Programs

Programming is a complicated task. Loosely speaking, a program can be thought of as mapping a set of input values to a set of output values. The mapping performed by a program is given as the specification for the programming task. It goes without saying that when the program is written, it should be verified to meet the specifications. In programming parlance, this activity is referred to as testing and validating the program.

Testing a program itself is a complicated task. Typically, test cases, selected to validate the program, should test each possible path in the program, boundary cases, and so on. During this process, errors ("bugs") are discovered. Once a bug is found, it is necessary to find the source code causing the error and fix it. This process is known by its colorful name, *debugging*.

Debugging is not an exact science. We have to rely on our intuition and experience. However, there are tools that can help us in this process. Several debuggers are available to help us in the debugging process. We will look at two such tools in this chapter—GDB and DDD. Note that our goal here is to introduce the basics of the debugging process, as the best way to get familiar with debugging is to use a debugger.

Finding bugs in a program is very much dependent on the individual program. Once an error is detected, there are some general ways of locating the source code lines causing the error. The basic principle that helps you in writing the source program in the first place—the divide and conquer technique—is also useful in the debugging process. Structured programming methodology facilitates debugging greatly.

A program typically consists of several modules, where each module may have several procedures. When developing a program, it is best to do incremental development. In this methodology, a few procedures are added to the program to add some specific functionality. The program must be tested before adding other functions to the program. In general, it is a bad idea to write the whole program and then testing it, unless the program is small. The best strategy is to write code that has as few bugs as possible. This can be achieved by using pseudocode and verifying the logic of the pseudocode even before you attempt to translate it into the assembly language program. This is a good way of catching many of the logical errors and saves a lot of debugging time. Never write an assembly language code with the pseudo-code in your head! Furthermore, don't be in a hurry to write assembly language code that appears to work. This is short sighted, as we end up spending more time in the debugging phase.

To isolate a bug, program execution should be observed in slow motion. Most debuggers provide a command to execute a program in single-step mode. In this mode, a program executes a single statement and pauses. Then we can examine contents of registers, data in memory, stack contents, and so on. In the single-step mode, a procedure call is treated as a single statement and the entire procedure is executed before pausing the program. This is useful if you know that the called procedure works correctly. Debuggers also provide another command to trace even the statements of a procedure call, which is useful in testing procedures.

Often we know that some parts of the program work correctly. In this case, it is a sheer waste of time to single step or trace the code. What we would like is to execute this part of the program and then stop for more careful debugging (perhaps by single stepping). Debuggers provide commands to set up breakpoints. The program execution stops at breakpoints, giving us a chance to look at the state of the program.

Another helpful feature that most debuggers provide is the watch facility. By using watches, it is possible to monitor the state (i.e., values) of the variables in the program as the execution progresses.

In the rest of the chapter, we discuss two debuggers and show how they are useful in debugging assembly language programs. Our debugging sessions use the following program, which is discussed in Chapter 11.

Program 8.1 An example program used to explain debugging

```
1:  ;Parameter passing via registers                    PROCEX1.ASM
2:  ;
3:  ;           Objective: To show parameter passing via registers.
4:  ;               Input: Requests two integers from the user.
```

```
 5:  ;                Output: Outputs the sum of the input integers.
 6:  %include "io.mac"
 7:  .DATA
 8:  prompt_msg1  DB    "Please input the first number: ",0
 9:  prompt_msg2  DB    "Please input the second number: ",0
10:  sum_msg      DB    "The sum is ",0
11:
12:  .CODE
13:        .STARTUP
14:        PutStr  prompt_msg1     ; request first number
15:        GetInt  CX              ; CX = first number
16:
17:        PutStr  prompt_msg2     ; request second number
18:        GetInt  DX              ; DX = second number
19:
20:        call    sum             ; returns sum in AX
21:        PutStr  sum_msg         ; display sum
22:        PutInt  AX
23:        nwln
24:  done:
25:        .EXIT
26:
27:  ;------------------------------------------------------------
28:  ;Procedure sum receives two integers in CX and DX.
29:  ;The sum of the two integers is returned in AX.
30:  ;------------------------------------------------------------
31:  sum:
32:        mov     AX,CX           ; sum = first number
33:        add     AX,DX           ; sum = sum + second number
34:        ret
```

Preparing Your Program

The assembly process described in the last chapter works fine if we just want to assemble and run our program. However, we need to prepare our program slightly differently to debug the program. More specifically, we would like to pass the source code and symbol table information so that we can debug using the source-level statements. This source-level debugging is much better than debugging using disassembled code.

To facilitate such symbolic debugging, we need to export symbolic information to the GNU debugger. This debugger expects the symbolic information in the stabs format. More details on this format are available in the GDB manual available online (see "Web Resources" section at the end of the chapter).

We can assemble and load a program (say, procex1.asm) for debugging as follows:

```
nasm -f elf -g -F stabs procex1.asm
ld -o procex1 procex1.o io.o
```

The executable program procex1 would have the necessary symbolic information to help us in the debugging process. Note that we need to include the I/O file io.o because our programs use the I/O routines described in the last chapter.

GNU Debugger

This section describes the GNU debugger gdb. It is typically invoked by

```
gdb file_name
```

For example, to debug the procex1 program, we can use

```
gdb procex1
```

We can also invoke gdb without giving the filename. We can specify the file to be debugged by using the file command inside the gdb. Details on the file command are available in the GDB manual. You know that gdb is running the show when you see the (gdb) prompt. At this prompt, it can accept one of several commands. Tables 8.1 and 8.2 show some of the commands useful in debugging programs.

Display Group

Displaying Source Code   When debugging, it is handy to keep a printed copy of the source code with line numbers. However, gdb has list commands that allow us to look at the source code. A simple list command takes no arguments. The command

```
list
```

displays the default number of lines. The default is 10 lines. If we issue this command again, it displays the next 10 lines. We can use list - to print lines before the last printed lines. We can abbreviate this command to l.

We can specify a line number as an argument. In this case, it displays 10 lines centered on the specified line number. For example, the command

```
l 20
```

displays lines 15 through 24, as shown in Program 8.2 on page 178. The list command can also take other arguments. For example,

```
l first,last
```

displays the lines from first to last.

The default number of lines displayed can be changed to n with the following command:

```
set listsize n
```

The command show listsize gives the current default value.

Displaying Register Contents   When debugging an assembly language program, we often need to look at the contents of the registers. The info can be used for this purpose. The

```
info registers
```

displays the contents of the integer registers. To display all registers including the floating-point registers, use

Table 8.1 Some of the GDB display commands

Display Commands

Source code display commands

list	Lists default number of source code lines from the last displayed lines (default is 10 lines). It can be abbreviated as l.
list -	Lists default number of source code lines preceding the last displayed lines (default is 10 lines)
list linenum	Lists default number of lines centered around the specified line number linenum
list first,last	Lists the source code lines from first to last

Register display commands

info registers	Displays the contents of registers except floating-point registers
info all-registers	Displays the contents of registers
info register ...	Displays contents of the specified registers

Memory display commands

x address	Displays the contents of memory at address (uses defaults)
x/nfu adddress	Displays the contents of memory at address

Stack frame display commands

backtrace	Displays backtrace of the entire stack (one line for each stack frame). It can be abbreviated as bt.
backtrace n	Displays backtrace of the innermost n stack frames
backtrace -n	Displays backtrace of the outermost n stack frames
frame n	Select frame n (frame zero is the innermost frame i.e., currently executing frame). It can be abbreviated as f.
info frame	Displays a description of the selected stack frame (details include the frame address, program counter saved in it, addresses of local variable and arguments, addresses of the next and previous frames, and so on)

```
info all-registers
```

Often we are interested in a select few registers. To avoid cluttering the display, gdb allows specification of the registers in the command. For example, we can use

```
info eax ecx edx
```

to check the contents of the eax, ecx, and edx registers.

Displaying Memory Contents   We can examine memory contents by using the x command (x stands for examine). It has the following syntax:

Table 8.2 Some of the GDB commands (continued on the next page)

Execution Commands

Breakpoint commands

`break linenum`	Sets a breakpoint at the specified line number in the current source file.
`break function`	Sets a breakpoint at entry to the specified function in the current source file.
`break *address`	Sets a breakpoint at the specified address. This command is useful if the debugging information or the source files are not available.
`info breakpoints`	Gives information on the breakpoints set. The information includes the breakpoint number, where the breakpoint is set in the source code, address, status (enabled or disabled), and so on.
`delete`	Deletes all breakpoints. By default, gdb runs this in query mode asking for confirmation for each breakpoint to be deleted. We can also specify a range as arguments (`delete range`). This command can be abbreviated as d.
`tbreak arg`	Sets a breakpoint as in break. The `arg` can be a line number, function name, or address as in the `break` command. However, the breakpoint is deleted after the first hit.
`disable range`	Disables the specified breakpoints. If no range is given, all breakpoints are disabled.
`enable range`	Enables the specified breakpoints. If no range is given, all breakpoints are enabled.
`enable once range`	Enables the specified breakpoints once i.e., when the breakpoint is hit, it is disabled. If no range is given, all breakpoints are enabled once.

Program execution commands

`run`	Executes the program under gdb. To be useful, you should set up appropriate breakpoints before issuing this command. It can be abbreviated as r.
`continue`	Continues execution from where the program has last stopped (e.g., due to a breakpoint). It can be abbreviated as c.

```
x/nfu address
```

where n, f, and u are optional parameters that specify the amount of memory to be displayed starting at address and its format. If the optional parameters are not given, the x command can be written as

```
x address
```

Table 8.2 (*continued*)

Single stepping commands

step	Single-steps execution of the program (i.e., one source line at a time). In case of a procedure call, it single-steps into the procedure code. It can be abbreviated as s.
step count	Single-steps program execution count times. If it encounters a break-point before reaching the count, it stops execution.
next	Single-steps as the step command does; however, procedure call is treated as a single statement (does not jump into the procedure code). As in the step command, we can specify a count value. It can be abbreviated as n.
next count	Single-steps program execution count times. If it encounters a break-point before reaching the count, it stops execution.
stepi	Executes one machine instruction. Like the step command, it single-steps into the procedure body. For assembly language programs, both step and stepi tend to behave the same. As in the step command, we can specify a count value. It can be abbreviated as si.
nexti	Executes one machine instruction. Like the next command, it treats a procedure call as a single machine instruction and executes the whole procdure. As in the next command, we can specify a count value. It can be abbreviated as ni.

Miscellaneous Commands

set listsize n	Sets the default list size to n lines
show listsize	Shows the default list size
q	Quits gdb

In this case the default values are used for the three optional parameters. Details about these parameters are given in Table 8.3.

Next we look at some examples of the x command. When gdb is invoked with Program 8.1, we can examine the contents of the memory at prompt_msg1 by using the following x command:

```
(gdb) x/1sb &prompt_msg1
0x80493e4 <prompt_msg1>:        "Please input the first number: "
```

This command specifies the three optional parameters as n = 1, f = s, and u = b. We get the following output when we change the n value to 3:

```
(gdb) x/3sb &prompt_msg1
0x80493e4 <prompt_msg1>:    "Please input the first number: "
0x8049404 <prompt_msg2>:    "Please input the second number: "
0x8049425 <sum_msg>:        "The sum is "
```

Table 8.3 Details about the optional parameters

n	Repeat count (decimal integer) Specifies the number of units (in u) of memory to be displayed. Default value is 1.
f	Display format

      x   displays in hexadecimal
      d   displays in decimal
      u   displays in unsigned decimal
      o   displays in octal
      t   displays in binary (t for two)
      a   displays address both in hexadecimal and as an offset
                from the nearest preceding symbol
      c   displays as a character
      s   displays as a null-terminated string
      t   displays as a floating-point number
      i   displays as a machine instruction
      Initial default is x. The default changes each time x is used.

u	Unit size

      b   bytes
      h   halfwords (2 bytes)
      w   words (4 bytes)
      g   giant words (8 bytes)
      Initial default is w. The default changes when a unit is specified
      with an x command.

As you can see from the program listing, it matches the three strings we declared in procex1. asm program.

Displaying Stack Frame Contents   This group of display commands helps us trace the history of procedure invocations. The backtrace command gives a list of procedure invocations at that point. This list consists of one line for each stack frame of the stack. As an example, consider a program that calls a procedure sum that calls another procedure compute, which in turn calls a third procedure get_values. If we stop the program in the get_values procedure and issue a backtrace command, we see the following output:

```
(gdb) bt
#0  get_values () at testex.asm:50
#1  0x080480bc in compute () at testex.asm:41
#2  0x080480a6 in sum () at testex.asm:27
```

This output clearly shows the invocation sequence of procedure calls with one line per invocation. The innermost stack frame is labelled #0, the next stack frame as #1, and so on. Each line gives the source code line that invoked the procedure. For example, the call instruction on line 27 (in the source file testex.asm) invoked the compute procedure. The program counter value

0x080480a6 gives the return address. As we shall discuss in Chapter 11, this is the address of
the instruction following the

```
call     compute
```

instruction in the sum procedure. Similarly, the call instruction on line 41 in the compute procedure invoked the get_values procedure. The return address for the get_values procedure
is 0x080480bc.

We can also restrict the number of stack frames displayed in the backtrace command by
giving an optional argument. Details on this optional argument are given in Table 8.1. For example,
bt 2 gives the innermost two stack frames as shown below:

```
(gdb) bt 2
#0   get_values () at testex.asm:50
#1   0x080480bc in compute () at testex.asm:41
(More stack frames follow...)
```

To display the outermost two stack frames, we can issue bt -2. This command produces the
following output for our example program:

```
(gdb) bt -2
#1   0x080480bc in compute () at testex.asm:41
#2   0x080480a6 in sum () at testex.asm:27
```

The frame and info frame commands allow us to examine the contents of a frame. We
can select a frame by using the frame command. For our test program, frame 1 gives the
following output:

```
(gdb) frame 1
#1   0x080480bc in compute () at testex.asm:41
41         call get_values
```

Once a frame is selected, we can issue the info frame command to look at the contents of this
stack frame. Note that if no frame is selected using the frame command, it defaults to frame 0.
The output produced for our example is shown below:

```
(gdb) info f
Stack level 1, frame at 0xbffffa00:
 eip = 0x80480bc in compute (testex.asm:41); saved eip 0x80480a6
 called by frame at 0xbffffa08, caller of frame at 0xbffff9f8
 source language unknown.
 Arglist at 0xbffffa00, args:
 Locals at 0xbffffa00, Previous frame's sp is 0x0
 Saved registers:
  ebp at 0xbffffa00, eip at 0xbffffa04
(gdb)
```

In our example, each stack frame consists of the return address (4 bytes) and the EBP value stored
by enter 0,0 instruction on entering a procedure. The details given here indicate that the
current stack frame is at 0xbffffa00 and previous and next frames are at 0xbffffa08 and
0xbffff9f8, respectively. It also shows where the arguments and locals are located as well as
the registers saved on the stack. In our example, only the return address (EIP) and stack pointer
(EBP) are stored on the stack for a total of 8 bytes.

Execution Group

Breakpoint Commands   Breakpoints can be inserted using the break commands. As indicated in Table 8.2, breakpoints can be specified using the source code line number, function name, or the address. For example, the following commands insert breakpoint at line 20 and function sum on line 32 in the procex1.asm program:

```
(gdb) b 20
Breakpoint 1 at 0x80480b0: file procex1.asm, line 20.
(gdb) b sum
Breakpoint 2 at 0x80480db: file procex1.asm, line 32.
(gdb)
```

Note that each breakpoint is assigned a sequence number in the order we establish them.

We can use info breakpoints (or simply info b) to get a summary of the breakpoints and their status. For example, after establishing the above two breakpoints, if we issue the info command, we get the following output:

```
(gdb) info b
Num Type           Disp Enb Address    What
1   breakpoint     keep y   0x080480b0 procex1.asm:20
2   breakpoint     keep y   0x080480db procex1.asm:32
(gdb)
```

The Disp (Disposition) column indicates the action needed to be taken (keep, disable, or delete) when hit. By default, all breakpoints are of 'keep' type as in our example here. The enb column indicates whether the breakpoint is enabled or disabled. A 'y' in this column indicated that the breakpoint is enabled.

We can use tbreak command to set a breakpoint with 'delete' disposition as shown below:

```
(gdb) tbreak 22
Breakpoint 3 at 0x80480c1: file procex1.asm, line 22.
(gdb) info b
Num Type           Disp Enb Address    What
1   breakpoint     keep y   0x080480b0 procex1.asm:20
2   breakpoint     keep y   0x080480db procex1.asm:32
3   breakpoint     del  y   0x080480c1 procex1.asm:22
(gdb)
```

We can use the enable and disable commands to enable or disable the breakpoints. The following example disables breakpoint 2:

```
(gdb) disable 2
(gdb) info b
Num Type           Disp Enb Address    What
1   breakpoint     keep y   0x080480b0 procex1.asm:20
2   breakpoint     keep n   0x080480db procex1.asm:32
3   breakpoint     del  y   0x080480c1 procex1.asm:22
(gdb)
```

If we want to enable this breakpoint, we do so by the following command:

```
(gdb) enable 2
```

We use the enable once command to set a breakpoint with 'disable' disposition as shown below:

```
(gdb) enable once 2
(gdb) info b
Num Type           Disp Enb Address    What
1   breakpoint     keep y   0x080480b0 procex1.asm:20
2   breakpoint     dis  y   0x080480db procex1.asm:32
3   breakpoint     del  y   0x080480c1 procex1.asm:22
(gdb)
```

Program Execution Commands   Program execution command run is used to start the execution of a program. To be able to debug the program, breakpoints must be established before issuing the run command.

The continue command resumes program execution from the last stop point (typically due to a breakpoint).

Single-Stepping Commands

The gdb debugger provides two basic single-stepping commands: step and next. The step command executes one source line at a time. In case of a procedure call, it traces procedure execution in the single-step mode. The next command is similar to the step command except that it does not single-step through the procedure body. Instead, it executes the entire procedure. Both step and next commands can take a count argument as shown in Table 8.2 on page 173. This table also gives details on the machine instruction version of these step and next commands (see the stepi and nexti commands).

Miscellaneous Group

The commands in Table 8.2 are useful to manipulate the list size and exit gdb.

An Example

A sample gdb session on procex1.asm is shown in Program 8.2. The l 20 command on line 9 displays the source code centered on the source code line 20. Before issuing the r command on line 22, we insert a breakpoint at source code line 20 using the break command on line 20. The run command executes the program until it hits line 20. Then it stops and prints breakpoint information. Note that we entered two input numbers (1234 and 5678) before hitting the breakpoint.

To check that these two input numbers are read into ECX and EDX registers, we issue the info registers command specifying these two registers (see line 28). The output of this command shows that these registers have indeed received the two input numbers.

We run the sum procedure in single-step mode (see commands on lines 31, 33, and 35). To see if the result in EAX is the sum of the two input values, we display the contents of the three registers (lines 38–40) using the info registers command on line 37. After verifying, we let the program continue its execution using the continue command on line 41. Finally, on line 46, we used the quit command to exit gdb.

Program 8.2 A sample `gdb` `session`

```
 1: GNU gdb Red Hat Linux (5.2.1-4)
 2: Copyright 2002 Free Software Foundation, Inc.
 3: GDB is free software, covered by the GNU General Public License, and
 4: you are welcome to change it and/or distribute copies of it under
 5: certain conditions. Type "show copying" to see the conditions.
 6: There is absolutely no warranty for GDB.
 7: Type "show warranty" for details.
 8: This GDB was configured as "i386-redhat-linux"...
 9: (gdb) l 20
10: 15         GetInt  CX                ; CX = first number
11: 16
12: 17         PutStr  prompt_msg2       ; request second number
13: 18         GetInt  DX                ; DX = second number
14: 19
15: 20         call    sum               ; returns sum in AX
16: 21         PutStr  sum_msg           ; display sum
17: 22         PutInt  AX
18: 23         nwln
19: 24 done:
20: (gdb) break 20
21: Breakpoint 1 at 0x80480b0: file procex1.asm, line 20.
22: (gdb) r
23: Starting program: /mnt/hgfs/winXP_D/temp/gdb_test/procex1
24: Please input the first number: 1234
25: Please input the second number: 5678
26: Breakpoint 1, _start () at procex1.asm:20
27: 20         call    sum               ; returns sum in AX
28: (gdb) info registers ecx edx
29: ecx             0x4d2   1234
30: edx             0x162e  5678
31: (gdb) si
32: 32         mov     AX,CX             ; sum = first number
33: (gdb) si
34: 33         add     AX,DX             ; sum = sum + second number
35: (gdb) si
36: 34         ret
37: (gdb) info registers eax ecx edx
38: eax             0x1b00  6912
39: ecx             0x4d2   1234
40: edx             0x162e  5678
41: (gdb) c
42: Continuing.
43: The sum is 6912
44:
45: Program exited normally.
46: (gdb) q
```

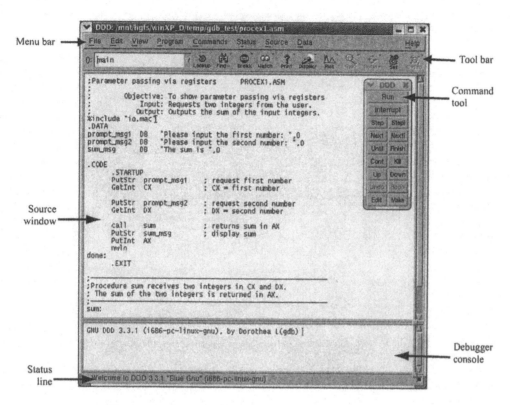

Menu bar

Tool bar

Command tool

Source window

Debugger console

Status line

Figure 8.1 DDD window at the start of `procex1` program.

Data Display Debugger

The Data Display Debugger (DDD) acts as a front-end to a command-line debugger. DDD supports several command line debuggers including GDB, DBX, JDB, and so on. Our interest here is in using DDD as a front-end for the GDB debugger discussed in the last section.

If you installed your Linux following the directions given in Chapter 5, DDD is already installed. However, if you did not install it as part of the Linux installation, or if you want the latest version, you can install it using the Linux package manager. Also the DDD Web page has details on the installation process (see the Web Resources section at the end of the chapter for details).

Because DDD is a front-end to GDB, we prepare our program exactly as we do for the GDB (see "Preparing Your Program" section on page 169). We can invoke DDD on the `procex1` executable by

```
ddd  procex1
```

Figure 8.1 shows the initial screen that appears after invoking DDD. The screen consists of the Source Window that displays the source program, Debugger Console, Status Line, Command Tool window, Menu Bar, and Tool Bar. The debugger console acts as the program's input/output console to display messages, to receive input, and so on.

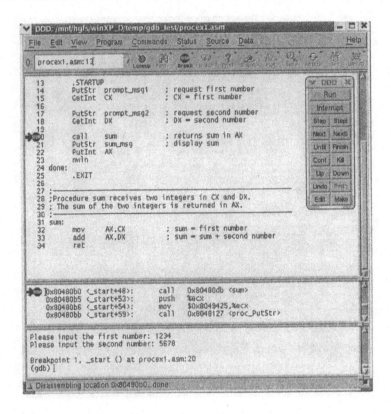

Figure 8.2 DDD window at the breakpoint on line 20. This screenshot also shows the machine code window and the source code line numbers.

We can insert a breakpoint using the Tool Bar. For example, to insert a breakpoint on line 20, place the cursor to the left of line 20 and click the breakpoint (red stop sign) on the Tool Bar. This inserts a breakpoint on line 20, which is indicated by the red stop sign on line 20 as shown in Figure 8.2. This figure also shows source code line numbers and the Machine Code window. Both of these can be selected from the Source pull down menu in the Menu Bar.

Once this breakpoint is inserted, we can run the program by clicking Run in the Command Tool. The big arrow next to the stop sign (on line 20) indicates that the program execution stopped at that line. While executing the program before reaching the breakpoint on line 20, the program takes two input numbers as shown in the Debugger Console (see Figure 8.2). We can get information on the breakpoints set in the program by selecting Breakpoints... in the Source pull-down menu. For our example program, it gives details on the single breakpoint we set on line 20 (see Figure 8.3). The details provided in this window are the same as those discussed in the last section. The breakpoint information also includes the number hits as shown in Figure 8.3.

All the execution commands of gdb, discussed in the last section, are available in the Program pull-down menu (see Figure 8.4). Figure 8.5 shows the screen after single stepping through the sum procedure. The program is stopped at the ret instruction on line 34. To verify

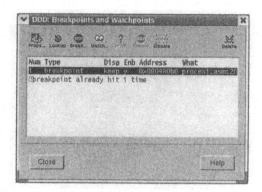

Figure 8.3 Breakpoints window.

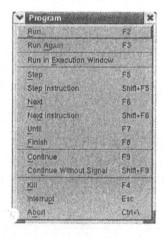

Figure 8.4 Details of the Program pull-down menu.

the functionality of the procedure, we can display the contents of the registers. This is done by selecting Registers... in the Status pull-down menu. The contents of the registers, shown in Figure 8.6, clearly indicate that the sum of the two input numbers (in the ECX and EDX registers) is in the EAX register.

The examination commands of gdb are available under Data pull-down menu. A sample memory examination window is shown in Figure 8.7. This window allows us to specify the memory location, format to be used to display the contents, size of the data, and the number of data items to be examined. In the window of Figure 8.7, we specified &prompt_msg1 as the location and string as the output format. The size is given as bytes and the number of strings to be examined is set to 1.

By clicking Display, the contents are displayed in the Data Window that appears above the Source Window as shown in Figure 8.8. We can pick the windows we want to see by selecting them

Figure 8.5 DDD window after single stepping from the breakpoint on line 20.

Figure 8.6 Register window after the single stepping shown in Figure 8.5.

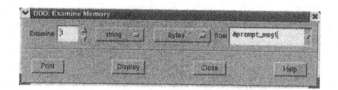

Figure 8.7 Memory examination window to display three strings.

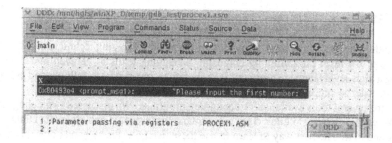

Figure 8.8 Memory examination window.

from the View pull-down menu. The View menu gives control to select any of the four windows: Debuger Console Window, Machine Code Window, Source Window, and Data Window.

We can also select to display the contents in the Debugger Console Window using the Print command. Figure 8.9 shows how we can display the three strings in our program in the Console window. This Examine Memory window is similar to that shown in Figure 8.7 except that we set the number of strings to be displayed as 3. The result of executing this x command is shown in Figure 8.10, which shows the three strings in our program.

Both gdb and DDD provide several other features that are useful in debugging programs. Our intent here is to introduce some of the basic features of these debuggers. More details on these debuggers are available from their web sites. We provide pointers to these Web sites at the end of this chapter.

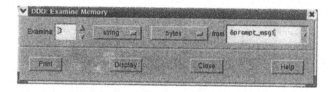

Figure 8.9 Memory examination window.

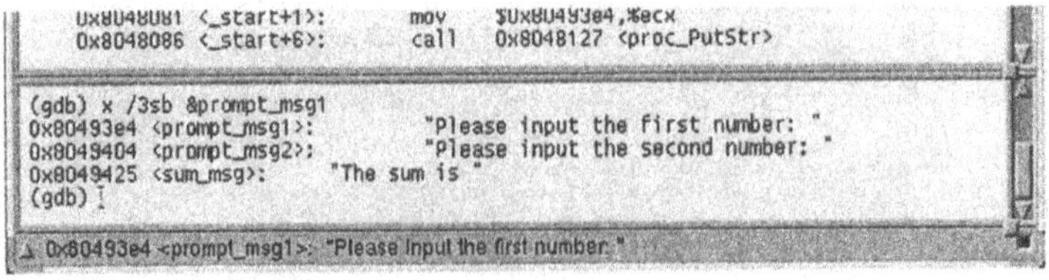

```
0x8048081 <_start+1>:      mov     $0x80493e4,%ecx
0x8048086 <_start+6>:      call    0x8048127 <proc_PutStr>

(gdb) x /3sb &prompt_msg1
0x80493e4 <prompt_msg1>:            "Please input the first number: "
0x8049404 <prompt_msg2>:            "Please input the second number: "
0x8049425 <sum_msg>:       "The sum is "
(gdb)

0x80493e4 <prompt_msg1>: "Please input the first number: "
```

Figure 8.10 CPU window after executing `Goto...` command.

Summary

We started this chapter with a brief discussion of the basic debugging techniques. Since assembly language is a low-level programming language, debugging tends to be even more tedious than debugging a high-level language program. It is, therefore, imperative to follow good programming practices in order to simplify debugging of assembly language programs.

There are several tools available for debugging programs. We discussed two debuggers—gdb and DDD—in this chapter. While gdb is a command line-oriented debugger, the DDD provides a nice front-end to it. The best way to learn to use these debuggers is by hands-on experience.

Web Resources

Details on gdb are available from `http://www.gnu.org/software/gdb`. The *GDB User Manual* is available from `http://www.gnu.org/software/gdb/documentation`.

Details on DDD are available from `http://www.gnu.org/software/ddd`. The *DDD Manual* is available from `http://www.gnu.org/manual/ddd/`.

PART V

Assembly Language

9

A First Look at Assembly Language

The objective of this chapter is to introduce the basics of the assembly language. Assembly language statements can either instruct the processor to perform a task, or direct the assembler during the assembly process. The latter statements are called assembler directives. We start this chapter with a discussion of the format and types of assembly language statements. A third type of assembly language statements called macros is covered in the next chapter.

Assemblers provide several directives to reserve storage space for variables. These directives are discussed in detail. The instructions of the processor consist of an operation code to indicate the type of operation to be performed, and the specification of the data required (also called the addressing mode) by the operation. Here we describe a few basic addressing modes. A thorough discussion of this topic is in Chapter 13.

The IA-32 instruction set can be divided into several groups of instructions. This chapter provides an overview of some of the instructions while the next chapter gives details on some more instructions. Later chapters discuss these instructions in more detail. The chapter concludes with a summary.

Introduction

Assembly language programs are created out of three different classes of statements. Statements in the first class tell the processor what to do. These statements are called *executable instructions*, or *instructions* for short. Each executable instruction consists of an *operation code* (*opcode* for short). Executable instructions cause the assembler to generate machine language instructions. As stated in Chapter 1, each executable statement typically generates one machine language instruction.

The second class of statements provides information to the assembler on various aspects of the assembly process. These instructions are called *assembler directives* or *pseudo-ops*. Assembler directives are nonexecutable and do not generate any machine language instructions.

The last class of statements, called *macros*, provide a sophisticated text substitution mechanism. Macros are discussed in detail in the next chapter.

Assembly language statements are entered one per line in the source file. All three classes of the assembly language statements use the same format:

```
[label]    mnemonic    [operands]    [;comment]
```

The fields in the square brackets are optional in some statements. As a result of this format, it is a common practice to align the fields to aid readability of assembly language programs. The assembler does not care about spaces between the fields.

Now let us look at some sample assembly language statements.

```
repeat:  inc     result  ;increment result by 1
```

The label `repeat` can be used to refer to this particular statement. The mnemonic `inc` indicates increment operation to be done on the data stored in memory at a location identified by `result`. Certain reserved words that have special meaning to the assembler are not allowed as labels. These include mnemonics such as `inc`.

The fields in a statement must be separated by at least one space or tab character. More spaces and tabs can be used at the programmer's discretion, but the assembler ignores them.

It is a good programming practice to use blank lines and spaces to improve the readability of assembly language programs. As a result, you rarely see in this book a statement containing all four fields in a single line. In particular, we almost always write labels on a separate line unless doing so destroys the program structure. Thus, our first example assembly language statement is written on two lines as

```
repeat:
    inc     result  ;increment result by 1
```

The NASM assembler provides several directives to reserve space for variables. These directives are discussed in the next section. Assembly language instructions typically require one or more operands. These operands can be at different locations. There are several different ways we can specify the location of the operands. These are referred to as the addressing modes. We introduce four simple addressing modes in this chapter. These addressing modes are sufficient to write simple but meaningful assembly language programs. Chapter 13 gives complete details on the addressing modes available in 16- and 32-bit modes. Following our discussion of the addressing modes, we give an overview of some of the instructions available in the IA-32 instruction set.

Starting with this chapter, we give several programming examples in each chapter. We give a simple example in the "Our First Example" section. A later "Illustrative Examples" section gives more examples. To understand the structure of these programs, you need to understand the information presented in Chapter 7. That chapter gives details about the structure of the assembly language programs presented in this book, the I/O routines we use, and how you can assemble and link them to create an executable file. If you have skipped that chapter, it is a good time to go back and review the material presented there.

Data Allocation

In high-level languages, allocation of storage space for variables is done indirectly by specifying the data types of each variable used in the program. For example, in C, the following declarations allocate different amounts of storage space for each variable.

```
char        response;    /* allocates 1 byte  */
int         value;       /* allocates 4 bytes */
float       total;       /* allocates 4 bytes */
double      temp;        /* allocates 8 bytes */
```

These variable declarations not only specify the amount of storage required, but also indicate how the stored bit pattern should be interpreted. As an example, consider the following two statements in C:

```
unsigned    value_1;
int         value_2;
```

Both variables use four bytes of storage. However, the bit pattern stored in them would be interpreted differently. For instance, the bit pattern (8FF08DB9H)

```
1000 1111 1111 0000 1000 1101 1011 1001
```

stored in the four bytes allocated for `value_1` is interpreted as representing $+2.4149 \times 10^9$, while the same bit pattern stored in `value_2` would be interpreted as -1.88006×10^9.

In the assembly language, allocation of storage space is done by the define assembler directive. The define directive can be used to reserve and initialize one or more bytes. However, no interpretation (as in a C variable declaration) is attached to the contents of these bytes. It is entirely up to the program to interpret the bit pattern stored in the space reserved for data.

The general format of the storage allocation statement for initialized data is

```
[variable-name] define-directive initial-value [,initial-value],···
```

The square brackets indicate optional items. The `variable-name` is used to identify the storage space allocated. The assembler associates an offset value for each variable name defined in the data segment. Note that no colon (:) follows the variable name (unlike a label identifying an executable statement).

The define directive takes one of the five basic forms:

```
DB      Define Byte           ; allocates 1 byte
DW      Define Word           ; allocates 2 bytes
DD      Define Doubleword     ; allocates 4 bytes
DQ      Define Quadword       ; allocates 8 bytes
DT      Define Ten Bytes      ; allocates 10 bytes
```

Let us look at some examples now.

```
sorted      DB      'y'
```

This statement allocates a single byte of storage and initializes it to character `y`. Our assembly language program can refer to this character location by its name `sorted`. We can also use numbers to initialize. For example,

```
sorted      DB      79H
```

or

```
sorted      DB      1111001B
```

is equivalent to

```
sorted    DB    'y'
```

Note that the ASCII value for y is 79H. The following data definition statement allocates two bytes of contiguous storage and initializes it to 25159.

```
value    DW    25159
```

The decimal value 25159 is automatically converted to its 16-bit binary equivalent (6247H). Since the processor uses the little-endian byte ordering (see Chapter 3), this 16-bit number is stored in memory as

```
address:    x    x+1
contents:   47   62
```

You can also use negative values, as in the following example:

```
balance    DW    -29255
```

Since the 2's complement representation is used to store negative values, $-29,255$ is converted to 8DB9H and is stored as

```
address:    x    x+1
contents:   B9   8D
```

The statement

```
total    DD    542803535
```

would allocate four contiguous bytes of memory and initialize it to 542803535 (205A864FH), as shown below:

```
address:    x    x+1   x+2   x+3
contents:   4F   86    5A    20
```

Short and long floating-point numbers are represented using 32 or 64 bits, respectively (see Appendix A for details). We can use DD and DQ directives to assign real numbers, as shown in the following examples:

```
float1    DD    1.234
real2     DQ    123.456
```

Uninitialized Data

To reserve space for uninitialized data, we use RESB, RESW, and so on. Each reserve directive takes a single operand that specifies the number of units of space (bytes, words, ...) to be reserved. There is a reserve directive for each define directive.

```
RESB    Reserve a Byte
RESW    Reserve a Word
RESD    Reserve a Doubleword
RESQ    Reserve a Quadword
REST    Reserve Ten Bytes
```

Here are some examples:

```
response    RESB    1
buffer      RESW    100
total       RESD    1
```

The first statement reserves a byte while the second reserves space for an array of 100 words. The last statement reserves space for a doubleword.

Multiple Definitions

Assembly language programs typically contain several data definition statements. For example, look at the following assembly language program fragment:

```
sort    DB    'y'          ; ASCII of y = 79H
value   DW    25159        ; 25159D = 6247H
total   DD    542803535    ; 542803535D = 205A864FH
```

When several data definition statements are used as above, the assembler allocates contiguous memory for these variables. The memory layout for these three variables is

address:	x	x+1	x+2	x+3	x+4	x+5	x+6
contents:	79	47	62	4F	86	5A	20
	sort	value			total		

Multiple data definitions can be abbreviated. For example, the following sequence of eight DB directives

```
message    DB    'W'
           DB    'E'
           DB    'L'
           DB    'C'
           DB    'O'
           DB    'M'
           DB    'E'
           DB    '!'
```

can be abbreviated as

```
message    DB    'W','E','L','C','O','M','E','!'
```

or even more compactly as

```
message    DB    'WELCOME!'
```

Here is another example showing how abbreviated forms simplify data definitions. The definition

```
message    DB    'B'
           DB    'y'
           DB    'e'
           DB    0DH
           DB    0AH
```

can be written as

```
message     DB      'Bye',0DH,0AH
```

Similar abbreviated forms can be used with the other define directives. For instance, a `marks` array of size 8 can be defined and initialized to zero by

```
marks   DW      0
        DW      0
        DW      0
        DW      0
        DW      0
        DW      0
        DW      0
        DW      0
```

which can be abbreviated as

```
marks   DW      0, 0, 0, 0, 0, 0, 0, 0
```

The initialization values of define directives can also be expressions as shown in the following example.

```
max_marks   DW      7*25
```

This statement is equivalent to

```
max_marks   DW      175
```

The assembler evaluates such expressions at assembly time and assigns the resulting value. Use of expressions to specify initial values is not preferred, because it affects the readability of programs. However, there are certain situations where using an expression actually helps clarify the code. In our example, if `max_marks` represents the sum of seven assignment marks where each assignment is marked out of 25 marks, it is preferable to use the expression 7 *25 rather than 175.

Multiple Initializations

In the previous example, if the class size is 90, it is inconvenient to define the array as described. The `TIMES` directive allows multiple initializations to the same value. Using `TIMES`, the `marks` array can be defined as

```
marks   TIMES 8  DW  0
```

The `TIMES` directive is useful in defining arrays and tables.

Symbol Table

When we allocate storage space using a data definition directive, we usually associate a symbolic name to refer to it. The assembler, during the assembly process, assigns an offset value for each symbolic name. For example, consider the following data definition statements:

```
.DATA
value      DW    0
sum        DD    0
marks      TIMES 10  DW   0
message    DB    'The grade is:',0
char1      DB    ?
```

As noted before, the assembler assigns contiguous memory space for the variables. The assembler also uses the same ordering of variables that is present in the source code. Then, finding the offset value of a variable is a simple matter of counting the number of bytes allocated to all the variables preceding it. For example, the offset value of marks is 6 because value and sum are allocated 2 and 4 bytes, respectively. The symbol table for the data segment is shown below:

Name	Offset
value	0
sum	2
marks	6
message	26
char1	40

Where Are the Operands

Most assembly language instructions require operands. There are several ways to specify the location of the operands. These are called the *addressing modes*. This section is a brief overview of some of the addressing modes required to do basic assembly language programming. A complete discussion is given in Chapter 13.

An operand required by an instruction may be in any one of the following locations:

- in a register internal to the processor;
- in the instruction itself;
- in main memory (usually in the data segment);
- at an I/O port (discussed in Chapter 20).

Specification of an operand that is in a register is called *register addressing mode*, while *immediate addressing mode* refers to specifying an operand that is part of the instruction. Several addressing modes are available to specify the location of an operand residing in memory. The motivation for providing these addressing modes comes from the perceived need to efficiently support high-level language constructs (see Chapter 13 for details).

Register Addressing Mode

In this addressing mode, processor's internal registers contain the data to be manipulated by the instruction. For example, the instruction

```
mov    EAX,EBX
```

requires two operands and both are in the processor registers. The syntax of the mov instruction is

```
mov    destination,source
```

The mov instruction copies contents of source to destination. The contents of source are not destroyed. Thus,

```
mov     EAX,EBX
```

copies the contents of the EBX register into the EAX register. Note that the original contents of EAX are lost. In this example, the mov instruction is operating on 32-bit data. However, it can also work on 16- and 8-bit data, as shown below:

```
mov     BX,CX
mov     AL,CL
```

Register-addressing mode is the most efficient way of specifying operands because they are within the processor and, therefore, no memory access is required.

Immediate Addressing Mode

In this addressing mode, data is specified as part of the instruction itself. As a result, even though the data is in memory, it is located in the code segment, not in the data segment. This addressing mode is typically used in instructions that require at least two data items to manipulate. In this case, this mode can only specify the source operand and immediate data is always a constant, either given directly or via the EQU directive (discussed in the next chapter). Thus, instructions typically use another addressing mode to specify the destination operand.

In the following example,

```
mov     AL,75
```

the source operand 75 is specified in the immediate addressing mode and the destination operand is specified in the register addressing mode. Such instructions are said to use mixed-mode addressing.

The remainder of the addressing modes we discuss here deal with operands that are located in the data segment. These are called the *memory addressing modes*. We discuss two memory addressing modes here: *direct* and *indirect*. The remaining memory addressing modes are discussed in Chapter 13.

Direct Addressing Mode

Operands specified in a memory-addressing mode require access to the main memory, usually to the data segment. As a result, they tend to be slower than either of the two previous addressing modes.

Recall that to locate a data item in the data segment, we need two components: the segment start address and an offset value within the segment. The start address of the segment is typically found in the DS register. Thus, various memory-addressing modes differ in the way the offset value of the data is specified. The offset value is often called the *effective address*.

In the direct addressing mode, the offset value is specified directly as part of the instruction. In an assembly language program, this value is usually indicated by the variable name of the data item. The assembler translates this name into its associated offset value during the assembly process. To facilitate this translation, assembler maintains a symbol table. As discussed before, symbol table stores the offset values of all variables in the assembly language program.

This addressing mode is the simplest of all the memory addressing modes. A restriction associated with the memory addressing modes is that these can be used to specify only one operand. The examples that follow assume the following data definition statements in the program.

```
response   DB      'Y'        ; allocates a byte, initializes to Y
table1     TIMES 20 DW 0      ; allocates 40 bytes, initializes to 0
name1      DB      'Jim Ray'  ; 7 bytes are initialized to Jim Ray
```

Here are some examples of the mov instruction:

```
mov    AL, [response]     ; copies Y into AL register
mov    [response],'N'     ; N is written into response
mov    [name1],'K'        ; write K as the first character of name1
mov    [table1],56        ; 56 is written in the first element
```

This last statement is equivalent to table1[0] = 56 in the C language.

Indirect Addressing Mode

The direct addressing mode can be used in a straightforward way but is limited to accessing simple variables. For example, it is not useful in accessing the second element of table1 as in the following C statement:

```
table1[1] = 99
```

The indirect addressing mode remedies this deficiency. In this addressing mode, the offset or effective address of the data is in one of the general registers. For this reason, this addressing mode is sometimes referred to as the register indirect addressing mode.

The indirect addressing mode is not required for variables having only a single element (e.g., response). But for variables like table1 containing several elements, the starting address of the data structure can be loaded into, say, the EBX register and then EBX acts as a pointer to an element in table1. By manipulating the contents of the EBX register, we can access different elements of table1.

The following code assigns 100 to the first element and 99 to the second element of table1. Note that EBX is incremented by 2 because each element of table1 requires two bytes.

```
mov    EBX,table1     ; copy address of table1 to EBX
mov    [EBX],100      ; table1[0] = 100
add    EBX,2          ; EBX = EBX + 2
mov    [EBX],99       ; table1[1] = 99
```

Chapter 13 discusses other memory addressing modes that can perform this task more efficiently.

The effective address can also be loaded into a register by the lea (load effective address) instruction. The syntax of this instruction is

```
lea    register,source
```

Thus,

```
lea    EBX, [table1]
```

can be used in place of the

```
mov     EBX,table1
```

instruction. The difference is that lea computes the offset values at run time, whereas the mov version resolves the offset value at assembly time. For this reason, we will try to use the latter whenever possible. However, lea offers more flexibility as to the types of source operands. For example, we can write

```
lea     EBX, [array+ESI]
```

to load EBX with the address of an element of array whose index is in the ESI register. However, we cannot write

```
mov     EBX, [array+ESI]     ; illegal
```

as the contents of ESI are known at assembly time.

Overview of Assembly Language Instructions

This section briefly reviews some of the remaining assembly language instructions. The discussion presented here would provide sufficient exposure to the assembly language so that you can write meaningful assembly language programs.

The MOV Instruction

We have already introduced the mov instruction, which requires two operands and has the syntax

```
mov     destination,source
```

The data is copied from source to destination and the source operand remains unchanged. Both operands should be of the same size. The mov instruction can take one of the following five forms:

```
mov     register,register
mov     register,immediate
mov     memory,immediate
mov     register,memory
mov     memory,register
```

There is no move instruction to transfer data from memory to memory. However, as we will see in Chapter 17, memory-to-memory data transfer is possible using the string instructions.
Here are some example mov statements:

```
mov     AL, [response]
mov     DX, [table1]
mov     [response],'N'
mov     [name1+4],'K'
```

Ambiguous Moves   Moving immediate value into memory sometimes causes ambiguity as to the type of operand. For example, in the statements

```
mov     EBX,[table1]
mov     ESI,[name1]
mov     [EBX],100
mov     [ESI],100
```

it is not clear, for example, whether a word (2 bytes) or a byte equivalent of 100 is to be written in the memory. We can clarify this ambiguity by using a type specifier. For example, we can use WORD type specifier to identify a word operation and BYTE for a byte operation. Using the type specifiers, we can write

```
mov     WORD [EBX],100
mov     BYTE [ESI],100
```

We can also write these statements as

```
mov     [EBX],WORD 100
mov     [ESI],BYTE 100
```

Some of the type specifiers available are given below:

Type specifier	Bytes addressed
BYTE	1
WORD	2
DWORD	4
QWORD	8
TBYTE	10

Simple Arithmetic Instructions

The instructin set provides several instructions to perform simple arithmetic operations. In this section, we describe a few instructions to perform addition and subtraction. We defer a full discussion until Chapter 14.

The INC and DEC Instructions   These instructions can be used to either increment or decrement the operands by one. The inc (INCrement) instruction adds one to its operand and the dec (DECrement) instruction subtracts one from its operand. Both instructions require a single operand. The operand can be either in a register or in memory. It does not make sense to use an immediate operand such as inc 55 or dec 109.

The general format of these instructions is

```
inc     destination
dec     destination
```

where destination may be an 8-, 16- or 32-bit operand.

```
inc     EBX          ; increment 32-bit register
dec     DL           ; decrement 8-bit register
```

Let us assume that EBX and DL have 1057H and 5AH, respectively. After executing the above two instructions, EBX and DL would have 1058H and 59H, respectively. If the initial values of EBX and DL are FFFFH and 00H, after executing the two statements the contents of EBX and DL are changed to 0000H and FFH, respectively.

Now consider the following program:

```
.DATA
count    DW    0
value    DB    25

.CODE
    inc    [count]        ;unambiguous
    dec    [value]        ;unambiguous
    move   EBX,count
    inc    [EBX]          ;ambiguous
    mov    ESI,value
    dec    [ESI]          ;ambiguous
```

In the above example,

```
    inc    [count]
    dec    [value]
```

are unambiguous because the assembler knows from the definition of count and value that they are WORD and BYTE operands. However,

```
    inc    [EBX]
    dec    [ESI]
```

are ambiguous because EBX and ESI merely point to an object in memory but the actual object type (whether a WORD, BYTE, etc.) is not clear. We have to use a type specifier to clarify, as shown below:

```
    inc    WORD [EBX]
    dec    BYTE [ESI]
```

The ADD Instruction   The add instruction can be used to add two 8-, 16- or 32-bit operands. The syntax is

```
    add    destination,source
```

As with the mov instruction, add can also take the five basic forms depending on how the two operands are specified. The semantics of the add instruction are

```
    destination = destination + source
```

Some examples of add instruction are givn in Table 9.1. In general,

```
    inc    EAX
```

is preferred to

```
    add    EAX,1
```

as the inc version improves readability and requires less memory space to store the instruction. However, both instructions execute at the same speed.

Table 9.1 Some examples of the add instruction

| Instruction | Before add | | After add |
	source	destination	destination
add AX,DX	DX = AB62H	AX = 1052H	AX = BBB4H
add BL,CH	BL = 76H	CH = 27H	BL = 9DH
add value,10H	—	value = F0H	value = 00H
add DX,count	count = 3746H	DX = C8B9H	DX = FFFFH

Table 9.2 Some examples of the sub instruction

| instruction | Before sub | | After sub |
	source	destination	destination
sub AX,DX	DX = AB62H	AX = 1052H	AX = 64F0H
sub BL,CH	CH = 27H	BL = 76H	BL = 4FH
sub value,10H	—	value = F0H	value = E0H
sub DX,count	count = 3746H	DX = C8B9H	DX = 9173H

The SUB and CMP Instructions   The sub (SUBtract) instruction can be used to subtract two 8-, 16- or 32-bit numbers. The syntax is

```
sub     destination,source
```

The source operand is subtracted from the destination operand and the result is placed in the destination.

```
destination = destination — source
```

Table 9.2 gives examples of the sub instruction.

The cmp (CoMPare) instruction is used to compare two operands (equal, not equal, and so on). The cmp instruction performs the same operation as the sub except that the result of subtraction is not saved. Thus, cmp does not disturb the source and destination operands. The cmp instruction is typically used in conjunction with a conditional jump instruction for decision making. This is the topic of the next section.

Conditional Execution

The instruction set has several branching and looping instructions to construct programs that require conditional execution. In this section, we discuss a subset of these instructions. A detailed discussion is in Chapter 15.

Unconditional Jump The unconditional jump instruction jmp, as its name implies, tells the processor that the next instruction to be executed is located at the label that is given as part of the instruction. This jump instruction has the form

```
jmp     label
```

where label identifies the next instruction to be executed. The following example

```
        mov     EAX,1
inc_again:
        inc     EAX
        jmp     inc_again
        mov     EBX,EAX
        . . .
```

results in an infinite loop incrementing EAX repeatedly. The instruction

```
mov     EBX,EAX
```

and all the instructions following it are never executed!

From this example, the jmp instruction appears to be useless. Later, we show some examples that illustrate the use of this instruction.

Conditional Jump In conditional jump instructions, program execution is transferred to the target instruction only when the specified condition is satisfied. The general format is

```
j<cond>    label
```

where <cond> identifies the condition under which the target instruction at label should be executed. Usually, the condition being tested is the result of the last arithmetic or logic operation. For example, the following code

```
read_char:
        mov     DL,0
        . . .
        (code for reading a character into AL)
        . . .
        cmp     AL,0DH        ;compare the character to CR
        je      CR_received   ;if equal, jump to CR_received
        inc     CL            ;otherwise, increment CL and
        jmp     read_char     ;go back to read another
                              ;character from keyboard
CR_received:
        mov     DL,AL
        . . .
```

reads characters from the keyboard until the carriage return (CR) key is pressed. The character count is maintained in the CL register. The two instructions

```
cmp     AL,0DH        ;0DH is ASCII for carriage return
je      CR_received   ;je stands for jump on equal
```

perform the required conditional execution. How does the processor remember the result of the previous cmp operation when it is executing the je instruction? One of the purposes of the flags register is to provide such short-term memory between instructions. Let us look at the actions taken by the processor in executing these two instructions.

Remember that the cmp instruction subtracts 0DH from the contents of the AL register. While the result is not saved anywhere, the operation sets the zero flag (ZF = 1) if the two operands are the same. If not, ZF = 0. The zero flag retains this value until another instruction that affects ZF is executed. Note that not all instructions affect all the flags. In particular, the mov instruction does not affect any of the flags.

Thus, at the time of the je instruction execution, the processor checks ZF and program execution jumps to the labeled instruction if and only if ZF = 1. To cause the jump, the processor loads the EIP register with the target instruction address. Recall that the EIP register always points to the next instruction to be executed. Therefore, when the input character is CR, instead of fetching the instruction

```
inc     CL
```

it will fetch the

```
mov     DL,AL
```

instruction. Here are some of the conditions tested by the conditional jump instructions:

je	jump if equal
jg	jump if greater
jl	jump if less
jge	jump if greater or equal
jle	jump if less than or equal
jne	jump if not equal

Conditional jumps can also test the values of flags. Some examples are

jz	jump if zero (i.e., if ZF = 1)
jnz	jump if not zero (i.e., if ZF = 0)
jc	jump if carry (i.e., if CF = 1)
jnc	jump if not carry (i.e., if CF = 0)

Example 9.1 *Conditional jump examples.*
Consider the following code.

```
go_back:
        inc     AL
        . . .

        . . .
        cmp     AL,BL
        statement_1
        mov     BL,77H
```

Table 9.3 shows the actions taken depending on statement_1.   □

Table 9.3 Some conditional jump examples

statement_1	AL	BL	Action taken
je go_back	56H	56H	Program control is transferred to inc AL
jg go_back	56H	55H	Program control is transferred to inc AL
jg go_back jl go_back	56H	56H	No jump; executes mov BL,77H
jle go_back jge go_back	56H	56H	Program control is transferred to inc AL
jne go_back jg go_back jge go_back	27H	26H	Program control is transferred to inc AL

These conditional jump instructions assume that the operands compared were treated as signed numbers. There is another set of conditional jump instructions for operands that are unsigned numbers. But until these instructions are discussed in Chapter 15, these six conditional jump instructions are sufficient for writing simple assembly language programs.

When you use these conditional jump instructions, your assembler sometimes complains that the destination of the jump is "out of range". If you find yourself in this situation, you can use the trick described on page 326.

Iteration Instruction

Iteration can be implemented with jump instructions. For example, the following code can be used to execute <loop body> 50 times.

```
        mov     CL,50
repeat1:
        <loop body>
        dec     CL
        jnz     repeat1  ;jumps back to repeat1 if CL is not 0
        . . .
        . . .
```

The instruction set, however, includes a group of loop instructions to support iteration. Here we describe the basic loop instruction. The syntax of this instruction is

```
    loop    target
```

where target is a label that identifies the target instruction as in the jump instructions.

This instruction assumes that the ECX register contains the loop count. As part of executing the loop instruction, it decrements the ECX register and jumps to the target instruction if ECX ≠ 0. Using this instruction, we can write the previous example as

```
        mov     ECX,50
repeat1:
        <loop body>
        loop    repeat1
                . . .
                . . .
```

Logical Instructions

The instruction set provides several logical instructions including and, or, xor and not. The syntax of these instructions is

```
and     destination,source
or      destination,source
xor     destination,source
not     destination
```

The first three are binary operators and perform bitwise and, or and xor logical operations, respectively. The not is a unary operator that performs bitwise complement operation. Truth tables for the logical operations and, or and xor are shown in Table 9.4. Some examples that explain the operation of these logical instructions are shown in Table 9.5. In this table, all numbers are expressed in binary.

Logical instructions set some of the flags and therefore can be used in conditional jump instructions to implement high-level language decision structures in the assembly language. Until we fully discuss the flags in Chapter 14, the following usage should be sufficient to write and understand the assembly language programs.

In the following example, we test the least significant bit of the data in the AL register, and the program control is transferred to the appropriate code depending on the value of this bit.

```
              . . .
        and     AL,01H
        je      bit_is_zero
        <code to be executed
         when the bit is one>
        jmp     skip1
bit_is_zero:
        <code to be executed
         when the bit is zero>
skip1:
        <rest of the code>
```

To understand how the jump is effective in this example, let us assume that AL = 10101110B. The instruction

```
        and     AL,01H
```

would make the result 00H and is stored in the AL register. At the same time, the logical operation sets the zero flag (i.e., ZF = 1) because the result is zero. Recall that je tests the ZF and jumps to the target location if ZF = 1. In this example, it is more appropriate to use jz (jump if zero). Thus,

```
        jz      bit_is_zero
```

can replace the

Table 9.4 Truth tables for the logical operations

and operation

Input bits		Output bit
source b_i	destination b_i	destination b_i
0	0	0
0	1	0
1	0	0
1	1	1

or operation

Input bits		Output bit
source b_i	destination b_i	destination b_i
0	0	0
0	1	1
1	0	1
1	1	1

xor operation

Input bits		Output bit
source b_i	destination b_i	destination b_i
0	0	0
0	1	1
1	0	1
1	1	0

```
je    bit_is_zero
```

instruction. In fact, the conditional jump je is an alias for jz.

A problem with using the and instruction for testing, as used in the previous example, is that it modifies the destination operand. For instance, in the last example,

```
and    AL,01H
```

changes the contents of AL to either 0 or 1 depending on whether the least significant bit is 0 or 1, respectively. To avoid this problem, a test instruction is provided. The syntax is

Table 9.5 Some logical instruction examples

		and AL,BL	or AL,BL	xor AL,BL	not AL
AL	BL	AL	AL	AL	AL
10101110	11110000	10100000	11111110	01011110	01010001
01100011	10011100	00000000	11111111	11111111	10011100
11000110	00000011	00000010	11000111	11000101	00111001
11110000	00001111	00000000	11111111	11111111	00001111

```
test      destination,source
```

The test instruction performs logical bitwise **and** operation like the and instruction except that the source and destination operands are not modified. However, test sets the flags just like the and instruction. Therefore, we can use

```
test    AL,01H
```

instead of

```
and     AL,01H
```

in the last example.

Our First Program

This is a simple program that adds up to 10 integers and outputs the sum. The program shown below follows the assembly language template given in Chapter 7 (see page 155). The program reads up to 10 integers from the user using GetLInt on line 20. Each input integer is read as a long integer into the EDX register. The maximum number of input values is enforced by the loop instruction on line 28. The loop iteration count is initialized to 10 in ECX on line 16. The user can terminate the input earlier by entering a zero. Each input value is compared with zero (line 21) and if it is equal to zero, the conditional branch instruction (je) on line 22 terminates the read loop. When the read loop terminates, the sum in EAX is output using PutLInt on line 32.

Program 9.1 An example program to find the sum of a set of integers

```
1:  ;Adds a set of integers                     ADDITION.ASM
2:  ;
3:  ;         Objective: To find the sum of a set of integers.
4:  ;             Input: Requests integers from the user.
5:  ;            Output: Outputs the sum of the input numbers.
6:  %include  "io.mac"
7:
```

```
 8:     .DATA
 9:     input_prompt   db   "Please enter at most 10 numbers: ",0
10:     end_msg        db   "No more numbers? Enter 0 to end: ",0
11:     sum_msg        db   "The sum is: ",0
12:
13:     .CODE
14:         .STARTUP
15:         PutStr   input_prompt   ; prompt for input numbers
16:         mov      ECX,10         ; loop count = 10
17:         sub      EAX,EAX        ; sum = 0
18:
19:     read_loop:
20:         GetLInt  EDX            ; read the input number
21:         cmp      EDX,0          ; is it zero?
22:         je       reading_done   ; if yes, stop reading input
23:         add      EAX,EDX
24:         cmp      ECX,1          ; if 10 numbers are input
25:         je       skip_msg       ; skip displaying end_msg
26:         PutStr   end_msg
27:     skip_msg:
28:         loop     read_loop
29:
30:     reading_done:
31:         PutStr   sum_msg
32:         PutLInt  EAX            ; write the sum
33:         nwln
34:         .EXIT
```

Note that after reading each input value, the program displays "No more numbers? Enter 0 to end:" message to inform the user of the other termination condition. However, if 10 numbers have been read, this message is skipped. This skipping is implemented by the code on lines 24 and 25.

Another point to note is that we used the loop count directly to initialize the ECX register on line 16. However, from the program maintenance point of view, it is better if we define this as a constant using the EQU directive, which is discussed in the next chapter.

Illustrative Examples

This section presents several examples that illustrate the use of the assembly language instructions discussed in this chapter. In order to follow these examples, you should be able to understand the difference between binary values and character representations. For example, when using a byte to store a number, number 5 is stored as

```
00000101B
```

On the other hand, character 5 is stored as

```
00110101B
```

Character manipulation is easier if you understand this difference and the key characteristics of ASCII, as discussed in Appendix A.

Example 9.2 *Conversion of lowercase letters to uppercase.*

This program demonstrates how indirect addressing can be used to access elements of an array. It also illustrates how character manipulation can be used to convert lowercase letters to uppercase. The program receives a character string from the user and converts all lowercase letters to uppercase and displays the string. Characters other than the lowercase letters are not changed in any way. The pseudocode of Program 9.2 is as follows:

```
main()
     display prompt message
     read input string
     index := 0
     char := string[index]
     while (char ≠ NULL)
          if ((char ≥ 'a') AND (char ≤ 'z'))
          then
               char := char + 'A' − 'a'
          end if
          display char
          index := index + 1
          char := string[index]
     end while
end main
```

You can see from Program 9.2 that the compound **if** condition requires two cmp instructions (lines 27 and 29). Also the program uses the EBX register in indirect addressing mode and always holds the pointer value of the character to be processed. In Chapter 13 we will see a better way of accessing the elements of an array. The end of the string is detected by

```
cmp     AL,0       ; check if AL is NULL
je      done
```

and is used to terminate the **while** loop (lines 25 and 26).

Program 9.2 Conversion to uppercase by character manipulation

```
 1:  ;Uppercase conversion of characters                    TOUPPER.ASM
 2:  ;
 3:  ;          Objective: To convert lowercase letters to
 4:  ;                     corresponding uppercase letters.
 5:  ;              Input: Requests a char. string from the user.
 6:  ;             Output: Prints the input string in uppercase.
 7:  %include "io.mac"
 8:
 9:  .DATA
10:  name_prompt      db    "Please type your name: ",0
11:  out_msg          db    "Your name in capitals is: ",0
12:
13:  .UDATA
14:  in_name          resb  31
```

```
15:
16:     .CODE
17:         .STARTUP
18:         PutStr    name_prompt      ; request character string
19:         GetStr    in_name,31       ; read input character string
20:
21:         PutStr    out_msg
22:         mov       EBX,in_name      ; EBX = pointer to in_name
23: process_char:
24:         mov       AL,[EBX]         ; move the char. to AL
25:         cmp       AL,0             ; if it is the NULL character
26:         je        done             ; conversion done
27:         cmp       AL,'a'           ; if (char < 'a')
28:         jl        not_lower_case   ; not a lowercase letter
29:         cmp       AL,'z'           ; if (char > 'z')
30:         jg        not_lower_case   ; not a lowercase letter
31: lower_case:
32:         add       AL,'A'-'a'       ; convert to uppercase
33: not_lower_case:
34:         PutCh     AL               ; write the character
35:         inc       EBX              ; EBX points to the next char.
36:         jmp       process_char     ; go back to process next char.
37: done:
38:         nwln
39:     .EXIT
```

Example 9.3 *Sum of the individual digits of a number.*
This last example shows how decimal digits can be converted from their character representations to the equivalent binary. The program receives a number (maximum 10 digits) and displays the sum of the individual digits of the input number. For example, if the input number is 45213, the program displays 15. Since ASCII assigns a special set of contiguous values to the digit characters, it is straightforward to get their numerical value (as discussed in Appendix A). All we have to do is to mask off the upper half of the byte, as is done in Program 9.3 (line 28) by

```
and    AL,0FH
```

Alternatively, we can also subtract the character code for 0

```
sub    AL,'0'
```

instead of masking the upper half byte. For the sake of brevity, we leave writing the pseudocode of Program 9.3 as an exercise.

Program 9.3 Sum of individual digits of a number

```
1:  ;Add individual digits of a number              ADDIGITS.ASM
2:  ;
3:  ;         Objective: To find the sum of individual digits of
```

```
 4:  ;                    a given number. Shows character to binary
 5:  ;                    conversion of digits.
 6:  ;             Input: Requests a number from the user.
 7:  ;             Output: Prints the sum of the individual digits.
 8:  %include  "io.mac"
 9:
10:  .DATA
11:  number_prompt   db  "Please type a number (<11 digits): ",0
12:  out_msg         db  "The sum of individual digits is: ",0
13:
14:  .UDATA
15:  number          resb  11
16:
17:  .CODE
18:       .STARTUP
19:       PutStr  number_prompt ; request an input number
20:       GetStr  number,11     ; read input number as a string
21:
22:       mov     EBX,number    ; EBX = address of number
23:       sub     DX,DX         ; DX = 0 -- DL keeps the sum
24:  repeat_add:
25:       mov     AL,[EBX]      ; move the digit to AL
26:       cmp     AL,0          ; if it is the NULL character
27:       je      done          ;   sum is done
28:       and     AL,0FH        ; mask off the upper 4 bits
29:       add     DL,AL         ; add the digit to sum
30:       inc     EBX           ; update EBX to point to next digit
31:       jmp     repeat_add
32:  done:
33:       PutStr  out_msg
34:       PutInt  DX            ; write sum
35:       nwln
36:       .EXIT
```

Summary

The structure of the stand-alone assembly language program is described in Chapter 7. In this chapter, we presented basics of the assembly language programming. We discussed two types of assembly language statements: (a) Executable statements that instruct the CPU as to what to do; (b) Assembler directives that facilitate the assembly process.

We have discussed the assembler directives to reserve space for variables. For initialized variables, we can use a define directive (DB, DW, and so on). To reserve space for uninitialized data, we use RESB, RESW, and so on. The TIMES directive can be used for multiple initializations.

We introduced some simple addressing modes to specify the location of the operands. The register addressing mode specifies the operands located in a processor register. The immediate addressing mode is used to specify constants. The remaining addressing modes specify the operands located in the memory. We discussed two memory addressing modes—direct and indirect. The remaining addressing modes are discussed in Chapter 13.

The instruction set consists of several groups of instructions—arithmetic, logical, shift, and so on. We presented a few instructions in each group so that we can write meaningful assembly language programs. We will introduce some more instructions in the next chapter.

10

More on Assembly Language

This chapter continues the assembly language overview from the last chapter. After the introduction, we discuss the data exchange and translate instructions. Then we describe the assembler directives to define constants—numeric as well as string constants. Next we discuss macros supported by NASM. Macros provide a sophisticated text substitution mechanism and are useful in program maintenance. NASM allows definition of macros with parameters. We use several examples to illustrate the application of the instructions discussed here. The performance advantage of the translation instruction is demonstrated in the last section. The chapter concludes with a summary.

Introduction

As mentioned in the last chapter, three types of statements are used in assembly language programs: instructions, assembler directives, and macros. We have discussed several instructions and directives in the last chapter. For example, we used assembler directives to allocate storage space for variables. This chapter continues our discussion from the last chapter and covers a few more processor instructions, some assembler directives to define constants, and macros.

We present some more instructions of the IA-32 instruction set. We describe two instructions for data exchange and translation: xchg and xlat. The xchg instruction exchanges two data values. These values can be 8, 16, or 32 bit values. This instruction is particularly useful in sort applications. The xlat instruction translates a byte value. We also discuss the shift and rotate family of instructions. We illustrate the use of these instructions by means of several examples.

Next we discuss the NASM directives to define constants. If you have used the C language, you already know the utility of %define in program maintenance. We describe three NASM directives: EQU, %assign and %define. The EQU can be used to define numeric constants. This directive does not allow redefinition. For example, the following assembler directive defines a constant CR. The ASCII carriage-return value is assigned to it by the EQU directive.

```
CR      EQU     0DH        ;carriage-return character
```

As mentioned, we cannot redefine CR to a different value later in the program. The %assign can also be used to define numeric constants. However, it allows redefinition. The %define directive can be used to define both string and numeric constants.

The last topic introduces the macros supported by the NASM assembler. Macros are used as a shorthand notation for a group of statements. Macros permit the assembly language programmer to name a group of statements and refer to the group by the macro name. During the assembly process, each macro is replaced by the group of statements that it represents and assembled in place. This process is referred to as *macro expansion*. We use macros to provide the basic input and output capabilities to our stand-alone assembly language programs.

Data Exchange and Translate Instructions

This section describes the data exchange (xchg) and translation (xlat) instructions. Other data transfer instructions such as movsx and movzx are discussed in Chapter 14.

The XCHG Instruction

The xchg instruction exchanges 8-, 16-, or 32-bit source and destination operands. The syntax is similar to that of the mov instruction. Some examples are

```
xchg     EAX,EDX
xchg     [response],CL
xchg     [total],DX
```

As in the mov instruction, both operands cannot be located in memory. Note that this restriction is applicable to most instructions. Thus,

```
xchg     [response],[name1]     ; illegal
```

is invalid. The xchg instruction is convenient because we do not need a third register to hold a temporary value in order to swap two values. For example, we need three mov instructions

```
mov     ECX,EAX
mov     EAX,EDX
mov     EDX,ECX
```

to perform xchg EAX,EDX. This instruction is especially useful in sorting applications. It is also useful to swap the two bytes of 16-bit data to perform conversions between little-endian and big-endian forms, as in the following example:

```
xchg     AL,AH
```

Another instruction, bswap, can be used to perform such conversions on 32-bit data. The format is

```
bswap   register
```

This instruction works only on the data located in a 32-bit register.

The XLAT Instruction

The xlat (translate) instruction can be used to perform character translation. The format of this instruction is shown below:

```
xlatb
```

To use this instruction, the EBX register must to be loaded with the starting address of the translation table and AL must contain an index value into the table. The xlat instruction adds contents of AL to EBX and reads the byte at the resulting address. This byte replaces the index value in the AL register. Since the 8-bit AL register provides the index into the translation table, the number of entries in the table is limited to 256. An application of xlat is given in Example 10.6.

Shift and Rotate Instructions

This section describes some of the shift and rotate instructions supported by the instruction set. The remaining instructions in this family are discussed in Chapter 16.

Shift Instructions

The instruction set provides several shift instructions. We discuss the following two instructions here: shl (SHift Left) and shr (SHift Right). The shl instruction can be used to left shift a destination operand. Each shift to the left by one bit position causes the leftmost bit to move to the carry flag (CF). The vacated rightmost bit is filled with a zero. The bit that was in CF is lost as a result of this operation.

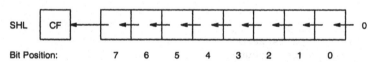

The shr instruction works similarly but shifts bits to the right as shown below:

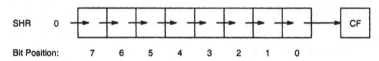

The general formats of these instructions are

```
shl   destination,count      shr   destination,count
shl   destination,CL         shr   destination,CL
```

The destination can be an 8-, 16- or 32-bit operand stored either in a register or in memory. The second operand specifies the number of bit positions to be shifted. The first format specifies the shift count directly. The shift count can range from 0 to 31. The second format can be used to indirectly specify the shift count, which is assumed to be in the CL register. The CL register contents are not changed by either the shl or shr instructions. In general, the first format is faster!

Even though the shift count can be between 0 and 31, it does not make sense to use count values of zero or greater than 7 (for an 8-bit operand), or 15 (for a 16-bit operand), or 31 (for a

Table 10.1 Some examples of the shift instructions

Instruction	Before shift	After shift	
	AL or AX	AL or AX	CF
shl AL,1	1010 1110	0101 1100	1
shr AL,1	1010 1110	0101 0111	0
mov CL,3 shl AL,CL	0110 1101	0110 1000	1
mov CL,5 shr AX,CL	1011 1101 0101 1001	0000 0101 1110 1010	1

32-bit operand). As indicated, shift count cannot be greater than 31. If a greater value is specified, only the least significant 5 bits of the number are taken as the shift count. Table 10.1 shows some examples of the shl and shr instructions.

The following code shows another way of testing the least significant bit of the data in the AL register.

```
        . . .
        . . .
     shr    AL,1
     jnc    bit_is_zero
     <code to be executed
      when the bit is one>
     jmp    skip1
bit_is_zero:
        <code to be executed
         when the bit is zero>
skip1:
        <rest of the code>
        . . .
        . . .
```

If the value in the AL register has a 1 in the least significant bit position, this bit will be in the carry flag after the shr instruction has been executed. Then we can use a conditional jump instruction that tests the carry flag. Recall that the jc (jump if carry) would cause the jump if CF = 1 and jnc (jump if no carry) causes jump only if CF = 0.

Rotate Instructions

A drawback with the shift instructions is that the bits shifted out are lost. There may be situations where we want to keep these bits. The rotate family of instructions provides this facility. These instructions can be divided into two types: rotate without involving the carry flag, or through the carry flag. We will briefly discuss these two types of instructions next.

Table 10.2 Some examples of the rotate instructions

Instruction	Before execution	After execution	
	AL or AX	AL or AX	CF
rol AL,1	1010 1110	0101 1101	1
ror AL,1	1010 1110	0101 0111	0
mov CL,3 rol AL,CL	0110 1101	0110 1011	1
mov CL,5 ror AX,CL	1011 1101 0101 1001	1100 1101 1110 1010	1

Rotate Without Carry   There are two instructions in this group:

    rol (ROtate Left)
    ror (ROtate Right)

The format of these instructions is similar to the shift instructions and is given below:

```
rol     destination,count     ror     destination,count
rol     destination,CL        ror     destination,CL
```

The rol instruction performs left rotation with the bits falling off on the left placed on the right side, as shown below:

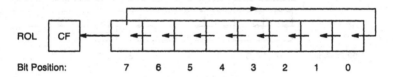

The ror instruction performs right rotation as shown below:

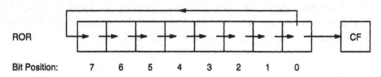

For both of these instructions, the CF will catch the last bit rotated out of the destination. The examples in Table 10.2 illustrate the rotate operation.

Rotate Through Carry   The instructions

    rcl (Rotate through Carry Left)
    rcr (Rotate through Carry Right)

Table 10.3 Some rotate through carry examples

Instruction	Before execution		After execution	
	AL or AX	CF	AL or AX	CF
rcl AL,1	1010 1110	0	0101 1100	1
rcr AL,1	1010 1110	1	1101 0111	0
mov CL,3 rcl AL,CL	0110 1101	1	0110 1101	1
mov CL,5 rcr AX,CL	1011 1101 0101 1001	0	1001 0101 1110 1010	1

include the carry flag in the rotation process. That is, the bit that is rotated out at one end goes into the carry flag and the bit that was in the carry flag is moved into the vacated bit, as shown below:

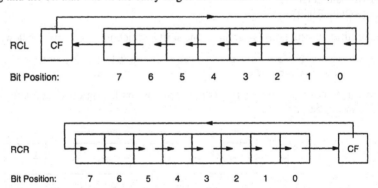

Some examples of the rcl and rcr instructions are given in Table 10.3.

The rcl and rcr instructions provide flexibility in bit rearranging. Furthermore, these are the only two instructions that take the carry flag bit as an input. This feature is useful in multiword shifts. As an example, suppose that we want to right shift the 64-bit number stored in EDX:EAX (the lower 32 bits are in EAX) by one bit position. This can be done by

```
shr    EDX,1
rcr    EAX,1
```

The shr instruction moves the least significant bit of EDX into the carry flag. The rcr instruction copies this carry flag value into the most significant bit of EAX. Chapter 16 introduces two doubleshift instructions to facilitate shifting of 64-bit numbers.

Defining Constants

NASM provides several directives to define constants. In this section, we discuss three directives—EQU, %assign and %define.

The EQU Directive

The syntax of the EQU directive is

```
name     EQU     expression
```

which assigns the result of the expression to name. For example, we can use

```
NUM_OF_STUDENTS     EQU     90
```

to assign 90 to NUM_OF_STUDENTS. It is customary to use capital letters for these names in order to distinguish them from variable names. Then, we can write

```
       .  .  .
mov    ECX,NUM_OF_STUDENTS
       .  .  .
cmp    EAX,NUM_OF_STUDENTS
       .  .  .
```

to move 90 into the ECX register and to compare EAX with 90. Defining constants this way has two advantages:

1. Such definitions increase program readability. This can be seen by comparing the statement

    ```
    mov    ECX,NUM_OF_STUDENTS
    ```

    with

    ```
    mov    ECX,90
    ```

    The first statement clearly indicates that we are moving the class size into the ECX register.

2. Multiple occurrences of a constant can be changed from a single place. For example, if the class size changes from 90 to 100, we just need to change the value in the EQU statement. If we didn't use the EQU directive, we have to scan the source code and make appropriate changes—a risky and error-prone process!

The operand of an EQU statement can be an expression that evaluates at assembly time. We can, for example, write

```
NUM_OF_ROWS     EQU     50
NUM_OF_COLS     EQU     10
ARRAY_SIZE      EQU     NUM_OF_ROWS * NUM_OF_COLS
```

to define ARRAY_SIZE to be 500.

The symbols that have been assigned a value cannot be reassigned another value in a given source module. If such redefinitions are required, you should use %assign directive, which is discussed next.

The %assign Directive

This directive can be used to define numeric constants like the EQU directive. However, %assign allows redefinition. For example, we define

```
%assign   i    j+1
```

and later in the code we can redefine it as

```
%assign   i    j+2
```

Like the EQU directive, it is evaluated once when %assign is processed.

The %assign is case sensitive. That is, i and I are treated as different. We can use %iassign for case insensitive definition.

Both EQU and %assign directives can be used to define numeric constants. The next directive removes this restriction.

The %define Directive

This directive is similar to the #define in C. It can be used to define numeric as well as string constants. For example

```
%define   X1    [EBP+4]
```

replaces X1 by [EBP+4]. Like the last directive, it allows redefinition. For example, we can redefine X1 as

```
%define   X1    [EBP+20]
```

The %define directive is case sensitive. If you want the case insensitive version, you should use the %idefine directive.

Macros

Macros provide a means by which a block of text (code, data, etc.) can be represented by a name (called the *macro name*). When the assembler encounters that name later in the program, the block of text associated with the macro name is substituted. This process is referred to as *macro expansion*. In simple terms, macros provide a sophisticated text substitution mechanism.

In NASM, macros can be defined with %macro and %endmacro directives. The macro text begins with the %macro directive and ends with the %endmacro directive. The macro definition syntax is

```
%macro    macro_name   para_count
              <macro body>
%endmacro
```

The para_count specifies the number parameters used in the macro. The macro_name is the name of the macro that, when used later in the program, causes *macro expansion*. To invoke or call a macro, use the macro_name and supply the necessary parameter values.

Example 10.1 *A parameterless macro.*

Here is our first macro example that does not require any parameters. Since using left-shift to multiply by a power of two is more efficient than using multiplication, let us write a macro to do this.

```
%macro  multEAX_by_16
        sal    EAX,4
%endmacro
```

The macro code consists of a single sal instruction, which will be substituted whenever the macro is called. Now we can invoke this macro by using the macro name multEAX_by_16, as in the following example:

```
        . . .
mov    EAX,27
multEAX_by_16
        . . .
```

When the assembler encounters the macro name multEAX_by_16, it is replaced (i.e., text substituted) by the macro body. Thus, after the macro expansion, the assembler finds the code

```
        . . .
mov    EAX,27
sal    EAX,4
        . . .
```

□

Macros with Parameters   Just as with procedures, using parameters with macros aids in writing more flexible and useful macros. The previous macro always multiplies EAX by 16. By using parameters, we can generalize this macro to operate on a byte, word, or doubleword located either in a general-purpose register or memory. The modified macro is

```
%macro   mult_by_16  1
         sal    %1,4
%endmacro
```

This macro takes one parameter, which can be any operand that is valid in the sal instruction. Within the macro body, we refer to the parameters by their number as in %1. To multiply a byte in the DL register

```
mult_by_16    DL
```

can be used. This causes the following macro expansion:

```
sal    DL,4
```

Similarly, a memory variable count, whether it is a byte, word, or doubleword, can be multiplied by 16 using

```
mult_by_16    count
```

Such a macro call will be expanded as

```
sal     count,4
```

Now, at least superficially, `mult_by_16` looks like any other assembly language instruction, except that it is defined by us. These are referred to as *macro-instructions*.

Example 10.2 *Memory-to-memory data transfer macro.*
We know that memory-to-memory data transfers are not allowed. We have to use an intermediate register to facilitate such a data transfer. We can write a macro to perform memory-to-memory data transfers using the basic instructions of the processor. Let us call this macro, which exchanges the values of two memory variables, `mxchg` to exchange doublewords of data in memory.

```
%macro     mxchg   2
           xchg    EAX,%1
           xchg    EAX,%2
           xchg    EAX,%1
%endmacro
```

For example, when this macro is invoked as

```
mxchg      value1,value2
```

it exchanges the memory words `value1` and `value2` while leaving EAX unaltered.   □

To end this section, we give couple of examples from the `io.mac` file.

Example 10.3 `PutInt` *macro definition from* `io.mac` *file.*
This macro is used to display a 16-bit integer, which is given as the argument to the macro, by calling `proc_PutInt` procedure. The macro definition is shown below:

```
%macro     PutInt  1
           push    AX
           mov     AX,%1
           call    proc_PutInt
           pop     AX
%endmacro
```

The `PutInt` procedure expects the integer to be in AX. Thus, in the macro body, we moves the input integer to AX before calling the procedure. Note that by using the `push` and `pop`, we preserve the AX register.   □

Example 10.4 `GetStr` *macro definition from* `io.mac` *file.*
This macro takes one or two parameters: a pointer to a buffer and an optional buffer length. The input string is read into the buffer. If the buffer length is given, it will read a string that is one less than the buffer length (one byte is reserved for the NULL character). If the buffer length is not specified, a default value of 81 is assumed. This macro calls `proc_GetStr` procedure to read the string. This procedure expects the buffer pointer in EDI and buffer length in ESI register. The macro definition is given below:

```
%macro   GetStr   1-2 81
         push     ESI
         push     EDI
         mov      EDI,%1
         mov      ESI,%2
         call     proc_GetStr
         pop      EDI
         pop      ESI
%endmacro
```

This macro is different from the previous one in that the number of parameters can be between 1 and 2. This condition is indicated by specifying the range of parameters (1-2 in our example). A further complication is that, if the second parameter is not specified, we have to use the default value (81 in our example). As shown in our example, we include this default value in the macro definition. Note that this default value is used only if the buffer length is not specified.   □

Our coverage of macros is a small sample of what is available in NASM. You should refer to the latest version of the NASM manual for complete details on macros.

Our First Program

This program reads a key from the input and displays its ASCII code in binary. It then queries the user as to whether he/she wants to quit. Depending on the response, the program either requests another character input from the user, or terminates.

To display the binary value of the ASCII code of the input key, we test each bit starting with the most significant bit (i.e., leftmost bit). The mask is initialized to 80H (=10000000B), which tests only the most significant bit of the ASCII value. If this bit is 0, the instruction on line 28

```
test    AL,mask
```

sets the zero flag (assuming that the ASCII value is in the AL register). In this case, a 0 is displayed by directing the program flow using the jz instruction (line 29). Otherwise, a 1 is displayed. The mask is then divided by 2, which is equivalent to right shifting mask by one bit position. Thus, we are ready for testing the second most significant bit. The process is repeated for each bit of the ASCII value. The pseudocode of the program is given below:

```
main()
read_char:
    display prompt message
    read input character into char
    display output message text
    mask := 80H {AH is used to store mask}
    count := 8 {CX is used to store count}
    repeat
        if ((char AND mask) = 0)
        then
            write 0
        else
            write 1
        end if
```

mask := mask/2 {can be done by shr}
count := count − 1
until (count = 0)
display query message
read response
if (response = 'Y')
then
    goto done
else
    goto read_char
end if
done:
    return
end main

The assembly language program, shown in Program 10.1, follows the pseudocode in a straight-forward way. Note that the instruction set provides an instruction to perform integer division. However, to divide a number by 2, shr is much faster than the divide instruction. More details about the division instructions are given in Chapter 14.

Program 10.1 Conversion of ASCII to binary representation

```
 1:  ;Binary equivalent of characters              BINCHAR.ASM
 2:  ;
 3:  ;          Objective: To print the binary equivalent of
 4:  ;                     ASCII character code.
 5:  ;             Input: Requests a character from the user.
 6:  ;            Output: Prints the ASCII code of the
 7:  ;                     input character in binary.
 8:  %include "io.mac"
 9:
10:  .DATA
11:  char_prompt    db   "Please input a character: ",0
12:  out_msg1       db   "The ASCII code of '",0
13:  out_msg2       db   "' in binary is ",0
14:  query_msg      db   "Do you want to quit (Y/N): ",0
15:
16:  .CODE
17:      .STARTUP
18:  read_char:
19:      PutStr  char_prompt   ; request a char. input
20:      GetCh   AL            ; read input character
21:
22:      PutStr  out_msg1
23:      PutCh   AL
24:      PutStr  out_msg2
25:      mov     AH,80H        ; mask byte = 80H
26:      mov     CX,8          ; loop count to print 8 bits
27:  print_bit:
```

```
28:          test    AL,AH        ; test does not modify AL
29:          jz      print_0      ; if tested bit is 0, print it
30:          PutCh   '1'          ; otherwise, print 1
31:          jmp     skip1
32:  print_0:
33:          PutCh   '0'          ; print 0
34:  skip1:
35:          shr     AH,1         ; right shift mask bit to test
36:                               ;  next bit of the ASCII code
37:          loop    print_bit
38:          nwln
39:          PutStr  query_msg    ; query user whether to terminate
40:          GetCh   AL           ; read response
41:          cmp     AL,'Y'       ; if response is not 'Y'
42:          jne     read_char    ; read another character
43:  done:                        ; otherwise, terminate program
44:          .EXIT
```

Illustrative Examples

This section presents two examples that perform ASCII to hex conversion. One example uses character manipulation for the conversion while the other uses the xlat instruction.

Example 10.5 *ASCII to hexadecimal conversion using character manipulation.*
The objective of this example is to show how numbers can be converted to characters by using character manipulation. In order to get the least significant hex digit, we have to mask off the upper half of the byte and then perform integer to hex digit conversion. The example shown below assumes that the input character is L, whose ASCII value is 4CH.

$$L \xrightarrow{\text{ASCII}} 01001100B \xrightarrow[\text{upper half}]{\text{mask off}} 00001100B \xrightarrow{\text{convert}} C$$

Similarly, to get the most significant hex digit we have to isolate the upper half of the byte and move these four bits to the lower half, as shown below:

$$L \xrightarrow{\text{ASCII}} 01001100B \xrightarrow[\text{lower half}]{\text{mask off}} 01000000B \xrightarrow[\text{4 positions}]{\text{shift right}} 00000100B \xrightarrow{\text{convert}} 4$$

Notice that shifting right by four bit positions is equivalent to performing integer division by 16. The pseudocode of the program shown in Program 10.2 is as follows:

```
main()
read_char:
    display prompt message
    read input character into char
    display output message text
    temp := char
```

```
      char := char AND F0H {mask off lower half}
      char := char/16 {shift right by 4 positions}
            {The last two steps can be done by shr}
      convert char to hex equivalent and display
      char := temp {restore char }
      char := char AND 0FH {mask off upper half}
      convert char to hex equivalent and display
      display query message
      read response
      if (response = 'Y')
      then
            goto done
      else
            goto read_char
      end if
done:
      return
end main
```

To convert a number between 0 and 15 to its equivalent in hex, we have to divide the process into two parts depending on whether the number is below 10 or not. The conversion using character manipulation can be summarized as follows:

```
if (number ≤ 9)
then
      write (number + '0')
then
      write (number + 'A' − 10)
end if
```

If the number is between 0 and 9, we add the ASCII value for character 0 to convert the number to its character equivalent. For instance, if the number is 5 (00000101B), it should be converted to character 5, whose ASCII value is 35H (00110101B). Therefore, we have to add 30H, which is the ASCII value of character 0. This is done in Program 10.2 by

```
add     AL,'0'
```

on line 31. If the number is between 10 and 15, we have to convert it to a hex digit between A and F. You can verify that the required translation is achieved by

```
number − 10 + ASCII value for character A
```

In Program 10.2, this is done by

```
add     AL,'A'-10
```

on line 34.

Program 10.2 Conversion to hexadecimal by character manipulation

```
 1:  ;Hex equivalent of characters                HEX1CHAR.ASM
 2:  ;
 3:  ;          Objective: To print the hex equivalent of
 4:  ;                     ASCII character code.
 5:  ;              Input: Requests a character from the user.
 6:  ;             Output: Prints the ASCII code of the
 7:  ;                     input character in hex.
 8:  %include "io.mac"
 9:
10:  .DATA
11:  char_prompt      db   "Please input a character: ",0
12:  out_msg1         db   "The ASCII code of '",0
13:  out_msg2         db   "' in hex is ",0
14:  query_msg        db   "Do you want to quit (Y/N): ",0
15:
16:  .CODE
17:        .STARTUP
18:  read_char:
19:        PutStr   char_prompt   ; request a char. input
20:        GetCh    AL            ; read input character
21:
22:        PutStr   out_msg1
23:        PutCh    AL
24:        PutStr   out_msg2
25:        mov      AH,AL         ; save input character in AH
26:        shr      AL,4          ; move upper 4 bits to lower half
27:        mov      CX,2          ; loop count - 2 hex digits to print
28:  print_digit:
29:        cmp      AL,9          ; if greater than 9
30:        jg       A_to_F        ; convert to A through F digits
31:        add      AL,'0'        ; otherwise, convert to 0 through 9
32:        jmp      skip
33:  A_to_F:
34:        add      AL,'A'-10     ; subtract 10 and add 'A'
35:                               ; to convert to A through F
36:  skip:
37:        PutCh    AL            ; write the first hex digit
38:        mov      AL,AH         ; restore input character in AL
39:        and      AL,0FH        ; mask off the upper half byte
40:        loop     print_digit
41:        nwln
42:        PutStr   query_msg     ; query user whether to terminate
43:        GetCh    AL            ; read response
44:
45:        cmp      AL,'Y'        ; if response is not 'Y'
46:        jne      read_char     ; read another character
47:  done:                        ; otherwise, terminate program
48:        .EXIT
```

Example 10.6 *ASCII to hexadecimal conversion using the xlat instruction.*

The objective of this example is to show how the use of xlat simplifies the solution of the last example. In this example, we use the xlat instruction to convert a number between 0 and 15 to its equivalent hex digit. The program is shown in Program 10.3. To use xlat we have to construct a translation table, which is done by the following statement (line 17):

```
hex_table    db    '0123456789ABCDEF'
```

We can then use the number as an index into the table. For example, 10 points to A, which is the equivalent hex digit. In order to use the xlat instruction, EBX should point to the base of the hex_table and AL should have the number. The instructin on line 29 loads the hex_table address into EBX. The rest of the program is straightforward to follow.

Program 10.3 Conversion to hexadecimal by using the xlat instruction

```
 1:  ;Hex equivalent of characters              HEX2CHAR.ASM
 2:  ;
 3:  ;           Objective: To print the hex equivalent of
 4:  ;                      ASCII character code. Demonstrates
 5:  ;                      the use of xlat instruction.
 6:  ;              Input: Requests a character from the user.
 7:  ;             Output: Prints the ASCII code of the
 8:  ;                      input character in hex.
 9:  %include "io.mac"
10:
11:  .DATA
12:  char_prompt    db  "Please input a character: ",0
13:  out_msg1       db  "The ASCII code of '",0
14:  out_msg2       db  "' in hex is ",0
15:  query_msg      db  "Do you want to quit (Y/N): ",0
16:  ; translation table: 4-bit binary to hex
17:  hex_table      db  "0123456789ABCDEF"
18:
19:  .CODE
20:       .STARTUP
21:  read_char:
22:       PutStr  char_prompt  ; request a char. input
23:       GetCh   AL           ; read input character
24:
25:       PutStr  out_msg1
26:       PutCh   AL
27:       PutStr  out_msg2
28:       mov     AH,AL        ; save input character in AH
29:       mov     EBX,hex_table; EBX = translation table
30:       shr     AL,4         ; move upper 4 bits to lower half
31:       xlatb                ; replace AL with hex digit
32:       PutCh   AL           ; write the first hex digit
33:       mov     AL,AH        ; restore input character to AL
34:       and     AL,0FH       ; mask off upper 4 bits
35:       xlatb
```

```
36:          PutCh   AL              ; write the second hex digit
37:          nwln
38:          PutStr  query_msg       ; query user whether to terminate
39:          GetCh   AL              ; read response
40:
41:          cmp     AL,'Y'          ; if response is not 'Y'
42:          jne     read_char       ; read another character
43:   done:                          ; otherwise, terminate program
44:          .EXIT
```

When to Use the XLAT Instruction

The xlat instruction is convenient to perform character conversions. Proper use of xlat would produce an efficient assembly language program. In this section, we demonstrate by means of two examples when xlat is beneficial from the performance point of view.

In general, xlat is not really useful if, for example, there is a straightforward method or a "formula" for the required conversion. This is true for conversions that exhibit a regular structure. An example of this type of conversion is the case conversion between uppercase and lowercase letters in ASCII. As you know, the ASCII encoding makes this conversion rather simple. Experiment 1 takes a look at this type of example.

The use of the xlat instruction, however, produces efficient code if the conversion does not have a regular structure. Conversion from EBCDIC to ASCII is one example that can benefit from using the xlat instruction. Conversion to hex is another example, as shown in Examples 10.5 and 10.6. This example is used in Experiment 2 to show the performance benefit that can be obtained from using the xlat instruction for the conversion.

Experiment 1

In this experiment, we show how using the xlat instruction for case conversion of letters deteriorates the performance. We have transformed the code of Example 9.2 to a procedure that can be called from a C main program. This program keeps track of the execution time. All interaction with the display is suppressed for these experiments. This case-conversion procedure is called several times to convert a string of lowercase letters. The string length is fixed at 1000 characters.

We used two versions of the case conversion procedure. The first version does not use the xlat instruction for case conversion. Instead, it uses the statement

```
add     AL,'A'-'a'
```

as shown in Program 9.2.

The other version uses the xlat instruction for case conversion. In order to do so, we have to set up the following conversion table in the data section:

```
upper_table     db      'ABCDEFGHIJKLMNOPQRSTUVWXYZ'
```

Furthermore, after initializing EBX to upper_table, the following code

```
sub     AL,'a'
xlatb
```

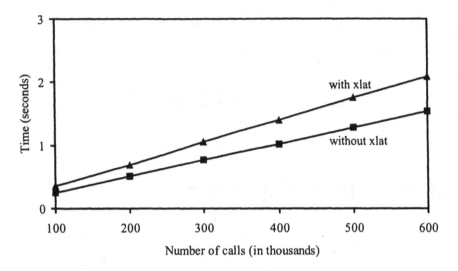

Figure 10.1 Performance of the case conversion program.

replaces the code

```
add    AL,'A'-'a'
```

You can clearly see the disadvantage of the xlat version of the code. First of all, it requires additional space to store the translation table upper_table. More important than this is the fact that the xlat version requires additional time. Note that the add and sub instructions take the same amount of time to execute. Therefore, the xlat version requires additional time to execute xlat, which generates a memory read to get the byte from upper_table located in the data segment.

The performance superiority of the first version (i.e., the version that does not use the xlat instruction) is clearly shown in Figure 10.1. These results were obtained on a 2.4-GHz Pentium 4 system. In this plot, the x-axis gives the number of times the case conversion procedure is called to convert a lowercase string of 1,000 characters. The data show that using the xlat instruction deteriorates the performance by about 35 percent! For the reasons discussed before, this is clearly a bad example to use the xlat instruction.

Experiment 2

In this experiment, we use the hex conversion examples presented in the last section to show the benefits of the xlat instruction. As shown in Example 10.5, without using the xlat, we have to test the input number to see if it falls in the range of 0–9 or 10–15. However, such testing and hence the associated overhead can be avoided by using a translation table along with xlat.

The two programs of Examples 10.5 and 10.6 have been converted to C callable procedures as in the last experiment. Each procedure receives a string and converts the characters in the input string to their hex equivalents. However, the hex code is not displayed. The input test string in this experiment consists of lowercase and uppercase letters, digits, and special symbols for a total of 100 characters.

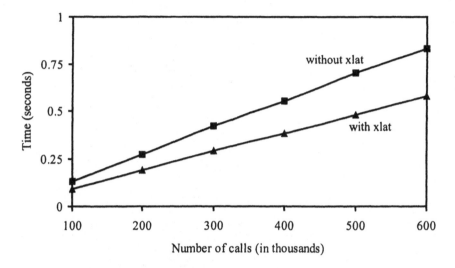

Figure 10.2 Performance of the hex conversion program.

The results, obtained on a 2.4-GHz Pentium 4 system, are shown in Figure 10.2. The data presented in this figure clearly demonstrate the benefit of using the xlat in this example. The procedure that does not use the xlat instruction is about 45% slower!

The moral of the story is that judicious use of assembly language instructions is necessary in order to reap the benefits of the assembly language.

Summary

We presented two instructions for data exchange and translation: xchg and xlat. The first instruction, which exchanges two data values, is useful in sort applications. The xlat instruction translates a byte value. We also discussed the shift and rotate family of instructions.

We presented the NASM directives to define constants—both numeric and string. We described three NASM directives: EQU, %assign and %define. The EQU directive can be used to define numeric constants. This directive does not allow redefinition. The %assign can also be used to define numeric constants. However, it allows redefinition. The %define directive can be used to define both string and numeric constants.

We introduced the macros supported by the NASM assembler. Macros permit the assembly language programmer to name a group of statements and refer to the group by the macro name. The NASM assembler supports macros with parameters to allow additional flexibility. We used several examples to illustrate how macros are defined in the assembly language programs.

We also demonstrated the performance advantage of the xlat instruction under certain conditions. The results show that judicious use of the xlat instruction provides significant performance advantages.

11

Writing Procedures

The last two chapters introduced the basics of the assembly language. Here we discuss how procedures are written in the assembly language. Procedure is an important programming construct that facilitates modular programming. In the IA-32 architecture, the stack plays an important role in procedure invocation and execution. We start this chapter by giving details on the stack, its uses, and how it is implemented. We also describe the assembly language instructions to manipulate the stack.

After this introduction to the stack, we look at the assembly language instructions for procedure invocation and return. Unlike high-level languages, there is not much support in the assembly language. For example, we cannot include the arguments in the procedure call. Thus parameter passing is more involved than in high-level languages. There are two parameter passing methods—one uses the registers and the other the stack. We discuss these two parameter passing methods in detail. The last section provides a summary of the chapter.

Introduction

A procedure is a logically self-contained unit of code designed to perform a particular task. These are sometimes referred to as *subprograms* and play an important role in modular program development. In high-level languages, there are two types of subprograms: *procedures* and *functions*. A function receives a list of arguments and performs a computation based on the arguments passed onto it and returns a single value. In this sense, these functions are very similar to the mathematical functions.

Procedures also receive a list of arguments just as the functions do. However, procedures, after performing their computation, may return zero or more results back to the calling procedure. In the C language, both these subprogram types are combined into a single function construct.

In the C function

```
int sum (int x, int y)
{
    return (x + y);
}
```

the parameters x and y are called formal parameters or simply parameters and the function body is defined based on these parameters. When this function is called (or invoked) by a statement like

```
total = sum(number1, number2);
```

the actual parameters or arguments—`number1` and `number2`—are used in the computation of the sum function.

There are two types of parameter passing mechanisms: *call-by-value* and *call-by-reference*. In the call-by-value mechanism, the called function (sum in our example) is provided only the current values of the arguments for its use. Thus, in this case, the values of these arguments are not changed in the called function; these values can only be used as in a mathematical function. In our example, the sum function is invoked by using the call-by-value mechanism, as we simply pass the values of `number1` and `number2` to the called sum function.

In the call-by-reference mechanism, the called function actually receives the addresses (i.e., pointers) of the parameters from the calling function. The function can change the contents of these parameters—and these changes will be seen by the calling function—by directly manipulating the argument storage space. For instance, the following swap function

```
void swap (int *a, int *b)
{
    int temp;
    temp = *a;
    *a = *b;
    *b = temp;
}
```

assumes that it receives the addresses of the two parameters from the calling function. Thus, we are using the call-by-reference mechanism for parameter passing. Such a function can be invoked by

```
swap (&data1, &data2);
```

Often both types of parameter passing mechanisms are used in the same function. As an example, consider finding the roots of the quadratic equation

$$ax^2 + bx + c = 0.$$

The two roots are defined as

$$\text{root1} = \frac{-b + \sqrt{b^2 - 4ac}}{2a},$$

$$\text{root2} = \frac{-b - \sqrt{b^2 - 4ac}}{2a}.$$

The roots are real if $b^2 \geq 4ac$, and imaginary otherwise.

Suppose that we want to write a function that receives a, b, and c and returns the values of the two roots (if real) and indicates whether the roots are real or imaginary (see Figure 11.1). The roots function receives parameters a, b, and c using the call-by-value mechanism, and root1 and root2 parameters are passed using the call-by-reference mechanism. A typical invocation of roots is

```
root_type = roots (a, b, c, &root1, &root2);
```

```
int roots (double a, double b, double c,
           double *root1, double *root2)
{
    int root_type = 1;
    if (4 * a * c <= b * b){  /* roots are real */
        *root1 = (-b + sqrt(b*b - 4*a*c))/(2*a);
        *root2 = (-b - sqrt(b*b - 4*a*c))/(2*a);
    }
    else    /* roots are imaginary */
        root_type = 0;
    return (root_type);
}
```

Figure 11.1 C function for the quadratic equation

In summary, procedures receive a list of arguments, which may be passed either by the call-by-value or by the call-by-reference mechanism. If more than one result is to be returned by a called procedure, the call-by-reference mechanism should be used.

In the assembly language we do not get as much help as we do in high-level languages. The instruction set provides only the basic support to invoke a procedure. However, there is no support to pass arguments in the procedure call. If we want to pass arguments to the called procedure, we have to use some shared space between the callee and caller. Typically, we use either registers or the stack for this purpose. This leads to the two basic parameter passing mechanisms: register-based or stack-based. Later we give more details on these mechanisms along with some examples.

Our goal in this chapter is to introduce assembly language procedures. We continue our discussion of procedures in the next chapter, which discusses passing a variable number of arguments, local variables, and multimodule programs.

What Is a Stack?

Conceptually, a stack is a last-in-first-out (LIFO) data structure. The operation of a stack is analogous to the stack of trays you find in cafeterias. The first tray removed from the stack of trays would be the last tray that had been placed on the stack. There are two operations associated with a stack: insertion and deletion. If we view the stack as a linear array of elements, stack insertion and deletion operations are restricted to one end of the array. Thus, the only element that is directly accessible is the element at the top-of-stack (TOS). In stack terminology, insert and delete operations are referred to as *push* and *pop* operations, respectively.

There is another related data structure, the *queue*. A queue can be considered as a linear array with insertions done at one end of the array and deletions at the other end. Thus, a queue is a first-in-first-out (FIFO) data structure.

As an example of a stack, let us assume that we are inserting numbers 1000 through 1003 into a stack in ascending order. The state of the stack can be visualized as shown in Figure 11.2. The arrow points to the top-of-stack. When the numbers are deleted from the stack, the numbers will come out in the reverse order of insertion. That is, 1003 is removed first, then 1002, and so on. After the deletion of the last number, the stack is said to be in the empty state (see Figure 11.3).

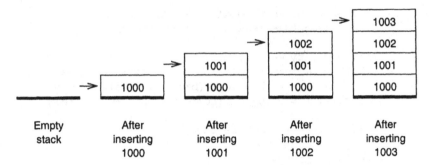

Figure 11.2 An example showing stack growth: Numbers 1000 through 1003 are inserted in ascending order. The arrow points to the top-of-stack.

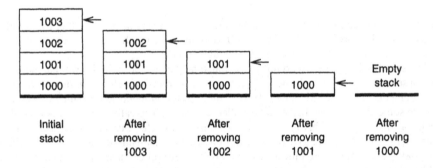

Figure 11.3 Deletion of data items from the stack: The arrow points to the top-of-stack.

In contrast, a queue maintains the order. Suppose that the numbers 1000 through 1003 are inserted into a queue as in the stack example. When removing the numbers from the queue, the first number to enter the queue would be the one to come out first. Thus, the numbers deleted from the queue would maintain their insertion order.

Implementation of the Stack

The memory space reserved in the stack segment is used to implement the stack. The registers SS and ESP are used to implement the stack. The top-of-stack, which points to the last item inserted into the stack, is indicated by SS:ESP, with the SS register pointing to the beginning of the stack segment, and the ESP register giving the offset value of the last item inserted.

The key stack implementation characteristics are as follows:

- Only words (i.e., 16-bit data) or doublewords (i.e., 32-bit data) are saved on the stack, never a single byte.
- The stack grows toward lower memory addresses. Since we graphically represent memory with addresses increasing from the bottom of a page to the top, we say that the stack grows *downward*.

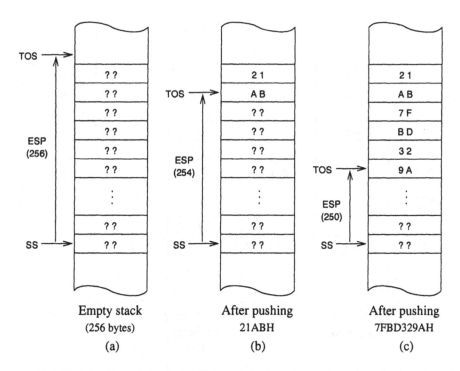

Figure 11.4 Stack implementation in the IA-32 architecture: SS:ESP points to the top-of-stack.

- Top-of-stack (TOS) always points to the last data item placed on the stack. The TOS always points to the lower byte of the last word pushed onto the stack. For example, when we push 21ABH onto the stack, the TOS points to ABH byte as shown in Figure 11.4.

Figure 11.4a shows an empty stack with 256 bytes of memory for stack operations. When the stack is initialized, TOS points to a byte just outside the reserved stack area. It is an error to read from an empty stack as this causes a *stack underflow*.

When a word is pushed onto the stack, ESP is first decremented by two, and then the word is stored at SS:ESP. Since the IA-32 processors use the little-endian byte order, the higher-order byte is stored in the higher memory address. For instance, when we push 21ABH, the stack expands by two bytes, and ESP is decremented by two to point to the last data item, as shown in Figure 11.4b. The stack shown in Figure 11.4c results when we expand the stack further by four more bytes by pushing the doubleword 7FBD329AH onto the stack.

The stack full condition is indicated by the zero offset value (i.e., ESP = 0). If we try to insert a data item into a full stack, *stack overflow* occurs. Both stack underflow and overflow are programming errors and should be handled with care.

Retrieving a 32-bit data item from the stack causes the offset value to increase by four to point to the next data item on the stack. For example, if we retrieve a doubleword from the stack shown in Figure 11.5a, we get 7FBD329AH from the stack and ESP is updated, as shown in Figure 11.5b. Notice that the four memory locations retain their values. However, since TOS is updated, these four locations will be used to store the next data value pushed onto the stack, as shown in Figure 11.5c.

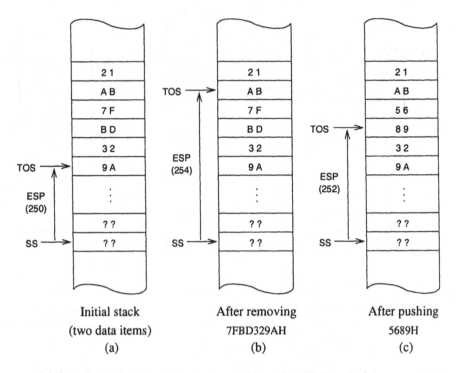

Initial stack   After removing   After pushing

(two data items)   7FBD329AH   5689H

(a)   (b)   (c)

Figure 11.5 An example showing stack insert and delete operations.

Stack Operations

Basic Instructions

The stack data structure allows two basic operations: insertion of a data item into the stack (called the *push* operation) and deletion of a data item from the stack (called the *pop* operation). These two operations are allowed on word or doubleword data items. The syntax is

```
push    source
pop     destination
```

The operand of these two instructions can be a 16- or 32-bit general-purpose register, segment register, or a word or doubleword in memory. In addition, source for the push instruction can be an immediate operand of size 8, 16, or 32 bits. Table 11.1 summarizes the two stack operations.

On an empty stack shown in Figure 11.4a the statements

```
push    21ABH
push    7FBD329AH
```

would result in the stack shown in Figure 11.5a. Executing the statement

```
pop     EBX
```

on this stack would result in the stack shown in Figure 11.5b with the register EBX receiving 7FBD329AH.

Table 11.1 Stack operations on 16- and 32-bit data

push source16	ESP = ESP − 2 SS:ESP = source16	ESP is first decremented by 2 to modify TOS. Then the 16-bit data from source16 is copied onto the stack at the new TOS. The stack expands by 2 bytes.
push source32	ESP = ESP − 4 SS:ESP = source32	ESP is first decremented by 4 to modify TOS. Then the 32-bit data from source32 is copied onto the stack at the new TOS. The stack expands by 4 bytes.
pop dest16	dest16 = SS:ESP ESP = ESP + 2	The data item located at TOS is copied to dest16. Then ESP is incremented by 2 to update TOS. The stack shrinks by 2 bytes.
pop dest32	dest32 = SS:ESP ESP = ESP + 4	The data item located at TOS is copied to dest32. Then ESP is incremented by 4 to update TOS. The stack shrinks by 4 bytes.

Additional Instructions

The instruction set supports two special instructions for stack manipulation. These instructions can be used to save or restore the flags and general-purpose registers.

Stack Operations on Flags The push and pop operations cannot be used to save or restore the flags register. For this, two special versions of these instructions are provided:

```
pushfd    (push 32-bit flags)
popfd     (pop 32-bit flags)
```

These instructions do not need any operands. For operating on the 16-bit flags register (FLAGS), we can use pushfw and popfw instructions. If we use pushf the default operand size selects either pushfd or pushfw. In our programs, since our default is 32-bit operands, pushf is used as an alias for pushfd. However, we use pushfd to make the operand size explicit. Similarly, popf can be used as an alias for either popfd or popfw.

Stack Operations on All General-Purpose Registers The instruction set also has special pusha and popa instructions to save and restore the eight general-purpose registers. The pushad saves the 32-bit general-purpose registers EAX, ECX, EDX, EBX, ESP, EBP, ESI, and EDI. These registers are pushed in the order specified. The last register pushed is the EDI register. The popad restores these registers except that it will not copy the ESP value (i.e., the ESP value is not loaded into the ESP register as part of the popad instruction). The corresponding instructions for the 16-bit registers are pushaw and popaw. These instructions are useful in procedure calls, as we will show later. Like the pushf and popf instructions, we can use pusha and popa as aliases.

Uses of the Stack

The stack is used for three main purposes: as a scratchpad to temporarily store data, for transfer of program control, and for passing parameters during a procedure call.

Temporary Storage of Data

The stack can be used as a scratchpad to store data on a temporary basis. For example, consider exchanging the contents of two 32-bit variables that are in the memory: `value1` and `value2`. We cannot use

```
xchg    value1,value2        ; illegal
```

because both operands of `xchg` are in the memory. The code

```
mov     EAX,value1
mov     EBX,value2
mov     value1,EBX
mov     value2,EAX
```

works, but it uses two 32-bit registers. This code requires four memory operations. However, due to the limited number of general-purpose registers, finding spare registers that can be used for temporary storage is nearly impossible in almost all programs.

What if we need to preserve the contents of the EAX and EBX registers? In this case, we need to save these registers before using them and restore them later as shown below:

```
        . . .
;save EAX and EBX registers on the stack
    push    EAX
    push    EBX
    ;EAX and EBX registers can now be used
    mov     EAX,value1
    mov     EBX,value2
    mov     value1,EBX
    mov     value2,EAX
;restore EAX and EBX registers from the stack
    pop     EBX
    pop     EAX
        . . .
```

This code requires eight memory accesses. Because the stack is a LIFO data structure, the sequence of `pop` instructions is a mirror image of the `push` instruction sequence.

An elegant way of exchanging the two values is

```
push    value1
push    value2
pop     value1
pop     value2
```

Notice that the above code does not use any general-purpose registers and requires eight memory operations as in the other example. Another point to note is that `push` and `pop` instructions allow movement of data from memory to memory (i.e., between data and stack segments). This is a special case because mov instructions do not allow memory-to-memory data transfer. Stack operations are an exception. String instructions, discussed in Chapter 17, also allow memory-to-memory data transfer.

Stack is frequently used as a scratchpad to save and restore registers. The necessity often arises when we need to free up a set of registers so they can be used by the current code. This is often the case with procedures as we will show later.

It should be clear from these examples that the stack grows and shrinks during the course of a program execution. It is important to allocate enough storage space for the stack, as stack overflow and underflow could cause unpredictable results, often causing system errors.

Transfer of Control

The previous discussion concentrated on how we, as programmers, can use the stack to store data temporarily. The stack is also used by some instructions to store data temporarily. In particular, when a procedure is called, the return address of the instruction is stored on the stack so that the control can be transferred back to the calling program. A detailed discussion of this topic is in the next section.

Parameter Passing

Another important use of the stack is to act as a medium to pass parameters to the called procedure. The stack is extensively used by high-level languages to pass parameters. A discussion on the use of the stack for parameter passing is deferred to a later section.

Procedure Instructions

The instruction set provides call and ret (return) instructions to write procedures in the assembly language. The call instruction can be used to invoke a procedure, and has the format

```
call     proc-name
```

where proc-name is the name of the procedure to be called. The assembler replaces proc-name by the offset value of the first instruction of the called procedure.

How Is Program Control Transferred?

The offset value provided in the call instruction is not the absolute value (i.e., offset is not relative to the start of the code segment pointed to by the CS register), but a relative displacement in bytes from the instruction following the call instruction. Let us look at the example in Figure 11.6.

After the call instruction of main has been fetched, the EIP register points to the next instruction to be executed (i.e., EIP = 00000007H). This is the instruction that should be executed after completing the execution of sum procedure. The processor makes a note of this by pushing the contents of the EIP register onto the stack.

Now, to transfer control to the first instruction of the sum procedure, the EIP register would have to be loaded with the offset value of the

```
push     EBP
```

instruction in sum. To do this, the processor adds the 32-bit relative displacement found in the call instruction to the contents of the EIP register. Proceeding with our example, the machine

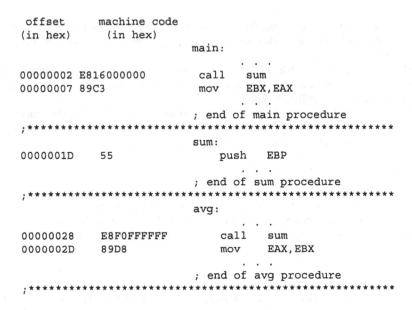

```
        offset       machine code
        (in hex)     (in hex)
                                       main:
                                          . . .
        00000002 E816000000            call   sum
        00000007 89C3                  mov    EBX,EAX
                                          . . .
                                    ; end of main procedure
;***********************************************************
                                       sum:
        0000001D    55                    push   EBP
                                          . . .
                                    ; end of sum procedure
;***********************************************************
                                       avg:
                                          . . .
        00000028    E8F0FFFFFF         call   sum
        0000002D    89D8               mov    EAX,EBX
                                          . . .
                                    ; end of avg procedure
;***********************************************************
```

Figure 11.6 An example to illustrate the transfer of program control.

language encoding of the `call` instruction, which requires five bytes, is E816000000H. The first byte E8H is the opcode for the `call` and the next four bytes give the (signed) relative displacement in bytes. In this example, it is the difference between 0000001DH (offset of the `push EBP` instruction in `sum`) and 00000007H (offset of the instruction `mov EBX,EAX` in `main`). Therefore, the displacement should be 0000001DH − 00000007H = 00000016H. This is the displacement value encoded in the `call` instruction. Note that this displacement value in this instruction is shown in the little-endian order, which is equal to 00000016H. Adding this difference to the contents of the EIP register leaves the EIP register pointing to the first instruction of `sum`.

Note that the procedure call in `main` is a forward call, and therefore the relative displacement is a positive number. As an example of a backward procedure call, let us look at the `sum` procedure call in the `avg` procedure. In this case, the program control has to be transferred back. That is, the displacement is a negative value. Following the explanation given in the last paragraph, we can calculate the displacement as 0000001DH − 0000002DH = FFFFFFF0H. Since negative numbers are expressed in 2's complement notation, FFFFFFF0H corresponds to −10H (i.e., −16D), which is the displacement value in bytes.

The following is a summary of the actions taken during a procedure call:

```
ESP = ESP − 2                    ; push return address onto the stack
SS:ESP = EIP
EIP = EIP + relative displacement    ; update EIP to point to the procedure
```

The relative displacement is a signed 32-bit number to accommodate both forward and backward procedure calls.

The ret Instruction

The ret (return) instruction is used to transfer control from the called procedure to the calling procedure. Return transfers control to the instruction following the call (the mov EBX, EAX instruction in our example). How will the processor know where this instruction is located? Remember that the processor made a note of this when the call instruction was executed. When the ret instruction is executed, the return address from the stack is recovered. The actions taken during the execution of the ret instruction are

EIP = SS:ESP   ; pop return address at TOS into IP
ESP = ESP + 4   ; update TOS by adding 4 to ESP

An optional integer may be included in the ret instruction, as in

ret 8

The details on this optional number are covered later.

Our First Program

In our first procedure example, two parameter values are passed onto the called procedure via the general-purpose registers. The procedure sum receives two integers in the CX and DX registers and returns the sum of these two integers via AX. No check is done to detect the overflow condition. The main program, shown in Program 11.1, requests two integers from the user and displays the sum on the screen.

Program 11.1 Parameter passing by call-by-value using registers

```
 1:  ;Parameter passing via registers            PROCEX1.ASM
 2:  ;
 3:  ;        Objective: To show parameter passing via registers.
 4:  ;            Input: Requests two integers from the user.
 5:  ;           Output: Outputs the sum of the input integers.
 6:  %include "io.mac"
 7:  .DATA
 8:  prompt_msg1  DB    "Please input the first number: ",0
 9:  prompt_msg2  DB    "Please input the second number: ",0
10:  sum_msg      DB    "The sum is ",0
11:
12:  .CODE
13:       .STARTUP
14:       PutStr  prompt_msg1    ; request first number
15:       GetInt  CX             ; CX = first number
16:
17:       PutStr  prompt_msg2    ; request second number
18:       GetInt  DX             ; DX = second number
19:
20:       call    sum            ; returns sum in AX
21:       PutStr  sum_msg        ; display sum
22:       PutInt  AX
23:       nwln
```

```
24:    done:
25:        .EXIT
26:
27:    ;-------------------------------------------------------------
28:    ;Procedure sum receives two integers in CX and DX.
29:    ;The sum of the two integers is returned in AX.
30:    ;-------------------------------------------------------------
31:    sum:
32:        mov     AX,CX          ; sum = first number
33:        add     AX,DX          ; sum = sum + second number
34:        ret
```

Parameter Passing

Parameter passing in assembly language is different and more complicated than that used in high-level languages. In the assembly language, the calling procedure first places all the parameters needed by the called procedure in a mutually accessible storage area (usually registers or memory). Only then can the procedure be invoked. There are two common methods depending on the type of storage area used to pass parameters: *register method* or *stack method*. As their names imply, the register method uses general-purpose registers to pass parameters, and the stack is used in the other method.

Register Method

In the register method, the calling procedure places the necessary parameters in the general-purpose registers before invoking the procedure, as we did in the last example. Next, let us look at the advantages and disadvantages of passing parameters using the register method.

Pros and Cons of the Register Method   The register method has its advantages and disadvantages. These are summarized here.

Advantages

1. The register method is convenient and easier for passing a small number of arguments.

2. This method is also faster because all the arguments are available in registers.

Disadvantages

1. The main disadvantage is that only a few arguments can be passed by using registers, as there are a limited number of general-purpose registers available in the CPU.

2. Another problem is that the general-purpose registers are often used by the calling procedure for some other purpose. Thus, it is necessary to temporarily save the contents of these registers on the stack to free them for use in parameter passing before calling a procedure, and restore them after returning from the called procedure. In this case, it is difficult to realize the second advantage listed above, as the stack operations involve memory access.

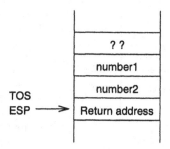

Figure 11.7 Stack state after the sum procedure call: Return address is the EIP value pushed onto the stack as part of executing the call instruction.

Stack Method

In this method of parameter passing, all arguments required by a procedure are pushed onto the stack before the procedure is called. As an example, let us consider passing the two parameters required by the sum procedure shown in Program 11.1. This can be done by

```
push    number1
push    number2
call    sum
```

After executing the call instruction, which automatically pushes the EIP contents onto the stack, the stack state is shown in Figure 11.7.

Reading the two arguments—number1 and number2—is tricky. Since the parameter values are buried inside the stack, first we have to pop the EIP value to read the two arguments. This, for example, can be done by

```
pop     EAX
pop     EBX
pop     ECX
```

in the sum procedure. Since we have removed the return address (EIP) from the stack, we will have to restore it by

```
push    EAX
```

so that TOS is pointing to the return address.

The main problem with this code is that we need to set aside general-purpose registers to copy parameter values. This means that the calling procedure cannot use these registers for any other purpose. Worse still, what if you want to pass 10 parameters? One way to free up registers is to copy the parameters from the stack to local data variables, but this is impractical and inefficient.

The best way to get parameter values is to leave them on the stack and read them from the stack as needed. Since the stack is a sequence of memory locations, ESP + 4 points to number2, and ESP + 6 to number1. Note that both number1 and number2 are 16-bit values. For instance,

```
mov     EBX, [ESP+4]
```

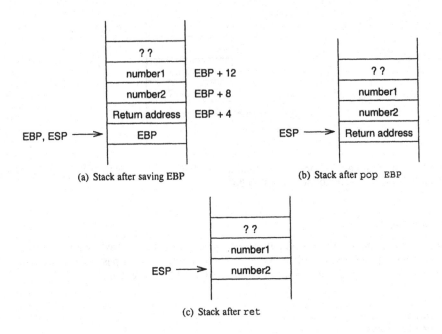

(a) Stack after saving EBP

(b) Stack after pop EBP

(c) Stack after ret

Figure 11.8 Changes in stack state during a procedure execution.

can be used to access number2, but this causes a problem. The stack pointer register is updated by the push and pop instructions. As a result, the relative offset changes with the stack operations performed in the called procedure. This is not a desirable situation.

There is a better alternative: we can use the EBP register instead of ESP to specify an offset into the stack segment. For example, we can copy the value of number2 into the EAX register by

```
mov     EBP,ESP
mov     EAX,[EBP+4]
```

This is the usual way of pointing to the parameters on the stack. Since every procedure uses the EBP register to access parameters, the EBP register should be preserved. Therefore, we should save the contents of the EBP register before executing the

```
mov     EBP,ESP
```

statement. We, of course, use the stack for this. Note that

```
push    EBP
mov     EBP,ESP
```

causes the parameter displacement to increase by four bytes, as shown in Figure 11.8a.

The information stored in the stack—parameters, return address, and the old EBP value—is collectively called the *stack frame*. As we show on page 256, the stack frame also consists of local variables if the procedure uses them. The EBP value is referred to as the *frame pointer* (FP). Once the EBP value is known, we can access all items in the stack frame.

Before returning from the procedure, we should use

```
pop     EBP
```

to restore the original value of EBP. The resulting stack state is shown in Figure 11.8*b*.

The `ret` statement causes the return address to be placed in the EIP register, and the stack state after `ret` is shown in Figure 11.8*c*.

Now the problem is that the four bytes of the stack occupied by the two arguments are no longer useful. One way to free these four bytes is to increment ESP by four after the call statement, as shown below:

```
push    number1
push    number2
call    sum
add     ESP,4
```

For example, C compilers use this method to clear parameters from the stack. The above assembly language code segment corresponds to the

```
sum(number2, number1);
```

function call in C.

Rather than adjusting the stack by the calling procedure, the called procedure can also clear the stack. Note that we cannot write

```
sum:
        . . .
add     ESP,4
ret
```

because when `ret` is executed, ESP should point to the return address on the stack. The solution lies in the optional operand that can be specified in the `ret` statement. The format is

```
ret     optional-value
```

which results in the following sequence of actions:

$$EIP = SS:ESP$$
$$ESP = ESP + 4 + \text{optional-value}$$

The `optional-value` should be a number (i.e., 16-bit immediate value). Since the purpose of the optional value is to discard the parameters pushed onto the stack, this operand takes a positive value.

Who Should Clean Up the Stack?

We have discussed the following ways of discarding the unwanted parameters on the stack:

1. clean-up is done by the calling procedure, or
2. clean-up is done by the called procedure.

If procedures require a fixed number of parameters, the second method is preferred. In this case, we write the clean-up code only once in the called procedure independent of the number of times this procedure is called. We follow this convention in our assembly language programs. However, if a procedure receives a variable number of parameters, we have to use the first method. We discuss this topic in detail in a later section.

Preserving Calling Procedure State

It is important to preserve the contents of the registers across a procedure call. The necessity for this is illustrated by the following code:

```
                . . .
            mov     ECX, count
    repeat:
            call    compute
                . . .

                . . .
            loop    repeat
                . . .
```

The code invokes the compute procedure count times. The ECX register maintains the number of remaining iterations. Recall that, as part of the loop instruction execution, the ECX register is decremented by 1 and, if not 0, starts another iteration.

Suppose, now, that the compute procedure uses the ECX register during its computation. Then, when compute returns control to the calling program, ECX would have changed, and the program logic would be incorrect.

Since there are a limited number of registers and registers should be used for writing efficient code, registers should be preserved. The stack is used to save registers temporarily.

Which Registers Should Be Saved?

The answer to this question is simple: Save those registers that are used by the calling procedure but changed by the called procedure. This leads to the following question: Which procedure, the calling or the called, should save the registers?

Usually, one or two registers are used to return a value by the called procedure. Therefore, such register(s) do not have to be saved. For example, the EAX register is often used to return integer values.

In order to avoid the selection of the registers to be saved, we could save, blindly, all registers each time a procedure is invoked. For instance, we could use the pushad instruction (see page 237). But such an action results in unnecessary overhead.

If the calling procedure were to save the necessary registers, it needs to know the registers used by the called procedure. This causes two serious difficulties:

1. Program maintenance would be difficult because, if the called procedure were modified later on and a different set of registers used, every procedure that calls this procedure would have to be modified.
2. Programs tend to be longer because if a procedure is called several times, we have to include the instructions to save and restore the registers each time the procedure is called.

For these reasons, we assume that the called procedure saves the registers that it uses and restores them before returning to the calling procedure. This also conforms to the modular program design principles.

When to Use pusha

The pusha instruction is useful in certain instances, but not all. We identify some instances where pusha is not useful. First, what if some of the registers saved by pusha are used for returning

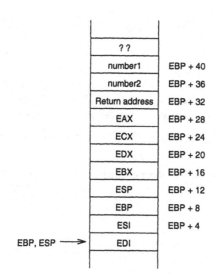

Figure 11.9 Stack state after `pusha`.

results? For instance, EAX register is often used to return integer results. In this case `pusha` is not really useful, as `popa` destroys the result to be returned to the calling procedure. Second, since `pusha` introduces more overhead, it may be worthwhile to use the `push` instruction if we want to save only one or two registers. Of course, the other side of the coin is that `pusha` improves readability of code and reduces memory required for the instructions.

When `pusha` is used to save registers, it modifies the offset of the parameters. Note that

```
pusha
mov     EBP,ESP
```

causes the stack state, shown in Figure 11.9, to be different from that shown in Figure 11.8a on page 244. You can see that the offset of `number1` and `number2` increases.

ENTER and LEAVE Instructions

The instruction set has two instructions to facilitate stack frame allocation and release on procedure entry and exit. The `enter` instruction can be used to allocate a stack frame on entering a procedure. The format is

```
enter   bytes,level
```

The first operand `bytes` specifies the number of bytes of local variable storage we want on the new stack frame. We discuss local variables in the next chapter. Until then, we set the first operand to zero. The second operand `level` gives the nesting level of the procedure. If we specify a nonzero level, it copies `level` stack frame pointers into the new frame from the preceding stack frame. In all our examples, we set the second operand to zero. Thus the statement

```
enter   XX,0
```

is equivalent to

```
push    EBP
mov     EBP,ESP
sub     ESP,XX
```

The `leave` instruction releases the stack frame allocated by the `enter` instruction. It does not take any operands. The `leave` instruction effectively performs the following:

```
mov     ESP,EBP
pop     EBP
```

We use the `leave` instruction before the `ret` instruction as shown in the following template for procedures:

```
proc-name:
    enter   XX,0
        . . .
    procedure body
        . . .
    leave
    ret     YY
```

As we show in the next chapter (page 259), the XX value is nonzero only if our procedure needs some local variable space on the stack frame. The value YY is used to clear the arguments passed on to the procedure.

Illustrative Examples

In this section, we use several examples to illustrate register-based and stack-based parameter passing.

Example 11.1 *Parameter passing by call-by-reference using registers.*
This example shows how parameters can be passed by call-by-reference using the register method. The program requests a character string from the user and displays the number of characters in the string (i.e., string length). The string length is computed by the `str_len` function. This function scans the input string for the NULL character while keeping track of the number of characters in the string. The pseudocode is shown below:

```
str_len (string)
    index := 0
    length := 0
    while (string[index] ≠ NULL)
        index := index + 1
        length := length + 1     { AX is used for string length}
    end while
    return (length)
end str_len
```

The `str_len` function receives a pointer to the string in EBX and returns the string length in the EAX register. The program listing is given in Program 11.2. The `main` procedure executes

```
mov     EBX,string
```

to place the address of `string` in EBX (line 22) before invoking the procedure on line 23. Note that even though the procedure modifies the EBX register during its execution, it restores the original value of EBX by saving its value initially on the stack (line 35) and restoring it (line 44) before returning to the `main` procedure.

Program 11.2 Parameter passing by call-by-reference using registers

```
 1:  ;Parameter passing via registers                    PROCEX2.ASM
 2:  ;
 3:  ;           Objective: To show parameter passing via registers
 4:  ;               Input: Requests a character string from the user.
 5:  ;              Output: Outputs the length of the input string.
 6:
 7:  %include "io.mac"
 8:  BUF_LEN         EQU 41              ; string buffer length
 9:
10:  .DATA
11:  prompt_msg  db  "Please input a string: ",0
12:  length_msg  db  "The string length is ",0
13:
14:  .UDATA
15:  string          resb BUF_LEN        ;input string < BUF_LEN chars.
16:
17:  .CODE
18:       .STARTUP
19:       PutStr  prompt_msg          ; request string input
20:       GetStr  string,BUF_LEN      ; read string from keyboard
21:
22:       mov     EBX,string          ; EBX = string address
23:       call    str_len             ; returns string length in AX
24:       PutStr  length_msg          ; display string length
25:       PutInt  AX
26:       nwln
27:  done:
28:       .EXIT
29:
30:  ;-----------------------------------------------------------------
31:  ;Procedure str_len receives a pointer to a string in BX.
32:  ;String length is returned in AX.
33:  ;-----------------------------------------------------------------
34:  str_len:
35:       push    EBX
36:       sub     AX,AX               ; string length = 0
37:  repeat:
38:       cmp     byte [EBX],0        ; compare with NULL char.
39:       je      str_len_done        ; if NULL we are done
40:       inc     AX                  ; else, increment string length
41:       inc     EBX                 ; point BX to the next char.
```

```
42:          jmp     repeat          ;  and repeat the process
43:  str_len_done:
44:          pop     EBX
45:          ret
```

Example 11.2 *Parameter passing by call-by-value using the stack.*

This is the stack counterpart of Program 11.1, which passes two integers to the procedure sum. The procedure returns the sum of these two integers in the AX register. The program listing is given in Program 11.3.

The program requests two integers from the user. It reads the two numbers into the CX and DX registers using GetInt (lines 16 and 19). Since the stack is used to pass the two numbers, we have to place them on the stack before calling the sum procedure (see lines 21 and 22). The state of the stack after the control is transferred to sum is shown in Figure 11.7 on page 243.

As discussed before, the EBP register is used to access the two parameters from the stack. Therefore, we have to save EBP itself on the stack. We do this by using the enter instruction (line 35), which changes the stack state to that in Figure 11.8*a* on page 244.

The original value of EBP is restored at the end of the procedure using the leave instruction (line 38). Accessing the two numbers follows the explanation given in Section 11. Note that the first number is at EBP + 10, and the second one at EBP + 8. As in our first example on page 241, no overflow check is done by sum. Control is returned to main by

```
ret     4
```

because sum has received two parameters requiring a total space of four bytes on the stack. This ret statement clears number1 and number2 from the stack.

Program 11.3 Parameter passing by call-by-value using the stack

```
 1:  ;Parameter passing via the stack                    PROCEX3.ASM
 2:  ;
 3:  ;          Objective: To show parameter passing via the stack.
 4:  ;              Input: Requests two integers from the user.
 5:  ;             Output: Outputs the sum of the input integers.
 6:  %include "io.mac"
 7:
 8:  .DATA
 9:  prompt_msg1   db   "Please input the first number: ",0
10:  prompt_msg2   db   "Please input the second number: ",0
11:  sum_msg       db   "The sum is ",0
12:
13:  .CODE
14:      .STARTUP
15:      PutStr  prompt_msg1     ; request first number
16:      GetInt  CX              ; CX = first number
17:
18:      PutStr  prompt_msg2     ; request second number
19:      GetInt  DX              ; DX = second number
```

```
20:
21:            push    CX              ; place first number on stack
22:            push    DX              ; place second number on stack
23:            call    sum             ; returns sum in AX
24:            PutStr  sum_msg         ; display sum
25:            PutInt  AX
26:            nwln
27:   done:
28:            .EXIT
29:
30:   ;------------------------------------------------------------
31:   ;Procedure sum receives two integers via the stack.
32:   ;The sum of the two integers is returned in AX.
33:   ;------------------------------------------------------------
34:   sum:
35:            enter   0,0             ; save EBP
36:            mov     AX, [EBP+10]    ; sum = first number
37:            add     AX, [EBP+8]     ; sum = sum + second number
38:            leave                   ; restore EBP
39:            ret     4               ; return and clear parameters
```

Example 11.3 *Parameter passing by call-by-reference using the stack.*

This example shows how the stack can be used for parameter passing using the call-by-reference mechanism. The procedure swap receives two pointers to two characters and interchanges them. The program, shown in Program 11.4, requests a string from the user and displays the input string with the first two characters interchanged.

Program 11.4 Parameter passing by call-by-reference using the stack

```
1:  ;Parameter passing via the stack                    PROCSWAP.ASM
2:  ;
3:  ;          Objective: To show parameter passing via the stack.
4:  ;              Input: Requests a character string from the user.
5:  ;             Output: Outputs the input string with the first
6:  ;                     two characters swapped.
7:
8:  BUF_LEN        EQU 41              ; string buffer length
9:  %include "io.mac"
10:
11: .DATA
12: prompt_msg  db      "Please input a string: ",0
13: output_msg  db      "The swapped string is: ",0
14:
15: .UDATA
16: string          resb  BUF_LEN         ;input string < BUF_LEN chars.
17:
18: .CODE
```

```
19:            .STARTUP
20:            PutStr   prompt_msg      ; request string input
21:            GetStr   string,BUF_LEN  ; read string from the user
22:
23:            mov      EAX,string      ; EAX = string[0] pointer
24:            push     EAX
25:            inc      EAX             ; EAX = string[1] pointer
26:            push     EAX
27:            call     swap            ; swaps the first two characters
28:            PutStr   output_msg      ; display the swapped string
29:            PutStr   string
30:            nwln
31:    done:
32:            .EXIT
33:
34:    ;-----------------------------------------------------------
35:    ;Procedure swap receives two pointers (via the stack) to
36:    ;characters of a string. It exchanges these two characters.
37:    ;-----------------------------------------------------------
38:    .CODE
39:    swap:
40:            enter    0,0
41:            push     EBX             ; save EBX - procedure uses EBX
42:            ; swap begins here. Because of xchg, AL is preserved.
43:            mov      EBX,[EBP+12]    ; EBX = first character pointer
44:            xchg     AL,[EBX]
45:            mov      EBX,[EBP+8]     ; EBX = second character pointer
46:            xchg     AL,[EBX]
47:            mov      EBX,[EBP+12]    ; EBX = first character pointer
48:            xchg     AL,[EBX]
49:            ; swap ends here
50:            pop      EBX             ; restore registers
51:            leave
52:            ret      8               ; return and clear parameters
```

In preparation for calling swap, the main procedure places the addresses of the first two characters of the input string on the stack (lines 23 to 26). The swap procedure, after saving the EBP register as in the last example, can access the pointers of the two characters at EBP + 8 and EBP + 12. Since the procedure uses the EBX register, we save it on the stack as well. Note that, once the EBP is pushed onto the stack and the ESP value is copied to EBP, the two parameters (i.e., the two character pointers in this example) are available at EBP + 8 and EBP + 12, irrespective of the other stack push operations in the procedure. This is important from the program maintenance point of view.

Summary

The stack is a last-in-first-out data structure that plays an important role in procedure invocation and execution. It supports two operations: push and pop. Only the element at the top-of-stack is directly accessible through these operations. The stack segment is used to implement the stack. The top-of-stack is represented by SS:ESP. In the implementation, the stack grows toward lower memory addresses (i.e., grows downward).

The stack serves three main purposes: temporary storage of data, transfer of control during a procedure call and return, and parameter passing.

When writing procedures in the assembly language, parameter passing has to be explicitly handled. Parameter passing can be done via registers or the stack. Although the register method is efficient, the stack-based method is more general. We have used several examples to illustrate the register-based and stack-based parameter passing.

12

More on Procedures

We introduced the basics of the assembly language procedures in the last chapter. We have discussed the two parameter passing mechanisms used in invoking procedures. However, we did not discuss how local variables, declared in a procedure, are handled in the assembly language. We start this chapter with a discussion of this topic.

Although short assembly language programs can be stored in a single file, real application programs are likely to be broken into several files, called modules. The issues involved in writing and assembling multiple source program modules are discussed in detail.

Most high-level languages use procedures that receive a fixed number of arguments. However, languages like C support variable number of arguments. By means of an example, we look at how we can pass a variable number of arguments to a procedure. It turns out that passing a variable number of arguments is straightforward using the stack. The last section provides a summary of the chapter.

Introduction

This chapter builds on the material presented in the last chapter. Specifically, we focus on three issues: handling local variables, splitting a program into multiple modules, and passing a variable number of arguments.

In the last chapter, we did not consider how local variables can be used in a procedure. To focus our discussion, let us look at the following C code:

```
int compute(int a, int b)
{
    int    temp, N;
         . . .
         . . .
}
```

The variables temp and N are local variables whose scope is limited to the compute procedure. These variable come into existence when the compute procedure is invoked and disappear when the procedure terminates. Like the parameter passing mechanism, we can use either registers or the stack to store the local variables. We discuss these two methods and their pros and cons in the next section.

In the assembly language programs we have seen so far, the entire assembly language program is in a single file. This is fine for short example programs. Real application programs, however, tend to be large, consisting of hundreds of procedures. Rather than keeping such a massive source program in a single file, it is advantageous to break it up into several small pieces, where each piece of the source code is stored in a separate file or *module*. There are three advantages associated with multimodule programs:

- The chief advantage is that, after modifying a source module, it is only necessary to re-assemble that module. On the other hand, if you keep only a single file, the whole file has to be reassembled.
- Making modifications to the source code is easier with several small files.
- It is safer to edit a short file; any unintended modifications to the source file are limited to a single small file.

After discussing the local variable issues, we describe in detail the mechanism involved in creating programs with multiple modules.

Most of the procedures we write receive a fixed number of arguments. These procedures always receive the same number of arguments. However, procedures in C can be defined with a variable number of parameters. In these procedures, the number of arguments passed can vary from call to call. For example, a procedure may receive only two arguments in one call but may receive five arguments in another. The input and output functions, scanf and printf, are the two common procedures that take a variable number of arguments. In this type of procedures, the called procedure does not know the number of arguments passed onto it. Usually, the first argument specifies this number. Using an example, we show how we can write assembly language procedures that can receive a variable number of arguments.

Local Variables

In the compute procedure, the local variables temp and N are dynamic. How do we store them in our assembly language programs? One alternative is to use the processor registers. Even though this method is efficient, it is not suitable for all procedures. The register method can be used for the leaf procedures[1]. Even here, the limited number of registers may cause problems.

To avoid these problems, we could reserve space for the local variables in our data segment. However, such a space allocation is not desirable for two main reasons:

1. Space allocation done in the data segment is static and remains active even when the proce-dure is not. However, these local variables are supposed to disappear when the procedure is terminated.

2. More importantly, it does not work with nonleaf and recursive procedures. Note that the recursive procedures call themselves either directly or indirectly. We discuss recursive pro-cedures in Chapter 19.

For these reasons, space for local variables is reserved on the stack. For the C compute function, Figure 12.1 shows the contents of the stack frame. In high-level languages, it is also referred to as the *activation record* because each procedure activation requires all this information. The EBP value, also called the *frame pointer*, allows us to access the contents of the stack frame.

---

[1] A leaf procedure is a procedure that does not call another procedure while a nonleaf procedure does.

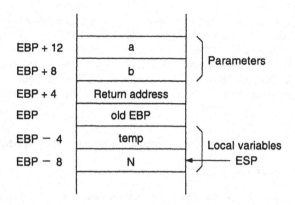

Figure 12.1 Activation record for the compute function.

For example, parameters a and b can be accessed at EBP + 12 and EBP + 8, respectively. Local variables temp and N can be accessed at EBP − 4 and EBP − 8, respectively.

To aid program readability, we can use the %define directive to name the stack locations. Then we can write

```
mov     EBX,a
mov     temp,EAX
```

instead of

```
mov     EBX, [EBP+12]
mov     [EBP-4],EAX
```

after establishing temp and a labels by using the %define directive, as shown below.

```
%define    a       dword [EBP+12]
%define    temp    dword [EBP-4]
```

Next we look at an example that computes the Fibonacci numbers.

Our First Program

In this example, we write a procedure to compute the largest Fibonacci number that is less than or equal to a given input number. The Fibonacci sequence of numbers is defined as

$$\text{fib}(1) = 1,$$
$$\text{fib}(2) = 1,$$
$$\text{fib}(n) = \text{fib}(n-1) + \text{fib}(n-2) \text{ for } n > 2.$$

In other words, the first two numbers in the Fibonacci sequence are 1. The subsequent numbers are obtained by adding the previous two numbers in the sequence. Thus,

$$1, 1, 2, 3, 5, 8, 13, 21, 34, \ldots,$$

is the Fibonacci sequence of numbers.

The listing for this example is given in Program 12.1. The main procedure requests the input number and passes it on to the fibonacci procedure. The fibonacci procedure keeps the last two Fibonacci numbers in local variables. We use the stack for storing these two Fibonacci numbers. The variable FIB_LO corresponds to fib(n − 1) and FIB_HI to fib(n).

The fib_loop on lines 43–50 successively computes the Fibonacci number until it is greater than or equal to the input number. Then the Fibonacci number in EAX is returned to the main procedure.

Program 12.1 Fibonacci number computation with local variables mapped to the stack

```
 1:  ;Fibonacci numbers                                    PROCFIB.ASM
 2:  ;
 3:  ;           Objective: To compute Fibonacci number using the stack
 4:  ;                      for local variables.
 5:  ;               Input: Requests a positive integer from the user.
 6:  ;              Output: Outputs the largest Fibonacci number that
 7:  ;                      is less than or equal to the input number.
 8:  %include "io.mac"
 9:
10:  .DATA
11:  prompt_msg   db   "Please input a positive number (>1): ",0
12:  output_msg1  db   "The largest Fibonacci number less than "
13:               db   "or equal to ",0
14:  output_msg2  db   " is ",0
15:
16:  .CODE
17:       .STARTUP
18:       PutStr    prompt_msg      ; request input number
19:       GetLInt   EDX             ; EDX = input number
20:       call      fibonacci
21:       PutStr    output_msg1     ; print Fibonacci number
22:       PutLInt   EDX
23:       PutStr    output_msg2
24:       PutLInt   EAX
25:       nwln
26:  done:
27:       .EXIT
28:
29:  ;-----------------------------------------------------------
30:  ;Procedure fibonacci receives an integer in EDX and computes
31:  ;the largest Fibonacci number that is less than the input
32:  ;number. The Fibonacci number is returned in EAX.
33:  ;-----------------------------------------------------------
34:  %define FIB_LO  dword [EBP-4]
35:  %define FIB_HI  dword [EBP-8]
36:  fibonacci:
37:       enter   8,0              ; space for two local variables
38:       push    EBX
39:       ; FIB_LO maintains the smaller of the last two Fibonacci
40:       ;  numbers computed; FIB_HI maintains the larger one.
```

```
41:          mov      FIB_LO,1       ; initialize FIB_LO and FIB_HI to
42:          mov      FIB_HI,1       ;   first two Fibonacci numbers
43:   fib_loop:
44:          mov      EAX,FIB_HI     ; compute next Fibonacci number
45:          mov      EBX,FIB_LO
46:          add      EBX,EAX
47:          mov      FIB_LO,EAX
48:          mov      FIB_HI,EBX
49:          cmp      EBX,EDX        ; compare with input number in EDX
50:          jle      fib_loop       ; if not greater, find next number
51:          ; EAX contains the required Fibonacci number
52:          pop      EBX
53:          leave                   ; clears local variable space
54:          ret
```

The code

```
push    EBP
mov     EBP,ESP
sub     ESP,8
```

saves the EBP value and copies the ESP value into the EBP as usual. It also decrements the ESP by 8, thus creating 8 bytes of storage space for the two local variables FIB_LO and FIB_HI. This three-instruction sequence can be replaced by the

```
enter   8,0
```

instruction (line 37). As mentioned before, the first operand specifies the number of bytes reserved for local variables. At this point, the stack allocation is

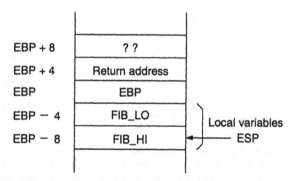

The two local variables can be accessed at EBP − 4 and EBP − 8. The two %define statements, on lines 34 and 35, conveniently establish labels for these two locations. We can clear the local variable space and restore the EBP value by

```
mov     ESP,EBP
pop     EBP
```

instructions. The `leave` instruction performs exactly the same. Thus, the `leave` instruction on line 53 automatically clears the local variable space. The rest of the code is straightforward to follow.

Multiple Source Program Modules

We discussed the advantages of multimodule programs at the beginning of this chapter. If we want to write multimodule assembly language programs, we have to precisely specify the intermodule interface. For example, if a procedure is called in the current module but is defined in another module, we have to state this fact so that the assembler does not flag such procedure calls as errors. Assemblers provide two directives—`global` and `extern`—to facilitate separate assembly of source modules. These two directives are discussed next.

GLOBAL Directive   The `global` directive makes the associated label(s) available to other modules of the program. The format is

```
global    label1, label2, ...
```

Almost any label can be made public. This includes procedure names, memory variables, and equated labels, as shown in the following example:

```
global  error_msg, total, sample
                . . .
                . . .
.DATA
error_msg    db    'Out of range!',0
total        dw    0
                . . .
                . . .
.CODE
                . . .
                . . .
sample:
                . . .
                . . .
             ret
```

Microsoft and Borland assemblers use PUBLIC directive for this purpose.

EXTERN Directive   The `extern` directive can be used to tell the assembler that certain labels are not defined in the current source file (i.e., module), but can be found in other modules. Thus, the assembler leaves "holes" in the corresponding object file that the linker will fill in later. The format is

```
extern    label1, label2, ...
```

where `label1` and `label2` are labels that are made public by a `global` directive in some other module.

Illustrative Examples

We present two examples to show how the global and extern directives are used to create multimodule programs in the assembly language.

Example 12.1 *A two-module example to find string length.*
We now present a simple example that reads a string from the user and displays the string length (i.e., number of characters in the string). The source code consists of two procedures: main and string_length. The main procedure is responsible for requesting and displaying the string length information. It uses GetStr, PutStr, and PutInt I/O routines. The string_length procedure computes the string length.

The source program is split into two modules: the main procedure is in the module1.asm file, and the string_length procedure is in the module2.asm file. Program 12.2 gives a listing of module1.asm. Notice that on line 18, we declare string_length as an externally defined procedure by using the extern directive.

Program 12.2 The main procedure defined in module1.asm calls the sum procedure defined in module2.asm

```
 1:  ;Multimodule program for string length          MODULE1.ASM
 2:  ;
 3:  ;         Objective: To show parameter passing via registers.
 4:  ;             Input: Requests two integers from keyboard.
 5:  ;            Output: Outputs the sum of the input integers.
 6:
 7:  BUF_SIZE   EQU  41   ; string buffer size
 8:  %include "io.mac"
 9:
10:  .DATA
11:  prompt_msg   db   "Please input a string: ",0
12:  length_msg   db   "String length is: ",0
13:
14:  .UDATA
15:  string1      resb   BUF_SIZE
16:
17:  .CODE
18:  extern    string_length
19:       .STARTUP
20:       PutStr   prompt_msg     ; request a string
21:       GetStr   string1,BUF_SIZE  ; read string input
22:
23:       mov      EBX,string1    ; EBX := string pointer
24:       call     string_length  ; returns string length in AX
25:       PutStr   length_msg     ; display string length
26:       PutInt   AX
27:       nwln
28:  done:
29:       .EXIT
```

Program 12.3 gives the `module2.asm` program listing. This module consists of a single procedure. By using the `global` directive, we make this procedure global (line 10) so that other modules can access it. The `string_length` procedure receives a pointer to a NULL-terminated string in EBX and returns the length of the string in EAX. The procedure preserves all registers except for EAX.

Program 12.3 This module defines the `sum` procedure called by `main`

```
 1:   ;String length procedure                        MODULE2.ASM
 2:   ;
 3:   ;         Function: To write a procedure to compute string
 4:   ;                   length of a NULL-terminated string.
 5:   ;         Receives: String pointer in the EBX register.
 6:   ;          Returns: Returns string length in AX.
 7:   %include "io.mac"
 8:
 9:   .CODE
10:   global string_length
11:   string_length:
12:         ; all registers except AX are preserved
13:         push    ESI          ; save ESI
14:         mov     ESI,EBX      ; ESI = string pointer
15:   repeat:
16:         cmp     byte [ESI],0 ; is it NULL?
17:         je      done         ; if so, done
18:         inc     ESI          ; else, move to next character
19:         jmp     repeat       ;       and repeat
20:   done:
21:         sub     ESI,EBX      ; compute string length
22:         mov     AX,SI        ; return string length in AX
23:         pop     ESI          ; restore ESI
24:         ret
```

We can assemble each source code module separately producing the corresponding object file. We can then link the object files together to produce a single executable file. For example, using the NASM assembler, the following sequence of commands

```
nasm  -f elf module1.asm                    ← Produces module1.o
nasm  -f elf module2.asm                    ← Produces module2.o
ld -s -o module module1.o module2.o io.o    ← Produces module
```

produces the executable file `module`. Note that the above sequence assumes that you have the `io.o` file in your current directory.

Example 12.2 *Bubble sort procedure.*

There are several algorithms to sort an array of numbers. The algorithm we use here is called the *bubble sort* algorithm. We assume that the array is to be sorted in ascending order. The bubble

```
              Initial state:   4 3 5 1 2
      After 1st comparison:   3 4 5 1 2 (4 and 3 swapped)
      After 2nd comparison:   3 4 5 1 2 (no swap)
      After 3rd comparison:   3 4 1 5 2 (5 and 1 swapped)
         End of first pass:   3 4 1 2 5 (5 and 2 swapped)
```

Figure 12.2 Actions taken during the first pass of the bubble sort algorithm.


```
            Initial state:   4 3 5 1 2
         After 1st pass:   3 4 1 2 5 (5 in its final position)
         After 2nd pass:   3 1 2 4 5 (4 in its final position)
         After 3rd pass:   1 2 3 4 5 (array in sorted order)
   After the final pass:   1 2 3 4 5 (final pass to check)
```

Figure 12.3 Behavior of the bubble sort algorithm.

sort algorithm consists of several passes through the array. Each pass scans the array, performing the following actions:

- Compare adjacent pairs of data elements;
- If they are out of order, swap them.

The algorithm terminates if, during a pass, no data elements are swapped. Even if a single swap is done during a pass, it will initiate another pass to scan the array.

Figure 12.2 shows the behavior of the algorithm during the first pass. The algorithm starts by comparing the first and second data elements (4 and 3). Since they are out of order, 4 and 3 are interchanged. Next, the second data element 4 is compared with the third data element 5, and no swapping takes place as they are in order. During the next step, 5 and 1 are compared and swapped and finally 5 and 2 are swapped. This terminates the first pass. The algorithm has performed $N - 1$ comparisons, where N is the number of data elements in the array. At the end of the first pass, the largest data element 5 is moved to its final position in the array.

Figure 12.3 shows the state of the array after each pass. Notice that after the first pass, the largest number (5) is in its final position. Similarly, after the second pass, the second largest number (4) moves to its final position, and so on. This is why this algorithm is called the bubble sort: during the first pass, the largest element bubbles to the top, the second largest bubbles to the top during the second pass, and so on. Even though the array is in sorted order after the third pass, one more pass is required by the algorithm to detect this.

The number of passes required to sort an array depends on how unsorted the initial array is. If the array is in sorted order, only a single pass is required. At the other extreme, if the array is completely unsorted (i.e., elements are initially in the descending order), the algorithm requires the maximum number of passes equal to one less than the number of elements in the array. The pseudocode for the bubble sort algorithm is shown in Figure 12.4.

The bubble sort program requests a set of up to 20 nonzero integers from the user and displays them in sorted order. The input can be terminated earlier by typing a zero.

We divide the bubble sort program into four modules, surely an overkill but it gives us an opportunity to practice multimodule programming. The main program calls three procedures to perform the bubble sort:

```
bubble_sort (arrayPointer, arraySize)
    status := UNSORTED
    #comparisons := arraySize
    while (status = UNSORTED)
        #comparisons := #comparisons − 1
        status := SORTED
        for (i = 0 to #comparisons)
            if (array[i] > array[i+1])
                swap ith and (i + 1)th elements of the array
                status := UNSORTED
            end if
        end for
    end while
end bubble_sort
```

Figure 12.4 Pseudocode for the bubble sort algorithm.

- `array_read` procedure: This procedure reads the input numbers into the array to be sorted.
- `array_output` procedure: This procedure outputs the sorted array.
- `bubble_sort` procedure: This procedure sorts the array in ascending order using the bubble sort algorithm.

The main program listing is shown in Program 12.4. It first calls the read_array procedure to fill the array with nonzero integers. The read_array procedure returns the actual number of values read into the array in the EAX register. If this value is zero, implying that no input was given, the program terminates after displaying an appropriate message. Otherwise, the array pointer and its size are passed onto the bubble sort procedure. After returning from this procedure, the array_output procedure is called to display the sorted array.

Program 12.4 Main program of the bubble sort program

```
 1: ;Bubble sort procedure                          BBLMAIN.ASM
 2: ;      Objective: To implement the bubble sort algorithm.
 3: ;         Input: A set of nonzero integers to be sorted.
 4: ;                Input is terminated by entering zero.
 5: ;        Output: Outputs the numbers in ascending order.
 6:
 7: %define    CRLF  0DH,0AH
 8: MAX_SIZE   EQU   20
 9: %include "io.mac"
10: .DATA
11: prompt_msg db  "Enter nonzero integers to be sorted.",CRLF
12:            db  "Enter zero to terminate the input.",0
13: output_msg db  "Input numbers in ascending order:",0
14: error_msg  db  "No input entered.",0
15:
```

```
16:    .UDATA
17:    array          resd  MAX_SIZE    ; input array for integers
18:
19:    .CODE
20:    extern    bubble_sort
21:    extern    read_array
22:    extern    output_array
23:
24:         .STARTUP
25:         PutStr    prompt_msg      ; request input numbers
26:         nwln
27:         mov       EBX,array       ; EBX = array pointer
28:         mov       ECX,MAX_SIZE    ; ECX = array size
29:
30:         call      read_array      ; reads input into the array
31:         ; returns the number of values read in EAX
32:
33:         cmp       EAX,0           ; if no input is given
34:         ja        input_OK        ; display error message
35:         PutStr    error_msg
36:         nwln
37:         jmp       short done
38:    input_OK:
39:         push      EAX             ; push array size onto stack
40.         push      array           ; place array pointer on stack
41:         call      bubble_sort
42:
43:         PutStr    output_msg      ; display sorted input numbers
44:         nwln
45:         mov       EBX,array
46:         mov       ECX,EAX         ; EAX has the number count
47:         call      output_array
48:    done:
49:         .EXIT
```

The read_array procedure, shown in Program 15.1, receives the array pointer in EBX and the maximum array size in the ECX register. It reads at most maximum array size values. The loop instruction on line 24 takes care of this condition. The input can also be terminated earlier by entering a zero. The zero input condition is detected and the loop is terminated by the statements on lines 19 and 20. The EDX register is used to keep track of the number of input values received from the user. This value is returned to the main program via the EAX register (line 26).

Program 12.5 Read array procedure

```
1:  ;Array read procedure                              BBLREAD.ASM
2:  ;         Function: To read a set of nonzero integers values
3:  ;                   into an array.
4:  ;                   Input is terminated by entering zero.
5;  ;         Receives: EBX = array pointer
```

```
 6:    ;                     ECX = array size
 7:    ;          Returns: EAX = number of values read.
 8:    %include "io.mac"
 9:
10:    .CODE
11:    global    read_array
12:
13:    read_array:
14:          push    EDX
15:          push    EBX
16:          sub     EDX,EDX        ; number count = 0
17:    read_loop:
18:          GetLInt EAX            ; read input number
19:          cmp     EAX,0          ; if the number is zero
20:          je      read_done      ; no more numbers to read
21:          mov     [EBX],EAX      ; copy the number into array
22:          add     EBX,4          ; EBX points to the next element
23:          inc     EDX            ; increment number count
24:          loop    read_loop      ; reads a max. of MAX_SIZE numbers
25:    read_done:
26:          mov     EAX,EDX        ; returns the # of values read
27:          pop     EBX
28:          pop     EDX
29:          ret
```

The array_output procedure (Program 12.6) receives the array pointer in the EBX register and the array size in the ECX register. It uses the loop on lines 14–18 to display the sorted array.

Program 12.6 Output array procedure

```
 1:    ;Array output procedure              BBLOUTPUT.ASM
 2:    ;      Function: To output the values of an array.
 3:    ;      Receives: EBX = array pointer
 4:    ;                ECX = array size
 5:    ;       Returns: None.
 6:    %include "io.mac"
 7:
 8:    .CODE
 9:    global    output_array
10:
11:    output_array:
12:          push    EBX
13:          push    ECX
14:    print_loop:
15:          PutLInt [EBX]
16:          nwln
17:          add     EBX,4
18:          loop    print_loop
19:          pop     ECX
```

```
20:            pop      EBX
21:            ret
```

The bubble_sort procedure receives the array size and a pointer to the array. In the bubble_sort procedure, the ECX register is used to keep track of the number of comparisons while EDX maintains the status information. The ESI register points to the *i*th element of the input array.

Program 12.7 Bubble sort procedure to sort integers in ascending order

```
 1:    ;-------------------------------------------------------------
 2:    ;This procedure receives a pointer to an array of integers
 3:    ;and the size of the array via the stack. It sorts the
 4:    ;array in ascending order using the bubble sort algorithm.
 5:    ;-------------------------------------------------------------
 6:    %include "io.mac"
 7:
 8:    SORTED       EQU    0
 9:    UNSORTED     EQU    1
10:    .CODE
11:    global   bubble_sort
12:    bubble_sort:
13:            pushad
14:            mov      EBP,ESP
15:
16:            ; ECX serves the same purpose as the end_index variable
17:            ; in the C procedure. ECX keeps the number of comparisons
18:            ; to be done in each pass. Note that ECX is decremented
19:            ; by 1 after each pass.
20:            mov      ECX, [EBP+40]   ; load array size into ECX
21:
22:    next_pass:
23:            dec      ECX             ; if # of comparisons is zero
24:            jz       sort_done       ; then we are done
25:            mov      EDI,ECX         ; else start another pass
26:
27:            ;DL is used to keep SORTED/UNSORTED status
28:            mov      DL,SORTED       ; set status to SORTED
29:
30:            mov      ESI,[EBP+36]    ; load array address into ESI
31:            ; ESI points to element i and ESI+4 to the next element
32:    pass:
33:            ; This loop represents one pass of the algorithm.
34:            ; Each iteration compares elements at [ESI] and [ESI+4]
35:            ; and swaps them if (([ESI]) < ([ESI+4])).
36:
37:            mov      EAX, [ESI]
38:            mov      EBX, [ESI+4]
39:            cmp      EAX,EBX
```

```
40:            jg      swap
41:
42:  increment:
43:            ; Increment ESI by 4 to point to the next element
44:            add     ESI,4
45:            dec     EDI
46:            jnz     pass
47:
48:            cmp     EDX,SORTED     ; if status remains SORTED
49:            je      sort_done      ; then sorting is done
50:            jmp     next_pass      ; else initiate another pass
51:
52:  swap:
53:            ; swap elements at [ESI] and [ESI+4]
54:            mov     [ESI+4],EAX    ; copy [ESI] in EAX to [ESI+4]
55:            mov     [ESI],EBX      ; copy [ESI+4] in EBX to [ESI]
56:            mov     EDX,UNSORTED   ; set status to UNSORTED
57:            jmp     increment
58:
59:  sort_done:
60:            popad
61:            ret     8
```

The while loop condition is tested by lines 48 to 50. The for loop body corresponds to lines 37 to 46 and 54 to 57. The rest of the code follows the pseudocode. Note that the array pointer is available in the stack at EBP + 36 and its size at EBP + 40, as we use pushad to save all registers.

Procedures with Variable Number of Parameters

In assembly language procedures, a variable number of parameters can be easily handled by the stack method of parameter passing. Only the stack size imposes a limit on the number of arguments that can be passed. The next example illustrates the use of the stack to pass a variable number of arguments in assembly language programs.

Example 12.3 *Passing a variable number of arguments via the stack.*
In this example, the variable_sum procedure receives a variable number of integers via the stack. The actual number of integers passed is the last argument pushed onto the stack before calling the procedure. The procedure finds the sum of the integers and returns this value in the EAX register.

The main procedure in Program 12.8 requests input from the user. Only nonzero values are accepted as valid input (entering a zero terminates the input). The read_number loop (lines 24 to 30) reads input numbers using GetLInt and pushes them onto the stack. The ECX register keeps a count of the number of input values, which is passed as the last parameter (line 32) before calling the variable_sum procedure. The state of the stack at line 53, after executing the enter instruction, is shown in Figure 12.5.

The variable_sum procedure first reads the number of parameters passed onto it from the stack at EBP + 8 into the ECX register. The add_loop (lines 60 to 63) successively reads each

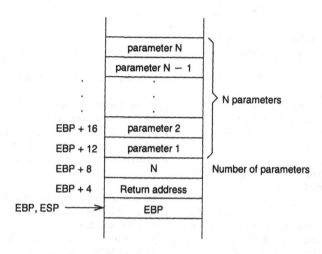

Figure 12.5 State of the stack after executing the `enter` statement.

integer from the stack and computes their sum in the EAX. Note that on line 61 we use a segment override prefix. If we write

```
add     EAX, [EBX]
```

the contents of the EBX are treated as the offset value into the data segment. However, our parameters are located in the stack segment. Therefore, it is necessary to indicate that the offset in EBX is relative to SS (and not DS) by using the SS: segment override prefix (line 61). The segment override prefixes—CS:, DS:, ES:, FS:, GS:, and SS:—can be placed in front of a memory operand to indicate a segment other than the default segment.

Program 12.8 A program to illustrate passing a variable number of parameters

```
 1: ;Variable number of parameters passed via stack    VARPARA.ASM
 2: ;
 3: ;          Objective: To show how variable number of parameters
 4: ;                     can be passed via the stack.
 5: ;              Input: Requests variable number of nonzero integers.
 6: ;                     A zero terminates the input.
 7: ;             Output: Outputs the sum of input numbers.
 8:
 9: %define CRLF    0DH,0AH     ; carriage return and line feed
10:
11: %include "io.mac"
12:
13: .DATA
14: prompt_msg  db  "Please input a set of nonzero integers.",CRLF
15:             db  "You must enter at least one integer.",CRLF
16:             db  "Enter zero to terminate the input.",0
17: sum_msg     db  "The sum of the input numbers is: ",0
18:
```

```
19:    .CODE
20:        .STARTUP
21:        PutStr  prompt_msg    ; request input numbers
22:        nwln
23:        sub     ECX,ECX       ; ECX keeps number count
24:    read_number:
25:        GetLInt EAX           ; read input number
26:        cmp     EAX,0         ; if the number is zero
27:        je      stop_reading  ; no more nuumbers to read
28:        push    EAX           ; place the number on stack
29:        inc     ECX           ; increment number count
30:        jmp     read_number
31:    stop_reading:
32:        push    ECX           ; place number count on stack
33:        call    variable_sum  ; returns sum in EAX
34:        ; clear parameter space on the stack
35:        inc     ECX           ; increment ECX to include count
36:        add     ECX,ECX       ; ECX = ECX * 4 (space in bytes)
37:        add     ECX,ECX
38:        add     ESP,ECX       ; update ESP to clear parameter
39:                              ; space on the stack
40:        PutStr  sum_msg       ; display the sum
41:        PutLInt EAX
42:        nwln
43:    done:
44:        .EXIT
45:
46:    ;-------------------------------------------------------------
47:    ;This procedure receives variable number of integers via the
48:    ;stack. The last parameter pushed on the stack should be
49:    ;the number of integers to be added. Sum is returned in EAX.
50:    ;-------------------------------------------------------------
51:    variable_sum:
52:        enter   0,0
53:        push    EBX           ; save EBX and ECX
54:        push    ECX
55:
56:        mov     ECX,[EBP+8]   ; ECX = # of integers to be added
57:        mov     EBX,EBP
58:        add     EBX,12        ; EBX = pointer to first number
59:        sub     EAX,EAX       ; sum = 0
60:    add_loop:
61:        add     EAX,[SS:EBX]  ; sum = sum + next number
62:        add     EBX,4         ; EBX points to the next integer
63:        loop    add_loop      ; repeat count in ECX
64:
65:        pop     ECX           ; restore registers
66:        pop     EBX
67:        leave
68:        ret                   ; parameter space cleared by main
```

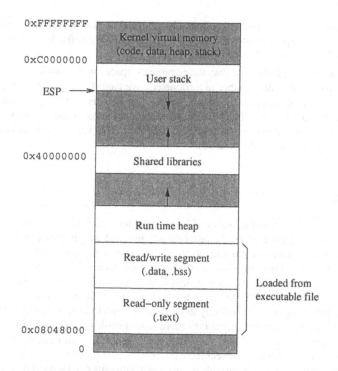

Figure 12.6 Memory layout of a Linux process.

A Few Notes

1. If you are running this program on a Linux system, you don't need the segment override prefix. The reason is that Linux and UNIX systems do not use the physical segmentation provided by the IA-32 architecture. Instead, these systems treat the memory as a single physical segment, which is partitioned into various logical segments. Figure 12.6 shows the memory layout for Linux. The bottom two segments are used for the code and data. For example, the code segment (.text) is placed in the bottom segment, which is a read-only segment. The next segment stores the data part (.data and .bss). The stack segment is placed below the kernel space.

2. In this example, we deliberately used the EBX to illustrate the use of segment override prefixes. We could have used the EBP itself to access the parameters. For example, the code

```
        add     EBP,12
        sub     EAX,EAX
add_loop:
        add     EAX,[EBP]
        add     EBP,4
        loop    add_loop
```

can replace the code at lines 58 to 63. A disadvantage of this modified code is that, since we have modified the EBP, we no longer can access, for example, the parameter count value in the stack. For this example, however, this method works fine. A better way is to use an index register to represent the offset relative to the EBP. We defer this discussion to the next chapter, which discusses the addressing modes.

3. Another interesting feature is that the parameter space on the stack is cleared by `main`. Since we pass a variable number of parameters, we cannot use `ret` to clear the parameter space. This is done in `main` by lines 35 to 38. The ECX is first incremented to include the count parameter (line 35). The byte count of the parameter space is computed on lines 36 and 37. These lines effectively multiply ECX by four. This value is added to the ESP register to clear the parameter space (line 38).

Summary

We started this chapter with a discussion of local variables. Such variables are dynamic as these variables come into existence when the procedure is invoked and disappear when the procedure terminates. As with parameter passing, local variables of a procedure can be stored either in registers or on the stack. Due to the limited number of registers available, only a few local variables can be mapped to registers. The stack avoids this limitation, but it is slow. Furthermore, we cannot use the registers for local variable storage in nonleaf and recursive procedures.

Real application programs are unlikely to be short enough to keep in a single file. It is advantageous to break large source programs into more manageable chunks. Then we can keep each chunk in a separate file (i.e., modules). We have discussed how such multimodule programs are written and assembled into a single executable file.

We have also discussed how a variable number of arguments can be passed onto procedures in the assembly language. When the stack is used for parameter passing, passing a variable number of arguments is straightforward. We have demonstrated this by means of an example.

13

Addressing Modes

In assembly language, specification of data required by instructions can be done in a variety of ways. In Chapter 9 we discussed four different addressing modes: register, immediate, direct, and indirect. The last two addressing modes specify operands in memory. However, such memory operands can be specified by several other addressing modes. Here we give a detailed description of these memory addressing modes.

Arrays are important for organizing a collection of related data. Although one-dimensional arrays are straightforward to implement, multidimensional arrays are more involved. This chapter discusses these issues in detail. Several examples are given to illustrate the use of the addressing modes in processing one- and two-dimensional arrays.

Introduction

Addressing mode refers how we specify the location of an operand that is required by an instruction. An operand can be at any of the following locations: in a register, in the instruction itself, in the memory, or at an I/O port. Chapter 20 discusses how operands located at an I/O port can be specified. Here we concentrate on how we can specify operands located in the first three locations. The three addressing modes are:

- *Register Addressing Mode:* In this addressing mode, as discussed in Chapter 9, processor registers provide the input operands and results are stored back in registers. Since the IA-32 architecture uses a two-address format, one operand specification acts as both source and destination. This addressing mode is the best way of specifying operands, as the delay in accessing the operands is minimal.

- *Immediate Addressing Mode:* This addressing mode can be used to specify at most one source operand. The operand value is encoded as part of the instruction. Thus, the operand is available as soon as the instruction is read.

- *Memory Addressing Modes:* When an operand is in memory, a variety of addressing modes is provided to specify it. Recall that we have to specify the logical address in order to specify the location of a memory operand. The logical address consists of two components: segment base and offset. Note that the offset is also referred to as the effective address. Memory addressing modes differ in how they specify the effective address.

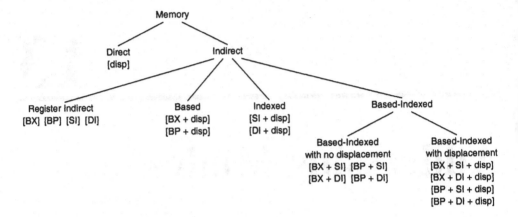

Figure 13.1 Memory addressing modes for 16-bit addresses.

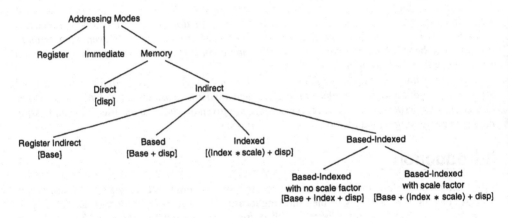

Figure 13.2 Addressing modes of the Pentium for 32-bit addresses.

We have already discussed the direct and register indirect addressing modes in Chapter 9. The direct addressing mode gives the effective address directly in the instruction. In the indirect addressing mode, the effective address is in one of the general-purpose registers. This chapter discusses the remaining memory addressing modes.

Memory Addressing Modes

The primary motivation for providing different addressing modes is to efficiently support high-level language constructs and data structures. The actual memory addressing modes available depend on the address size used (16 bits or 32 bits). The memory addressing modes available for 16-bit addresses are the same as those supported by the 8086. Figure 13.1 shows the default

Table 13.1 Differences between 16-bit and 32-bit addressing

	16-bit addressing	32-bit addressing
Base register	BX BP	EAX, EBX, ECX, EDX ESI, EDI, EBP, ESP
Index register	SI DI	EAX, EBX, ECX, EDX ESI, EDI, EBP
Scale factor	None	1, 2, 4, 8
Displacement	0, 8, 16 bits	0, 8, 32 bits

memory addressing modes available for 16-bit addresses. A more flexible set of addressing modes is supported for 32-bit addresses. These addressing modes are shown in Figure 13.2 and are summarized below:

Segment + Base + (Index * Scale) + displacement

```
CS      EAX     EAX     1       No displacement
SS      EBX     EBX     2       8-bit displacement
DS      ECX     ECX     4       32-bit displacement
ES      EDX     EDX     8
FS      ESI     ESI
GS      EDI     EDI
        EBP     EBP
        ESP
```

The differences between 16-bit and 32-bit addressing are summarized in Table 13.1. How does the processor know whether to use 16- or 32-bit addressing? As discussed in Chapter 4, it uses the D bit in the CS segment descriptor to determine if the address is 16 or 32 bits long (see page 70). It is, however, possible to override these defaults by using the size override prefixes:

66H   Operand size override prefix
67H   Address size override prefix

By using these prefixes, we can mix 16- and 32-bit data and addresses. Remember that our assembly language programs use 32-bit data and addresses. This, however, does not restrict us from using 16-bit data and addresses. For example, when we write

```
mov     EAX,123
```

the assembler generates the following machine language code:

```
B8  0000007B
```

However, when we use a 16-bit operand as in

```
mov     AX,123
```

the following code is generated by the assembler:

```
66 | B8 007B
```

The assembler automatically inserts the operand size override prefix (66H). Similarly, we can use 16-bit addresses. For instance, consider the following example:

```
mov    EAX, [BX]
```

The assembler automatically inserts the address size override prefix (67H) as shown below:

```
67 | 8B 07
```

It is also possible to mix both override prefixes as demonstrated by the following example. The assembly language statement

```
mov    AX, [BX]
```

causes the assembler to insert both operand and address size override prefixes:

```
66 | 67 | 8B 07
```

Based Addressing

In the based addressing mode, one of the registers acts as the base register in computing the effective address of an operand. The effective address is computed by adding the contents of the specified base register with a signed displacement value given as part of the instruction. For 16-bit addresses, the signed displacement is either an 8- or a 16-bit number. For 32-bit addresses, it is either an 8- or a 32-bit number.

Based addressing provides a convenient way to access individual elements of a structure. Typically, a base register can be set up to point to the base of the structure and the displacement can be used to access an element within the structure. For example, consider the following record of a course schedule:

Course number	Integer	2 bytes
Course title	Character string	38 bytes
Term offered	Single character	1 byte
Room number	Character string	5 bytes
Enrollment limit	Integer	2 bytes
Number registered	Integer	2 bytes
Total storage per record		50 bytes

In this example, suppose we want to find the number of available spaces in a particular course. We can let the EBX register point to the base address of the corresponding course record and use displacement to read the number of students registered and the enrollment limit for the course to compute the desired answer. This is illustrated in Figure 13.3.

This addressing mode is also useful in accessing arrays whose element size is not 2, 4, or 8 bytes. In this case, the displacement can be set equal to the offset to the beginning of the array, and the base register holds the offset of a specific element relative to the beginning of the array.

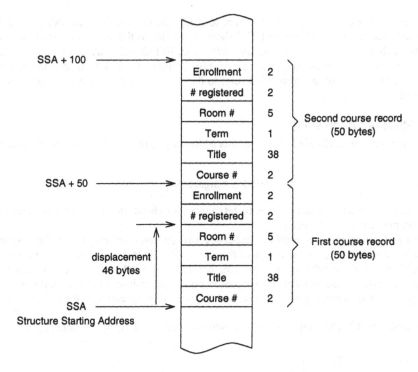

Figure 13.3 Course record layout in memory.

Indexed Addressing

In this addressing mode, the effective address is computed as

(Index * scale factor) + signed displacement.

For 16-bit addresses, no scaling factor is allowed (see Table 13.1 on page 275). For 32-bit addresses, a scale factor of 2, 4, or 8 can be specified. Of course, we can use a scale factor in the 16-bit addressing mode by using an address size override prefix.

The indexed addressing mode is often used to access elements of an array. The beginning of the array is given by the displacement, and the value of the index register selects an element within the array. The scale factor is particularly useful to access arrays whose element size is 2, 4, or 8 bytes.

The following are valid instructions using the indexed addressing mode to specify one of the operands.

```
add    EAX, [EDI+20]
mov    EAX, [marks_table+ESI*4]
add    EAX, [table1+ESI]
```

In the second instruction, the assembler would supply a constant displacement that represents the offset of marks_table in the data segment. Assume that each element of marks_table takes four bytes. Since we are using a scale factor of four, ESI should have the index value. For example, if we want to access the tenth element, ESI should have nine as the index value starts with zero.

If no scale factor is used as in the last instruction, ESI should hold the offset of the element in *bytes* relative to the beginning of the array. For example, if table1 is an array of four-byte elements, ESI register should have 36 to refer to the tenth element. By using the scale factor, we avoid such byte counting.

Based-Indexed Addressing

Based-Indexed with No Scale Factor   In this addressing mode, the effective address is computed as

$$\text{Base} + \text{Index} + \text{signed displacement.}$$

The displacement can be a signed 8- or 16-bit number for 16-bit addresses; it can be a signed 8- or 32-bit number for 32-bit addresses.

This addressing mode is useful in accessing two-dimensional arrays with the displacement representing the offset to the beginning of the array. This mode can also be used to access arrays of records where the displacement represents the offset to a field in a record. In addition, this addressing mode is used to access arrays passed on to a procedure. In this case, the base register could point to the beginning of the array, and an index register can hold the offset to a specific element.

Assuming that EBX points to table1, which consists of four-byte elements, we can use the code

```
mov     EAX, [EBX+ESI]
cmp     EAX, [EBX+ESI+4]
```

to compare two successive elements of table1. This type of code is particularly useful if the table1 pointer is passed as a parameter.

Based-Indexed with Scale Factor   In this addressing mode, the effective address is computed as

$$\text{Base} + (\text{Index} * \text{scale factor}) + \text{signed displacement.}$$

This addressing mode provides an efficient indexing mechanism into a two-dimensional array when the element size is 2, 4, or 8 bytes.

Arrays

Arrays are useful in organizing a collection of related data items, such as test marks of a class, salaries of employees, and so on. We have used arrays of characters to represent strings. Such arrays are one-dimensional: only a single subscript is necessary to access a character in the array. High-level languages support multidimensional arrays. In this section, we discuss both one-dimensional and multidimensional arrays.

One-Dimensional Arrays

A one-dimensional array of test marks can be declared in C as

```
int     test_marks [10];
```

In C, the subscript always starts at zero. Thus, `test_marks[0]` gives the first student's mark and `test_marks[9]` gives the last student's mark.

Array declaration in high-level languages specifies the following five attributes:

- Name of the array (`test_marks`),
- Number of the elements (10),
- Element size (4 bytes),
- Type of element (integer), and
- Index range (0 to 9).

From this information, the amount of storage space required for the array can be easily calculated. Storage space in bytes is given by

$$\text{Storage space} = \text{number of elements} * \text{element size in bytes.}$$

In our example, it is equal to $10 * 4 = 40$ bytes. In the assembly language, arrays are implemented by allocating the required amount of storage space. For example, the `test_marks` array can be declared as

```
test_marks     resd     10
```

An array name can be assigned to this storage space. But that is all the support you get in assembly language! It is up to you as a programmer to "properly" access the array taking the element size and the range of subscripts into account.

You need to know how the array is stored in memory in order to access elements of the array. For one-dimensional arrays, representation of the array in memory is rather direct: array elements are stored linearly in the same order as shown in Figure 13.4. In the remainder of this section, we use the convention used for arrays in C (i.e., subscripts are assumed to begin with 0).

To access an element we need to know its displacement value in bytes relative to the beginning of the array. Since we know the element size in bytes, it is rather straightforward to compute the displacement from the subscript value:

$$\text{displacement} = \text{subscript} * \text{element size in bytes.}$$

For example, to access the sixth student's mark (i.e., subscript is 5), you have to use $5 * 4 = 20$ as the displacement value into the `test_marks` array. Later we present an example that computes the sum of a one-dimensional integer array. If the array element size is 2, 4, or 8 bytes, we can use the scale factor to avoid computing displacement in bytes.

Multidimensional Arrays

Programs often require arrays of more than one dimension. For example, we need a two-dimensional array of size 50×3 to store test marks of a class of 50 students taking three tests during a semester. For most programs, arrays of up to three dimensions are adequate. In this section, we discuss how two-dimensional arrays are represented and manipulated in the assembly language. Our discussion can be generalized to higher-dimensional arrays.

For example, a 5×3 array to store test marks can be declared in C as

```
int     class_marks[5][3];    /* 5 rows and 3 columns */
```

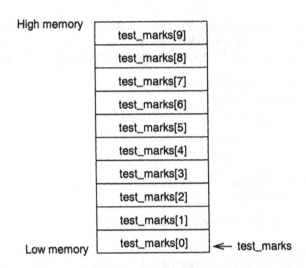

High memory

Low memory ← test_marks

Figure 13.4 One-dimensional array storage representation.

Storage representation of such arrays is not as direct as that for one-dimensional arrays. Since the memory is one-dimensional (i.e., linear array of bytes), we need to transform the two-dimensional structure to a one-dimensional structure. This transformation can be done in one of two common ways:

- Order the array elements row-by-row, starting with the first row, or
- Order the array elements column-by-column, starting with the first column.

The first method, called the *row-major ordering*, is shown in Figure 13.5*a*. Row-major ordering is used in most high-level languages including C. The other method, called the *column-major ordering*, is shown in Figure 13.5*b*. Column-major ordering is used in FORTRAN. In the remainder of this section, we focus on the row-major ordering scheme.

Why do we need to know the underlying storage representation? When we are using a high-level language, we really do not have to bother about the storage representation. Access to arrays is provided by subscripts: one subscript for each dimension of the array. However, when using assembly language, we need to know the storage representation in order to access individual elements of the array for reasons discussed next.

In the assembly language, we can allocate storage space for the class_marks array as

```
class_marks     resd     5*3
```

This statement simply allocates the 60 bytes required to store the array. Now we need a formula to translate row and column subscripts to the corresponding displacement. In the C language, which uses row-major ordering and subscripts start with zero, we can express displacement of an element at row i and column j as

$$displacement = (i * COLUMNS + j) * ELEMENT\_SIZE,$$

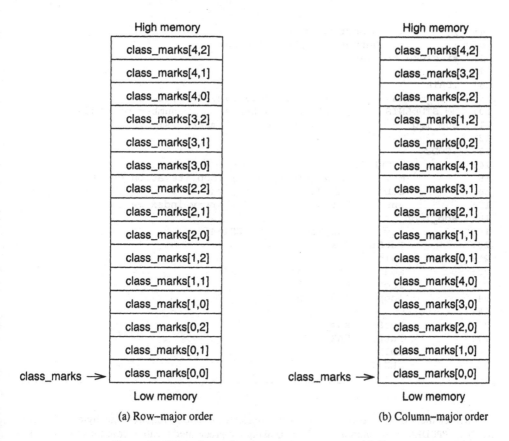

	High memory			High memory
	class_marks[4,2]			class_marks[4,2]
	class_marks[4,1]			class_marks[3,2]
	class_marks[4,0]			class_marks[2,2]
	class_marks[3,2]			class_marks[1,2]
	class_marks[3,1]			class_marks[0,2]
	class_marks[3,0]			class_marks[4,1]
	class_marks[2,2]			class_marks[3,1]
	class_marks[2,1]			class_marks[2,1]
	class_marks[2,0]			class_marks[1,1]
	class_marks[1,2]			class_marks[0,1]
	class_marks[1,1]			class_marks[4,0]
	class_marks[1,0]			class_marks[3,0]
	class_marks[0,2]			class_marks[2,0]
	class_marks[0,1]			class_marks[1,0]
class_marks →	class_marks[0,0]		class_marks →	class_marks[0,0]
	Low memory			Low memory
	(a) Row–major order			(b) Column–major order

Figure 13.5 Two-dimensional array storage representation.

where COLUMNS is the number of columns in the array and ELEMENT_SIZE is the number of bytes required to store an element. For example, displacement of class_marks[3,1] is (3 ∗ 3 + 1) ∗ 4 = 40. Later we give an example to illustrate how two-dimensional arrays are manipulated.

Our First Program

This example demonstrates how one-dimensional arrays can be manipulated. Program 13.1 finds the sum of the test_marks array and displays the result.

Program 13.1 Computing the sum of a one-dimensional array

```
1:  ;Sum of a long integer array                        ARRAY_SUM.ASM
2:  ;
3:  ;          Objective: To find sum of all elements of an array.
```

```
 4:  ;                Input:  None.
 5:  ;                Output: Displays the sum.
 6:  %include "io.mac"
 7:
 8:  .DATA
 9:  test_marks       DD   90,50,70,94,81,40,67,55,60,73
10:  NO_STUDENTS      EQU  ($-test_marks)/4      ; number of students
11:  sum_msg          DB   'The sum of test marks is: ',0
12:
13:  .CODE
14:          .STARTUP
15:          mov     CX,NO_STUDENTS    ; loop iteration count
16:          sub     EAX,EAX          ; sum := 0
17:          sub     ESI,ESI          ; array index := 0
18:  add_loop:
19:          mov     EBX,[test_marks+ESI*4]
20:          PutLInt EBX
21:          nwln
22:          add     EAX,[test_marks+ESI*4]
23:          inc     ESI
24:          loop    add_loop
25:
26:          PutStr  sum_msg
27:          PutLInt EAX
28:          nwln
29:          .EXIT
```

Each element of the test_marks array, declared on line 9, requires four bytes. The array size NO_STUDENTS is computed on line 10 using the predefined location counter symbol $. The predefined symbol $ is always set to the current offset in the segment. Thus, on line 10, $ points to the byte after the array storage space. Therefore, ($-test_marks) gives the storage space in bytes and dividing this by four gives the number of elements in the array. We are using the indexed addressing mode with a scale factor of four on lines 19 and 22. Remember that the scale factor is only allowed in the 32-bit mode.

Illustrative Examples

We now present several examples to illustrate the usefulness of the various addressing modes. The first example sorts an array of integers using the insertion sort algorithm, and the second example implements a binary search to locate a value in a sorted array. Our last example demonstrates how 2-dimensional array are manipulated in the assembly language.

Example 13.1 *Sorting an integer array using the insertion sort.*
This example requests a set of integers from the user and displays these numbers in sorted order. The main procedure reads a maximum of MAX_SIZE integers (lines 20 to 28). It accepts only nonnegative numbers. Entering a negative number terminates the input (lines 24 and 25).

The main procedure passes the array pointer and its size (lines 30 to 34) to the insertion sort procedure. The remainder of the main procedure displays the sorted array returned by the sort procedure. Note that the main procedure uses the indirect addressing mode on lines 26 and 41.

The basic principle behind the insertion sort is simple: insert a new number into the sorted array in its proper place. To apply this algorithm, we start with an empty array. Then insert the first number. Now the array is in sorted order with just one element. Next insert the second number in its proper place. This results in a sorted array of size two. Repeat this process until all the numbers are inserted. The pseudocode for this algorithm, shown below, assumes that the array index starts with 0:

> insertion_sort (array, size)
>   **for** ($i = 1$ to size-1)
>   temp := array[i]
> $j := i - 1$
>   **while** ((temp $<$ array[j]) AND ($j \geq 0$))
>   array[$j+1$] := array[j]
> $j := j - 1$
>   **end while**
>   array[$j+1$] := temp
>   **end for**
> **end** insertion_sort

Here, index i points to the number to be inserted. The array to the left of i is in sorted order. The numbers to be inserted are the ones located at or to the right of index i. The next number to be inserted is at i. The implementation of the insertion sort procedure, shown in Program 13.2, follows the pseudocode.

Program 13.2 Insertion sort

```
 1:  ;Sorting an array by insertion sort                    INS_SORT.ASM
 2:  ;
 3:  ;          Objective: To sort an integer array using insertion sort.
 4:  ;              Input: Requests numbers to fill array.
 5:  ;             Output: Displays sorted array.
 6:  %include "io.mac"
 7:
 8:  .DATA
 9:  MAX_SIZE          EQU 100
10:  input_prompt      db   "Please enter input array: "
11:                    db   " (negative number terminates input)",0
12:  out_msg           db   "The sorted array is:",0
13:
14:  .UDATA
15:  array             resd  MAX_SIZE
16:
17:  .CODE
18:          .STARTUP
19:          PutStr  input_prompt ; request input array
20:          mov     EBX,array
21:          mov     ECX,MAX_SIZE
```

```
22:   array_loop:
23:          GetLInt EAX          ; read an array number
24:          cmp     EAX,0         ; negative number?
25:          jl      exit_loop     ; if so, stop reading numbers
26:          mov     [EBX],EAX     ; otherwise, copy into array
27:          add     EBX,4         ; increment array address
28:          loop    array_loop    ; iterates a maximum of MAX_SIZE
29:   exit_loop:
30:          mov     EDX,EBX       ; EDX keeps the actual array size
31:          sub     EDX,array     ; EDX = array size in bytes
32:          shr     EDX,2         ; divide by 4 to get array size
33:          push    EDX           ; push array size & array pointer
34:          push    array
35:          call    insertion_sort
36:          PutStr  out_msg       ; display sorted array
37:          nwln
38:          mov     ECX,EDX
39:          mov     EBX,array
40:   display_loop:
41:          PutLInt [EBX]
42:          nwln
43:          add     EBX,4
44:          loop    display_loop
45:   done:
46:          .EXIT
47:
48:   ;----------------------------------------------------------------
49:   ; This procedure receives a pointer to an array of integers
50:   ; and the array size via the stack. The array is sorted by
51:   ; using insertion sort. All registers are preserved.
52:   ;----------------------------------------------------------------
53:   %define   SORT_ARRAY   EBX
54:   insertion_sort:
55:          pushad                    ; save registers
56:          mov     EBP,ESP
57:          mov     EBX,[EBP+36]      ; copy array pointer
58:          mov     ECX,[EBP+40]      ; copy array size
59:          mov     ESI,4             ; array left of ESI is sorted
60:   for_loop:
61:          ; variables of the algorithm are mapped as follows.
62:          ; EDX = temp, ESI = i, and EDI = j
63:          mov     EDX,[SORT_ARRAY+ESI] ; temp = array[i]
64:          mov     EDI,ESI           ; j = i-1
65:          sub     EDI,4
66:   while_loop:
67:          cmp     EDX,[SORT_ARRAY+EDI]   ; temp < array[j]
68:          jge     exit_while_loop
69:          ; array[j+1] = array[j]
70:          mov     EAX,[SORT_ARRAY+EDI]
71:          mov     [SORT_ARRAY+EDI+4],EAX
72:          sub     EDI,4             ; j = j-1
```

```
73:                cmp      EDI,0            ; j >= 0
74:                jge      while_loop
75:     exit_while_loop:
76:                ; array[j+1] = temp
77:                mov      [SORT_ARRAY+EDI+4],EDX
78:                add      ESI,4            ; i = i+1
79:                dec      ECX
80:                cmp      ECX,1            ; if ECX = 1, we are done
81:                jne      for_loop
82:     sort_done:
83:                popad                     ; restore registers
84:                ret      8
```

Since the sort procedure does not return any value to the main program in registers, we can use pushad (line 55) and popad (line 83) to save and restore registers. As pushad saves all eight registers on the stack, the offset is appropriately adjusted to access the array size and array pointer parameters (lines 57 and 58).

The while loop is implemented by lines 66 to 74, and the for loop is implemented by lines 60 to 81. Note that the array pointer is copied to the EBX (line 57), and line 53 assigns a convenient label to this. We have used the based-indexed addressing mode on lines 63, 67, and 70 without any displacement and on lines 71 and 77 with displacement. Based addressing is used on lines 57 and 58 to access parameters from the stack.

Example 13.2 *Binary search procedure.*
Binary search is an efficient algorithm to locate a value in a sorted array. The search process starts with the whole array. The value at the middle of the array is compared with the number we are looking for: if there is a match, its index is returned. Otherwise, the search process is repeated either on the lower half (if the number is less than the value at the middle), or on the upper half (if the number is greater than the value at the middle). The pseudocode of the algorithm is given below:

```
binary_search (array, size, number)
     lower := 0
     upper := size − 1
     while (lower ≤ upper)
          middle := (lower + upper)/2
          if (number = array[middle])
          then
               return (middle)
          else
               if (number < array[middle])
               then
                    upper := middle − 1
               else
                    lower := middle + 1
               end if
          end if
```

> **end while**
> **return** (0)   {number not found}
> **end** binary_search

The listing of the binary search program is given in Program 13.3. The main procedure is similar to that in the last example. In the binary search procedure, the lower and upper index variables are mapped to the AX and CX registers, respectively. The number to be searched is stored in the DX and the array pointer is in the EBX. Register SI keeps the middle index value.

Program 13.3 Binary search

```
 1:  ;Binary search of a sorted integer array       BIN_SRCH.ASM
 2:  ;
 3:  ;          Objective: To implement binary search of a sorted
 4:  ;                     integer array.
 5:  ;              Input: Requests numbers to fill array and a
 6:  ;                     number to be searched for from user.
 7:  ;             Output: Displays the position of the number in
 8:  ;                     the array if found; otherwise, not found
 9:  ;                     message.
10:  %include "io.mac"
11:
12:  .DATA
13:  MAX_SIZE       EQU 100
14:  input_prompt   db  "Please enter input array (in sorted order): "
15:                 db  "(negative number terminates input)",0
16:  query_number   db  "Enter the number to be searched: ",0
17:  out_msg        db  "The number is at position ",0
18:  not_found_msg  db  "Number not in the array!",0
19:  query_msg      db  "Do you want to quit (Y/N): ",0
20:
21:  .UDATA
22:  array          resw  MAX_SIZE
23:
24:  .CODE
25:          .STARTUP
26:          PutStr  input_prompt ; request input array
27:          nwln
28:          sub     ESI,ESI      ; set index to zero
29:          mov     CX,MAX_SIZE
30:  array_loop:
31:          GetInt  AX             ; read an array number
32:
33:          cmp     AX,0            ; negative number?
34:          jl      exit_loop       ; if so, stop reading numbers
35:          mov     [array+ESI*2],AX ; otherwise, copy into array
36:          inc     ESI             ; increment array index
37:          loop    array_loop      ; iterates a maximum of MAX_SIZE
38:  exit_loop:
39:  read_input:
40:          PutStr  query_number ; request number to be searched for
```

```
41:           GetInt  AX              ; read the number
42:           push    AX              ; push number, size & array pointer
43:           push    SI
44:           push    array
45:           call    binary_search
46:           ; binary_search returns in AX the position of the number
47:           ; in the array; if not found, it returns 0.
48:           cmp     AX,0            ; number found?
49:           je      not_found       ; if not, display number not found
50:           PutStr  out_msg         ; else, display number position
51:           PutInt  AX
52:           jmp     user_query
53:   not_found:
54:           PutStr  not_found_msg
55:   user_query:
56:           nwln
57:           PutStr  query_msg       ; query user whether to terminate
58:           GetCh   AL              ; read response
59:           cmp     AL,'Y'          ; if response is not 'Y'
60:           jne     read_input      ; repeat the loop
61:   done:                           ; otherwise, terminate program
62:           .EXIT
63:
64:   ;-------------------------------------------------------------
65:   ; This procedure receives a pointer to an array of integers,
66:   ; the array size, and a number to be searched via the stack.
67:   ; It returns in AX the position of the number in the array
68:   ; if found; otherwise, returns 0.
69:   ; All registers, except AX, are preserved.
70:   ;-------------------------------------------------------------
71:   binary_search:
72:           enter   0,0
73:           push    EBX
74:           push    ESI
75:           push    CX
76:           push    DX
77:           mov     EBX,[EBP+8]     ; copy array pointer
78:           mov     CX,[EBP+12]     ; copy array size
79:           mov     DX,[EBP+14]     ; copy number to be searched
80:           xor     AX,AX           ; lower = 0
81:           dec     CX              ; upper = size-1
82:   while_loop:
83:           cmp     AX,CX           ;lower > upper?
84:           ja      end_while
85:           sub     ESI,ESI
86:           mov     SI,AX           ; middle = (lower + upper)/2
87:           add     SI,CX
88:           shr     SI,1
89:           cmp     DX,[EBX+ESI*2]     ; number = array[middle]?
90:           je      search_done
91:           jg      upper_half
```

```
 92:    lower_half:
 93:            dec       SI              ; middle = middle-1
 94:            mov       CX,SI           ; upper = middle-1
 95:            jmp       while_loop
 96:    upper_half:
 97:            inc       SI              ; middle = middle+1
 98:            mov       AX,SI           ; lower = middle+1
 99:            jmp       while_loop
100:    end_while:
101:            sub       AX,AX           ; number not found (clear AX)
102:            jmp       skip1
103:    search_done:
104:            inc       SI              ; position = index+1
105:            mov       AX,SI           ; return position
106:    skip1:
107:            pop       DX              ; restore registers
108:            pop       CX
109:            pop       ESI
110:            pop       EBX
111:            leave
112:            ret       8
```

Since the binary search procedure returns a value in the AX register, we cannot use the pusha instruction as in the last example. On line 89, we use a scale factor of two to convert the index value in SI to byte count. Also, a single comparison (line 89) is sufficient to test multiple conditions (i.e., equal to, greater than, or less than). If the number is found in the array, the index value in SI is returned via AX (line 105).

Example 13.3 *Finding the sum of a column in a two-dimensional array.*
This example illustrates how two-dimensional arrays are manipuilated in the assembly language. This example also demonstrates the use of advanced addressing modes in accessing multidimensional arrays.

Consider the class_marks array representing the test scores of a class. For simplicity, assume that there are only five students in the class. Also, assume that the class is given three tests. As we have discussed before, we can use a 5 × 3 array to store the marks. Each row represents the three test marks of a student in the class. The first column represents the marks of the first test; the second column represents the marks of the second test, and so on. The objective of this example is to find the sum of the last test marks for the class. The program listing is given below.

Program 13.4 Finding the sum of a column in a two-dimensional array

```
1:    ;Sum of a column in a 2-dimensional array       TEST_SUM.ASM
2:    ;
3:    ;         Objective: To demonstrate array index manipulation
4:    ;                    in a two-dimensional array of integers.
5:    ;             Input: None.
6:    ;            Output: Displays the sum.
```

```
 7:    %include "io.mac"
 8:
 9:    .DATA
10:    NO_ROWS          EQU  5
11:    NO_COLUMNS       EQU  3
12:    NO_ROW_BYTES     EQU  NO_COLUMNS * 2   ; number of bytes per row
13:    class_marks      dw   90,89,99
14:                     dw   79,66,70
15:                     dw   70,60,77
16:                     dw   60,55,68
17:                     dw   51,59,57
18:
19:    sum_msg          db   "The sum of the last test marks is: ",0
20:
21:    .CODE
22:            .STARTUP
23:            mov     CX,NO_ROWS     ; loop iteration count
24:            sub     AX,AX          ; sum = 0
25:            ; ESI = index of class_marks[0,2]
26:            sub     EBX,EBX
27:            mov     ESI,NO_COLUMNS-1
28:    sum_loop:
29:            add     AX,[class_marks+EBX+ESI*2]
30:            add     EBX,NO_ROW_BYTES
31:            loop    sum_loop
32:
33:            PutStr  sum_msg
34:            PutInt  AX
35:            nwln
36:    done:
37:            .EXIT
```

To access individual test marks, we use based-indexed addressing with a displacement on line 29. Note that even though we have used

```
[class_marks+EBX+ESI*2]
```

it is translated by the assembler as

```
[EBX+(ESI*2)+constant]
```

where constant is the offset of class_marks. For this to work, the EBX should store the offset of the row in which we are interested. For this reason, after initializing the EBX to zero to point to the first row (line 29), NO_ROW_BYTES is added in the loop body (line 30). The ESI register is used as the column index. This works for row-major ordering.

Summary

The addressing mode refers to the specification of operands required by an assembly language instruction. We discussed several memory addressing modes supported by the IA-32 architecture.

We showed by means of examples how these addressing modes are useful in supporting features of high-level languages.

Arrays are useful for representing a collection of related data. In high-level languages, programmers do not have to worry about the underlying storage representation used to store arrays in the memory. However, when manipulating arrays in the assembly language, we need to know this information. This is so because accessing individual elements of an array involves computing the corresponding displacement value. Although there are two common ways of storing a multidimensional array—row-major or column-major order—most high-level languages, including C, use the row-major order. We presented examples to illustrate how one- and two-dimensional arrays are manipulated in the assembly language.

14

Arithmetic Instructions

We start this chapter with a detailed discussion of the six status flags—zero, carry, overflow, sign, parity, and auxiliary flags. We have already used these flags in our assembly language programs. The discussion here helps us understand how the processor executes some of the conditional jump instructions. The next section deals with multiplication and division instructions. The IA-32 instruction set includes multiplication and division instructions for both signed and unsigned integers. We then present several examples to illustrate the use of the instructions discussed in this chapter. The chapter concludes with a summary.

Introduction

We have discussed the flags register in Chapter 4. Six flags in this register are used to monitor the outcome of the arithmetic, logical, and related operations. By now you are familiar with the purpose of some of these flags. The six flags are the zero flag (ZF), carry flag (CF), overflow flag (OF), sign flag (SF), auxiliary flag (AF), and parity flag (PF). For obvious reasons, these six flags are called the *status* flags.

When an arithmetic operation is performed, some of the flags are updated (set or cleared) to indicate certain properties of the result of that operation. For example, if the result of an arithmetic operation is zero, the zero flag is set (i.e., ZF = 1). Once the flags are updated, we can use the conditional branch instructions to alter flow control. We have discussed several types of conditional jump instructions, including jump on less than or equal, greater than, and so on. However, we have not described how the jumps test for the condition. We discuss these details in this chapter.

The IA-32 instruction set provides several arithmetic instructions. We have already used some of these instructions (e.g., add and sub). The instruction set supports the four basic operations: addition, subtraction, multiplication, and division. The addition and subtraction operations do not require separate instructions for signed and unsigned numbers. In fact, we do not need even the subtract instructions as the subtract operation can be treated as adding a negative value.

Multiplication and division operations, however, need separate instructions. In addition, the format of these instructions is slightly different in the sense they typically specify only a single operand. The other operand is assumed to be in a designated register. Since we have covered the addition and subtraction instructions in Chapter 9, we will focus on the multiplication and division instructions in this chapter.

Status Flags

The six status flags are affected by most of the arithmetic instructions we discuss in this chapter. You should note that once a flag is set or cleared, it remains in that state until another instruction changes its value. Also note that not all assembly language instructions affect all the flags. Some instructions affect all six status flags, whereas other instructions affect none of the flags. And there are other instructions that affect only a subset of these flags. For example, the arithmetic instructions add and sub affect all six flags, but inc and dec instructions affect all but the carry flag. The mov, push, and pop instructions, on the other hand, do not affect any of the flags.

Here is an example illustrating how the zero flag changes with instruction execution.

```
        ;initially, assume that ZF is 0
        mov     EAX,55H    ; ZF is still 0
        sub     EAX,55H    ; result is zero
                           ; Thus, ZF is set (ZF = 1)
        push    EBX        ; ZF remains 1
        mov     EBX,EAX    ; ZF remains 1
        pop     EDX        ; ZF remains 1
        mov     ECX,0      ; ZF remains 1
        inc     ECX        ; result is 1
                           ; Thus, ZF is cleared (ZF = 0)
```

As we show later, these flags can be tested either individually or in combination to affect the flow control of a program.

In understanding the workings of these status flags, you should know how signed and unsigned integers are represented. At this point, it is a good idea to review the material presented in Appendix A.

The Zero Flag

The purpose of the zero flag is to indicate whether the execution of the last instruction that affects the zero flag has produced a zero result. If the result was zero, ZF = 1; otherwise, ZF = 0. This is slightly confusing! You may want to take a moment to see through the confusion.

Although it is fairly intuitive to understand how the sub instruction affects the zero flag, it is not so obvious with other instructions. The following examples show some typical cases.

The code

```
        mov     AL,0FH
        add     AL,0F1H
```

sets the zero flag (i.e., ZF = 1). This is because, after executing the add instruction, the AL would contain zero (all eight bits zero). In a similar fashion, the code

```
        mov     AX,0FFFFH
        inc     AX
```

also sets the zero flag. The same is true for the following code:

```
        mov     EAX,1
        dec     EAX
```

Related Instructions   The following two conditional jump instructions test this flag:

```
jz    jump if zero (jump is taken if ZF = 1)
jnz   jump if not zero (jump is taken if ZF = 0)
```

Usage   There are two main uses for the zero flag: testing for equality, and counting to a preset value.

Testing for Equality: The cmp instruction is often used to do this. Recall that cmp performs subtraction. The main difference between cmp and sub is that cmp does not store the result of the subtract operation. The cmp instruction performs the subtract operation only to set the status flags. Here are some examples:

```
cmp     char,'$'      ; ZF = 1 if char is $
```

Similarly, two registers can be compared to see if they both have the same value.

```
cmp     EAX,EBX
```

Counting to a Preset Value: Another important use of the zero flag is shown below. Consider the following code:

```
sum = 0
for (i = 1 to M)
    for (j = 1 to N)
        sum = sum + 1
    end for
end for
```

The equivalent code in the assembly language is written as follows (assume that both M and N are ≥ 1):

```
            sub     EAX,EAX    ; EAX = 0 (EAX stores sum)
            mov     EDX,M
outer_loop:
            mov     ECX,N
inner_loop:
            inc     EAX
            loop    inner_loop
            dec     EDX
            jnz     outer_loop
exit_loops:
            mov     sum,EAX
```

In the above example, the inner loop count is placed in the ECX register so that we can use the loop instruction to iterate. Incidentally, the loop instruction does not affect any of the flags.

Since we have two nested loops to handle, we are forced to use another register to keep the outer loop count. We use the dec instruction and the zero flag to see if the outer loop has executed M times. This code is more efficient than initializing the EDX register to one and using the code

```
inc     EDX
cmp     EDX,M
jle     outer_loop
```

in place of the dec/jnz instruction combination.

The Carry Flag

The carry flag records the fact that the result of an arithmetic operation on unsigned numbers is out of range (too big or too small) to fit the destination register or memory location. Consider the example

```
mov     AL,0FH
add     AL,0F1H
```

The addition of 0FH and F1H would produce a result of 100H that requires 9 bits to store, as shown below.

```
  00001111B   (0FH = 15D)
  11110001B   (F1H = 241D)
1 00000000B   (100H = 256D)
```

Since the destination register AL is only 8 bits long, the carry flag would be set to indicate that the result is too big to be held in AL.

To understand when the carry flag would be set, it is helpful to remember the range of unsigned numbers that can be represented. The range is given below for easy reference.

Size (bits)	Range
8	0 to 255
16	0 to 65,535
32	0 to 4,294,967,295

Any operation that produces a result that is outside this range sets the carry flag to indicate an underflow or overflow condition. It is obvious that any negative result is out of range, as illustrated by the following example:

```
mov     EAX,12AEH   ;EAX = 4782D
sub     EAX,12AFH   ;EAX = 4782D - 4783D
```

Executing the above code will set the carry flag because 12AFH − 12AFH produces a negative result (i.e., the subtract operation generates a borrow), which is too small to be represented using unsigned numbers. Thus, the carry flag is set to indicate this underflow condition.

Executing the code

```
mov     AL,0FFH
inc     AL
```

or the code

```
mov     EAX,0
dec     EAX
```

does not set the carry flag as we might expect because inc and dec instructions do not affect the carry flag.

Related Instructions   The following two conditional jump instructions test this flag:

```
jc      jump if carry (jump is taken if CF = 1)
jnc     jump if not carry (jump is taken if CF = 0)
```

Usage   The carry flag is useful in several situations:

* To propagate carry or borrow in multiword addition or subtraction operations.
* To detect overflow/underflow conditions.
* To test a bit using the shift/rotate family of instructions.

To Propagate Carry/Borrow: The assembly language arithmetic instructions can operate on 8-, 16-, or 32-bit data. If two operands, each more than 32 bits, are to be added, the addition has to proceed in steps by adding two 32-bit numbers at a time. The following example illustrates how we can add two 64-bit unsigned numbers. For convenience, we use the hex representation.

$$
\begin{array}{rl}
& \quad 1 \quad \leftarrow \text{carry from lower 32 bits} \\
x = & 3710\ 26A8\ 1257\ 9AE7H \\
y = & 489B\ A321\ FE60\ 4213H \\
\hline
& 7FAB\ C9CA\ 10B7\ DCFAH
\end{array}
$$

To accomplish this, we need two addition operations. The first operation adds the least significant (lower half) 32 bits of the two operands. This produces the lower half of the result. This addition operation could produce a carry that should be added to the upper 32 bits of the input. The other add operation performs the addition of the most significant (upper half) 32 bits and any carry generated by the first addition. This operation produces the upper half of the 64-bit result.

As an example consider adding two 64-bit numbers in the registers EBX:EAX and EDX:ECX with EAX and ECX holding the lower 32-bit values of the two numbers. Then we can use the following code to add these two values:

```
add     EAX,ECX
adc     EBX,EDX
```

It leaves the 64-bit result in the EBX:EAX register pair. Notice that we use adc to do the second addition as we want to add any carry generated by the first addition. An overflow occurs if there is a carry out of the second addition, which sets the carry flag.

We can extend this process to larger numbers. For example, adding two 128-bit numbers involves a four-step process, where each step adds two 32-bit words. The first addition can be done using add but the remaining three additions must be done with the adc instruction. Similarly, the sub and other operations also require multiple steps when the numbers require more than 32 bits.

To Detect Overflow/Underflow Conditions: In the previous example, if the second addition produces a carry, the result is too big to be held by 64 bits. In this case, the carry flag would be set to indicate the overflow condition. It is up to the programmer to handle such error conditions.

Testing a Bit: When using shift and rotate instructions (introduced in Chapter 9), the bit that has been shifted or rotated out is captured in the carry flag. This bit can be either the most significant bit (in the case of a left-shift or rotate), or the least significant bit (in the case of a right-shift or rotate). Once the bit is in the carry flag, conditional execution of the code is possible using conditional jump instructions that test the carry flag: jc (jump on carry) and jnc (jump if no carry).

Why inc and dec Do Not Affect the Carry Flag   We have stated that the inc and dec instructions do not affect the carry flag. The rationale for this is twofold:

1. The instructions inc and dec are typically used to maintain iteration or loop count. Using 32 bits, the number of iterations can be as high as 4,294,967,295. This number is sufficiently large for most applications. What if we need a count that is greater than this? Do we have to use add instead of inc? This leads to the second, and the main, reason.

2. The condition detected by the carry flag can also be detected by the zero flag. Why? Because inc and dec change the number only by 1. For example, suppose that the ECX register has reached its maximum value 4,294,967,295 (FFFFFFFFH). If we then execute

```
inc    ECX
```

we would normally expect the carry flag to be set to 1. However, we can detect this condition by noting that ECX = 0, which sets the zero flag. Thus, setting the carry flag is really redundant for these instructions.

The Overflow Flag

The overflow flag, in some respects, is the carry flag counterpart for the signed number arithmetic. The main purpose of the overflow flag is to indicate whether an operation on signed numbers has produced a result that is out of range. It is helpful to recall the range of signed numbers that can be represented using 8, 16, and 32 bits. For your convenience, this range is given below:

Size (bits)	Range
8	-128 to $+127$
16	$-32,768$ to $+32,767$
32	$-2,147,483,648$ to $+2,147,483,647$

Executing the code

```
mov    AL,72H    ; 72H = 114D
add    AL,0EH    ; 0EH = 14D
```

will set the overflow flag to indicate that the result 80H (128D) is too big to be represented as an 8-bit signed number. The AL register will contain 80H, the correct result if the two 8-bit operands are treated as unsigned numbers. But AL contains an incorrect answer for 8-bit signed numbers (80H represents -128 in signed representation, not $+128$ as required).

Here is another example that uses the sub instruction. The AX register is initialized to -5, which is FFFBH in 2's complement representation using 16 bits.

```
mov    AX,0FFFBH    ; AX = -5
sub    AX,7FFDH     ; subtract 32,765 from AX
```

Execution of the above code will set the overflow flag as the result

$$(-5)-(32,765) = -32,770$$

which is too small to be represented as a 16-bit signed number.

Note that the result will not be out of range (and hence the overflow flag will not be set) when we are adding two signed numbers of opposite sign or subtracting two numbers of the same sign.

Signed or Unsigned: How Does the System Know?   The values of the carry and overflow flags depend on whether the operands are unsigned or signed numbers. Given that a bit pattern can be treated both as representing a signed and an unsigned number, a question that naturally arises is: How does the system know how your program is interpreting a given bit pattern? The answer is that the processor does not have a clue. It is up to our program logic to interpret a given bit pattern correctly. The processor, however, assumes both interpretations and sets the carry and overflow flags. For example, when executing

```
mov     AL,72H
add     AL,0EH
```

the processor treats 72H and 0EH as unsigned numbers. And since the result 80H (128) is within the range of 8-bit unsigned numbers (0 to 255), the carry flag is cleared (i.e., CF = 0). At the same time, 72H and 0EH are also treated as representing signed numbers. Since the result 80H (128) is outside the range of 8-bit signed numbers (-128 to $+127$), the overflow flag is set.

Thus, after executing the above two lines of code, CF = 0 and OF = 1. It is up to our program logic to take whichever flag is appropriate. If you are indeed representing unsigned numbers, disregard the overflow flag. Since the carry flag indicates a valid result, no exception handling is needed.

```
        mov     AL,72H
        add     AL,0EH
        jc      overflow
no_overflow:
        (no overflow code here)
            . . .
overflow:
        (overflow code here)
            . . .
```

If, on the other hand, 72H and 0EH are representing 8-bit signed numbers, we can disregard the carry flag value. Since the overflow flag is 1, our program will have to handle the overflow condition.

```
        mov     AL,72H
        add     AL,0EH
        jo      overflow
no_overflow:
        (no overflow code here)
            . . .
overflow:
        (overflow code here)
            . . .
```

Related Instructions   The following two conditional jump instructions test this flag:

jo   jump on overflow (jump is taken if OF = 1)

jno   jump on no overflow (jump is taken if OF = 0)

In addition, a special software interrupt instruction

into interrupt on overflow

is provided to test the overflow flag. Interrupts are discussed in Chapter 20.

Usage The main purpose of the overflow flag is to indicate whether an arithmetic operation on signed numbers has produced an out-of-range result. The overflow flag is also affected by shift, multiply, and divide operations. More details on some of these instructions can be found in later sections of this chapter.

The Sign Flag

As the name implies, the sign flag indicates the sign of the result of an operation. Therefore, it is useful only when dealing with signed numbers. Recall that the most significant bit is used to represent the sign of a number: 0 for positive numbers and 1 for negative numbers. The sign flag gets a copy of the sign bit of the result produced by arithmetic and related operations. The following sequence of instructions

```
mov     EAX,15
add     EAX,97
```

will clear the sign flag (i.e., SF = 0) because the result produced by the add instruction is a positive number: 112D (which is 01110000 in binary).

The result produced by

```
mov     EAX,15
sub     EAX,97
```

is a negative number and sets the sign flag to indicate this fact. Remember that negative numbers are represented in 2s complement notation (see Appendix A). As discussed in Appendix A, the subtract operation can be treated as the addition of the corresponding negative number. Thus, $15 - 97$ is treated as $15 + (-97)$, where, as usual, -97 is expressed in 2s complement form. Therefore, after executing the above two instructions, the EAX register contains AEH, as shown below:

```
    00001111B      (8-bit signed form of 15)
  + 10011111B      (8-bit signed number for -97)
    ─────────
    10101110B
```

Since the sign bit of the result is 1, the result is negative and is in 2s complement form. You can easily verify that AEH is the 8-bit signed form of -82, which is the correct answer.

Related Instructions The following two conditional jump instructions test this flag:

```
js   jump on sign (jump is taken if SF = 1)
jns  jump on no sign (jump is taken if SF = 0)
```

The js instruction causes the jump if the last instruction that updated the sign flag produced a negative result. The jns instruction causes the jump if the result was nonnegative.

Usage The main use of the sign flag is to test the sign of the result produced by arithmetic and related instructions. Another use for the sign flag is in implementing counting loops that should iterate until (and including) the control variable is zero. For example, consider the following code:

for (i = M downto 0)
        <loop body>
end for

This loop can be implemented without using a cmp instruction as follows:

```
        mov     ECX,M
for_loop:
        . . .
        <loop body>
        . . .
        dec     ECX
        jns     for_loop
```

If we do not use the jns instruction, we have to use

```
        cmp     ECX,0
        jl      for_loop
```

in its place.

From the user point of view, the sign bit of a number can be easily tested by using a logical or shift instruction. Compared to the other three flags we have discussed so far, the sign flag is used relatively infrequently in user programs. However, the processor uses the sign flag when executing conditional jump instructions on signed numbers (details are in Chapter 15 on page 322).

The Auxiliary Flag

The auxiliary flag indicates whether an operation has produced a result that has generated a carry out of or a borrow into the low-order four bits of 8-, 16-, or 32-bit operands. In computer jargon, four bits are referred to as a nibble. The auxiliary flag is set if there is such a carry or borrow; otherwise it is cleared.

In the example

```
        mov     AL,43
        add     AL,94
```

the auxiliary flag is set because there is a carry out of bit 3, as shown below:

```
              1  ← carry generated from lower to upper nibble
    43D  = 00101011B
    94D  = 01011110B
   137D  = 10001001B
```

You can verify that executing the following code clears the auxiliary flag:

```
        mov     AL,43
        add     AL,84
```

Since the following instruction sequence

```
        mov     AL,43
        sub     AL,92
```

generates a borrow into the low-order 4 bits, the auxiliary flag is set. On the other hand, the instruction sequence

```
        mov     AL,43
        sub     AL,87
```

clears the auxiliary flag.

Related Instructions and Usage   There are no conditional jump instructions that test the auxiliary flag. However, arithmetic operations on numbers expressed in decimal form or binary coded decimal (BCD) form use the auxiliary flag. Some related instructions are as follows:

aaa	ASCII adjust for addition
aas	ASCII adjust for subtraction
aam	ASCII adjust for multiplication
aad	ASCII adjust for division
daa	Decimal adjust for addition
das	Decimal adjust for subtraction

For details on these instructions and BCD numbers, see Chapter 18.

The Parity Flag

This flag indicates the parity of the 8-bit result produced by an operation; if this result is 16 or 32 bits long, only the lower-order 8 bits are considered to set or clear the parity flag. The parity flag is set if the byte contains an even number of 1 bits; if there are an odd number of 1 bits, it is cleared. In other words, the parity flag indicates an even parity condition of the byte.

Thus, executing the code

```
mov     AL,53
add     AL,89
```

will set the parity flag because the result contains an even number of 1s (four 1 bits), as shown below:

```
  53D = 00110101B
  89D = 01011001B
─────────────────
 142D = 10001110B
```

The instruction sequence

```
mov     AX,23994
sub     AX,9182
```

on the other hand, clears the parity flag, as the low-order 8 bits contain an odd number of 1s (five 1 bits), as shown below:

```
    23994D = 01011101 10111010B
+   -9182D = 11011100 00100010B
──────────────────────────────
    14813D = 00111001 11011100B
```

Related Instructions   The following two conditional jump instructions test this flag:

jp	jump on parity (jump is taken if PF = 1)
jnp	jump on no parity (jump is taken if PF = 0)

The jp instruction causes the jump if the last instruction that updated the parity flag produced an even parity byte; the jnp instruction causes the jump for an odd parity byte.

Usage This flag is useful for writing data encoding programs. As a simple example, consider transmission of data via modems using the 7-bit ASCII code. To detect simple errors during data transmission, a single parity bit is added to the 7-bit data. Assume that we are using even parity encoding. That is, every 8-bit character code transmitted will contain an even number of 1 bits. Then, the receiver can count the number of 1s in each received byte and flag transmission error if the byte contains an odd number of 1 bits. Such a simple encoding scheme can detect single bit errors (in fact, it can detect an odd number of single bit errors).

To encode, the parity bit is set or cleared depending on whether the remaining 7 bits contain an odd or even number of 1s, respectively. For example, if we are transmitting character A, whose 7-bit ASCII representation is 41H, we set the parity bit to 0 so that there is an even number of 1s. In the following examples, the parity bit is the leftmost bit:

```
A = 01000001
```

For character C, the parity bit is set because its 7-bit ASCII code is 43H.

```
C = 11000011
```

Here is a procedure that encodes the 7-bit ASCII character code present in the AL register. The most significant bit (i.e., leftmost bit) is assumed to be zero.

```
parity_encode PROC
        shl     AL
        jp      parity_zero
        stc             ; CF = 1
        jmp     move_parity_bit
parity_zero:
        clc             ; CF = 0
move_parity_bit:
        rcr     AL
parity_encode ENDP
```

Flag Examples

Here we present two examples to illustrate how the status flags are affected by the arithmetic instructions. You can verify the answers by using a debugger (see Chapter 8 for information on debuggers).

Example 14.1 *Add/subtract example.*

Table 14.1 gives some examples of add and sub instructions and how they affect the flags. Updating of ZF, SF, and PF is easy to understand. The ZF is set whenever the result is zero; SF is simply a copy of the most significant bit of the result; and PF is set whenever there are an even number of 1s in the result. In the rest of this example, we focus on the carry and overflow flags.

Example 1 performs $-5 - 123$. Note that -5 is represented internally as FBH, which is treated as 251 in unsigned representation. Subtracting 123 (=7BH) leaves 80H (=128) in AL. Since the result is within the range of unsigned 8-bit numbers, CF is cleared. For the overflow flag, the operands are interpreted as signed numbers. Since the result is -128, OF is also cleared.

Example 2 subtracts 124 from -5. For reasons discussed in the previous example, the CF is cleared. The OF, however, is set because the result is -129, which is outside the range of signed 8-bit numbers.

Table 14.1 Examples illustrating the effect on flags

	Code		AL	CF	ZF	SF	OF	PF
Example 1	mov	AL,-5						
	sub	AL,123	80H	0	0	1	0	0
Example 2	mov	AL,-5						
	sub	AL,124	7FH	0	0	0	1	0
Example 3	mov	AL,-5						
	add	AL,132	7FH	1	0	0	1	0
	add	AL,1	80H	0	0	1	1	0
Example 4	sub	AL,AL	00H	0	1	0	0	1
Example 5	mov	AL,127						
	add	AL,129	00H	1	1	0	0	1

In Example 3, the first add statement adds 132 to -5. However, when treating them as un-signed numbers, 132 is actually added to 251, which results in a number that is greater than 255D. Therefore, CF is set. When treating them as signed numbers, 132 is internally represented as 84H ($=-124$). Therefore, the result -129 is smaller than -128. Therefore, the OF is also set. After executing the first add instruction, AL will have 7FH. The second add instruction increments 7FH. This sets the OF, but not CF.

Example 4 causes the result to be zero irrespective of the contents of the AL register. This sets the zero flag. Also, since the number of 1s is even, PF is also set in this example.

The last example adds 127D to 129D. Treating them as unsigned numbers, the result 256D is just outside the range, and sets CF. However, if we treat them as representing signed numbers, 129D is stored internally as 81H ($=-127$). The result, therefore, is zero and the OF is cleared.

Example 14.2 *A compare example.*
This example shows how the status flags are affected by the compare instruction discussed in Chapter 9 on page 199. Table 14.2 gives some examples of executing the

```
cmp    AL,DL
```

instruction. We leave it as an exercise to verify (without using a debugger) the flag values.

Arithmetic Instructions

For the sake of completeness, we list the arithmetic instructions supported by the IA-32 instruction set:

```
Addition: add, adc, inc
Subtraction: sub, sbb, dec, neg, cmp
Multiplication: mul, imul
Division: div, idiv
Related instructions: cbw, cwd, cdq, cwde, movsx, movzx
```

Table 14.2 Some examples of `cmp AL, DL`

AL	DL	CF	ZF	SF	OF	PF	AF
56	57	1	0	1	0	1	1
200	101	0	0	0	1	1	0
101	200	1	0	1	1	0	1
200	200	0	1	0	0	1	0
−105	−105	0	1	0	0	1	0
−125	−124	1	0	1	0	1	1
−124	−125	0	0	0	0	0	0

We have already looked at the addition and subtraction instructions in Chapter 9. Here we discuss the remaining instructions. There are a few other arithmetic instructions that operate on decimal and BCD numbers. Details of these instructions can be found in Chapter 18.

Multiplication Instructions

Multiplication is more complicated than the addition and subtraction operations for two reasons:

1. First, multiplication produces double-length results. That is, multiplying two n-bit values produces a $2n$-bit result. To see that this is indeed the case, consider multiplying two 8-bit numbers. Assuming unsigned representation, FFH (255D) is the maximum number that the source operands can take. Thus, the multiplication produces the maximum result, as shown below:

$$11111111 \times 11111111 = 11111110\,11111111.$$
$$\text{(255D)} \qquad \text{(255D)} \qquad \text{(65025D)}$$

Similarly, multiplication of two 16-bit numbers requires 32 bits to store the result, and two 32-bit numbers require 64 bits for the result.

2. Second, unlike the addition and subtraction operations, multiplication of signed numbers should be treated differently from that of unsigned numbers. This is because the resulting bit pattern depends on the type of input, as illustrated by the following example:

We have just seen that treating FFH as the unsigned number results in multiplying 255D × 255D.

$$11111111 \times 11111111 = 11111110\,11111111.$$

Now, what if FFH is representing a signed number? In this case, FFH is representing −1D and the result should be 1, as shown below:

$$11111111 \times 11111111 = 00000000\,00000001.$$

As you can see, the resulting bit patterns are different for the two cases.

Thus, the instruction set provides two multiplication instructions: one for unsigned numbers and the other for signed numbers. We first discuss the unsigned multiplication instruction, which has the format

```
mul     source
```

The `source` operand can be in a general-purpose register or in memory. Immediate operand specification is not allowed. Thus,

```
mul     10          ; invalid
```

is an invalid instruction. The `mul` instruction works on 8-, 16-, and 32-bit unsigned numbers. But, where is the second operand? The instruction assumes that it is in the accumulator. If the source operand is a byte, it is multiplied by the contents of the AL register. The 16-bit result is placed in the AX register, as shown below:

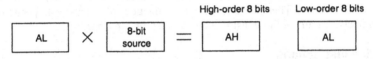

If the source operand is a word, it is multiplied by the contents of the AX register and the doubleword result is placed in DX:AX, with the AX register holding the lower-order 16 bits, as shown below:

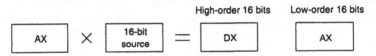

If the source operand is a doubleword, it is multiplied by the contents of the EAX register and the 64-bit result is placed in EDX:EAX, with the EAX register holding the lower-order 32 bits, as shown below:

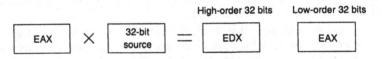

The `mul` instruction affects all six status flags. However, it updates only the carry and overflow flags. The remaining four flags are undefined. The carry and overflow flags are set if the upper half of the result is nonzero; otherwise, they are both cleared.

Setting of the carry and overflow flags does not indicate an error condition. Instead, this condition implies that AH, DX, or EDX contains significant digits of the result.

For example, the code

```
mov     AL,10
mov     DL,25
mul     DL
```

clears both the carry and overflow flags, as the result of the `mul` instruction is 250, which can be stored in the AL register (and the AH register contains 00000000). On the other hand, executing

```
mov     AL,10
mov     DL,26
mul     DL
```

sets the carry and overflow flags indicating that the result is more than 255.

For signed numbers, we have to use the imul (integer multiplication) instruction, which has the same format[1] as the mul instruction

```
imul    source
```

The behavior of the imul instruction is similar to that of the mul instruction. The only difference to note is that the carry and overflow flags are set if the upper half of the result is not the sign extension of the lower half. To understand sign extension in signed numbers, consider the following example. We know that −66 is represented using 8 bits as

10111110.

Now, suppose that we can use 16 bits to represent the same number. Using 16 bits, −66 is represented as

1111111110111110.

The upper 8 bits are simply sign-extended (i.e., the sign bit is copied into these bits), and doing so does not change the magnitude.

Following the same logic, the positive number 66, represented using 8 bits as

01000010

can be sign-extended to 16 bits by adding eight leading zeros as shown below:

0000000001000010.

As with the mul instruction, setting of the carry and overflow flags does not indicate an error condition; it simply indicates that the result requires double length.

Here are some examples of the imul instruction. Execution of the following code

```
mov     DL,0FFH    ; DL = -1
mov     AL,42H     ; AL = 66
imul    DL
```

causes the result

1111111110111110

to be placed in the AX register. The carry and overflow flags are cleared, as AH contains the sign extension of the AL value. This is also the case for the following code:

```
mov     DL,0FFH    ; DL = -1
mov     AL,0BEH    ; AL = -66
imul    DL
```

[1] The imul instruction supports several other formats, including specification of an immediate value. We do not discuss these details; see Intel's *IA-32 Architecture Software Developer's Manual*.

which produces the result

    0000000001000010   (+66)

in the AX register. Again, both the carry and overflow flags are cleared.
    In contrast, both flags are set for the following code:

```
mov    DL,25   ; DL = 25
mov    AL,0F6H ; AL = -10
imul   DL
```

which produces the result

    1111111100000110   (−250).

A Note on Multiplication   The multiplication instruction is an expensive one in the sense it takes
more time than the other arithmetic instructions like add and sub. (Of course, the division instructions take even more time.) Thus, for some multiplications, we get better performance by not
using the multiplication instructions. For example, to multiply the value in EAX by 2, we do better
by using

```
add    EAX,EAX
```

The add instruction takes only one clock cycle whereas the multiplication instruction takes 10+
clock cycles.
    As another example, consider multiplication by 10, which is often needed in number conver-
sion routines. We can do this multiplication by using a sequence of additions more efficiently than
the multiplication instruction. For example, if we want to multiply y (in EAX) by 10, we can use
the following code:

```
add    EAX,EAX    ; EAX = 2y
mov    EBX,EAX    ; EBX = 2y
add    EAX,EAX    ; EAX = 4y
add    EAX,EAX    ; EAX = 8y
add    EAX,EBX    ; EAX = 10y
```

Since the mov and add instructions take only one clock cycle, this sequence takes only 5 clocks
compared to 10+ clocks for the multiplication instruction. We can do even better by using a mix
of shift and add instructions. If we want to multiply a number by a power of 2, it is better to use
the shift instructions (see our discussion in Chapter 16 on page 351).

Division Instructions

The division operation is even more complicated than multiplication for two reasons:

1. Division generates two result components: a quotient and a remainder.
2. In multiplication, by using double-length registers, overflow never occurs. In division, divide overflow is a real possibility. The processor generates a special software interrupt when
   a divide overflow occurs.

As with the multiplication instruction, two versions of the divide instruction are provided to work
on unsigned and signed numbers.

```
div    source   (unsigned)
idiv   source   (signed)
```

The source operand specified in the instruction is used as the divisor. As with the multiplication instruction, both division instructions can work on 8-, 16-, or 32-bit numbers. All six status flags are affected and are *undefined*. None of the flags are updated. We first consider the unsigned version.

If the source operand is a byte, the dividend is assumed to be in the AX register and 16 bits long. After the division, the quotient is returned in the AL register and the remainder in the AH register, as shown below:

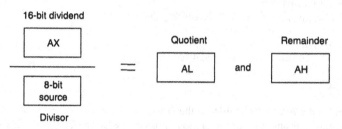

For word operands, the dividend is assumed to be 32 bits long and in DX:AX (upper 16 bits in DX). After the division, the 16-bit quotient will be in AX and the 16-bit remainder in DX, as shown below:

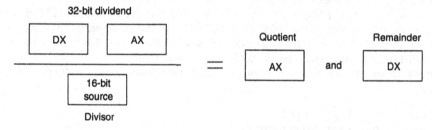

For 32-bit operands, the dividend is assumed to be 64 bits long and in EDX:EAX. After the division, the 32-bit quotient will be in the EAX and the 32-bit remainder in the EDX, as shown below:

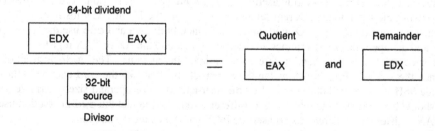

Example 14.3 *8-bit division.*

Consider dividing 251 by 12 (i.e., 251/12), which produces 20 as the quotient and 11 as the remainder. The code

```
mov    AX,251
mov    CL,12
div    CL
```

leaves 20 (14H) in the AL register and 11 (0BH) in the AH register.   □

Example 14.4 *16-bit division.*

Consider the 16-bit division: 5147/300. Executing the code

```
xor    DX,DX      ; clear DX
mov    AX,141BH   ; AX = 5147D
mov    CX,012CH   ; CX = 300D
div    CX
```

leaves 17 (12H) in the AX and 47 (2FH) in the DX.   □

Now let us turn our attention to the signed division operation. The `idiv` instruction has the same format and behavior as the unsigned `div` instruction including the registers used for the dividend, quotient, and remainder.

The `idiv` instruction introduces a slight complication when the dividend is a negative number. For example, assume that we want to perform the 16-bit division: −251/12. Since −251 = FF14H, the AX register is set to FF14H. However, the DX register has to be initialized to FFFFH by sign-extending the AX register. If the DX is set to 0000H as we did in the unsigned `div` operation, the dividend 0000FF14H is treated as a positive number 65300D. The 32-bit equivalent of −251 is FFFFFF14H. If the dividend is positive, DX should have 0000H.

To aid sign extension in instructions such as `idiv`, the instruction set provides several instructions:

```
cbw    (convert byte to word)
cwd    (convert word to doubleword)
cdq    (convert doubleword to quadword)
```

These instructions take no operands. The first instruction can be used to sign-extend the AL register into the AH register and is useful with the 8-bit `idiv` instruction. The `cwd` instruction sign extends the AX into the DX register and is useful with the 16-bit `idiv` instruction. The `cdq` instruction sign extends the EAX into the EDX. In fact, both `cwd` and `cdq` use the same opcode 99H, and the operand size determines whether to sign-extend the AX or EAX register.

For completeness, we mention three other related instructions. The `cwde` instruction sign extends the AX into EAX much as the `cbw` instruction. Just like the `cwd` and `cdq`, the same opcode 98H is used for both `cbw` and `cwde` instructions. The operand size determines which one should be applied. Note that `cwde` is different from `cwd` in that the `cwd` instruction uses the DX:AX register pair, whereas `cwde` uses the EAX register as the destination.

The instruction set also provides the following two move instructions:

```
movsx    dest,src    (move sign-extended src to dest)
movzx    dest,src    (move zero-extended src to dest)
```

In both these instructions, dest has to be a register, whereas the src operand can be in a register or memory. If the source is an 8-bit operand, the destination has to be either a 16- or 32-bit register. If the source is a 16-bit operand, the destination must be a 32-bit register.

Here are some examples of the idiv instruction.

Example 14.5 *Signed 8-bit division.*
The following sequence of instructions perform the signed 8-bit division −95/12:

```
mov     AL,-95
cbw                 ; AH = FFH
mov     CL,12
idiv    CL
```

The idiv instruction leaves −7 (F9H) in the AL register and −11 (F5H) in the AH register.   □

Example 14.6 *Signed 16-bit division.*
Suppose that we want to divide −5147 by 300. The instruction sequence

```
mov     AX,-5147
cwd                 ; DX = FFFFH
mov     CX,300
idiv    CX
```

performs this division and leaves −17 (FFEFH) in the AX register and −47 (FFD1H) in the DX register as the remainder.   □

Our First Program

In the previous chapters, we looked at how the add and subtract instructions are used in assembly language programs. Since we introduced the multiplication instructions in this chapter, we look at how they are used in assembly language programs. Program 14.1 is a simple to program to multiply two 32-bit integers and display the result.

Program 14.1 Multiplication program to multiply two 32-bit signed integers

```
 1: ;Multiplies two 32-bit signed integerts       MULT.ASM
 2: ;
 3: ;         Objective: To use the multiply instruction.
 4: ;             Input: Requests two integers N and M.
 5: ;            Output: Outputs N*M if no overflow.
 6: %include "io.mac"
 7:
 8: .DATA
 9: prompt_msg  db    "Enter two integers: ",0
10: output_msg  db    "The product = ",0
11: oflow_msg   db    "Sorry! Result out of range.",0
12: query_msg   db    "Do you want to quit (Y/N): ",0
13:
14: .CODE
15:         .STARTUP
```

```
16:   read_input:
17:         PutStr    prompt_msg
18:         GetLInt   EAX
19:         GetLInt   EBX
20:         imul      EBX          ; signed multiply
21:         jc        overflow
22:         PutStr    output_msg   ; no overflow
23:         PutLInt   EAX          ; display result
24:         nwln
25:         jmp       short user_query
26:   overflow:
27:         PutStr    oflow_msg
28:         nwln
29:   user_query:
30:         ; query user whether to terminate
31:         PutStr    query_msg
32:         GetCh     AL
33:         cmp       AL,'Y'       ; if response is not 'Y'
34:         jne       read_input   ; repeat the loop
35:   done:
36:         .EXIT
```

An example interaction with the program is shown below:

```
Enter two integers: 65535
32768
The product = 2147450880
Do you want to quit (Y/N): n
Enter two integers: 65535
32769
Sorry! Result out of range.
Do you want to quit (Y/N): Y
```

If there is no overflow, the result is displayed; otherwise, an error message is displayed. In both cases, the user is queried if the program is to be continued.

The two input numbers are read into the EAX and EBX registers using GetLInt on lines 18 and 19. Since the two values are signed integers, we use imul to multiply these two integers. Recall that the multiply instructions set the carry flag if the result requires more than 32 bits. While this condition is technically not an error, for practical purposes we treat this as an overflow. We use the conditional jump instruction on line 21 to detect this overflow condition. If there is no overflow, we display the 32-bit result (line 23). The rest of the program is straightforward to follow.

Illustrative Examples

To demonstrate the application of the arithmetic instructions and flags, we write two procedures to input and output signed 8-bit integers in the range of −128 to +127. These procedures are as follows:

PutInt8   Displays a signed 8-bit integer that is in the AL register;
GetInt8   Reads a signed 8-bit integer from the keyboard into the AL register.

The following two subsections describe these procedures in detail.

Example 14.7 *PutInt8 procedure.*
Our objective here is to write a procedure that displays the signed 8-bit integer that is in the AL register. In order to do this, we have to separate individual digits of the number to be displayed and convert them to their ASCII representation. The steps involved are illustrated by the following example, which assumes that AL has 108.

separate 1 → convert to ASCII (31H) → display
separate 0 → convert to ASCII (30H) → display
separate 8 → convert to ASCII (38H) → display

Separating individual digits is the heart of the procedure. This step is surprisingly simple! All we have to do is repeatedly divide the number by 10, as shown below (for a related discussion, see Appendix A):

		Quotient	Remainder
108/10	=	10	8
10/10	=	1	0
1/10	=	0	1

The only problem with this step is that the digits come out in the reverse order. Therefore, we need to buffer them before displaying. The pseudocode for the PutInt8 procedure is shown below:

```
PutInt8 (number)
    if (number is negative)
    then
        display '−' sign
        number = −number {reverse sign}
    end if
    index = 0
    repeat
        quotient = number/10 {integer division}
        remainder = number % 10 {% is the modulo operator}
        buffer[index] = remainder + 30H
        {save the ASCII character equivalent of remainder}
        index = index + 1
        number = quotient
    until (number = 0)
    repeat
        index = index − 1
        display digit at buffer[index]
    until (index = 0)
end PutInt8
```

Program 14.2 The `PutInt8` procedure to display an 8-bit signed number (in `getput.asm` file)

```
 1:   ;------------------------------------------------------------
 2:   ;PutInt8 procedure displays a signed 8-bit integer that is
 3:   ;in the AL register. All registers are preserved.
 4:   ;------------------------------------------------------------
 5:   PutInt8:
 6:         enter    3,0                ; reserves 3 bytes of buffer space
 7:         push     AX
 8:         push     BX
 9:         push     ESI
10:         test     AL,80H            ; negative number?
11:         jz       positive
12:   negative:
13:         PutCh    '-'               ; sign for negative numbers
14:         neg      AL                ; convert to magnitude
15:   positive:
16:         mov      BL,10             ; divisor = 10
17:         sub      ESI,ESI          ; ESI = 0 (ESI points to buffer)
18:   repeat1:
19:         sub      AH,AH            ; AH = 0 (AX is the dividend)
20:         div      BL
21:         ; AX/BL leaves AL = quotient & AH = remainder
22:         add      AH,'0'            ; convert remainder to ASCII
23:         mov      [EBP+ESI-3],AH ; copy into the buffer
24:         inc      ESI
25:         cmp      AL,0              ; quotient = zero?
26:         jne      repeat1           ; if so, display the number
27:   display_digit:
28:         dec      ESI
29:         mov      AL,[EBP+ESI-3]; display digit pointed by ESI
30:         PutCh    AL
31:         jnz      display_digit ; if ESI<0, done displaying
32:   display_done:
33:         pop      ESI               ; restore registers
34:         pop      BX
35:         pop      AX
36:         leave                      ; clears local buffer space
37:         ret
```

The `PutInt8` procedure shown in Program 14.2 follows the logic of the pseudocode. Some points to note are the following:

- The buffer is considered as a local variable. Thus, we reserve three bytes on the stack using the `enter` instruction (see line 6).
- The code

```
test    AL,80H
jz      positive
```

tests whether the number is negative or positive. Remember that the sign bit (the leftmost bit) is 1 for a negative number.

- Reversal of sign is done by the

```
neg    AL
```

instruction on line 14.

- Note that we have to initialize AH with 0 (line 19), as the div instruction assumes a 16-bit dividend in the AX register when the divisor is an 8-bit number.
- Conversion to ASCII character representation is done on line 22 using

```
add    AH,'0'
```

- The ESI register is used as the index into the buffer, which starts at [BP − 3]. Thus, [BP + ESI − 3] points to the current byte in the buffer (line 29).
- The repeat- while condition (index = 0) is tested by

```
jnz    display_digit
```

on line 31.

Example 14.8 *GetInt8 procedure.*

The GetInt8 procedure reads a signed integer and returns the number in the AL register. Since only 8 bits are used to represent the number, the range is limited to −128 to +127 (both inclusive). The key part of the procedure converts a sequence of input digits received in the character form to its binary equivalent. The conversion process, which involves repeated multiplication by 10, is illustrated for the number 158:

Input digit	Numeric value	Number = number * 10 + numeric value
Initial value	—	0
'1' (31H)	1	$0 * 10 + 1 = 1$
'5' (35H)	5	$1 * 10 + 5 = 15$
'8' (38H)	8	$15 * 10 + 8 = 158$

The pseudocode of the GetInt8 procedure is as follows:

```
GetInt8()
    read input character into char
    if ((char = '−') OR (char = '+'))
    then
        sign = char
        read the next character into char
    end if
    number = char − '0' {convert to numeric value}
    count = 2 {number of remaining digits to read}
repeat
    read the next character into char
    if (char ≠ carriage return)
    then
```

$$number = number * 10 + (char - '0')$$

        else
             goto `convert_done`
        end if
        count = count − 1
    until (count = 0)
`convert_done`:
    {check for out-of-range error}
    if ((number > 128) OR ((number = 128) AND (sign ≠ '−')))
    then
        out of range error
        set carry flag
    else {number is OK}
        clear carry flag
    end if
    if (sign = '−')
    then
        number = −number {reverse sign}
    end if
end `GetInt8`

Program 14.3 The `GetInt8` procedure to read a signed 8-bit integer (in `getput.asm` file)

```
1:    ;-------------------------------------------------------------
2:    ;GetInt8 procedure reads an integer from the keyboard and
3:    ;stores its equivalent binary in AL register. If the number
4:    ;is within -128 and +127 (both inclusive), CF is cleared;
5:    ;otherwise, CF is set to indicate out-of-range error.
6:    ;No error check is done to see if the input consists of
7:    ;digits only. All registers are preserved except for AX.
8:    ;-------------------------------------------------------------
9:    GetInt8:
10:          push    BX              ; save registers
11:          push    CX
12:          push    DX
13:          push    ESI
14:          sub     DX,DX           ; DX = 0
15:          sub     BX,BX           ; BX = 0
16:          GetStr  number,5        ; get input number
17:          mov     ESI,number
18:   get_next_char:
19:          mov     DL,[ESI]        ; read input from buffer
20:          cmp     DL,'-'          ; is it negative sign?
21:          je      sign            ; if so, save the sign
22:          cmp     DL,'+'          ; is it positive sign?
23:          jne     digit           ; if not, process the digit
24:   sign:
25:          mov     BH,DL           ; BH keeps sign of input number
26:          inc     ESI
```

```
27:            jmp        get_next_char
28:    digit:
29:            sub        AX,AX          ; AX = 0
30:            mov        BL,10          ; BL holds the multiplier
31:            sub        DL,'0'         ; convert ASCII to numeric
32:            mov        AL,DL
33:            mov        CX,2           ; maximum two more digits to read
34:    convert_loop:
35:            inc        ESI
36:            mov        DL,[ESI]
37:            cmp        DL,0           ; NULL?
38:            je         convert_done   ; if so, done reading the number
39:            sub        DL,'0'         ; else, convert ASCII to numeric
40:            mul        BL             ; multiply total (in AL) by 10
41:            add        AX,DX          ; and add the current digit
42:            loop       convert_loop
43:    convert_done:
44:            cmp        AX,128
45:            ja         out_of_range   ; if AX > 128, number out of range
46:            jb         number_OK      ; if AX < 128, number is valid
47:            cmp        BH,'-'         ; if AX = 128, must be a negative;
48:            jne        out_of_range   ; otherwise, an invalid number
49:    number_OK:
50:            cmp        BH,'-'         ; number negative?
51:            jne        number_done    ; if not, we are done
52:            neg        AL             ; else, convert to 2's complement
53:    number_done:
54:            clc                       ; CF = 0 (no error)
55:            jmp        done
56:    out_of_range:
57:            stc                       ; CF = 1 (range error)
58:    done:
59:            pop        ESI            ; restore registers
60:            pop        DX
61:            pop        CX
62:            pop        BX
63:            ret
```

The assembly language code for the GetInt8 procedure is given in Program 14.3. The procedure uses GetStr to read the input digits into a buffer number. This buffer is 5 bytes long so that it can hold the sign, 3 digits, and a null character. Thus, we specify 5 in GetStr on line 16.

- The character input digits are converted to their numeric equivalent by subtracting '0' on lines 31 and 39.
- The multiplication is done on line 40, which produces a 16-bit result in AX. Note that the numeric value of the current digit (in DX) is added (line 41) to detect the overflow condition rather than the 8-bit value in DL.
- When the conversion is done, AX will have the absolute value of the input number. Lines 44 to 48 perform the out-of-range error check. To do this check, the following conditions are tested:

> AX > 128   ⇒   out of range
>
> AX = 128   ⇒   input must be a negative number to be a valid
>   number; otherwise, out of range

The `ja` (jump if above) and `jb` (jump if below) on lines 45 and 46 are conditional jumps for unsigned numbers.

- If the input is a negative number, the value in AL is converted to the 2's complement representation by using the `neg` instruction (line 52).
- The `clc` (clear CF) and `stc` (set CF) instructions are used to indicate the error condition (lines 54 and 57).

Summary

The status flags register the outcome of arithmetic and logical operations. Of the six status flags, zero flag, carry flag, overflow flag, and sign flag are the most important. The zero flag records whether the result of an operation is zero or not. The sign flag monitors the sign of the result. The carry and overflow flags record the overflow conditions of the arithmetic operations. The carry flag is set if the result on unsigned numbers is out of range; the overflow flag is used to indicate the out-of-range condition on the signed numbers.

The IA-32 instruction set includes instructions for addition, subtraction, multiplication, and division. While the add and subtract instructions work on both unsigned and signed data, separate instructions are required for signed and unsigned numbers for performing multiplication and division operations.

The arithmetic instructions can operate on 8-, 16-, or 32-bit operands. If numbers are represented using more than 32 bits, we need to devise methods for performing the arithmetic operations on multiword operands. We gave an example to illustrate how multiword addition could be implemented.

We demonstrated that multiplication by special values (for example, multiplication by 10) can be done more efficiently by using addition. Chapter 16 discusses how the shift operations can be used to implement multiplication by a power of 2.

15

Conditional Execution

Assembly language provides several instructions to facilitate conditional execution. We have discussed some of these instructions like jmp *and* loop *in Chapter 9. Our discussion here complements that discussion. In this chapter, we give more details on these instructions including how the target address is specified, how the flags register is used to implement conditional jumps, and so on. The jump instructions we have used so far specify the target address directly. It is also possible to specify the target of jump indirectly. We describe how the target can be specified indirectly and illustrate its use of such indirect jumps by means of an example.*

Introduction

Modern high-level languages provide a variety of decision structures. These structures include selection structures such as if-then-else and iterative structures such as while and for loops. Assembly language, being a low-level language, does not provide these structures directly. However, assembly language provides several basic instructions that could be used to construct these high-level language selection and iteration structures. These assembly language instructions include the unconditional jump, compare, conditional jump, and loop. We briefly introduced some of these instructions in Chapter 9. In this chapter, we give more details on these instructions.

As we have seen in the previous chapters, we can specify the target address directly. In assembly language programs, we do this by specifying a label associated with the target instruction. The assembler replaces the label with the address. In general, this address can be a relative address or an absolute address. If the address is relative, the offset of the target is specified relative to the current instruction. In the absolute address case, target address is given. We start this with a discussion of these details.

We can also specify the target address indirectly, just like the address given in the indirect addressing mode. In these indirect jumps, the address is specified via a register or memory. We describe the indirect jump mechanism toward the end of the chapter. We also illustrate how the indirect jump instructions are useful in implementing multiway switch or case statements.

The IA-32 instruction set provides three types of conditional jump instructions. These include the jump instructions that test the individual flag values, jumps based on signed comparisons, and jumps based on unsigned comparisons. Our discussion of these conditional jump instructions on page 322 throws light on how the processor uses the flags to test for the various conditions.

Unconditional Jump

We introduced the unconditional jump instruction in Chapter 9. It unconditionally transfers control to the instruction located at the target address. The general format, as we have seen before, is

```
jmp     target
```

There are several versions of the jmp instruction depending on how the target address is specified and where the target instruction is located.

Specification of Target

There are two distinct ways by which the target address of the jmp instruction can be specified: *direct* and *indirect*. The vast majority of jumps are of the direct type. We have used these types of unconditional jumps in the previous chapters. Therefore, we focus our attention on the direct jump instructions and discuss the indirect jumps toward the end of the chapter.

Direct Jumps   In the direct jump instruction, the target address is specified directly as part of the instruction. In the following code fragment

```
              . . .
            mov     CX,10
            jmp     CX_init_done
init_CX_20:
            mov     CX,20
CX_init_done:
            mov     AX,CX
repeat1:
            dec     CX
              . . .
            jmp     repeat1
              . . .
```

both the jmp instructions directly specify the target. As an assembly language programmer, you only specify the target address by using a label; the assembler figures out the exact value by using its symbol table.

The instruction

```
jmp   CX_init_done
```

transfers control to an instruction that follows it. This is called the *forward jump*. On the other hand, the instruction

```
jmp     repeat1
```

is a *backward jump*, as the control is transferred to an instruction that precedes the jump instruction.

Relative Address   The address specified in a jump instruction is not the absolute address of the target. Rather, it specifies the relative displacement in bytes between the target instruction and the instruction following the jump instruction (and not from the jump instruction itself!).

In order to see why this is so, we have to understand how jumps are executed. Recall that the EIP register always points to the next instruction to be executed (see Chapter 4). Thus, after fetching the jmp instruction, the EIP is automatically advanced to point to the instruction following the jmp instruction. Execution of jmp involves changing the EIP from where it is currently pointing to the target instruction location. This is achieved by adding the difference (i.e., the relative displacement) to the EIP contents. This works fine because the relative displacement is a signed number—a positive displacement implies a forward jump and a negative displacement indicates a backward jump.

The specification of relative address as opposed to absolute address of the target instruction is appropriate for dynamically relocatable code (i.e., for position-independent code).

Where Is the Target? If the target of a jump instruction is located in the same segment as the jump itself, it is called an *intrasegment jump*; if the target is located in another segment, it is called an *intersegment jump*.

Our previous discussion has assumed an intrasegment jump. In this case, the jmp simply performs the following action:

EIP = EIP + relative-displacement

In the case of an intersegment jump, called *far jump*, the CS is also changed to point to the target segment, as shown below:

CS = target-segment
EIP = target-offset

Both target-segment and target-offset are specified directly in the instruction. Thus, for 32-bit segments, the instruction encoding for the intersegment jump takes seven bytes: one byte for the specification of the opcode, two bytes for the target-segment, and four bytes for the target-offset specification.

The majority of jumps are of the intrasegment type. Therefore, more flexibility is provided to specify the target in intrasegment jump instructions. These instructions can have *short* and *near* format, depending on the distance of the target location from the instruction following the jump instruction—that is, depending on the value of the relative displacement.

If the relative displacement, which is a signed number, can fit in a byte, a jump instruction is encoded using just two bytes: one byte for the opcode and the other for the relative displacement. This means that the relative displacement should be within -128 to $+127$ (the range of a signed 8-bit number). This form is called the *short jump*.

If the target is outside this range, 2 or 4 bytes are used to specify the relative displacement. A two-byte displacement is used for 16-bit segments, and 4-byte displacement for 32-bit segments. As a result, the jump instruction requires either 3 or 5 bytes to encode in the machine language. This form is called the *near jump*.

If you want to use the short jump form, you can inform the assembler of your intention by using the operator SHORT, as shown below:

```
jmp     SHORT CX_init_done
```

The question that naturally arises at this point is: What if the target is not within -128 or $+127$ bytes? The assembler will inform you with an error message that the target can't be reached with a short jump.

In fact, specification of SHORT in a statement like

. . .

```
 8 0005  EB 0C            jmp     SHORT CX_init_done
 9 0007  B9 000A          mov     CX,10
10 000A  EB 07 90         jmp     CX_init_done
11                   init_CX_20:
12 000D  B9 0014          mov     CX,20
13 0010  E9 00D0          jmp     near_jump
14                   CX_init_done:
15 0013  8B C1            mov     AX,CX
16                   repeat1:
17 0015  49              dec     CX
18 0016  EB FD           jmp     repeat1
```

. . .

. . .

```
84 00DB  EB 03           jmp     SHORT short_jump
85 00DD  B9 FF00         mov     CX, 0FF00H
86                  short_jump:
87 00E0  BA 0020         mov     DX, 20H
88                  near_jump:
89 00E3  E9 FF27         jmp     init_CX_20
```

. . .

Figure 15.1 Example encoding of jump instructions.

```
jmp    SHORT repeat1
```

in the example code on page 318 is redundant, as the assembler can automatically select the SHORT jump, if appropriate, for all backward jumps. However, for forward jumps, the assembler needs your help. This is because the assembler does not know the relative displacement of the target when it must decide whether to use the short form. Therefore, use the SHORT operator only for forward jumps if appropriate.

Example 15.1 *Example encodings of short and near jumps.*
Figure 15.1 shows some example encodings for short and near jump instructions. The forward short jump on line 8 is encoded in the machine language as EB 0C, where EB represents the opcode for the short jump. The relative offset to target CX_init_done is 0CH. From the code, it can be seen that this is the difference between the address of the target (address 0013H) and the instruction following the jump instruction on line 9 (address 0007H). Another example of a forward short jump is given on line 84.

The backward jump instruction on line 18 also uses the short jump form. In this case, the assembler can decide whether the short or near jump is appropriate. The relative offset is given by FDH, which is −3 in decimal. This is the offset from the instruction following the jump instruction at address 18H to repeat1 at 15H.

For near jumps, the opcode is E9H, and the relative offset is a 16-bit signed integer. The relative offset of the forward near jump on line 13 is 00D0H, which is equal to 00E3H − 0013H. The relative offset of the backward near jump on line 89 is given by 000DH − 00E6H = FF27H, which is equal to −217 in decimal.

Table 15.1 Some examples of cmp AL,DL

AL	DL	CF	ZF	SF	OF	PF	AF
56	57	1	0	1	0	1	1
200	101	0	0	0	1	1	0
101	200	1	0	1	1	0	1
200	200	0	1	0	0	1	0
−105	−105	0	1	0	0	1	0
−125	−124	1	0	1	0	1	1
−124	−125	0	0	0	0	0	0

The jump instruction encoding on line 10 requires some explanation. Since this is a forward jump and we have not specified that it could be a short jump, assembler reserves 3 bytes for a near jump (the worst case scenario). At the time of actual encoding, the assembler knows the target location and therefore uses the short jump version. Thus, EB 07 represents the encoding, and the third byte is not used and contains a nop (no operation). □

Compare Instruction

Implementation of high-level language decision structures like if-then-else in assembly language is a two step process:

1. An arithmetic or comparison instruction updates one or more arithmetic flags;
2. A conditional jump instruction causes selective execution of the appropriate code fragment based on the values of the flags.

We discussed the compare (cmp) instruction on page 199. The main purpose of the cmp instruction is to update the flags so that a subsequent conditional jump instruction can test these flags.

Example 15.2 *Some examples of the compare instruction.*
The four flags that are useful in establishing a relationship ($<$, $\leq$, $>$, and so on) between two integers are CF, ZF, SF, and OF. Table 15.1 gives some examples of executing the

```
cmp     AL,DL
```

instruction. Recall that CF is set if the result is out of range when treating the operands as unsigned numbers. Since the operands are 8 bits in our example, this range is 0 to 255D. Similarly, the OF is set if the result is out of range for signed numbers (for our example, this range is −128D to +127D).

In general, the value of ZF and SF can be obtained in a straightforward way. Therefore, let us focus on the carry and overflow flags. In the first example, since $56-57 = -1$, CF is set but not OF.

The second example is not so simple. Treating the operands in AL and DL as unsigned numbers, $200-101 = 99$, which is within the range of unsigned numbers. Therefore, CF = 0. However, when treating 200D (= C8H) as a signed number, it represents -56D. Therefore, compare performs $-56-101 = -157$, which is out of range for signed numbers resulting in setting OF. We will leave verification of the rest of the examples as an exercise.   □

Conditional Jumps

Conditional jump instructions can be divided into three groups:

1. Jumps based on the value of a single arithmetic flag;
2. Jumps based on unsigned comparisons;
3. Jumps based on signed comparisons.

Jumps Based on Single Flags

The IA-32 instruction set provides two conditional jump instructions—one for jumps if the flag tested is set, and the other for jumps when the flag is cleared—for each arithmetic flag except the auxiliary flag. These instructions are summarized in Table 15.2.

As shown in Table 15.2, the jump instructions that test the zero and parity flags have aliases (e.g., je is an alias for jz). These aliases are provided to improve program readability. For example,

> **if** (count = 100)
> **then**
>   <statement1>
> **end if**

can be written in the assembly language as

```
        cmp     count,100
        jz      S1
                . . .
S1:
        <statement1 code here>
                . . .
```

But our use of jz does not convey that we are testing for equality. This meaning is better conveyed by

```
        cmp     count,100
        je      S1
                . . .
S1:
        <statement1 code here>
                . . .
```

The assembler, however, treats both jz and je as synonymous instructions.

The only surprising instruction in Table 15.2 is the jecxz instruction. This instruction does not test any flag but tests the contents of the ECX register for zero. It is often used in conjunction with the loop instruction. Therefore, we defer a discussion of this instruction to a later section that deals with the loop instruction.

Table 15.2 Jumps based on single flag value

Mnemonic		Meaning	Jumps if
Testing for zero:			
	jz	jump if zero	ZF = 1
	je	jump if equal	
	jnz	jump if not zero	ZF = 0
	jne	jump if not equal	
	jecxz	jump if ECX = 0	ECX = 0 (no flags tested)
Testing for carry:			
	jc	jump if carry	CF = 1
	jnc	jump if no carry	CF = 0
Testing for overflow:			
	jo	jump if overflow	OF = 1
	jno	jump if no overflow	OF = 0
Testing for sign:			
	js	jump if (negative) sign	SF = 1
	jns	jump if no (negative) sign	SF = 0
Testing for parity:			
	jp	jump if parity	PF = 1
	jpe	jump if parity is even	
	jnp	jump if not parity	PF = 0
	jpo	jump if parity is odd	

Jumps Based on Unsigned Comparisons

When comparing two numbers

```
cmp     num1,num2
```

it is necessary to know whether these numbers num1 and num2 represent singed or unsigned numbers in order to establish a relationship between them. As an example, assume that AL = 10110111B and DL = 01101110B. Then the statement

```
cmp     AL,DL
```

should appropriately update flags to yield that AL > DL if we treat their contents as representing unsigned numbers. This is because, in unsigned representation, AL = 183D and DL = 110D. However, if the contents of AL and DL registers are treated as representing signed numbers, AL < DL

Table 15.3 Jumps based on unsigned comparison

Mnemonic	Meaning	condition tested
je	jump if equal	ZF = 1
jz	jump if zero	
jne	jump if not equal	ZF = 0
jnz	jump if not zero	
ja	jump if above	CF = 0 and ZF = 0
jnbe	jump if not below or equal	
jae	jump if above or equal	CF = 0
jnb	jump if not below	
jb	jump if below	CF = 1
jnae	jump if not above or equal	
jbe	jump if below or equal	CF = 1 or ZF = 1
jna	jump if not above	

as the AL register has a negative number ($-73D$) while the DL register has a positive number ($+110D$).

Note that when using a cmp statement like

```
cmp     num1,num2
```

we compare num1 to num2 (e.g., num1 < num2, num1 > num2, and so on). There are six possible relationships between two numbers:

$$num1 = num2$$
$$num1 \neq num2$$
$$num1 > num2$$
$$num1 \geq num2$$
$$num1 < num2$$
$$num1 \leq num2$$

For the unsigned numbers, the carry and the zero flags record the necessary information in order to establish one of the above six relationships.

The six conditional jump instructions (along with six aliases) and the flag conditions tested are shown in Table 15.3. Note that "above" and "below" are used for > and < relationships for the unsigned comparisons, reserving "greater" and "less" for signed comparisons, as we shall see next.

Jumps Based on Signed Comparisons

The = and ≠ comparisons work with either signed or unsigned numbers, as we essentially compare the bit pattern for a match. For this reason, je and jne also appear in Table 15.4 for signed comparisons.

For signed comparisons, three flags record the necessary information: the sign flag (SF), the overflow flag (OF), and the zero flag (ZF). Testing for = and ≠ simply involves testing whether the ZF is set or cleared, respectively. With the singed numbers, establishing < and > relationships is somewhat tricky. Let us assume that we are executing the cmp instruction

```
cmp     Snum1, Snum2
```

Conditions for Snum1 > Snum2   The following table shows several examples in which Snum1 > Snum2 holds.

Snum1	Snum2	ZF	OF	SF
56	55	0	0	0
56	−55	0	0	0
−55	−56	0	0	0
55	−75	0	1	1

It appears from these examples that Snum1 > Snum2 if

ZF	OF	SF
0	0	0

or

ZF	OF	SF
0	1	1

That is, ZF = 0 and OF = SF. We cannot use just OF = SF because if two numbers are equal, ZF = 1 and OF = SF = 0. In fact, these conditions do imply the "greater than" relationship between Snum1 and Snum2. As shown in Table 15.4, these are the conditions tested for the jg conditional jump.

Conditions for Snum1 < Snum2   Again, as in the previous case, we develop our intuition by means of a few examples. The following table shows several examples in which the Snum1 < Snum2 holds.

Snum1	Snum2	ZF	OF	SF
55	56	0	0	1
−55	56	0	0	1
−56	−55	0	0	1
−75	55	0	1	0

Table 15.4 Jumps based on signed comparison

Mnemonic	Meaning	condition tested
je jz	jump if equal jump if zero	ZF = 1
jne jnz	jump if not equal jump if not zero	ZF = 0
jg jnle	jump if greater jump if not less or equal	ZF = 0 and SF = OF
jge jnl	jump if greater or equal jump if not less	SF = OF
jl jnge	jump if less jump if not greater or equal	SF ≠ OF
jle jng	jump if less or equal jump if not greater	ZF = 1 or SF ≠ OF

It appears from these examples that Snum1 < Snum2 holds if the following conditions are true:

	ZF	OF	SF
	0	0	1
or			
	0	1	0

That is, ZF = 0 and OF ≠ SF. In this case, ZF = 0 is redundant and the condition reduces to OF ≠ SF. As indicated in Table 15.4, this is the condition tested by the jl conditional jump instruction.

A Note on Conditional Jumps

All conditional jump instructions are encoded into the machine language using only 2 bytes (like the short jump instruction). As a consequence, all jumps should be short jumps. That is, the target instruction of a conditional jump must be 128 bytes before or 127 bytes after the instruction following the conditional jump instruction.

What if the target is outside this range? If the target is not reachable by using a short jump, you can use the following trick to overcome this limitation of the conditional jump instructions. For example, in the instruction sequence

```
target:
        . . .
        cmp     EAX,EBX
        je      target   ; target is not a short jump
        mov     ECX,10
        . . .
```

if `target` is not reachable by a short jump, it should be replaced by

```
target:
        . . .
        cmp     EAX,EBX
        jne     skip1    ; skip1 is a short jump
        jmp     target
skip1:
        mov     ECX,10
        . . .
```

What we have done here is negated the test condition (`je` becomes `jne`) and used an unconditional jump to transfer control to target. Recall that `jmp` instruction has both *short* and *near* versions.

Looping Instructions

Instructions in this group use the CX or ECX register to maintain repetition count. The CX register is used if the operand size is 16 bits; ECX is used for 32-bit operands. In the following discussion, we assume that the operand size is 32 bits. The three loop instructions decrement the ECX register before testing it for zero. Decrementing ECX does not affect any of the flags. The format of these instructions along with the action taken is shown below.

Mnemonic		Meaning	Action
`loop`	`target`	loop	$ECX = ECX - 1$ if $CX \neq 0$ jump to target
`loope`	`target`	loop while equal	$ECX = ECX - 1$
`loopz`	`target`	loop while zero	if ($ECX \neq 0$ and $ZF = 1$) jump to target
`loopne`	`target`	loop while not equal	$ECX = ECX - 1$
`loopnz`	`target`	loop while not zero	if ($ECX \neq 0$ and $ZF = 0$) jump to target

The destination specified in these instructions should be reachable by a short jump. This is a consequence of using the two-byte encoding with a single byte indicating the relative displacement, which should be within -128 to $+127$.

We have seen how the `loop` instruction is useful in constructing loops. The other two loop instructions are useful in writing loops that require two termination conditions. The following example illustrates this point.

Our First Program

Let us say that we want to write a loop that reads a series of nonzero integers into an array. The input can be terminated either when the array is full, or when the user types a zero, whichever occurs first. The program is given below.

Program 15.1 A program to read long integers into an array

```
1:  ;Reading long integers into an array          READ_ARRAY.ASM
2:  ;
3:  ;          Objective: To read long integers into an array;
4:  ;                     demonstrates the use of loopne.
5:  ;              Input: Requests nonzero values to fill the array;
6:  ;                     a zero input terminated input.
7:  ;             Output: Displays the array contents.
8:
9:  %include "io.mac"
10:
11: MAX_SIZE       EQU     20
12:
13: .DATA
14: input_prompt   db      "Enter at most 20 nonzero values "
15:                db      "(entering zero terminates input):",0
16: out_msg        db      "The array contents are: ",0
17: empty_msg      db      "The array is empty. ",0
18: query_msg      db      "Do you want to quit (Y/N): ",0
19:
20: .UDATA
21: array          resd    MAX_SIZE
22:
23: .CODE
24:         .STARTUP
25: read_input:
26:         PutStr  input_prompt ; request input array
27:         xor     ESI,ESI      ; ESI = 0 (ESI is used as an index)
28:         mov     ECX,MAX_SIZE
29: read_loop:
30:         GetLInt EAX
31:         mov     [array+ESI*4],EAX
32:         inc     ESI          ; increment array index
33:         cmp     EAX,0        ; number = zero?
34:         loopne  read_loop    ; iterates a maximum of MAX_SIZE
35: exit_loop:
36:         ; if the input is terminated by a zero,
37:         ; decrement ESI to keep the array size
```

```
38:              jnz     skip
39:              dec     ESI
40:     skip:
41:              mov     ECX,ESI      ; ESI has the actual array size
42:              jecxz   empty_array  ; if ecx = 0, empty array
43:              xor     ESI,ESI      ; initalize index to zero
44:              PutStr  out_msg
45:     write_loop:
46:              PutLInt [array+ESI*4]
47:              nwln
48:              inc     ESI
49:              loop    write_loop
50:              jmp     short user_query
51:     empty_array:
52:              PutStr  empty_msg    ; output empty array message
53:              nwln
54:     user_query:
55:              PutStr  query_msg    ; query user whether to terminate
56:              GetCh   AL
57:              cmp     AL,'Y'       ; if response is not 'Y'
58:              jne     read_input   ; repeat the loop
59:     done:
60:              .EXIT
```

The program has two loops: a read loop and a write loop. The read loop consists of lines 29–34. The loop termination conditions are implemented by the loopne instruction on line 34. To facilitate termination of the loop after reading a maximum of MAX_SIZE integers, the ECX register is initialized to MAX_SIZE on line 28. The other termination condition is tested on line 33.

The write loop consists of the code on lines 45–49. It uses the loop instruction (line 49) to iterate the loop where the loop count in ECX is the number of valid integers given by the user. However, we have a problem with the loop instruction: if the user did not enter any nonzero integers, the count in ECX is zero. In this case, the write loop iterates the maximum number of times (not zero times) because it decrements ECX before testing for zero. This is not what we want!

The instruction jecxz provides a remedy for this situation by testing the ECX register. The syntax of this instruction is

```
jecxz    target
```

which tests the ECX register and if it is zero, control is transferred to the target instruction. Thus, it is equivalent to

```
cmp    ECX,0
jz     target
```

except that jecxz does not affect any of the flags, while the cmp/jz combination affects the status flags. If the operand size is 16 bits, we can use the jcxz instruction instead of jecxz. Both instructions, however, use the same opcode E3H. The operand size determines the register—CX or ECX—used. We use this instruction on line 42 to test for an empty array. The rest of the code is straightforward to follow.

Notes on Execution Times of loop and jecxz Instructions

1. The functionality of the loop instruction can be replaced by

```
dec     ECX
jnz     target
```

   Surprisingly, the loop instruction is slower than the corresponding dec/jnz instruction pair.

2. Similarly, the jecxz instruction is slower than the code shown below:

```
cmp     ECX,0
jz      target
```

   Thus, for code optimization, these complex instructions should be avoided. However, for illustrative purposes, we use these instructions in the following examples.

Illustrative Examples

In this section, we present two examples to show the use of the selection and iteration instructions discussed in this chapter. The first example uses linear search for locating a number in an unsorted array, and the second example sorts an array of integers using the selection sort algorithm.

Example 15.3 *Linear search of an integer array.*
In this example, the user is asked to input an array of non-negative integers and then query whether a given number is in the array or not. The program, shown below, uses a procedure that implements the linear search to locate a number in an unsorted array.

The main procedure initializes the input array by reading a maximum of MAX_SIZE number of non-negative integers into the array. The user, however, can terminate the input by entering a negative number. The loop instruction (line 36), with ECX initialized to MAX_SIZE (line 29), is used to iterate a maximum of MAX_SIZE times. The other loop termination condition (i.e., entering a negative number) is tested on lines 32 and 33. The rest of the main program queries the user for a number and calls the linear search procedure to locate the number. This process is repeated as long as the user appropriately answers the query.

Program 15.2 Linear search of an integer array

```
 1:  ;Linear search of integer array                    LIN_SRCH.ASM
 2:  ;
 3:  ;              Objective: To implement linear search on an integer
 4:  ;                         array.
 5:  ;                  Input: Requests numbers to fill array and a
 6:  ;                         number to be searched for from user.
 7:  ;                 Output: Displays the position of the number in
 8:  ;                         the array if found; otherwise, not found
 9:  ;                         message.
10:  %include "io.mac"
11:
12:  MAX_SIZE          EQU    20
```

```
13:
14:     .DATA
15:     input_prompt    db      "Please enter input values "
16:                     db      "(a negative value terminates input):",0
17:     query_number    db      "Enter the number to be searched: ",0
18:     out_msg         db      "The number is at position ",0
19:     not_found_msg   db      "Number not in the array!",0
20:     query_msg       db      "Do you want to quit (Y/N): ",0
21:
22:     .UDATA
23:     array           resw    MAX_SIZE
24:
25:     .CODE
26:             .STARTUP
27:             PutStr  input_prompt
28:             xor     ESI,ESI         ; index = 0
29:             mov     ECX,MAX_SIZE
30:     array_loop:
31:             GetInt  AX
32:             cmp     AX,0            ; negative number?
33:             jl      read_input      ; if so, stop reading numbers
34:             mov     [array+ESI*2],AX
35:             inc     ESI             ; increment array index
36:             loop    array_loop      ; iterates a maximum of MAX_SIZE
37:     read_input:
38:             PutStr  query_number    ; request a number to be searched
39:             GetInt  AX
40:             push    AX              ; push number, size & array pointer
41:             push    ESI
42:             push    array
43:             call    linear_search
44:             ; linear_search returns in AX the position of the number
45:             ; in the array; if not found, it returns 0.
46:             cmp     AX,0            ; number found?
47:             je      not_found       ; if not, display number not found
48:             PutStr  out_msg         ; else, display number position
49:             PutInt  AX
50:             jmp     SHORT user_query
51:     not_found:
52:             PutStr  not_found_msg
53:     user_query:
54:             nwln
55:             PutStr  query_msg       ; query user whether to terminate
56:             GetCh   AL
57:             cmp     AL,'Y'          ; if response is not 'Y'
58:             jne     read_input      ; repeat the loop
59:     done:
60:             .EXIT
61:
62:     ;--------------------------------------------------------------
63:     ; This procedure receives a pointer to an array of integers,
```

```
64:    ; the array size, and a number to be searched via the stack.
65:    ; If found, it returns in AX the position of the number in
66:    ; the array; otherwise, returns 0.
67:    ; All registers, except EAX, are preserved.
68:    ;-----------------------------------------------------------
69:    linear_search:
70:            enter   0,0
71:            push    EBX             ; save registers
72:            push    ECX
73:            mov     EBX,[EBP+8]     ; copy array pointer
74:            mov     ECX,[EBP+12]    ; copy array size
75:            mov     AX,[EBP+16]     ; copy number to be searched
76:            sub     EBX,2           ; adjust pointer to enter loop
77:    search_loop:
78:            add     EBX,2           ; update array pointer
79:            cmp     AX,[EBX]        ; compare the numbers
80:            loopne  search_loop
81:            mov     AX,0            ; set return value to zero
82:            jne     number_not_found
83:            mov     EAX,[EBP+12]    ; copy array size
84:            sub     EAX,ECX         ; compute array index of number
85:    number_not_found:
86:            pop     ECX             ; restore registers
87:            pop     EBX
88:            leave
89:            ret     10
```

The linear search procedure receives a pointer to an array, its size, and the number to be searched via the stack. The search process starts at the first element of the array and proceeds until either the element is located or the array is exhausted. We use the loopne instruction on line 80 to test these two conditions for the termination of the search loop. The ECX is initialized (line 74) to the size of the array. In addition, a compare (line 79) tests if there is a match between the two numbers. If so, the zero flag is set and loopne terminates the search loop. If the number is found, the index of the number is computed (lines 83 and 84) and returned in the EAX register.

Example 15.4 *Sorting of an integer array using the selection sort algorithm.*
The main program is very similar to that in the last example, except for the portion that displays the sorted array. The sort procedure receives a pointer to the array to be sorted and its size via the stack. It uses the selection sort algorithm to sort the array in ascending order. The basic idea is as follows:

1. Search the array for the smallest element;
2. Move the smallest element to the first position by exchanging values of the first and smallest element positions;
3. Search the array for the smallest element from the second position of the array;
4. Move this element to position 2 by exchanging values as in Step 2;
5. Continue this process until the array is sorted.

The selection sort procedure implements the following pseudocode:

```
       selection_sort (array, size)
           for (position = 0 to size−2)
                   min_value := array[position]
                   min_position := position
                   for (j = position+1 to size−1)
                       if (array[j] < min_value)
                       then
                               min_value := array[j]
                               min_position := j
                       end if
                   end for
                   if (position ≠ min_position)
                   then
                               array[min_position] := array[position]
                               array[position] := min_value
                   end if
           end for
       end selection_sort
```

The selection sort procedure, shown in Program 15.3, implements this pseudocode with the following mapping of variables: `position` is maintained in ESI, and EDI is used for the index variable j. The `min_value` variable is maintained in DX and `min_position` in AX. The number of elements to be searched for finding the minimum value is kept in ECX.

Program 15.3 Sorting of an integer array using the selection sort algorithm

```
 1:  ;Sorting an array by selection sort            SEL_SORT.ASM
 2:  ;
 3:  ;         Objective: To sort an integer array using
 4:  ;                    selection sort.
 5:  ;             Input: Requests numbers to fill array.
 6:  ;            Output: Displays sorted array.
 7:  %include "io.mac"
 8:
 9:  MAX_SIZE        EQU    100
10:
11:  .DATA
12:  input_prompt        db      "Please enter input array (a negative "
13:                      db      "number terminates the input):",0
14:  out_msg             db      "The sorted array is:",0
15:  empty_array_msg db      "Empty array!",0
16:
17:  .UDATA
18:  array               resw   MAX_SIZE
19:
20:  .CODE
21:              .STARTUP
22:              PutStr  input_prompt ; request input array
23:              xor     ESI,ESI      ; array index = 0
```

```
24:            mov      ECX,MAX_SIZE
25:  array_loop:
26:            GetInt   AX
27:            cmp      AX,0            ; negative number?
28:            jl       exit_loop       ; if so, stop reading numbers
29:            mov      [array+ESI*2],AX
30:            inc      ESI             ; increment array index
31:            loop     array_loop      ; iterates a maximum of MAX_SIZE
32:  exit_loop:
33:            push     ESI             ; push array size & array pointer
34:            push     array
35:            call     selection_sort
36:            mov      ECX,ESI         ; ECX = array size
37:            jecxz    empty_array     ; check for empty array
38:            PutStr   out_msg         ; display sorted array
39:            nwln
40:            mov      EBX,array
41:            xor      ESI,ESI
42:  display_loop:
43:            PutInt   [array+ESI*2]
44:            nwln
45:            inc      ESI
46:            loop     display_loop
47:            jmp      short done
48:  empty_array:
49:            PutStr   empty_array_msg
50:            nwln
51:  done:
52:            .EXIT
53:
54:  ;----------------------------------------------------------------
55:  ; This procedure receives a pointer to an array of integers
56:  ; and the array size via the stack. The array is sorted by
57:  ; using the selection sort. All registers are preserved.
58:  ;----------------------------------------------------------------
59:  %define SORT_ARRAY   EBX
60:  selection_sort:
61:            pushad                   ; save registers
62:            mov      EBP,ESP
63:            mov      EBX,[EBP+36]    ; copy array pointer
64:            mov      ECX,[EBP+40]    ; copy array size
65:            cmp      ECX,1
66:            jle      sel_sort_done
67:            sub      ESI,ESI         ; array left of ESI is sorted
68:  sort_outer_loop:
69:            mov      EDI,ESI
70:            ; DX is used to maintain the minimum value and AX
71:            ; stores the pointer to the minimum value
72:            mov      DX,[SORT_ARRAY+ESI*2]   ; min. value is in DX
73:            mov      EAX,ESI         ; EAX = pointer to min. value
74:            push     ECX
```

```
75:            dec      ECX                ; size of array left of ESI
76: sort_inner_loop:
77:            inc      EDI                ; move to next element
78:            cmp      DX,[SORT_ARRAY+EDI*2] ; less than min. value?
79:            jle      skip1              ; if not, no change to min. value
80:            mov      DX,[SORT_ARRAY+EDI*2]; else, update min. value (DX)
81:            mov      EAX,EDI                 ; & its pointer (EAX)
82: skip1:
83:            loop     sort_inner_loop
84:            pop      ECX
85:            cmp      EAX,ESI    ; EAX = ESI?
86:            je       skip2      ; if so, element at ESI is in its place
87:            mov      EDI,EAX    ; otherwise, exchange
88:            mov      AX,[SORT_ARRAY+ESI*2]  ; exchange min. value
89:            xchg     AX,[SORT_ARRAY+EDI*2]  ; & element at ESI
90:            mov      [SORT_ARRAY+ESI*2],AX
91: skip2:
92:            inc      ESI                ; move ESI to next element
93:            dec      ECX
94:            cmp      ECX,1              ; if ECX = 1, we are done
95:            jne      sort_outer_loop
96: sel_sort_done:
97:            popad                       ; restore registers
98:            ret      8
```

Indirect Jumps

So far, we have used only the direct jump instruction. In direct jump, the target address (i.e., its relative offset value) is encoded into the jump instruction itself (see Figure 15.1 on page 320). We now look at indirect jumps. We limit our discussion to jumps within a segment.

In an indirect jump, the target address is specified indirectly either through memory or a general-purpose register. Thus, we can write

```
jmp    [ECX]
```

if the ECX register contains the offset of the target. In indirect jumps, the target offset is the absolute value (unlike the direct jumps, which use a relative offset value). The next example shows how indirect jumps can be used with a jump table stored in memory.

Example 15.5 *An example with an indirect jump.*
The objective here is to show how we can use the indirect jump instruction. To this end, we show a simple program that reads a digit from the user and prints the corresponding choice represented by the input. The listing is shown in Program 15.4. An input between 0 and 9 is valid. If the input is 0, 1, or 2, it displays a simple message to indicate the class selection. Other digit inputs terminate the program. If a nondigit input is given to the program, it displays an error message and requests a valid digit input.

Program 15.4 An example demonstrating the use of the indirect jump

```
 1:  ;Sample indirect jump example                        IJUMP.ASM
 2:  ;
 3:  ;        Objective: To demonstrate the use of indirect jump.
 4:  ;            Input: Requests a digit character from the user.
 5:  ;           Output: Appropriate class selection message.
 6:  %include "io.mac"
 7:
 8:  .DATA
 9:  jump_table  dd  code_for_0    ; indirect jump pointer table
10:              dd  code_for_1
11:              dd  code_for_2
12:              dd  default_code ; default code for digits 3-9
13:              dd  default_code
14:              dd  default_code
15:              dd  default_code
16:              dd  default_code
17:              dd  default_code
18:              dd  default_code
19:
20:  prompt_msg  db  "Type a digit: ",0
21:  msg_0       db  "Economy class selected.",0
22:  msg_1       db  "Business class selected.",0
23:  msg_2       db  "First class selected.",0
24:  msg_default db  "Not a valid code!",0
25:  msg_nodigit db  "Not a digit! Try again.",0
26:
27:  .CODE
28:          .STARTUP
29:  read_again:
30:          PutStr    prompt_msg    ; request a digit
31:          sub       EAX,EAX       ; EAX = 0
32:          GetCh     AL            ; read input digit and
33:          cmp       AL,'0'        ; check to see if it is a digit
34:          jb        not_digit
35:          cmp       AL,'9'
36:          ja        not_digit
37:          ; if digit, proceed
38:          sub       AL,'0'        ; convert to numeric equivalent
39:          mov       ESI,EAX       ; ESI is index into jump table
40:          jmp       [jump_table+ESI*4] ; indirect jump based on ESI
41:  test_termination:
42:          cmp       AL,2
43:          ja        done
44:          jmp       read_again
45:  code_for_0:
46:          PutStr    msg_0
47:          nwln
48:          jmp       test_termination
49:  code_for_1:
50:          PutStr    msg_1
```

```
51:              nwln
52:              jmp        test_termination
53:  code_for_2:
54:              PutStr     msg_2
55:              nwln
56:              jmp        test_termination
57:  default_code:
58:              PutStr     msg_default
59:              nwln
60:              jmp        test_termination
61:
62:  not_digit:
63:              PutStr     msg_nodigit
64:              nwln
65:              jmp        read_again
66:  done:
67:              .EXIT
```

In order to use the indirect jump, we have to build a jump table of pointers (see lines 9–18). The input is tested for its validity on lines 33 to 36. If the input is a digit, it is converted to act as an index into the jump table and stored in ESI. This value is used in the indirect jump instruction (line 40). The rest of the program is straightforward to follow.

Multiway Conditional Statements

In high-level languages, a two- or three-way conditional execution can be controlled easily by using if statements. For large multiway conditional execution, writing the code with nested if statements is tedious and error prone. High-level languages like C provide a special construct for multiway conditional execution. In this section we look at the C switch construct for multiway conditional execution.

Example 15.6 *Multiway conditional execution in C.*

As an example of the switch statement, consider the following code:

```
switch (ch)
{
    case 'a':
            count[0]++; /* increment count[0] */
            break;
    case 'b':
            count[1]++;
            break;
    case 'c':
            count[2]++;
            break;
    case 'd':
            count[3]++;
            break;
    case 'e':
            count[4]++;
```

```
                    break;
        default:
                    count[5]++;
    }
```

The semantics of the switch statement are as follows: If character ch is a, it executes the count[0]++ statement. The break statement is necessary to escape out of the switch statement. Similarly, if ch is b, count[1] is incremented, and so on. The default case statement is executed if ch is not one of the values specified in the other case statements.

The assembly language code generated by gcc (with −s option) is shown below. Note that gcc uses AT&T syntax, which is different from the syntax we have been using here. The assembly code is embellished for easy reading. We will discuss the AT&T syntax in Chapter 21 (see page 434).

```
 1:  main:
 2:                  . . .
 3:                  . . .
 4:          mov     EAX,ch
 5:          sub     EAX,97      ; 97 = ASCII for 'a'
 6:          cmp     EAX,4
 7:          ja      default
 8:          jmp     [jump_table+EAX*4]
 9:
10:          section  .rodata
11:          .align  4
12:  jump_table:
13:                  dd      case_a
14:                  dd      case_b
15:                  dd      case_c
16:                  dd      case_d
17:                  dd      case_e
18:          .text
19:  case_a:
20:                  inc     dword ptr[EBP-56]
21:  end_switch:
22:                  . . .
23:                  . . .
24:                  leave
25:                  ret
26:  case_b:
27:                  inc     dword ptr[EBP-52]
28:                  jmp     end_switch
29:  case_c:
30:                  inc     dword ptr[EBP-48]
31:                  jmp     end_switch
32:  case_d:
33:                  inc     dword ptr[EBP-44]
34:                  jmp     end_switch
35:  case_e:
36:                  inc     dword ptr[EBP-40]
37:                  jmp     end_switch
```

```
38:   default:
39:           inc    WORD PTR [EBP-20]
40:           jmp    end_switch
41:                  . . .
42:                  . . .
```

The character to be tested is moved to the EAX register. The subtract and compare instructions on lines 5 and 6 check if the character is within the range of the case values (i.e., between a and e). If not, the conditional jump instruction on line 7 transfers control to the default case. If it is one of the five lowercase letters, the indirect jump instruction on line 8 transfers control to the appropriate case using the jump table on lines 12–17. Since each entry in this jump table is four bytes long, we use a scale factor of 4 in this jump instruction.   □

Summary

We discussed unconditional and conditional jump instructions as well as compare and loop instructions in detail. These assembly language instructions are useful in implementing high-level language selection and iteration constructs such as if-then-else and while loops. Through detailed examples, we have shown how these instructions are used in the assembly language.

In the previous chapters, we extensively used direct jump instructions. In this chapter, we introduced the indirect jump instruction. In this jump instruction, the target of the jump is specified indirectly. Indirect jumps are useful to implement multiway conditional statements such as the switch statement in C. By means of an example, we have shown how such multiway statements of high-level languages are implemented in the assembly language.

16

Logical and Bit Operations

Bit manipulation is an important aspect of many high-level languages. This chapter discusses the logical and bit manipulation instructions supported by the assembly language. Assembly language provides several logical instructions to implement logical expressions. These instructions are also useful in implementing bitwise logical operations. In addition, several shift and rotate instructions are provided to facilitate bit manipulation. A few instructions are also provided to test and modify bits. These four types of instructions are discussed in this chapter. After describing these instructions, we give several examples to illustrate their application. The chapter concludes with a summary.

Introduction

Modern high-level languages provide several conditional and loop constructs. These constructs require Boolean or logical expressions for specifying conditions. Assembly language provides several logical instructions to express these conditions. These instructions manipulate logical data just like the arithmetic instructions manipulate arithmetic data (e.g., integers) with operations such as addition and subtraction. The logical data can take one of two possible values: `true` or `false`.

As the logical data can assume only one of two values, a single bit is sufficient to represent these values. Thus, all logical instructions that we discuss here operate on a bit-by-bit basis. By convention, if the value of the bit is 0 it represents `false`, and a value of 1 represents `true`.

We have discussed the assembly language logical instructions in Chapter 9, we devote part of this chapter to look at the typical uses for these logical instructions. The assembly language also provides several shift and rotate instructions. The shift instructions are very efficient in performing multiplication and division of signed and unsigned integers by a power of 2. We use examples to illustrate how this can be done using the shift instructions. Several bit manipulation instructions are also provided by the assembly language. These instructions can be used to test a specific bit, to scan for a bit, and so on. A detailed discussion of these instructions is provided in the later part of this chapter.

Logical Instructions

Assembly language provides a total of five logical instructions: and, or, not, xor, and test. Except for the not operator, all of the logical operators are binary operators (i.e., they require two operands). These instructions operate on 8-, 16-, or 32-bit operands.

All of these logical instructions affect the status flags. Since operands of these instructions are treated as a sequence of independent bits, these instructions do not generate carry or overflow. Therefore, the carry (CF) and overflow (OF) flags are cleared, and the status of the auxiliary flag (AF) is undefined.

Only the remaining three arithmetic flags—the zero flag (ZF), the sign flag (SF), and the parity flag (PF)—record useful information about the results of these logical instructions. Since we discussed these instructions in Chapter 9, we look at their typical use in this chapter.

The logical instructions are useful in implementing logical expressions of high-level languages. For example, C provides the following two logical operators:

C operator	Meaning
&&	AND
||	OR

These logical operators can be implemented using the corresponding assembly language logical instructions.

Some high-level languages provide bitwise logical operators. For example, C provides bitwise and (&), or (|), xor (^), and not (~) operators. These can be implemented by using the logical instructions provided in the assembly language.

Table 16.1 shows how the logical instructions are used to implement the bitwise logical operators of the C language. The variable mask is assumed to be in the ESI register.

Table 16.1 Examples of C bitwise logical operators

C statement	Assembly language instruction
mask = ~mask (complement mask)	not ESI
mask = mask & 85 (bitwise and)	and ESI,85
mask = mask | 85 (bitwise or)	or ESI,85
mask = mask ^ 85 (bitwise xor)	xor ESI,85

The and Instruction

The and instruction is useful mainly in three situations:

1. To support compound logical expressions and bitwise and operations of high-level languages;
2. To clear one or more bits;
3. To isolate one or more bits.

As we have already discussed the first use, here we concentrate on how and can be used to clear and isolate selected bits of an operand.

Clearing Bits   If you look at the truth table of the and operation (see page 204), you will notice that the source b_i acts as a *masking* bit: if the masking bit is 0, the output is 0 no matter what the other input bit is; if the masking bit is 1, the other input bit is passed to the output. Consider the following example:

$$
\begin{aligned}
\text{AL} &= 11010110 \leftarrow \text{operand to be manipulated} \\
\text{BL} &= \underline{11111100} \leftarrow \text{mask byte} \\
\text{and} \quad \text{AL,BL} &= 11010100
\end{aligned}
$$

Here, AL contains the operand to be modified by bit manipulation and BL contains a set of masking bits. Let us say that we want to force the least significant two bits to 0 without altering any of the remaining 6 bits. We select our mask in BL such that it contains 0's in those two bit positions and 1's in the remainder of the masking byte. As you can see from this example, the and instruction produces the desired result.

Here is another example that utilizes the bit clearing capability of the and instruction.

Example 16.1 *Even-parity generation (partial code).*
Let us consider generation of even parity. Assume that the most significant bit of a byte represents the parity bit; the rest of the byte stores the data bits. The parity bit can be set or cleared so as to make the number of 1's in the whole byte even.

If the number of 1's in the least significant 7 bits is even, the parity bit should be 0. Assuming that the byte to be parity-encoded is in the AL register, the following statement

```
and     AL,7FH
```

clears the parity bit without altering the remaining 7 bits. Notice that the mask 7FH has a 0 only in the parity bit position.   □

Isolating Bits   Another typical use of the and instruction is to isolate selected bit(s) for testing. This is done by masking out all the other bits, as shown in the next example.

Example 16.2 *Finding an odd or even number.*
In this example, we want to find out if the unsigned 8-bit number in the AL register is an odd or an even number. A simple test to determine this is to check the least significant bit of the number: if this bit is 1, it is an odd number; otherwise, an even number. Here is the code to perform this test using the and instruction.

```
            and     AL,1      ; mask = 00000001B
            jz      even_number
odd_number:
```

```
        . . .
    <code for processing odd number>
        . . .
even_number:
        . . .
    <code for processing even number>
        . . .
```

If AL has an even number, the least significant bit of AL is 0. Therefore,

```
and    AL,1
```

would produce a zero result in AL and sets the zero flag. The jz instruction is then used to test the status of the zero flag and to selectively execute the appropriate code fragment. This example shows the use of and to isolate a bit—the least significant bit in this case. □

The or Instruction

Like the and instruction, the or instruction is useful in two applications:

1. To support compound logical expressions and bitwise or operations of high-level languages;
2. To set one or more bits.

The use of the or instruction to express compound logical expressions and to implement bitwise or operations has been discussed before. We now discuss how the or instruction can be used to set a given set of bits.

As you can see from the truth table for the or operation (see page 204), when the source b_i is 0, the other input is passed on to the output; when the source b_i is 1, the output is forced to take a value of 1 irrespective of the other input. This property is used to set bits in the output. This is illustrated in the following example.

$$AL = 11010110B \leftarrow \text{operand to be manipulated}$$
$$BL = \underline{00000011B} \leftarrow \text{mask byte}$$
$$or \quad AL,BL = 11010111B$$

The mask value in the BL register causes the least significant two bits to change to 1. Here is another example.

Example 16.3 *Even-parity encoding (partial code).*
Consider the even-parity encoding discussed in Example 16.1. If the number of 1's in the least significant 7 bits is odd, we have to make the parity bit 1 so that the total number of 1's is even. This is done by

```
or    AL,80H
```

assuming that the byte to be parity-encoded is in the AL register. This or operation forces the parity bit to 1 while leaving the remainder of the byte unchanged. □

Cutting and Pasting Bits   The and and or instructions can be used together to "cut and paste" bits from two or more operands. We have already seen that and can be used to isolate selected bits—analogous to the "cut" operation. The or instruction can be used to "paste" the bits. For example, the following code creates a new byte in AL by combining odd bits from AL and even bits from BL registers.

```
and    AL,55H    ; cut odd bits
and    BL,0AAH   ; cut even bits
or     AL,BL     ; paste them together
```

The first and instruction selects only the odd bits from the AL register by forcing all even bits to 0 by using the mask 55H (01010101B). The second and instruction selects the even bits by using the mask AAH (10101010B). The or insstruction simply pastes these two bytes together to produce the desired byte in the AL register.

The xor Instruction

The xor instruction is useful mainly in three different situations:

1. To support compound logical expressions of high-level languages;
2. To toggle one or more bits;
3. To initialize registers to zero.

The use of the xor instruction to express compound logical expression has been discussed before. Here we focus on the use of xor to toggle bits and to initialize registers to zero.

Toggling Bits Using the xor instruction, we can toggle a specific set of bits. To do this, the mask should have 1 in the bit positions that are to be flipped. The following example illustrates this application of the xor instruction.

Example 16.4 *Parity conversion.*
Suppose we want to change the parity encoding of incoming data—if even parity, change to odd parity and vice versa. To accomplish this change, all we have to do is flip the parity bit, which can be done by

```
xor    AL,80H
```

Thus, an even-parity encoded ASCII character A—01000001B—is transformed into its odd-parity encoding, as shown below:

$$
\begin{array}{ll}
& \texttt{01000001B} \leftarrow \text{even-parity encoded ASCII character A} \\
\text{xor} & \underline{\texttt{10000000B}} \leftarrow \text{mask byte} \\
& \texttt{11000001B} \leftarrow \text{odd-parity encoded ASCII character A}
\end{array}
$$

Notice that if we perform the same xor operation on odd-parity encoding of A, we get back the even-parity encoding! This is an interesting property of the xor operation: xoring twice gives back the original value. This is not hard to understand, as xor behaves like the not operation by selectively flipping bits. This property is used in the following example to encrypt a byte. □

Example 16.5 *Encryption of data.*

Data encryption is useful in applications that deal with sensitive data. We can write a simple encryption program by using the xor instruction. The idea is that we will use the encryption key as the mask byte of the xor instruction as shown below. Assume that the byte to be encrypted is in the AL register and the encryption key is A6H.

```
; read a data byte into AL
xor     AL,0A6H
; write the data byte back from AL
```

Suppose we have received character B, whose ASCII code is 01000010B. After encryption, the character becomes d in ASCII, as shown below.

```
01000010B  ← ASCII character B
00100110B  ← encryption key (mask)
```
```
01100100B  ← ASCII character d
```

An encrypted data file can be transformed back into normal form by running the encrypted data through the same encryption process again. To continue with our example, if the above encrypted character code 64H (representing d) is passed through the encryption procedure, we get 42H, which is the ASCII code for character B. □

Initialization of Registers Another use of the xor instruction is to initialize registers to 0. We can, of course, do this by

```
mov     EAX,0
```

but the same result can be achieved by

```
xor     EAX,EAX
```

This works no matter what the contents of the EAX register are. To see why this is so, look at the truth table for the xor operation given on page 204. Since we are using the same operand as both inputs, the input can be either both 0 or 1. In both cases, the result bit is 0—see the first and last rows of the xor truth table.

These two instructions, however, are not exactly equivalent. The xor instruction affects flags, whereas the mov instruction does not. Of course, we can also use the sub instruction to do the same. All three instructions take one clock cycle to execute, even though the mov instruction requires more bytes to encode the instruction.

The not Instruction

The not instruction is used for complementing bits. Its main use is in supporting logical expressions of high-level languages and bitwise-NOT operations.

Another possible use for the not instruction is to compute 1's complement. Recall that 1's complement of a number is simply the complement of the number. Since most systems use the 2's complement number representation system, generating 2's complement of an 8-bit signed number using not involves

```
not     AL
inc     AL
```

However, the IA-32 instruction set also provides the neg instruction to reverse the sign of a number. Thus, the not instruction is not useful for this purpose.

The test Instruction

The test instruction is the logical equivalent of the compare (cmp) instruction. It performs the logical and operation but, unlike the and instruction, test does not alter the destination operand. That is, test is a nondestructive and instruction.

This instruction is used only to update the flags, and a conditional jump instruction normally follows it. For instance, in Example 16.2 on page 343, the instruction

```
and    AL,1
```

destroys the contents of the AL register. If our purpose is to test whether the unsigned number in the AL register is an odd number, we can do this using test without destroying the original number. For convenience, the example is reproduced below with the test instruction.

```
        test   AL,1     ; mask = 00000001B
        jz     even_number
odd_number:
                . . .
even_number:
                . . .
```

Shift Instructions

The instruction set provides two types of shift instructions: one for logical shifts, and the other for arithmetic shifts. The logical shift instructions are:

shl (SHift Left)
shr (SHift Right)

and the arithmetic shift instructions are

sal (Shift Arithmetic Left)
sar (Shift Arithmetic Right)

Another way of looking at these two types of shift instructions is that the logical type instructions work on unsigned binary numbers, and the arithmetic type work on signed binary numbers. We will get back to this discussion later in this section.

Effect on Flags As in the logical instructions, the auxiliary flag is undefined following a shift instruction. The carry flag (CF), zero flag (ZF), and parity flag (PF) are updated to reflect the result of a shift instruction. The CF always contains the bit last shifted out of the operand. The OF is undefined following a multibit shift. In a single-bit shift, OF is set if the sign bit has been changed as a result of the shift operation; OF is cleared otherwise. The OF is rarely tested in a shift operation; we often test the CF and ZF flags.

Logical Shift Instructions

Since we discussed the logical shift instructions in Chapter 9, we discuss their usage here. These instructions are useful mainly in two situations:

1. To implement the shift operations of high-level languages;
2. To manipulate bits;
3. To multiply and divide unsigned numbers by a power of 2.

Table 16.2 Examples of bitwise logical operators

C statement	Assembly language instruction
mask = mask>>2 (right-shift mask by two bit positions)	shr SI,2
mask = mask<<4 (left-shift mask by four bit positions)	shl SI,4

Shift Operations Some high level languages provide left- and right-shift operations. For example, the C language provides two shift operators: left shift (<<) and right shift (>>). These operators can be implemented with the assembly language shift instructions.

Table 16.2 shows how the shift instructions are used to implement the shift operators of the C language. The variable mask is assumed to be in the SI register.

Bit Manipulation The shift operations provide flexibility to manipulate bits as illustrated by the following example.

Example 16.6 *Another encryption example.*
Consider the encryption example discussed on page 346. In this example, we use the following encryption algorithm: encrypting a byte involves exchanging the upper and lower nibbles (i.e., 4 bits). This algorithm also allows the recovery of the original data by applying the encryption twice, as in the xor example on page 346.

Assuming that the byte to be encrypted is in the AL register, the following code implements this algorithm:

```
; AL contains the byte to be encrypted
mov     AH,AL
shl     AL,4      ; move lower nibble to upper
shr     AH,4      ; move upper nibble to lower
or      AL,AH     ; paste them together
; AL has the encrypted byte
```

To understand this code, let us trace the execution by assuming that AL has the ASCII character A. Therefore,

```
AH = AL = 01000001B
```

The idea is to move the upper nibble to lower in the AH register, and the other way around in the AL register. To do this, we use shl and shr instructions. The shl instruction replaces the shifted bits by 0's and after the shl

```
AL = 00010000B
```

Similarly, shr introduces 0's in the vacated bits on the left. Thus, after the shr instruction

```
AH = 00000100B
```

Table 16.3 Doubling and halving of unsigned numbers

Binary number	Decimal value
00011100	28
00111000	56
01110000	112
11100000	224
10101000	168
01010100	84
00101010	42
00010101	21

The or instruction pastes these two bytes together, as shown below:

$$AL = 00010000B$$
$$AH = 00000100B$$
$$or \quad AL,AH = 00010100B$$

We show later that this encryption can be done better by using a rotate instruction (see Example 16.7 on page 353). □

Multiplication and Division Shift operations are very effective in performing doubling or halving of unsigned binary numbers. More generally, they can be used to multiply or divide unsigned binary numbers by a power of 2.

In the decimal number system, we can easily perform multiplication and division by a power of 10. For example, if we want to multiply 254 by 10, we will simply append a 0 at the right (analogous to shifting left by a digit with the vacated digit receiving a 0). Similarly, division of 750 by 10 can be accomplished by throwing away the 0 on the right (analogous to right shift by a digit).

Since computers use the binary number system, they can perform multiplication and division by a power of 2. This point is further clarified in Table 16.3. The first half of this table shows how shifting a binary number to the left by one bit position results in multiplying it by 2. Note that the vacated bits are replaced by 0's. This is exactly what the shl instruction does. Therefore, if we want to multiply a number by 8 (i.e., 2^3), we can do so by shifting the number left by three bit positions.

Similarly, as shown in the second half of the table, shifting the number right by one bit position is equivalent to dividing it by 2. Thus, we can use the shr instruction to perform division by a power of 2. For example, to divide a number by 32 (i.e., 2^5), we right shift the number by five bit positions. Remember that this division process corresponds to integer division, which discards any fractional part of the result.

Table 16.4 Doubling of signed numbers

Signed binary number	Decimal value
00001011	+11
00010110	+22
00101100	+44
01011000	+88
11110101	−11
11101010	−22
11010100	−44
10101000	−88

Arithmetic Shift Instructions

This set of shift instructions

> sal (Shift Arithmetic Left)
> sar (Shift Arithmetic Right)

can be used to shift signed numbers left or right, as shown below.

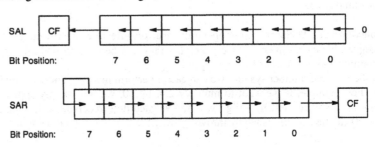

As with the logical shift instructions, the CL register can be used to specify the count value. The general format is

```
sal    destination,count        sar    destination,count
sal    destination,CL           sar    destination,CL
```

Doubling Signed Numbers   Doubling a signed number by shifting it left by one bit position may appear to cause problems because the leftmost bit is used to represent the sign of the number. It turns out that this is not a problem at all. See the examples presented in Table 16.4 to develop your intuition. The first group presents the doubling effect on positive numbers and the second group on negative numbers. In both cases, a 0 replaces the vacated bit. Why isn't shifting the sign bit out causing problems? The reason is that signed numbers are sign-extended to fit a larger-than-required number of bits. For example, if we want to represent numbers in the range of +3 and

Table 16.5 Division of signed numbers by 2

Signed binary number	Decimal value
01011000	+88
00101100	+44
00010110	+22
00001011	+11
10101000	−88
11010100	−44
11101010	−22
11110101	−11

−4, 3 bits are sufficient to represent this range. If we use a byte to represent the same range, the number is sign-extended by copying the sign bit into the higher order five bits, as shown below.

$$+3 = \overbrace{00000}^{\substack{\textit{sign bit}\\\textit{copied}}} 011\text{B}$$

$$-3 = \overbrace{11111}^{\substack{\textit{sign bit}\\\textit{copied}}} 101\text{B}$$

Clearly, doubling a signed number is no different than doubling an unsigned number. Thus, no special shift left instruction is needed for the signed numbers. In fact, sal and shl are one and the same instruction—sal is an alias for shl.

Halving Signed Numbers   Can we also forget about treating the signed numbers differently in halving a number? Unfortunately, we cannot! When we right shift a signed number, the vacated left bit should be replaced by a copy of the sign bit. This rules out the use of shr for signed numbers. See the examples presented in Table 16.5. The sar instruction precisely does this—it copies the sign bit into the vacated bit on the left.

Remember that the shift right operation performs integer division. For example, right shifting 00001011B (+11D) by a bit results in 00000101B (+5D).

Why Use Shifts for Multiplication and Division?

Shifts are more efficient than the corresponding multiplication and division instructions. As an example, consider dividing an unsigned 16-bit number in the AX register by a power of 2 that is BX. Using the div instruction, we can write

```
; dividend is assumed to be in DX:AX
div     BX
```

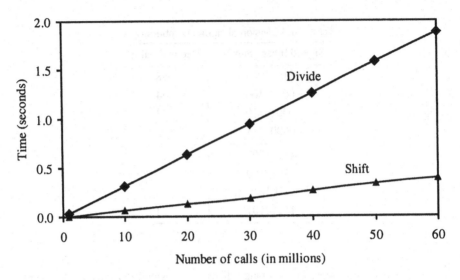

Figure 16.1 Execution time comparison of implementing division by a power of 2 using the shift and divide instructions.

Now let us look at how we can perform this multiplication with the shr instruction. If we place the bit shift count in the CL register, we can use this shift instruction to perform the division operation. In the following code

```
bsr    CX,BX
shr    AX,CL
```

the bsr instruction places this shift count in the CX register. We give details of this instruction on page 355.

Figure 16.1 shows the execution of these two versions on a 2.8 GHz Pentium 4 machine running the Red Hat Linux. The x-axis gives the number times (in millions) the division operation is performed. The y-axis gives the execution time in seconds. The "Shift" line is the execution time of the version that uses shr to perform the division 40000/1024. The corresponding execution time for the div version is shown by the "Divide" line. Clearly, the shift version is much more efficient than the divide version.

Doubleshift Instructions

The IA-32 instruction set also provides two doubleshift instructions for 32-bit and 64-bit shifts. These two instructions operate on either word or doubleword operands and produce a word or doubleword result, respectively. The doubleshift instructions require three operands, as shown below:

```
shld    dest,src,count   ; left shift
shrd    dest,src,count   ; right shift
```

dest and src can be either a word or a doubleword. While the dest operand can be in a register or memory, the src operand must be in a register. The shift count can be specified as in the shift instructions—either as an immediate value or in the CL register.

A significant difference between the shift and doubleshift instructions is that the src operand supplies the bits in doubleshift instructions, as shown below:

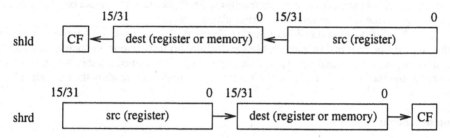

Note that the bits shifted out of the src operand go into the dest operand. However, the src operand itself is not modified by the doubleshift instructions. Only the dest operand is updated appropriately. As in the shift instructions, the last bit shifted out is stored in the carry flag. Later we present an example that demonstrates the use of the doubleshift instructions (see Example 16.8 on page 354).

Rotate Instructions

A drawback with the shift instructions is that the bits shifted out are lost. There are situations where we want to keep these bits. While the doubleshift instructions provide this capability on word and doubleword operands, the rotate instructions remedy this drawback for a variety of operands. These instructions can be divided into two types: rotate without involving the carry flag (CF), or rotate through the carry flag. Since we presented these two types of rotate instructions in Chapter 9, we discuss their typical usage next.

Rotate Without Carry

The rotate instructions are useful in rearranging bits of a byte, word, or doubleword. This is illustrated below by revisiting the data encryption example given on page 348.

Example 16.7 *Encryption example revisited.*
In Example 16.6, we encrypted a byte by interchanging the upper and lower nibbles. This can be done easily either by

```
mov     CL,4
ror     AL,CL
```

or by

```
mov     CL,4
rol     AL,CL
```

This is a much simpler solution than the one using shifts.   □

Rotate Through Carry

The rcl and rcr instructions provide flexibility in bit rearranging. Furthermore, these are the only two instructions that take the carry flag bit as an input. This feature is useful in multiword shifts, as illustrated by the following example.

Example 16.8 *Shifting 64-bit numbers.*

We have seen that multiplication and division by a power of 2 is faster if we use shift operations rather than multiplication or division instructions. Shift instructions operate on operands of size up to 32 bits. What if the operand to be manipulated is bigger?

Since the shift instructions do not involve the carry flag as input, we have two alternatives: either use `rcl` or `rcr` instructions, or use the double shift instructions for such multiword shifts. As an example, assume that we want to multiply a 64-bit unsigned number by 16. The 64-bit number is assumed to be in the EDX:EAX register pair with EAX holding the least significant 32 bits.

Rotate version:

```
      mov    CX,4        ; 4 bit shift
   shift_left:
      shl    EAX,1       ; moves leftmost bit of AX to CF
      rcl    EDX,1       ; CF goes to rightmost bit of DX
      loop   shift_left
```

Doubleshift version:

```
      shld   EDX,EAX,4 ; EAX is unaffected by shld
      shl    EAX,4
```

Similarly, if we want to divide the same number by 16, we can use the following code:

Rotate version:

```
      mov    CX,4        ; 4 bit shift
   shift_right:
      shr    EDX,1       ; moves rightmost bit of DX to CF
      rcr    EAX,1       ; CF goes to leftmost bit of AX
      loop   shift_right
```

Doubleshift version:

```
      shrd   EAX,EDX,4 ; EDX is unaffected by shld
      shr    EDX,4
```

Clearly, the doubleshift instruction avoids the need for a loop.   □

Bit Instructions

The IA-32 instruction set includes several bit test and modification instructions as well as bit scan instructions. This section discusses these two groups of instructions. The programming examples given later illustrate the use of these instructions.

Bit Test and Modify Instructions

There are four bit test instructions. Each instruction takes the position of the bit to be tested. The least significant bit is considered as bit position zero. A summary of the four instructions is given below:

Instruction	Effect on Selected Bit
bt (Bit Test)	No effect
bts (Bit Test and Set)	Selected bit← 1
btr (Bit Test and Reset)	Selected bit← 0
btc (Bit Test and Complement)	Selected bit← NOT(Selected bit)

All four instructions copy the selected bit into the carry flag. The format of all four instructions is the same. We use the bt instruction to illustrate the format of these instructions.

```
bt      operand,bit_pos
```

where operand can be a word or doubleword located either in a register or in memory. The bit_pos specifies the bit position to be tested. It can be specified as an immediate value or in a 16- or 32-bit register. Instructions in this group affect only the carry flag. The other five status flags are undefined following a bit test instruction.

Bit Scan Instructions

Bit scan instructions scan the operand for a 1 bit and return its bit position in a register. There are two instructions—one to scan forward and the other to scan backward. The format is

```
bsf     dest_reg,operand      ;bit scan forward
bsr     dest_reg,operand      ;bit scan reverse
```

where operand can be a word or doubleword located either in a register or in memory. The dest_reg receives the bit position. It must be a 16- or 32-bit register. The zero flag is set if all bits of operand are 0; otherwise, the ZF is cleared and the dest_reg is loaded with the bit position of the first 1 bit while scanning forward (for bsf), or reverse (for bsr). Like the bit test and modify instructions, these two instructions affect only the zero flag; the other five status flags are undefined.

Our First Program

As our first program, we look at how we can use the sar instruction to perform signed integer division. In this program, we divide a signed 32-bit integer by a power of 2. The program listing is given in Program 16.1. It requests two numbers from the user. The numerator can be a signed 32-bit integer. This is read using GetLint on line 20. The user is then prompted to enter the denominator. After validating the denominator, the program outputs the result of the division operation. After displaying the result, it queries whether the user wants to quit. Based on the response received, the program either terminates or repeats the process.

Program 16.1 Integer division using the shift instruction

```
 1:  ;Division using shifts                    SAR_DIVIDE.ASM
 2:  ;
 3:  ;          Objective: To divide a 32-bit signed number
 4:  ;                     by a power of 2 using SAR.
 5:  ;              Input: Requests two numbers from the user.
 6:  ;             Output: Prints the division result.
 7:  %include "io.mac"
 8:  .DATA
 9:  prompt1     db  'Please input numerator: ',0
10:  prompt2     db  'Please input denominator: ',0
11:  out_msg1    db  'The integer division result is: ',0
12:  query_msg   db  'Do you want to quit (Y/N): ',0
13:  error_msg   db  'Denominator is zero. ',
14:              db  'Enter a nonzero value: ',0
15:
16:  .CODE
17:      .STARTUP
18:  read_input:
19:      PutStr  prompt1      ; request numerator
20:      GetLInt EAX
21:      PutStr  prompt2      ; request denominator
22:  read_denom:
23:      GetLInt EBX
24:      bsr     ECX,EBX      ; ECX receives the position of
25:                          ; the leftmost 1 bit in EBX
26:      ; bsr clears ZF if there is at least 1 bit
27:      ; in denominator; ZF = 0 if all the bits are zero
28:      jnz     nonZero
29:      PutStr  error_msg    ; if denominator is zero,
30:      jmp     read_denom   ; read again
31:  nonZero:
32:      sar     EAX,CL
33:      PutStr  out_msg1     ; output the result
34:      PutLInt EAX
35:      nwln
36:      PutStr  query_msg    ; query whether to terminate
37:      GetCh   AL
38:      cmp     AL,'Y'       ; if response is not 'Y'
39:      jne     read_input   ; repeat the loop
40:  done:
41:      .EXIT
```

The division is done by the `sar` instruction. To do this, we need to find out the number bit positions the numerator needs to be shifted right. If we assume that the denominator is a power of 2, it will have a single 1 bit. We use `bsr` to find the position of this 1 bit. The instruction

```
bsr     ECX,EBX
```

scans the denominator in EBX from the most significant bit (i.e., it scans the value in EBX from left to right). The first 1 bit position is returned in the ECX register. If the denominator is zero, the `bsr` instruction sets the zero flag (ZF = 1). Otherwise, it is cleared. We use this condition to detect if the denominator is zero (line 28). If it is zero, an error message is displayed and the user is prompted for a nonzero value. If the denominator is not a power of 2, the most significant bit that has 1 is returned by the `bsr` instruction. For example, if the denominator is 10, it divides the numerator by 8.

Illustrative Examples

This section presents two examples that use the instructions introduced in this chapter.

Example 16.9 *Multiplication using only shifts and adds.*
The objective of this example is to show how multiplication can be done entirely by using the shift and add operations. We consider multiplication of two unsigned 8-bit numbers. In order to use the shift operation, we have to express the multiplier as a power of 2. For example, if the multiplier is 64, the result can be obtained by shifting the multiplicand left by six bit positions because $2^6 = 64$.

What if the multiplier is not a power of 2? In this case, we have to express this number as a sum of powers of 2. For example, if the multiplier is 10, it can be expressed as 8+2, where each term is a power of 2. Then the required multiplication can be done by two shifts and one addition.

The question now is: How do we express the multiplier in this form? If we look at the binary representation of the multiplicand (10D = 00001010B), there is a 1 in bit positions with weights 8 and 2. Thus, for each 1 bit in the multiplier, the multiplicand should be shifted left by a number of positions equal to the bit position number. In the above example, the multiplicand should be shifted left by 3 and 1 bit positions and then added. This procedure is formalized in the following algorithm:

```
mult8 (number1, number2)
    result = 0
    for (i = 7 downto 0)
        if (bit(number2, i) = 1)
            result = result + number1 * 2^i
        end if
    end for
end mult8
```

The function `bit` returns the *i*th bit of `number2`. The program listing is given in Program 16.2. The main program requests two numbers from the user and calls the procedure `mult8` and displays the result. As in the previous program, it queries the user whether to quit and proceeds according to the response.

Program 16.2 Multiplication of two 8-bit numbers using only shifts and adds

```
 1:  ;8-bit multiplication using shifts              SHL_MLT.ASM
 2:  ;
 3:  ;         Objective: To multiply two 8-bit unsigned numbers
 4:  ;                    using SHL rather than MUL instruction.
 5:  ;             Input: Requests two unsigned numbers.
 6:  ;            Output: Prints the multiplication result.
 7:  %include "io.mac"
 8:  .DATA
 9:  input_prompt   db  'Please input two short numbers: ',0
10:  out_msg1       db  'The multiplication result is: ',0
11:  query_msg      db  'Do you want to quit (Y/N): ',0
12:
13:  .CODE
14:      .STARTUP
15:  read_input:
16:      PutStr  input_prompt ; request two numbers
17:      GetInt  AX           ; AX = first number
18:      GetInt  BX           ; BX = second number
19:      call    mult8        ; mult8 leaves result in AX
20:      PutStr  out_msg1
21:      PutInt  AX
22:      nwln
23:      PutStr  query_msg    ; query whether to terminate
24:      GetCh   AL
25:      cmp     AL,'Y'       ; if the response is not 'Y'
26:      jne     read_input   ; repeat the loop
27:  done:
28:      .EXIT
29:
30:  ;-------------------------------------------------------------
31:  ; mult8 multiplies two 8-bit unsigned numbers passed on
32:  ; to it in AL and BL. The 16-bit result is returned in AX.
33:  ; This procedure uses the SHL instruction to do the
34:  ; multiplication. All registers, except AX, are preserved.
35:  ;-------------------------------------------------------------
36:  mult8:
37:      push    CX           ; save registers
38:      push    DX
39:      push    SI
40:      xor     DX,DX        ; DX = 0 (keeps mult. result)
41:      mov     CX,7         ; CX = # of shifts required
42:      mov     SI,AX        ; save original number in SI
43:  repeat1:        ; multiply loop - iterates 7 times
44:      rol     BL,1         ; test number2 bits from left
45:      jnc     skip1        ; if 0, do nothing
46:      mov     AX,SI        ; else, AX = number1*bit weight
47:      shl     AX,CL
48:      add     DX,AX        ; update running total in DX
49:  skip1:
50:      dec     CX
```

```
51:        jnz      repeat1
52:        rol      BL,1              ; test the rightmost bit of AL
53:        jnc      skip2             ; if 0, do nothing
54:        add      DX,SI             ; else, add number1
55:  skip2:
56:        mov      AX,DX             ; move final result into AX
57:        pop      SI                ; restore registers
58:        pop      DX
59:        pop      CX
60:        ret
```

The mult8 procedure multiplies two 8-bit unsigned numbers and returns the result in AX. It follows the algorithm discussed on page 357. The multiply loop (lines 43–51) tests the most significant 7 bits of the multiplier. The least significant bit is tested on lines 52 and 53. Notice that the procedure uses rol rather than shl to test each bit (lines 44 and 52). The use of rol automatically restores the BL register after 8 rotates.   □

Example 16.10 *Multiplication using only shifts and adds—version 2.*
In this example, we rewrite the mult8 procedure of the last example by using the bit test and scan instructions. In the previous version, we used a loop (see lines 43–50) to test each bit. Since we are interested only in 1 bits, we can use a bit scan instruction to do this job. The modified mult8 procedure is shown below.

```
 1:  ;--------------------------------------------------------------
 2:  ; mult8 multiplies two 8-bit unsigned numbers passed on
 3:  ; to it in AL and BL. The 16-bit result is returned in AX.
 4:  ; This procedure uses the SHL instruction to do the
 5:  ; multiplication. All registers, except AX, are preserved.
 6:  ; Demonstrates the use of bit instructions BSF and BTC.
 7:  ;--------------------------------------------------------------
 8:  mult8:
 9:        push     CX                ; save registers
10:        push     DX
11:        push     SI
12:        xor      DX,DX             ; DX = 0 (keeps mult. result)
13:        mov      SI,AX             ; save original number in SI
14:  repeat1:
15:        bsf      CX,BX             ; CX = first 1 bit position
16:        jz       skip1             ; if ZF=1, no 1 bit in B
17:        mov      AX,SI             ; else, AX = number1*bit weight
18:        shl      AX,CL
19:        add      DX,AX             ; update running total in DX
20:        btc      BX,CX             ; complement the bit found by BSF
21:        jmp      repeat1
22:  skip1:
23:        mov      AX,DX             ; move final result into AX
24:        pop      SI                ; restore registers
25:        pop      DX
26:        pop      CX
27:        ret
```

The modified loop (lines 14–21) replaces the loop in the previous version. This code is more efficient because the number of times the loop iterates is equal to the number of 1's in BX. The previous version, on the other hand, always iterates seven times. Also note that we can replace the btc instruction on line 20 by a btr instruction. Similarly, the bsf instruction on line 15 can be replaced by a brf instruction.   □

Summary

We discussed logical, shift, and rotate instructions available in the assembly language. Logical instructions are useful to implement bitwise logical operators and Boolean expressions. However, in some instances Boolean expressions can also be implemented by using conditional jump instructions without using the logical instructions.

Shift and rotate instructions provide flexibility to bit manipulation operations. There are two types of shift instructions: one works on logical and unsigned values, and the other is meant for signed values. There are also two types of rotate instructions: rotate without, or rotate through carry. Rotate through carry is useful in shifting multiword data.

The instruction set also provides two doubleshift instructions that work on either word or doubleword operands. In addition, four instructions for testing and modifying bits and two instructions to scan for a bit are available.

We discussed how the logical and shift instructions are used to implement logical expressions and bitwise logical operations in high-level languages. Shift instructions can be used to multiply or divide by a number that is a power of 2. We have demonstrated that the shift instructions for such arithmetic operations are much more efficient than the corresponding arithmetic instructions.

PART VI

Advanced Assembly Language

17

String Processing

String manipulation is an important aspect of any programming task. Strings are represented in a variety of ways. We start the chapter with a discussion of the two representation schemes used to store strings. The IA-32 instruction set supports string processing by a special set of instructions. We describe these instructions in detail. Several examples are presented to illustrate the use of string instructions in developing procedures for string processing. We also describe a program to test the procedures developed here. A novelty of this program is that it demonstrates the use of indirect procedure calls. Even though these instructions are called string instructions, they can be used for processing other types data. We demonstrate this aspect by means of an example. The chapter concludes with a summary.

String Representation

A string can be represented either as a *fixed-length* string or as a *variable-length* string. In the fixed-length representation, each string occupies exactly the same number of character positions. That is, each string has the same length, where the length of a string refers to the number of characters in the string. In this representation, if a string has fewer characters, it is extended by padding, for example, with blank characters. On the other hand, if a string has more characters, it is usually truncated to fit the storage space available.

Clearly, if we want to avoid truncation of larger strings, we need to fix the string length carefully so that it can accommodate the largest string that the program will ever handle. A potential problem with this representation is that we should anticipate this value, which may cause difficulties with program maintenance. A further disadvantage of using fixed-length representation is that memory space is wasted if majority of the strings are shorter than the length used.

The variable-length representation avoids these problems. In this scheme, a string can have as many characters as required (usually, within some system-imposed limit). Associated with each string, there is a string length attribute giving the number of characters in the string. This length attribute is given in one of two ways:

1. Explicitly storing string length, or
2. Using a sentinel character.

These two methods are discussed next.

Explicitly Storing String Length

In this method, string length attribute is explicitly stored along with the string, as shown in the following example:

```
string    DB    'Error message'
str_len   DW    $-string
```

where $ is the location counter symbol that represents the current value of the location counter. In this example, $ points to the byte after the last character of `string`. Therefore,

```
$-string
```

gives the length of the string. Of course, we could also write

```
string    DB    'Error message'
str_len   DW    13
```

However, if we modify the contents of `string` later, we have to update the string length value as well. On the other hand, by using `$-string`, we let the assembler do the job for us at assembly time.

Using a Sentinel Character

In this method, strings are stored with a trailing sentinel character to delimit a string. Therefore, there is no need to store the string length explicitly. The assumption here is that the sentinel character is a special character that does not appear within a string. We normally use a special, nonprintable character that does not appear in strings. We have been using the ASCII NULL-character (00H) to terminate strings. Such NULL-terminated strings are called *ASCIIZ strings*. Here are some examples:

```
string1   DB    'This is OK',0
string2   DB    'Price = $9.99',0
```

The C language, for example, uses this representation to store strings. In the remainder of this chapter, we use this representation for strings.

String Instructions

There are five main string-processing instructions. These can be used to copy a string, to compare two strings, and so on. It is important to note that these instructions are not just for the strings. We can use them for other types of data. For example, we could use them to copy arrays of doublewords, as we shall see later. The five basic instructions are shown in Table 17.1.

Specifying Operands

As indicated, each string instruction may require a source operand, a destination operand, or both. For 32-bit segments, string instructions use ESI and EDI registers to point to the source and destination operands, respectively. The source operand is assumed to be at DS:ESI in memory, and the destination operand at ES:EDI in memory. For 16-bit segments, SI and DI registers are used instead of ESI and EDI registers. If both the operands are in the same data segment, we can let both DS and ES point to the data segment to use the string instructions.

Table 17.1 String Instructions

Mnemonic	Meaning	Operand(s) required
LODS	LOaD String	source
STOS	STOre String	destination
MOVS	MOVe String	source & destination
CMPS	CoMPare Strings	source & destination
SCAS	SCAn String	destination

Variations

Each string instruction can operate on 8-, 16-, or 32-bit operands. As part of execution, string instructions automatically update (i.e., increment or decrement) the index register(s) used by them. For byte operands, source and destination index registers are updated by 1. These registers are updated by 2 and 4 for word and doubleword operands, respectively. In this chapter, we focus mostly on byte operand strings.

String instructions derive much of their power from the fact that they can accept a repetition prefix to repeatedly execute the operation. These prefixes are discussed next. The direction of string processing—forward or backward—is controlled by the direction flag (discussed later).

Repetition Prefixes

String instructions can be repeated by using a repetition prefix. As shown in Table 17.2, the three prefixes are divided into two categories: *unconditional* or *conditional* repetition. None of the flags is affected by these instructions.

Table 17.2 Repetition Prefixes

unconditional repeat	
rep	REPeat
conditional repeat	
repe/repz	REPeat while Equal
	REPeat while Zero
repne/repnz	REPeat while Not Equal
	REPeat while Not Zero

rep This is an unconditional repeat prefix and causes the instruction to repeat according to the value in the ECX register. Note that for 16-bit addresses, CX register is used. The semantics of the rep prefix are

while (ECX $\neq$ 0)
        execute the string instruction;
        ECX := ECX–1;
end while

The ECX register is first checked and if it is not 0, only then is the string instruction executed. Thus, if ECX is 0 to start with, the string instruction is not executed at all. This is in contrast to the `loop` instruction, which first decrements and then tests if ECX is 0. Thus, with `loop`, ECX = 0 results in a maximum number of iterations, and usually a `jecxz` check is needed.

repe/repz   This is one of the two conditional repeat prefixes. Its operation is similar to that of `rep` except that the repetition is also conditional on the zero flag (ZF), as shown below:

while (ECX $\neq$ 0)
        execute the string instruction;
        ECX := ECX–1;
        if (ZF = 0)
        then
                exit loop
        end if
end while

The maximum number of times the string instruction is executed is determined by the contents of ECX, as in the `rep` prefix. But the actual number of times the instruction is repeated is determined by the status of ZF. Conditional repeat prefixes are useful with `cmps` and `scas` string instructions.

repne/repnz   This prefix is similar to the `repe/repz` prefix except that the condition tested is ZF = 1 as shown below:

while (ECX $\neq$ 0)
        execute the string instruction;
        ECX := ECX–1;
        if (ZF = 1)
        then
                exit loop
        end if
end while

Direction Flag

The direction of string operations depends on the value of the direction flag. Recall that this is one of the bits of the flag's register (see Figure 4.4 on page 65). If the direction flag (DF) is clear (i.e., DF = 0), string operations proceed in the forward direction (from head to tail of a string); otherwise, string processing is done in the opposite direction.

Two instructions are available to explicitly manipulate the direction flag:

`std`   set direction flag (DF = 1)
`cld`   clear direction flag (DF = 0)

Both of these instructions do not require any operands. Each instruction is encoded using a single byte.

Usually, it does not matter whether a string is processed in the forward or backward direction. For sentinel character-terminated strings, forward direction is preferred. However, there are situations where one particular direction is mandatory. For example, if we want to shift a string right by one position, we have to start with the tail and proceed toward the head (i.e., move backward) as in the following example.

Initial string →	a	b	c	0	?	
After one shift →	a	b	c	0	0	
After two shifts →	a	b	c	c	0	
After three shifts→	a	b	b	c	0	
Final string →	a	a	b	c	0	

String Move Instructions

There are three basic instructions in this group—movs, lods, and stos. Each instruction can take one of four forms. We start our discussion with the first instruction.

Move a String (movs)   The format of the movs instruction is:

```
movs      dest_string,source_string
movsb
movsw
movsd
```

Using the first form, we can specify the source and destination strings. This specification will be sufficient to determine whether it is a byte, word, or doubleword operand. However, this form is not used frequently.

In the other three forms, the suffix b, w, or d is used to indicate byte, word, or doubleword operands. This format applies to all the string instructions of this chapter.

The movs instruction is used to copy a value (byte, word, or doubleword) from the source string to the destination string. As mentioned earlier, the source string value is pointed to by DS:ESI and the destination string location is indicated by ES:EDI in memory. After copying, the ESI and EDI registers are updated according to the value of the direction flag and the operand size. Thus, before executing the movs instruction, all four registers should be set up appropriately. (This is necessary even if you use the first format.) Note that our focus is on 32-bit segments. For 16-bit segments, we use the SI and DI registers.

```
movsb — move a byte string
     ES:EDI := (DS:ESI)      ; copy a byte
     if (DF = 0)             ; forward direction
     then
           ESI := ESI+1
           EDI := EDI+1
```

```
        else                    ; backward direction
                ESI := ESI–1
                EDI := EDI–1
        end if
    Flags affected: none
```

For word and doubleword operands, the index registers are updated by 2 and 4, respectively. This instruction, along with the rep prefix, is useful to copy a string. More generally, we can use them to perform memory-to-memory block transfers. Here is an example that copies string1 to string2.

```
    .DATA
    string1     db      'The original string',0
    strLen      EQU     $-string1
    .UDATA
    string2     resb    80
    .CODE
        .STARTUP
        mov     ECX,strLen      ; strLen includes NULL
        mov     ESI,string1
        mov     EDI,string2
        cld                     ; forward direction
        rep     movsb
```

Since the movs instruction does not change any of the flags, conditional repeat (repe or repne) should not be used with this instruction.

Load a String (lods) This instruction copies the value from the source string (pointed to by DS:ESI) in memory to AL (for byte operands—lodsb), AX (for word operands—lodsw), or EAX (for doubleword operands—lodsd).

```
    lodsb — load a byte string
                AL := (DS:ESI)     ; copy a byte
                if (DF = 0)        ; forward direction
                then
                        ESI := ESI+1
                else                ; backward direction
                        ESI := ESI–1
                end if
    Flags affected: none
```

Use of the rep prefix does not make sense, as it will leave only the last value in AL, AX, or EAX. This instruction, along with the stos instruction, is often used when processing is required while copying a string. This point is elaborated after we describe the stos instruction.

Store a String (stos) This instruction performs the complementary operation. It copies the value in AL (for stosb), AX (for stosw), or EAX (for stosd) to the destination string (pointed to by ES:EDI) in memory.

```
stosb — store a byte string
        ES:EDI := AL      ; copy a byte
        if (DF = 0)       ; forward direction
        then
                EDI := EDI+1
        else              ; backward direction
                EDI := EDI−1
        end if
Flags affected: none
```

We can use the `rep` prefix with the `stos` instruction if our intention is to initialize a block of memory with a specific character, word, or doubleword value. For example, the following code initializes `array1` with −1.

```
.UDATA
array1    resw    100
.CODE
    .STARTUP
    mov     ECX,100
    mov     EDI,array1
    mov     AX,-1
    cld                     ; forward direction
    rep     stosw
```

In general, the `rep` prefix is not useful with `lods` and `stos` instructions. These two instructions are often used in a loop to do value conversions while copying data. For example, if `string1` only contains letters and blanks, the following code

```
    mov     ECX,strLen
    mov     ESI,string1
    mov     EDI,string2
    cld                     ; forward direction
loop1:
    lodsb
    or      AL,20H
    stosb
    loop    loop1
done:
        .  .  .
```

can convert it to a lowercase string. Note that blank characters are not affected because 20H represents blank in ASCII, and the

```
or      AL,20H
```

instruction does not have any effect on it. The advantage of `lods` and `stos` is that they automatically increment ESI and EDI registers.

String Compare Instruction

The `cmps` instruction can be used to compare two strings.

> `cmpsb` — compare two byte strings
> > Compare the two bytes at DS:ESI and ES:EDI and set flags
> > **if** (DF = 0)   ; forward direction
> > **then**
> > > ESI := ESI+1
> > > EDI := EDI+1
> > **else**   ; backward direction
> > > ESI := ESI−1
> > > EDI := EDI−1
> > **end if**
> Flags affected: As per `cmp` instruction

The `cmps` instruction compares the two bytes, words, or doublewords at DS:ESI and ES:EDI and sets the flags just like the `cmp` instruction. Like the `cmp` instruction, `cmps` performs

```
(DS:ESI) - (ES:EDI)
```

and sets the flags according to the result. The result itself is not stored. We can use conditional jumps like `ja`, `jg`, `jc`, etc. to test the relationship of the two values. As usual, the ESI and EDI registers are updated according to the value of the direction flag and the operand size. The `cmps` instruction is typically used with the `repe/repz` or `repne/repnz` prefix.

The following code

```
.DATA
string1     db      'abcdfghi',0
strLen      EQU     $-string1
string2     db      'abcdefgh',0
.CODE
   .STARTUP
   mov      ECX,strLen
   mov      ESI,string1
   mov      EDI,string2
   cld                       ; forward direction
   repe     cmpsb
```

leaves ESI pointing to `g` in `string1` and EDI to `f` in `string2`. Therefore, adding

```
   dec      ESI
   dec      EDI
```

leaves ESI and EDI pointing to the last character that differs. Then we can use, for example,

```
   ja       str1Above
```

to test if `string1` is greater (in the collating sequence) than `string2`. This, of course, is true in this example. A more concrete example is given later (see the string comparison procedure on page 375).

The `repne/repnz` prefix can be used to continue comparison as long as the comparison fails and the loop terminates when a matching value is found. For example,

```
.DATA
string1     db      'abcdfghi',0
strLen      EQU     $-string1-1
string2     db      'abcdefgh',0
.CODE
    .STARTUP
    mov     ECX,strLen
    mov     ESI,string1 + strLen - 1
    mov     EDI,string2 + strLen - 1
    std                 ; backward direction
    repne   cmpsb
    inc     ESI
    inc     EDI
```

leaves ESI and EDI pointing to the first character that matches in the backward direction.

Scanning a String

The scas (scanning a string) instruction is useful in searching for a particular value or character in a string. The value should be in AL (for scasb), AX (for scasw), or EAX (for scasd), and ES:EDI should point to the string to be searched.

> scasb — scan a byte string
> > Compare AL to the byte at ES:EDI and set flags
> > **if** (DF = 0)   ; forward direction
> > **then**
> > > EDI := EDI+1
> > **else**   ; backward direction
> > > EDI := EDI−1
> > **end if**
> Flags affected: As per cmp instruction

Like with the cmps instruction, the repe/repz or repne/repnz prefix can be used.

```
.DATA
string1     db      'abcdefgh',0
strLen      EQU     $ - string1
.CODE
    .STARTUP
    mov     ECX,strLen
    mov     EDI,string1
    mov     AL,'e'      ; character to be searched
    cld                 ; forward direction
    repne   scasb
    dec     EDI
```

This program leaves the EDI register pointing to e in string1. The following example can be used to skip the initial blanks.

```
.DATA
string1     db      '       abc',0
strLen      EQU     $-string1
.CODE
```

```
        .STARTUP
        mov     ECX,strLen
        mov     EDI,string1
        mov     AL,' '          ; character to be searched
        cld                     ; forward direction
        repe    scasb
        dec     EDI
```

This program leaves the EDI register pointing to the first nonblank character in string1, which is a in our example.

Our First Program

The string instructions we have discussed so far are not restricted to string operations only. For example, they can be used for general-purpose memory-to-memory copy operations. To demonstrate this aspect, we write a program to perform a memory-to-memory copy operation. In this program, we copy the contents of a doubleword array to another array. Of course, we can do this without the string instructions. Program 17.1 shows how this can be done using the string instructions.

Program 17.1 Memory-to-memory copy using the string instructions

```
 1: ;Memory-to-memory copy                    MEM_COPY.ASM
 2: ;
 3: ;         Objective: To demonstrate memory-to-memory copy
 4: ;                    using the string instructions.
 5: ;             Input: None.
 6: ;            Output: Outputs the copied array.
 7:
 8: %include "io.mac"
 9:
10: .DATA
11: in_array       dd  10,20,30,40,50,60,70,80,90,100
12: ARRAY_SIZE     EQU ($-in_array)/4
13: out_msg        db  'The copied array is: ',0
14:
15: .UDATA
16: out_array      resd  ARRAY_SIZE
17:
18: .CODE
19:         .STARTUP
20:             mov     ECX,ARRAY_SIZE   ; ECX = array size
21:             mov     ESI,in_array     ; ESI = in array pointer
22:             mov     EDI,out_array    ; EDI = out array pointer
23:             cld                      ; forward direction
24:             rep     movsd
25:
26:             PutStr  out_msg
27:             mov     ECX,ARRAY_SIZE
28:             mov     ESI,out_array
29: repeat1:
```

```
30:             lodsd
31:             PutLInt EAX
32:             nwln
33:             loop    repeat1
34:             .EXIT
```

This program's structure follows the example we have seen in Chapter 13 (see Example 13 on page 281). The source array (in_array) is initialized with 10 values, each is a 32-bit value. The array size is determined on line 12 by using the predefined location counter symbol $. For a discussion of how the array size is computed, see Example 13 on page 281.

To copy the array, we store the array size in ECX (line 20) and the source and destination array pointers in ESI and EDI registers, respectively (lines 21 and 22). Once these registers are set up, we clear the direction flag using cld on line 23. Copying of the array is done using the movsd instruction along with the rep prefix on line 24.

In operating systems that use segmentation provided by the IA-32 architecture, we have to make sure that the ES segment register points to the data segment. This, for example, can be done by the following code:

```
mov     AX,DS
mov     ES,AX
```

We have to resort to an indirect means to copy the DS contents to ES as

```
mov     ES,DS
```

is not a valid instruction. Since the Linux operating system does not use the segmentation and initializes the DS and ES registers to the same value, we don't need this code in our programs.

To display the contents of the destination array (out_array), we use the lodsd instruction, which loads the value into the EAX register. This value is displayed using the PutLInt on line 31. We cannot use the rep prefix with the lodsd instruction as we need to display the value. Instead, we use a loop to display the array values.

Illustrative Examples

We now give some examples to illustrate the use of the string instructions discussed in this chapter. These procedures along with several others are available in the string.asm file. These procedures receive the parameters via the stack. The pointer to a string is received in segment:offset form. A string pointer is loaded into either DS and ESI or ES and EDI using the lds or les instructions, the details of which are discussed next.

LDS and LES Instructions   The syntax of these instructions is

```
lds     register,source
les     register,source
```

where register is a 32-bit general-purpose register, and source is a pointer to a 48-bit memory operand. The instructions perform the following actions:

```
lds
        register := (source)
                DS := (source + 4)
les
        register := (source)
                ES := (source + 4)
```

The 32-bit value at source in memory is copied to register and the next 16-bit value (i.e., at source+4) is copied to the DS or ES register. Both instructions affect none of the flags. By specifying ESI as the register operand, lds can be conveniently used to set up a source string. Similarly, a destination string can be set up by specifying EDI with les. For completeness, you should note that lfs, lgs, and lss instructions are available to load the other segment registers.

Examples

We will next present two simple string processing procedures. These functions are available in high-level languages such as C. All procedures use the carry flag (CF) to report input error—*not a string*. This error results if the input passed is not a string whose length is less than the STR_MAX constant defined in string.asm. The carry flag is set (i.e., CF = 1) if there is an input error; otherwise, the carry flag is cleared.

The following constants are defined in string.asm:

```
STR_MAX     EQU         128
%define     STRING1     [EBP+8]
%define     STRING2     [EBP+16]
```

Example 17.1 *String length procedure to return the length of* string1.

String length is the number of characters in a string, excluding the NULL character. We use the scasb instruction and search for the NULL character. Since scasb works on the destination string, les is used to load the string pointer to the ES and EDI registers from the stack. STR_MAX, the maximum length of a string, is moved into ECX, and the NULL character (i.e., 0) is moved into the AL register. The direction flag is cleared to initiate a forward search. The string length is obtained by taking the difference between the end of the string (pointed to by EDI) and the start of the string available at [EBP+8]. The EAX register is used to return the string length value. This procedure is similar to the C function strlen.

```
;-------------------------------------------------------------
;String length procedure. Receives a string pointer
;(seg:offset) via the stack. If not a string, CF is set;
;otherwise, string length is returned in EAX with CF = 0.
;Preserves all registers.
;-------------------------------------------------------------
str_len:
        enter   0,0
        push    ECX
        push    EDI
        push    ES
        les     EDI,STRING1  ; copy string pointer to ES:EDI
        mov     ECX,STR_MAX  ; need to terminate loop if EDI
                             ; is not pointing to a string
        cld                  ; forward search
```

```
        mov     AL,0            ; NULL character
        repne   scasb
        jcxz    sl_no_string    ; if ECX = 0, not a string
        dec     EDI             ; back up to point to NULL
        mov     EAX,EDI
        sub     EAX,[EBP+8]     ; string length in EAX
        clc                     ; no error
        jmp     SHORT sl_done
sl_no_string:
        stc                     ; carry set => no string
sl_done:
        pop     ES
        pop     EDI
        pop     ECX
        leave
        ret     8               ; clear stack and return
```

Example 17.2 *String compare procedure to compare two strings.*
This function uses the cmpsb instruction to compare two strings. It returns in EAX a negative value if string1 is lexicographically less than string2, 0 if string1 is equal to string2, and a positive value if string1 is lexicographically greater than string2.

To implement this procedure, we have to find the first occurrence of a character mismatch between the corresponding characters in the two strings (when scanning strings from left to right). The relationship between the strings is the same as that between these two differing characters. When we include the NULL character in this comparison, this algorithm works correctly even when the two strings are of different length.

The str_cmp instruction finds the length of string2 using the str_len procedure. It does not really matter whether we find the length of string2 or string1. We use this value (plus one to include NULL) to control the number of times the cmpsb instruction is repeated. Conditional jump instructions are used to test the relationship between the differing characters to return an appropriate value in the EAX register. The corresponding function in C is strcmp, which can be invoked by strcmp(sting1,string2). This function also returns the same values (negative, 0, or positive value) depending on the comparison.

```
;-----------------------------------------------------------
;String compare procedure. Receives two string pointers
;(seg:offset) via the stack - string1 and string2.
;If string2 is not a string, CF is set;
;otherwise, string1 and string2 are compared and returns a
;a value in EAX with CF = 0 as shown below:
;    EAX = negative value  if string1 < string2
;    EAX = zero            if string1 = string2
;    EAX = positive value  if string1 > string2
;Preserves all registers.
;-----------------------------------------------------------
str_cmp:
        enter   0,0
        push    ECX
        push    EDI
        push    ESI
```

```
        push    DS
        push    ES
        ; find string length first
        les     EDI,STRING2  ; string2 pointer
        push    ES
        push    EDI
        call    str_len
        jc      sm_no_string

        mov     ECX,EAX      ; string1 length in ECX
        inc     ECX          ; add 1 to include NULL
        lds     ESI,STRING1  ; string1 pointer
        cld                  ; forward search
        repe    cmpsb
        je      same
        ja      above
below:
        mov     EAX,-1       ; EAX = -1 => string1 < string2
        clc
        jmp     SHORT sm_done
same:
        xor     EAX,EAX      ; EAX = 0 => string match
        clc
        jmp     SHORT sm_done
above:
        mov     EAX,1        ; EAX = 1 => string1 > string2
        clc
        jmp     SHORT sm_done
sm_no_string:
        stc                  ; carry set => no string
sm_done:
        pop     ES
        pop     DS
        pop     ESI
        pop     EDI
        pop     ECX
        leave
        ret     16           ; clear and return
```

In addition to these two functions, several other string processing functions such as string copy and string concatenate are available in the string.asm file.

Testing String Procedures

Now let us turn our attention to testing the string procedures developed in the last section. A partial listing of this program is given in Program 17.2. The full program can be found in the str_test.asm file.

Our main interest in this section is to show how using an indirect procedure call would substantially simplify calling the appropriate procedure according to the user request. Let us first look at the *indirect call* instruction for 32-bit segments.

Program 17.2 Part of string test program `str_test.asm`

```
        . . .
        . . .
.DATA
proc_ptr_table    dd   str_len_fun,str_cpy_fun,str_cat_fun
                  dd   str_cmp_fun,str_chr_fun,str_cnv_fun
MAX_FUNCTIONS     EQU  ($ - proc_ptr_table)/4

choice_prompt     db   'You can test several functions.',CR,LF
                  db   '     To test          enter',CR,LF
                  db   'String length         1',CR,LF
                  db   'String copy           2',CR,LF
                  db   'String concatenate    3',CR,LF
                  db   'String compare        4',CR,LF
                  db   'Locate character      5',CR,LF
                  db   'Convert string        6',CR,LF
                  db   'Invalid response terminates program.',CR,LF
                  db   'Please enter your choice: ',0
        . . .
        . . .
.UDATA
string1           resb  STR_MAX
string2           resb  STR_MAX

.CODE
        . . .
        . . .
        .STARTUP
query_choice:
        xor     EBX,EBX
        PutStr  choice_prompt    ; display menu
        GetCh   BL               ; read response
        sub     BL,'1'
        cmp     BL,0
        jb      invalid_response
        cmp     BL,MAX_FUNCTIONS
        jb      response_ok
invalid_response:
        PutStr  invalid_choice
        nwln
        jmp     SHORT done
response_ok:
        shl     EBX,2                     ; multiply EBX by 4
        call    [proc_ptr_table+EBX]; indirect call
        jmp     query_choice
done:
        .EXIT
        . . .
        . . .
```

Indirect Procedure Call

In our discussions so far, we have been using only the direct procedure calls, where the offset of the target procedure is provided directly. Recall that, even though we write only the procedure name, the assembler generates the appropriate offset value at the assembly time.

In indirect procedure calls, this offset is given with one level of indirection. That is, the call instruction contains either a memory word address (through a label) or a 32-bit general-purpose register. The actual offset of the target procedure is obtained from the memory word or the register referenced in the call instruction. For example, we could use

```
call    EBX
```

if EBX contains the offset of the target procedure. As part of executing this `call` instruction, the contents of the EBX register are used to load EIP to transfer control to the target procedure. Similarly, we can use

```
call    [target_proc_ptr]
```

if the memory at `target_proc_ptr` contains the offset of the target procedure. As we have seen in Chapter 15, the `jmp` is another instruction that can be used for indirect jumps in exactly the same way as the indirect `call`.

Back to the Example   We maintain a procedure pointer table `proc_ptr_table` to facilitate calling the appropriate procedure. The user query response is used as an index into this table to get the target procedure offset. The EBX register is used as the index into this table. The instruction

```
call    [proc_ptr_table+EBX]
```

causes the indirect procedure call. The rest of the program is straightforward to follow.

Summary

We started this chapter with a brief discussion of various string representation schemes. Strings can be represented as either fixed-length or variable-length. Each representation has advantages and disadvantages. Variable-length strings can be stored either by explicitly storing the string length or by using a sentinel character to terminate the string. High-level programming languages like C use the NULL-terminated storage representation for strings. We have also used the same representation to store strings.

There are five basic string instructions—`movs`, `lods`, `stos`, `cmps`, and `scas`. Each of these instructions can work on byte, word, or doubleword operands. These instructions do not require the specification of any operands. Instead, the required operands are assumed to be at DS:ESI and/or ES:EDI for 32-bit segments. For 16-bit segments, SI and DI registers are used instead of the ESI and EDI registers, respectively. In addition, the direction flag is used to control the direction of string processing (forward or backward). Efficient code can be generated by combining string instructions with the repeat prefixes. Three repeat prefixes—`rep`, `repe`/`repz`, and `repne`/`repnz`—are provided.

We also demonstrated, by means of an example, how indirect procedure calls can be used. Indirect procedure calls give us a powerful mechanism by which, for example, we can pass a procedure to be executed as an argument using the standard parameter passing mechanisms.

18

ASCII and BCD Arithmetic

In the previous chapters, we used the binary representation and discussed several instructions that operate on binary data. In this chapter, we present two alternative representations—ASCII and BCD—that avoid or reduce the conversion overhead. We start this chapter with a brief introduction to these two representations. The next two sections discuss how arithmetic operations can be done in these two representations.

While the ASCII and BCD representations avoid/reduce the conversion overhead, processing numbers in these two representations is slower than in the binary representation. This inherent tradeoff between conversion overhead and processing overhead among the three representations is explored toward the end of the chapter. The chapter ends with a summary.

Introduction

We normally represent the numeric data in the binary system. We have discussed several arithmetic instructions that operate on such data. The binary representation is used internally for manipulation (e.g., arithmetic and logical operations).

When numbers are entered from the keyboard or displayed, they are in the ASCII form. Thus, it is necessary to convert numbers from ASCII to binary at the input end; we have to convert from binary to ASCII to output results as shown below:

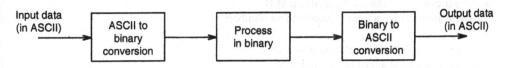

We used `GetInt`/`GetLint` and `PutInt`/`PutLint` to perform these two conversions, respectively. These conversions represent an overhead, but we can process numbers much more efficiently in the binary form.

In some applications where processing of numbers is quite simple (for example, a single addition), the overhead associated with the two conversions might not be justified. In this case, it is probably more efficient to process numbers in the decimal form.

Another reason for processing numbers in decimal form is that we can use as many digits as necessary, and we can control rounding-off errors. This is important when representing dollars and cents for financial records.

Decimal numbers can be represented in one of two forms: ASCII or binary-coded-decimal (BCD). These two representations are discussed next.

ASCII Representation

In this representation, numbers are stored as strings of ASCII characters. For example, 1234 is represented as

    31 32 33 34H

where 31H is the ASCII code for 1, 32H for 2, etc. As you can see, arithmetic on decimal numbers represented in the ASCII form requires special care. There are two instructions to handle these numbers:

    aaa — ASCII adjust after addition
    aas — ASCII adjust after subtraction

We discuss these two instructions after introducing the BCD representation.

BCD Representation

There are two types of BCD representation: unpacked BCD and packed BCD. In the unpacked BCD representation, each digit is stored in a byte, while two digits are packed into a byte in the packed representation.

Unpacked BCD   This representation is similar to the ASCII representation except that each byte stores the binary equivalent of a decimal digit. Note that the ASCII codes for digits 0 through 9 are 30H through 39H. Thus, if we mask off the upper four bits, we get the unpacked BCD representation. For example, 1234 is stored in this representation as

    01 02 03 04H

We deal with only positive numbers in this chapter. Thus, there is no need to represent the sign. But if a sign representation is needed, an additional byte can be used for the sign. The number is positive if this byte is 00H and negative if 80H.

There are two instructions to handle these numbers:

    aam — ASCII adjust after multiplication
    aad — ASCII adjust before division

Since this representation is similar to the ASCII representation, the four instructions—aaa, aas, aam, and aad—can be used with the ASCII and unpacked BCD representations.

Packed BCD   In the last two representations, each digit of a decimal number is stored in a byte. The upper four bits of each byte contain redundant information. In packed BCD representation, each digit is stored using only four bits. Thus, two decimal digits can be packed into a byte. This reduces the memory requirement by half compared to the other two representations. For example, the decimal number 1234 is stored in the packed BCD representation as

12 34H

which requires only two bytes as opposed to four in the other two representations. There are only two instructions that support addition and subtraction of packed BCD numbers:

daa — decimal adjust after addition
das — decimal adjust after subtraction

There is no support for multiplication or division operations. These two instructions are discussed later.

Processing in ASCII Representation

As mentioned before, four instructions are available to process numbers in the ASCII representation:

aaa — ASCII adjust after addition
aas — ASCII adjust after subtraction
aam — ASCII adjust after multiplication
aad — ASCII adjust before division

These instructions do not take any operands. They assume that the required operand is in the AL register.

ASCII Addition

To understand the need for the aaa instruction, look at the next two examples.

Example 18.1 *An ASCII addition example.*
Consider adding two ASCII numbers 4 (34H) and 5 (35H).

```
34H = 00110100B
35H = 00110101B
69H = 01101001B
```

The sum 69H is not correct. The correct value should be 09H in unpacked BCD representation. In this example, we get the right answer by setting the upper four bits to 0. This scheme, however, does not work in cases where the result digit is greater than 9, as shown in the next example.   □

Example 18.2 *Another ASCII addition example.*
In this example, consider the addition of two ASCII numbers, 6 (36H) and 7 (37H).

```
36H = 00110110B
37H = 00110111B
6DH = 01101101B
```

Again, the sum 6DH is incorrect. We would expect the sum to be 13 (01 03H). In this case, ignore 6 as in the last example. But we have to add 6 to D to get 13. We add 6 because that is the difference between the bases of hex and decimal number systems. □

The aaa instruction performs these adjustments. This instruction is used after performing an addition operation by using either an add or adc instruction. The resulting sum in AL is adjusted to unpacked BCD representation. The aaa instruction works as follows.

1. If the least significant four bits of AL are greater than 9 or if the auxiliary flag is set, it adds 6 to AL and 1 to AH. Both CF and AF are set.
2. In all cases, the most significant four bits of AL are cleared (i.e., zeroed).

Here is an example that illustrates the use of the aaa instruction.

Example 18.3 *A typical use of the aaa instruction.*
```
sub    AH,AH    ; clear AH
mov    AL,'6'   ; AL = 36H
add    AL,'7'   ; AL = 36H+37H = 6DH
aaa             ; AX = 0103H
or     AL,30H   ; AL = 33H
```

To convert the result in AL to an ASCII result, we have to insert 3 into the upper four bits of the AL register. □

To add multidigit decimal numbers, we have to use a loop that adds one digit at a time starting from the rightmost digit. Program 18.1 shows how the addition of two 10-digit decimal numbers is done in ASCII representation.

ASCII Subtraction

The aas instruction is used to adjust the result of a subtraction operation (sub or sbb) and works like aaa. The actions taken by aas are

1. If the least significant four bits of AL are greater than 9 or if the auxiliary flag is set, it subtracts 6 from AL and 1 from AH. Both CF and AF are set.
2. In all cases, the most significant four bits of AL are cleared (i.e., zeroed).

It is straightforward to see that the adjustment is needed only when the result is negative, as shown in the following examples.

Example 18.4 *ASCII subtraction (positive result).*
```
sub    AH,AH    ; clear AH
mov    AL,'9'   ; AL = 39H
sub    AL,'3'   ; AL = 39H-33H = 6H
aas             ; AX = 0006H
or     AL,30H   ; AL = 36H
```

Notice that the aas instruction does not change the contents of the AL register, as the result is a positive number. □

Example 18.5 *ASCII subtraction (negative result).*
```
sub    AH,AH      ; clear AH
mov    AL,'3'     ; AL = 33H
sub    AL,'9'     ; AL = 33H-39H = FAH
aas               ; AX = FF04H
or     AL,30H     ; AL = 34H
```

The AL result indicates the magnitude; the aas instruction sets the carry flag to indicate that a borrow has been generated.   □

Is the last result, FF04H, generated by aas useful? It is when you consider multidigit subtraction. For example, if we are subtracting 29 from 53 (i.e., 53−29), the first loop iteration performs 3−9 as in the last example. This gives us the result 4 in AL and the carry flag is set. Next we perform 5−2 using sbb to include the borrow generated by the previous subtraction. This leaves 2 as the result. After ORing with 30H, we will have 32 34H, which is the correct answer (24).

ASCII Multiplication

The aam instruction is used to adjust the result of a mul instruction. Unlike addition and subtraction, multiplication should not be performed on ASCII numbers but on unpacked BCD numbers. The aam works as follows: AL is divided by 10 and the quotient is stored in AH and the remainder in AL.

Example 18.6 *ASCII multiplication.*
```
mov    AL,3       ; multiplier in unpacked BCD form
mov    BL,9       ; multiplicand in unpacked BCD form
mul    BL         ; result 001BH is in AX
aam               ; AX = 0207H
or     AX,3030H   ; AX = 3237H
```

Notice that the multiplication should be done using unpacked BCD numbers—not on ASCII numbers! If the digits in AL and BL are in ASCII as in the following code, we have to mask off the upper four bits.

```
mov    AL,'3'     ; multiplier in ASCII
mov    BL,'9'     ; multiplicand in ASCII
and    AL,0FH     ; multiplier in unpacked BCD form
and    BL,0FH     ; multiplicand in unpacked BCD form
mul    BL         ; result 001BH is in AX
aam               ; AX = 0207H
or     AL,30H     ; AL = 37H
```

The aam instruction works only with the mul instruction, not with the imul instruction.   □

ASCII Division

The aad instruction adjusts the numerator in AX *before* dividing two unpacked decimal numbers. The denominator has to be a single byte unpacked decimal number. The aad instruction multiplies AH by 10 and adds it to AL and sets AH to zero. For example, if AX = 0207H before aad, AX changes to 001BH after executing aad. As you can see from the last example, aad reverses the operation of aam.

Example 18.7 *ASCII division.*
Consider dividing 27 by 5.

```
mov     AX,0207H ; dividend in unpacked BCD form
mov     BL,05H   ; divisor in unpacked BCD form
aad              ; AX = 001BH
div     BL       ; AX = 0205H
```

The `aad` instruction converts the unpacked BCD number in AX to the binary form so that `div` can be used. The `div` instruction leaves the quotient (05H) in the AL register and the remainder (02H) in the AH register.   □

Our First Program

As our first example of the chapter, let us see how we can perform multidigit ASCII addition. Addition of multidigit numbers in the ASCII representation is done one digit at a time starting with the rightmost digit. To illustrate the process involved, we discuss how addition of two 10-digit numbers is done (see the program listing below).

Program 18.1 ASCII addition of two 10-digit numbers

```
 1:  ;Addition of two integers in ASCII form    ASCIIADD.ASM
 2:  ;
 3:  ;         Objective: To demonstrate addition of two integers
 4:  ;                    in the ASCII representation.
 5:  ;             Input: None.
 6:  ;            Output: Displays the sum.
 7:  %include "io.mac"
 8:
 9:  .DATA
10:  sum_msg    db   'The sum is: ',0
11:  number1    db   '1234567890'
12:  number2    db   '1098765432'
13:  sum        db   '          ',0 ; add NULL char. to use PutStr
14:
15:  .CODE
16:      .STARTUP
17:      ; ESI is used as index into number1, number2, and sum
18:      mov     ESI,9          ; ESI points to rightmost digit
19:      mov     ECX,10         ; iteration count (# of digits)
20:      clc                    ; clear carry (we use ADC not ADD)
21:  add_loop:
22:      mov     AL,[number1+ESI]
23:      adc     AL,[number2+ESI]
24:      aaa                    ; ASCII adjust
25:      pushf                  ; save flags because OR
26:      or      AL,30H         ;  changes CF that we need
27:      popf                   ;  in the next iteration
28:      mov     [sum+ESI],AL   ; store the sum byte
29:      dec     ESI            ; update ESI
```

```
30:            loop     add_loop
31:            PutStr   sum_msg          ; display sum
32:            PutStr   sum
33:            nwln
34:            .EXIT
```

The program adds two numbers number1 and number2 and displays the sum. We use ESI as an index into the input numbers, which are in the ASCII representation. The ESI register is initialized to point to the rightmost digit (line 18). The loop count 10 is set up in ECX (line 19). The addition loop (lines 21–30) adds one digit by taking any carry generated during the previous iteration into account. This is done by using the adc rather than the add instruction. Since the adc instruction is used, we have to make sure that the carry is clear initially. This is done on line 20 using the clc (clear carry) instruction.

Note that the aaa instruction produces the result in unpacked BCD form. To convert to the ASCII form, we have to or the result with 30H (line 26). This ORing, however, destroys the carry generated by the adc instruction that we need in the next iteration. Therefore, it is necessary to save (line 25) and restore (line 27) the flags.

The overhead in performing the addition is obvious. If the input numbers were in binary, only a single add instruction would have performed the required addition. This conversion-overhead versus processing-overhead tradeoff is discussed later.

Processing Packed BCD Numbers

In this representation, as indicated earlier, two decimal numbers are packed into a byte. There are two instructions to process packed BCD numbers:

daa — Decimal adjust after addition
das — Decimal adjust after subtraction

There is no support for multiplication or division. For these operations, we will have to unpack the numbers, perform the operation, and repack them.

Packed BCD Addition
The daa instruction can be used to adjust the result of an addition operation to conform to the packed BCD representation. To understand the sort of adjustments required, let us look at some examples next.

Example 18.8 *A packed BCD addition example.*
Consider adding two packed BCD numbers 29 and 69.

```
29H  = 00101001B
69H  = 01101001B
92H  = 10010010B
```

The sum 92 is not the correct value. The result should be 98. We get the correct answer by adding 6 to 92. We add 6 because the carry generated from bit 3 (i.e., auxiliary carry) represents an overflow above 16, not 10, as is required in BCD.   □

Example 18.9 *Another packed BCD addition example.*
Consider adding two packed BCD numbers 27 and 34.

```
27H = 00100111B
34H = 00110100B
─────────────────
5BH = 01011011B
```

Again, the result is incorrect. The sum should be 61. The result 5B requires correction, as the first digit is greater than 9. To correct the result add 6, which gives us 61.   □

Example 18.10 *A final packed BCD addition example.*
Consider adding two packed BCD numbers 52 and 61.

```
52H = 01010010B
61H = 01100001B
─────────────────
B3H = 10110011B
```

This result also requires correction. The first digit is correct, but the second digit requires a correction. The solution is the same as that used in the last example—add 6 to the second digit (i.e., add 60H to the result). This gives us 13 as the result with a carry (effectively equal to 113).   □

The daa instruction exactly performs adjustments like these to the result of add or adc instructions. More specifically, the following actions are taken by daa:

- If the least significant four bits of AL are greater than 9 or if the auxiliary flag is set, it adds 6 to AL and sets AF;
- If the most significant four bits of AL are greater than 9 or if the carry flag is set, it adds 60H to AL and sets CF.

Example 18.11 *Code for packed BCD addition.*
Consider adding two packed BCD numbers 71 and 43.

```
mov    AL,71H
add    AL,43H      ; AL = B4H
daa               ; AL = 14H and CF = 1
```

As indicated, the daa instruction restores the result in AL to the packed BCD representation. The result including the carry (i.e., 114H) is the correct answer in packed BCD.   □

As in the ASCII addition, multibyte BCD addition requires a loop. After discussing the packed BCD subtraction, we present an example to add two 10-byte packed BCD numbers.

Packed BCD Subtraction

The das instruction can be used to adjust the result of a subtraction (i.e., the result of sub or sbb). It works similar to daa and performs the following actions:

- If the least significant four bits of AL are greater than 9 or if the auxiliary flag is set, it subtracts 6 from AL and sets AF;

- If the most significant four bits of AL are greater than 9 or if the carry flag is set, it subtracts 60H from AL and sets CF.

Here is an example that illustrates the use of the das instruction.

Example 18.12 *Code for packed BCD subtraction.*
Consider subtracting 43 from 71 (i.e., 71 − 43).

```
mov     AL,71H
sub     AL,43H      ; AL = 2EH
das                 ; AL = 28H
```

The das instruction restores the result in AL to the packed BCD representation.   □

Illustrative Example

In this example, we consider multibyte packed BCD addition. As in the ASCII representation, when adding two multibyte packed BCD numbers, we have to use a loop that adds a pair of decimal digits in each iteration, starting from the rightmost pair. The program, given below, adds two 10-byte packed BCD numbers, number1 and number2.

Program 18.2 Packed BCD addition of two 10-digit numbers

```
 1:  ;Addition of integers in packed BCD form    BCDADD.ASM
 2:  ;
 3:  ;          Objective: To demonstrate addition of two integers
 4:  ;                     in the packed BCD representation.
 5:  ;              Input: None.
 6:  ;             Output: Displays the sum.
 7:
 8:  %define SUM_LENGTH     10
 9:
10:  %include "io.mac"
11:
12:  .DATA
13:  sum_msg     db    'The sum is: ',0
14:  number1     db    12H,34H,56H,78H,90H
15:  number2     db    10H,98H,76H,54H,32H
16:  ASCIIsum    db    '            ',0    ; add NULL char.
17:
18:  .UDATA
19:  BCDsum      resb    5
20:
21:  .CODE
22:          .STARTUP
23:          mov     ESI,4
24:          mov     ECX,5                ; loop iteration count
25:          clc                          ; clear carry (we use ADC)
26:  add_loop:
27:          mov     AL,[number1+ESI]
```

```
28:            adc     AL,[number2+ESI]
29:            daa                       ; ASCII adjust
30:            mov     [BCDsum+ESI],AL   ; store the sum byte
31:            dec     ESI               ; update index
32:            loop    add_loop
33:            call    ASCII_convert
34:            PutStr  sum_msg           ; display sum
35:            PutStr  ASCIIsum
36:   nwln
37:            .EXIT
38:
39:   ;-----------------------------------------------------------------
40:   ; Converts the packed decimal number (5 digits) in BCDsum
41:   ; to ASCII represenation and stores it in ASCIIsum.
42:   ; All registers are preserved.
43:   ;-----------------------------------------------------------------
44:   ASCII_convert:
45:            pushad                    ; save registers
46:            ; ESI is used as index into ASCIIsum
47:            mov     ESI,SUM_LENGTH-1
48:            ; EDI is used as index into BCDsum
49:            mov     EDI,4
50:            mov     ECX,5             ; loop count (# of BCD digits)
51:   cnv_loop:
52:            mov     AL,[BCDsum+EDI]   ; AL = BCD digit
53:            mov     AH,AL             ; save the BCD digit
54:            ; convert right digit to ASCII & store in ASCIIsum
55:            and     AL,0FH
56:            or      AL,30H
57:            mov     [ASCIIsum+ESI],AL
58:            dec     ESI
59:            mov     AL,AH             ; restore the BCD digit
60:            ; convert left digit to ASCII & store in ASCIIsum
61:            shr     AL,4              ; right-shift by 4 positions
62:            or      AL,30H
63:            mov     [ASCIIsum+ESI],AL
64:            dec     ESI
65:            dec     EDI               ; update EDI
66:            loop    cnv_loop
67:            popad                     ; restore registers
68:            ret
```

The two numbers to be added are initialized on lines 14 and 15. The space for the sum (BCDsum) is reserved using resb on line 19.

The code is similar to that given in Program 18.1. However, since we add two decimal digits during each loop iteration, only five iterations are needed to add the 10-digit numbers. Thus, processing numbers in the packed BCD representation is faster than in the ASCII representation. In any case, both representations are considerably slower in processing numbers than the binary representation.

Table 18.1 Tradeoffs associated with the three representations

Representation	Storage overhead	Conversion overhead	Processing overhead
Binary	Nil	High	Nil
Packed BCD	Medium	Medium	Medium
ASCII	High	Nil	High

At the end of the loop, the sum is stored in BCDsum as a packed BCD number. To display this number, we have to convert it to the ASCII form (an overhead that is not present in the ASCII version).

The procedure ASCII_convert takes BCDsum and converts it to equivalent ASCII string and stores it in ASCIIsum. For each byte read from BCDsum, two ASCII digits are generated. Note that the conversion from packed BCD to ASCII can be done by using only logical and shift operations. On the other hand, conversion from binary to ASCII requires a more expensive division operation (thus increasing the conversion overhead).

Decimal Versus Binary Arithmetic

Now you know three representations to perform arithmetic operations: binary, ASCII, and BCD. The majority of operations are done in binary. However, there are tradeoffs associated with these three representations.

First we will look at the storage overhead. The binary representation is compact and the most efficient one. The ASCII and unpacked BCD representations incur high overhead as each decimal digit is stored in a byte (see Table 18.1). The packed BCD representation, which stores two decimal digits per byte, reduces this overhead by approximately half. For example, using two bytes, we can represent numbers from 0 to 65,535 in the binary representation and from 0 to 9999 in the packed BCD representation, but only from 0 to 99 in the ASCII and unpacked BCD representations.

In applications where the input data is in ASCII form and the output is required to be in ASCII, binary arithmetic may not always be the best choice. This is because there are overheads associated with the conversion between ASCII and binary representations. However, processing numbers in binary can be done much more efficiently than in either ASCII or BCD representations. Table 18.1 shows the tradeoffs associated with these three representations.

When the input and output use the ASCII form and there is little processing, processing numbers in ASCII is better. This is so because ASCII version does not incur any conversion overhead. On the other hand, due to high overhead in converting numbers between ASCII and binary, the binary version takes more time than the ASCII version. The BCD version also takes substantially more time than the ASCII version but performs better than the binary version mainly because conversions between BCD and ASCII are simpler.

When there is significant processing of numbers, the binary version tends to perform better than the ASCII and BCD versions. In this scenario, the ASCII version provides the worst performance as its processing overhead is high (see Table 18.1). The BCD version, while slower than the binary version, performs much better than the ASCII version.

The moral of the story is that a careful analysis of the application should be done before deciding on the choice of representation for numbers in some applications. This is particularly true for business applications, where the data might come in the ASCII form.

Summary

In previous chapters we converted decimal data into binary for storing internally as well as for manipulation. This chapter introduced two alternative representations for storing the decimal data—ASCII and BCD. The BCD representation can be either unpacked or packed.

In the ASCII and unpacked BCD representations, one decimal digit is stored per byte, whereas the packed BCD representation stores two digits per byte. Thus, the storage overhead is substantial in ASCII and unpacked BCD. Packed BCD representation uses the storage space more efficiently (typically requiring half as much space). The binary representation, on the other hand, does not introduce any overhead.

There are two main overheads that affect the execution time of a program: conversion overhead and processing overhead. When the ASCII form is used for data input and output, the data should be converted between ASCII and binary/BCD. This conversion overhead for the binary representation can be substantial, as multiplication and division are required. There is much less overhead for the BCD representations, as only logical and shift operations are needed. On the other hand, number processing in binary is much faster than in ASCII or BCD representations. Packed BCD representation is better than ASCII representation, as each byte stores two decimal digits.

19

Recursion

We can use recursion as an alternative to iteration. This chapter first introduces the basics of recursion. After that we give some examples to illustrate how recursive procedures are written in the assembly language. The advantages and pitfalls associated with a recursive solution as opposed to an iterative solution are discussed toward the end of the chapter. The last section gives a summary.

Introduction

A recursive procedure calls itself, either directly or indirectly. In direct recursion, a procedure calls itself directly. In indirect recursion, procedure P makes a call to procedure Q, which in turn calls procedure P. The sequence of calls could be longer before a call is made to procedure P.

Recursion is a powerful tool that allows us to express our solution elegantly. Some solutions can be naturally expressed using recursion. Computing a factorial is a classic example. Factorial n, denoted $n!$, is the product of positive integers from 1 to n. For example,

$$5! = 1 \times 2 \times 3 \times 4 \times 5.$$

The factorial can be formally defined as

$$\text{factorial}(0) = 1$$
$$\text{factorial}(n) = n * \text{factorial}(n - 1) \text{ for } n > 0.$$

Recursion shows up in this definition as we define factorial(n) in terms of factorial($n - 1$). Every recursive function should have a termination condition to end the recursion. In this example, when $n = 0$, recursion stops. How do we express such recursive functions in programming languages? Let us first look at how this function is written in C:

```
int fact(int n)
{
    if (n == 0)
        return(1);
    return(n * fact(n-1));
}
```

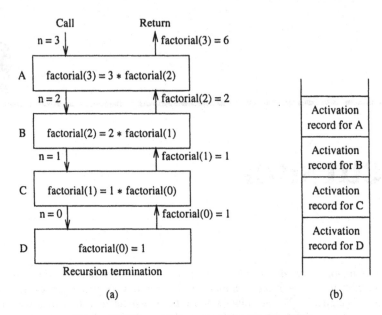

Figure 19.1 Recursive computation of factorial(3).

This is an example of direct recursion. How is this function implemented? At the conceptual level, its implementation is not any different from implementing other procedures. Once you understand that each procedure call instance is distinct from the others, the fact that a recursive procedure calls itself does not make a big difference.

Each active procedure maintains an activation record, which is stored on the stack. The activation record, as explained on page 256, consists of the arguments, return address, and local variables. The activation record comes into existence when a procedure is invoked and disappears after the procedure is terminated. Thus, for each procedure that is not terminated, an activation record that contains the state of that procedure is stored. The number of activation records, and hence the amount of stack space required to run the program, depends on the depth of recursion.

Figure 19.1 shows the stack activation records for factorial(3). As you can see from this figure, each call to the factorial function creates an activation record. Stack is used to keep these activation records.

Our First Program

To illustrate the principles of recursion, we look at an example that computes the factorial function. An implementation of the factorial function is shown in Program 19.1. The main function provides the user interface. It requests a positive number n from the user. If a negative number is given as input, the user is prompted to try again (lines 20–24). The positive number, which is read into the BX register, is passed on to the fact procedure (line 27). This procedure returns factorial(n) in the AX register, which is output with an appropriate message (lines 29–31).

Program 19.1 Recursive computation of factorial(N)

```
 1:  ;Factorial - Recursive version              FACTORIAL.ASM
 2:  ;
 3:  ;          Objective: To compute factoral using recursion.
 4:  ;             Input: Requests an integer N from the user.
 5:  ;             Output: Outputs N!
 6:
 7:  %include "io.mac"
 8:
 9:  .DATA
10:  prompt_msg  db  "Please enter a positive integer: ",0
11:  output_msg  db  "The factorial is: ",0
12:  error_msg   db  "Not a positive number. Try again.",0
13:
14:  .CODE
15:       .STARTUP
16:       PutStr  prompt_msg      ; request the number
17:
18:  try_again:
19:       GetInt  BX              ; read number into BX
20:       cmp     BX,0            ; test for a positive number
21:       jge     num_ok
22:       PutStr  error_msg
23:       nwln
24:       jmp     try_again
25:
26:  num_ok:
27:       call    fact
28:
29:       PutStr  output_msg      ; output result
30:       PutInt  AX
31:       nwln
32:
33:  done:
34:       .EXIT
35:
36:  ;-------------------------------------------------------
37:  ;Procedure fact receives a positive integer N in BX.
38:  ;It returns N! in the AX register.
39:  ;-------------------------------------------------------
40:
41:  fact:
42:       cmp     BL,1            ; if N > 1, recurse
43:       jg      one_up
44:       mov     AX,1            ; return 1 for N < 2
45:       ret                     ; terminate recursion
46:
47:  one_up:
48:       dec     BL              ; recurse with (N-1)
```

```
49:              call     fact
50:              inc      BL
51:              mul      BL                        ; AX = AL * BL
52:
53:              ret
```

The fact procedure receives the number n in the BL register. It essentially implements the C code given before. One minor difference is that this procedure terminates when $n \leq 1$. This termination would save us one recursive call. When the value in BL is less than or equal to 1, the AX register is set to 1 to terminate the recursion. The activation record in this example consists of the return address pushed onto the stack by the call instruction. Since we are using the BL register to pass n, it is decremented before the call (line 48) and restored after the call (line 50). The multiply instruction

```
     mul      BL
```

multiplies the contents of the BL and AL registers and places the 16-bit result in the AX register. This is the value returned by the fact procedure.

Illustrative Examples

We give two examples to further illustrate the principles of recursion. The first one computes a Fibonacci number and the second one implements the popular quicksort algorithm.

Example 19.1 *Computes the Nth Fibonacci number.*
The Fibonacci sequence of numbers is defined as

$$\text{fib}(1) = 1,$$
$$\text{fib}(2) = 1,$$
$$\text{fib}(n) = \text{fib}(n - 1) + \text{fib}(n - 2) \text{ for } n > 2.$$

In other words, the first two numbers in the Fibonacci sequence are 1. The subsequent numbers are obtained by adding the previous two numbers in the sequence. Thus,

$$1, 1, 2, 3, 5, 8, 13, 21, 34, 55, \ldots,$$

is the Fibonacci sequence of numbers. From this definition, you can see the recursive nature of the computation.

Program 19.1 shows the program to compute the Nth Fibonacci number. The value N is requested from the user as in the last program. The main program checks the validity of the input value. If the number is less than 1, an error message is displayed and the user is asked to enter a valid number (lines 20–24). If the input number is a valid one, it calls the fib procedure, which returns the Nth Fibonacci number in the EAX register. This value is output using PutLInt on line 30.

Program 19.2 A program to compute the Fibonacci numbers

```
 1:   ;Fibonacci number - Recursive version          FIB.ASM
 2:   ;
 3:   ;          Objective: To compute the Fibonacci number.
 4:   ;              Input: Requests an integer N from the user.
 5:   ;             Output: Outputs fib(N).
 6:
 7:   %include "io.mac"
 8:
 9:   .DATA
10:   prompt_msg  db  "Please enter a number > 0: ",0
11:   output_msg  db  "fib(N) is: ",0
12:   error_msg   db  "Not a valid number. Try again.",0
13:
14:   .CODE
15:         .STARTUP
16:         PutStr  prompt_msg      ; request the number
17:
18:   try_again:
19:         GetInt  BX              ; read number into BX
20:         cmp     BX,0            ; test if N>0
21:         jg      num_ok
22:         PutStr  error_msg
23:         nwln
24:         jmp     try_again
25:
26:   num_ok:
27:         call    fib
28:
29:         PutStr  output_msg      ; output result
30:         PutLInt EAX
31:         nwln
32:
33:   done:
34:         .EXIT
35:
36:   ;-------------------------------------------------------
37:   ;Procedure fib receives a positive integer N in BX.
38:   ;It returns fib(N) in the EAX register.
39:   ;-------------------------------------------------------
40:
41:   fib:
42:         cmp     BX,2            ; if N > 2, recurse
43:         jg      one_up
44:         mov     EAX,1           ; return 1 if N = 1 or 2
45:         ret                     ; terminate recursion
46:
47:   one_up:
48:         push    EDX
49:         dec     BX              ; recurse with (N-1)
```

```
50:          call     fib
51:          mov      EDX,EAX         ; save fib(N-1) in EDX
52:          dec      BX              ; recurse with (N-2)
53:          call     fib
54:          add      EAX,EDX         ; EAX = fib(N-2) + fib(N-1)
55:
56:          add      BX,2            ; restore BX and EDX
57:          pop      EDX
58:
59:          ret
```

The fib procedure uses recursion to compute the required Fibonacci number. The N value is received in the BX register. The recursion termination condition is implemented by lines 42–44. This procedure returns 1 in EAX if N is 1 or 2.

The recursion is implemented on lines 47–57. It decrements BX by one before calling the fib procedure to compute fib(N-1). The value returned by this call is stored in the EDX register (line 51). The BX value is decremented again before calling fib on line 53 to compute fib(N-2). The two fib values are added on line 54 to compute the fib(N) value. The procedure preserves both BX (line 56) and EDX (lines 48 and 57).

Example 19.2 *Implementation of the quicksort algorithm using recursion.*

Quicksort is one of the most popular sorting algorithms; it was proposed by C.A.R. Hoare in 1960. Once you understand the basic principle of the quicksort, you will see why recursion naturally expresses it.

At its heart, quicksort uses a divide-and-conquer strategy. The original sort problem is reduced to two smaller sort problems. This is done by selecting a partition element x and partitioning the array into two subarrays: all elements less than x are placed in one subarray and all elements greater than x are in the other. Now, we have to sort these two subarrays, which are smaller than the original array. We apply the same procedure to sort these two subarrays. This is where the recursive nature of the algorithm shows up. The quicksort procedure to sort an N-element array is summarized below:

1. Select a partition element x.

2. Assume that we know where this element x should be in the final sorted array. Let it be at array[i]. We give details of this step shortly.

3. Move all elements that are less than x into positions array[0] $\cdots$ array[i-1]. Similarly, move those elements that are greater than x into positions array[i+1] $\cdots$ array[N-1]. Note that these two subarrays are not sorted.

4. Now apply the quicksort procedure recursively to sort these two subarrays until the array is sorted.

How do we know the final position of the partition element x without sorting the array? We don't have to sort the array; we just need to know the number of elements either before or after it. To clarify the working of the quicksort algorithm, let us look at an example. In this example, and in our quicksort implementation, we pick the last element as the partition value. Obviously, the selection of the partition element influences performance of the quicksort. There are several better ways of selecting the partition value; you can get these details in any textbook on sorting.

```
Initial state:    2 9 8 1 3 4 7 6   ←—    Partition element;
After 1st pass:   2 1 3 4 6 7 9 8         Partition element 6 is in its final place.
```

The second pass works on the following two subarrays.

```
                        1st subarray:   2  1  3  4;
                        2nd subarray:   7  9  8.
```

To move the partition element to its final place, we use two pointers i and j. Initially, i points to the first element and j points to the second-to-the-last element. Note that we are using the last element as the partition element. The index i is advanced until it points to an element that is greater than or equal to x. Similarly, j is moved backward until it points to an element that is less than or equal to x. Then we exchange the two values at i and j. We continue this process until i is greater than or equal to j. The quicksort pseudocode is shown below:

```
quick_sort (array, lo, hi)
    if (hi > lo)
          x := array[hi]
          i := lo
          j := hi
          while (i < j)
                while (array[i] < x)
                      i := i + 1
                end while
                while (array[j] > x)
                      j := j – 1
                end while
                if (i < j)
                      array[i] ⟺ array[j]          /* exchange values */
                end if
          end while
          array[i] ⟺ array[hi]          /* exchange values */
          quick_sort (array, lo, i–1)
          quick_sort (array, i+1, hi)
    end if
end quick_sort
```

The quicksort program is shown in Program 19.3. The input values are read by the read loop (lines 25 to 31). This loop terminates if the input is zero. As written, this program can cause problems if the user enters more than 200 integers. You can easily remedy this problem by initializing the ECX with 200 and using the loop instruction on line 31. The three arguments are placed in the EBX (array pointer), ESI (lo), and EDI (hi) registers (lines 35 to 37). After the quicksort call on line 38, the program outputs the sorted array (lines 41 to 50).

Program 19.3 Sorting integers using the recursive quicksort algorithm

```
 1: ;Sorting integers using quicksort              QSORT.ASM
 2: ;
 3: ;         Objective: Sorts an array of integers using
 4: ;                    quick sort. Uses recursion.
 5: ;             Input: Requests integers from the user.
 6: ;                    Terminated by entering zero.
 7: ;            Output: Outputs the sorted arrray.
 8:
 9: %include "io.mac"
10:
11: .DATA
12: prompt_msg  db  "Please enter integers. ",0DH,0AH
13:             db  "Entering zero terminates the input.",0
14: output_msg  db  "The sorted array is: ",0
15:
16: .UDATA
17: array1      resw  200
18:
19: .CODE
20:      .STARTUP
21:      PutStr  prompt_msg      ; request the number
22:      nwln
23:      mov     EBX,array1
24:      xor     EDI,EDI         ; EDI keeps a count of
25: read_more:                   ;      input numbers
26:      GetInt  AX
27:      mov     [EBX+EDI*2],AX ; store input # in array
28:      cmp     AX,0            ; test if it is zero
29:      je      exit_read
30:      inc     EDI
31:      jmp     read_more
32:
33: exit_read:
34:      ; prepare arguments for procedure call
35:      mov     EBX,array1
36:      xor     ESI,ESI         ; ESI = lo index
37:      dec     EDI             ; EDI = hi index
38:      call    qsort
39:
40:      PutStr  output_msg      ; output sorted array
41: write_more:
42:      ; since qsort preserves all registers, we will
43:      ; have valid EBX and ESI values.
44:      mov     AX,[EBX+ESI*2]
45:      cmp     AX,0
46:      je      done
47:      PutInt  AX
48:      nwln
49:      inc     ESI
```

```
 50:          jmp     write_more
 51:
 52: done:
 53:          .EXIT
 54:
 55: ;------------------------------------------------------------
 56: ;Procedure qsort receives a pointer to the array in BX.
 57: ;LO and HI are received in ESI and EDI, respectively.
 58: ;It preserves all the registers.
 59: ;------------------------------------------------------------
 60:
 61: qsort:
 62:          pushad
 63:          cmp     EDI,ESI
 64:          jle     qsort_done      ; end recursion if hi <= lo
 65:
 66:          ; save hi and lo for later use
 67:          mov     ECX,ESI
 68:          mov     EDX,EDI
 69:
 70:          mov     AX,[EBX+EDI*2] ; AX = xsep
 71:
 72: lo_loop:                        ;
 73:          cmp     [EBX+ESI*2],AX  ;
 74:          jge     lo_loop_done    ; LO while loop
 75:          inc     ESI             ;
 76:          jmp     lo_loop         ;
 77: lo_loop_done:
 78:
 79:          dec     EDI             ; hi = hi-1
 80: hi_loop:
 81:          cmp     EDI,ESI         ;
 82:          jle     sep_done        ;
 83:          cmp     [EBX+EDI*2],AX  ; HI while loop
 84:          jle     hi_loop_done    ;
 85:          dec     EDI             ;
 86:          jmp     hi_loop         ;
 87: hi_loop_done:
 88:
 89:          xchg    AX,[EBX+ESI*2]  ;
 90:          xchg    AX,[EBX+EDI*2]  ; x[i] <=> x[j]
 91:          xchg    AX,[EBX+ESI*2]  ;
 92:          jmp     lo_loop
 93:
 94: sep_done:
 95:          xchg    AX,[EBX+ESI*2]  ;
 96:          xchg    AX,[EBX+EDX*2]  ; x[i] <=> x[hi]
 97:          xchg    AX,[EBX+ESI*2]  ;
 98:
 99:          dec     ESI
100:          mov     EDI,ESI         ; hi = i-1
```

```
101:        ; We modify the ESI value in the next statement.
102:        ; Since the original ESI value is in EDI, we use
103:        ; EDI to get i+1 value for the second qsort call.
104:        mov     ESI,ECX
105:        call    qsort
106:
107:        ; EDI has the i value
108:        inc     EDI
109:        inc     EDI
110:        mov     ESI,EDI            ; lo = i+1
111:        mov     EDI,EDX
112:        call    qsort
113:
114: qsort_done:
115:        popad
116:        ret
```

The quicksort procedure follows the pseudocode. Since we are not returning any values, we use pushad to preserve all registers (line 62). The two inner **while** loops are implemented by the LO_LOOP and HI_LOOP. The exchange of elements is done by using three xchg instructions (lines 89 to 91 and 95 to 97). The rest of the program is straightforward to follow.

Recursion Versus Iteration

In theory, every recursive function has an iterative counterpart. To see this, let us write in C the iterative version to compute the factorial function.

```
int fact_iterative(int n)
{
    int    i, result;

    if (n == 0)
        return (1);

    result = 1;
    for(i = 1; i <= n; i++)
        result = result * i;
    return(result);
}
```

Comparing this code with the recursive version given on page 391, it is obvious that the recursive version is concise and reflects the mathematical definition of the factorial function. Once you get through the initial learning problems with recursion, recursive code is easier to understand for those functions that are defined recursively. Some such examples are the factorial function, Fibonacci number computation, binary search, and quicksort.

This leads us to the question of when to use recursion. To answer this question, we need to look at the potential problems recursion can cause. There are two main problems with recursion:

- *Inefficiency:* In most cases, recursive versions tend to be inefficient. You can see this point by comparing the recursive and iterative versions of the factorial function. The recursive version induces more overheads to invoke and return from procedure calls. To compute $N!$, we need to call the factorial function about N times. In the iterative version, the loop iterates about N times.

  Recursion could also introduce duplicate computation. For example, to compute the Fibonacci number `fib(5)`

  ```
  fib(5) = fib(4) + fib(3)
  ```

  a recursive procedure computes `fib(3)` twice, `fib(2)` twice, and so on.

- *Increased memory requirement:* Recursion tends to demand more memory. This can be seen from the simple factorial example. For large N, the demand for stack memory can be excessive. In some cases, the limit on the available memory may make the recursive version unusable.

On the positive side, however, note that recursion leads to better understanding of the code for those naturally recursive problems. In this case, recursion aids in program maintenance.

Summary

We can use recursive procedures as an alternative to iterative ones. A procedure that calls itself, whether directly or indirectly, is called a recursive procedure. In direct recursion, a procedure calls itself, as in our factorial example. In indirect recursion, a procedure may initiate a sequence of calls that eventually results in calling the procedure itself.

For some applications, we can write an elegant solution because recursion is a natural fit. We illustrated the principles of recursion using a few examples: factorial, Fibonacci number, and quicksort. We presented recursive versions of these functions in the assembly language. In the last section we identified the tradeoffs associated with recursion as opposed to iteration.

20

Protected-Mode Interrupt Processing

Interrupts, like procedures, can be used to alter a program's control flow to a procedure called an interrupt service routine. Unlike procedures, which can be invoked by a `call` *instruction, interrupt service routines can be invoked either in software (called software interrupts) or by hardware (called hardware interrupts). After introducing the interrupts we discuss the taxonomy of the IA-32 interrupts. We describe the interrupt invocation mechanism in the protected mode before describing the exceptions. The next two sections deal with software interrupts and file I/O. We use the Linux system calls to illustrate how we can access I/O devices like the keyboard and display. Hardware interrupts along with the I/O instructions are briefly introduced toward the end of the chapter. The last section summarizes the chapter.*

Introduction

Interrupt is a mechanism by which a program's flow control can be altered. We have seen two other mechanisms to do the same: *procedures* and *jumps*. While jumps provide a one-way transfer of control, procedures provide a mechanism to return control to the point of calling when the called procedure is completed.

Interrupts provide a mechanism similar to that of a procedure call. Causing an interrupt transfers control to a procedure, which is referred to as an *interrupt service routine* (ISR). An ISR is sometimes called a *handler*. When the ISR is completed, the interrupted program resumes execution as if it were not interrupted. This behavior is analogous to a procedure call. There are, however, some basic differences between procedures and interrupts that make interrupts almost indispensable.

One of the main differences is that interrupts can be initiated by both software and hardware. In contrast, procedures are purely software-initiated. The fact that interrupts can be initiated by hardware is the principal factor behind much of the power of interrupts. This capability gives us an efficient way by which external devices (outside the processor) can get the processor's attention.

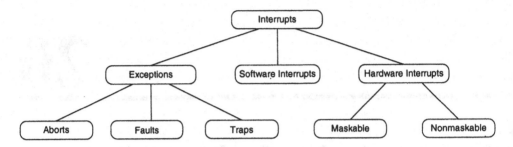

Figure 20.1 A taxonomy of the IA-32 interrupts.

Software-initiated interrupts—called simply *software interrupts*—are caused by executing the int instruction. Thus these interrupts, like procedure calls, are anticipated or planned events. For example, when you are expecting a response from the user (e.g., Y or N), you can initiate an interrupt to read a character from the keyboard. What if an unexpected situation arises that requires immediate attention of the processor? For example, you have written a program to display the first 90 Fibonacci numbers on the screen. While running the program, however, you realized that your program never terminates because of a simple programming mistake (e.g., you forgot to increment the index variable controlling the loop). Obviously, you want to abort the program and return control to the operating system. As you know, this can be done by ctrl-c in Linux (ctrl-break on Windows). The important point is that this is not an anticipated event—so it cannot be effectively programmed into the code.

The interrupt mechanism provides an efficient way to handle such unanticipated events. Referring to the previous example, the ctrl-c could cause an interrupt to draw the attention of the processor away from the user program. The interrupt service routine associated with ctrl-c can terminate the program and return control to the operating system.

Another difference between procedures and interrupts is that ISRs are normally memory-resident. In contrast, procedures are loaded into memory along with application programs. Some other differences—such as using numbers to identify interrupts rather than names, using an invocation mechanism that automatically pushes the flags register onto the stack, and so on—are pointed out in later sections.

A Taxonomy of Interrupts

We have already identified two basic categories of interrupts—software-initiated and hardware-initiated (see Figure 20.1). The third category is called *exceptions*. Exceptions handle instruction faults. An example of an exception is the divide error fault, which is generated whenever divide by 0 is attempted. This error condition occurs during the div or idiv instruction execution if the divisor is 0. We discuss exceptions later.

Software interrupts are written into a program by using the int instruction. The main use of software interrupts is in accessing I/O devices such as the keyboard, printer, display screen, disk drive, etc. Software interrupts can be further classified into *system-defined* and *user-defined*.

Hardware interrupts are generated by hardware devices to get the attention of the processor. For example, when you strike a key, the keyboard hardware generates an external interrupt, causing the processor to suspend its present activity and execute the keyboard interrupt service routine to process the key. After completing the keyboard ISR, the processor resumes what it was doing before the interruption.

Hardware interrupts can be either *maskable* or *nonmaskable*. The processor always attends the nonmaskable interrupt (NMI) immediately. One example of NMI is the RAM parity error indicating memory malfunction.

Maskable interrupts can be delayed until execution reaches a convenient point. As an example, let us assume that the processor is executing a `main` program. An interrupt occurs. As a result, the processor suspends `main` as soon as it finishes the current instruction and transfers control to the ISR1 interrupt service routine. If ISR1 has to be executed without any interruption, the processor can mask further interrupts until it is completed. Suppose that, while executing ISR1, another maskable interrupt occurs. Service to this interrupt would have to wait until ISR1 is completed. We discuss hardware interrupts toward the end of the chapter.

Interrupt Processing in the Protected Mode

Let's now look at interrupt processing in the protected mode. Unlike procedures, where a name is given to identify a procedure, interrupts are identified by a type number. The IA-32 architecture supports 256 different interrupt types. The interrupt type ranges from 0 to 255. The interrupt type number, which is also called a *vector*, is used as an index into a table that stores the addresses of ISRs. This table is called the *interrupt descriptor table* (IDT). Like the global and local descriptor tables GDT and LDT (discussed in Chapter 4), each descriptor is essentially a pointer to an ISR and requires eight bytes. The interrupt type number is scaled by 8 to form an index into the IDT.

The IDT may reside anywhere in physical memory. The location of the IDT is maintained in an IDT register IDTR. The IDTR is a 48-bit register that stores the 32-bit IDT base address and a 16-bit IDT limit value as shown in Figure 20.2. However, the IDT does not require more than 2048 bytes, as there can be at most 256 descriptors. In a system, the number of descriptors could be much smaller than the maximum allowed. In this case, the IDT limit can be set to the required size. If the referenced descriptor is outside the IDT limit, the processor enters the shutdown mode. In this mode, instruction execution is stopped until either a nonmaskable interrupt or a reset signal is received.

There are two special instructions to load (`lidt`) and store (`sidt`) the contents of the IDTR register. Both instructions take the address of a 6-byte memory as the operand.

The IDT can have three types of descriptors: interrupt gate, trap gate, and task gate. We will not discuss task gates, as they are not directly related to the interrupt mechanism that we are interested in. The format of the other two gates is shown in Figure 20.3. Both gates store identical information: a 16-bit segment selector, a 32-bit offset, a descriptor privilege level (DPL), and a P bit to indicate whether the segment is present or not.

When an interrupt occurs, the segment selector is used to select a segment descriptor that is in either the GDT or the current LDT. Recall from our discussion in Chapter 4 that the TI bit of the segment descriptor identifies whether the GDT or the current LDT should be used. The segment descriptor provides the base address of segment that contains the interrupt service routine as shown in Figure 20.4. The offset part comes from the interrupt gate.

What happens when an interrupt occurs depends on whether there is a privilege change or not. In the remainder of the chapter, we look at the simple case of no privilege change. In this case, the following actions are taken on an interrupt:

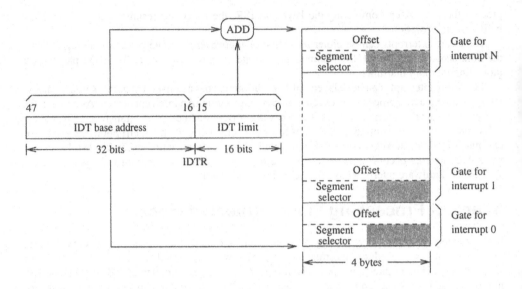

Figure 20.2 Organization of the IDT. The IDTR register stores the 32-bit IDT base address and a 16-bit value indicating the IDT size.

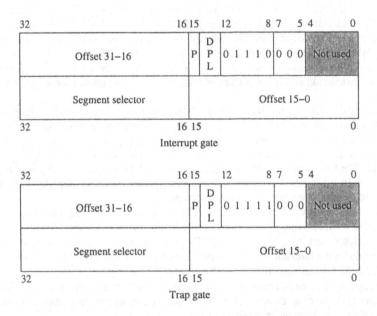

Figure 20.3 The IA-32 interrupt descriptors.

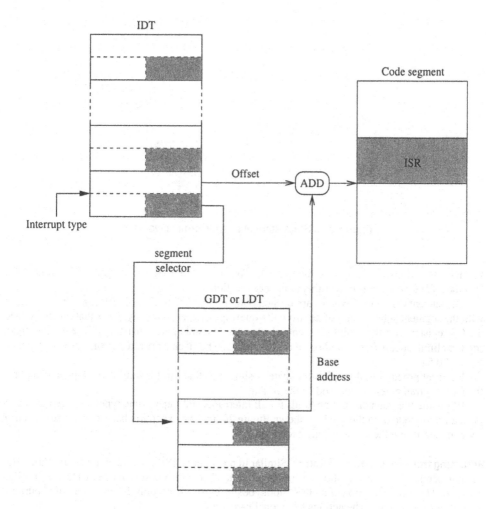

Figure 20.4 Protected-mode interrupt invocation.

1. Push the EFLAGS register onto the stack;
2. Clear the interrupt and trap flags;
3. Push CS and EIP registers onto the stack;
4. Load CS with the 16-bit segment selector from the interrupt gate;
5. Load EIP with the 32-bit offset values from the interrupt gate.

On receiving an interrupt, the flags register is automatically saved on the stack. The interrupt and trap flags are cleared to disable further interrupts. Usually, this flag is set in ISRs unless there is a special reason to disable other interrupts. The interrupt flag can be set by sti and cleared by cli assembly language instructions. Both of these instructions require no operands. There are no

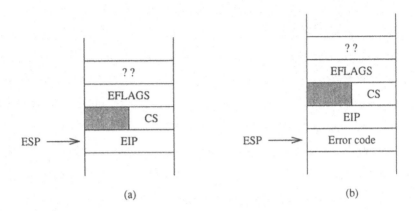

Figure 20.5 Stack state after an interrupt invocation.

special instructions to manipulate the trap flag. We have to use popf and pushf to modify the trap flag. We give an example of this in the next section.

The current CS and EIP values are pushed onto the stack. The CS and EIP registers are loaded with the segment selector and offset from the interrupt gate, respectively. Note that when we load the CS register with the 16-bit segment selector, the invisible part consisting of the base address, segment limit, access rights, and so on is also loaded. The stack state after an interrupt is shown in Figure 20.5a.

Interrupt processing through a trap gate is similar to that through an interrupt gate except for the fact that trap gates do not modify the IF flag.

While the previous discussion holds for all interrupts and traps, some types of exceptions also push an error code onto the stack as shown Figure 20.5b. The exception handler can use this error code in identifying the cause for the exception.

Returning from an interrupt handler Similar to procedures, ISRs should end with a return statement to send control back to the interrupted program. The interrupt return (iret) is used for this purpose. The last instruction of an ISR should be the iret instruction. It serves the same purpose as ret for procedures. The actions taken on iret are

1. Pop the 32-bit value on top of the stack into the EIP register;
2. Pop the 16-bit value on top of the stack into the CS register;
3. Pop the 32-bit value on top of the stack into the EFLAGS register.

Exceptions

The exceptions are classified into *faults*, *traps*, and *aborts* depending on the way they are reported and whether the interrupted instruction is restarted. Faults and traps are reported at instruction boundaries. Faults use the boundary before the instruction during which the exception was detected. When a fault occurs, the system state is restored to the state before the current instruction so that the instruction can be restarted. The divide error, for instance, is a fault detected during the div or idiv instruction. The processor, therefore, restores the state to correspond to the one

Table 20.1 The First Five Dedicated Interrupts

Interrupt type	Purpose
0	Divide error
1	Single-step
2	Nonmaskable interrupt (NMI)
3	Breakpoint
4	Overflow

before the divide instruction that caused the fault. Furthermore, the instruction pointer is adjusted to point to the divide instruction so that, after returning from the exception handler, the divide instruction is reexecuted.

Another example of a fault is the *segment-not-present* fault. This exception is caused by a reference to data in a segment that is not in memory. Then, the exception handler must load the missing segment from the disk and resume program execution starting with the instruction that caused the exception. In this example, it clearly makes sense to restart the instruction that caused the exception.

Traps, on the other hand, are reported at the instruction boundary immediately following the instruction during which the exception was detected. For instance, the overflow exception (interrupt 4) is a trap. Therefore, no instruction restart is done. User-defined interrupts are also examples of traps.

Aborts are exceptions that report severe errors. Examples include hardware errors and inconsistent values in system tables.

There are several predefined interrupts. These are called *dedicated* interrupts. These include the first five interrupts as shown in Table 20.1. The NMI is a hardware interrupt and is discussed in Section 20. A brief description of the remaining four interrupts is given here.

Divide Error Interrupt The processor generates a type 0 interrupt whenever executing a divide instruction—either `div` (divide) or `idiv` (integer divide)—results in a quotient that is larger than the destination specified. The default interrupt handler on Linux displays a *Floating point exception* message and terminates the program.

Single-Step Interrupt Single-stepping is a useful debugging tool to observe the behavior of a program instruction by instruction. To start single-stepping, the trap flag (TF) bit in the flags register should be set (i.e., TF = 1). When TF is set, the CPU automatically generates a type 1 interrupt after executing each instruction. Some exceptions do exist, but we do not worry about them here.

The interrupt handler for the type 1 interrupt can be used to display relevant information about the state of the program. For example, the contents of all registers could be displayed.

To end single stepping, the TF should be cleared. The instruction set, however, does not have instructions to directly manipulate the TF bit. Instead, we have to resort to an indirect means. You have to push flags register using `pushf` and manipulate the TF bit and use `popf` to store this value back in the flags register. Here is an example code fragment that sets the trap flag:

```
pushf                    ; copy the flag register
pop      AX              ; into AX
or       AX,100H         ; set the trap flag bit (TF = 1)
push     AX              ; copy the modified flag bits
popf                     ; back into the flags register
```

Recall that bit 8 of the flags register is the trap flag (see Figure 4.4 on page 65). We can use the following code to clear the trap flag:

```
pushf                    ; copy the flags register
pop      AX              ; into AX
and      AX,0FEFFH       ; clear trap flag bit (TF = 0)
push     AX              ; write back into
popf                     ; the flags register
```

Breakpoint Interrupt   If you have used a debugger, which you should have by now, you already know the usefulness of inserting breakpoints while debugging a program. The type 3 interrupt is dedicated to the breakpoint processing. This type of interrupt can be generated by using the special single-byte form of int 3 (opcode CCH). Using the int 3 instruction automatically causes the assembler to encode the instruction into the single-byte version. Note that the standard encoding for the int instruction is two bytes long.

Inserting a breakpoint in a program involves replacing the program code byte by CCH while saving the program byte for later restoration to remove the breakpoint. The standard 2-byte version of int 3 can cause problems in certain situations, as there are instructions that require only a single byte to encode.

Overflow Interrupt   The type 4 interrupt is dedicated to handle overflow conditions. There are two ways by which a type 4 interrupt can be generated: either by int 4 or by into. Like the breakpoint interrupt, into requires only one byte to encode, as it does not require the specification of the interrupt type number as part of the instruction. Unlike int 4, which unconditionally generates a type 4 interrupt, into generates a type 4 interrupt only if the overflow flag is set. We do not normally use into, as the overflow condition is usually detected and processed by using the conditional jump instructions jo and jno.

Software Interrupts

Software interrupts are initiated by executing an interrupt instruction. The format of this instruction is

```
int      interrupt-type
```

where interrupt-type is an integer in the range 0 through 255 (both inclusive). Thus a total of 256 different types is possible. This is a sufficiently large number, as each interrupt type can be parameterized to provide several services. For example, Linux provides a large number of services via int 0x80. In fact, it provides more than 180 different system calls! All these system calls are invoked by int 0x80. The required service is identified by placing the system call number in the EAX register. If the number of arguments required for a system call is less than six, these are placed in other registers. Usually, the system call also returns values in registers. We give details on some of the file access services provided by int 0x80 in the next section.

Linux System Calls   Of the 256 interrupt vectors available, Linux uses the first 32 vectors (i.e., from 0 to 31) for exceptions and nonmaskable interrupts. The next 16 vectors (from 32 to 47) are used for hardware interrupts generated through interrupt request lines (IRQs) (discussed in the next chapter). It uses one vector (128 or 0x80) for software interrupt to provide system services. Even though only one interrupt vector is used for system services, Linux provides several services using this interrupt.

File I/O

In this section we give several examples to perform file I/O operations. In Linux as in UNIX, the keyboard and display are treated as stream files. So reading from the keyboard is not any different from reading a file from the disk. If you have done some file I/O in C, it is relatively easy to understand the following examples. Don't worry if you are not familiar with the file I/O; we give enough details here.

The system sees the input and output data as a stream of bytes. It does not make any logical distinction whether the byte stream is coming from a disk file or the keyboard. This makes it easy to interface with the I/O devices like keyboard and display. Three standard file streams are defined: standard input (stdin), standard output (stdout), and standard error (stderr). The default association for the standard input is the keyboard; for the other two, it is the display.

File Descriptor

For each open file, a small 16-bit integer is assigned as a file id. These magic numbers are called the *file descriptors*. Before accessing a file, it must first be opened or created. To open or create a file, we need the file name, mode in which it should be opened or created, and so on. The file descriptor is returned by the file open or create system calls. Once a file is open or created, we use the file descriptor to access the file.

We don't have to open the three standard files mentioned above. They are automatically opened for us. These files are assigned the lowest three integers: stdin (0), stdout (1), and stderr (2).

File Pointer

A file pointer is associated with each open file. The file pointer specifies an offset in bytes into the file relative to the beginning of the file. A file itself is viewed as a sequence of bytes or characters. The file pointer specifies the location in the file for the subsequent read or write operation.

When a file is opened, the file pointer of that file is set to zero. In other words, the file pointer points to the first byte of the file. Sequential access to the file is provided by updating the file pointer to move past the data read or written. Direct access, as opposed to sequential access, to a file is provided by simply manipulating the file pointer.

File System Calls

System calls described in this section provide access to the data in disk files. As discussed previously, before accessing the data stored in a file, we have to open the file. We can only open a file if it already exists. Otherwise, we have to create a new file, in which case there is no data and our intent should be to write something into the file. Linux provides two separate functions—one to open an existing file (system call 5) and the other to create a new file (system call 8).

Once a file is opened or created, the data from that file can be read or data can be written into the file. We can use system call 3 to read data from a file and data can be written to a file by using system call 4. In addition, since disks allow direct access to the data stored, data contained in a disk file can be accessed directly or randomly. To provide direct access to the data stored in a file, the file pointer should be moved to the desired position in the file. The system call 19 facilitates this process. Finally, when processing of data is completed we should close the file. We use system call number 6 to close an open file.

A file name (you can include the path if you wish) is needed only to open or create file. Once a file is opened or created, a file descriptor is returned and all subsequent accesses to the file should use this file descriptor.

The remainder of this section describes some of the file system calls.

System call 8 — Create and open a file

Inputs:	EAX = 8
	EBX = file name
	ECX = file permissions
Returns:	EAX = file descriptor
Error:	EAX = error code

This system call can be used to create a new file. The EBX should point to the file name string, which can include the path. The ECX should be loaded with file permissions for owner, group and others as you would in the Linux (using chmod command) to set the file permissions. File permissions are represented by three groups of three bits as shown below:

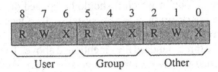

For each group, you can specify read (R), write (W), and execute (X) permissions. For example, if you want to give read, write, and execute for the owner but no access to anyone else, set the three owner permission bits to 1 and other bits to 0. Using the octal number system, we represent this number as 0700. If you want to give read, write, and execute for the owner, read permission to the group, and no access to others, you can set the permissions as 0740. (Note that octal numbers are indicated by prefixing them with a zero as in the examples here.)

The file is opened in read/write access mode and a file descriptor (a positive integer) is returned in EAX if there is no error. In case of an error, the error code (a negative integer) is placed in EAX. For example, a create error may occur due to a nonexistent directory in the specified path, or if there are device access problems or the specified file already exists, and so on. As we see next, we can also use file open to create a file.

System call 5 — Open a file

Inputs:	EAX	=	5
	EBX	=	file name
	ECX	=	file access mode
	EDX	=	file permissions
Returns:	EAX	=	file descriptor
Error:	EAX	=	error code

This function can be used to open an existing file. It takes the file name and file mode information as in the file-create system call. In addition, it takes the file access mode in ECX register. This field gives information on how the file can be accessed. Some interesting values are read-only (0), write-only (1), and read-write (2). Why is access mode specification important? The simple answer is to provide security. A file that is used as an input file to a program can be opened as a read-only file. Similarly, an output file can be opened as a write-only file. This eliminates accidental writes or reads. This specification facilitates, for example, access to files for which you have read-only access permission.

We can use this system call to create a file by specifying 0100 for file access mode. This is equivalent to the file-create system call we discussed before. We can erase contents of a file by specifying 01000 for the access mode. This leaves the file pointer at the beginning of the file. If we want to append to the existing contents, we can specify 02000 to leave the file pointer at the end.

As with the create system call, file descriptor and error code values are returned in the EAX register.

System call 3 — Read from a file

Inputs:	EAX	=	3
	EBX	=	file descriptor
	ECX	=	pointer to input buffer
	EDX	=	buffer size
			(maximum number of bytes to read)
Returns:	EAX	=	number of bytes read
Error:	EAX	=	error code

Before calling this function to read data from a previously opened or created file, the number of bytes to read should be specified in EDX and ECX should point to a data buffer into which the data read from the file is placed. The file is identified by giving its descriptor in EBX.

The system attempts to read EDX bytes from the file starting from the current file pointer location. Thus, by manipulating the file pointer (see lseek system call discussed later), we can use this function to read data from a random location in a file.

After the read is complete, the file pointer is updated to point to the byte after the last byte read. Thus, successive calls would give us sequential access to the file.

Upon completion, if there is no error, EAX contains the actual number of bytes read from the file. If this number is less than that specified in EDX, the only reasonable explanation is that the end of file has been reached. Thus, we can use this condition to detect end-of-file.

System call 4 — Write to a file

Inputs:	EAX =	4
	EBX =	file descriptor
	ECX =	pointer to output buffer
	EDX =	buffer size (number bytes to write)
Returns:	EAX =	number of bytes written
Error:	EAX =	error code

This function can be used to write to a file that is open in write or read/write access mode. Of course, if a file is created, it is automatically opened in read/write access mode. The input parameters have similar meaning as in the read system call. On return, if there is no error, EAX contains the actual number of bytes written to the file. This number should normally be equal to that specified in EDX. If not, there was an error—possibly due to disk full condition.

System call 6 — Close a file

Inputs:	EAX =	6
	EBX =	file descriptor
Returns:	EAX =	—
Error:	EAX =	error code

This function can be used to close an open file. It is not usually necessary to check for errors after closing a file. The only reasonable error scenario is when EBX contains an invalid file descriptor.

System call 19 — lseek (Updates file pointer)

Inputs:	EAX =	19
	EBX =	file descriptor
	ECX =	offset
	EDX =	whence
Returns:	EAX =	byte offset from the beginning of file
Error:	EAX =	error code

Thus far, we processed files sequentially. The file pointer remembers the position in the file. As we read from or write to the file, the file pointer is advanced accordingly. If we want to have random access to a file rather than accessing sequentially, we need to manipulate the file pointer.

This system call allows us to reposition the file pointer. As usual, the file descriptor is loaded into EBX. The offset to be added to the file pointer is given in ECX. This offset can added relative to the beginning of file, end of file, or current position. The whence value in EDX specifies this reference point:

Reference position	whence value
Beginning of file	0
Current position	1
End of file	2

These system calls allow us to write file I/O programs. Since keyboard and display are treated as files as well, we can write assembly language programs to access these I/O devices.

Our First Program

As our first example, we look at the PutCh procedure we used to write a character to the display. This is done by using the write system call. We specify stdout as the file to be written. The procedure is shown in Program 20.1. Since the character to be displayed is received in the AL register, we store it in temp_char before loading EAX with system call number 4. We load the temp_char pointer in ECX. Since we want to read just one character, we load 1 into EDX (line 10). We preserve the registers by using pusha and popa on lines 5 and 12.

Program 20.1 Procedure to write a character

```
 1:    ;------------------------------------------------------------
 2:    ; Put character procedure receives the character in AL.
 3:    ;------------------------------------------------------------
 4:    putch:
 5:            pusha
 6:            mov     [temp_char],AL
 7:            mov     EAX,4              ; 4 = write
 8:            mov     EBX,1             ; 1 = std output (display)
 9:            mov     ECX,temp_char     ; pointer to char buffer
10:            mov     EDX,1             ; # bytes = 1
11:            int     0x80
12:            popa
13:            ret
```

Illustrative Examples

We present two examples that use the file I/O system calls described before. As in the last example, the first one is taken from the I/O routines we have used (see Chapter 7 for details).

Example 20.1 *Procedure to read a string.*

In this example, we look at the string read function getstr. We can read a string by using a single file read system call as shown in Program 20.2. Since we use the dec instruction, which modifies the flags register, we preserve its contents by saving and restoring the flags register using pushf (line 7) and popf (line 16). Since the file read system call returns the number of characters read in EAX, we can add this value (after decrementing) to the buffer pointer to append a NULL character (line 15). This returns the string in the NULL-terminated format.

Program 20.2 Procedure to read a string

```
 1:    ;------------------------------------------------------------
 2:    ; Get string procedure receives input buffer pointer in
 3:    ; EDI and the buffer size in ESI.
 4:    ;------------------------------------------------------------
 5:    getstr:
 6:            pusha
```

```
 7:            pushf
 8:            mov     EAX,3          ; file read service
 9:            mov     EBX,0          ; 0 = std input (keyboard)
10:            mov     ECX,EDI        ; pointer to input buffer
11:            mov     EDX,ESI        ; input buffer size
12:            int     0x80
13:            dec     EAX
14: done_getstr:
15:            mov     byte[EDI+EAX],0  ; append NULL character
16:            popf
17:            popa
18:            ret
```

Example 20.2 *A file copy program.*

This example uses file copy to show how disk files can be manipulated using the file I/O system calls. The program requests the input and output file names (lines 27–31). It opens the input file in read-only mode using the open file system call (lines 33–39). If the call is successful, it returns the file descriptor (a positive integer) in EAX. In case of an error, a negative value is returned in EAX. This error check is done on line 41. If there is an error in opening the file, the program displays the error message and quits. Otherwise, it creates the output file (lines 47–53). A similar error check is done for the output file (lines 55–59).

File copy is done by reading a block of data from the input file and writing it to the output file. The block size is determined by the buffer size allocated for this purpose (see line 23). The copy loop on lines 61–79 consists of three parts:

- Read a block of BUF_SIZE bytes from the input file (lines 62–67);
- Write the block to the output file (lines 69–74);
- Check to see if the end of file has been reached. As discussed before, this check is done by comparing the number of bytes read by the file-read system call (which is copied to EDX) to BUF_SIZE. If the number of bytes read is less than BUF_SIZE, we know we have reached the end of file (lines 76 and 77).

After completing the copying process, we close the two open files (lines 81–85).

Program 20.3 File copy program using the file I/O services

```
 1: ;A file copy program                        file_copy.asm
 2: ;
 3: ; Objective: To copy a file using the int 0x80 services.
 4: ;      Input: Requests names of the input and output files.
 5: ;     Output: Creates a new output file and copies contents
 6: ;             of the input file.
 7:
 8: %include "io.mac"
 9:
10: %define    BUF_SIZE    256
11:
```

```
12:      .DATA
13:      in_fn_prompt      db   'Enter the input file name: ',0
14:      out_fn_prompt     db   'Enter the output file name: ',0
15:      in_file_err_msg   db   'Input file open error.',0
16:      out_file_err_msg  db   'Cannot create output file.',0
17:
18:      .UDATA
19:      in_file_name      resb   30
20:      out_file_name     resb   30
21:      fd_in             resd   1
22:      fd_out            resd   1
23:      in_buf            resb   BUF_SIZE
24:
25:      .CODE
26:          .STARTUP
27:          PutStr   in_fn_prompt      ; request input file name
28:          GetStr   in_file_name,30   ; read input file name
29:
30:          PutStr   out_fn_prompt     ; request output file name
31:          GetStr   out_file_name,30  ; read output file name
32:
33:          ;open the input file
34:          mov      EAX,5             ; file open
35:          mov      EBX,in_file_name  ; input file name pointer
36:          mov      ECX,0             ; access bits (read only)
37:          mov      EDX,0700          ; file permissions
38:          int      0x80
39:          mov      [fd_in],EAX       ; store fd for use in
40:                                     ;      read routine
41:          cmp      EAX,0             ; open error if fd < 0
42:          jge      create_file
43:          PutStr   in_file_err_msg
44:          nwln
45:          jmp      done
46:
47:  create_file:
48:          ;create output file
49:          mov      EAX,8             ; file create
50:          mov      EBX,out_file_name ; output file name pointer
51:          mov      ECX,0700          ; r/w/e by owner only
52:          int      0x80
53:          mov      [fd_out],EAX      ; store fd for use in
54:                                     ;      write routine
55:          cmp      EAX,0             ; create error if fd < 0
56:          jge      repeat_read
57:          PutStr   out_file_err_msg
58:          nwln
59:          jmp      close_exit        ; close input file & exit
60:
61:  repeat_read:
62:          ; read input file
```

```
63:        mov       EAX, 3               ; file read
64:        mov       EBX, [fd_in]         ; file descriptor
65:        mov       ECX, in_buf          ; input buffer
66:        mov       EDX, BUF_SIZE        ; size
67:        int       0x80
68:
69:        ; write to output file
70:        mov       EDX, EAX             ; byte count
71:        mov       EAX, 4               ; file write
72:        mov       EBX, [fd_out]        ; file descriptor
73:        mov       ECX, in_buf          ; input buffer
74:        int       0x80
75:
76:        cmp       EDX, BUF_SIZE        ; EDX = # bytes read
77:        jl        copy_done            ; EDX < BUF_SIZE
78:                                       ; indicates end-of-file
79:        jmp       repeat_read
80: copy_done:
81:        mov       EAX, 6               ; close output file
82:        mov       EBX, [fd_out]
83: close_exit:
84:        mov       EAX, 6               ; close input file
85:        mov       EBX, [fd_in]
86: done:
87:        .EXIT
```

Hardware Interrupts

We have seen how interrupts can be caused by the software instruction int. Since these instructions are placed in a program, software interrupts are called *synchronous* events. Hardware interrupts, on the other hand, are of hardware origin and *asynchronous* in nature. These interrupts are used by I/O devices such as the keyboard to get the processor's attention.

As discussed before, hardware interrupts can be further divided into either *maskable* or *nonmaskable* interrupts (see Figure 20.1). A nonmaskable interrupt (NMI) can be triggered by applying an electrical signal on the NMI pin of the processor. This interrupt is called nonmaskable because the CPU always responds to this signal. In other words, this interrupt cannot be disabled under program control. The NMI causes a type 2 interrupt.

Most hardware interrupts are of maskable type. To cause this type of interrupt, an electrical signal should be applied to the INTR (INTerrupt Request) input of the processor. The processor recognizes the INTR interrupt only if the interrupt enable flag (IF) bit of the flags register is set to 1. Thus, these interrupts can be masked or disabled by clearing the IF bit. Note that we can use sti and cli to set and clear this bit in the flags register, respectively.

How Does the Processor Know the Interrupt Type?   Recall that every interrupt should be identified by a vector (a number between 0 and 255), which is used as an index into the interrupt vector table to obtain the corresponding ISR address. This interrupt invocation procedure is common to all interrupts, whether caused by software or hardware.

In response to a hardware interrupt request on the INTR pin, the processor initiates an interrupt acknowledge sequence. As part of this sequence, the processor sends out an interrupt acknowledge (INTA) signal, and the interrupting device is expected to place the interrupt vector on the data bus. The processor reads this value and uses it as the interrupt vector.

How Can More Than One Device Interrupt?   From the above description, it is clear that all interrupt requests from external devices should be input via the INTR pin of the processor. While it is straightforward to connect a single device, computers typically have more than one I/O device requesting interrupt service. For example, the keyboard, hard disk, and floppy disk all generate interrupts when they require the attention of the processor.

When more than one device interrupts, we have to have a mechanism to prioritize these interrupts (if they come simultaneously) and forward only one interrupt request at a time to the processor while keeping the other interrupt requests pending for their turn. This mechanism can be implemented by using a special APIC (Advanced Programmable Interrupt Controller) chip.

Hardware interrupts provide direct access to the I/O devices. The next section discusses some of the instructions available to access I/O ports.

Direct Control of I/O Devices

When we want to access an I/O device for which there is no such support available from the operating system, or when we want a nonstandard access, we have to access these devices directly.

At this point, it is useful to review the material presented in Chapter 4. As described in that chapter, the IA-32 architecture uses a separate I/O address space of 64K. This address space can be used for 8-bit, 16-bit, or 32-bit I/O ports. However, the combination cannot be more than the total I/O space. For example, we can have 64K 8-bit ports, 32K 16-bit ports, 16K 32-bit ports, or a combination of these that fits the I/O address space.

Devices that transfer data 8 bits at a time can use 8-bit ports. These devices are called 8-bit devices. An 8-bit device can be located anywhere in the I/O space without any restrictions. On the other hand, a 16-bit port should be aligned to an even address so that 16 bits can be simultaneously transferred in a single bus cycle. Similarly, 32-bit ports should be aligned at addresses that are multiples of four. The architecture, however, supports unaligned I/O ports, but there is a performance penalty (see page 59 for a related discussion).

Accessing I/O Ports

To facilitate access to the I/O ports, the instruction set provides two types of instructions: register I/O instructions and block I/O instructions. Register I/O instructions are used to transfer data between a register and an I/O port. Block I/O instructions are used for block transfer of data between memory and I/O ports.

Register I/O Instructions   There are two register I/O instructions: in and out. The in instruction is used to read data from an I/O port, and the out instruction to write data to an I/O port. A port address can be any value in the range 0 to FFFFH. The first 256 ports are directly addressable—address is given as part of the instruction.

Both instructions can be used to operate on 8-, 16-, or 32-bit data. Each instruction can take one of two forms, depending on whether a port is directly addressable or not. The general format of the in instruction is

```
in      accumulator,port8 — direct addressing format
in      accumulator,DX     — indirect addressing format
```

The first form uses the direct addressing mode and can only be used to access the first 256 ports. In this case, the I/O port address, which is in the range 0 to FFH, is given by the port8 operand. In the second form, the I/O port address is given indirectly via the DX register. The contents of the DX register are treated as the port address.

In either form, the first operand accumulator must be AL, AX, or EAX. This choice determines whether a byte, word, or doubleword is read from the specified port.

The format for the out instruction is

```
out     port8,accumulator — direct addressing format
out     DX,accumulator     — indirect addressing format
```

Notice the placement of the port address. In the in instruction, it is the source operand and in the out instruction, it is the destination operand signifying the direction of data movement.

Block I/O Instructions   The instruction set has two block I/O instructions: ins and outs. These instructions can be used to move blocks of data between I/O ports and memory. These I/O instructions are, in some sense, similar to the string instructions discussed in Chapter 17. For this reason, block I/O instructions are also called string I/O instructions. Like the string instructions, ins and outs do not take any operands. Also, we can use the repeat prefix rep as in the string instructions.

For the ins instruction, the port address should be placed in DX and the memory address should be pointed to by ES:(E)DI. The address size determines whether the DI or EDI register is used (see Chapter 4 for details). Block I/O instructions do not allow the direct addressing format.

For the outs instruction, the memory address should be pointed by DS:(E)SI, and the I/O port should be specified in DX. You can see the similarity between the block I/O instructions and the string instructions.

You can use the rep prefix with ins and outs instructions. However, you cannot use the other two prefixes—repe and repne—with the block I/O instructions. The semantics of rep are the same as those in the string instructions. The directions flag (DF) determines whether the index register in the block I/O instruction is decremented (DF is 1) or incremented (DF is 0). The increment or decrement value depends on the size of the data unit transferred. For byte transfers, the index register is updated by 1. For word and doubleword transfers, the corresponding values are 2 and 4, respectively. The size of the data unit involved in the transfers can be specified as in the string instructions. Use insb and outsb for byte transfers, insw and outsw for word transfers, and insd and outsd for doubleword transfers.

Summary

Interrupts provide a mechanism to transfer control to an interrupt service routine. The mechanism is similar to that of a procedure call. However, while procedures can be invoked only by a procedure call in software, interrupts can be invoked by both hardware and software.

Software interrupts are generated using the int instruction. Hardware interrupts are generated by I/O devices. These interrupts are used by I/O devices to interrupt the processor to service their requests.

Software interrupts are often used to support access to the system I/O devices. Linux provides a high-level interface to the hardware with software interrupts. We introduced Linux system calls and discussed how these calls can be used to access I/O devices. The system calls are invoked using int   0x80. We used several examples to illustrate the utility of these calls in reading from the keyboard, writing to the screen, and accessing files.

All interrupts, whether hardware-initiated or software-initiated, are identified by an interrupt type number that is between 0 and 255. This interrupt number is used to access the interrupt vector table to get the associated interrupt vector.

21

High-Level Language Interface

Thus far, we have written standalone assembly language programs. This chapter considers mixed-mode programming, which refers to writing parts of a program in different programming languages. We use the C and assembly languages to illustrate how such mixed-mode programs are written. We begin the chapter with discussion of the motivation for writing mixed-mode programs. Next we give an overview of mixed-mode programming, which can be done either by inline assembly code or by separate assembly modules. We describe both methods with some example programs. The last section summarizes the chapter.

Introduction

In this chapter we focus on mixed-mode programming that involves C and assembly languages. Thus, we write part of the program in C and the other part in the assembly language. We use the gcc compiler and NASM assembler to explain the principles involved in mixed-mode programming. This discussion can be easily extended to a different set of languages and compilers/assemblers.

In Chapter 1 we discussed several reasons why one would want to program in the assembly language. Although it is possible to write a program entirely in the assembly language, there are several disadvantages in doing so. These include

- Low productivity
- High maintenance cost
- Lack of portability

Low productivity is due to the fact that assembly language is a low-level language. As a result, a single high-level language instruction may require several assembly language instructions. It has been observed that programmers tend to produce the same number of lines of debugged and tested source code per unit time irrespective of the level of the language used. As the assembly language requires more lines of source code, programmer productivity tends to be low.

Programs written in the assembly language are difficult to maintain. This is a direct consequence of it's being a low-level language. In addition, assembly language programs are not portable. On the other hand, the assembly language provides low-level access to system hardware. In addition, the assembly language may help us reduce the execution time.

As a result of these pros and cons, some programs are written in mixed mode using both high-level and low-level languages. System software often requires mixed-mode programming. In such programs, it is possible for a high-level procedure to call a low-level procedure, and vice versa. The remainder of the chapter discusses how mixed-mode programming is done in C and assembly languages. Our goal is to illustrate only the principles involved. Once these principles are understood, the discussion can be generalized to any type of mixed-mode programming.

Overview

There are two ways of writing mixed-mode C and assembly programs: inline assembly code or separate assembly modules. In the inline assembly method, the C program module contains assembly language instructions. Most C compilers including `gcc` allow embedding assembly language instructions within a C program by prefixing them with **asm** to let the compiler know that it is an assembly language instruction. This method is useful if you have only a small amount of assembly code to embed. Otherwise, separate assembly modules are preferred. We discuss the inline assembly method later (see page 434).

When separate modules are used for C and assembly languages, each module can be translated into the corresponding object file. To do this translation, we use a C compiler for the C modules and an assembler for the assembly modules, as shown in Figure 21.1. Then the linker can be used to produce the executable file from these object files.

Suppose our mixed-mode program consists of two modules:

- One C module, file `sample1.c`, and
- One assembly module, file `sample2.asm`.

The process involved in producing the executable file is shown in Figure 21.1. We can invoke the NASM assembler as

```
nasm -f elf sample2.asm
```

This creates the `sample2.o` object file. We can compile and link the files with the following command:

```
gcc -o sample1.out sample1.c sample2.o
```

This command instructs the compiler to first compile `sample1.c` to `sample1.o`. The linker is automatically invoked to link `sample1.o` and `sample2.o` to produce the executable file `sample1.out`.

Calling Assembly Procedures from C

Let us now discuss how we can call an assembly language procedure from a C program. The first thing we have to know is what communication medium is used between the C and assembly language procedures, as the two procedures may exchange parameters and results. You are right if you guessed it to be the stack.

Given that the stack is used for communication purposes, we still need to know a few more details as to how the C function places the parameters on the stack, and where it expects the

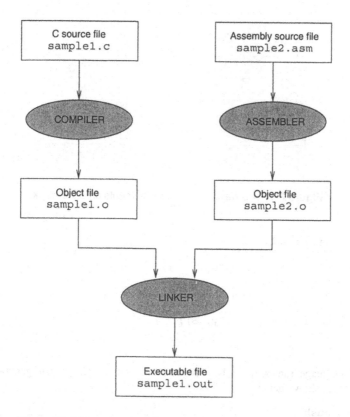

Figure 21.1 Steps involved in compiling mixed-mode programs.

assembly language procedure to return the result. In addition, we should also know which registers we can use freely without worrying about preserving their values. Next we discuss these issues in detail.

Parameter Passing   There are two ways in which arguments (i.e., parameter values) are pushed onto the stack: from left to right or from right to left. Most high-level languages push the arguments from left to right. These are called *left-pusher* languages. C, on the other hand, pushes arguments from right to left. Thus, C is a *right-pusher* language. The stack state after executing

```
sum(a,b,c,d)
```

is shown in Figure 21.2. From now on, we consider only right-pushing of arguments, as we focus on the C language.

To see how gcc pushes arguments onto the stack, take a look at the following C program (this is a partial listing of Program 21.1 on page 428):

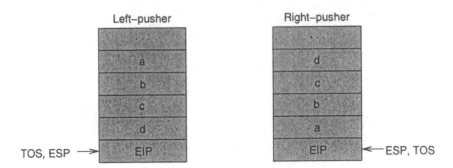

Figure 21.2 Two ways of pushing arguments onto the stack.

```
int main(void)
{
    int     x=25, y=70;
    int     value;
    extern  int test(int, int, int);

    value = test (x, y, 5);
    . . .
}
```

The assembly language translation of the procedure call (use the -S option to generate the assembly source code) is shown below:[1]

```
push    5
push    70
push    25
call    test
add     ESP,12
mov     [EBP-12],EAX
```

This program is compiled with -O2 optimization. This optimization is the reason for pushing constants 70 and 25 instead of variables x and y. If you don't use this optimization, gcc produces the following code:

```
push    5
push    [EBP-8]
push    [EBP-4]
call    test
add     ESP,12
mov     [EBP-12],EAX
```

It is obvious from this code fragment that the compiler assigns space for variables x, y, and value on the stack at EBP−4, EBP−8, and EBP−12, respectively. When the test function is called, the arguments are pushed from right to left, starting with the constant 5. Also notice that the stack is cleared of the arguments by the C program after the call by the following statement:

---

[1]Note that gcc uses AT&T syntax for the assembly language—not the Intel syntax we have been using in this book. To avoid any confusion, the contents are reported in our syntax. The AT&T syntax is introduced on page 434.

```
add    ESP,12
```

So, when we write our assembly procedures, we should not bother clearing the arguments from the stack as we did in our programs in the previous chapters. This convention is used because C allows a variable number of arguments to be passed in a function call (see our discussion on page 268).

Returning Values   We can see from the previous assembly language code that the EAX register is used to return the function value. In fact, the EAX register is used to return 8-, 16-, and 32-bit values. To return a 64-bit value, use the EDX:EAX pair with the EDX holding the upper 32 bits.

We have not discussed how floating-point values are returned. For example, if a C function returns a double value, how do we return this value? We discuss this issue in the next chapter.

Preserving Registers   In general, the called assembly language procedure can use the registers as needed, except that the following registers should be preserved:

```
EBP, EBX, ESI, EDI
```

The other registers, if needed, must be preserved by the calling function.

Globals and Externals   Mixed-mode programming involves at least two program modules: a C module and an assembly module. Thus, we have to declare those functions and procedures that are not defined in the same module as external. Similarly, those procedures that are accessed by another module should be declared as global, as discussed in Chapter 11. Before proceeding further, you may want to review the material on multimodule programs presented in Chapter 11 (see our discussion on page 260). Here we mention only those details that are specific to the mixed-mode programming involving the C and assembly languages.

In most C compilers, external labels should start with an underscore character (_). The C and C++ compilers automatically append the required underscore character to all external functions and variables. A consequence of this characteristic is that when we write an assembly procedure that is called from a C program, we have to make sure that we prefix an underscore character to its name. However, gcc does not follow this convention by default. Thus, we don't have to worry about the underscore.

Our First Program

To illustrate the principles involved in writing mixed-mode programs, we look at a simple example that passes three parameters to the test1 assembly language function. The C code is shown in Program 21.1 and the assembly code in Program 21.2. The function test1 is declared as external in the C program (line 12) and global in the assembly program (line 8). Since C clears the arguments from the stack, the assembly procedure uses a simple ret to transfer control back to the C program. Other than these differences, the assembly procedure is similar to several others we have written before.

Program 21.1 An example illustrating assembly calls from C: C code (in file `hll_ex1c.c`)

```
 1:   /*********************************************************
 2:    * A simple program to illustrate how mixed-mode programs
 3:    * are written in C and assembly languages. The main C
 4:    * program calls the assembly language procedure test1.
 5:    *********************************************************/
 6:   #include        <stdio.h>
 7:
 8:   int main(void)
 9:   {
10:           int    x = 25, y = 70;
11:           int    value;
12:           extern int test1 (int, int, int);
13:
14:           value = test1(x, y, 5);
15:           printf("Result = %d\n", value);
16:
17:           return 0;
18:   }
```

Program 21.2 An example illustrating assembly calls from C: assembly language code (in file `hll_test.asm`)

```
 1:   ;------------------------------------------------------------
 2:   ; This procedure receives three integers via the stack.
 3:   ; It adds the first two arguments and subtracts the
 4:   ; third one. It is called from the C program.
 5:   ;------------------------------------------------------------
 6:   segment .text
 7:
 8:   global  test1
 9:
10:   test1:
11:           enter   0,0
12:           mov     EAX, [EBP+8]        ; get argument1 (x)
13:           add     EAX, [EBP+12]       ; add argument 2 (y)
14:           sub     EAX, [EBP+16]       ; subtract argument3 (5)
15:           leave
16:           ret
```

Illustrative Examples

In this section, we give two more examples to illustrate the interface between C and assembly language programs.

Example 21.1 *An example to show parameter passing by call-by-value as well as call-by-reference.*

This example shows how pointer parameters are handled. The C main function requests three integers and passes them to the assembly procedure. The C program is given in Program 21.3. The assembly procedure min_max, shown in Program 21.4, receives the three integer values and two pointers to variables minimum and maximum. It finds the minimum and maximum of the three integers and returns them to the main C function via these two pointers. The minimum value is kept in EAX and the maximum in EDX. The code given on lines 28 to 31 in Program 21.4 stores the return values by using the EBX register in the indirect addressing mode.

Program 21.3 An example with the C program passing pointers to the assembly program: C code (in file hll_minmaxc.c)

```
 1:   /**********************************************************
 2:    * An example to illustrate call-by-value and            *
 3:    * call-by-reference parameter passing between C and      *
 4:    * assembly language modules. The min_max function is     *
 5:    * written in assembly language (in hll_minmaxa.asm).     *
 6:    **********************************************************/
 7:   #include <stdio.h>
 8:   int main(void)
 9:   {
10:           int     value1, value2, value3;
11:           int     min, max;
12:           extern  void min_max (int, int, int, int*, int*);
13:
14:           printf("Enter number 1 = ");
15:           scanf("%d", &value1);
16:           printf("Enter number 2 = ");
17:           scanf("%d", &value2);
18:           printf("Enter number 3 = ");
19:           scanf("%d", &value3);
20:
21:           min_max(value1, value2, value3, &min, &max);
22:           printf("Minimum = %d, Maximum = %d\n", min, max);
23:           return 0;
24:   }
```

Program 21.4 An example with the C program passing pointers to the assembly program: assembly language code (in file `hll_minmaxa.asm`)

```
 1:  ;-----------------------------------------------------------------
 2:  ; Assembly program for the min_max function - called from
 3:  ; the C program in the file hll_minmaxc.c. This function
 4:  ; finds the minimum and maximum of the three integers it
 5:  ; receives.
 6:  ;-----------------------------------------------------------------
 7:  global   min_max
 8:
 9:  min_max:
10:          enter    0,0
11:          ; EAX keeps minimum number and EDX maximum
12:          mov      EAX, [EBP+8]      ; get value 1
13:          mov      EDX, [EBP+12]     ; get value 2
14:          cmp      EAX,EDX           ; value 1 < value 2?
15:          jl       skip1             ; if so, do nothing
16:          xchg     EAX,EDX           ; else, exchange
17:  skip1:
18:          mov      ECX, [EBP+16]     ; get value 3
19:          cmp      ECX,EAX           ; value 3 < min in EAX?
20:          jl       new_min
21:          cmp      ECX,EDX           ; value 3 < max in EDX?
22:          jl       store_result
23:          mov      EDX,ECX
24:          jmp      store_result
25:  new_min:
26:          mov      EAX,ECX
27:  store_result:
28:          mov      EBX, [EBP+20]     ; EBX = &min
29:          mov      [EBX],EAX
30:          mov      EBX, [EBP+24]     ; EBX = &max
31:          mov      [EBX],EDX
32:          leave
33:          ret
```

Example 21.2 *Array sum example.*

This example illustrates how arrays, declared in C, are accessed by assembly language procedures. The array `value` is declared in the C program, as shown in Program 21.5 (line 12). The assembly language procedure computes the sum as shown in Program 21.6. As in the other programs in this chapter, the C program clears the parameters off the stack. We will redo this example using inline assembly on page 439. In addition, a floating-point version of this example is given in the next chapter.

Program 21.5 An array sum example: C code (in file `hll_arraysumc.c`)

```
 1:  /**********************************************************
 2:   * This program reads 10 integers into an array and calls
 3:   * an assembly language program to compute the array sum.
 4:   * The assembly program is in "hll_arraysuma.asm" file.
 5:   **********************************************************/
 6:  #include        <stdio.h>
 7:
 8:  #define  SIZE  10
 9:
10:  int main(void)
11:  {
12:      int    value[SIZE], sum, i;
13:      extern int array_sum(int*, int);
14:
15:      printf("Input %d array values:\n", SIZE);
16:      for (i = 0; i < SIZE; i++)
17:          scanf("%d",&value[i]);
18:
19:      sum = array_sum(value,SIZE);
20:      printf("Array sum = %d\n", sum);
21:
22:      return 0;
23:  }
```

Program 21.6 An array sum example: assembly language code (in file `hll_arraysuma.asm`)

```
 1:  ;-------------------------------------------------------------
 2:  ; This procedure receives an array pointer and its size
 3:  ; via the stack. It computes the array sum and returns it.
 4:  ;-------------------------------------------------------------
 5:  segment .text
 6:
 7:  global  array_sum
 8:
 9:  array_sum:
10:      enter   0,0
11:      mov     EDX, [EBP+8]     ; copy array pointer to EDX
12:      mov     ECX, [EBP+12]    ; copy array size to ECX
13:      sub     EBX, EBX         ; array index = 0
14:      sub     EAX, EAX         ; sum = 0 (EAX keeps the sum)
15:  add_loop:
16:      add     EAX, [EDX+EBX*4]
17:      inc     EBX              ; increment array index
18:      cmp     EBX, ECX
19:      jl      add_loop
20:      leave
21:      ret
```

Calling C Functions from Assembly

So far, we have considered how a C function can call an assembler procedure. Sometimes it is desirable to call a C function from an assembler procedure. This scenario often arises when we want to avoid writing assembly language code for a complex task. Instead, a C function could be written for those tasks. This section illustrates how we can access C functions from assembly procedures. Essentially, the mechanism is the same: we use the stack as the communication medium, as shown in the next example.

Example 21.3 *An example to illustrate a C function call from an assembly procedure.*

In previous chapters, we used simple I/O routines to facilitate input and output in our assembly language programs. If we want to use the C functions like printf() and scanf(), we have to pass the arguments as required by the function. In this example, we show how we can use these two C functions to facilitate input and output of integers. This discussion can be generalized to other types of data.

Here we compute the sum of an array passed onto the array_sum assembly language procedure. This example is similar to Example 21.2, except that the C program does not read the array values; instead, the assembly program does this by calling the printf() and scanf() functions as shown in Program 21.8. In this program, the prompt message is declared as a string on line 9 (including the newline). The assembly language version implements the equivalent of the following printf statement we used in Program 21.5:

```
printf("Input %d array values:\n", SIZE);
```

Before calling the printf function on line 21, we push the array size (which is in ECX) and the string onto the stack. The stack is cleared on line 22.

The array values are read using the read loop on lines 26 to 36. It uses the scanf function, the equivalent of the following statement:

```
scanf("%d",&value[i]);
```

The required arguments (array and format string pointers) are pushed onto the stack on lines 28 and 29 before calling the scanf function on line 30. The array sum is computed using the add loop on lines 41 to 45 as in Program 21.6.

Program 21.7 An example to illustrate C calls from assembly programs: C code (in file hll_arraysum2c.c)

```
 1:   /**********************************************************
 2:    * This program calls an assembly program to read the
 3:    * array input and compute its sum. It prints the sum.
 4:    * The assembly program is in "hll_arraysum2a.asm" file.
 5:    **********************************************************/
 6:   #include        <stdio.h>
 7:
 8:   #define  SIZE   10
 9:
10:   int main(void)
11:   {
```

```
12:        int     value[SIZE];
13:        extern int array_sum(int*, int);
14:
15:        printf("sum = %d\n",array_sum(value,SIZE));
16:
17:        return 0;
18: }
```

Program 21.8 An example to illustrate C calls from assembly programs: assembly language code (in file hll_arraysum2a.asm)

```
1:  ;------------------------------------------------------------
2:  ; This procedure receives an array pointer and its size
3:  ; via the stack. It first reads the array input from the
4:  ; user and then computes the array sum.
5:  ; The sum is returned to the C program.
6:  ;------------------------------------------------------------
7:  segment .data
8:  scan_format     db    "%d",0
9:  printf_format   db    "Input %d array values:",10,13,0
10:
11: segment .text
12:
13: global  array_sum
14: extern  printf,scanf
15:
16: array_sum:
17:        enter   0,0
18:        mov     ECX,[EBP+12]    ; copy array size to ECX
19:        push    ECX             ; push array size
20:        push    dword printf_format
21:        call    printf
22:        add     ESP,8           ; clear the stack
23:
24:        mov     EDX,[EBP+8]     ; copy array pointer to EDX
25:        mov     ECX,[EBP+12]    ; copy array size to ECX
26: read_loop:
27:        push    ECX             ; save loop count
28:        push    EDX             ; push array pointer
29:        push    dword scan_format
30:        call    scanf
31:        add     ESP,4           ; clear stack of one argument
32:        pop     EDX             ; restore array pointer in EDX
33:        pop     ECX             ; restore loop count
34:        add     EDX,4           ; update array pointer
35:        dec     ECX
36:        jnz     read_loop
37:
38:        mov     EDX,[EBP+8]     ; copy array pointer to EDX
```

```
39:          mov      ECX,[EBP+12]     ; copy array size to ECX
40:          sub      EAX,EAX          ; EAX = 0 (EAX keeps the sum)
41: add_loop:
42:          add      EAX,[EDX]
43:          add      EDX,4            ; update array pointer
44:          dec      ECX
45:          jnz      add_loop
46:          leave
47:          ret
```

Inline Assembly

In this section we look at writing inline assembly code. In this method, we embed assembly language statements within the C code. We identify assembly language statements by using the asm construct. (You can use __asm__ if asm causes a conflict, e.g., for ANSI C compatibility.)

We now have a serious problem: the gcc syntax for the assembly language statements is different from the syntax we have been using so far. We have been using the Intel syntax (NASM, TASM, and MASM use this syntax). The gcc compiler uses the AT&T syntax, which is used by GNU assemblers. It is different in several aspects from the Intel syntax. But don't worry! We give an executive summary of the differences so that you can understand the syntactical differences without spending too much time.

The AT&T Syntax

This section gives a summary of some of the key differences from the Intel syntax.

Register Naming   In the AT&T syntax, we have to prefix register names with %. For example, the EAX register is specified as %eax.

Source and Destination Order   The source and destination operands order is reversed in the AT&T syntax. In this format, source operand is on the left-hand side. For example, the instruction

```
mov      eax,ebx
```

is written as

```
movl     %ebx,%eax
```

Operand Size   As demonstrated by the last example, the instructions specify the operand size. The instructions are suffixed with b, w, and l for byte, word, and longword operands, respectively. With this specification, we don't have to use byte, word, and dword to clarify the operand size (see our discussion on page 197).

The operand size specification is not strictly necessary. You can let the compiler guess the size of the operand. However, if you specify, it takes the guesswork out and we don't have to worry about the compiler making an incorrect guess. Here are some examples:

```
movb     %bl,%al      ; moves contents of bl to al
movw     %bx,%ax      ; moves contents of bx to ax
movl     %ebx,%eax    ; moves contents of ebx to eax
```

Immediate and Constant Operands   In the AT&T syntax, immediate and constant operands are specified by prefixing with $. Here are some examples:

```
movb    $255,%al
movl    $0xFFFFFFFF,%eax
```

The following statement loads the address of the C global variable `total` into the EAX register:

```
movl    $total,%eax
```

This works only if `total` is declared as a global variable. Otherwise, we have to use the extended `asm` construct that we discuss later.

Addressing   To specify indirect addressing, the AT&T syntax uses brackets (not square brackets). For example, the instruction

```
mov     eax, [ebx]
```

is written in AT&T syntax as

```
movl    (%ebx),%eax
```

The full 32-bit protected-mode addressing format is shown below:

```
imm32(base,index,scale)
```

The address is computed as

```
imm32 + base + index * scale
```

If we declared `marks` as a global array of integers, we can load `marks[5]` into EAX register using

```
movl    $5,%ebx
movl    marks(,%ebx,4),%eax
```

For example, if the pointer to `marks` is in the EAX register, we can load `marks[5]` into the EAX register using

```
movl    $5,%ebx
movl    (%eax,%ebx,4),%eax
```

We use a similar technique in the array sum example discussed later. We have covered enough details to work with the AT&T syntax.

Simple Inline Statements

At the basic level, introducing assembly statements is not difficult. Here is an example that increments the EAX register contents:

```
asm("incl %eax");
```

Multiple assembly statements like these

```
asm("pushl    %eax");
asm("incl     %eax");
asm("popl     %eax");
```

can be grouped into a single compound asm statement as shown below:

```
asm("pushl    %eax; incl    %eax; popl    %eax");
```

If you want to add structure to this compound statement, you can write the above statement as follows:

```
asm("pushl    %eax;"
    "incl     %eax;"
    "popl     %eax");
```

We have one major problem in accessing the registers as we did here: How do we know if gcc is not keeping something useful in the register that we are using? More importantly, how do we get access to C variables that are not global to manipulate in our inline assembly code? The answers are provided by the extended asm statement. This is where we are going next.

Extended Inline Statements

The format of the asm statement consists of four components as shown below:

```
asm(assembly code
    :outputs
    :inputs
    :clobber list);
```

Each component is separated by a colon (:). The last three components are optional. These four components are described next.

Assembly Code   This component consists of the assembly language statements to be inserted into the C code. This may have a single instruction or a sequence of instructions, as discussed in the last subsection. If no compiler optimization should be done to this code, add the keyword volatile after asm (i.e., use asm volatile). The instructions typically use the operands specified in the next two components.

Outputs   This component specifies the output operands for the assembly code. The format for specifying each operand is shown below:

```
"=op-constraint" (C-expression)
```

The first part specifies an operand constraint, and the part in brackets is a C expression. The = identifies that it is an output constraint. For some strange reason we have to specify = even though we separate inputs and outputs with a colon. The following example

```
"=r" (sum)
```

specifies that the C variable sum should be mapped to a register as indicated by r in the constraint. Multiple operands can be specified by separating them with commas. We give some examples later.

Depending on the processor, several other choices are allowed including m (memory), i (immediate), rm (register or memory), ri (register or immediate), or g (general). The last one is typically equivalent to rim. You can also specify a particular register by using a, b, and so on. The following table summarizes the register letters used to specify which registers that gcc may use:

Letter	Register set
a	EAX register
b	EBX register
c	ECX register
d	EDX register
S	ESI register
D	EDI register
r	Any of the eight general registers (EAX, EBX, ECX, EDX, ESI, EDI, EBP, ESP)
q	Any of the four data registers (EAX, EBX, ECX, EDX)
A	A 64-bit value in EAX and EDX
f	Floating-point registers
t	Top floating-point register
u	Second top floating-point register

The last three letters are used to specify floating-point registers. We discuss floating-point operations in the next chapter.

Inputs The inputs are also specified in the same way, except for the = sign. The operands specified in the output and input parts are assigned sequence numbers 0, 1, 2, ... starting with the leftmost output operand. There can be a total of 10 operands, inputs and outputs combined. Thus, 9 is the maximum sequence number allowed.

In the assembly code, we can refer to the output and input operands by their sequence number prefixed with %. In the following example

```
asm("movl %1,%0"
      :"=r"(sum)      /* output */
      :"r"(number1)   /* input  */
    );
```

the C variables sum and number1 are both mapped to registers. In the assembly code statement, sum is identified by %0 and number1 by %1. Thus, this statement copies the value of number1 to sum.

Sometimes, an operand provides input and receives the result as well (e.g., x in x = x + y). In this case, the operand should be in both lists. In addition, you should use its output sequence number as its input constraint specifier. The following example clarifies what we mean.

```
asm("addl %1,%0"
    :"=r"(sum)                    /* output */
    :"r"(number1), "0"(sum)      /* inputs */
    );
```

In this example, we want to perform sum = sum + number1. In this expression, the variable sum provides one of the inputs and also receives the result. Thus, sum is in both lists. However, note that the constraint specifier for it in the input list is "0", not "r".

The assembly code can use specific registers prefixing the register with %. Since the AT&T syntax prefixes registers with %, we end up using %% as in %%eax to refer to the EAX register.

Clobber List   This last component specifies the list of registers modified by the assembly instructions in the asm statement. This lets gcc know that it cannot assume that the contents of these registers are valid after the asm statement. The compiler may use this information to reload their values after executing the asm statement.

In case the assembly code modifies the memory, use the keyword "memory" to indicate this fact. Even though it may not be needed, you may want to specify "cc" in the clobber list if the flags register is modified (e.g., by an arithmetic instruction). Here is an example that includes the clobber list:

```
asm("movl %0,%%eax"
    : /* no output */
    :"r"(number1)   /* inputs */
    :"%eax"         /* clobber list */
    );
```

In this example, there is no output list; thus, the input operand (number1) is referred by %0. Since we copy the value of number1 into EAX register, we specify EAX in the clobber list so that gcc knows that our asm statement modifies this register.

Inline Examples

We now give some examples to illustrate how we can write mixed-mode programs using the inline assembly method.

Example 21.4 *Our first inline assembly example.*
As our first example, we rewrite the code of the example given on page 428 using inline assembly. The inline code is given in Program 21.9. The procedure test1 is written using inline assembly code. We use the EAX register to compute the sum as in Program 21.2 (see lines 22–24). Since there are no output operands, we explicitly state this by the comment on line 25. The three input operands x, y, and z, specified on line 26, are referred in the assembly code as %0, %1, and %2, respectively. The clobbered list consists of the EAX register and the flags register ("cc") as the add and sub instructions modify the flags register. Since the result is available in the EAX register, we simply return from the function.

Program 21.9 Our first inline assembly code example (in file hll_ex1_inline.c)

```
 1:    /*******************************************************
 2:     * A simple program to illustrate how mixed-mode programs
 3:     * are written in C and assembly languages. This program
 4:     * uses inline assembly code in the test1 function.
 5:     *******************************************************/
 6:    #include        <stdio.h>
 7:
 8:    int main(void)
 9:    {
10:            int     x = 25, y = 70;
11:            int     value;
12:            extern int test1 (int, int, int);
13:
14:            value = test1(x, y, 5);
15:            printf("Result = %d\n", value);
16:
17:            return 0;
18:    }
19:
20:    int test1(int x, int y, int z)
21:    {
22:            asm("movl   %0,%%eax;"
23:                "addl   %1,%%eax;"
24:                "subl   %2,%%eax;"
25:                :/* no outputs */         /* outputs */
26:                : "r"(x), "r"(y), "r"(z)  /* inputs */
27:                :"cc","%eax");            /* clobber list */
28:    }
```

Example 21.5 *Array sum example—inline version.*
This is the inline assembly version of the array sum example we did in Example 21.2. The program is given in Program 21.10. In the array_sum procedure, we replace the C statement

```
sum += value[i];
```

by the inline assembly code. The output operand specifies sum. The input operand list consists of the array value, array index variable i, and sum. Since sum is also in the output list, we use "0" as explained before. Since we use the add instruction, we specify "cc" in the clobber list as in the last example.

The assembly code consists of a single addl instruction. The source operand of this add instruction is given as (%1,%2,4). From our discussion on page 435 it is clear that this operand refers to value[i]. The rest of the code is straightforward to follow.

Program 21.10 Inline assembly version of the array sum example (in file hll_arraysum_inline.c)

```
 1:  /********************************************************
 2:   * This program reads 10 integers into an array and calls
 3:   * an assembly language program to compute the array sum.
 4:   * It uses inline assembly code in array_sum function.
 5:   ********************************************************/
 6:  #include          <stdio.h>
 7:
 8:  #define  SIZE  10
 9:
10:  int main(void)
11:  {
12:       int    value[SIZE], sum, i;
13:       int    array_sum(int*, int);
14:
15:       printf("Input %d array values:\n", SIZE);
16:       for (i = 0; i < SIZE; i++)
17:            scanf("%d",&value[i]);
18:
19:       sum = array_sum(value,SIZE);
20:       printf("Array sum = %d\n", sum);
21:
22:       return 0;
23:  }
24:
25:  int array_sum(int* value, int size)
26:  {
27:       int  i, sum=0;
28:       for (i = 0; i < size; i++)
29:            asm("addl (%1,%2,4),%0"
30:                :"=r"(sum)                          /* output */
31:                :"r"(value),"r"(i),"0"(sum)   /* inputs */
32:                :"cc");                       /* clobber list */
33:       return(sum);
34:  }
```

Example 21.6 *Array sum example—inline version 2.*

In the last example, we just replaced the statement

```
sum += value[i];
```

of the array_sum function by the assembly language statement. In this example, we rewrite the array_sum function completely in the assembly language. The rewritten function is shown in Program 21.11. This code illustrates some of the features we have not used in the previous examples.

As you can see from line 10, we receive the two input parameters (value and size) in specific registers (value in EBX and size in ECX). We compute the sum directly in the EAX register, so there are no outputs in the asm statement (see line 9). We don't use "%0" and "%1" to refer to the input operands. Since these are mapped to specific registers, we can use the register names in our assembly language code (see lines 5 and 6).

We use the EAX register to keep the sum. This register is initialized to zero on line 3. We use jecxz to test if ECX is zero. This is the termination condition for the loop. This code also shows how we can use jump instructions and labels.

Program 21.11 Another inline assembly version of the array sum function (This function is in file hll_arraysum_inline2.c)

```
 1:  int array_sum(int* value, int size)
 2:  {
 3:              asm("       xorl  %%eax,%%eax;"    /* sum = 0 */
 4:              "rep1: jecxz done;         "
 5:              "      decl  %%ecx;         "
 6:              "      addl  (%%ebx,%%ecx,4),%%eax;"
 7:              "      jmp   rep1;          "
 8:              "done:                      "
 9:              : /* no outputs */
10:              :"b"(value),"c"(size)             /* inputs */
11:              :"%eax","cc");            /* clobber list */
12:  }
```

Summary

We introduced the principles involved in mixed-mode programming. We discussed the main motivation for writing mixed-mode programs. This chapter focused on mixed-mode programming involving C and the assembly language. Using the gcc compiler and NASM assembler, we demonstrated how assembly language procedures are called from C, and vice versa. Once you understand the principles discussed in this chapter, you can easily handle any type of mixed-mode programming activity.

22

Floating-Point Operations

In this chapter we introduce the floating-point instructions. After giving a brief introduction to the floating-point numbers, we describe the registers of the floating-point unit. The floating-point unit supports several floating-point instructions. We describe a subset of these instructions in detail. We then give a few examples to illustrate the application of these floating-point instructions. We conclude the chapter with a summary.

Introduction

In the previous chapters, we represented numbers using integers. As you know, these numbers cannot be used to represent fractions. We use floating-point numbers to represent fractions. For example, in C, we use the `float` and `double` data types for the floating-point numbers.

One key characteristic of integers is that operations on these numbers are always precise. For example, when we add two integers, we always get the exact result. In contrast, operations on floating-point numbers are subjected to rounding-off errors. This tends to make the result approximate, rather than precise. However, floating-point numbers have several advantages.

Floating-point numbers can be used to represent both very small numbers and very large numbers. To achieve this, these numbers use the scientific notation to represent numbers. The number is divided into three parts: the *sign*, the *mantissa*, and the *exponent*. The sign bit identifies whether the number is positive (0) or negative (1). The magnitude is given by

$$\text{magnitude} = \text{mantissa} \times 2^{\text{exponent}}$$

Implementation of floating-point numbers on computer systems vary from this generic format—usually for efficiency reasons or to conform to a standard. The Intel 32-bit processors, like most other processors, follow the IEEE 754 floating-point standard. Such standards are useful, for example, to exchange data among several different computer systems and to write efficient numerical software libraries.

The floating-point unit (FPU) supports three formats for floating-point numbers. Two of these are for external use and one for internal use. The external format defines two precision types: the single-precision format uses 32 bits while the double-precision format uses 64 bits. In C, we use float for single-precision and double for double-precision floating-point numbers. The internal format uses 80 bits and is referred to as the extended format. As we see in the next section, all internal registers of the floating-point unit are 80 bits so that they can store floating-point numbers in the extended format. More details on the floating-point numbers are given in Appendix A.

The number-crunching capability of a processor can be enhanced by using a special hardware to perform floating-point operations. The 80X87 numeric coprocessors were designed to work with the 80X86 family of processors. The 8087 coprocessor was designed for the 8086 and 8088 processors to provide extensive high-speed numeric processing capabilities. The 8087, for example, provided about a hundredfold improvement in execution time compared to that of an equivalent software function on the 8086 processor. The 80287 and 80387 coprocessors were designed for use with the 80286 and 80386 processors, respectively. Starting with the 80486 processor, the floating-point unit has been integrated into the processor itself, avoiding the need for external numeric processors.

In the remainder of this chapter, we discuss the floating-point unit organization and its instructions. Toward the end of the chapter, we give a few example programs that use the floating-point instructions.

Floating-Point Unit Organization

The floating-point unit provides several registers, as shown in Figure 22.1. These registers are divided into three groups: data registers, control and status registers, and pointer registers. The last group consists of the instruction and data pointer registers, as shown in Figure 22.1. These pointers provide support for programmed exception handlers. Since this topic is beyond the scope of this book, we do not discuss details of these registers.

Data Registers

The FPU has eight floating-point registers to hold the floating-point operands. These registers supply the necessary operands to the floating-point instructions. Unlike the processor's general-purpose registers such as the EAX and EBX registers, these registers are organized as a register stack. In addition, we can access these registers individually using ST0, ST1, and so on.

Since these registers are organized as a register stack, these names are not statically assigned. That is, ST0 does not refer to a specific register. It refers to whichever register is acting as the top-of-stack (TOS) register. The next register is referred to as ST1, and so on; the last register as ST7. There is a 3-bit top-of-stack pointer in the status register to identify the TOS register.

Each data register can hold an extended-precision floating-point number. This format uses 80 bits as opposed to single-precision (32 bits) or double-precision (64 bits) formats. The rationale is that these registers typically hold intermediate results and using the extended format improves the accuracy of the final result.

The status and contents of each register is indicated by a 2-bit tag field. Since we have eight registers, we need a total of 16 tag bits. These 16 bits are stored in the tag register (see Figure 22.1). We discuss the tag register details a little later.

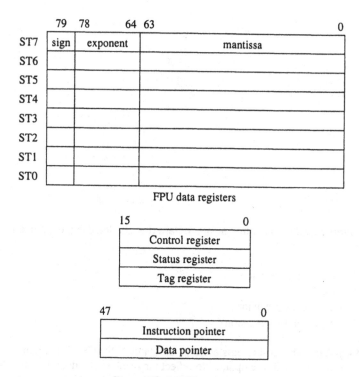

Figure 22.1 FPU registers.

Control and Status Registers

This group consists of three 16-bit registers: the control register, the status register, and the tag register, as shown in Figure 22.1.

FPU Control Register This register is used to provide control to the programmer on several processing options. Details about the control word are given in Figure 22.2. The least significant six bits contain masks for the six floating-point exceptions. The PC and RC bits control precision and rounding. Each uses two bits to specify four possible controls. The options for the rounding control are

- 00 — Round to nearest
- 01 — Round down
- 10 — Round up
- 11 — Truncate

The precision control can be used to set the internal operating precision to less than the default precision. These bits are provided for compatibility to earlier FPUs with less precision. The options for precision are

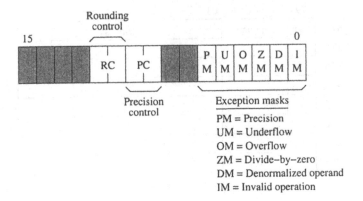

Figure 22.2 FPU control register details (the shaded bits are not used).

- 00 — 24 bits (single precision)
- 01 — Not used
- 10 — 53 bits (double precision)
- 11 — 64 bits (extended precision)

FPU Status Register   This 16-bit register keeps the status of the FPU (see Figure 22.3). The four condition code bits (C0 − C3) are updated to reflect the result of the floating-point arithmetic operations. These bits are similar to the flags register of the processor. The correspondence between three of these four bits and the flag register is shown below:

FPU flag	CPU flag
C0	CF
C2	PF
C3	ZF

The missing C1 bit is used to indicate stack underflow/overflow (discussed below). These bits are used for conditional branching just like the corresponding CPU flag bits.

To facilitate this branching, the status word should be copied into the CPU flags register. This copying is a two-step process. First, we use the fstsw instruction to store the status word in the AX register. We can then load these values into the flags register by using the sahf instruction. Once loaded, we can use conditional jump instructions. We demonstrate an application of this in Example 22.1.

The status register uses three bits to maintain the top-of-stack (TOS) information. The eight floating-point registers are organized as a circular buffer. The TOS identifies the register that is at the top. Like the CPU stack, this value is updated as we push and pop from the stack.

The least significant six bits give the status of the six exceptions shown in Figure 22.3. The invalid operation exception may occur due to either a stack operation or an arithmetic operation. The stack fault bit gives information as to the cause of the invalid operation. If this bit is 1, the stack fault is caused by a stack operation that resulted in a stack overflow or underflow condition; otherwise, the stack fault is due to an arithmetic instruction encountering an invalid operand.

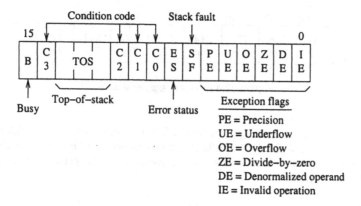

Figure 22.3 FPU status register details. The busy bit is included for 8087 compatibility only.

We can use the C1 bit to further distinguish between the stack underflow (C1 = 0) and overflow (C1 = 1).

The overflow and underflow exceptions occur if the number is too big or too small. These exceptions usually occur when we execute floating-point arithmetic instructions.

The precision exception indicates that the result of an operation could not be represented exactly. This, for example, would be the case when we want to represent a fraction like 1/3. This exception indicates that we lost some accuracy in representing the result. In most cases, this loss of accuracy is acceptable.

The divide-by-zero exception is similar to the divide error exception generated by the processor (see our discussion on page 409). The denormal exception is generated when an arithmetic instruction attempts to operate on a denormal operand (denormals are explained later—see page 452).

Tag Register This register stores information on the status and content of the data registers. The tag register details are shown in Figure 22.4. For each register, two bits are used to give the following information:

- 00 — valid
- 01 — zero
- 10 — special (invalid, infinity, or denormal)
- 11 — empty

The least significant two bits are used for the ST0 register, and the next two bits for the ST1 register, and so on. This tag field identifies whether the associated register is empty or not. If not empty, it identifies the contents: valid number, zero, or some special value like infinity.

Floating-Point Instructions

The FPU provides several floating-point instructions for data movement, arithmetic, comparison, and transcendental operations. In addition, there are instructions for loading frequently used constants like π as well as processor control words. In this section we look at some of these instructions.

15	14	13	12	11	10	9	8	7	6	5	4	3	2	1	0
ST7 Tag		ST6 Tag		ST5 Tag		ST4 Tag		ST3 Tag		ST2 Tag		ST1 Tag		ST0 Tag	

Figure 22.4 FPU tag register details.

Unless otherwise specified, these instructions affect the four FPU flag bits as follows: the flag bits C0, C2, and C3 are undefined; the C1 flag is updated as described before to indicate the stack overflow/underflow condition. Most instructions we discuss next, except the compare instructions, affect the flags this way.

Data Movement

Data movement is supported by two types of instructions: load and store. We start our discussion with the load instructions. The general load instruction has the following format:

```
fld     src
```

This instruction pushes src onto the FPU stack. That is, it decrements the TOS pointer and stores src at ST0. The src operand can be in a register or in memory. If the source operand is in memory, it can be a single-precision (32-bit), double-precision (64-bit), or extended (80-bit) floating-point number. Since the registers hold the numbers in the extended format, a single- or double-precision number is converted to the extended format before storing it in ST0.

There are also instructions to push constants onto the stack. These instructions do not take any operands. Here is a list of these instructions:

Instruction	Description
fldz	Push +0.0 onto the stack
fld1	Push +1.0 onto the stack
fldpi	Push π onto the stack
fldl2t	Push $\log_2 10$ onto the stack
fldl2e	Push $\log_2 e$ onto the stack
fldlg2	Push $\log_{10} 2$ onto the stack
fldln2	Push $\log_e 2$ onto the stack

To load an integer, we can use

```
fild    src
```

The src operand must be a 16- or 32-bit integer located in memory. The instruction converts the integer to the extended format and pushes onto the stack (i.e., loads in ST0).

The store instruction has the following format:

```
fst     dest
```

It stores the top-of-stack values at dest. The destination can be one of the FPU registers or memory. Like the load instruction, the memory operand can be single-precision, double-precision, or extended floating-point number. As usual, if the destination is a single- or double-precision operand, the register value is converted to the destination format. It is important to note this instruction does not remove the value from the stack; it simply copies its value. If you want the value to be copied as well as pop it off the stack, use the following instruction (i.e., use the suffix p):

```
fstp    dest
```

There is an integer version of the store instruction. The instruction

```
fist    dest
```

converts the value in ST0 to a signed integer and stores it at dest in memory. It uses the RC (rounding control) field in the conversion (see the available rounding options on page 445).

The pop version of this instruction

```
fistp    dest
```

performs similar conversion as the fist instruction; the difference is that it also pops the value from the stack.

Addition

The basic add instruction has the following format:

```
fadd    src
```

It adds the floating-point number in memory (at src) to that in ST0 and stores the result back in ST0. The value at src can be a single- or double-precision number. This instruction does not pop the stack.

The two-operand version of the instruction allows us to specify the destination register:

```
fadd    dest,src
```

In this instruction, both src and dest must be FPU registers. Like the last add instruction, it does not pop the stack. For this, you have to use the pop version:

```
faddp    dest,src
```

We can add integers using the following instruction:

```
fiadd    src
```

Here src is a memory operand that is either a 16- or 32-bit integer.

Subtraction

The subtract instruction has a similar instruction format as the add instruction. The subtract instruction

```
fsub    src
```

performs the following operation:

```
STO = STO-src
```

As in the add instruction, we can use the two-operand version to specify two registers. The instruction

```
fsub    dest,src
```

performs $dest = dest - src$. We can also have a pop version of this instruction:

```
fsubp   dest,src
```

Since subtraction is not commutative (i.e., $A - B$ is not the same as $B - A$), there is a reverse subtract operation. It is reverse in the sense that operands of this instruction are reversed from the previous subtract instructions. The instruction

```
fsubr   src
```

performs the operation $STO = src - STO$. Note that the fsub performs $STO - src$. Now you know why this instruction is called the reverse subtract! Like the fsub instruction, there is a two-operand version as well as a pop version (for the pop version, use fsubrp opcode).

If you want to subtract an integer, you can use fisub for the standard subtraction, or fisubr for reverse subtraction. As in the fiadd instruction, the 16- or 32-bit integer must be in memory.

Multiplication

The multiplication instruction has several versions similar to the fadd instruction. We start with the memory operand version:

```
fmul    src
```

where the source (src) can be a 32- or 64-bit floating-point number in memory. It multiplies this value with that in STO and stores the result in STO.

As in the add and subtract instructions, we can use the two-operand version to specify two registers. The instruction

```
fmul    dest,src
```

performs $dest = dest * src$. The pop version of this instruction is also available:

```
fmulp   dest,src
```

There is also a special pop version that does not take any operands. The operands are assumed to be the top two values on the stack. The instruction

```
fmulp
```

is similar to the last one except that it multiplies STO and ST1.

To multiply the contents of STO by an integer stored in memory, we can use

```
fimul   src
```

The value at src can be a 32- or 64-bit integer.

Division

The division instruction has several versions like the subtract instruction. The memory version of the divide instruction is

```
fdiv    src
```

It divides the contents of ST0 by src and stores the result in ST0:

```
ST0 = ST0/src
```

The src operand can be a single- or double-precision floating-point value in memory.
The two-operand version

```
fdiv    dest,src
```

performs dest = dest/src. As in the previous instructions, both operands must be in the floating-point registers. The pop version uses fdivp instead of fdiv. To divide ST0 by an integer, use the fidiv instruction.

Like the subtract instruction, there is a reverse variation for each of these divide instructions. The rationale is simple: A/B is not the same as B/A. For example, the reverse divide instruction

```
fdivr    src
```

performs

```
ST0 = src/ST0
```

As shown in this instruction, we get the reverse version by suffixing r to the opcode.

Comparison

This instruction can be used to compare two floating-point numbers. The format is

```
fcom    src
```

It compares the value in ST0 with src and sets the FPU flags. The src operand can be in memory or in a register. As mentioned before, the C1 bit is used to indicate stack overflow/underflow condition. The other three flags—C0, C2, and C3—are used to indicate the relationship as follows:

ST0 > src	C3 C2 C0 = 0 0 0
ST0 = src	C3 C2 C0 = 1 0 0
ST0 < src	C3 C2 C0 = 0 0 1
Not comparable	C3 C2 C0 = 1 1 1

If no operand is given in the instruction, the top two values are compared (i.e., ST0 is compared with ST1). The pop version is also available (fcomp).

The compare instruction also comes in a double-pop flavor. The instruction

```
fcompp
```

takes no operands. It compares ST0 with ST1 and updates the FPU flags as discussed before. In addition, it pops the two values off the stack, effectively removing the two numbers it just compared.

To compare the top of stack with an integer value in memory, we can use

```
ficom    src
```

The src can be a 16- or 32-bit integer. There is also the pop version of this instruction (ficomp).
    A special case of comparison that is often required is the comparison with zero. The instruction

```
ftst
```

can used for this purpose. It takes no operands and compares the stack top value to 0.0 and updates
the FPU flags as in the fcmp instruction.
    The last instruction we discuss here allows us to examine the type of number. The instruction

```
fxam
```

examines the number in ST0 and returns its sign in C1 flag bit (0 for positive and 1 for negative).
In addition, it returns the following information in the remaining three flag bits (C0, C2, and C3):

Type	C3	C2	C0
Unsupported	0	0	0
NaN	0	0	1
Normal	0	1	0
Infinity	0	1	1
Zero	1	0	0
Empty	1	0	1
Denormal	1	1	0

The *unsupported* type is a format that is not part of the IEEE 754 standard. The *NaN* represents
Not-a-Number, as discussed in Appendix A. The meaning of *Normal, Infinity*, and *Zero* does not
require an explanation. A register that does not have a number is identified as *Empty*.
    Denormals are used for numbers that are very close to zero. Recall that normalized numbers
have 1.XX...XX as the mantissa. In single- and double-precision numbers, the integer 1 is not
explicitly stored (it is implied to save a bit). Thus, we store only XX...XX in mantissa. This
integer bit is explicitly stored in the extended format.
    When the number is very close to zero, we may underflow the exponent when we try to normal-
ize it. Therefore, in this case, we leave the integer bit as zero. Thus, a denormal has the following
two properties:

- The exponent is zero;
- The integer bit of the mantissa is zero as well.

Miscellaneous

We now give details on some of the remaining floating-point instructions. Note that there are
several other instructions that are not covered in our discussion here. The NASM manual gives a
complete list of the floating-point instructions implemented in NASM.
    The instruction

```
fchs
```

changes the sign of the number in ST0. We use this instruction in our quadratic roots example to
invert the sign. A related instruction

```
fabs
```

replaces the value in ST0 with its absolute value.

Two instructions are available for loading and storing the control word. The instruction

```
fldcw    src
```

loads the 16-bit value in memory at `src` into the FPU control word register. To store the control word, we use

```
fstcw    dest
```

Following this instruction, all four flag bits (C0 – C3) are undefined.

To store the status word, we can use the instruction

```
fstsw    dest
```

It stores the status word at `dest`. Note that the `dest` can be a 16-bit memory location or the AX register. Combining this instruction with `sahf`, which copies AH into the processor flags register, gives us the ability to use the conditional jump instructions. We use these two instructions in the quadratic roots example given later. After executing this instruction, all four flag bits (C0 – C3) are undefined.

Our First Program

All the examples in this chapter follow the mixed-mode programs discussed in the last chapter. Thus, you need to understand the material presented in the last chapter in order to follow these examples.

As our introductory floating-point example, we write an assembly language program to compute the sum of an array of doubles. We have done an integer version of this program in the last chapter (see Example 21.2 on page 430). Here we use a separate assembly language module. In the next section, we will redo this example using the inline assembly method.

The C program, shown in Program 22.1, takes care of the user interface. It requests values to fill the array and then calls the `array_fsum` assembly language procedure to compute the sum.

The `array_fsum` procedure is given in Program 22.2. It copies the array pointer to EDX (line 11) and the array size to ECX (line 12). We initialize ST0 to zero by using the `fldz` instruction on line 13. The add loop consists of the code on lines 14–18. We use the `jecxz` instruction to exit the loop if the index is zero at the start of the loop.

We use the `fadd` instruction to compute the sum in ST0. Also note that the based-indexed addressing mode with a scale factor of 8 is used to read the array elements (line 17). Since C programs expect floating-point return values in ST0, we simply return from the procedure as the result is already in ST0.

Program 22.1 Array sum program—C program

```
 1:  /*********************************************************
 2:   * This program reads SIZE values into an array and calls
 3:   * an assembly language program to compute the array sum.
 4:   * The assembly program is in the file "arrayfsuma.asm".
 5:   *********************************************************/
 6:  #include        <stdio.h>
 7:
 8:  #define   SIZE   10
 9:
10:  int main(void)
11:  {
12:      double      value[SIZE];
13:      int         i;
14:      extern double array_fsum(double*, int);
15:
16:      printf("Input %d array values:\n", SIZE);
17:      for (i = 0; i < SIZE; i++)
18:          scanf("%lf",&value[i]);
19:
20:      printf("Array sum = %lf\n", array_fsum(value,SIZE));
21:
22:      return 0;
23:  }
```

Program 22.2 Array sum program—assembly language procedure

```
 1:  ;----------------------------------------------------------
 2:  ; This procedure receives an array pointer and its size
 3:  ; via the stack. It computes the array sum and returns
 4:  ; it via ST0.
 5:  ;----------------------------------------------------------
 6:  segment .text
 7:  global   array_fsum
 8:
 9:  array_fsum:
10:      enter   0,0
11:      mov     EDX, [EBP+8]        ; copy array pointer
12:      mov     ECX, [EBP+12]       ; copy array size
13:      fldz                        ; ST0 = 0 (sum is in ST0)
14:  add_loop:
15:      jecxz   done
16:      dec ECX                     ; update the array index
17:      fadd    qword[EDX+ECX*8]    ; ST0 = ST0 + arrray_element
18:      jmp     add_loop
19:  done:
20:      leave
21:      ret
```

Illustrative Examples

To further illustrate the application of the floating-point instructions, we give a couple of examples here. The first example uses separate assembly language modules as in the last example. The second example uses inline assembly code.

Example 22.1 *Quadratic equation solution.*
In this example, we find roots of the quadratic equation

$$ax^2 + bx + c = 0 \,.$$

The two roots are defined as follows:

$$\text{root1} = \frac{-b + \sqrt{b^2 - 4ac}}{2a} \,,$$

$$\text{root2} = \frac{-b - \sqrt{b^2 - 4ac}}{2a} \,.$$

The roots are real if $b^2 \geq 4ac$, and imaginary otherwise.

As in the last example, our C program takes care of the user interface (see Program 22.3). It requests the user to input constants a, b, and c. It then passes these three values to the quad_roots assembly language procedure along with two pointers to root1 and root2. This procedure returns 0 if the roots are not real; otherwise it returns 1. If the roots are real, the two roots are returned in root1 and root2.

The assembly language procedure, shown in Program 22.4, receives five arguments: three constants and two pointers to return the two roots. These five arguments are assigned convenient labels on lines 7–11. The comments included in the code make it easy to follow the body of the procedure. On each line, we indicate the contents on the stack with the leftmost value being at the top of the stack.

We use the ftst instruction to see if $(b^2 - 4ac)$ is negative (line 30). We move the FPU flag bits to AX and then to the processor flags register using the fstsw and sahf instructions on lines 31 and 32. Once these bits are copied into the flags register, we can use the conditional jump instruction jb (line 33). The rest of the procedure body is straightforward to follow.

Program 22.3 Quadratic equation solution—C program

```
 1:   /**********************************************************
 2:    * This program reads three constants (a, b, c) and calls
 3:    * an assembly language program to compute the roots of
 4:    * the quadratic equation.
 5:    * The assembly program is in the file "quada.asm".
 6:    **********************************************************/
 7:   #include        <stdio.h>
 8:
 9:   int main(void)
10:   {
11:         double     a, b, c, root1, root2;
12:         extern int quad_roots(double, double, double,
```

```
13:                                    double*, double*);
14:
15:      printf("Enter quad constants a, b, c: ");
16:      scanf("%lf %lf %lf",&a, &b, &c);
17:
18:      if (quad_roots(a, b, c, &root1, &root2))
19:          printf("Root1 = %lf and root2 = %lf\n",
20:                                        root1, root2);
21:      else
22:          printf("There are no real roots.\n");
23:
24:      return 0;
25:  }
```

Program 22.4 Quadratic equation solution—assembly language procedure

```
 1:  ;-----------------------------------------------------------
 2:  ; It receives three constants a, b, c and pointers to two
 3:  ; roots via the stack. It computes the two real roots if
 4:  ; they exist and returns them in root1 & root2. In this
 5:  ; case, EAX = 1. If no real roots exist, EAX = 0.
 6:  ;-----------------------------------------------------------
 7:  %define    a          qword[EBP+8]
 8:  %define    b          qword[EBP+16]
 9:  %define    c          qword[EBP+24]
10:  %define    root1      dword[EBP+32]
11:  %define    root2      dword[EBP+36]
12:
13:  segment .text
14:  global   quad_roots
15:
16:  quad_roots:
17:          enter    0,0
18:          fld      a           ; a
19:          fadd     ST0         ; 2a
20:          fld      a           ; a,2a
21:          fld      c           ; c,a,2a
22:          fmulp    ST1         ; ac,2a
23:          fadd     ST0         ; 2ac,2a
24:          fadd     ST0         ; 4ac,2a
25:          fchs                 ; -4ac,2a
26:          fld      b           ; b,-4ac,2a
27:          fld      b           ; b,b,-4ac,2a
28:          fmulp    ST1         ; b*b,-4ac,2a
29:          faddp    ST1         ; b*b-4ac,2a
30:          ftst                 ; compare (b*b-4ac) with 0
31:          fstsw    AX          ; store status word in AX
32:          sahf
33:          jb       no_real_roots
```

```
34:            fsqrt                ; sqrt(b*b-4ac),2a
35:            fld       b          ; b,sqrt(b*b-4ac),2a
36:            fchs                 ; -b,sqrt(b*b-4ac),2a
37:            fadd      ST1        ; -b+sqrt(b*b-4ac),sqrt(b*b-4ac),2a
38:            fdiv      ST2        ; -b+sqrt(b*b-4ac)/2a,sqrt(b*b-4ac),2a
39:            mov       EAX,root1
40:            fstp      qword[EAX]  ; store root1
41:            fchs                 ; -sqrt(b*b-4ac),2a
42:            fld       b          ; b,sqrt(b*b-4ac),2a
43:            fsubp     ST1        ; -b-sqrt(b*b-4ac),2a
44:            fdivrp    ST1        ; -b-sqrt(b*b-4ac)/2a
45:            mov       EAX,root2
46:            fstp      qword[EAX]  ; store root2
47:            mov       EAX,1       ; real roots exist
48:            jmp       short done
49: no_real_roots:
50:            sub       EAX,EAX     ; EAX = 0 (no real roots)
51: done:
52:            leave
53:            ret
```

Example 22.2 *Array sum example—inline version.*

In this example we rewrite the code for the `array_fsum` procedure using the inline assembly method. Remember that when we use this method, we have to use AT&T syntax. In this syntax, the operand size is explicitly indicated by suffixing a letter to the opcode. For the floating-point instructions, the following suffixes are used:

s   Single-precision

l   Double-precision

t   Extended-precision

The inline assembly code, shown in Program 22.5, is similar to that in Program 22.2. You will notice that on line 10 we use =t output specifier to indicate that variable sum is mapped to a floating-point register (see page 437 for a discussion of these specifiers). Since we map value to EBX and size to ECX (line 11), we use these registers in the assembly language code to access the array elements (see line 7). The rest of the code is straightforward to follow.

Program 22.5 Array sum example—inline version

```
 1:  double array_fsum(double* value, int size)
 2:  {
 3:       double sum;
 4:       asm ("            fldz;                    "  /* sum = 0 */
 5:           "add_loop: jecxz    done;            "
 6:           "          decl     %%ecx;           "
 7:           "          faddl    (%%ebx,%%ecx,8); "
 8:           "          jmp      add_loop;        "
 9:           "done:                               "
10:           : "=t" (sum)                     /* output */
11:           : "b" (value), "c" (size)       /* inputs */
12:           : "cc");                        /* clobber list */
13:       return (sum);
14:  }
```

Summary

We presented a brief description of the floating-point unit organization. Specifically, we concentrated on the registers provided by the FPU. It provides eight floating-point data registers that are organized as a stack. The floating-point instructions include several arithmetic and nonarithmetic instructions. We discussed some of these instructions. Finally, we presented some examples that used the floating-point instructions discussed.

APPENDICES

Number Systems

This appendix introduces background material on various number systems and representations. We start the appendix with a discussion of various number systems, including the binary and hexadecimal systems. When we use multiple number systems, we need to convert numbers from system to another. We present details on how such number conversions are done. We then give details on integer representations. We cover both unsigned and signed integer representations. We close the appendix with a discussion of the floating-point numbers.

Positional Number Systems

The number systems that we discuss here are based on positional number systems. The decimal number system that we are already familiar with is an example of a positional number system. In contrast, the Roman numeral system is not a positional number system.

Every positional number system has a *radix* or *base*, and an *alphabet*. The base is a positive number. For example, the decimal system is a base-10 system. The number of symbols in the alphabet is equal to the base of the number system. The alphabet of the decimal system is 0 through 9, a total of 10 symbols or digits.

In this appendix, we discuss four number systems that are relevant in the context of computer systems and programming. These are the *decimal* (base-10), *binary* (base-2), *octal* (base-8), and *hexadecimal* (base-16) number systems. Our intention in including the familiar decimal system is to use it to explain some fundamental concepts of positional number systems.

Computers internally use the binary system. The remaining two number systems—octal and hexadecimal—are used mainly for convenience to write a binary number even though they are number systems on their own. We would have ended up using these number systems if we had 8 or 16 fingers instead of 10.

In a positional number system, a sequence of digits is used to represent a number. Each digit in this sequence should be a symbol in the alphabet. There is a weight associated with each position. If we count position numbers from right to left starting with zero, the weight of position n in a base b number system is b^n. For example, the number 579 in the decimal system is actually interpreted as

$$5 \times (10^2) + 7 \times (10^1) + 9 \times (10^0).$$

(Of course, $10^0 = 1$.) In other words, 9 is in unit's place, 7 in 10's place, and 5 in 100's place. More generally, a number in the base b number system is written as

$$d_n d_{n-1} \ldots d_1 d_0 ,$$

where d_0 represents the least significant digit (LSD) and d_n represents the most significant digit (MSD). This sequence represents the value

$$d_n b^n + d_{n-1} b^{n-1} + \cdots + d_1 b^1 + d_0 b^0 . \tag{A.1}$$

Each digit d_i in the string can be in the range $0 \le d_i \le (b-1)$. When we use a number system with $b \le 10$, we use the first b decimal digits. For example, the binary system uses 0 and 1 as its alphabet. For number systems with $b > 10$, the initial letters of the English alphabet are used to represent digits greater than 9. For example, the alphabet of the hexadecimal system, whose base is 16, is 0 through 9 and A through F, a total of 16 symbols representing the digits of the hexadecimal system. We treat lowercase and uppercase letters used in a number system such as the hexadecimal system as equivalent.

The number of different values that can be represented using n digits in a base b system is b^n. Consequently, since we start counting from 0, the largest number that can be represented using n digits is $(b^n - 1)$. This number is written as

$$\underbrace{(b-1)(b-1)\ldots(b-1)(b-1)}_{\text{total of } n \text{ digits}} .$$

The minimum number of digits (i.e., the length of a number) required to represent X different values is given by $\lceil \log_b X \rceil$, where $\lceil \ \rceil$ represents the ceiling function. Note that $\lceil m \rceil$ represents the smallest integer that is greater than or equal to m.

Notation   The commonality in the alphabet of several number systems gives rise to confusion. For example, if we write 100 without specifying the number system in which it is expressed, different interpretations can lead to assigning different values, as shown below:

Number		Decimal value
100	$\xrightarrow{\text{binary}}$	4
100	$\xrightarrow{\text{decimal}}$	100
100	$\xrightarrow{\text{octal}}$	64
100	$\xrightarrow{\text{hexadecimal}}$	256

Thus, it is important to specify the number system (i.e., specify the base). One common notation is to append a single letter—uppercase or lowercase—to the number to specify the number system. For example, D is used for decimal, B for binary, Q for octal, and H for hexadecimal number systems. Using this notation, 10110111B is a binary number and 2BA9H is a hexadecimal number. Some assemblers use prefix 0x for hexadecimal and prefix 0 for octal.

Decimal Number System   We use the decimal number system in everyday life. This is a base-10 system presumably because we have 10 fingers and toes to count. The alphabet consists of 10 symbols, digits 0 through 9.

Binary Number System The binary system is a base-2 number system that is used by computers for internal representation. The alphabet consists of two digits, 0 and 1. Each binary digit is called a bit (standing for *binary digit*). Thus, 1021 is not a valid binary number. In the binary system, using n bits, we can represent numbers from 0 through $(2^n - 1)$ for a total of 2^n different values.

Octal Number System This is a base-8 number system with the alphabet consisting of digits 0 through 7. Thus, 181 is not a valid octal number. The octal numbers are often used to express binary numbers in a compact way. For example, we need 8 bits to represent 256 different values. The same range of numbers can be represented in the octal system by using only 3 digits.

For example, the number 230Q is written in the binary system as 10011000B, which is difficult to read and error prone. In general, we can reduce the length by a factor of 3. As we show later, it is straightforward to go back to the binary equivalent, which is not the case with the decimal system.

Hexadecimal Number System This is a base-16 number system. The alphabet consists of digits 0 through 9 and letters A through F. In this text, we use capital letters consistently, even though lowercase and uppercase letters can be used interchangeably. For example, FEED is a valid hexadecimal number, whereas GEFF is not.

The main use of this number system is to conveniently represent long binary numbers. The length of a binary number expressed in the hexadecimal system can be reduced by a factor of 4. Consider the previous example again. The binary number 10011000B can be represented as 98H. Debuggers, for example, display information—addresses, data, and so on—in hexadecimal representation.

Conversion to Decimal

When we are dealing with several number systems, there is often a need to convert numbers from one system to another. Let us first look at how a number expressed in the base-b system can be converted to the decimal system. To do this conversion, we merely perform the arithmetic calculations of Equation A.1 given on page 462; that is, multiply each digit by its weight, and add the results. Here is an example.

Example A.1 *Conversion from binary to decimal.*
Convert the binary number 10100111B into its equivalent in the decimal system.

$$10100111B = 1 \cdot 2^7 + 0 \cdot 2^6 + 1 \cdot 2^5 + 0 \cdot 2^4$$
$$+ 0 \cdot 2^3 + 1 \cdot 2^2 + 1 \cdot 2^1 + 1 \cdot 2^0$$
$$= 167D$$

Conversion from Decimal

There is a simple method that allows conversions from the decimal to a target number system. The procedure is as follows:

Divide the decimal number by the base of the target number system and keep track of the quotient and remainder. Repeatedly divide the successive quotients while keeping track of the remainders generated until the quotient is zero. The remainders generated during the process, written in the reverse order of generation from left to right, form the equivalent number in the target system.

Let us look at an example now.

Example A.2 *Conversion from decimal to binary.*
Convert the decimal number 167 into its equivalent binary number.

		Quotient	Remainder
167/2	=	83	1
83/2	=	41	1
41/2	=	20	1
20/2	=	10	0
10/2	=	5	0
5/2	=	2	1
2/2	=	1	0
1/2	=	0	1

The desired binary number can be obtained by writing the remainders generated in the reverse order from left to right. For this example, the binary number is 10100111B. This agrees with the result of Example A.1.   □

Binary/Octal/Hexadecimal Conversion

Conversion among binary, octal, and hexadecimal number systems is relatively easier and more straightforward. Conversion from binary to octal involves converting three bits at a time, whereas binary to hexadecimal conversion requires converting four bits at a time.

Binary/Octal Conversion   To convert a binary number into its equivalent octal number, form 3-bit groups starting from the right. Add extra 0s at the left-hand side of the binary number if the number of bits is not a multiple of 3. Then replace each group of 3 bits by its equivalent octal digit. Why three bit groups? Simply because $2^3 = 8$. Here is an example.

Example A.3 *Conversion from binary to octal.*
The following examples illustrate this conversion process.

$$1000101B = \overbrace{001}^{1}\ \overbrace{000}^{0}\ \overbrace{101}^{5}\ B$$
$$= 105Q.$$

$$10100111B = \overset{2}{\overbrace{010}} \overset{4}{\overbrace{100}} \overset{7}{\overbrace{111}} B$$
$$= 247Q.$$

Note that we have added leftmost 0s (shown in bold) so that the number of bits is 9. Adding 0s on the left-hand side does not change the value of a number. For example, in the decimal system, 35 and 0035 represent the same value. □

We can use the reverse process to convert numbers from octal to binary. For each octal digit, write the equivalent 3 bits. You should write exactly 3 bits for each octal digit even if there are leading 0s. For example, for octal digit 0, write the three bits 000.

Example A.4 *Conversion from octal to binary.*
The following two examples illustrate conversion from octal to binary:

$$105Q = \overset{1}{\overbrace{001}} \overset{0}{\overbrace{000}} \overset{5}{\overbrace{101}} B,$$
$$247Q = \overset{2}{\overbrace{010}} \overset{4}{\overbrace{100}} \overset{7}{\overbrace{111}} B.$$

If you want an 8-bit binary number, throw away the leading 0 in the binary number. □

Binary/Hexadecimal Conversion The process for conversion from binary to hexadecimal is similar except that we use 4-bit groups instead of 3-bit groups because $2^4 = 16$. For each group of 4 bits, replace it by the equivalent hexadecimal digit. If the number of bits is not a multiple of 4, pad 0s at the left. Here is an example.

Example A.5 *Binary to hexadecimal conversion.*
Convert the binary number 1101011111 into its equivalent hexadecimal number.

$$1101011111B = \overset{3}{\overbrace{0011}} \overset{5}{\overbrace{0101}} \overset{F}{\overbrace{1111}} B$$
$$= 35FH.$$

As in the octal to binary example, we have added two 0s on the left to make the total number of bits a multiple of 4 (i.e., 12). □

The process can be reversed to convert from hexadecimal to binary. Each hex digit should be replaced by exactly four binary bits that represent its value. An example follows:

Example A.6 *Hex to binary conversion.*
Convert the hexadecimal number B01D into its equivalent binary number.

$$B01DH = \overset{B}{\overbrace{1011}} \overset{0}{\overbrace{0000}} \overset{1}{\overbrace{0001}} \overset{D}{\overbrace{1101}} B.$$
□

Unsigned Integers

Now that you are familiar with different number systems, let us turn our attention to how integers (numbers with no fractional part) are represented internally in computers. Of course, we know that the binary number system is used internally. Still, there are a number of other details that need to be sorted out before we have a workable internal number representation scheme.

We begin our discussion by considering how unsigned numbers are represented using a fixed number of bits. We then proceed to discuss the representation for signed numbers in the next section.

The most natural way to represent unsigned (i.e., nonnegative) numbers is to use the equivalent binary representation. As discussed before, a binary number with n bits can represent 2^n different values, and the range of the numbers is from 0 to $(2^n - 1)$. Padding of 0s on the left can be used to make the binary conversion of a decimal number equal exactly N bits. For example, we can represent 16D as 10000B using 5 bits. However, this can be extended to a byte (i.e., $N = 8$) as 00010000B or to 16 bits as 0000000000010000B. This process is called *zero extension* and is suitable for unsigned numbers.

A problem arises if the number of bits required to represent an integer in binary is more than the N bits we have. Clearly, such numbers are outside the range of numbers that can be represented using N bits. Recall that using N bits, we can represent any integer X such that $0 \le X \le 2^N - 1$.

Signed Integers

There are several ways in which signed numbers can be represented. These include

- Signed magnitude,
- Excess-M,
- 1's complement, and
- 2's complement.

Signed Magnitude Representation

In signed magnitude representation, one bit is reserved to represent the sign of a number. The most significant bit is used as the sign bit. Conventionally, a sign bit value of 0 is used to represent a positive number and 1 for a negative number. Thus, if we have N bits to represent a number, $(N - 1)$ bits are available to represent the magnitude of the number. For example, when N is 4, Table A.1 shows the range of numbers that can be represented. For comparison, the unsigned representation is also included in this table. The range of n-bit signed magnitude representation is $-2^{n-1} + 1$ to $+2^{n-1} - 1$. Note that in this method, 0 has two representations: $+0$ and -0.

Excess-M Representation

In this method, a number is mapped to a nonnegative integer so that its binary representation can be used. This transformation is done by adding a value called *bias* to the number to be represented. For an n bit representation, the bias should be such that the mapped number is less than 2^n.

To find out the binary representation of a number in this method, simply add the bias M to the number and find the corresponding binary representation. That is, the representation for number

Table A.1 Number representation using 4-bit binary (All numbers except Binary column in decimal)

Unsigned representation	Binary pattern	Signed magnitude	Excess-7	1's Complement	2's Complement
0	0000	0	−7	0	0
1	0001	1	−6	1	1
2	0010	2	−5	2	2
3	0011	3	−4	3	3
4	0100	4	−3	4	4
5	0101	5	−2	5	5
6	0110	6	−1	6	6
7	0111	7	0	7	7
8	1000	−0	1	−7	−8
9	1001	−1	2	−6	−7
10	1010	−2	3	−5	−6
11	1011	−3	4	−4	−5
12	1100	−4	5	−3	−4
13	1101	−5	6	−2	−3
14	1110	−6	7	−1	−2
15	1111	−7	8	−0	−1

X is the binary representation for the number $X + M$, where M is the bias. For example, in the excess-7 system, $-3D$ is represented as

$$-3 + 7 = +4 = 0100B.$$

Numbers represented in excess-M are called *biased integers* for obvious reasons. Table A.1 gives examples of biased integers using 4-bit binary numbers. This representation, for example, is used to store the exponent values in the floating-point representation (discussed in the next section).

1's Complement Representation

As in the excess-M representation, negative values are biased in 1's complement and 2's complement representations. For positive numbers, the standard binary representation is used. As in the signed magnitude representation, the most significant bit indicates the sign (0 = positive and 1 = negative). In 1's complement representation, negative values are biased by $b^n - 1$, where b is the base or radix of the number system. For the binary case that we are interested in here, the bias is $2^n - 1$. For the negative value $-X$, the representation used is the binary representation for $(2^n - 1) - X$. For example, if n is 4, we can represent -5 as

$$
\begin{aligned}
2^4 - 1 &= 1111B \\
-5 &= \underline{-0101B} \\
&\ \ 1010B
\end{aligned}
$$

As you can see from this example, the 1's complement of a number can be obtained by simply complementing individual bits (converting 0s to 1s and vice versa) of the number. Table A.1 shows

1's complement representation using 4 bits. In this method also, 0 has two representations. The most significant bit is used to indicate the sign. To find the magnitude of a negative number in this representation, apply the process used to obtain the 1's complement (i.e., complement individual bits) again.

Representation of signed numbers in 1's complement representation allows the use of simpler circuits for performing addition and subtraction than the other two representations we have seen so far (signed magnitude and excess-M). Some older computer systems used this representation for integers. An irritant with this representation is that 0 has two representations. Furthermore, the carry bit generated out of the sign bit will have to be added to the result. The 2's complement representation avoids these pitfalls. As a result, 2's complement representation is the choice of current computer systems.

2's Complement Representation

In 2's complement representation, positive numbers are represented the same way as in the signed magnitude and 1's complement representations. The negative numbers are biased by 2^n, where n is the number of bits used for number representation. Thus, the negative value $-A$ is represented by $(2^n - A)$ using n bits. Since the bias value is one more than that in the 1's complement representation, we have to add 1 after complementing to obtain the 2's complement representation of a negative number. We can, however, discard any carry generated out of the sign bit. For example, -5 can be represented as

$$
\begin{aligned}
5D = 0101B &\longrightarrow \text{complement} \longrightarrow 1010B \\
&\quad\quad \text{add 1} \quad\quad\quad\quad\quad \underline{1B} \\
&\quad\quad\quad\quad\quad\quad\quad\quad\quad\quad 1011B
\end{aligned}
$$

Therefore, `1011B` represents $-5D$ in 2's complement representation. Table A.1 shows the 2's complement representation of numbers using 4 bits. Notice that there is only one representation for 0. The range of an n-bit 2's complement integer is -2^{n-1} to $+2^{n-1} - 1$. For example, using 8 bits, the range is -128 to $+127$.

To find the magnitude of a negative number in the 2's complement representation, as in the 1's complement representation, simply reverse the sign of the number. That is, use the same conversion process i.e., complement and add 1 and discard any carry generated out of the leftmost bit.

Sign Extension

How do we extend a signed number? For example, we have shown that -5 can be represented in the 2's complement representation as `1011B`. Suppose we want to save this as a byte. How do extend these four bits into eight bits? We have seen on page 466 that, for unsigned integers, we add zeros on the left to extend the number. However, as cannot use this technique for signed numbers because the most significant bit represents the sign. To extend a signed number, we have to copy the sign bit. In our example, -5 is represented using eight bits as

$$
-5D = \overbrace{1111}^{\text{sign bit}} 1011
$$

We have copied the sign bit to extend the four-bit value to eight bits. Similarly, we can express -5 using 16 bits by extending it as follows:

$$-5D = \overbrace{1111111111111}^{\text{sign bit}}1011$$

This process is referred to as *sign extension*.

Floating-Point Representation

Using the decimal system for a moment, we can write very small and very large numbers in scientific notation as follows:

$$1.2345 \times 10^{45},$$

$$9.876543 \times 10^{-37}.$$

Expressing such numbers using the positional number notation is difficult to write and understand, errorprone, and requires more space. In a similar fashion, binary numbers can be written in the scientific notation. For example,

$$+1101.101 \times 2^{+11001} = 13.625 \times 2^{25}$$
$$= 4.57179 \times 10^{8}.$$

As indicated, numbers expressed in this notation have two parts: a *mantissa* (or *significand*), and an *exponent*. There can be a sign ($+$ or $-$) associated with each part.

Numbers expressed in this notation can be written in several equivalent ways, as shown below:

$$1.2345 \times 10^{45},$$
$$123.45 \times 10^{43},$$
$$0.00012345 \times 10^{49}.$$

This causes implementation problems to perform arithmetic operations, comparisons, and the like. This problem can be avoided by introducing a standard form called the *normal form*. Reverting to the binary case, a normalized binary form has the format

$$\pm 1.X_1 X_2 \cdots X_{M-1} X_M \times 2^{\pm Y_{N-1} Y_{N-2} \cdots Y_1 Y_0},$$

where X_i and Y_j represent a bit, $1 \leq i \leq M$, and $0 \leq j < N$. The normalized form of

$$+1101.101 \times 2^{+11010}$$

is

$$+1.101101 \times 2^{+11101}.$$

We normally write such numbers as

$$+1.101101\text{E}11101.$$

To represent such normalized numbers, we might use the format shown below:

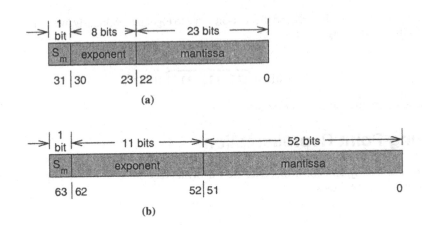

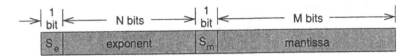

Figure A.1 Floating-point formats (a) Single-precision (b) Double-precision.

where S_m and S_e represent the sign of mantissa and exponent, respectively.

Implementation of floating-point numbers varies from this generic format, usually for efficiency reasons or to conform to a standard. From here on, we discuss the format of the IEEE 754 floating-point standard. Such standards are useful, for example, to exchange data among several different computer systems and to write efficient numerical software libraries.

The single-precision and double-precision floating-point formats are shown in Figure A.1. Certain points are worth noting about these formats:

1. The mantissa stores only the fractional part of a normalized number. The 1 to the left of the binary point is not explicitly stored but implied to save a bit. Since this bit is always 1, there is really no need to store it. However, representing 0.0 requires special attention, as we show later.

2. There is no sign bit associated with the exponent. Instead, the exponent is converted to an excess-M form and stored. For the single-precision numbers, the bias used is 127D (= 7FH), and for the double-precision numbers, 1023 (= 3FFH).

Special Values The representations of 0 and infinity (∞) require special attention. Table A.2 shows the values of the three components to represent these values. Zero is represented by a zero exponent and fraction. We can have a -0 or $+0$ depending on the sign bit. An exponent of all ones indicates a special floating-point value. An exponent of all ones with a zero mantissa indicates infinity. Again, the sign bit indicates the sign of the infinity. An exponent of all ones with a nonzero mantissa represents a not-a-number (NaN). The NaN values are used to represent operations like 0/0 and $\sqrt{-1}$.

The last entry in Table A.2 shows how *denormalized values* are represented. The denormals are used to represent values smaller than the smallest value that can be represented with normalized

Table A.2 Representation of special values in the floating-point format

Special number	Sign	Exponent (biased)	Mantissa
+0	0	0	0
−0	1	0	0
+∞	0	FFH	0
−∞	1	FFH	0
NaN	0/1	FFH	$\neq 0$
Denormals	0/1	0	$\neq 0$

floating-point numbers. For denormals, the implicit 1 to the left of the binary point becomes a 0. The smallest normalized number has a 1 for the exponent (note zero is not allowed) and 0 for the fraction. Thus, the smallest number is 1×2^{-126}. The largest denormalized number has a zero exponent and all 1s for the fraction. This represents approximately $0.9999999 \times 2^{-127}$. The smallest denormalized number would have zero as the exponent and a 1 in the last bit position (i.e., position 23). Thus, it represents $2^{-23} \times 2^{-127}$, which is approximately 10^{-45}. For a thorough discussion of floating-point numbers, see D. Goldberg, "What Every Computer Scientist Should Know About Floating-Point Arithmetic," *ACM Computing Surveys*, Vol. 23, No. 1, March 1991, pp. 5–48.

Summary

We discussed how numbers are represented using the positional number system. Positional number systems are characterized by a base and an alphabet. The familiar decimal system is a base-10 system with the alphabet 0 through 9. Computer systems use the binary system for internal storage. This is a base-2 number system with 0 and 1 as the alphabet. The remaining two number systems—octal (base-8) and hexadecimal (base-16)—are mainly used for convenience to write a binary number. For example, debuggers use the hexadecimal numbers to display address and data information.

When we use several number systems, there is often a need to convert numbers from one system to another. Conversion among binary, octal, and hexadecimal systems is simple and straightforward. We also discussed how numbers are converted from decimal to binary and vice versa.

The remainder of the chapter was devoted to internal representation of numbers. Representation of unsigned integers is straightforward and uses binary representation. There are, however, several ways of representing signed integers. We discussed four methods to represent signed integers. Of these four methods, current computer systems use the 2's complement representation.

Floating-point representation on most computers follows the IEEE 754 standard. There are three components of a floating-point number: mantissa, exponent, and the sign of the mantissa. There is no sign associated with the exponent. Instead, the exponent is stored as a biased number.

B

Character Representation

This appendix discusses character representation. We identify some desirable properties that a character-encoding scheme should satisfy in order to facilitate efficient character processing. Our focus is on the ASCII encoding; we don't discuss other character sets such as UCS and Unicode. The ASCII encoding, which is used by most computers, satisfies the requirements of an efficient character code.

Character Representation

As computers have the capability to store and understand the alphabet 0 and 1, characters should be assigned a sequence over this alphabet i.e., characters should be encoded using this alphabet. For efficient processing of characters, several guidelines have been developed. Some of these are mentioned here:

1. Assigning a contiguous sequence of numbers (if treated as unsigned binary numbers) to letters in alphabetical order is desired. Upper and lowercase letters (A through Z and a through z) can be treated separately, but a contiguous sequence should be assigned to each case. This facilitates efficient character processing such as case conversion, identifying lowercase letters, and so on.
2. In a similar fashion, digits should be assigned a contiguous sequence in the numerical order. This would be useful in numeric-to-character and character-to-numeric conversions.
3. A space character should precede all letters and digits.

These guidelines allow for efficient character processing including sorting by names or character strings. For example, to test if a given character code corresponds to a lowercase letter, all we have to do is to see if the code of the character is between that of a and z. These guidelines also aid in applications requiring sorting—for instance, sorting a class list by last name.

Since computers are rarely used in isolation, exchange of information is an important concern. This leads to the necessity of having some standard way of representing characters. Most computers use the American Standard Code for Information Interchange (ASCII) for character representation. The standard ASCII uses 7 bits to encode a character. Thus, $2^7 = 128$ different characters can be represented. This number is sufficiently large to represent uppercase and lower-case characters, digits, special characters such as !,^ and control characters such as CR (carriage return), LF (linefeed), etc.

Since we store the bits in units of a power of 2, we end up storing 8 bits for each character—even though ASCII requires only 7 bits. The eighth bit is put to use for two purposes.

1. *To parity encode for error detection:* The eighth bit can be used to represent the parity bit. This bit is made 0 or 1 such that the total number of 1's in a byte is even (for even parity) or odd (for odd parity). This can be used to detect simple errors in data transmission.

2. *To represent an additional 128 characters:* By using all eight bits we can represent a total of $2^8 = 256$ different characters. This is referred to as the extended ASCII. These additional codes are used for special graphics symbols, Greek letters, etc. make up the additional 128 characters.

The standard ASCII character code is presented in two tables on the next two pages. You will notice from these tables that ASCII encoding satisfies the three guidelines mentioned earlier. For instance, successive bit patterns are assigned to uppercase letters, lowercase letters, and digits. This assignment leads to some good properties. For example, the difference between the uppercase and lowercase characters is constant. That is, the difference between the character codes of a and A is the same as that between n and N, which is 32. This characteristic can be exploited for efficient case conversion.

Another interesting feature of ASCII is that the character codes are assigned to the 10 digits such that the lower order four bits represent the binary equivalent of the corresponding digit. For example, digit 5 is encoded as 0110101. If you take the rightmost four bits (0101), they represent 5 in binary. This feature, again, helps in writing an efficient code for character-to-numeric conversion. Such a conversion, for example, is required when you type a number as a sequence of digit characters.

ASCII Character Set

The next two pages give the standard ASCII character set. We divide the character set into control and printable characters. The control character codes are given on the next page and the printable ASCII characters are on page 476.

Control Codes

Hex	Decimal	Character	Meaning
00	0	NUL	NULL
01	1	SOH	Start of heading
02	2	STX	Start of text
03	3	ETX	End of text
04	4	EOT	End of transmission
05	5	ENQ	Enquiry
06	6	ACK	Acknowledgment
07	7	BEL	Bell
08	8	BS	Backspace
09	9	HT	Horizontal tab
0A	10	LF	Line feed
0B	11	VT	Vertical tab
0C	12	FF	Form feed
0D	13	CR	Carriage return
0E	14	SO	Shift out
0F	15	SI	Shift in
10	16	DLE	Data link escape
11	17	DC1	Device control 1
12	18	DC2	Device control 2
13	19	DC3	Device control 3
14	20	DC4	Device control 4
15	21	NAK	Negative acknowledgment
16	22	SYN	Synchronous idle
17	23	ETB	End of transmission block
18	24	CAN	Cancel
19	25	EM	End of medium
1A	26	SUB	Substitute
1B	27	ESC	Escape
1C	28	FS	File separator
1D	29	GS	Group separator
1E	30	RS	Record separator
1F	31	US	Unit separator
7F	127	DEL	Delete

Printable Character Codes

Hex	Decimal	Character	Hex	Decimal	Character	Hex	Decimal	Character
20	32	Space	40	64	@	60	96	`
21	33	!	41	65	A	61	97	a
22	34	"	42	66	B	62	98	b
23	35	#	43	67	C	63	99	c
24	36	$	44	68	D	64	100	d
25	37	%	45	69	E	65	101	e
26	38	&	46	70	F	66	102	f
27	39	'	47	71	G	67	103	g
28	40	(	48	72	H	68	104	h
29	41	)	49	73	I	69	105	i
2A	42	*	4A	74	J	6A	106	j
2B	43	+	4B	75	K	6B	107	k
2C	44	,	4C	76	L	6C	108	l
2D	45	–	4D	77	M	6D	109	m
2E	46	.	4E	78	N	6E	110	n
2F	47	/	4F	79	O	6F	111	o
30	48	0	50	80	P	70	112	p
31	49	1	51	81	Q	71	113	q
32	50	2	52	82	R	72	114	r
33	51	3	53	83	S	73	115	s
34	52	4	54	84	T	74	116	t
35	53	5	55	85	U	75	117	u
36	54	6	56	86	V	76	118	v
37	55	7	57	87	W	77	119	w
38	56	8	58	88	X	78	120	x
39	57	9	59	89	Y	79	121	y
3A	58	:	5A	90	Z	7A	122	z
3B	59	;	5B	91	[	7B	123	{
3C	60	<	5C	92	\	7C	124		
3D	61	=	5D	93	]	7D	125	}
3E	62	>	5E	94	^	7E	126	~
3F	63	?	5F	95	_			

Note that 7FH (127 in decimal) is a control character listed on the previous page.

C

Programming Exercises

This appendix gives several programming exercises. These exercises can be used to practice writing programs in the assembly language.

1. Modify the `addigits.asm` program given in Example 9.3 such that it accepts a string from the keyboard consisting of digit and nondigit characters. The program should display the sum of the digits present in the input string. All nondigit characters should be ignored. For example, if the input string is

   ```
   ABC1?5wy76:~2
   ```

   the output of the program should be

   ```
   sum of individual digits is: 21
   ```

2. Write an assembly language program to encrypt digits as shown below:

input digit:	0 1 2 3 4 5 6 7 8 9
encrypted digit:	4 6 9 5 0 3 1 8 7 2

   Your program should accept a string consisting of digit and nondigit characters. The encrypted string should be displayed in which only the digits are affected. Then the user should be queried whether he/she wants to terminate the program. If the response is either 'y' or 'Y' you should terminate the program; otherwise, you should request another input string from the keyboard.

   The encryption scheme given here has the property that when you encrypt an already encrypted string, you get back the original string. Use this property to verify your program.

3. Write a program to accept a number in the hexadecimal form and display the decimal equivalent of the number. A typical interaction of your program is (user input is shown in bold):

   Please input a positive number in hex (4 digits max.): **A10F**
   The decimal equivalent of A10FH is 41231
   Do you want to terminate the program (Y/N): **Y**

   You can refer to Appendix A for an algorithm to convert from base *b* to decimal. You should do the required multiplication by the left shift instruction. Once you have converted the hex number into the equivalent in binary, you can use the `print_int` system call to display the decimal equivalent.

4. Write a program that reads an input number (given in decimal) between 0 and 65,535 and displays the hexadecimal equivalent. You can read the input using `read_int` system call.

5. Modify the above program to display the octal equivalent instead of the hexadecimal equivalent of the input number.

6. Write a procedure `locate` to locate a character in a given string. The procedure receives a pointer to a NULL-terminated character string and the character to be located. When the first occurrence of the character is located, its position is returned to `main`. If no match is found, a negative value is returned. The `main` procedure requests a character string and a character to be located and displays the position of the first occurrence of the character returned by the `locate` procedure. If there is no match, a message should be displayed to that effect.

7. Write a procedure that receives a string and removes all leading blank characters in the string. For example, if the input string is (⊔ indicates a blank character)

    ⊔ ⊔ ⊔ ⊔ ⊔Read⊔⊔my⊔lips.

it will be modified by removing all leading blanks as

    Read⊔⊔my⊔lips.

Write a main program to test your procedure.

8. Write a procedure that receives a string and removes all leading and duplicate blank characters in the string. For example, if the input string is (⊔ indicates a blank character)

    ⊔ ⊔ ⊔ ⊔ ⊔Read⊔ ⊔ ⊔my⊔ ⊔ ⊔ ⊔ ⊔lips.

it will be modified by removing all leading and duplicate blanks as

    Read⊔my⊔lips.

Write a main program to test your procedure.

9. Write a procedure to read a string, representing a person's name, in the format

    first-name⊔MI⊔last-name

and displays the name in the format

    last-name,⊔first-name⊔MI

where ⊔ indicates a blank character. As indicated, you can assume that the three names— first name, middle initial, and last name—are separated by single spaces. Write a main program to test your procedure.

10. Modify the last exercise to work on an input that can contain multiple spaces between the names. Also, display the name as in the last exercise but with the last name in all capital letters.

11. Write a complete assembly language program to read two matrices **A** and **B** and display the result matrix **C**, which is the sum of **A** and **B**. Note that the elements of **C** can be obtained as

$$C[i, j] = A[i, j] + B[i, j].$$

Your program should consist of a main procedure that calls the `read_matrix` procedure twice to read data for **A** and **B**. It should then call the `matrix_add` procedure, which receives pointers to **A**, **B**, **C**, and the size of the matrices. Note that both **A** and **B** should have the same size. The `main` procedure calls another procedure to display **C**.

12. Write a procedure to perform multiplication of matrices **A** and **B**. The procedure should receive pointers to the two input matrices (**A** of size $l \times m$, **B** of size $m \times n$), the product matrix **C**, and values l, m, and n. Also, the data for the two matrices should be obtained from the user. Devise a suitable user interface to read these numbers.

13. Modify the program of the last exercise to work on matrices stored in the column-major order.

14. Write a program to read a matrix (maximum size 10×10) from the user and display the transpose of the matrix. To obtain the transpose of matrix **A**, write rows of **A** as columns. Here is an example:

If the input matrix is

$$\begin{bmatrix} 12 & 34 & 56 & 78 \\ 23 & 45 & 67 & 89 \\ 34 & 56 & 78 & 90 \\ 45 & 67 & 89 & 10 \end{bmatrix},$$

the transpose of the matrix is

$$\begin{bmatrix} 12 & 23 & 34 & 45 \\ 34 & 45 & 56 & 67 \\ 56 & 67 & 78 & 89 \\ 78 & 89 & 90 & 10 \end{bmatrix}.$$

15. Write a program to read a matrix (maximum size 10×15) from the user and display the subscripts of the maximum element in the matrix. Your program should consist of two procedures: main is responsible for reading the input matrix and for displaying the position of the maximum element. Another procedure mat_max is responsible for finding the position of the maximum element. For example, if the input matrix is

$$\begin{bmatrix} 12 & 34 & 56 & 78 \\ 23 & 45 & 67 & 89 \\ 34 & 56 & 78 & 90 \\ 45 & 67 & 89 & 10 \end{bmatrix}$$

the output of the program should be

The maximum element is at (2,3),

which points to the largest value (90 in our example).

16. Write a program to read a matrix of integers, perform cyclic permutation of rows, and display the result matrix. Cyclic permutation of a sequence $a_0, a_1, a_2, \ldots, a_{n-1}$ is defined as $a_1, a_2, \ldots, a_{n-1}, a_0$. Apply this process for each row of the matrix. Your program should be able to handle up to 12×15 matrices. If the input matrix is

$$\begin{bmatrix} 12 & 34 & 56 & 78 \\ 23 & 45 & 67 & 89 \\ 34 & 56 & 78 & 90 \\ 45 & 67 & 89 & 10 \end{bmatrix},$$

the permuted matrix is

$$\begin{bmatrix} 34 & 56 & 78 & 12 \\ 45 & 67 & 89 & 23 \\ 56 & 78 & 90 & 34 \\ 67 & 89 & 10 & 45 \end{bmatrix}.$$

17. Generalize the last exercise to cyclically permute by a user-specified number of elements.

18. Write a complete assembly language program to do the following:

   - Read the names of students in a class into a one-dimensional array.
   - Read test scores of each student into a two-dimensional marks array.
   - Output a letter grade for each student in the format:

     ```
     student name     letter grade
     ```

   You can use the following information in writing your program:

   - Assume that the maximum class size is 20.
   - Assume that the class is given four tests of equal weight (i.e., 25 points each).
   - Test marks are rounded to the nearest integer so you can treat them as integers.
   - Use the following table to convert percentage marks (i.e, sum of all four tests) to a letter grade.

Marks range	Grade
85–100	A
70–84	B
60–69	C
50–59	D
0–49	F

19. Modify the program for the last exercise to also generate a class summary stating the number of students receiving each letter grade in the following format:

   A = number of students receiving A,
   B = number of students receiving B,
   C = number of students receiving C,
   D = number of students receiving D,
   F = number of students receiving F.

20. If we are given a square matrix (i.e., a matrix with the number of rows equal to the number of columns), we can classify it as the diagonal matrix if only its diagonal elements are nonzero; as an upper triangular matrix if all the elements below the diagonal are 0; and as a lower triangular matrix if all elements above the diagonal are 0. Some examples are:

Diagonal matrix:

$$\begin{bmatrix} 28 & 0 & 0 & 0 \\ 0 & 87 & 0 & 0 \\ 0 & 0 & 97 & 0 \\ 0 & 0 & 0 & 65 \end{bmatrix}.$$

Upper triangular matrix:

$$\begin{bmatrix} 19 & 26 & 35 & 98 \\ 0 & 78 & 43 & 65 \\ 0 & 0 & 38 & 29 \\ 0 & 0 & 0 & 82 \end{bmatrix}.$$

Lower triangular matrix:

$$\begin{bmatrix} 76 & 0 & 0 & 0 \\ 44 & 38 & 0 & 0 \\ 65 & 28 & 89 & 0 \\ 87 & 56 & 67 & 54 \end{bmatrix}.$$

Write an assembly language program to read a matrix and output the type of matrix.

21. In Appendix A, we discussed the format of the single-precision floating-point numbers. Write a program that reads the floating-point internal representation from the user as a string of eight hexadecimal digits and displays the three components—mantissa, exponent, and sign—in binary. For example, if the input to the program is 429DA000, the output should be:

```
sign = 0
mantissa = 1.0011101101
exponent = 110
```

22. Modify the program for the last exercise to work with the double-precision floating-point representation.

23. Ackermann's function $A(m, n)$ is defined for $m \geq 0$ and $n \geq 0$ as

$$\begin{aligned} A(0, n) &= N + 1 & &\text{for } n \geq 0 \\ A(m, 0) &= A(m - 1, 1) & &\text{for } m \geq 1 \\ A(m, n) &= A(m - 1, A(m, n - 1)) & &\text{for } m \geq 1, n \geq 1. \end{aligned}$$

Write a recursive procedure to compute this function. Your main program should handle the user interface to request m and n and display the final result.

24. Write a program to solve the Towers of Hanoi puzzle. The puzzle consists of three pegs and N disks. Disk 1 is smaller than disk 2, which is smaller than disk 3, and so on. Disk N is the largest. Initially, all N disks are on peg 1 such that the largest disk is at the bottom and the smallest at the top (i.e., in the order N, $N - 1$, ..., 3, 2, 1 from bottom to top). The problem is to move these N disks from peg 1 to peg 2 under two constraints: You can move only one disk at a time and you must not place a larger disk on top of a smaller one. We can express a solution to this problem by using recursion. The function

```
move (N, 1, 2, 3)
```

moves N disks from peg 1 to peg 2 using peg 3 as the extra peg. There is a simple solution if you concentrate on moving the bottom disk on peg 1. The task move (N, 1, 2, 3) is equivalent to

```
move (N-1, 1, 3, 2)
move the remaining disk from peg 1 to 2
move (N-1, 3, 2, 1)
```

Even though the task appears to be complex, we write a very elegant and simple solution to solve this puzzle. Here is a version in C.

```c
void move (int n, int x, int y, int z)
{
    if (n == 1)
        printf("Move the top disk from peg %d to %d\n",x,y};
    else
        move(n-1, x, z, y)
        printf("Move the top disk from peg %d to %d\n",x,y);
        move(n-1, z, y, x)
}


int main (void)
{
    int    disks;

    scanf("%d", &disks);
    move(disks, 1, 2, 3);
}
```

Test your program for a very small number of disks (say, less than 6). Even for 64 disks, it takes hundreds of years on whatever PC you have!

25. Write a procedure `str_str` that receives two pointers to strings `string` and `substring` and searches for `substring` in `string`. If a match is found, it returns the starting position of the first match. Matching should be case sensitive. A negative value is returned if no match is found. For example, if

> string = Good things come in small packages.

and

> substring = in

the procedure should return 8 indicating a match of in in things.

26. Write a procedure `str_ncpy` to mimic the `strncpy` function provided by the C library. The function `str_ncpy` receives two strings, `string1` and `string2`, and a positive integer num. Of course, the procedure receives only the string pointers but not the actual strings. It should copy at most the first num characters from `string2` to `string1`.

27. A *palindrome* is a word, verse, sentence, or a number that reads the same both backward and forward. Blanks, punctuation marks, and capitalization do not count in determining palindromes. Here are some examples:

> 1991
> Able was I ere I saw Elba
> Madam! I'm Adam

Write a program to determine if a given string is a palindrome. The procedure returns 1 if the string is a palindrome; otherwise, it returns 0.

28. Write an assembly language program to read a string of characters from the user and that prints the vowel count. For each vowel, the count includes both uppercase and lowercase letters. For example, the input string

Advanced Programming in UNIX Environment

produces the following output:

Vowel	Count
a or A	3
e or E	3
i or I	4
o or O	2
u or U	1

29. Merge sort is a technique to combine two sorted arrays. Merge sort takes two sorted input arrays X and Y—say of size m and n—and produces a sorted array Z of size $m + n$ that contains all elements of the two input arrays. The pseudocode of merge sort is as follows:

```
mergesort (X, Y, Z, m, n)
    i := 0 {index variables for arrays X, Y, and Z}
    j := 0
    k := 0
    while ((i < m) AND (j < n))
        if (X[i] ≤ Y[j]) {find largest of two}
        then
            Z[k] := X[i] {copy and update indices}
            k := k+1
            i := i+1
        else
            Z[k] := Y[j] {copy and update indices}
            k := k+1
            j := j+1
        end if
    end while
    if (i < m) {copy remainder of input array}
        while (i < m)
            Z[k] := X[i]
            k := k+1
            i := i+1
        end while
    else
        while (j < n)
            Z[k] := Y[j]
            k := k+1
            j := j+1
        end while
    end if
end mergesort
```

The merge sort algorithm scans the two input arrays while copying the smallest of the two elements from X and Y into Z. It updates indices appropriately. The first while loop terminates when one of the arrays is exhausted. Then the other array is copied into Z.

Write a merge sort procedure and test it with two sorted arrays. Assume that the user enters the two input arrays in sorted (ascending) order.

D

IA-32 Instruction Set

Instruction format and encoding encompass a variety of factors: addressing modes, number of operands, number of registers, sources of operands, etc. Instructions can be of fixed length or variable length. In a fixed-length instruction set, all instructions are of the same length. The IA-32 instruction set uses variable-length instructions to accommodate the complexity of the instructions. This appendix first gives the IA-32 instruction format. A subset of the IA-32 instruction set is described next.

Instruction Format

In the IA-32 architecture, instruction length varies between 1 and 16 bytes. The instruction format is shown in Figure D.1. The general instruction format is shown in Figure D.1b. In addition, instructions can have several optional instruction prefixes shown in Figure D.1a. The next two subsections discuss the instruction format in detail.

Instruction Prefixes

There are four instruction prefixes, as shown in Figure D.1a. These prefixes can appear in any order. All four prefixes are optional. When a prefix is present, it takes a byte.

- *Instruction Prefixes*: Instruction prefixes such as rep were discussed in Chapter 17. This group of prefixes consists of rep, repe/repz, repne/repnz, and lock. The three repeat prefixes were discussed in detail in Chapter 17. The lock prefix is useful in multiprocessor systems to ensure exclusive use of shared memory.
- *Segment Override Prefixes*: These prefixes are used to override the default segment association. For example, DS is the default segment for accessing data. We can override this by using a segment prefix. We saw an example of this in Chapter 11 (see Program 12.8 on page 269). The following segment override prefixes are available: CS, SS, DS, ES, FS, and GS.
- *Address-Size Override Prefix*: This prefix is useful in overriding the default address size. As discussed in Chapter 4, the D bit indicates the default address and operand size. A D bit of 0 indicates the default address and operand sizes of 16 bits and a D bit of 1 indicates 32 bits. The address size can be either 16 bits or 32 bits long. This prefix can be used to switch between the two sizes.

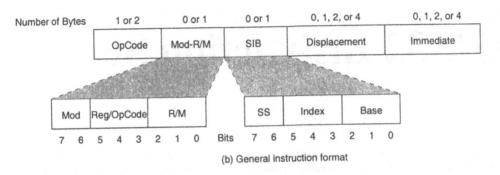

Figure D.1 The IA-32 instruction format.

- *Operand-Size Override Prefix*: The use of this prefix allows us to switch from the default operand size to the other. For example, in the 16-bit operand mode, using a 32-bit register, for example, is possible by prefixing the instruction with the operand-size override prefix.

These four prefixes can be used in any combination, and in any order.

General Instruction Format

The general instruction format consists of the Opcode, an optional address specifier consisting of a Mod R/M byte and SIB (scale-index-base) byte, an optional displacement, and an immediate data field, if required. Next we briefly discuss these five fields.

- *Opcode*: This field can be 1 or 2 bytes long. This is the only field that must be present in every instruction. For example, the opcode for the popa instruction is 61H and takes only one byte. On the other hand, the opcode for the shld instruction with an immediate value for the shift count takes two bytes (the opcode is 0FA4H). The opcode field also contains other smaller encoding fields. These fields include the register encoding, direction of operation (to or from memory), the size of displacement, and whether the immediate data must be sign-extended. For example, the instructions

```
push    EAX
push    ECX
push    EDX
push    EBX
```

are encoded as 50H, 51H, 52H, and 53H, respectively. Each takes only one byte that includes the operation code (push) as well as the register encoding (EAX, ECX, EDX, or EBX).

- *Mod R/M*: This byte and the SIB byte together provide addressing information. The Mod R/M byte consists of three fields, as shown in Figure D.1.
  - *Mod*: This field (2 bits) along with the R/M field (3 bits) specify one of 32 possible choices: 8 registers and 24 indexing modes.
  - *Reg/Opcode*: This field (3 bits) specifies either a register number or three more bits of opcode information. The first byte of the instruction determines the meaning of this field.
  - *R/M*: This field (3 bits) either specifies a register as the location of operand or forms part of the addressing-mode encoding along with the Mod field.
- *SIB*: The based indexed and scaled indexed modes of 32-bit addressing require the SIB byte. The presence of the SIB byte is indicated by certain encodings of the Mod R/M byte. The SIB byte consists of three fields, as shown in Figure D.1. The SS field (2 bits) specifies the scale factor (1, 2, 4, or 8). The index and base fields (3 bits each) specify the index and base registers, respectively.
- *Displacement*: If an addressing mode requires a displacement value, this field provides the required value. When present, it is an 8-, 16- or 32-bit signed integer. For example

```
jg     SHORT done
pop    EBX
done:
```

generates the code 7F 01 for the jg conditional jump instruction. The opcode for jg is 7FH and the displacement is 01 because the pop instruction encoding takes only a single byte.
- *Immediate*: The immediate field is the last one in the instruction. It is present in those instructions that specify an immediate operand. When present, it is an 8-, 16- or 32-bit operand. For example

```
mov    EAX,256
```

is encoded as B8 00000100. Note that the first byte B8 not only identifies the instruction as mov but also specifies the destination register as EAX (by the least significant three bits of the opcode byte). The following encoding is used for the 32-bit registers:

EAX = 0	ESP = 4
ECX = 1	EBP = 5
EDX = 2	ESI = 6
EBX = 3	EDI = 7

The last four bytes represent the immediate value 256, which is equal to 00000100H. If we change the register from EAX to EBX, the opcode byte changes from B8 to BB.

Selected Instructions

This section gives selected instructions in alphabetical order. For each instruction, instruction mnemonic, flags affected, format, and a description are given. For a more detailed description, please refer to the *Pentium Processor Family Developer's Manual—Volume 3: Architecture and Programming Manual*. The clock cycles reported are for the Pentium processor. While most of the components are self explanatory, flags section requires some explanation regarding the notation used. An instruction can affect a flag bit in one of several ways. We use the following notation to represent the effect of an instruction on a flag bit.

0 — Cleared
1 — Set
– — Unchanged
M — Updated according to the result
* — Undefined

---

aaa — ASCII adjust after addition

C	O	Z	S	P	A
M	*	*	*	*	M

Format: aaa

Description: ASCII adjusts AL register contents after addition. The AF and CF are set if there is a decimal carry, cleared otherwise. See Chapter 18 for details. Clock cycles: 3.

---

aad — ASCII adjust before division

C	O	Z	S	P	A
*	*	M	M	M	*

Format: aad

Description: ASCII adjusts AX register contents before division. See Chapter 18 for details. Clock cycles: 10.

---

aam — ASCII adjust after Multiplication

C	O	Z	S	P	A
*	*	M	M	M	*

Format: aam

Description: ASCII adjusts AX register contents after multiplication. See Chapter 18 for details. Clock cycles: 18.

---

aas — ASCII adjust after subtraction

C	O	Z	S	P	A
M	*	*	*	*	M

Format: aas

Description: ASCII adjusts AL register contents after subtraction. The AF and CF are set if there is a decimal carry, cleared otherwise. See Chapter 18 for details. Clock cycles: 3.

adc — Add with carry

C	O	Z	S	P	A
M	M	M	M	M	M

Format: adc   dest,src

Description: Performs integer addition of src and dest with the carry flag. The result (dest + src + CF) is assigned to dest. Clock cycles: 1–3.

---

add — Add without carry

C	O	Z	S	P	A
M	M	M	M	M	M

Format: add   dest,src

Description: Performs integer addition of src and dest. The result (dest + src) is assigned to dest. Clock cycles: 1–3.

---

and — Logical bitwise and

C	O	Z	S	P	A
0	0	M	M	M	*

Format: and   dest,src

Description: Performs logical bitwise **and** operation. The result src **and** dest is stored in dest. Clock cycles: 1–3

---

bsf — Bit scan forward

C	O	Z	S	P	A
*	*	M	*	*	*

Format: bsf   dest,src

Description: Scans the bits in src starting with the least significant bit. The ZF flag is set if all bits are 0; otherwise, ZF is cleared and the dest register is loaded with the bit index of the first set bit. Note that dest and src must be either both 16- or 32-bit operands. While the src operand can be either in a register or memory, dest must be a register. Clock cycles: 6–35 for 16-bit operands and 6–43 for 32-bit operands.

C	O	Z	S	P	A
*	*	M	*	*	*

bsr — Bit scan reverse

Format: bsr   dest,src

Description: Scans the bits in src starting with the most significant bit. The ZF flag is set if all bits are 0; otherwise, ZF is is cleared and the dest register is loaded with the bit index of the first set bit when scanning src in the reverse direction. Note that dest and src must be either both 16- or 32-bit operands. While the src operand can be either in a register or memory, dest must be a register. Clock cycles: 7–40 for 16-bit operands and 7–72 for 32-bit operands.

C	O	Z	S	P	A
–	–	–	–	–	–

bswap — Byte swap

Format: bswap   src

Description: Reverses the byte order of a 32-bit register src. This effectively converts a value from little endian to big endian, and vice versa. Note that src must be a 32-bit register. Result is undefined if a 16-bit register is used. Clock cycles: 1.

C	O	Z	S	P	A
M	–	–	–	–	–

bt — Bit test

Format: bt   src1,src2

Description: The value of the bit in src1, whose position is indicated by src2, is saved in the carry flag. The first operand src1 can be a 16- or 32-bit value that is either in a register or in memory. The second operand src2 can be a 16- or 32-bit value located in a register or an 8-bit immediate value. Clock cycles: 4–9.

C	O	Z	S	P	A
M	–	–	–	–	–

btc — Bit test and complement

Format: btc   src1,src2

Description: The value of the bit in src1, whose position is indicated by src2, is saved in the carry flag and then the bit in src1 is complemented. The first operand src1 can be a 16- or 32-bit value that is either in a register or in memory. The second operand src2 can be a 16- or 32-bit value located in a register or an 8-bit immediate value. Clock cycles: 7–13.

btr — Bit test and reset

C	O	Z	S	P	A
M	–	–	–	–	–

Format: btr   src1,src2

Description: The value of the bit in src1, whose position is indicated by src2, is saved in the carry flag and then the bit in src1 is reset (i.e., cleared). The first operand src1 can be a 16- or 32-bit value that is either in a register or in memory. The second operand src2 can be a 16- or 32-bit value located in a register or an 8-bit immediate value. Clock cycles: 7–13.

bts — Bit test and set

C	O	Z	S	P	A
M	–	–	–	–	–

Format: bts   src1,src2

Description: The value of the bit in src1, whose position is indicated by src2, is saved in the carry flag and then the bit in src1 is set (i.e., stores 1). The first operand src1 can be a 16- or 32-bit value that is either in a register or in memory. The second operand src2 can be a 16- or 32-bit value located in a register or an 8-bit immediate value. Clock cycles: 7–13.

call — Call procedure

C	O	Z	S	P	A
–	–	–	–	–	–

Format: call   dest

Description: The call instruction causes the procedure in the operand to be executed. There are a variety of call types. We indicated that the flags are not affected by call. This is true only if there is no task switch. For more details on the call instruction, see Chapter 11. For details on other forms of call, see the Pentium data book. Clock cycles: vary depending on the type of call.

cbw — Convert byte to word

C	O	Z	S	P	A
–	–	–	–	–	–

Format: cbw

Description: Converts the signed byte in AL to a signed word in AX by copying the sign bit of AL (the most significant bit) to all bits of AH. Clock cycles: 3.

cdq — Convert doubleword to quadword

C	O	Z	S	P	A
–	–	–	–	–	–

Format: cdq

Description: Converts the signed doubleword in EAX to a signed quadword in EDX:EAX by copying the sign bit of EAX (the most significant bit) to all bits of EDX. Clock cycles: 2.

---

clc — Clear carry flag

C	O	Z	S	P	A
0	–	–	–	–	–

Format: clc

Description: Clears the carry flag. Clock cycles: 2.

---

cld — Clear direction flag

C	O	Z	S	P	A
–	–	–	–	–	–

Format: cld

Description: Clears the direction flag. Clock cycles: 2.

---

cli — Clear interrupt flag

C	O	Z	S	P	A
–	–	–	–	–	–

Format: cli

Description: Clears the interrupt flag. Note that maskable interrupts are disabled when the interrupt flag is cleared. Clock cycles: 7.

---

cmc — Complement carry flag

C	O	Z	S	P	A
M	–	–	–	–	–

Format: cmc

Description: Complements the carry flag. Clock cycles: 2.

cmp — Compare two operands

C	O	Z	S	P	A
M	M	M	M	M	M

Format: cmp   dest,src

Description: Compares the two operands specified by performing dest − src. However, the result of this subtraction is not stored (unlike the sub instruction) but only the flags are updated to reflect the result of the subtract operation. This instruction is typically used in conjunction with conditional jumps. If an operand greater than 1 byte is compared to an immediate byte, the byte value is first sign-extended. Clock cycles: 1 if no memory operand is involved; 2 if one of the operands is in memory.

---

cmps — Compare string operands

C	O	Z	S	P	A
M	M	M	M	M	M

Format: cmps   dest,src
cmpsb
cmpsw
cmpsd

Description: Compares the byte, word, or doubleword pointed by the source index register (SI or ESI) with an operand of equal size pointed by the destination index register (DI or EDI). If the address size is 16 bits, SI and DI registers are used; ESI and EDI registers are used for 32-bit addresses. The comparison is done by subtracting operand pointed by the DI or EDI register from that by SI or ESI register. That is, the cmps instructions performs either [SI]−[DI] or [ESI]−[EDI]. The result is not stored but used to update the flags, as in the cmp instruction. After the comparison, both source and destination index registers are automatically updated. Whether these two registers are incremented or decremented depends on the direction flag (DF). The registers are incremented if DF is 0 (see the cld instruction to clear the direction flag); if the DF is 1, both index registers are decremented (see the std instruction to set the direction flag). The two registers are incremented or decremented by 1 for byte comparisons, 2 for word comparisons, and 4 for doubleword comparisons.

Note that the specification of the operands in cmps is not really required as the two operands are assumed to be pointed by the index registers. The cmpsb, cmpsw, and cmpsd are synonyms for the byte, word, and doubleword cmps instructions, respectively.

The repeat prefix instructions (i.e., rep, repe or repne) can precede the cmps instructions for array or string comparisons. See rep instruction for details. Clock cycles: 5.

C	O	Z	S	P	A
–	–	–	–	–	–

cwd — Convert word to doubleword

Format: cwd

Description: Converts the signed word in AX to a signed doubleword in DX:AX by copying the sign bit of AX (the most significant bit) to all bits of DX. In fact, cdq and this instruction use the same opcode (99H). Which one is executed depends on the default operand size. If the operand size is 16 bits, cwd is performed; cdq is performed for 32-bit operands. Clock cycles: 2.

C	O	Z	S	P	A
–	–	–	–	–	–

cwde — Convert word to doubleword

Format: cwde

Description: Converts the signed word in AX to a signed doubleword in EAX by copying the sign bit of AX (the most significant bit) to all bits of the upper word of EAX. In fact, cbw and cwde are the same instructions (i.e., share the same opcode of 98H). The action performed depends on the operand size. If the operand size is 16 bits, cbw is performed; cwde is performed for 32-bit operands. Clock cycles: 3.

C	O	Z	S	P	A
M	*	M	M	M	M

daa — Decimal adjust after addition

Format: daa

Description: The daa instruction is useful in BCD arithmetic. It adjusts the AL register to contain the correct two-digit packed decimal result. This instruction should be used after an addition instruction, as described in Chapter 18. Both AF and CF flags are set if there is a decimal carry; these two flags are cleared otherwise. The ZF, SF, and PF flags are set according to the result. Clock cycles: 3.

das — Decimal adjust after subtraction

C	O	Z	S	P	A
M	*	M	M	M	M

Format: das

Description: The das instruction is useful in BCD arithmetic. It adjusts the AL register to contain the correct two-digit packed decimal result. This instruction should be used after a subtract instruction, as described in Chapter 18. Both AF and CF flags are set if there is a decimal borrow; these two flags are cleared otherwise. The ZF, SF, and PF flags are set according to the result. Clock cycles: 3.

---

dec — Decrement by 1

C	O	Z	S	P	A
–	M	M	M	M	M

Format: dec   dest

Description: The dec instruction decrements the dest operand by 1. The carry flag is not affected. Clock cycles: 1 if dest is a register; 3 if dest is in memory.

---

div — Unsigned divide

C	O	Z	S	P	A
*	*	*	*	*	*

Format: div   divisor

Description: The div instruction performs unsigned division. The divisor can be an 8-, 16-, or 32-bit operand, located either in a register or in memory. The dividend is assumed to be in AX (for byte divisor), DX:AX (for word divisor), or EDX:EAX (for doubleword divisor). The quotient is stored in AL, AX, or EAX for 8-, 16-, and 32-bit divisors, respectively. The remainder is stored in AH, DX, or EDX for 8-, 16-, and 32-bit divisors, respectively. It generates interrupt 0 if the result cannot fit the quotient register (AL, AX, or EAX), or if the divisor is zero. See Chapter 14 for details. Clock cycles: 17 for an 8-bit divisor, 25 for a 16-bit divisor, and 41 for a 32-bit divisor.

C	O	Z	S	P	A
–	–	–	–	–	–

enter — Allocate stack frame

Format: enter   bytes,level

Description: This instruction creates a stack frame at procedure entry. The first operand bytes specifies the number of bytes for the local variable storage in the stack frame. The second operand level gives the nesting level of the procedure. If we specify a nonzero level, it copies level stack frame pointers into the new frame from the preceding stack frame. In all our examples, we set the second operand to zero. Thus the

```
enter    XX,0
```

statement is equivalent to

```
push    EBP
mov     EBP,ESP
sub     ESP,XX
```

See Chapter 11 for more details on its usage. Clock cycles: 11 if level is zero.

C	O	Z	S	P	A
–	–	–	–	–	–

hlt — Halt

Format: hlt

Description: This instruction halts instruction execution indefinitely. An interrupt or a reset will enable instruction execution. Clock cycles: ∞.

idiv — Signed divide

C	O	Z	S	P	A
*	*	*	*	*	*

Format: idiv   divisor

Description: Similar to div instruction except that idiv performs signed division. The divisor can be an 8-, 16-, or 32-bit operand, located either in a register or in memory. The dividend is assumed to be in AX (for byte divisor), DX:AX (for word divisor), or EDX:EAX (for doubleword divisor). The quotient is stored in AL, AX, or EAX for 8-, 16-, and 32-bit divisors, respectively. The remainder is stored in AH, DX, or EDX for 8-, 16-, and 32-bit divisors, respectively. It generates interrupt 0 if the result cannot fit the quotient register (AL, AX, or EAX), or if the divisor is zero. See Chapter 14 for details. Clock cycles: 22 for an 8-bit divisor, 30 for a 16-bit divisor, and 46 for a 32-bit divisor.

imul — Signed multiplication

C	O	Z	S	P	A
M	M	*	*	*	*

Format: imul   src
            imul   dest,src
            imul   dest,src,constant

Description: This instruction performs signed multiplication. The number of operands for imul can be between 1 and 3, depending on the format used. In the one-operand format, the other operand is assumed to be in the AL, AX, or EAX register depending on whether the src operand is 8, 16, or 32 bits long, respectively. The src operand can be either in a register or in memory. The result, which is twice as long as the src operand, is placed in AX, DX:AX, or EDX:EAX for 8-, 16-, or 32-bit src operands, respectively. In the other two forms, the result is of the same length as the input operands.

The two-operand format specifies both operands required for multiplication. In this case, src and dest must both be either 16-bit or 32-bit operands. While src can be either in a register or in memory, dest must be a register.

In the three-operand format, a constant can be specified as an immediate operand. The result (src × constant) is stored in dest. As in the two-operand format, the dest operand must be a register. The src can be either in a register or in memory. The immediate constant can be an 8-, 16-, or 32-bit value. For additional restrictions, refer to the Pentium data book. Clock cycles: 10 (11 if the one-operand format is used with either 8- or 16-bit operands).

in — Input from a port

C	O	Z	S	P	A
–	–	–	–	–	–

Format: in   dest,port
           in   dest,DX

Description: This instruction has two formats. In both formats, dest must be the AL, AX, or EAX register. In the first format, it reads a byte, word, or double-word from port into the AL, AX, or EAX register, respectively. Note that port is an 8-bit immediate value. This format is restrictive in the sense that only the first 256 ports can be accessed. The other format is more flexible and allows access to the complete I/O space (i.e., any port between 0 and 65,535). In this format, the port number is assumed to be in the DX register. Clock cycles: varies—see Pentium data book.

---

inc — Increment by 1

C	O	Z	S	P	A
–	M	M	M	M	M

Format: inc   dest

Description: The inc instruction increments the dest operand by 1. The carry flag is not affected. Clock cycles: 1 if dest is a register; 3 if dest is in memory.

---

ins — Input from a port to string

C	O	Z	S	P	A
–	–	–	–	–	–

Format: insb
           insw
           insd

Description: This instruction transfers an 8-, 16-, or 32-bit data from the input port specified in the DX register to a location in memory pointed by ES:(E)DI. The DI index register is used if the address size is 16 bits and EDI index register for 32-bit addresses. Unlike the in instruction, the ins instruction does not allow the specification of the port number as an immediate value. After the data transfer, the index register is updated automatically. The index register is incremented if DF is 0; it is decremented if DF is 1. The index register is incremented or decremented by 1, 2, or 4 for byte, word, double-word operands, respectively. The repeat prefix can be used along with the ins instruction to transfer a block of data (the number of data transfers is indicated by the CX register—see the rep instruction for details). Clock cycles: varies—see Pentium data book.

int — Interrupt

C	O	Z	S	P	A
–	–	–	–	–	–

Format: int   interrupt-type

Description: The int instruction calls an interrupt service routine or handler associated with interrupt-type. The interrupt-type is an immediate 8-bit operand. This value is used as an index into the Interrupt Descriptor Table (IDT). See Chapter 20 for details on the interrupt invocation mechanism. Clock cycles: varies—see Pentium data book.

into — Interrupt on overflow

C	O	Z	S	P	A
–	–	–	–	–	–

Format: into

Description: The into instruction is a conditional software interrupt identical to int 4 except that the int is implicit and the interrupt handler is invoked conditionally only when the overflow flag is set. Clock cycles: varies—see Pentium data book.

iret — Interrupt return

C	O	Z	S	P	A
M	M	M	M	M	M

Format: iret
       iretd

Description: The iret instruction returns control from an interrupt handler. In real address mode, it loads the instruction pointer and the flags register with values from the stack and resumes the interrupted routine. Both iret and iretd are synonymous (and use the opcode CFH). The operand size in effect determines whether the 16-bit or 32-bit instruction pointer (IP or EIP) and flags (FLAGS or EFLAGS) are to be used. See Chapter 20 for more details. This instruction affects all flags as the flags register is popped from stack. Clock cycles: varies—see Pentium data book.

C	O	Z	S	P	A
–	–	–	–	–	–

jcc — Jump if condition cc is satisfied

Format: `jcc     target`

Description: The `jcc` instruction alters program execution by transferring control conditionally to the `target` location in the same segment. The `target` operand is a relative offset (relative to the instruction following the conditional jump instruction). The relative offset can be a signed 8-, 16-, or 32-bit value. Most efficient instruction encoding results if 8-bit offsets are used. With 8-bit offsets, the target should be within -128 to $+127$ of the first byte of the next instruction. For 16- and 32-bit offsets, the corresponding values are 2^{15} to $2^{15} - 1$ and 2^{31} to $2^{31} - 1$, respectively. When the target is in another segment, test for the opposite condition and use the unconditional `jmp` instruction, as explained in Chapter 15. See Chapter 15 for details on the various conditions tested like `ja`, `jbe`, etc. The `jcxz` instruction tests the contents of the CX or ECX register and jumps to the target location only if (E)CX = 0. The default operand size determines whether CX or ECX is used for comparison. Clock cycles: 1 for all conditional jumps (except `jcxz`, which takes 5 or 6 cycles).

C	O	Z	S	P	A
–	–	–	–	–	–

jmp — Unconditional jump

Format: `jmp     target`

Description: The `jmp` instruction alters program execution by transferring control unconditionally to the `target` location. This instruction allows jumps to another segment. In direct jumps, the `target` operand is a relative offset (relative to the instruction following the `jmp` instruction). The relative offset can be an 8-, 16-, or 32-bit value as in the conditional jump instruction. In addition, the relative offset can be specified indirectly via a register or memory location. See Chapter 15 for an example. For other forms of the `jmp` instruction, see the Pentium data book. Note: Flags are not affected unless there is a task switch, in which case all flags are affected. Clock cycles: 1 for direct jumps, 2 for indirect jumps (more clock cycles for other types of jumps).

lahf — Load flags into AH register

C	O	Z	S	P	A
–	–	–	–	–	–

Format: `lahf`

Description: The `lahf` instruction loads the AH register with the low byte of the flags register. AH := SF, ZF, *, AF, *, PF, *, CF where * represent indeterminate value. Clock cycles: 2.

---

lds/les/lfs/lgs/lss — Load full pointer

C	O	Z	S	P	A
–	–	–	–	–	–

Format:
```
lds     dest,src
les     dest,src
lfs     dest,src
lgs     dest,src
lss     dest,src
```

Description: These instructions read a full pointer from memory (given by the `src` operand) and load the corresponding segment register (e.g., DS register for the `lds` instruction, ES register for the `les` instruction, etc.) and the `dest` register. The `dest` operand must be a 16- or 32-bit register. The first 2 or 4 bytes (depending on whether the `dest` is a 16- or 32-bit register) at the effective address given by the `src` operand are loaded into the `dest` register and the next 2 bytes into the corresponding segment register. Clock cycles: 4 (except `lss`).

---

lea — Load effective address

C	O	Z	S	P	A
–	–	–	–	–	–

Format: `lea     dest,src`

Description: The `lea` instruction computes the effective address of a memory operand given by `src` and stores it in the `dest` register. The `dest` must be either a 16- or 32-bit register. If the `dest` register is a 16-bit register and the address size is 32, only the lower 16 bits are stored. On the other hand, if a 32-bit register is specified when the address size 16 bits, the effective address is zero-extended to 32 bits. Clock cycles: 1.

		C	O	Z	S	P	A
leave — Procedure exit		–	–	–	–	–	–

Format: `leave`

Description: The `leave` instruction takes no operands. Effectively, it reverses the actions of the `enter` instruction. It performs two actions:

- Releases the local variable stack space allocated by the `enter` instruction;
- Old frame pointer is popped into (E)BP register.

This instruction is typically used just before the `ret` instruction. Clock cycles: 3.

		C	O	Z	S	P	A
lods — Load string operand		–	–	–	–	–	–

Format: `lodsb`
`lodsw`
`lodsd`

Description: The `lods` instruction loads the AL, AX, or EAX register with the memory byte, word, or doubleword at the location pointed by DS:SI or DS:ESI. The address size attribute determines whether the SI or ESI register is used. The `lodsw` and `loadsd` instructions share the same opcode (ADH). The operand size is used to load either a word or a doubleword. After loading, the source index register is updated automatically. The index register is incremented if DF is 0; it is decremented if DF is 1. The index register is incremented or decremented by 1, 2, or 4 for byte, word, doubleword operands, respectively. The `rep` prefix can be used with this instruction but is not useful, as explained in Chapter 17. This instruction is typically used in a loop (see the `loop` instruction). Clock cycles: 2.

loop/loope/loopne — Loop control

C	O	Z	S	P	A
–	–	–	–	–	–

Format:
```
loop      target
loope/loopz      target
loopne/loopnz      target
```

Description: The `loop` instruction decrements the count register (CX if the address size attribute is 16 and ECX if it is 32) and jumps to `target` if the count register is not zero. This instruction decrements the (E)CX register without changing any flags. The operand `target` is a relative 8-bit offset (i.e., the target must be in the range −128 to +127 bytes).

The `loope` instruction is similar to `loop` except that it also checks the ZF value to jump to the `target`. That is, control is transferred to `target` if, after decrementing the (E)CX register, the count register is not zero and ZF = 1. The `loopz` is a synonym for the `loope` instruction.

The `loopne` instruction is similar to `loopne` except that it transfers control to `target` if ZF is 0 (instead of 1 as in the `loope` instruction). See Chapter 15 for more details on these instructions. Clock cycles: 5 or 6 for `loop` and 7 or 8 for the other two.

Note that the unconditional `loop` instruction takes longer to execute than a functionally equivalent two-instruction sequence that decrements the (E)CX register and jumps conditionally.

---

mov — Copy data

C	O	Z	S	P	A
–	–	–	–	–	–

Format:
```
mov      dest,src
```

Description: Copies data from `src` to `dest`. Clock cycles: 1 for most `mov` instructions except when copying into a segment register, which takes more clock cycles.

movs — Copy string data

C	O	Z	S	P	A
–	–	–	–	–	–

Format:
```
movs      dest,src
movsb
movsw
movsd
```

Description: Copies the byte, word, or doubleword pointed by the source index register (SI or ESI) to the byte, word, or doubleword pointed by the destination index register (DI or EDI). If the address size is 16 bits, SI and DI registers are used; ESI and EDI registers are used for 32-bit addresses. The default segment for the source is DS and ES for the destination. Segment override prefix can be used only for the source operand. After the move, both source and destination index registers are automatically updated as in the cmps instruction.

The rep prefix instruction can precede the movs instruction for block movement of data. See rep instruction for details. Clock cycles: 4.

movsx — Copy with sign extension

C	O	Z	S	P	A
–	–	–	–	–	–

Format:
```
movsx     reg16,src8
movsx     reg32,src8
movsx     reg32,src16
```

Description: Copies the sign-extended source operand src8/src16 into the destination reg16/reg32. The destination can be either a 16-bit or 32-bit register only. The source can be a register or memory byte or word operand. Note that reg16 and reg32 represent a 16- and 32-bit register, respectively. Similarly, src8 and src16 represent a byte and word operand, respectively. Clock cycles: 3.

movzx — Copy with zero extension

C	O	Z	S	P	A
–	–	–	–	–	–

Format:
```
movzx     reg16,src8
movzx     reg32,src8
movzx     reg32,src16
```

Description: Similar to movsx instruction except movzx copies the zero-extended source operand into destination. Clock cycles: 3.

mul — Unsigned multiplication

C	O	Z	S	P	A
M	M	*	*	*	*

Format: mul   AL,src8
mul   AX,src16
mul   EAX,src32

Description: Performs unsigned multiplication of two 8-, 16-, or 32-bit operands. Only one of the operand needs to be specified; the other operand, matching in size, is assumed to be in the AL, AX, or EAX register.

- For an 8-bit multiplication, the result is in the AX register. CF and OF are cleared if AH is zero; otherwise, they are set.
- For a 16-bit multiplication, the result is in the DX:AX register pair. The higher-order 16 bits are in DX. CF and OF are cleared if DX is zero; otherwise, they are set.
- For a 32-bit multiplication, the result is in the EDX:EAX register pair. The higher-order 32 bits are in EDX. CF and OF are cleared if EDX is zero; otherwise, they are set.

Clock cycles: 11 for 8- or 16-bit operands and 10 for 32-bit operands.

---

neg — Negate sign (two's complement)

C	O	Z	S	P	A
M	M	M	M	M	M

Format: neg   operand

Description: Performs 2's complement negation (sign reversal) of the operand specified. The operand specified can be 8, 16, or 32 bits in size and can be located in a register or memory. The operand is subtracted from zero and the result is stored back in the operand. The CF flag is set for nonzero result; cleared otherwise. Other flags are set according to the result. Clock cycles: 1 for register operands and 3 for memory operands.

---

nop — No operation

C	O	Z	S	P	A
–	–	–	–	–	–

Format: nop

Description: Performs no operation. Interestingly, the nop instruction is an alias for the xchg (E)AX,(E)AX instruction. Clock cycles: 1.

not — Logical bitwise not

C	O	Z	S	P	A
–	–	–	–	–	–

Format: not   operand

Description: Performs 1's complement bitwise **not** operation (a 1 becomes 0 and vice versa). Clock cycles: 1 for register operands and 3 for memory operands.

or — Logical bitwise or

C	O	Z	S	P	A
0	0	M	M	M	*

Format: or   dest,src

Description: Performs bitwise **or** operation. The result (dest **or** src) is stored in dest. Clock cycles: 1 for register and immediate operands and 3 if a memory operand is involved.

out — Output to a port

C	O	Z	S	P	A
–	–	–	–	–	–

Format: out   port,src
              out   DX,src

Description: Like the in instruction, this instruction has two formats. In both formats, src must be in the AL, AX, or EAX register. In the first format, it outputs a byte, word, or doubleword from src to the I/O port specified by the first operand port. Note that port is an 8-bit immediate value. This format limits access to the first 256 I/O ports in the I/O space. The other format is more general and allows access to the full I/O space (i.e., any port between 0 and 65,535). In this format, the port number is assumed to be in the DX register. Clock cycles: varies—see Pentium data book.

outs — Output from a string to a port

C	O	Z	S	P	A
–	–	–	–	–	–

Format: `outsb`
              `outsw`
              `outsd`

Description: This instruction transfers an 8-, 16-, or 32-bit data from a string (pointed by the source index register) to the output port specified in the DX register. Similar to the `ins` instruction, it uses the SI index register for 16-bit addresses and the ESI register if the address size is 32. The (E)SI register is automatically updated after the transfer of a data item. The index register is incremented if DF is 0; it is decremented if DF is 1. The index register is incremented or decremented by 1, 2, or 4 for byte, word, or doubleword operands, respectively. The repeat prefix can be used with `outs` for block transfer of data. Clock cycles: varies—see Pentium data book.

---

pop — Pop a word from the stack

C	O	Z	S	P	A
–	–	–	–	–	–

Format: `pop      dest`

Description: Pops a word or doubleword from the top of the stack. If the address size attribute is 16 bits, SS:SP is used as the top of the stack pointer; otherwise, SS:ESP is used. `dest` can be a register or memory operand. In addition, it can also be a segment register DS, ES, SS, FS, or GS (e.g., `pop DS`). The stack pointer is incremented by 2 (if the operand size is 16 bits) or 4 (if the operand size is 32 bits). Note that `pop CS` is not allowed. This can be done only indirectly by the `ret` instruction. Clock cycles: 1 if `dest` is a general register; 3 if `dest` is a segment register or memory operand.

---

popa — Pop all general registers

C	O	Z	S	P	A
–	–	–	–	–	–

Format: `popa`
              `popad`

Description: Pops all eight 16-bit (`popa`) or 32-bit (`popad`) general registers from the top of the stack. The `popa` loads the registers in the order DI, SI, BP, discard next two bytes (to skip loading into SP), BX, DX, CX, and AX. That is, DI is popped first and AX last. The `popad` instruction follows the same order on the 32-bit registers. Clock cycles: 5.

popf — Pop flags register

C	O	Z	S	P	A
M	M	M	M	M	M

Format: popf
              popfd

Description: Pops the 16-bit (popf) or 32-bit (popfd) flags register (FLAGS or EFLAGS) from the top of the stack. Bits 16 (VM flag) and 17 (RF flag) of the EFLAGS register are not affected by this instruction. Clock cycles: 6 in the real mode and 4 in the protected mode.

---

push — Push a word onto the stack

C	O	Z	S	P	A
–	–	–	–	–	–

Format: push   src

Description: Pushes a word or doubleword onto the top of the stack. If the address size attribute is 16 bits, SS:SP is used as the top of the stack pointer; otherwise, SS:ESP is used. src can be (i) a register, or (ii) a memory operand, or (iii) a segment register (CS, SS, DS, ES, FS, or GS), or (iv) an immediate byte, word, or doubleword operand. The stack pointer is decremented by 2 (if the operand size is 16 bits) or 4 (if the operand size is 32 bits). The push ESP instruction pushes the ESP register value before it was decremented by the push instruction. On the other hand, push SP pushes the decremented SP value onto the stack. Clock cycles: 1 (except when the operand is in memory, in which case it takes 2 clock cycles).

---

pusha — Push all general registers

C	O	Z	S	P	A
–	–	–	–	–	–

Format: pusha
              pushad

Description: Pushes all eight 16-bit (pusha) or 32-bit (pushad) general registers onto the stack. The pusha pushes the registers onto the stack in the order AX, CX, DX, BX, SP, BP, SI, and DI. That is, AX is pushed first and DI last. The pushad instruction follows the same order on the 32-bit registers. It decrements the stack pointer SP by 16 for word operands; decrements ESP by 32 for doubleword operands. Clock cycles: 5.

pushf — Push flags register

C	O	Z	S	P	A
–	–	–	–	–	–

Format: `pushf`
`pushfd`

Description: Pushes the 16-bit (`pushf`) or 32-bit (`pushfd`) flags register (FLAGS or EFLAGS) onto the stack. Decrements SP by 2 (`pushf`) for word operands and decrements ESP by 4 (`pushfd`) for doubleword operands. Clock cycles: 4 in the real mode and 3 in the protected mode.

---

rep/repe/repz/repne/repnz — Repeat instruction

C	O	Z	S	P	A
–	–	M	–	–	–

Format: `rep      string-inst`
`repe/repz      string-inst`
`repne/repnz      string-inst`

Description: These three prefixes repeat the specified string instruction until the conditions are met. The `rep` instruction decrements the count register (CX or ECX) each time the string instruction is executed. The string instruction is repeatedly executed until the count register is zero. The `repe` (repeat while equal) has an additional termination condition: ZF = 0. The `repz` is an alias for the `repe` instruction. The `repne` (repeat while not equal) is similar to `repe` except that the additional termination condition is ZF =1. The `repnz` is an alias for the `repne` instruction. The ZF flag is affected by the `rep cmps` and `rep scas` instructions. For more details, see Chapter 17. Clock cycles: varies—see Pentium data book for details.

---

ret — Return form a procedure

C	O	Z	S	P	A
–	–	–	–	–	–

Format: `ret`
`ret value`

Description: Transfers control to the instruction following the corresponding `call` instruction. The optional immediate `value` specifies the number of bytes (for 16-bit operands) or number of words (for 32-bit operands) that are to be cleared from the stack after the return. This parameter is usually used to clear the stack of the input parameters. See Chapter 11 for more details. Clock cycles: 2 for near return and 3 for far return; if the optional `value` is specified, add one more clock cycle. Changing privilege levels takes more clocks—see Pentium data book.

		C	O	Z	S	P	A
rol/ror/rcl/rcr — Rotate instructions		M	M	–	–	–	–

Format: rol/ror/rcl/rcr   src,1
                rol/ror/rcl/rcr   src,count
                rol/ror/rcl/rcr   src,CL

Description: This group of instructions supports rotation of 8-, 16-, or 32-bit data. The rol (rotate left) and ror (rotate right) instructions rotate the src data as explained in Chapter 16. The second operand gives the number of times src is to be rotated. This operand can be given as an immediate value (a constant 1 or a byte value count) or preloaded into the CL register. The other two rotate instructions rcl (rotate left including CF) and rcr (rotate right including CF) rotate the src data with the carry flag (CF) included in the rotation process, as explained in Chapter 16. The OF flag is affected only for single bit rotates; it is undefined for multibit rotates. Clock cycles: rol and ror take 1 (if src is a register) or 3 (if src is a memory operand) for the immediate mode (constant 1 or count) and 4 for the CL version; for the other two instructions, it can take as many as 27 clock cycles—see Pentium data book for details.

		C	O	Z	S	P	A
sahf — Store AH into flags register		M	–	M	M	M	M

Format: sahf

Description: The AH register bits 7, 6, 4, 2, and 0 are loaded into flags SF, ZF, AF, PF, and CF, respectively. Clock cycles: 2.

sal/sar/shl/shr — Shift instructions

C	O	Z	S	P	A
M	M	M	M	M	–

Format:
```
sal/sar/shl/shr    src,1
sal/sar/shl/shr    src,count
sal/sar/shl/shr    src,CL
```

Description: This group of instructions supports shifting of 8-, 16-, or 32-bit data. The format is similar to the rotate instructions. The `sal` (shift arithmetic left) and its synonym `shl` (shift left) instructions shift the `src` data left. The shifted out bit goes into CF and the vacated bit is cleared, as explained in Chapter 16. The second operand gives the number of times `src` is to be shifted. This operand can be given as an immediate value (a constant 1 or a byte value `count`) or preloaded into the CL register. The `shr` (shift right) is similar to `shl` except for the direction of the shift. The `sar` (shift arithmetic right) is similar to `sal` except for two differences: the shift direction is right and the sign bit is copied into the vacated bits. If shift count is zero, no flags are affected. The CF flag contains the last bit shifted out. The OF flag is defined only for single shifts; it is undefined for multibit shifts. Clock cycles: 1 (if `src` is a register) or 3 (if `src` is a memory operand) for the immediate mode (constant 1 or `count`) and 4 for the CL version.

sbb — Subtract with borrow

C	O	Z	S	P	A
M	M	M	M	M	M

Format: `sbb    dest,src`

Description: Performs integer subtraction with borrow. The `dest` is assigned the result of `dest - (src+CF)`. Clock cycles: 1–3.

C	O	Z	S	P	A
M	M	M	M	M	M

scas — Compare string operands

Format: scas   operand
scasb
scasw
scasd

Description: Subtracts the memory byte, word, or doubleword pointed by the destination index register (DI or EDI) from the AL, AX, or EAX register, respectively. The result is not stored but used to update the flags. The memory operand must be addressable from the ES register. Segment override is not allowed in this instruction. If the address size is 16 bits, DI register is used; EDI register is used for 32-bit addresses. After the subtraction, the destination index register is updated automatically. Whether the register is incremented or decremented depends on the direction flag (DF). The register is incremented if DF is 0 (see the cld instruction to clear the direction flag); if the DF is 1, the index register is decremented (see the std instruction to set the direction flag). The amount of increment or decrement is 1 (for byte operands), 2 (for word operands), or 4 (for doubleword operands).

Note that the specification of the operand in scas is not really required as the memory operand is assumed to be pointed by the index register. The scasb, scasw, and scasd are synonyms for the byte, word, and doubleword scas instructions, respectively.

The repeat prefix instructions (i.e., repe or repne) can precede the scas instructions for array or string comparisons. See the rep instruction for details. Clock cycles: 4.

C	O	Z	S	P	A
–	–	–	–	–	–

setCC — Byte set on condition operands

Format: setCC   dest

Description: Sets dest byte to 1 if the condition CC is met; otherwise, sets to zero. The operand dest must be either an 8-bit register or a memory operand. The conditions tested are similar to the conditional jump instruction (see jcc instruction). The conditions are A, AE, B, BE, E, NE, G, GE, L, LE, NA, NAE, NB, NBE, NG, NGE, NL, NLE, C, NC, O, NO, P, PE, PO, NP, O, NO, S, NS, Z, NZ. The conditions can specify signed and unsigned comparisons as well as flag values. Clock cycles: 1 for register operand and 2 for memory operand.

shld/shrd — Double precision shift

C	O	Z	S	P	A
M	M	M	M	M	*

Format: shld/shrd   dest,src,count

Description: The shld instruction performs left shift of dest by count times. The second operand src provides the bits to shift in from the right. In other words, the shld instruction performs a left shift of dest concatenated with src and the result in the upper half is copied into dest. dest and src operands can both be either 16- or 32-bit operands. While dest can be a register or memory operand, src must be a register of the same size as dest. The third operand count can be an immediate byte value or the CL register can be used as in the shift instructions. The contents of the src register are not altered.

The shrd instruction (double precision shift right) is similar to shld except for the direction of the shift.

If the shift count is zero, no flags are affected. The CF flag contains the last bit shifted out. The OF flag is defined only for single shifts; it is undefined for multibit shifts. The SF, ZF, and PF flags are set according to the result. Clock cycles: 4 (5 if dest is a memory operand and the CL register is used for count).

---

stc — Set carry flag

C	O	Z	S	P	A
1	–	–	–	–	–

Format: stc

Description: Sets the carry flag to 1. Clock cycles: 2.

---

std — Set direction flag

C	O	Z	S	P	A
–	–	–	–	–	–

Format: std

Description: Sets the direction flag to 1. Clock cycles: 2.

---

sti — Set interrupt flag

C	O	Z	S	P	A
–	–	–	–	–	–

Format: sti

Description: Sets the interrupt flag to 1. Clock cycles: 7.

C	O	Z	S	P	A
–	–	–	–	–	–

stos — Store string operand

Format: `stosb`
               `stosw`
               `stosd`

Description: Stores the contents of the AL, AX, or EAX register at the memory byte, word, or doubleword pointed by the destination index register (DI or EDI), respectively. If the address size is 16 bits, DI register is used; EDI register is used for 32-bit addresses. After the load, the destination index register is automatically updated. Whether this register is incremented or decremented depends on the direction flag (DF). The register is incremented if DF is 0 (see the `cld` instruction to clear the direction flag); if the DF is 1, the index register is decremented (see the `std` instruction to set the direction flag). The amount of increment or decrement depends on the operand size (1 for byte operands, 2 for word operands, and 4 for doubleword operands).
The repeat prefix instruction `rep` can precede the `stos` instruction to fill a block of CX/ECX bytes, words, or doublewords. Clock cycles: 3.

C	O	Z	S	P	A
M	M	M	M	M	M

sub — Subtract

Format: `sub`   `dest,src`

Description: Performs integer subtraction. The `dest` is assigned the result of `dest` − `src`. Clock cycles: 1–3.

C	O	Z	S	P	A
0	0	M	M	M	*

test — Logical compare

Format: `test`   `dest,src`

Description: Performs logical **and** operation (`dest` **and** `src`). However, the result of the **and** operation is discarded. The `dest` operand can be either in a register or in memory. The `src` operand can be either an immediate value or a register. Both `dest` and `src` operands are not affected. Sets SF, ZF, and PF flags according to the result. Clock cycles: 1 if `dest` is a register operand and 2 if it is a memory operand.

xchg — Exchange data

C	O	Z	S	P	A
–	–	–	–	–	–

Format: xchg   dest,src

Description: Exchanges the values of the two operands src and dest. Clock cycles: 2 if both operands are registers or 3 if one of them is a memory operand.

---

xlat — Translate byte

C	O	Z	S	P	A
–	–	–	–	–	–

Format: xlat   table-offset
           xlatb

Description: Translates the data in the AL register using a table lookup. It changes the AL register from the table index to the corresponding table contents. The contents of the BX (for 16-bit addresses) or EBX (for 32-bit addresses) registers are used as the offset to the the translation table base. The contents of the AL register are treated as an index into this table. The byte value at this index replaces the index value in AL. The default segment for the translation table is DS. This is used in both formats. However, in the operand version, a segment override is possible. Clock cycles: 4.

---

xor — Logical bitwise exclusive-or

C	O	Z	S	P	A
0	0	M	M	M	*

Format: xor   dest,src

Description: Performs logical bitwise exclusive-or (xor) operation (dest **xor** src) and the result is stored in dest. Sets the SF, ZF, and PF flags according to the result. Clock cycles: 1–3.

E

Glossary

Aborts See *Exceptions*

Access permissions Unix and Linux systems provide a sophisticated security mechanism to control access to individual files and directories. Each file and directory has certain access permissions that indicate who can access and in what mode (read-only, read/write, and so on). With these permissions the system can protect, for example, users from accessing other user's files. Linux, like the UNIX systems, associates three types of access permissions to files and directories: read (r), write (w), and execute (x). As the names indicate, the read permission allows read access and the write permission allows writing into the file or directory. The execute permission is required to execute a file and, for obvious reasons, should be used with binary and script files that contain executable code or commands. The Linux system uses nine bits to keep the access permissions as there are three types of users, each of which can have three types of permissions.

Address bus A group of parallel wires that carry the address of a memory location or I/O port. The width of the address bus determines the memory addressing capacity of a processor. Typically, 32-bit processors support 32-bit addresses. Thus, these processors can address up to 4 GB (2^{32} bytes) of main memory.

Addressing mode Most assembly language instructions require operands. There are several ways to specify the location of the operands. These are called the *addressing modes*. A complete discussion of the addressing modes is given in Chapter 13.

ALU see *Arithmetic and logic unit*

Arithmetic and logic unit This unit forms the computational core of a processor. It performs the basic arithmetic and logical operations such as integer addition, subtraction, and logical AND and OR functions.

Assembler Assembler is a program that translates an assembly language source program to its machine language equivalent (usually into an object file format such as ELF).

Assembler directives These directives provide information to the assembler on various aspects of the assembly process. These instructions are also called pseudo-ops. Assembler directives are nonexecutable and do not generate any machine language instructions.

Auxiliary flag   The auxiliary flag indicates whether an operation has produced a result that has generated a carry out of or a borrow into the low-order four bits of 8-, 16-, or 32-bit operands. The auxiliary flag is set if there is such a carry or borrow; otherwise it is cleared.

Based addressing mode   In this addressing mode, one of the registers acts as the base register in computing the effective address of an operand. The effective address is computed by adding the contents of the specified base register with a signed displacement value given as part of the instruction. For 16-bit addresses, the signed displacement is either an 8- or a 16-bit number. For 32-bit addresses, it is either an 8- or a 32-bit number. Based addressing provides a convenient way to access individual elements of a structure. Typically, a base register can be set up to point to the base of the structure and the displacement can be used to access an element within the structure.

Based-indexed addressing mode   In this addressing mode, the effective address is computed as

$$\text{Base} + \text{Index} + \text{signed displacement.}$$

The displacement can be a signed 8- or 16-bit number for 16-bit addresses; it can be a signed 8- or 32-bit number for 32-bit addresses. This addressing mode is useful in accessing two-dimensional arrays with the displacement representing the offset to the beginning of the array. This mode can also be used to access arrays of records where the displacement represents the offset to a field in a record. In addition, this addressing mode is used to access arrays passed on to a procedure. In this case, the base register could point to the beginning of the array, and an index register can hold the offset to a specific element.

Based-indexed addressing mode with a scale factor   In this addressing mode, the effective address is computed as

$$\text{Base} + (\text{Index} * \text{scale factor}) + \text{signed displacement.}$$

This addressing mode provides an efficient indexing mechanism into a two-dimensional array when the element size is 2, 4, or 8 bytes.

Big-endian byte order   When storing multibyte data, the big-endian byte order stores the data from the most-significant byte to the least-significant byte.

Breakpoint   Breakpoint is a debugging technique. Often we know that some parts of the program work correctly. In this case, it is a sheer waste of time to single step or trace the code. What we would like is to execute this part of the program and then stop for more careful debugging (perhaps by single stepping). Debuggers provide commands to set up breakpoints. The program execution stops at breakpoints, giving us a chance to look at the state of the program.

Bus protocol   When there is more than one master device, which is typically the case, the device requesting the use of the bus sends a bus request signal to the bus arbiter using the bus request control line. If the bus arbiter grants the request, it notifies the requesting device by sending a signal on the bus grant control line. The granted device, which acts as the master, can then use the bus for data transfer. The bus-request-grant procedure is called *bus protocol*. Different buses use different bus protocols. In some protocols, permission to use the bus is granted for only one bus cycle; in others, permission is granted until the bus master relinquishes the bus.

Bus transaction   A bus transaction refers to the data transfers taking place on the system bus. Some examples of bus transactions are memory read, memory write, I/O read, I/O write, and interrupt. Depending on the processor and the type of bus used, there may be other types of transactions. For example, the Pentium processor supports a burst mode of data transfer in which up to four 64 bits of data can be transferred in a burst cycle. Every bus transaction involves a *master* and a *slave*. The master is the initiator of the transaction and the slave is the target of the transaction. The processor usually acts as the master of the system bus, while components like memory are usually slaves. Some components may act as slaves for some transactions and as masters for other transactions.

Call-by-value parameter passing   In the call-by-value mechanism, the called function is provided only the current values of the arguments for its use. Thus, in this case, the values of these arguments are not changed in the called function; these values can only be used as in a mathematical function.

Call-by-reference parameter passing   In the call-by-reference mechanism, the called function actually receives the addresses (i.e., pointers) of the parameters from the calling function. The function can change the contents of these parameters—and these changes will be seen by the calling function—by directly manipulating the argument storage space.

Carry flag   The carry flag records the fact that the result of an arithmetic operation on unsigned numbers is out of range (too big or too small) to fit the destination register or memory location.

Clock   A clock is a sequence of 1s and 0s. We refer to the period during which the clock is 1 as the ON period and the period with 0 as the OFF period. Even though we normally use symmetric clock signals with equal ON and OFF periods, clock signals can take asymmetric forms.

Clock cycle   A clock cycle is defined as the time between two successive rising edges or between successive falling edges.

Clock frequency   Clock frequency is measured in number of cycles per second. This number is referred to as Hertz (Hz). The abbreviation MHz refers to millions of cycles per second.

Clock period   The clock period is defined as the time represented by one clock cycle.

Column-major order   As the memory is a one-dimensional structure, we need to transform a multidimensional array to a one-dimensional structure. In the column-major order, array elements are stored column by column. This ordering is shown Figure 13.5b. Column-major ordering is used in FORTRAN.

Combinational circuits   The output of a combinational circuit depends only on the current inputs applied to the circuit. The adder is an example of a combinational circuit.

Control bus   The control bus consists of a set of control signals. Typical control signals include memory read, memory write, I/O read, I/O write, interrupt, interrupt acknowledge, bus request, and bus grant. These control signals indicate the type of action taking place on the system bus. For example, when the processor is writing data into the memory, the memory write signal is asserted. Similarly, when the processor is reading from an I/O device, the I/O read signal is asserted.

Data bus   A group of parallel wires that carry the data between the processor and memory or I/O device. The width of data bus indicates the size of the data transferred between the processor and memory or I/O device.

DDD   The Dynamic Data Display (DDD) provides a nice visual interface to command-line debuggers like GDB. For more details on this debugger interface, see Chapter 8.

Decoder   A decoder is useful in selecting one-out-of-N lines. The input to a decoder is an I-bit binary (i.e., encoded) number and the output is 2^I bits of decoded data. Among the 2^I outputs of a decoder, only one output line is 1 at any time.

Define directive   In the assembly language, allocation of storage space is done by the define assembler directive. The define directive can be used to reserve and initialize one or more bytes. However, no interpretation (as in a C variable declaration) is attached to the contents of these bytes. It is entirely up to the program to interpret the bit pattern stored in the space reserved for data.

Demultiplexer   A demultiplexer has n selection inputs, 2^n data outputs, and one data input. Depending on the value of the selection input, the data input is connected to the corresponding data output.

Direct addressing mode   This is a memory addressing mode. In this addressing mode, the offset value is specified directly as part of the instruction. In an assembly language program, this value is usually indicated by the variable name of the data item. The assembler translates this name into its associated offset value during the assembly process. To facilitate this translation, assembler maintains a symbol table. This addressing mode is the simplest of all the memory addressing modes. A restriction associated with the memory addressing modes is that these can be used to specify only one operand.

Direction flag   The direction flag determines the direction of string processing done by the string instructions. If the direction flag is clear, string operations proceed in the forward direction (from head to tail of a string); otherwise, string processing is done in the opposite direction.

Effective address   To locate a data item in the data segment, we need two components: the segment start address and an offset value within the segment. The start address of the segment is typically found in the DS register. The offset value is often called the effective address.

Executable instructions   These instructions tell the processor what to do. Each executable instruction consists of an *operation code* (*opcode* for short). Executable instructions cause the assembler to generate machine language instructions. As stated in Chapter 1, each executable statement typically generates one machine language instruction.

Exceptions   An exception is a type of interrupt that is generated by the processor. The exceptions are classified into *faults*, *traps*, and *aborts* depending on the way they are reported and whether the interrupted instruction is restarted. Faults and traps are reported at instruction boundaries. Faults use the boundary before the instruction during which the exception was detected. When a fault occurs, the system state is restored to the state before the current instruction so that the instruction can be restarted. The divide error, for instance, is a fault detected during the `div` or `idiv` instruction. Traps are reported at the instruction boundary immediately following the instruction during which the exception was detected. For instance, the overflow exception (interrupt 4) is a trap. Aborts are exceptions that report severe errors. Examples include hardware errors and inconsistent values in system tables.

EXTERN directive   The `extern` directive is used to tell the assembler that certain labels are not defined in the current source file (i.e., module), but can be found in other modules. Thus, the assembler leaves "holes" in the corresponding object file that the linker will fill in later. This directive and the `global` directive facilitate separate assembly of source modules.

Fanin   Fanin specifies the maximum number of inputs a logic gate can have.

Fanout   Fanout refers to the driving capacity of an output. Fanout specifies the maximum number of gates that the output of a gate can drive.

Faults   See *Exceptions*

Fetch-decode-execute cycle   See *Processor execution cycle*

Full mapping   Full mapping is useful in mapping a memory module to the memory address space. It refers to a one-to-one mapping function between the memory address and the address in memory address space. Thus, for each address value in memory address space that has a memory location mapped, there is one and only one memory location responding to the address. Full mapping, however, requires a more complex circuit to generate the chip select signal that is often not necessary.

GDB   GDB is a GNU debugger. This is a command-line debugger. For more details on this debugger, see Chapter 8.

GLOBAL directive   NASM provides the `global` directive to make the associated label(s) available to other modules of the program. This directive is useful in writing multimodule programs. Microsoft and Borland assemblers use `public` directive for this purpose. This directive and the `extern` directive facilitate separate assembly of source modules.

Hardware interrupts   Hardware interrupts are of hardware origin and *asynchronous* in nature. These interrupts are used by I/O devices such as the keyboard to get the processor's attention. Hardware interrupts can be divided into either *maskable* or *nonmaskable* interrupts (see Figure 20.1). A nonmaskable interrupt (NMI) can be triggered by applying an electrical signal on the NMI pin of the processor. This interrupt is called nonmaskable because the processor always responds to this signal. In other words, this interrupt cannot be disabled under program control. Most hardware interrupts are of maskable type. To cause this type of interrupt, an electrical signal should be applied to the INTR (INTerrupt Request) input of the processor. The processor recognizes the INTR interrupt only if the interrupt enable flag (IF) bit of the flags register is set to 1. Thus, these interrupts can be masked or disabled by clearing the IF bit.

I/O port   An I/O port can be thought of as the address of a register associated with an I/O controller.

Immediate addressing mode   In this addressing mode, data is specified as part of the instruction itself. As a result, even though the data is in memory, it is located in the code segment, not in the data segment. This addressing mode is typically used in instructions that require at least two data items to manipulate. In this case, this mode can only specify the source operand and immediate data is always a constant. Thus, instructions typically use another addressing mode to specify the destination operand.

Indexed addressing mode   In this addressing mode, the effective address is computed as

$$(\text{Index} * \text{scale factor}) + \text{signed displacement}.$$

For 16-bit addresses, no scaling factor is allowed (see Table 13.1 on page 275). For 32-bit addresses, a scale factor of 2, 4, or 8 can be specified. Of course, we can use a scale factor in the 16-bit addressing mode by using an address size override prefix. The indexed addressing mode is often used to access elements of an array. The beginning of the array is given by the displacement, and the value of the index register selects an element within the array. The scale factor is particularly useful to access arrays whose element size is 2, 4, or 8 bytes.

Indirect addressing mode   This is a memory addressing mode. In this addressing mode, the offset or effective address of the data is in one of the general registers. For this reason, this addressing mode is sometimes referred to as the register indirect addressing mode.

Interrupt enable flag   See *Hardware interrupts*

Interrupts   Interrupt is a mechanism by which a program's flow control can be altered. Interrupts provide a mechanism similar to that of a procedure call. Causing an interrupt transfers control to a procedure, which is referred to as an *interrupt service routine* (ISR). An ISR is sometimes called a *handler*. When the ISR is completed, the interrupted program resumes execution as if it were not interrupted. This behavior is analogous to a procedure call. There are, however, some basic differences between procedures and interrupts that make interrupts almost indispensable. One of the main differences is that interrupts can be initiated by both software and hardware. In contrast, procedures are purely software-initiated. The fact that interrupts can be initiated by hardware is the principal factor behind much of the power of interrupts. This capability gives us an efficient way by which external devices can get the processor's attention.

Isolated I/O   In isolated I/O, I/O ports are mapped to an I/O address space that is separate from the memory address space. In architectures such as the IA-32, which use the isolated I/O, special I/O instructions are needed to access the I/O address space. The IA-32 instruction set provides two instructions—in and out—to access I/O ports. The in instruction can be used to read from an I/O port and the out for writing to an I/O port.

Linker   Linker is a program that takes one or more object programs as its input and produces executable code.

Little-endian byte order   When storing multibyte data, the little-endian byte order stores the data from the least-significant byte to the most-significant byte. The Intel 32-bit processors such as the Pentium use this byte order.

Machine language   Machine language is a close relative of the assembly language. Typically, there is a one-to-one correspondence between the assembly language and machine language instructions. The processor understands only the machine language, whose instructions consist of strings of 1s and 0s.

Macros   Macros provide a sophisticated text substitution mechanism. Macros permit the assembly language programmer to name a group of statements and refer to the group by the macro name. During the assembly process, each macro is replaced by the group of statements that it represents and assembled in place. This process is referred to as macro expansion. Macros are discussed in detail in Chapter 10.

Maskable interrupts   See *Hardware interrupts*

Memory address space   This refers to the amount of memory that a processor can address. Memory address space depends on the system address bus width. Typically, 32-bit processors support 32-bit addresses. Thus, these processors can address up to 4 GB (2^{32} bytes) of main memory. The actual memory in a system, however, is always less than or equal to the memory address space. The amount of memory in a system is determined by how much of this memory address space is populated with memory chips.

Memory-mapped I/O   In memory-mapped I/O, I/O ports are mapped to memory addresses. In systems that use memory mapped I/O, writing to an I/O port is similar to writing to a memory location.

Multiplexer   A multiplexer is characterized by 2^n data inputs, n selection inputs, and a single output. It connects one of 2^n inputs, selected by the selection inputs, to the output.

Nonmaskable interrupts   See *Hardware interrupts*

Offset See *Effective address*

Overflow flag The overflow flag is the carry flag counterpart for the signed number arithmetic. The main purpose of the overflow flag is to indicate whether an operation on signed numbers has produced a result that is out of range.

PALs see *Programmable array logic device*

Parameter passing Parameter passing in assembly language is different and more complicated than that used in high-level languages. In the assembly language, the calling procedure first places all the parameters needed by the called procedure in a mutually accessible storage area (usually registers or memory). Only then can the procedure be invoked. There are two common methods depending on the type of storage area used to pass parameters: register method or stack method. As their names imply, the register method uses general-purpose registers to pass parameters, and the stack is used in the other method.

Parity flag The parity flag indicates the parity of the 8-bit result produced by an operation; if this result is 16 or 32 bits long, only the lower-order 8 bits are considered to set or clear the parity flag. The parity flag is set if the byte contains an even number of 1 bits; if there are an odd number of 1 bits, it is cleared. In other words, the parity flag indicates an even parity condition of the byte.

Partial mapping Partial mapping is useful in mapping a memory module to the memory address space. This mapping reduces the complexity associated with full mapping by mapping each memory location to more than one address in the memory address space. Typically, the number of addresses a location is mapped to is a power of 2.

Path name A path name specifies the location of a file or directory in hierarchical file system. A path can be specified as the absolute path or a relative path. In the former specification, you give the location of a file/directory starting from the root directory. Absolute path always begins with the root directory (/). In contrast, a relative path specifies the path relative to your current directory.

Pipe Linux provides several commands, which can be treated as the basic building blocks. Often, we may need several commands to accomplish a complicated task. We may have to feed the output of one command as input to another to accomplish a task. The shell provides the pipe operator (|) to achieve this. The syntax is

```
command1 | command2
```

The output of the first command (`command1`) is fed as input to the second command (`command2`). The output of `command2` is the final output. Of course, we can generalize this to connect several commands.

Processor execution cycle The processor execution cycle consists of the following: (i) Fetch an instruction from the memory; (ii) Decode the instruction (i.e., identify the instruction); (iii) Execute the instruction (i.e., perform the action specified by the instruction).

Programmable array logic device A programmable array logic device is very similar to the PLA except that there is no programmable OR array. Instead, the OR connections are fixed. This reduces the complexity by cutting down the set of fuses in the OR array. Due to their cost advantage, most manufacturers produce only PALs.

Programmable logic array A programmable logic array is a field programmable device to implement sum-of-product expressions. It consists of an AND array and an OR array. A PLA takes N inputs and produces M outputs. Each input is a logical variable. Each output of a PLA represents a logical function output. Internally, each input is complemented, and a total of $2N$ inputs is connected to each AND gate in the AND array through a fuse. Each AND gate can be used to implement a product term in the sum-of-products expression. The OR array is organized similarly except that the inputs to the OR gates are the outputs of the AND array. Thus, the number of inputs to each OR gate is equal to the number of AND gates in the AND array. The output of each OR gate represents a function output.

PLA   See *Programmable logic array*

Propagation delay   Propagation delay represents the time required for the output of a circuit to react to an input. The propagation delay depends on the complexity of the circuit and the technology used.

Protected-mode memory architecture   The IA-32 architecture supports a sophisticated memory architecture under real and protected modes. The protected mode uses 32-bit addresses and is the native mode of the IA-32 architecture. In the protected mode, both segmentation and paging are supported. Paging is useful in implementing virtual memory; it is transparent to the application program, but segmentation is not.

Queue   A queue is a first-in-first-out (FIFO) data structure. A queue can be considered as a linear array with insertions done at one end of the array and deletions at the other end.

Real-mode memory architecture   The IA-32 architecture supports a sophisticated memory architecture under real and protected modes. The real mode, which uses 16-bit addresses, is provided to run programs written for the 8086 processor. In this mode, it supports the segmented memory architecture of the 8086 processor.

Register addressing mode   In this addressing mode, processor's internal registers contain the data to be manipulated by an instruction. Register addressing mode is the most efficient way of specifying operands because they are within the processor and, therefore, no memory access is required.

Row-major order   As the memory is a one-dimensional structure, we need to transform a multidimensional array to a one-dimensional structure. In the row-major order, array elements are stored row by row. This ordering is shown Figure 13.5a. Row-major ordering is used in most high-level languages including C.

Segment descriptors   A segment descriptor provides the attributes of a segment. These attributes include its 32-bit base address, 20-bit segment size, as well as control and status information.

Segment registers   In the IA-32 architecture, these registers support the segmented memory organization. In this organization, memory is partitioned into segments, where each segment is a small part of the memory. The processor, at any point in time, can only access up to six segments of the main memory. The six segment registers point to where these segments are located in the memory.

Sequential circuits   The output of a sequential circuit depends not only on the current inputs but also on the past inputs. That is, output depends both on the current inputs as well as on how it got to the current state. For example, in a binary counter, the output depends on the current value. The next value is obtained by incrementing the current value (in a way, the current state represents a snapshot of the past inputs). That is, we cannot say what the output of a counter will be unless we know its current state. Thus, the counter is a sequential circuit.

Shell The shell can be thought of as the user's interface to the operating system. It acts as the command line interpreter. Several popular shells including the Bourne shell (sh), C-shell (csh), Korn shell (ksh), and Bourne Again shell (bash) are available. However, bash is the default shell in Fedora 3.

Sign flag The sign flag indicates the sign of the result of an operation. Therefore, it is useful only when dealing with signed numbers. Note that the most significant bit is used to represent the sign of a number: 0 for positive numbers and 1 for negative numbers. The sign flag gets a copy of the sign bit of the result produced by arithmetic and related operations.

Single-stepping Single-stepping is a debugging technique. To isolate a bug, program execution should be observed in slow motion. Most debuggers provide a command to execute the program in single-step mode. In this mode, a program executes a single statement and pauses. Then we can examine contents of registers, data in memory, stack contents, and so on.

Software interrupts Software interrupts are caused by executing the int instruction. Thus these interrupts, like procedure calls, are anticipated or planned events. The main use of software interrupts is in accessing I/O devices such as the keyboard, printer, display screen, disk drive, and so on.

Stack A stack is a last-in-first-out (LIFO) data structure. The operation of a stack is analogous to the stack of trays you find in cafeterias. The first tray removed from the stack of trays would be the last tray that had been placed on the stack. There are two operations associated with a stack: insertion and deletion. In stack terminology, insert and delete operations are referred to as push and pop operations, respectively.

Status flags Status flags are used to monitor the outcome of the arithmetic, logical, and related operations. There are six status flags. These are the zero flag (ZF), carry flag (CF), overflow flag (OF), sign flag (SF), auxiliary flag (AF), and parity flag (PF). When an arithmetic operation is performed, some of the flags are updated (set or cleared) to indicate certain properties of the result of that operation. For example, if the result of an arithmetic operation is zero, the zero flag is set (i.e., ZF = 1). Once the flags are updated, we can use conditional branch instructions to alter flow control.

Symbolic debugging Symbolic debugging allows us to debug using the source-level statements. However, to facilitate symbolic debugging, we need to pass the source code and symbol table information to the debugger. The GNU debugger expects the symbolic information in the stabs format. More details on this topic are given in Chapter 8.

System bus A system bus interconnects the three main components of a computer system: a central processing unit (CPU) or processor, a memory unit, and input/output (I/O) devices. The three major components of the system bus are the address bus, data bus, and control bus (see Figure 2.1).

Top of stack If we view the stack as a linear array of elements, stack insertion and deletion operations are restricted to one end of the array. The top-of-stack (TOS) identifies the only element that is directly accessible from the stack.

TOS see *Top of stack*

Trace Tracing is a debugging technique similar to the single stepping. In the single-step mode, a procedure call is treated as a single statement and the entire procedure is executed before pausing the program. This is useful if you know that the called procedure works correctly. Trace, on the other hand, can be used to single-step even the statements of a procedure call, which is useful to test procedures.

Traps See *Exceptions*

Tristate buffers Tristate buffers can be in three states: 0, 1, or Z state. A tristate buffer output can be in state 0 or 1 just as with a normal logic gate. In addition, the output can also be in a high impedance (Z) state, in which the output floats. Thus, even though the output is physically connected to the bus, it behaves as though it is electrically and logically disconnected from the bus. Tristate buffers use a separate control signal so that the output can be in a high impedance state, independent of the data input. This particular feature makes them suitable for bus connections.

Web browser An Internet application that allows you to surf the web. Netscape Navigator, Mozilla Fire Fox, and Microsoft Internet Explorer are some of the popular Web browsers.

Zero flag The purpose of the zero flag (ZF) is to indicate whether the execution of the last instruction that affects the zero flag has produced a zero result. If the result was zero, ZF = 1; otherwise, ZF = 0.

Index

The GNU General Public License

Version 2, June 1991
Copyright © 1989, 1991 Free Software Foundation, Inc.

59 Temple Place - Suite 330, Boston, MA 02111-1307, USA

PREAMBLE

The licenses for most software are designed to take away your freedom to share and change it. By contrast, the GNU General Public License is intended to guarantee your freedom to share and change free software—to make sure the software is free for all its users. This General Public License applies to most of the Free Software Foundation's software and to any other program whose authors commit to using it. (Some other Free Software Foundation software is covered by the GNU Library General Public License instead.) You can apply it to your programs, too.

When we speak of free software, we are referring to freedom, not price. Our General Public Licenses are designed to make sure that you have the freedom to distribute copies of free software (and charge for this service if you wish), that you receive source code or can get it if you want it, that you can change the software or use pieces of it in new free programs; and that you know you can do these things.

To protect your rights, we need to make restrictions that forbid anyone to deny you these rights or to ask you to surrender the rights. These restrictions translate to certain responsibilities for you if you distribute copies of the software, or if you modify it.

For example, if you distribute copies of such a program, whether gratis or for a fee, you must give the recipients all the rights that you have. You must make sure that they, too, receive or can get the source code. And you must show them these terms so they know their rights.

We protect your rights with two steps: (1) copyright the software, and (2) offer you this license which gives you legal permission to copy, distribute and/or modify the software.

Also, for each author's protection and ours, we want to make certain that everyone understands that there is no warranty for this free software. If the software is modified by someone else and passed on, we want its recipients to know that what they have is not the original, so that any problems introduced by others will not reflect on the original authors' reputations.

Finally, any free program is threatened constantly by software patents. We wish to avoid the danger that redistributors of a free program will individually obtain patent licenses, in effect making the program proprietary. To prevent this, we have made it clear that any patent must be licensed for everyone's free use or not licensed at all.

The precise terms and conditions for copying, distribution and modification follow.

Terms and Conditions For Copying, Distribution and Modification

0. This License applies to any program or other work which contains a notice placed by the copyright holder saying it may be distributed under the terms of this General Public License. The "Program", below, refers to any such program or work, and a "work based on the Program" means either the Program or any derivative work under copyright law: that is to say, a work containing the Program or a portion of it, either verbatim or with modifications and/or translated into another language. (Hereinafter, translation is included without limitation in the term "modification".) Each licensee is addressed as "you".

    Activities other than copying, distribution and modification are not covered by this License; they are outside its scope. The act of running the Program is not restricted, and the output from the Program is covered only if its contents constitute a work based on the Program (independent of having been made by running the Program). Whether that is true depends on what the Program does.

1. You may copy and distribute verbatim copies of the Program's source code as you receive it, in any medium, provided that you conspicuously and appropriately publish on each copy an appropriate copyright notice and disclaimer of warranty; keep intact all the notices that refer to this License and to the absence of any warranty; and give any other recipients of the Program a copy of this License along with the Program.

    You may charge a fee for the physical act of transferring a copy, and you may at your option offer warranty protection in exchange for a fee.

2. You may modify your copy or copies of the Program or any portion of it, thus forming a work based on the Program, and copy and distribute such modifications or work under the terms of Section 1 above, provided that you also meet all of these conditions:

    (a) You must cause the modified files to carry prominent notices stating that you changed the files and the date of any change.

    (b) You must cause any work that you distribute or publish, that in whole or in part contains or is derived from the Program or any part thereof, to be licensed as a whole at no charge to all third parties under the terms of this License.

    (c) If the modified program normally reads commands interactively when run, you must cause it, when started running for such interactive use in the most ordinary way, to print or display an announcement including an appropriate copyright notice and a notice that there is no warranty (or else, saying that you provide a warranty) and that users may redistribute the program under these conditions, and telling the user how to view a copy of this License. (Exception: if the Program itself is interactive but does not normally print such an announcement, your work based on the Program is not required to print an announcement.)

    These requirements apply to the modified work as a whole. If identifiable sections of that work are not derived from the Program, and can be reasonably considered independent and separate works in themselves, then this License, and its terms, do not apply to those sections when you distribute them as separate works. But when you distribute the same sections as part of a whole which is a work based on the Program, the distribution of the whole must be on the terms of this License, whose permissions for other licensees extend to the entire whole, and thus to each and every part regardless of who wrote it.

Thus, it is not the intent of this section to claim rights or contest your rights to work written entirely by you; rather, the intent is to exercise the right to control the distribution of derivative or collective works based on the Program.

In addition, mere aggregation of another work not based on the Program with the Program (or with a work based on the Program) on a volume of a storage or distribution medium does not bring the other work under the scope of this License.

3. You may copy and distribute the Program (or a work based on it, under Section 2) in object code or executable form under the terms of Sections 1 and 2 above provided that you also do one of the following:

   (a) Accompany it with the complete corresponding machine-readable source code, which must be distributed under the terms of Sections 1 and 2 above on a medium customarily used for software interchange; or,

   (b) Accompany it with a written offer, valid for at least three years, to give any third party, for a charge no more than your cost of physically performing source distribution, a complete machine-readable copy of the corresponding source code, to be distributed under the terms of Sections 1 and 2 above on a medium customarily used for software interchange; or,

   (c) Accompany it with the information you received as to the offer to distribute corresponding source code. (This alternative is allowed only for noncommercial distribution and only if you received the program in object code or executable form with such an offer, in accord with Subsection b above.)

The source code for a work means the preferred form of the work for making modifications to it. For an executable work, complete source code means all the source code for all modules it contains, plus any associated interface definition files, plus the scripts used to control compilation and installation of the executable. However, as a special exception, the source code distributed need not include anything that is normally distributed (in either source or binary form) with the major components (compiler, kernel, and so on) of the operating system on which the executable runs, unless that component itself accompanies the executable.

If distribution of executable or object code is made by offering access to copy from a designated place, then offering equivalent access to copy the source code from the same place counts as distribution of the source code, even though third parties are not compelled to copy the source along with the object code.

4. You may not copy, modify, sublicense, or distribute the Program except as expressly provided under this License. Any attempt otherwise to copy, modify, sublicense or distribute the Program is void, and will automatically terminate your rights under this License. However, parties who have received copies, or rights, from you under this License will not have their licenses terminated so long as such parties remain in full compliance.

5. You are not required to accept this License, since you have not signed it. However, nothing else grants you permission to modify or distribute the Program or its derivative works. These actions are prohibited by law if you do not accept this License. Therefore, by modifying or distributing the Program (or any work based on the Program), you indicate your acceptance of this License to do so, and all its terms and conditions for copying, distributing or modifying the Program or works based on it.

6. Each time you redistribute the Program (or any work based on the Program), the recipient automatically receives a license from the original licensor to copy, distribute or modify the Program subject to these terms and conditions. You may not impose any further restrictions on the recipients' exercise of the rights granted herein. You are not responsible for enforcing compliance by third parties to this License.

7. If, as a consequence of a court judgment or allegation of patent infringement or for any other reason (not limited to patent issues), conditions are imposed on you (whether by court order, agreement or otherwise) that contradict the conditions of this License, they do not excuse you from the conditions of this License. If you cannot distribute so as to satisfy simultaneously your obligations under this License and any other pertinent obligations, then as a consequence you may not distribute the Program at all. For example, if a patent license would not permit royalty-free redistribution of the Program by all those who receive copies directly or indirectly through you, then the only way you could satisfy both it and this License would be to refrain entirely from distribution of the Program.

   If any portion of this section is held invalid or unenforceable under any particular circumstance, the balance of the section is intended to apply and the section as a whole is intended to apply in other circumstances.

   It is not the purpose of this section to induce you to infringe any patents or other property right claims or to contest validity of any such claims; this section has the sole purpose of protecting the integrity of the free software distribution system, which is implemented by public license practices. Many people have made generous contributions to the wide range of software distributed through that system in reliance on consistent application of that system; it is up to the author/donor to decide if he or she is willing to distribute software through any other system and a licensee cannot impose that choice.

   This section is intended to make thoroughly clear what is believed to be a consequence of the rest of this License.

8. If the distribution and/or use of the Program is restricted in certain countries either by patents or by copyrighted interfaces, the original copyright holder who places the Program under this License may add an explicit geographical distribution limitation excluding those countries, so that distribution is permitted only in or among countries not thus excluded. In such case, this License incorporates the limitation as if written in the body of this License.

9. The Free Software Foundation may publish revised and/or new versions of the General Public License from time to time. Such new versions will be similar in spirit to the present version, but may differ in detail to address new problems or concerns.

   Each version is given a distinguishing version number. If the Program specifies a version number of this License which applies to it and "any later version", you have the option of following the terms and conditions either of that version or of any later version published by the Free Software Foundation. If the Program does not specify a version number of this License, you may choose any version ever published by the Free Software Foundation.

10. If you wish to incorporate parts of the Program into other free programs whose distribution conditions are different, write to the author to ask for permission. For software which is copyrighted by the Free Software Foundation, write to the Free Software Foundation; we sometimes make exceptions for this. Our decision will be guided by the two goals of preserving the free status of all derivatives of our free software and of promoting the sharing and reuse of software generally.

No Warranty

11. Because the program is licensed free of charge, there is no warranty for the program, to the extent permitted by applicable law. Except when otherwise stated in writing the copyright holders and/or other parties provide the program "as is" without warranty of any kind, either expressed or implied, including, but not limited to, the implied warranties of merchantability and fitness for a particular purpose. The entire risk as to the quality and performance of the program is with you. Should the program prove defective, you assume the cost of all necessary servicing, repair or correction.

12. In no event unless required by applicable law or agreed to in writing will any copyright holder, or any other party who may modify and/or redistribute the program as permitted above, be liable to you for damages, including any general, special, incidental or consequential damages arising out of the use or inability to use the program (including but not limited to loss of data or data being rendered inaccurate or losses sustained by you or third parties or a failure of the program to operate with any other programs), even if such holder or other party has been advised of the possibility of such damages.

End of Terms and Conditions

What is on the DVD-ROMs?

DVD-ROM 1

The first DVD-ROM (DVD 1) contains the complete Fedora 3 distribution. It is a copy of the distribution available at the Red Hat's Fedora Web site (www.fedora.redhat.com). If you have a DVD-ROM drive, you can install Fedora Core 3 using DVD 1. For more details, see Chapter 5.

"Red Hat" and "Fedora" are trademarks of Red Hat, Inc. "Linux" is a registered trademark of Linus Torvalds. All other trademarks are the property of their respective owners. For the Fedora trademark guidelines and policies, please see the Red Hat's Fedora Web site at the following URL: http://www.fedora.redhat.com/about/trademarks/. The GNU General Public License given on page 539.

DVD-ROM 2

The second DVD-ROM (DVD 2) contains the source code and CD-ROM images. If your target system does not have a DVD-ROM drive, you can make installation CD-ROMs from the image files on DVD 2. Of course, this step assumes that you have access to another system with a DVD-ROM drive and a CD writer. This DVD-ROM contains three CD-ROM ISO image files: FC3-i386-disc1.iso, FC3-i386-disc2.iso, and FC3-i386-disc3.iso. You can use these files to burn three CD-ROMs that can be used to install the Linux operating system. In addition, it has the FC3-i386-rescuecd.iso image file. For more details, see Chapter 5.

The following four source RPM ISO image files are also on this DVD-ROM: FC3-i386-SRPMS-disc1.iso, FC3-i386-SRPMS-disc2.iso, FC3-i386-SRPMS-disc3.iso, and FC3-i386-SRPMS-disc4.iso.

As mentioned in Chapter 5, the SystemRescueCD ISO image is included on this DVD-ROM. It is distributed under the GNU General Public License given on page 539. If you want to download the latest version of this image, which is about 100 MB, you can do so from the following URL: http://www.sysresccd.org.

The assembly language programs used in the book are in the asm_programs folder. You can also get these programs from the book's Web site.